Reflections by
Anthony Saunders

Financial Institutions, In and Out of Crisis

Reflections by Anthony Saunders

Financial Institutions, In and Out of Crisis

editor

Anthony Saunders

New York University, USA

World Scientific

NEW JERSEY • LONDON • SINGAPORE • BEIJING • SHANGHAI • HONG KONG • TAIPEI • CHENNAI

Published by

World Scientific Publishing Co. Pte. Ltd.
5 Toh Tuck Link, Singapore 596224
USA office: 27 Warren Street, Suite 401-402, Hackensack, NJ 07601
UK office: 57 Shelton Street, Covent Garden, London WC2H 9HE

Library of Congress Cataloging-in-Publication Data
Financial institutions, in and out of crisis : reflections by Anthony Saunders / edited by Anthony Saunders.
p. cm.
Includes bibliographical references.
ISBN-13: 978-9814374019
ISBN-10: 9814374016
1. Financial institutions. 2. Bank management. 3. Financial services industry. 4. Banks and banking, International. I. Saunders, Anthony, 1949–
HG173.F5126 2012
332.1--dc23

2011048305

British Library Cataloguing-in-Publication Data
A catalogue record for this book is available from the British Library.

In-house Editor: Agnes Ng

Printed in Singapore by B & Jo Enterprise Pte Ltd

PREFACE

There have been great strides made in research into financial intermediation over the past 15–20 years. Indeed, as a result of the recent financial crisis research in this area has become increasingly important. In this volume I have put together some of my papers published in the area that bears relevance to many broadly defined issues that arose during the crisis. First, I focus on regulatory issues such as universal banking and bank consolidation (via mergers and acquisitions) as well as the importance of deposit insurance and related too-big-to-fail guarantees, all of which became controversial issues during the recent crisis. Second, I focus on issues relating to relationship lending. It has been long argued that banks are "special" because they form long-term relationships with their borrowers and are willing to support those borrowers both in pricing, collateral requirements as well as credit availability under all economic conditions. Many argue that bank relationships have a "dark-side" in that they can tie a customer to a bank and make it harder for the customer to switch to alternative sources of funds. Moreover, supporting relationship borrowers during a crisis can potentially result in enhanced insolvency risk problems for a relationship bank as the creditworthiness of their borrowers deteriorate. Thirdly, I focus on issues of bank risk management, both the incentives for managerial risk taking as well as its control, which have proven to be so pivotal during the crisis and have given rise to numerous concerns about controlling management compensation and bank risk-taking activities.

1. Regulation: Universal Banking

One of the most important issues in the area of bank regulation is the degree to which banks should be allowed to enter into activities such as securities underwriting, insurance and ownership of corporate equity (thereby engaging in commerce). In my paper with Berlin and John (RFS 1996) we show that banks should be allowed to take either a limited or large stake in a borrowing firm's equity. That is, the bank's financial claim on a borrower has to be structured so that it doesn't have an incentive to collude with the firm's equity owners at the expense of its debt holders by claiming that a firm is healthy when it is not. Nevertheless, today in the US, if not in countries like Germany and Japan, the equity stakes of banks in firms remain highly limited.

In two related papers, with Gande *et al.* (RFS 1997) and (JFE 1998) [winner of the FAMA-DFA award for the best paper in corporate finance and asset pricing in the *Journal of Financial Economics* in 1998] we consider the case for allowing banks to undertake investment banking or securities underwriting activities. Specifically, between 1933 and 1999 the so-called Glass Steagall Act in US was in effect and that limited the ability of banks to underwrite corporate securities such as bonds and equity. However, just prior to the full liberalization of these activities, with the introduction of the Financial Service Modernization Act of 1999, banks were allowed to undertake limited corporate underwriting activities through special (so-from bad banks to good banks during that period. That is, whether depositors could distinguish good from bad banks prior to the introduction of deposit insurance. If they could, it would reduce the case for the introduction of deposit insurance in the first place. We found evidence of contagion for 1930–1932, while none seems to have existed in 1929 or 1933. In addition, the pace of contagion accelerated over 1930–1932. Nevertheless, we still found that even in the period of contagion 1930–1932, failing-bank deposit outflows exceeded those of a matched control sample of non-failing banks. This finding is consistent with the presence of a number of informed depositors who were able to distinguish among ex-ante failing and non-failing banks during a bank crisis. A second and related issue with deposit insurance is its pricing (the insurance premium) and the level or cap placed by the insurance agency on insured depositors' deposits. For example, when deposit insurance was introduced in the US in 1933, it had a flat or risk insensitive insurance premium paid by a bank as a percentage of its deposits and the level of deposit insurance coverage was capped at $2,500. This cap now stands at $250,000 as a consequence of the current crisis. It has long been argued that a non-risk sensitive deposit insurance premium and a relatively high cap on insured deposits can induce moral hazard, i.e., more rather than less risk taking by banks. In a paper with Wilson (JFI, 1995) we examined cross-subsidy, moral hazard, and bank liability issues related to the provision of federal deposit insurance by "rerunning" its implementation in the US, i.e., determining fair deposit insurance premium values, over the period 1927–1932. The pre-1933 period was characterized by historically high asset-price volatility, a large number of bank failures, and a weak federal safety net. In this environment, we found that there was a high degree of self-insurance on the part of the banks in our sample, both in terms of higher overall capital levels and a strong correlation between capital levels and asset volatility and the economically fair deposit insurance premium was relatively low.

In a paper with Dreyfus *et al.* (JMCB 1994) we examined the optimality of establishing specific caps on the level of insured deposits, given the existence of a flat (non-risk sensitive) premium schedule for deposit insurance. Importantly, if the premium income generated by a deposit insurer, using a flat premium schedule, is less than the insurer's actuarially calculated liability (so that the insurance is underpriced), a cost-minimizing insurer would prefer to limit the insurance coverage as much as possible. However, the existence of a flat premium schedule raises the possibility that deposit insurance might actually become overpriced if a bank is low risk. Since the extent of over or underpricing of deposit insurance depends on the scale of the coverage of insured deposits, that is, on the ratio of insured deposits to the bank's total liabilities, the choice of a cap on insured deposits is complex, trading off the revenue benefits to the insurer from a high deposit insurance coverage cap against enhanced moral hazard incentives of the bank as a result of a flat insurance premium.

A further important issue is that if deposit insurance premiums are to be related to bank risk, what variables can be used to measure that risk? In the US and other countries the variables have principally been insolvency related accounting and market–based measures such as return on assets and asset value volatility. In a paper with John *et al.* (RFS 2000) we show that concentrating bank regulation and deposit insurance pricing on bank capital ratios may be ineffective in controlling risk taking. We propose, instead, a more direct mechanism of influencing bank risk–taking incentives, in which the deposit insurance premium scheme depends on managerial compensation and the structure of that compensation. Managerial compensation was a controversial issue during the recent crisis. We show that if bank owners choose an optimal management compensation structure they can induce first-best, value-maximizing risk-taking choices by a bank's management. In the paper we explicitly characterize the parameters of the optimal management compensation structure and the fairly priced deposit insurance premium in the presence of single or multiple sources of agency problems.

4. Banks and Corporate Governance

One of the most important developments in corporate finance in recent years has been to recognize the benefits and costs to a firm's owners from having a "main" bank or a "relationship" bank from which to borrow. In a number of papers I have shown that a main bank relationship does not only affect the cost and availability of bank finance to a borrower, but also the control power of the equity owners and managers of the borrowing firm. In a paper with Ivashina *et al.* (RFS 2009) we investigate the disciplining role of banks and bank debt in the market for corporate control. We find that relationship bank lending intensity and bank client networks have positive effects on the probability of a borrowing firm becoming a takeover target. This effect is enhanced in cases where the target and acquirer have a relationship with the same bank. We also investigate reasons motivating a bank's informational role in the market for corporate control.

In two further papers with Bharath *et al.* (JFE 2007) and Bharath *et al.* (RFS 2009), we investigate particular contract specific effects of banks forming relationships with their customers. In the 2007 paper we show that one benefit to a lender of relationships arises from an enhanced probability of making a future loan to a relationship borrower. Specifically, a relationship bank has a 40% higher probability of making a loan to a prior borrower than an unrelated bank. Moreover, the relationship bank is likely to be selected to provide profitable non-bank services such as securities underwriting. In the 2009 paper we find that repeated borrowing from a relationship lender translates into a 10–17 bps lowering of loan spreads for a borrower and that relationships are particularly valuable in keeping spreads low, especially for small firms. Interestingly, relationship benefits disappear for the largest firms. An alternative way to look at the benefits and costs of relationship lending, from the perspective of lenders, is how the bank's equity returns are impacted when one of their relationship borrowers suffers from financial distress. In a paper with Dahiya *et al.* (JF 2003) we find a significant negative effect on relationship banks when a major corporate borrower announces default or bankruptcy. Finally, in a paper with Dahiya *et al.* (JB 2003) we examine the effect on relationship borrowers when investors learn that their relationship bank has actually sold one of their loans. Since the sale of a loan may carry negative connotations regarding the creditworthiness of a borrower, investors in the distressed firm appear to react in a strongly adverse fashion to such a sale.

Finally, relationships are not only important for corporate customers. Retail customers also face considerable switching costs in moving away from their relationship bank. In a paper with Massoud *et al.* (JB 2006) we show that retail customers are likely to break relationships with smaller banks if larger banks' fee and network structures create sufficient incentives to switch.

5. Banks and Risk Management

Since the onset of the recent financial crisis concerns have been raised about the causes of bank risk taking as well as its consequences. A common theme has been that banks face an agency problem in which managers tend to take more risk than is optimal for stockholders, thus subjecting a bank to a greater risk of failure. An alternative argument is that since managers have a relatively greater proportion of their human and non-human wealth invested in a bank, they are likely to take less risk than a bank's equity holders. In a paper with Strock *et al.* (JF 1990) we show that stockholder controlled banks exhibited significantly greater risk-taking behavior than managerially controlled banks during a period in which the US experimented with significant deregulation and gave banks expanded risk-taking powers. This suggests that managerial self preservation and related incentives may mitigate bank risk-taking behavior.

One way for banks to manage risk exposure is to charge a risk premium for loans to more risky borrowers. In recent years there has been a rapid growth in the highly leveraged transaction loan (HLT) market. In a paper with Angbazo *et al.* (JBF 1998) we show that while HLT loans do reflect the high risk of such loans, via higher risk premiums, these premiums are not of a similar magnitude as those found in the high yield (HY) bond market. One reason for this is that banks charge risky borrowers indirectly, through additional price terms such as fees for syndication, commitment provision and cancellation. Thus, banks augment risk premiums or spreads with a menu of additional fees. In a later paper with Altman *et al.* (JMCB 2010) we show that secondary market loan prices actually anticipate bad news regarding a borrower quicker than the bonds of the same firm.

An important way in which banks can manage risk and insulate themselves against risk is by building up their loan loss reserves (LLR) against which future losses can be charged. However, building loan loss reserves is not costless for shareholders since additional LLRs have to come from a bank's current income. As a result, a bank's announcement of LLR additions may be viewed as either good or bad news by a bank's stockholders. In a paper with Grammatikos (JME 1990) we examine stockholder reactions to LLR addition announcements by Citibank and 34 other banks in the aftermath of the Brazilian debt crisis. We find the results are quite heterogeneous. Importantly, however Citibank's announcement of additional LLRs in the face of mounting loan loss risk had a positive effect on its stock returns. This is consistent with LLR additions being viewed positively by investors overall, despite the negative impact that such additions pose to the current net income of a bank.

One important risk management issue is the degree of diversification of a bank's loan portfolio, i.e., "should it put all its eggs in one basket or should it spread them more widely?" More generally, the issue has been whether a bank should focus or diversify. This issue has been difficult to test because of a dearth of publicly available data on individual bank loan portfolios. However, in some countries such as Italy, data is available at the industry concentration level. Using these data, in a paper with Acharaya *et al.* (JB 2006), we find strong evidence that banks should focus on just a few industry areas of lending and that diversification across many areas is actually risk increasing.

Overall, these papers represent what I believe to be a partial selection of those issues that bear some relevance to the recent and any potential future banking industry crises.

CONTENTS

ACKNOWLEDGMENTS

Chapter 1
Bank Equity Stakes in Borrowing Firms and Financial Distress
Copyright © 1996 by Oxford University Press. Reprinted with permission from *The Review of Financial Studies*, Vol. 9, No. 3 (July 1996) pp. 889–919.

Chapter 2
Bank Underwriting of Debt Securities: Modern Evidence
Copyright © 1997 by Oxford University Press. Reprinted with permission from *The Review of Financial Studies*, Vol. 10, No. 4 (October 1997) pp. 1175–1202.

Chapter 3
Bank Entry, Competition, and the Market for Corporate Securities Underwriting
Copyright © 1999 by Elsevier. Reprinted with permission from the *Journal of Financial Economics*, Vol. 54, No. 2 (October 1999) pp. 165–195.

Chapter 4
The Effects of Bank Mergers and Acquisitions on Small Business Lending
Copyright © 1998 by Elsevier. Reprinted with permission from the *Journal of Financial Economics*, Vol. 50, No. 2 (November 1998) pp. 187–229.

Chapter 5
The Effects of Cross-Border Bank Mergers on Bank Risk and Value
Copyright © 2002 by Elsevier. Reprinted with permission from the *Journal of International Money and Finance*, Vol. 21, No. 6 (November 2002) pp.857–877.

Chapter 6
Contagious Bank Runs: Evidence from the 1929–1933 Period
Copyright © 1996 by Elsevier. Reprinted with permission from the *Journal of Financial Intermediation*, Vol. 5, No. 4 (October 1996) pp. 409–423.

Chapter 7
If History Could Be Rerun: The Provision and Pricing of Deposit Insurance in 1933
Copyright © 1995 by Elsevier. Reprinted with permission from the *Journal of Financial Intermediation*, Vol. 4, No. 4 (October 1995) pp. 396–413.

Chapter 8
Deposit Insurance and Regulatory Forbearance: Are Caps on Insured Deposits Optimal?
Copyright © 1994 by Ohio State University Press. Reprinted with permission from the *Journal of Money, Credit, and Banking*, Vol. 26, No. 3 (August 1994) pp. 411–438.

Chapter 9
A Theory of Bank Regulation and Management Compensation
Copyright © 2000 by Oxford University Press. Reprinted with permission from *The Review of Financial Studies*, Vol. 13, No. 1 (January 2000) pp. 95–125.

Chapter 10
Bank Debt and Corporate Governance
Copyright © 2009 by Oxford University Press. Reprinted with permission from *The Review of Financial Studies*, Vol. 22, No. 1 (January 2009) pp. 41–77.

Chapter 11
So What Do I Get? The Bank's View of Lending Relationships
Copyright © 2007 by Elsevier. Reprinted with permission from the *Journal of Financial Economics*, Vol. 85, No. 2 (August 2007) pp. 368–419.

Chapter 12
Lending Relationships and Loan Contract Terms
Copyright © 2011 by Oxford University Press. Reprinted with permission from *The Review of Financial Studies*, Vol. 24, No. 4 (April 2011) pp. 1141–1203.

Chapter 13
Financial Distress and Bank Lending Relationships
Copyright © 2003 by John Wiley and Sons. Reprinted with permission from *The Journal of Finance*, Vol. 58, No. 1 (February 2003) pp. 375–399.

Chapter 14
Bank Borrowers and Loan Sales: New Evidence on the Uniqueness of Bank Loans
Copyright © 2003 by the University of Chicago. Reprinted with permission from the *Journal of Business*, Vol. 76, No. 4 (October 2003) pp. 563–582.

Chapter 15
The Impact of ATM Surcharges on Large versus Small Banks: Is There a Switching Effect?
Copyright © 2006 by the University of Chicago. Reprinted with permission from the *Journal of Business*, Vol. 79, No. 4 (July 2006) pp. 2099–2125.

Chapter 16
Ownership Structure, Deregulation, and Bank Risk Taking
Copyright © 1990 by the American Finance Association. Reprinted with permission from *The Journal of Finance*, Vol. 45, No. 2 (June 1990) pp. 643–654.

Chapter 17
Credit Spreads in the Market for Highly Leveraged Transaction Loans
Copyright © 1998 by Elsevier. Reprinted with permission from the *Journal of Banking and Finance*, Vol. 22, No. 10–11 (October 1988) pp. 1249–1282.

Chapter 18
Bank Debt versus Bond Debt: Evidence from Secondary Market Prices
Copyright © 2010 by John Wiley and Sons. Reprinted with permission from the *Journal of Money, Credit and Banking*, Vol. 42, No. 4 (June 2010) pp. 755–767.

Chapter 19
Additions to Bank Loan-Loss Reserves: Good News or Bad News?
Copyright © 1990 by Elsevier. Reprinted with permission from the *Journal of Monetary Economics*, Vol. 25, No. 2 (March 1990) pp. 289–304.

Chapter 20
Should Banks Be Diversified? Evidence from Individual Bank Loan Portfolios
Copyright © 2006 by the University of Chicago. Reprinted with permission from the *Journal of Business*, Vol. 79, No. 3 (May 2006) pp. 1355–1412.

I. Regulation: Universal Banking

Bank Equity Stakes in Borrowing Firms and Financial Distress

Mitchell Berlin
Federal Reserve Bank of Philadelphia

Kose John
Anthony Saunders
New York University

We derive the optimal financial claim for a bank when the borrowing firm's uninformed stakeholders depend on the bank to establish whether the firm is distressed and whether concessions by stakeholders are necessary. The bank's financial claim is designed to ensure that it cannot collude with a healthy firm's owners to seek unnecessary concessions or to collude with a distressed firm's owners to claim that the firm is healthy. To prove that a request for concessions has not come from a healthy firm/bank coalition, the bank must hold either a very small or a very large equity stake when the firm enters distress. To prove that a distressed firm and the bank have not colluded to claim that the firm is healthy, the bank may need to hold equity under routine financial conditions.

We are grateful to Franklin Allen (the editor), Craig Holden, Loretta Mester, Manju Puri, Raghuram Rajan, Sherrill Shaffer, Anjan Thakor, Patricia Wilson, an anonymous referee, seminar participants at the Board of Governors, the 1993 BRC/JFI Symposium on Financial Institutions, and the 1993 BRC/JFI Symposium on Financial Institutions, and the 1993 Western Finance Association meetings for helpful comments and discussions. None of them are responsible for any remaining errors. We also thank Heidi English for our graphics. M. Berlin thanks the Leonard N. Stern School of Business and the Indiana University School of Business for financial support. K. John thanks the Charles William Gerstenberg Chair and the Bank and Financial Analysts Association Faculty Fellowship for financial support. A. Saunders thanks the John M. Schiff Chair for financial support. The views expressed here are ours and do not necessarily represent the views of the Federal Reserve Bank of Philadelphia or the Federal Reserve System. Address requests for reprints to Kose John, Suite 9-190/Finance Department, Stern School of Business, New York University, 44 West Fourth St., New York, NY 10012.

The Review of Financial Studies Fall 1996 Vol. 9, No. 3, pp. 889–919

Recent years have witnessed an increasing interest in the behavior of large investors and their influence on firm behavior. This interest has been stimulated by the growing size and influence of institutional investors in the U.S. economy and also by the perception that banks in Germany and Japan — so called "bank-centered" economies — have played an especially productive role in the successes of their respective economies. Thus, we now have a number of empirical studies seeking evidence for distinctive channels through which close bank ties might influence firm performance. Notably, researchers have found evidence that close ties between Japanese banks and firms may reduce the costs of financial distress for borrowing firms.[1] The evidence for Germany is more mixed.[2] Even granting the unsettled state of our empirical knowledge, it is natural to ask which aspects of firm-bank relationships may be important in improving firm performance.

It has often been suggested that bank equity holdings in the firms to which they lend — symptomatic of firm-bank relationships in Japan and Germany — may facilitate more effective bank interventions when firms are distressed. For example, a bank's ability to take an equity position in a distressed firm might reduce agency conflicts between the bank and the firm's shareholders that would lead to excessive liquidation or myopic investment decisions.[3] However, the empirical evidence for this view is mixed. For Germany, Edwards and Fischer (1994, chap. 7) report that bankers seldom take equity stakes when firms enter financial distress. For the United States, James (1993) dispels the common belief that regulatory restrictions prevent banks from taking equity positions in financially distressed firms, yet finds evidence that conflicts among fixed claimants restrict bank equity positions in distressed restructurings.[4] Nonetheless, recent studies suggest

[1] Researchers have documented that the costs of financial distress are lower for those firms that maintain close bank ties [Hodder (1986), Hoshi, Kashyap, and Scharfstein (1990), and Kester (1991)] and that firms with close bank ties are less likely to curtail investments when internal funds are low [Hoshi, Kashyap and Scharfstein (1991)].

[2] Edwards and Fischer (1994) argue quite strenuously against the view that German banks play a special role in reducing the costs of financial distress. On the other side, Harm (1993) finds evidence that close bank ties reduce liquidity constraints for small firms.

[3] It is straightforward that a bank equity share might help resolve conflicts of interest between the firm's shareholders and the bank about project risk or maturity. However, we do not subscribe to the common belief that there are any simple relationships between a bank's equity stake and (1) its information about the firm, or (2) its power to influence firm affairs. Information and power should flow to large investors whether or not their claim includes an equity component. This is especially true in distress, when creditors' influence is greatest. We do believe that the precise relationship between the debt-equity structure of the bank's claim and its power to influence firm behavior is an important topic for research.

[4] In James's (1993) sample, banks do take equity in 30% of the distressed restructurings, not an inconsequential number. At the same time, banks do not take equity in the vast majority of the cases, and the presence and weight of other creditors seem to be the most important constraint. Notably, for those cases in which banks do take equity as part of the distressed restructuring, the median share of public debt in the firm's total debt is zero. James's results are echoed in a

that banks in the U.S. — like banks in Japan — do play an important role in facilitating restructurings in the U.S. [For the U.S., see Gilson, John, and Lang (1990) and James (1993, 1994).]

Of course, taking larger equity stakes in financially distressed firms is not the only conceivable channel through which banks' equity powers might affect the costs of financial distress for borrowing firms. There is some evidence from Japan and Germany that bank equity stakes in healthy firms are associated with reduced agency costs and, perhaps, reduced costs of financial distress.[5] Although banks in the United States have broad rights to take equity stakes when their debt claims are impaired, they cannot hold equity on a routine basis.[6]

Against the steady accumulation of empirical work, there has been relatively little theoretical work that would shed any light on the potential efficiencies — or costs — of expanded equity powers for banks, or, for that matter, the optimal structure of the financial claim for any large institutional investor. Our article examines theoretically the effect of the structure of an informed lender's financial claim on its own behavior when a borrowing firm enters financial distress. In particular, we examine how the structure of an informed lender's financial claim affects its ability to resolve conflicts between a potentially distressed firm and the firm's nonequity stakeholders, such as suppliers and customers who have a direct interest in the firm's continuing viability and whose business is essential to the firm's existence.[7] Assuming no a priori regulatory restrictions on the bank's equity powers, we show how the debt-equity structure of the bank's claim affects its ability to play a constructive role in mitigating conflicts both between the firm's owners and its fixed claimants and also among the claimants themselves.[8]

---

number of other recent studies. For example, Gilson (1993) finds that firms exit from a distressed restructuring with surprisingly high debt-equity ratios and that a firm's debt-equity ratio coming out of a restructuring is positively related to the amount of the firm's bank debt entering distress. Gilson, John, and Lang (1990) find that bank and insurance company debt is converted into common stock less often than other creditors' debt.

[5] For Japan, see Flath (1993) and Prowse (1990, 1992). For Germany, see Harm (1993). Also see Cable (1985) and Gorton and Shmid (1994) for conflicting evidence that German banks' equity positions affect firm performance more generally.

[6] See James (1993) for a thorough description of current regulations in the United States.

[7] Hodder (1986) and Kester (1991) emphasize the role of Japanese banks in resolving conflicts between firm owners and nonequity stakeholders when firms enter into financial distress. Fama (1990) emphasizes that bankers play a key role in communicating relevant information to stakeholders in their lending decisions.

[8] Our emphasis on the bank's role in financial distress and on potential conflicts among claimants is broadly consistent with our reading of the empirical evidence as described above. It should be noted that while empirical work on financial distress has emphasized potential conflicts among financial claimants, it has not focused on stakeholders. As we proceed we will indicate how stakeholders in general might differ from public bondholders.

The Review of Financial Studies / v 9 n 3 1996

Specifically, a firm in financial distress may be unable to continue production profitably without concessions by its long-time suppliers and customers. At the same time, these stakeholders — who may face substantial costs of switching their business to other firms — will be suspicious of any plea by the firm for financial concessions, viewing it as an attempt by a healthy firm to renege on past contractual agreements and to capture rents at the stakeholders' expense. Of course, stakeholders might undertake the costs of monitoring the firm's true financial condition themselves. But as Fama (1990) and others have argued, bankers evaluate borrowers' financial health routinely in their capacity as lenders, so nonequity stakeholders need not duplicate the bank's efforts as long as the bank can be relied on to tell the truth about the firm's financial condition. Whether stakeholders can, in fact, rely on the bank to tell the truth crucially depends on the structure of the bank's financial claim on the firm. An equity stake in the firm — which gives the bank a residual claim on the firm's profits — tends to align the bank's interests with the firm's owners against the firm's nonequity stakeholders. This can create suspicions in stakeholders' minds that the bank and firm will collude to extract rents by seeking unwarranted reductions in the stakeholders' contractual claims.

On the other hand, nonequity stakeholders with fixed claims may also be suspicious of statements made by a bank holding a pure debt claim on the firm — if this debt claim has greater priority than their own. Specifically, a bank with a pure debt claim and a financially distressed firm may collude to convince nonequity stakeholders that the firm's prospects are healthy and that no concessions are necessary. This can occur when the distressed firm's owners have relatively weak bargaining power vis-á-vis the bank in contract negotiations and when deadweight bankruptcy costs are low. Then, given the high likelihood of bankruptcy if stakeholders do not scale down their claims, the bank's higher priority allows it to capture nearly all of the firm's revenues (net of the deadweight bankruptcy costs) and the stakeholders are effectively expropriated.

Although a subordinated debt claim would allay stakeholders' suspicions, it may be difficult for the bank to credibly subordinate its own debt claim to those of the firm's input suppliers and long-term customers for two reasons.[9] First, its superior information may permit the bank to take collateral when the firm's condition worsens (but before the deterioration becomes public information). Second, many of

[9] See White (1981) for a discussion of the reasons why banks can effectively increase the priority of their claims in financial distress. Also see Slovin, Sushka, and Waller (1993).

Bank Equity Stakes in Borrowing Firms and Financial Distress

these stakeholders have only implicit contracts with the firm. Hence, a bank equity claim on the firm may be the only means for the bank to credibly subordinate a sufficient fractions of its claim to uninformed stakeholders.

In the article we show that the optimal dynamic financial claim for an informed bank lender has the following characteristics: (1) Should a firm enter financial distress–where both the bank and the firm's stakeholders must make concessions for the firm to continue efficiently — there are strict limits on the bank's feasible equity stake. Specifically, the bank's equity share in the distressed firm must be either near zero or near one, but it cannot lie within some intermediate range. By not holding an equity share within some intermediate range, the bank assures stakeholders that it has not formed a coalition with a healthy firm to extract rents through unnecessary contractual concessions. (2) The bank's initial claim (its claim on the healthy firm) may require a minimum equity component to assure stakeholders that the bank and the firm will not collude to portray the firm as healthy even when it has entered distress. In our model, this type of collusion is possible if firm insiders' bargaining power in financial distress is weak and if deadweight bankruptcy costs are sufficiently small. If these conditions hold, and if the bank is unable to credibly subordinate its own debt claim to stakeholder claims, then the bank optimally holds an initial equity share and retains this equity share as long as the firm remains healthy.[10]

Beyond the particular banking setting we have chosen, our model of contract renegotiations is a particular example of a signaling model that, to our knowledge, has not been examined before. In this signaling model (1) two informed agents produce a signal about the state of the world to an uninformed third agent, and (2) the signal arises as the result of bargaining between the informed agents. The main insight of the model is that contracts can be designed to create conflicts of interest between informed agents, which generate a particular structure for the bargaining game and create signaling possibilities that would not otherwise arise. In turn, the contractually created conflicts of interest can be used to mitigate the informed agents' joint incentives to exploit the uninformed agents. In our setting, contracts are designed to create conflicts between the firm and the bank over the division of rents that might be expropriated from stakeholders, thereby overcoming the firm's and bank's joint interest in colluding to capture those

[10] Thus, our model provides a rationale for self-imposed constraints on substantial bank equity shares in financially distressed firms, rooted in conflicts of interest among fixed claimants and the bank's pivotal role in distressed restructurings. It also provides some support for arguments that bank equity holdings in healthy firms may enhance efficiency.

rents. We believe that variations of this signaling model might usefully be applied to settings other than our particular application.

Our article has a number of connections with various strands of the extant literature. The main connections are discussed in Section 2. In Section 2.2 we elaborate on the relationship between our article and others that examine firms' incentives to seek unnecessary concessions from uninformed creditors [Brown, James, and Mooradian (1993) and Heinkel and Zechner (1993)] and in which informed investors' contracts are designed to prevent the exploitation of uninformed outsider investors [Admati and Pfleiderer (1994)]. In Section 2.5 we discuss the relationship between our article and others that make predictions about the optimal priority for the claims of an informed lender [Berlin and Mester (1992), Brown, James and Mooradian (1993), Diamond (1993), Fama (1990), Gorton and Kahn (1993), and Rajan (1992)].[11]

Our article proceeds as follows. We describe the model in the first section. In Section 2 we derive the structure of the bank's optimal financial claim. The final section summarizes and concludes.

1. The Model

1.1 Agents

There are three risk-neutral agents: the firm's owners (the firm), the firm's banker (the bank), and the firm's nonequity stakeholders, whom we model as a single input supplier (the supplier). Throughout, we distinguish between the firm's owners and the bank, even though the bank may hold equity in the firm. Without loss of generality, we assume a zero risk-free interest rate. Both the loan market and the input market are competitive when the firm signs initial contracts with the bank and the supplier.

1.2 Production

The model has three dates: Initial investments are made on date 0, the continuation/liquidation decision is made on date 1, and revenues are produced on date 2. See Figure 1 for a time line representation of the model.

1.2.1 The firm. At date 0, the firm invests X_0 dollars; for simplicity we assume that all of the funds for the initial investment come from

[11] Two recent articles, Kim (1992) and Pozdena (1991) have models that show it is optimal for banks to hold equity in borrowing firms. In both cases, the bank — which is assumed to be the sole source of funds — is essentially a passive substitute for the firm's capital structure, rather than an independent actor whose behavior is affected by the structure of its claim. Thus, both models are essentially models of capital structure, rather than models of the optimal claim for an informed investor.

Bank Equity Stakes in Borrowing Firms and Financial Distress

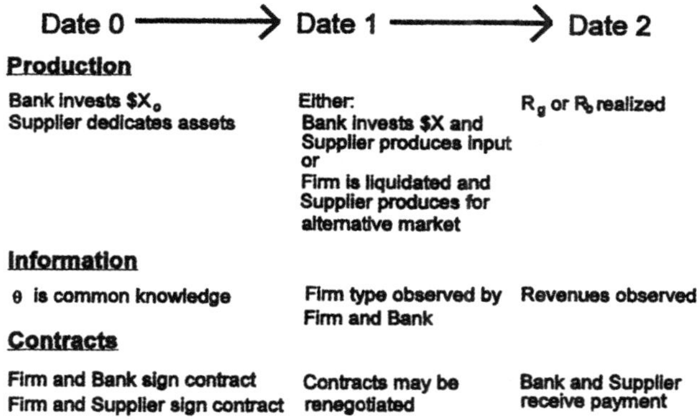

Figure 1
Sequence of events

the bank.[12] This initial investment allows the firm to learn more about the distribution of returns on a risky project at date 1. At this date, continued production requires X additional dollars from the firm's bank — which is assumed to be the sole source of such funds.[13] Projects do not produce any revenues until date 2.

Date 2 project revenues may take one of two values, R_g or R_b, with $R_g > R_b$. Uncertainty about ultimate project revenues is resolved sequentially (see Figure 1). Specifically, at time 0 the firm has a prior probability θ of being a healthy type ($t = t_h$) at date 1 and a $(1 - \theta)$ probability of being a distressed type ($t = t_d$) at date 1. Letting the subscript j index the firm's type, a type t_j firm has date 2 revenues R_g with probability p_j, and R_b with probability $(1 - p_j)$, where $p_h > p_d > 0$. Thus, at date 1 there remains some residual uncertainty about the firm's ultimate revenues. If a firm with revenues R_k, $k = g, b$, defaults on its contractual obligations at date 2, deadweight bankruptcy costs B are borne and date 2 revenues are $R_k - B$.[14]

In addition to extra funds (X) at date 1, continued production requires the purchase of an essential input from the supplier at date 1. If

[12] The assumption of a zero initial investment by the firm's owners is merely a scaling convention that could easily be relaxed at the cost of adding a period 0 participation constraint for the firm's owners.

[13] In our article, the availability of a less informed alternative funding source would affect none of our results in a material way. The bank's bargaining power derives from its superior information about the firm's financial health, not from its position as the firm's sole financier.

[14] In our model, the only role of bankruptcy costs is to ensure the inefficiency of an equilibrium where claims are not restructured in financial distress, that is, where there is no real need for an informed lender to facilitate restructurings.

sufficient funds cannot be secured, or if the supplier does not provide the input, the firm's assets must be liquidated at date 1 and production by the firm is discontinued. Since we are concerned about states where liquidation is inefficient, we assume for simplicity that the liquidation value of the firm at date 1 is zero. If the firm is liquidated early, the firm's owners have an outside employment opportunity between dates 1 and 2 that yields net income w at date 2. If managerial control rents are important, we might have $w < 0$.

1.2.2 The supplier (stakeholders). At date 0, the supplier decides whether or not it wishes to set up a supply relationship with the firm. A supply relationship requires dedicated assets; that is, the supplier's assets are oriented toward producing inputs for the firm rather than for other potential purchasers. If a relationship is established, the supplier can (but may not) choose to produce the input for the firm at cost c at date 1. If the supplier and firm have entered into a supply relationship, but the supplier chooses not to sell to the firm, the input can be sold elsewhere, but only for a net profit of v. If the supply relationship between the firm and the supplier is severed, the supplier's next best market is less profitable than if no such supply relationship had been established. We denote the supplier's net profits in the absence of a supply relationship by v_o, where $v_o > v$. Finally, although we model the stakeholder as a single supplier, it could also be thought of as a representative of stakeholders in general.

1.3 Information

At date 0, the probability of financial distress $(1-\theta)$ is common knowledge, as are all contractual agreements signed at date 0. At date 1, both the firm and the bank, but not the supplier, observe whether the firm is healthy or distressed. Thus, the bank is a fully informed investor, but neither the supplier nor any potential outside lender can observe the firm's actual financial condition.

This information structure captures two essential ideas, both of which derive from the costs of producing information. First, a bank that has evaluated a firm's initial prospects and maintained an ongoing relationship with the firm is likely to be at an informational advantage compared to other potential lenders. Second, although the firm's nonequity stakeholders have a substantial interest in information about the firm's prospects, having a single agent, such as a bank, produce information about the firm can reduce the costs of information production. Whether it is efficient for the supplier to delegate information production to the bank, and whether it is efficient for the firm to permit a single lender to have an informational monopoly will depend, in turn, on the types of contracts that the firm, the bank, and the supplier sign.[15]

1.4 Contracts

1.4.1 Contracts between the firm and the supplier. At date 0, the firm and supplier sign a contract that commits the firm to pay a price m_o at date 2 for the input. Thus, we assume (1) that the supplier cannot be paid up front for the promised input and (2) that the supplier has a fixed-price claim on the firm — the firm and the supplier cannot write explicit revenue contingent contracts at date 0. By mutual consent, however, the firm and the supplier may renegotiate the contract price at date 1. Recognizing the possibility that the final contract price might differ from the original contract price (m_o), we write the contract price that prevails when the firm is type t_j as m_j, $j = b, d$.

Although we do not derive explicitly the optimal contractual claim between the firm and the supplier, our supply contract is intended to capture the main features of many real-world supply relationships. Supply prices are typically inflexible in most states of the world, because of the high costs of writing detailed state-contingent contracts. At the same time, contracts are not totally inflexible and may be renegotiated when business conditions change significantly–such as when the firm enters into a state of financial distress. Our assumption that payments to suppliers can be made only at date 2 is a stylized description of a typical relationship between a firm and its trade creditors — where payments to suppliers are financed out of the revenues from firm sales.[16]

1.4.2 Contracts between the firm and the bank. The bank and the firm are assumed to sign a funding commitment at date 0. The contract states that the firm may draw down up to X dollars at date 1, subject to the bank's approval. We permit the bank's claim to be a mixture of debt and equity. That is, the funding commitment specifies a financial claim for the bank, $\{a_o, D_o\}$, where a_o (the bank's equity share) is the bank's contractual share of the firm's date 2 profits and D_o is the face value of the bank's debt claim, assuming that the firm draws down the X dollars and that is is not liquidated at date 1. Contracts

[15] Although the bank's informational monopoly gives the bank substantial market power, our model does not incorporate the types of distortions that can arise due to ex post market power as in Sharpe (1990) or Rajan (1992).

[16] With minor modeling changes, the stakeholder could also be a buyer of the firm's products. In this interpretation, the buyer must make a binding decision at date 1 whether to purchase the firm's product in preference to some standardized alternative, and delivery cannot occur until date 2.

may be renegotiated by mutual consent at date 1. We write the bank's claim when the firm is type t_j as $\{a_j, D_j\}$.

1.4.3 The relative priority of the bank's and the supplier's claims. The results in our article that suggest a positive role for routine bank equity holdings in the firm depend on the assumption that the bank cannot credibly subordinate its debt claim to that of the supplier. Thus, for much of this article, we view bank equity holdings as the only credible means for the bank to subordinate a portion of its total claim to that of the supplier. Our motivation for this assertion is twofold.

First, as an informed insider, the bank will typically learn about any deterioration in the firm's financial condition before uninformed stakeholders. This gives the bank ample opportunity to take collateral or to perfect a preexisting claim on assets out of view and out of the control of the firm's long-time suppliers and customers.[17] Second, although we have modeled the supply contract as a binding legal contract with a single contractual price, we might just as well view it as part of an implicit contingent contract with a higher price when the firm is healthy and a lower price when the firm is distressed. As long as the supplier can differentiate healthy from distressed firms — and the role of the bank in our model is to communicate this information to the supplier — then such implicit contracts will often be feasible. In this interpretation, the bank cannot credibly subordinate its own explicit contractual debt claim to that of stakeholders, who have implicit promises of dubious standing in court.

1.5 Contract renegotiations

Contracts between the firm, the bank, and the supplier may be renegotiated at date 1. Our stylized model of contract renegotiations is intended to capture two main ideas. The first idea is that the bank and the firm — as informed agents — might have opportunities to strike a deal to expropriate uninformed stakeholders and that the actual deliberations may be unobservable by stakeholders. Thus, the outcome of negotiations between the firm and the bank — for example, a proposal to restructure contracts — may be the supplier's

[17] In principle, we could imagine our uninformed stakeholders collateralizing their own claims or placing "no subordination" covenants in their supply contracts. Taking collateral–which requires continued monitoring to ensure the value and maintenance of the value of the assets — is foreclosed by precisely the same information costs that lead the stakeholders to defer information collection about the firm s financial condition to the bank. In the context of contracts to supply or purchase goods or services, the transaction costs and the operating inflexibility that would afflict any attempt to specify contractually those subsequent claims — real and financial — that can or cannot be given priority would be considerable.

only information to help judge the actual content of the negotiations. The second idea is that the bank's key role in financial distress gives it bargaining power that it does not have when the firm is healthy. Thus, both the firm and stakeholders are at a bargaining disadvantage vis-á-vis the bank when the firm is financially distressed and contracts must be restructured for efficient production.

We assume that negotiations at date 1 take place sequentially, as pictured in Figure 2. In stage 1, the firm and the bank negotiate over the bank's financial claim. Then, in stage 2, the firm-bank coalition negotiates with the supplier over the price of the input. In stage 1, the bank makes a single offer to the firm, which the firm may accept or refuse. If the firm refuses, the initial contract terms remain in effect. In either case, the firm and the bank then decide whether they wish to continue production or to liquidate the firm. If the firm and the bank reach agreement to continue production, they announce their contractual agreement to the supplier. This final agreement is the only aspect of stage 1 negotiations that can be observed by the supplier. In stage 2 the firm-bank coalition makes a single offer to the supplier, which it may accept or reject. If it rejects the offer, the original contract terms remain in force. At that time, all agents — the firm, the supplier, and the bank — decide whether they wish to continue production.[18]

1.6 Parametric restrictions

First, we assume that liquidation at date 1 is never efficient ex post,

$$p_d R_g + (1 - p_d)[R_b - B] > X + c + v + w. \tag{1}$$

The left-hand side of Equation (1) denotes the expected date 2 revenues for a financially distressed firm — assuming that the firm defaults when revenues are low. (Thus, the left-hand side assumes the worst possible date 2 outcome.) The right-hand side of Equation (1) is the sum of the additional funds needed at date 2 (X), the supplier's costs of supplying the input ($c + v$) — which includes both the direct production costs and the forgone profits in the alternative market — and the firm owners' opportunity cost — their income in alternative employment (w).

[18] Our qualitative results would hold for many other bargaining games (which would lead to less extreme distributions of the bargaining surplus). Only two features of our bargaining setup are essential: (1) The firm and the bank must be able to negotiate in private before an offer is made to the supplier — this introduces the possibility that the firm and the bank might form a coalition to expropriate the supplier. (2) The supplier and the firm must have some power to enforce the terms of the initial contract when the initial contract is feasible. If this were not the case, suppliers would never enter into initial supply relationships and firms would never contract with banks. We give the supplier and the firm bargaining power by assuming that they can always reject an offer in favor of the initial contract.

The Review of Financial Studies / v 9 n 3 1996

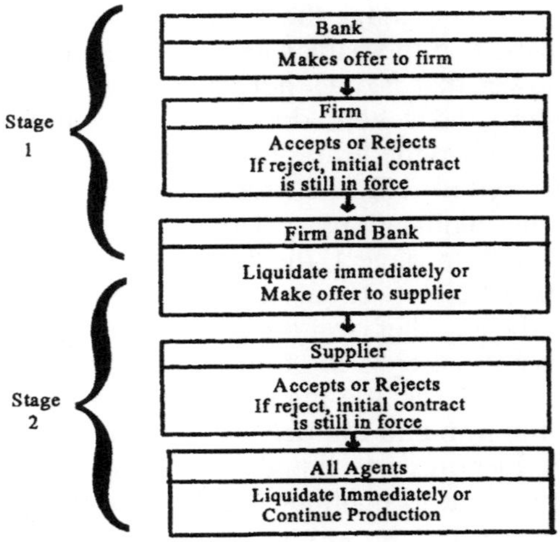

Figure 2
Bargaining

Second, we assume that the lowest possible date 2 revenues are too low to cover the supplier's costs of supplying the input (evaluated ate date 0),

$$R_b < c + v_o. \tag{2}$$

As we shall see, Equation (2) implies that stakeholders must make concessions to avoid inefficiencies when the firm enters financial distress.

1.7 Profit functions

It is convenient to think of the second stage of contract renegotiations as a game in which the bank announces the firm's type to the supplier at date 1. The following profit functions refer to each agent's expected date 2 payoff when the bank states that the firm is type i and the firm is actually type j. We denote the firm's total fixed claims by

$$F_i \equiv m_i + D_i,$$

and we use the indicator function to denote whether the firm can meet its fixed claims at date 2, that is,

$$\begin{aligned}\delta_{ki} &= 1 \text{ if } R_k \geq F_i, \\ &\ 0 \text{ if } R_k < F_i,\ k = g, b,\ i = h, d.\end{aligned}$$

Bank Equity Stakes in Borrowing Firms and Financial Distress

If the firm continues production at date 1, then its expected payoff is

$$\pi^f(i \mid j) = p_j(1 - a_i)[R_g - F_I, 0]^+ + (1 - p_j)(1 - a_i)[R_b - F_i, 0]^+,$$

and if the firm is liquidated its expected payoff is w.

If the firm continues production at date 1, and if the bank's fixed claim has priority over the supplier's claim, the bank's expected payoff (gross of its funding costs) is

$$\begin{aligned}\pi^b(i \mid j) &= p_j(a_i[R_g - F_i, 0]^+ + \delta_{gi}D_i + (1 - \delta_{gi})[R_g - B]) \\ &\quad + (1 - p_j)(a_i[R_b - F_i, 0]^+ + \delta_{bi}D_i + (1 - \delta_{bi})[R_b - B]).\end{aligned}$$

The third expressions on both the top and bottom line incorporate the priority assumption. If the firm defaults at date 2, the bank captures all of the revenues net of the deadweight bankruptcy costs, $[R_k - B]$, when its claim has higher priority than the supplier's. If the supplier's claim has priority over the bank's fixed claim, the bank's payoff is

$$\begin{aligned}\pi^b(i \mid j) &= p_j(a_i[R_g - F_i, 0]^+ + \delta_{gi}D_i + (1 - \delta_{gi})[R_g - B - m_i, 0]^+) \\ &\quad + (1 - p_j)(a_i[R_b - F_i, 0]^+ + \delta_{bi}D_i + (1 - \delta_{bi}) \\ &\quad \times [R_b - B - m_i, 0]^+).\end{aligned}$$

Again, the third expressions on both lines incorporate the priority assumption. If the firm defaults at date 2, the bank receives a return $[R_k - B - m_i]$ only if revenues net of bankruptcy costs exceed the supplier's claim.[19] If the firm is liquidated, the bank's payoff is zero.

If the firm continues production, and if the supplier's claim is subordinated to the bank's claim, the supplier's expected payoff is

$$\begin{aligned}\pi^s(i \mid j) &= p_j(\delta_{gi}m_i + (1 - \delta_{gi})[R_g - B - D_i, 0]^+) \\ &\quad + (1 - p_j)(\delta_{bi}m_i + (1 - \delta_{bi})[R_b - B - D_i, 0]^+) - c,\end{aligned}$$

and if the bank's fixed claim is subordinated, the supplier's expected payoff is

$$\begin{aligned}\pi^s(i \mid j) &= p_j(\delta_{gi}m_i + (1 - \delta_{gi})[R_g - B]) \\ &\quad + (1 - p_j)(\delta_{bi}m_i + (1 - \delta_{bi})[R_b - B]) - c.\end{aligned}$$

If the firm is liquidated, then the supplier produces elsewhere and receives v.

[19] Hopefully without confusion, we use the same notation for the agents' payoff functions under both assumptions about relative priority. In subsequent sections we will be clear about which assumption and which payoff functions are being used.

The Review of Financial Studies / v 9 n 3 1996

Finally we denote the profit functions when the bank is truthful by

$$\pi^n(j) \equiv \pi^n(j \mid j), \quad n = f, b, s, \text{ and } j = h, d.$$

2. The Structure of the Bank's Optimal Claim

In this section we show how the bank's financial claim can be structured to facilitate the efficient restructuring of claims when the firm is in financial distress. The underlying problem is that the firm and the bank have an incentive to form a coalition to expropriate the uninformed supplier. There are two potential conflicts of interest between the firm-bank coalition and the supplier to overcome.

First, the informed bank has an incentive to collude with a healthy firm to seek unnecessary concessions from suppliers. But the structure of the bank's financial claim on a distressed firm can be designed to prevent the possibility of collusion in healthy states. In essence, the bank and the firm use contracts to create a conflict of interest between themselves over the division of the surplus expropriated from the supplier. This contractually created conflict of interest between the bank and the firm permits the bank to signal credibly that the firm and bank are not seeking unnecessary concessions. More specifically, we show that the bank can establish the need for concessions in one of two ways. Its equity claim on the distressed firm must be sufficiently small — that is, below a ceiling level (a_d^c) — or else it must be sufficiently large — that is, above some floor (a_d^f), where $a_d^f > a_d^c$. Said differently, the bank's equity share on the distressed firm must lie outside the interval (a_d^c, a_d^f).

Second, the bank may have an incentive to collude with the distressed firm to claim that the firm is actually healthy, despite the presence of deadweight bankruptcy costs. This conflict arises when the bank cannot credibly subordinate its debt claim to that of the supplier. To ensure that the bank and the distressed firm have an incentive to seek a full restructuring of claims, the bank's claim on the healthy firm — its initial contractual claim — cannot be a pure debt claim.

We proceed in two steps. In Section 2.1 we derive restrictions on the bank's financial claim on the distressed firm, which prevent the firm and the bank from seeking unnecessary concessions from stakeholders (Proposition 1). The results in Proposition 1 hold for all parameter values and are independent of any assumptions about the relative priority of the bank's and supplier's fixed claims. In Section 2.3, we derive restrictions on the structure of the bank's initial financial claim, which ensure that the distressed firm and the bank will not claim falsely that the firm is healthy (Propositions 2 and 3).

2.1 Credibility and the bank's claim on the distressed firm

We begin with a lemma that states that the first-best outcome — the outcome that maximizes the joint profit of the firm, the bank, and the supplier — requires the restructuring of the supplier's claim when the firm is in financial distress. The formal proofs of this lemma and all following results are placed in the appendix.

Lemma 1. *Joint profits are maximized only if*

$$m_b > R_b > m_d. \tag{3}$$

Intuitively, the supplier will not enter into a supply relationship unless its expected profits are greater than v_o, which implies that $m_b > c + v_o > R_b$, the second inequality following from Equation (2). But this means that the distressed firm will be unable to cover its fixed payments at date 2 with probability $(1 - p_d)$ unless the supplier agrees to a concessionary claim in financial distress, that is, $m_d < R_b$. If the supplier will not restructure its claim in financial distress, then, depending on the value of the firm owners' outside employment opportunities (w), one of two inefficiencies will arise. If the firm owners' outside employment opportunities are sufficiently profitable, the firm owners will refuse to continue production — an inefficient outcome by Equation (1) — unless the supplier offers concessions. If the firm owners' outside employment opportunities are relatively unprofitable, both the bank and the distressed firm might be willing to continue production even if the supplier refuses to make concessions. However, this will lead to excessive deadweight bankruptcy costs, which raise expected input and funding costs and reduce the firm's date 0 expected profits.

In light of Lemma 1, we focus our attention on separating equilibria in which the supplier is willing to accept a concessionary supply price when the firm enters financial distress.[20] The following proposition states our first main result, the necessary restrictions on the bank's financial claim on the distressed firm to ensure that the supplier will make concessions. It also gives a partial description of the pure strategy sequential equilibrium contractual outcomes. Since Proposition 1 holds whatever the relative priority of claims, the payoff functions can refer to either the case where the bank's claim has higher priority than the supplier's or vice versa.

Proposition 1. *The supplier will accept concessions from the distressed firm only if the bank holds a contractual claim in financial distress*

[20] There also exist inefficient pooling equilibria in which the supplier always refuses to make concessions.

The Review of Financial Studies / v 9 n 3 1996

$\{a_d, D_d\} \neq \{a_o, D_o\}$, in which the bank's equity share a_d falls outside the interval (a_d^c, a_d^f), where,

$$a_d^c \equiv \left[\frac{\pi^b(h) - \pi^b(d)}{(p_h - p_d)(R_g - R_b)} \right], \tag{4}$$

and,

$$a_d^f \equiv a_d^c + \left[\frac{\pi^s(h) - (m_d - c)}{(p_h - p_d)(R_g - R_b)} \right] > a_d^c. \tag{5}$$

In financial distress, the renegotiated price for the supplier is

$$m_d = c + v, \tag{6}$$

and $\{a_d, D_d\}$ satisfies,

$$\pi^f(d) = [w, 0]^+, \text{ and } \pi^b(d) = p_d R_g + (1 - p_d) R_b - m_d - \pi^f(d). \tag{7}$$

The initial contract is not renegotiated when the firm is healthy, that is:

$$\{a_h, D_h m_h\} = \{a_o, D_o, m_o\}. \tag{8}$$

The intuition behind the separating equilibrium described in Equations (6)–(8) is straightforward. The supplier will be unwilling to make price concessions to the distressed firm unless the bank's claim on the distressed firm differs from its claim on the healthy firm. Since the bank's claim signals the underlying state in a separating equilibrium, a supplier confronted with a demand for concessions from a firm that it knows to be healthy will insist on its initial contractual price. As long as it does so, there are no rents to be shared between the healthy firm and the bank; and since the healthy firm can, in fact, continue without concessions, it will also insist on its initial contractual agreement with the bank. Thus, the initial contracts remain in force when the firm is healthy, as stated in Equation (8).

However, when the firm is distressed, neither the firm nor the supplier can insist on its initial contract. Given our bargaining structure, the firm-bank coalition will demand that the supplier accept a price (m_d) that leaves it indifferent between producing for the firm and severing the supply relationship; thus, $m_d = c + v$, as stated in Equation (6). The bank, which has an enhanced bargaining position when the firm is in distress, permits the firm's owners to retain just enough equity to keep them indifferent between continuing production and liquidation (in which case they could earn income w outside the firm), as stated in Equation (7).

But how can the supplier be sure that the demand for concessions has not come from a healthy firm colluding with the bank to extract

Bank Equity Stakes in Borrowing Firms and Financial Distress

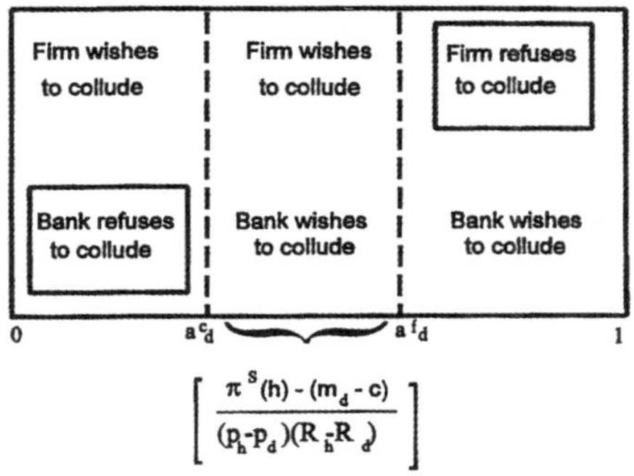

Figure 3
The bank's and the healthy firm's incentives to collude
Either the healthy firm or the bank will refuse to collude against the supplier if a_d falls outside the interval (a_d^c, c_d^f).

rents at the supplier's expense? The key is for the bank to hold a claim on the distressed firm that creates a conflict between the bank and the healthy firm over the distribution of any rents extracted from the supplier. The requirement that the bank's equity claim in financial distress fall outside the interval (a_d^c, a_d^f) provides two alternative contractual restrictions that create such a conflict and prevent the coalition from forming. The first alternative — a ceiling on the bank's equity share (a_d^c) — guarantees that the bank finds it unprofitable to collude with the healthy firm against the supplier. The second alternative — a floor under the bank's equity share (a_d^f) — guarantees that the healthy firm finds it unprofitable to collude with the bank.[21] The following discussion of the bank's and the healthy firm's incentives to collude is illustrated in Figure 3.

The ceiling (a_d^c) comes directly from the bank's truth-telling constraint:

$$\pi^b(h) \geq \pi^b(d \mid h) = \pi^b(d) + a_d(p_h - p_d)(R_g - R_b), \tag{9}$$

which says that when the firm is healthy the bank prefers its initial contractual claim to its concessionary claim.

Intuitively, an equity share gives the bank a residual claim on the firm's profits, which would increase with a concessionary reduction in the supplier's price. If the bank were permitted too large an equity share in the distressed firm, it would wish to collude with the healthy firm to extract rents from the supplier. Further, as long as the bank's

[21] The reader should note that $a_d^f > a_d^c$ follows directly from the supplier's date 0 participation constraint.

The Review of Financial Studies / v 9 n 3 1996

equity share in the distressed firm is not so large that it would capture a disproportionate share of the rents, the healthy firm would also find it profitable to collude against the supplier.

To see that such a coalition would form if the bank's equity claim on the distressed firm falls within the interval (a_d^c, a_d^f), note that the healthy firm would prefer its concessionary equity share $(1 - a_d)$ to its initial equity share $(1 - a_o)$ as long as,

$$\pi^f(h) < \pi^f(d \mid h), \tag{10}$$

which can be rewritten as a restriction on the size of the bank's equity claim:[22]

$$\begin{aligned} a_d &< \frac{[\pi^b(h) - \pi^b(d)] + [\pi^s(h) - (m_d - c)]}{(p_h - p_d)(R_g - R_b)} \\ &= a_d^c + \left[\frac{\pi^s(h) - (m_d - c)}{(p_h - p_d)(R_h - R_d)}\right]. \end{aligned} \tag{11}$$

So, if the bank's claim on the distressed firm exceeded the ceiling (a_d^c), both the bank and the firm would prefer to claim that the firm was in a distressed state and share the rents expropriated from the supplier for a_d over the interval

$$a_d \in \left(a_d^c, a_d^c + \left[\frac{\pi^s(h) - (m_d - c)}{R_h - R_d}\right]\right). \tag{12}$$

Of course, a rational supplier would always refuse to make price concessions demanded by a firm-bank coalition in which the bank holds an equity claim on the interval defined in Equation (12).

Simply reversing Equation (10) yields the second alternative restriction on the bank's claim, the floor (a_d^f) defined in Equation (5). If the bank takes a sufficiently large equity share when the firm is in financial distress, a healthy firm would always prefer the initial contract to forming a coalition with the bank to expropriate the supplier. Intuitively, when the bank's equity share in financial distress is very large, the bank would capture a disproportionate share of any rents captured from the supplier, so the healthy firm's profits are higher under the original contract and no coalition can form.

The main empirical prediction of this section is that banks face potentially severe restrictions on their ability to take equity positions

[22] The inequality in Equation (11) is derived by noting that $\pi^f(i \mid j) = p_j R_g + (1 - p_j)R_b - \pi^s(i \mid j) - \pi^b(i \mid j)$, and substituting the equality in Equation (9) and the value of a_d^c from Equation (4).

Bank Equity Stakes in Borrowing Firms and Financial Distress

in distressed firms in the presence of other fixed claimants.[23] This is consistent with the emerging literature on financial distress in the United States, which suggests that conflicts among fixed claimants — rather than regulatory restrictions — are the main constraint on bank equity positions in distressed restructurings. It is also consistent with evidence from Germany that banks seldom take equity positions in financially distressed firms.[24]

2.2 Related literature

Ours is a novel signaling model with two informed agents — the firm and the bank — in which the signal about the firm's type is the outcome of bargaining between the informed agents, and in which both the firm and the bank must agree to send a particular signal. Although the firm and the bank potentially have a common interest in seeking concessions from the supplier, they also have a conflict of interest concerning the distribution of the surplus. The bank's stronger bargaining position when the firm is truly financially distressed (compared to when the firm is healthy) restricts the gains that the healthy firm-bank coalition can achieve at the supplier's expense by lying. This follows since any proposal must mimic that which would arise in equilibrium were the firm truly distressed. Since the healthy firm and the bank's respective gains depend on the structure of the bank's financial claim on the distressed firm, this claim can be designed to make it impossible for a coalition to form when the firm is healthy, as described above.

Brown, James, and Mooradian (BJ&R) (1993) and Heinkel and Zechner (H&Z) (1993) also consider models in which firms have incentives to seek unnecessary concessions from uninformed creditors. In BJ&R's model of public restructurings, a distressed firm-bank coalition offers new securities to uninformed bondholders, which supports a signaling equilibrium in which better firms offer senior debt and worse firms offer equity. Unlike our model, the firm in BJ&R is assumed to be in default on its debt obligations from the outset, and the bank and the firm are assumed to maximize joint profits; that is, the existence of the firm-bank coalition — with some distribution of

[23] Although our model permits the bank to take large equity shares in distress, we prefer to focus on the ceiling (a^c_d) on the bank's possible equity share. While a pure debt claim in distress is always feasible, there is no assurance that $(a^f_d) < 1$, that is, an equity share large enough to prevent collusion may be infeasible. Further, if managerial effort (which we have not modeled) is important, a very large bank equity share may be infeasible for incentive reasons.

[24] See Footnotes 3 and 5 for the relevant references. The existing empirical literature emphasizes the role of conflicts among financial claimants. A direct test of the empirical importance of the factors driving model would examine how the outcomes of distressed restructurings are affected by the relative importance of dedicated supply relationships in firms' input and output markets.

bargaining power determined by the event of default — is also given from the outset. In our model, only the distressed firm requires concessions from the supplier, and our central question is how contracts can be designed to prevent collusion between the firm and the bank.

In a model without an informed creditor, H&Z show that for some parametric restrictions the firm can assure uninformed bondholders that they are seeking only necessary concessions by swapping convertible debt for straight debt, a possibility we rule out by assumption. Although H&Z's solution may be attractive as a means of restructuring the firm's debt, it is less so when the contracts that must be restructured are those of the firm's suppliers and customers. When an individual stakeholder's contribution to firm profitability is difficult to measure, and when total firm profitability depends on managerial decisions as well as the quality of inputs provided by other suppliers an purchasing decisions made by other customers, stakeholders may be loath to accept payments based on firm profits. These appropriation problems do not arise for bondholders, who do not maintain a continuing productive relationship with the firm.

In Admati and Pfleiderer's (A&P) (1994) model of a venture capitalist, the optimal venture capital contract requires uninformed outside investors to contribute a share of the subsequent funding for a project initially financed by an informed investor. The venture capitalist's fixed share contract ensures not only that interim investment incentives are correct, but also that the outside investors pay a fair price for their claims — as long as they refuse to invest when they observe a revision of the original contract between the firm and the venture capitalist. Thus, renegotiation never occurs; in fact, any attempt to renegotiate the initial contract would lead outside investors to shun investment in the firm. Unlike our stakeholders, A&P's uninformed investors have no initial investment in the firm. In our model, stakeholders' initial willingness to engage in a supply relationship requires an enforceable initial contract, and the need to reduce fixed claims in financial distress ensures that renegotiation actually occurs. Thus, we cannot rely on a nonnegotiable contract as a means of ensuring that uninformed stakeholders are not exploited.

2.3 Credibility and the bank's claim on the healthy firm

The separating equilibrium described in Proposition 1 is feasible only if the supplier has no reason to be suspicious of a bank's statement that the firm is healthy. And if the bank can credibly subordinate its own debt claim to the suppliers claim, the bank has a simple way to signal to the supplier that it would never falsely state that a distressed firm was healthy. Specifically, the bank can be a pure debtholder with a claim strictly subordinate to the supplier. In this case, a false statement that the distressed firm was healthy would lead to a high probability that the firm will default on its fixed claims, and the supplier would be paid out of the firm's revenues before the bank. Thus, the bank would have nothing to gain by denying that the firm was in distress.

Since Proposition 1 has already established that the bank cannot form a coalition with the healthy firm if it holds a pure debt claim when the firm is in distress — and since the restrictions on the bank's financial claim on the distressed firm do not depend on the relative priority of the bank's debt claim on the distressed firm — we have the following proposition:

Proposition 2. *No bank-firm coalition to expropriate the supplier can form if the bank holds a pure debt claim, as long as the bank's initial contractual debt claim (D_o) is subordinated to all other fixed claims.*

However, recognizing the bank's difficulties in subordinating its debt claim to all stakeholders, a bank equity share in the firm may serve a positive function under some conditions, as the following proposition states:

Proposition 3. *Assume that the bank's debt claim has priority over the supplier's claim. When firm owners' wage in alternative employment, w, is below a critical value w^* — to be defined below — the distressed firm would always seek to misrepresent itself as a healthy firm. Further, when*

$$(m_d - p_d m_o) - (1 - p_d)B > 0, \tag{13}$$

then the bank will reveal truthfully the distressed firm's financial condition only if the bank's initial claim includes some equity, that is, $\{a_o > 0, D_o \geq 0\}$.

Intuitively, when the firm is in financial distress there is a substantial probability of default, $(1 - p_d)$ — if the supplier's claims are not renegotiated. When the deadweight bankruptcy costs are not too large, a bank with no initial equity claim and an initial debt claim, $D_o > R_b - B$, can often profitably expropriate the supplier by claiming falsely that the distressed firm is healthy.[25,26] The bank would induce the supplier to produce the input at the original supply price, while the probability

[25] When the bank holds no equity, the inequality $D_o > R_b$ follows directly from the bank's date 0 participation constraint.

[26] The reader should note that the only role of deadweight bankruptcy costs in our model is to ensure that a pooling outcome without the restructuring of claims is inefficient. Without deadweight bankruptcy costs, there is an efficient pooling equilibrium where the supplier always refuses to renegotiate and the firm avoids liquidation whether it is healthy or distressed (if w is low enough). Note that our results hold even if bankruptcy costs are quite small. In fact, if bankruptcy costs are too large, the bank would always prefer to reveal truthfully that the firm is distressed — as Equation (13) states — and the priority of the bank's claim is irrelevant.

that the supplier will actually recover any payment is small — because of the high probability of default and the banker's higher priority in the event of default. Thus, with a high probability the bank captures all of the firm revenue (net of the deadweight bankruptcy costs) and the supplier is effectively expropriated.

Equation (13) is a necessary condition for the distressed firm and bank to collude profitably and misrepresent the firm as healthy. The condition shows the net gains to the distressed firm-bank coalition from expropriating the supplier in this way. The coalition avoids paying the supplier its restructured wage, m_d, but it must weigh against this gain the expected deadweight bankruptcy costs, $(1 - p_d)B$, and the expected payments to the supplier under the original contract, $p_d m_o$.

The distressed firm would agree to form a coalition with the bank as long as its payoff under a full restructuring of claims is sufficiently low. Specifically, the distressed firm would prefer to collude with the bank to expropriate the supplier as long as

$$\pi^s(h \mid d) = p_d(1 - a_o)[R_g - m_o - D_o] \geq \pi^s(d) = [0, w]^+. \tag{14}$$

Note, that since $m_o > R_b$, the firm defaults and receives no payoff with probability $(1 - p_d)$. Since the size of the bank's and the supplier's initial contractual claims are determined by their date 0 participation constraints, and since a defaulting firm cares nothing about the relative priority of the bank's and supplier's respective claims, the distressed firm is concerned only about the sum of the initial contractual payments to the bank and the supplier $(m_o + a_o[R_g - m_o - D_o] + D_o)$. Thus, the distressed firm's payoff under collusion is unaffected by the structure of the bank's claim. Using the bank's and the supplier's date 0 participation constraints and rearranging, Equation (14) can be rewritten,

$$w^* \equiv \left[\frac{p_d}{p_h\theta + p_d(1-\theta)}\right][E(R_k) - \theta(1 - p_h)B - (c + v_o) - (X_o + X)] \geq [0, w]^+, \tag{16}$$

where

$$E(R_k) \equiv (\theta p_h + (1-\theta)p_d)R_g + (\theta(1 - p_h) + (1-\theta)(1 - p_d))R_b.$$

Thus, as long as the firm's owners have only relatively unprofitable opportunities outside the firm — or if they benefit from substantial control rents — the distressed firm will be willing to collude with the bank to expropriate the supplier.

Under these conditions, the supplier must rely on the bank to reveal truthfully whether the firm is distressed. Here, a large enough initial bank equity claim allows the bank to subordinate enough of its total claim to that of the supplier to ensure that it will not collude with the distressed firm. Specifically, from the bank's truth-telling condition,

$$\pi^b(d) \geq \pi^b(h \mid d),$$

we can determine the minimum initial equity stake that would guarantee that the bank will not collude with the distressed firm:

$$a_o \geq \frac{\pi^b(h) - \pi^b(d)}{(p_h - p_d)(R_g - m_o - D_o)} + \frac{[R_b - B, D_o]^- - D_o}{R_g - m_o - D_o}. \tag{17}$$

2.4 Other factors affecting the structure of the bank's initial claim

To this point, our model yields limits on bank equity shares in financially distressed firms and provides conditions in which banks will optimally hold a least some equity under normal financial conditions. Yet it provides no upper bound on the bank's equity share under normal conditions. Strictly speaking, our bank might hold a pure equity claim as long as the firm is healthy, a possibility clearly inconsistent with prevailing bank practices anywhere. However, our simple model can be extended to ensure that the bank will optimally hold a debt claim when the firm is financially healthy.

In an earlier version of this article [Berlin, John, and Saunders (1993)], we examined an extension in which the firm's ultimate probability of financial distress is determined by its choice between a safe and a risky project and in which the bank can exercise a veto over the firm's project choice through its refusal to lend initial funds. In that model, we show that the bank's optimal initial claim will always include a strictly positive amount of debt. Intuitively, a pure equity claim would give the bank an excessive preference for projects that shift risks to the firm's other fixed claimants.[27]

Another potential difficulty with our model is our assumption that banks may write lending contracts that specify debt and equity shares. The available evidence suggests that banks initially accumulate equity

[27] Of course, there are other reasons outside our model why a bank's normal claim will include debt, even when the bank is well informed. Recent models of optimal capital structure as a means of assigning control rights in the presence of nontransferable sources of utility for managers [e.g., Aghion and Bolton (1992) and Hart and Moore (1989)] or prior uncertainty about managerial abilities [e.g., Kalay and Zender (1992)] would predict that even an informed investor will hold at least a partial debt claim. An attempt to integrate our emphasis on conflicts among claimants and the control rights literature would be an interesting (and difficult) avenue for future research.

stakes in a less systematic way than our model would predict.[28] We view our model as a stylization of a world in which banks may hold continuing equity positions, unconstrained by regulatory restrictions. Although the initial reason for a bank equity position may offer evidence about its function, the bank may maintain an equity stake for reasons — perhaps multiple reasons — unrelated to its origin. Nonetheless, the fact that banks do not write explicit debt-equity contracts under routine conditions suggests an underlying preference for debt claims not captured by our model.

2.5 Related literature

Other recent contributions have predictions about the optimal priority of an informed lender's claim. Some articles offer arguments that the informed investor's optimal claim is subordinate to uninformed creditors. For example, Fama (1990) argues than an informed bank's optimal claim is a subordinated debt claim, so that the bank can make credible statements about the firm's creditworthiness to uninformed stakeholders. Fama does not examine contract negotiations per se and he makes no attempt to formalize or prove his claim. In a sense, our model may be viewed as one possible formalization and elaboration of Fama's claim. Rajan (1992) also argues that the bank's claim should be subordinated, to reduce its bargaining power when contracts are renegotiated and thereby to increase the borrower's initial effort. Unlike our model, the relative priority of the bank's debt plays no role in conveying information to other creditors in Rajan. Similarly, in Brown, James, and Mooradian's (1993) model of private restructurings — in which the bank accepts subordinated claims only when firms' prospects are truly bad — the structure of the bank's claim is not used to affect its ability to convey credible information to uninformed creditors.

Other articles predict that the optimal claim for an informed lender has higher priority than uninformed creditors. In Diamond (1993), where banks have incentives to liquidate excessively (because of the existence of large nonappropriable control rents), a higher priority claim permits the bank to expropriate other creditors ex post and to internalize as much of the appropriable firm value as possible. In Berlin and Mester (1992) and Gorton and Kahn (1993), a higher priority bank claim enhances the bank's threat to liquidate the firm in the even of default, which reduces the firm's incentives to take

[28] For example, Baums (1994) cites a study that examines the reasons for German banks taking equity stakes of 25% or more in the period 1976–1989. Of 21 cases, one-half involve a desire by dominant shareholders (or their family members) to reduce their equity positions. Interestingly, only a small number (3) were banks taking equity stakes in distressed firms.

excessive risks. In each of these articles the central question in contract design is improving the efficiency of the informed lender's ability to make the correct liquidation decision, unlike our article, which emphasizes the informational role of the structure of the bank's claim for uninformed claimants.

3. Conclusion

In this article we have examined a model of the optimal claim for a bank in a world where uninformed nonequity stakeholders — it long-time suppliers and customers — depend on the bank for truthful information about a borrowing firm's financial condition. In particular, stakeholders rely on the bank to reveal whether the borrowing firm is financially distressed and whether concessions are necessary. The bank's financial claim is designed to ensure that it cannot form a coalition with the firm's owners either to seek unnecessary concessions when the firm is actually healthy or to claim that the firm is healthy when it is actually in financial distress.

We show that the optimal claim has the following characteristics. To ensure that a healthy firm and the bank will not seek unnecessary concessions from stakeholders, the bank cannot hold an equity stake within some intermediate range; that is, the bank's equity share must either by very small or very large. Thus, there are stringent constraints on the bank's ability to take equity stakes in distressed firms. To ensure that the financially distressed firm and bank will not collude to claim falsely that the firm is healthy — a possibility that arises when managers' bargaining power is weak and bankruptcy costs are relatively small — a sufficiently large portion of the bank's financial claim on the healthy firm must be subordinated to stakeholders' claims. Since banks may have difficulties in credibly subordinating their debt claims, a bank equity share when the firm is healthy may be necessary. Thus, our analysis offers limited support for often-made claims that bank equity stakes in borrowing firms may enhance efficiency.

Appendix

Proof of Lemma 1. Assume that $m_b < R_b$. Then the supplier's date 0 expected profits are no greater than $[R_b - c]$ and the supplier's participation constraint is violated since $R_b < c + v_o$, by assumption. We will show that $m_d < R_b$, so we must have $m_b > R_b$ or the supplier will not participate.

Assume that $m_d > R_b$. If this supply price leads to liquidation at date 1, we have an ex post inefficient outcome given Equation (1).

In Propositions 1–3, we show that liquidation can be avoided, so liquidation is also ex ante inefficient. If the firm is not liquidated, the joint expected profits are

$$\theta[p_b R_g + (1 - p_b)(R_b - B)] + (1 - \theta)[p_d R_g + (1 - p_d)(R_b - B)] \\ - (X_o + X) - (c + v_o).$$

If, on the other hand, $m_d < R_b$, joint expected profits are

$$\theta[p_b R_g + (1 - p_b)(R_b - B)] + (1 - \theta)[p_d R_g + (1 - p_d) R_b] - (X_o + X) - (c + v_o),$$

which are clearly larger, because expected deadweight bankruptcy costs $(1 - \theta)(1 - p_d)B$ are avoided. ■

Proof of Proposition 2. Step 1: In any efficient separating equilibrium,

$$\{a_d, D_d\} \neq \{a_j, D_j\},\ j = b, d. \tag{A.1}$$

Assume otherwise, and let $\{a, D\}$ be the bank's contractual claim in the stage 1 contractual agreement in both states and m_j be the offer to the supplier in state j. Thus, the bank's claim provides no information to the supplier. If the supplier were ever to accept $m_d < R_b$, the firm and bank would always collude to claim distress, and the supplier's participation constraint is violated. If the supplier always refuses to accept $m_d < R_b$, there is no restructuring, which is inefficient by Lemma 1.

Step 2: Confronted with a stage 1 contractual agreement $\{a_j, D_j\} \neq \{a_d, D_d\}$, the supplier's unique best response in stage 2 is to refuse any offer $m_j < m_o$.

Given Equation (A.1) and the restriction to pure strategies, a supplier that sees stage 1 agreement $\{a_j, D_j\} \neq \{a_d, D_d\}$ in equilibrium believes that the firm is healthy with probability 1. If it refuses any offer below m_o, the original contract is in effect, and all agents will agree to continue under contractual outcome $\{a_o, D_o, m_o\}$. Clearly, the supplier's expected profits are higher when the price is higher (as long as the firm continues production).

Step 3: When the firm is healthy, the unique stage 1 equilibrium contractual agreement is $\{a_o, D_o\}$.

If the supplier will reject any $m_j < m_o$, any revision of the initial contract reduces either the bank's or the healthy firm's profits. The bank would never propose a revision that reduces its own profits and the firm would always reject any revision that reduces its profits. Together, steps 2 and 3 establish that $\{a_j, D_j, m_j\} = \{a_o, D_o, m_o\}$, $j = b, s$.

Step 4: If the supplier accepts m_d when the stage 1 agreement is $\{a_d, D_d\}$, there will exist states where the bank and a healthy firm will agree to $\{a_d, D_d\}$ and propose m_d unless a_d satisfies one of the following two conditions:

$$a_d \le a_d^c \equiv \left[\frac{\pi^b(h) - \pi^b(d)}{(p_h - p_d)(R_g - R_b)}\right], \tag{A.2}$$

or

$$a_d \ge a_d^f \equiv a_d^c + \left[\frac{\pi^s(h) - (m_d - c)}{(p_h - p_d)(R_g - R_b)}\right] > a_d^c. \tag{A.3}$$

Equations (A.2) and (A.3) are merely restatements of Equations (4) and (5) in the text, where their derivations are explained.

Step 5: Confronted with stage 1 contractual agreement $\{a_d, D_d\}$, satisfying Equation (A.2) or (A.3), the supplier's best response is to accept any offer $m_d \ge c + v$.

Since the supplier knows that the firm is in distress and that concessions are necessary when it observes $\{a_d, D_d\}$ — given steps 3 and 4 — the supplier does at least as well producing for the firm as when the firm is liquidated, as long as $m_d \ge c + v$.

Step 6: In distress, the unique equilibrium stage 1 agreement satisfies $\pi^f(d) = [w, 0]^+$, and the unique stage 2 offer by the firm-bank coalition is $m_d = c + v$.

Assume that the stage 1 contractual agreement is $\{a_d, D_d\}$. Then, given step 5, the firm-bank coalition's maximizing offer is the lowest price that would be accepted by the supplier. Then in stage 1, the bank's profits are maximized by making the firm just indifferent between continuation and liquidation. This establishes Equations (7) and (8).

Step 7: This equilibrium can be sustained as long as the supplier adopts the strategy of rejecting $m < m_o$ for any stage 1 agreement other than $\{a_d, D_d\}$, supported by supplier beliefs that the firm is healthy with probability one whenever the stage 1 agreement is not $\{a_d, D_d\}$. ■

Proof of Proposition 2. Assume that the bank's contractual claim on the distressed firm is a pure debt claim — which satisfies Proposition 1 — so that the healthy firm and bank will not collude. Assume that the bank's initial claim is fully subordinated to the supplier's claim. The bank would never willingly claim that a distressed firm was healthy as long as

$$\pi^b(d) \ge \pi^b(h \mid d) = \pi^b(h) - (p_h - p_d)(\phi_o - [R_b - B - m_o, 0]^+, \tag{A.4}$$

The Review of Financial Studies / v 9 n 3 1996

where

$$\phi_o \equiv a_o[R_g - m_o - D_o] + D_o, \tag{A.5}$$

which is the value of the bank's initial financial claim when firm revenues are high. Since we have already shown that $m_o > R_b$, Equation (A.4) can be rewritten,

$$(p_h - p_d)\phi_o \geq \pi^b(h) - \pi^b(d). \tag{A.6}$$

Since ϕ_o is determined by the bank's initial contractual claim, its structure may be an object of design but its expected value is fully determined by the bank's date 0 participation constraint. Furthermore, its structure does not affect whether Equation (A.6) is satisfied. We conclude that the structure of the bank's initial claim is indeterminate; in particular, a pure debt claim will suffice. ■

Proof of Proposition 3. The distressed firm and the bank will not collude to claim falsely that the firm is actually healthy if either the firm's truth-telling condition holds — $\pi^f(d) \geq \pi^f(h \mid d)$ — or the bank's truth-telling condition holds — $\pi^b(d) \geq \pi^b(h \mid d)$ — or both hold. Equation (14) in the text shows that the distressed firm will be willing to collude for w sufficiently small, independent of the structure of the bank's claim or the relative priority of the bank's and stakeholder's fixed claims. Now assume that the bank's fixed claim has priority over the supplier's claim.

We can write

$$\pi^b(h) = p_h\phi_o + (1 - p_h)\mu_o, \tag{A.7}$$

where ϕ_o was defined in the previous proof, and

$$\mu_o \equiv [R_b - B, D_o]^-,$$

which is the value of the bank's initial contractual fixed claim when firm revenues are low and the bank has priority. Also,

$$\pi^b(h \mid d) = p_d\phi_o + (1 - p_d)\mu_o, \tag{A.8}$$

so the bank's truth-telling condition when the firm is distressed can be written

$$\phi_o - \mu_o \leq \frac{\pi^b(h) - \pi^b(d)}{p_h - p_d}, \tag{A.9}$$

and since

$$\pi^f(h \mid d) = p_d R_g + (1 - p_d)[R_b - B] - \pi^b(h \mid d) - \pi^f(h \mid d),$$

the distressed firm's truth-telling condition can be written

$$\frac{\pi^b(h) - \pi^b(d) - (m_d - p_d m_o) + (1 - p_d)B}{p_h - p_d} \geq \phi_o - \mu_o. \qquad \text{(A.10)}$$

Reversing Equations (A.9) and (A.10) and combining, we see that a necessary condition for the bank and distressed firm to agree to collude to claim that the firm is actually healthy is that

$$(m_d - p_d m_o) - (1 - p_d)B > 0, \qquad \text{(A.11)}$$

which is Equation (13) in the text.

Assume that $w \leq w^*$ and that Equation (A.11) holds so that the bank and the distressed firm might agree to collude, and assume that the bank holds no initial equity, i.e., $a_o = 0$. Then Equation (A.9) can be rewritten

$$D_o - \mu_o \geq \frac{\pi^b(h) - \pi^b(d)}{p_h - p_d}. \qquad \text{(A.12)}$$

If the bank holds no initial equity claim, the bank's date 0 participation requires that $D_o > R_b$, so with a little rearranging, Equation (A.12) can be rewritten

$$-\left(\frac{p_d}{p_h - p_d}\right)(D_o - [R_b - B]) \geq \frac{[R_b - B] - \pi^b(d)}{p_h - p_d}. \qquad \text{(A.13)}$$

To show that this cannot hold for B sufficiently small, take the limiting case as B approaches 0. Equation (A.13) can be written

$$-\left(\frac{p_d}{p_h - p_d}\right)(D_o - R_b) \geq \frac{R_b - \pi^b(d)}{p_d - p_h}, \qquad \text{(A.14)}$$

a contradiction since $R_b > \pi^b(d)$. Thus, we must have $a_o > 0$.

Using the definitions for ϕ_o and μ_o, Equation (A.9) can be rearranged to solve for the minimum initial equity share that will ensure that the bank will be truthful:

$$a_o \geq \frac{\pi^b(h) - \pi^b(d)}{(p_h - p_d)(R_g - m_o - D_o)} + \frac{[R_b - B, D_o]^- - D_o}{R_g - m_o - D_o}. \qquad \blacksquare$$

References

Admati, A., and P. Pfleiderer, 1994, "Robust Financial Contracting and the Role of Venture Capitalists," *Journal of Finance*, 49, 371–402.

Aghion, P., and P. Bolton, 1992, "An 'Incomplete Contract' Approach to Bankruptcy and the Financial Structure of the Firm," *Review of Economic Studies*, 59, 473–494.

The Review of Financial Studies / v 9 n 3 1996

Baums, T., 1994, "The German Banking System and Its Impacts on Corporate Finance and Governance," EDI Working Papers 94-13, Economic Development Institute.

Berlin, M., K. John, and A. Saunders, 1993, "Should Banks Hold Equity in Borrowing Firms?," working paper, New York University.

Berlin, M., and L. Mester, 1992, "Debt Covenants and Renegotiation," *Journal of Financial Intermediation*, 2, 95–133.

Brown, S., C. James, and R. Mooradian, 1993, "The Information Content of Distressed Restructurings Involving Public and Private Debt Claims," *Journal of Financial Economics*, 33, 93–118.

Cable,J., 1985, "Capital Market Information and Industrial Performance: The Role of West German Banks," *Economic Journal*, 95, 118–132.

Diamond, D., 1993, "Seniority and Maturity Structure of Bank Loans and Directly Placed Debt," *Journal of Financial Economics*, 33, 341–368.

Edwards, J., and K. Fischer, 1994, *Banks, Finance and Investment in Germany*, Cambridge University Press, Cambridge.

Fama, E., 1990, "Contract Costs and Financing Decisions," *Journal of Business*, 63, S71–S90.

Flath, D., 1993, "Shareholding in the Keiretsu, Japan's Financial Groups," *Review of Economics and Statistics*, 77, 249–257.

Gilson, S., 1993, "Debt Reduction, Optimal Capital Structure, and Renegotiation of Claims During Financial Distress," Working Paper 94-029, Harvard University.

Gilson, S., K. John, and L. Lang, 1990, "Troubled Debt Restructurings: An Empirical Study of Private Reorganizations of Firms in Default," *Journal of Financial Economics*, 27, 315–353.

Gorton, G., and J. Kahn, 1993, "The Design of Bank Loan Contracts, Collateral, and Renegotiation," working paper, University of Pennsylvania.

Gorton, G., and F. Shmid, 1994, "Universal Banking and the Performance of German Firms," working paper, University of Pennsylvania.

Harm, C., 1993, "The Role of Universal Banks and Majority Shareholders to Overcome Financial Constraints: Evidence from German Balance Sheet Data," working paper, New York University.

Hart, O., and J. Moore, 1989, "Default and Renegotiation: A Dynamic Model of Debt," working paper, Harvard University.

Heinkel, R., and J. Zechner, 1993, "Financial Distress and Optimal Capital Structure Adjustments," working paper, University of British Columbia.

Hodder, J., 1986, "Corporate Capital Structure in the U.S. and Japan: Financial Intermediation and Implications of Financial Deregulation," working paper, Stanford University.

Hoshi, T., A. Kashyap, and D. Scharfstein, 1990, "The Role of Banks in Reducing the Costs of Financial Distress in Japan," *Journal of Financial Economics*, 27, 67–88.

Hoshi, T., A. Kashyap, and D. Scharfstein, 1991, "Corporate Structure, Liquidity, and Investment: Evidence From Japanese Industrial Groups," *Quarterly Journal of Economics*, 106, 33–60.

James, C., 1993, "When Do Banks Take Equity? An Analysis of Bank Loan Restructurings and the Role of Debt," working paper, University of Florida.

James, C., 1994, "The Mix of Private and Public Debt Claims and Capital Structure Flexibility in Financial Distress," working paper, University of Florida.

Bank Equity Stakes in Borrowing Firms and Financial Distress

Kalay, A., and J. Zender, 1992, "Bankruptcy and State Contingent Changes in the Ownership of Control," working paper, University of Utah.

Kester, W., 1991, "Japanese Corporate Governance and the Conservation of Value in Financial Distress," *Journal of Applied Corporate Finance*, 4, 98–104.

Kim, S., 1992, "Corporate Financing Through a Shareholder Bank: Lessons From Japan," working paper PB92-03, Federal Reserve Bank of San Francisco.

Pozdena, R., 1991, "Why Banks Need Commerce Powers," *Economic Review*, Federal Reserve Bank of San Francisco, 18–30.

Prowse, S., 1990, "Institutional Investment Patterns and Corporate Financial Behavior in the U.S. and Japan," *Journal of Financial Economics*, 27, 43–66.

Prowse, S., 1992, "The Structure of Corporate Ownership in Japan," *Journal of Finance*, 47, 1121–1140.

Rajan, R., 1992, "Insiders and Outsiders: The Choice Between Relationship and Armslength Debt," *Journal of Finance*, 47, 1367–1400.

Sharpe, S., 1990, "Asymmetric Information, Bank Lending and Implicit Contracts: A Stylized Model of Customer Relationships," *Journal of Finance*, 45, 1069–1087.

Slovin, M., M. Sushka, and E. Waller, 1993, "Bankruptcy Resolution, Protection of Security, Priority Rules, and Private Creditors: Market Based Evidence From Chapter 11 Filing Announcements," working paper, Arizona State University.

White, M., 1981, "Economics of Bankruptcy: Liquidation and Reorganization," Working Paper 239, Salomon Brothers Center, New York University.

Bank Underwriting of Debt Securities: Modern Evidence

Amar Gande
Vanderbilt University

Manju Puri
Stanford University

Anthony Saunders
Ingo Walter
New York University

This article examines debt securities underwritten by Section 20 subsidiaries of bank holding companies relative to those underwritten by investment houses. Consistent with a net certification effect for banks, bank underwriting of lower credit rated firms to whom the bank lends results in relatively higher prices (lower yields). We find no evidence of conflicts of interest even when an issue is used to repay bank debt. Further, banks bring a relatively larger proportion of small issues to the market. Contrary to the contention that universal banking stunts availability of finance to small firms, bank underwritings appear to benefit small firms.

There has been an extensive debate in the United States regarding the degree and the form of partici-

We thank the editors Franklin Allen and Ravi Jagannathan, two anonymous referees, and the seminar participants at the American Finance Association meetings at San Francisco, Bank Structure Conference of the Federal Reserve Bank of Chicago, European Finance Association Conference in Milan, Financial Management Association Conference in New York, Salomon Center Universal Banking Conference, Financial Economics and Accounting Conference in Maryland, Venture Capital Conference at Stanford University, Western Finance Association meetings at Sunriver, London School of Economics, New York University, University of Washington, St. Louis, and VPI for their comments. Financial support from the NYU Salomon Center is gratefully acknowledged. M. Puri thanks the Financial Research Initiative at Stanford University for financial support. Address correspondence to Anthony Saunders, Department of Finance, Stern School of Business, New York University, MEC 9-190, 44 West 4th Street, New York, NY 10012.

The Review of Financial Studies Winter 1997 Vol. 10, No. 4, pp. 1175–1202

pation by commercial banks in the underwriting of corporate securities. Commercial banks have been effectively prohibited from underwriting corporate securities by the Glass–Steagall provisions of the Banking Act of 1933, amidst concerns that combining the underwriting of these securities with lending activities presented a potential conflict of interest that was detrimental to investors.

In 1987 the Glass–Steagall provisions were relaxed, with some banks (e.g., J. P. Morgan, Bankers Trust Co.) being allowed by the Federal Reserve to set up Section 20 subsidiaries which can underwrite corporate securities. These Section 20 subsidiaries (referred to as *banks* in this article) are subject to a substantial set of *firewalls*, that limit information, resource and financial linkages between them and their respective parent holding companies as well as with their commercial banking affiliates. In addition, these subsidiaries were also limited to generating a maximum of 10% of their gross revenues from underwriting corporate securities. Proposals by the Office of Comptroller of the Currency intend to make it even simpler for commercial banks to expand into other nonbanking businesses, such as trading securities, selling real estate, insurance, and computer services. Recently the Federal Reserve has raised the limit on revenue generation from securities activities of commercial bank holding companies to 25% from the current 10%. It also dropped some of the firewalls. These relaxations are a further indication of the likelihood of banks expanding their nonbanking businesses in the future.[1] This raises questions regarding the public benefits and costs of relaxing the Glass–Steagall provisions and other regulations limiting the ability of U.S. banking organizations to expand their nonbank product set.

This article contributes to this discussion by examining the pricing and other characteristics of bank and investment house underwritings in the post-Section 20 era. It also contributes to the discussion of the optimal organizational form for bank underwritings in the post-Section 20 era.

There is a limited literature on the pricing of public security issues based on whether an underwriter is a commercial bank or an investment house. On the theoretical front, Puri (1996b) finds conditions under which a commercial bank and an investment house would, in equilibrium, price the same issue differently. The intuition for this finding can be summarized in the following manner: when

[1] For a complete discussion of the scope and limitations of firewalls on activities of Section 20 subsidiaries, see GAO (1990). For the proposal by the Comptroller of Currency's office see the Business section of the *New York Times*, November 29, 1994; for recent relaxations in the regulations surrounding Section 20 subsidiaries see the Economy section of the *Wall Street Journal*, August 1, 1996. Initially banks expanded into commercial paper in 1987, corporate debt in 1989, with equity following in 1990.

the proceeds of a debt issue are being used to refinance existing bank debt, and the underwriter is a commercial bank whose loans are being refinanced, there is a potential conflict of interest present. The commercial bank, in its role as underwriter, could try to misrepresent the quality of the security to potential buyers.[2] If the potential buyers are not naive, they realize that such a conflict might exist and therefore will adjust the price they are willing to pay for the securities in a downward direction. On the other hand, a commercial bank with a lending relationship with the issuer has the potential to efficiently obtain more accurate information on the issuer than an investment house (which has no lending exposure to the issuer). Thus, there is a trade-off: a commercial bank underwriter might have better information than an investment bank underwriter, but it might misrepresent this information to the market. When the benefit of having better information outweighs the potential conflict of interest then the commercial bank underwriter can be viewed as providing a net certification effect to investors. For example, firms issuing junior and more information-sensitive securities may receive higher prices when a bank underwrites them than when such securities are underwritten by an investment house. This is because of the perceived monitoring advantages of the bank that are a by-product of its lending activities.

The empirical evidence on the conflicts of interest in the pre-Glass–Steagall period, when there were no firewalls between a bank and its securities subsidiary, has been studied in two ways. First, several studies examine the long-run performance of bank underwritten issues as compared to investment house underwritten issues [(see Ang and Richardson (1994), Kroszner and Rajan (1994), Puri (1994)]. These studies find that commercial bank underwritten securities had a better default record in the long term than investment house underwritten securities (despite the potential conflicts of interest that were present). Second, Puri (1996a) examines ex ante pricing of corporate debt in the immediate pre-Glass-Steagall period and finds that issuers of commercial bank underwritten securities obtained higher prices ex ante than those obtained by (similar) investment house underwritten securities. This supports banks having a net certification effect that dominated any conflict of interest effect. This evidence along with the long-run performance of these issues also supports the view that investors an-

[2] The basic distinction between a commercial bank and an investment house is that an investment house underwrites securities but does not make loans, whereas a commercial bank does both. Fama (1985) argues that bank loans are a form of inside debt since the commercial bank has access to information that is not publicly available. Commercial banks acquire such private information from monitoring loans. For example, they inspect factory premises and inventory or they may be privy to investment opportunities available to the firm. On the other hand, investment houses must expend resources in collecting information. For a detailed discussion of the various kinds of potential conflicts of interest, see Saunders (1985), Benston (1990), Saunders and Walter (1994), and Walter (1985).

ticipated correctly the higher quality of bank underwritten issues.

In the light of recent developments regarding the possible expansion of nonbanking activities of banks, and the possibility of conflicts of interest, an important policy question relates to the characteristics and pricing of securities underwritten by banks and investment houses in the post-Section 20 period. Specifically our article addresses the following issues: (i) What are the characteristics of the securities underwritten by banks as compared to those underwritten by investment houses? (ii) Is there a difference in the pricing of bank and investment house underwritings and, if so, what are the implications regarding conflicts of interest and certification effects? (iii) What evidence do our results provide regarding the efficacy of firewalls in the prevention of conflicts of interest?

This article differs from the previous empirical literature in the following ways: First, it focuses on the use of the proceeds of debt issues. In particular, we analyze the conflict of interest and the certification effects by examining separately the pricing of debt underwritings when the purpose of the issue is (i) to refinance existing bank debt, and (ii) not for refinancing existing bank debt (i.e., all other reasons). Such an analysis would be extremely difficult in the pre-Glass–Steagall era since information on the purpose of the issue, while stated, was extremely noisy, given that stringent disclosure rules (such as those provided in the Securities Act of 1934) did not exist. Second, in the analysis below we explicitly control for the underlying lending relationship of the bank (through its commercial banking affiliate). Third, our article provides evidence on the implications of organizational form for the pricing of debt securities underwritten by banks as compared to those underwritten by investment houses.

The main results of the article are as follows: We find that 31% of bank underwritings are of smaller issues (less than $75 million in size), whereas only 8% of investment house underwritings are of smaller issues. Further, over time, as banks have gained underwriting experience, the average issue size that banks have underwritten has declined in absolute terms as well as relative to the average size of issues underwritten by investment houses. This evidence is consistent with a positive role of banks in bringing smaller issuers to the market and is contrary to the contention that greater (universal) banking powers may stunt small firm access to the capital market. We also find that bank underwritings, where the bank holds a significant lending stake (through its commercial banking affiliate), reduces yield spreads by 27 basis points for lower-credit rated issues (Caa-Ba3).[3] This finding is consis-

[3] The reduction of 27 basis points is per unit of the natural log of the bank's outstanding loans to the firm.

tent with the view that bank association is valuable for such issuers due to the bank's dominant certification effect. Where debt securities are issued, for purposes other than repaying existing bank debt, and where the bank retains a significant lending stake (through its commercial banking affiliate), yield spreads are reduced by 42 basis points for lower-credit (Caa-Ba3) rated issues. Where the stated purpose of an issue is to refinance existing bank debt, there is no statistically significant difference between yield spreads on similar debt issues underwritten by banks and investment houses. These results are consistent with a dominant net-certification effect of bank underwritings.

The rest of the article is organized as follows. We describe the data and sample selection in Section 1. We develop testable hypotheses in Section 2. In Section 3 we explain our test methodology. Section 4 discusses the empirical results. Section 5 concludes.

1. Data and Sample Selection

We employ the following criteria for the selection of the sample period. First, the sample needs to consist of both bank and investment house underwritings — that is, the sample should begin no earlier than January 1989, when J. P. Morgan Securities (the Section 20 subsidiary of J. P. Morgan Inc.) underwrote the first public corporate bond issue by a bank since the Glass–Steagall Act. Second, to ensure that the test results are representative, the sample must have a nontrivial number of issues underwritten by banks. Third, in devising econometric tests examining bank-specific effects, it is necessary to control for other factors such as the issuer's credit rating, size of the issue, purpose of the issue, underlying security (collateral), underlying lending relationship, maturity, and the term structure of risk-free (treasury) yields. Data on these variables must also be available for the entire sample period. Finally, the sample should be selected from a period during which there was relative stability in economic and regulatory conditions.

Based on these considerations, we define our sample period as January 1, 1993 to March 31, 1995 — approximately $2\frac{1}{4}$ years. We exclude financial firms (one-digit SIC code 6) and firms in regulated industries (one-digit SIC code 4) from our study since: (i) the nature of any conflict of interest among financial firms may be significantly different from that among nonfinancial firms, and (ii) the absence of regulation contrasts firms in nonregulated industries from those in regulated industries. Additionally, we focus on the top 20 underwriters (rankings based on dollar value of underwritings) of fixed-rate nonconvertible debt. For our sample, 4 of the top 20 underwriters are Section 20 subsidiaries of money center banks, namely J. P. Morgan, Bankers Trust, Citibank, and Chase Manhattan Bank. Our sample consists of 670 fixed-rate U.S. nonconvertible debt issues. Of these 80 (approximately 12%) issues were underwritten by Section 20 subsidiaries.

Information about these issues, such as date of issuance, offering yield to maturity, the principal underwriter, syndicate members, the underlying collateral, the size of the issue, the maturity of the debt, etc., was obtained from the Securities Data Corporation, Inc. (SDC). The sample is constructed from the U.S. domestic public new-issues database of SDC. The SDC database is compiled from regulatory filings, news sources, company press releases, and prospectuses.[4]

However, the SDC database does not tell us which companies have bank loans outstanding. For this purpose we use the Dealscan database compiled by the Loan Pricing Corporation. This database comprises information about loans over $100,000 in size to firms filing SEC 13-Ds, 14-Ds, 13-Es, 10-Ks, 10-Qs, 8-Ks, and registration filings (S-series filings) which were outstanding at the beginning of our sample period.[5] The database consists largely of publicly held companies, and privately held companies with public debt outstanding, which are required to file these forms with the SEC.

The dependent and independent variables are explained in the next section. Appendix A.1 to this article provides a complete description of the construction of these variables from the SDC and the Dealscan databases.

Test Hypotheses

2.1 Characteristics

We examine the impact of greater universal banking powers on smaller firms in terms of their capital market access. A possible hypothesis is that greater universal banking powers stunt capital market access to smaller firms since larger banks tend to concentrate customer relationships on larger firms/clients.[6] Alternately, banks, through the private information at their disposal, and their certification role as monitors, can potentially help smaller firms gain greater access to the capital market.

[4] SDC claims that it double-checks public sources by surveying underwriters, financial advisors, law firms, and other deal makers.

[5] We thank Mark Carey for assisting us with the Dealscan database.

[6] This concern has been raised at various times regarding German universal banks.

2.2 Pricing of bank versus investment house underwritings

We also analyze the pricing of debt securities underwritten by Section 20 subsidiaries relative to those underwritten by investment houses. Specifically, the current organizational form of a Section 20 subsidiary is similar to a regular bank holding company affiliate, but with more restrictions on its activities. This is due to the presence of a set of firewalls which severely limit the informational, financial, and real resource interlinks among the Section 20 subsidiary, the bank holding company (parent), and its commercial banking affiliate. If these firewalls are binding — that is, if they prevent conflict of interest exploitation and informed certification — one may expect to find no significant difference in the pricing of similar securities among investment houses and Section 20 subsidiaries.[7] However, if these firewalls are nonbinding and if the informed certification effect of banks outweighs any potential conflict of interest effects, we should expect to find bank underwritings priced higher (have lower yields) than similar investment house underwritings. Alternatively, if potential conflicts of interest are perceived by investors to be greater than any informed certification effect, bank underwritings will be priced lower (have higher yields) than similar issues underwritten by investment houses. Thus our results provide insights regarding the relative strength of any certification and conflict of interest effects, as well as the efficacy of firewalls.

We hypothesize that, should conflicts of interest be present, they are most likely to be found in cases where the purpose of an issue is to refinance existing bank loans. In particular, yields should be highest on debt issues underwritten by banks (relative to those of similar underwritings by investment houses) whose purpose is to refinance bank loans. Further, since any potential conflict of interest will depend on the extent of the underlying lending exposure of the commercial banking affiliate — the higher the lending exposure of the commercial banking affiliate the higher will be required yield spreads (since rational investors impound any such potential conflicts of interest into a security's price).

We also hypothesize that where conflict of interest incentives are potentially small or are absent, that is, where debt securities are not issued for the purpose of refinancing bank loans, there may be a positive role for an informed certification effect by banks. In other words, yields should be lowest on bank underwritings (relative to those of similar underwritings by investment houses) of those debt

[7] This assumes similar distributional abilities across banks and investment houses. The fact that our sample period starts 4 years after the granting of debt underwriting powers gives Section 20 subsidiaries sufficient time to have established distributional channels for underwriting new issues by themselves.

The Review of Financial Studies / v 10 n 4 1997

issues whose purpose is not to refinance existing bank debt. Further, such informed certification will depend on the extent of the underlying lending exposure of the commercial banking affiliate, that is, the higher its lending exposure, the higher is the informed certification effect and hence the lower will be yield spreads (since rational investors are willing to pay more for the informed certification of the issuer).

Methodology

3.1 Characteristics

In our study we use univariate *t* tests and probit regression models to examine the characteristics of bank versus investment house underwritings. The dependent variable for the probit regressions is BANK which is a dummy variable that takes the value of 1 if the lead underwriter is a bank (Section 20 subsidiary) and 0 otherwise (an investment house). The independent variables for the probit regression are the same as those for the linear regressions (described in the next section 3.2).

3.2 Pricing of bank versus investment house underwritings

We use linear regression models to examine the determinants of ex ante yield premiums on debt securities. The construction of the variables from the SDC and Dealscan databases is explained in Appendix A.1. The dependent variable BPS (basis points spread) is the premium of the ex ante yield spread of a debt security over the ex ante yield of a U.S. Treasury security of comparable maturity. The independent variables used to explain this spread are

LN(STAKE): The natural log of 1 plus STAKE, the outstanding lending exposure to the issuer (in millions of dollars) by the commercial banking affiliate of the Section 20 subsidiary.[8]

EXCHANGE: A dummy variable that takes the value 1 if the firm is listed on an exchange and 0 otherwise.

LN(AMOUNT): The natural log of the size of the issue (in millions of dollars).

REF BK DEBT: A dummy variable that is 1 if the purpose of the issue is to refinance existing bank debt and 0 otherwise.

[8] By construction, STAKE is positive for all bank underwritings with outstanding lending exposure by the commercial banking affiliate of the underwriting Section 20 subsidiary and 0 for all other underwritings (including all investment house underwritings). We also use another measure PROP(STAKE) = STAKE/AMOUNT for the outstanding lending exposure, where STAKE is the outstanding lending exposure to the issuer by the commercial banking affiliate of the underwriting Section 20 subsidiary and AMOUNT is the size of the issue.

SECURED: A dummy variable that is 1 if the issue has underlying collateral and 0 otherwise. This variable is created based on the description of the security.

NEW ISSUE: A dummy variable that is 1 if the issue is a first-time issue by the firm (a debt IPO). This variable is created in the following manner: If the company did not have a debt issue during the 20 years prior to the sample period, it is assumed to be a first-time issue.

INDUSTRY: Stands for a set of industry dummy variables based on one-digit primary SIC codes. For example, if the primary SIC code is 861, the one-digit primary SIC code is 8. The corresponding dummy variable is 1 and all other industry dummy variables are 0.

CREDIT RATING: Stands for a set of seven credit rating dummy variables (Caa-C, B1-B3, Ba1-Ba3, Baa1-Baa3, A1-A3, Aa1-Aa3, Aaa) based on Moody's credit rating for the debt issue. For example, B1–B3 is a dummy variable which is 1 if Moody's credit rating for the issue is B1, B2, or B3. The dummy variable is 0 otherwise.

REPUTATION: Three dummy variables based on the market share rank of dollar volume of underwritings of debt issues in our sample. LOWREP is 1 if the rank based on market share is between 16 and 20. MEDREP is 1 if the rank is between 11 and 15. HIREP is 1 if the rank is between 1 and 10. The dummy variables are 0 otherwise.

MATURITY: Stands for three dummy variables based on the maturity of the security. We classify the security issues into three separate categories based on the maturity and form three dummy variables. LOWMAT is 1 if the security matures in less than 5 years. MEDMAT is 1 if it matures in 5 to 15 years. HIMAT is 1 if the maturity is greater than 15 years. The dummy variables are 0 otherwise.

3.3 Discussion of variables

The credit rating of the issue is clearly important. One would expect that higher-credit rated issues should have lower yield spreads over Treasuries than lower-credit rated issues. As larger offerings are likely to be associated with less uncertainty than smaller offerings, be more liquid, and have more public information associated with them, one would also expect larger issues to have lower yields. A new (debt IPO) issue is potentially associated with greater uncertainty than a seasoned issue and should result in relatively higher yield spreads. Underlying security (collateral) may affect the yield spread either positively or negatively. The practitioner's view associates a large amount of collateral with a higher degree of issuer riskiness, and hence should be associated with higher yields, that is, collateral and ex ante yield spread are positively related [see, e.g., Berger and Udell (1990)]. Alternatively, a large amount of collateral enhances the amount investors expect to receive in the event of an issuer default. In such a case, collateral and ex ante yield spread may be negatively related. The purpose (or use of funds) of the issue can also potentially affect the ex ante yield spread. In particular, where the purpose is to refinance existing bank debt, and investors believe firewalls are nonbinding (i.e., that the firm has been induced to issue new public debt to pay down existing bank loans that are at risk), one would expect a positive effect on the yield spread.[9] Underwriter reputation is also important [see Beatty and Ritter (1986)] and one would expect a high reputation to reduce yield spreads. Further, one might also expect reputation to, in part, proxy for placing ability and/or distribution network. Maturity is another variable potentially affecting spreads. In particular, if the probability of default increases with debt maturity [see Flannery (1986)] then we should expect to see higher yield spreads with longer maturity issues. A firm listed on an exchange is associated with more information production, and one would expect a debt issue of such a firm to have lower yield spreads (priced higher). Finally, the impact on yield spreads of a bank underwriting a debt issue while an underlying lending relationship exists (through its commercial banking affiliate) relative to a similar issue underwritten by an investment house with no direct or indirect lending powers[10] is measured by the magnitude and the significance of the coefficient on the LN(STAKE) variable [and alternatively, of the coefficient on PROP(STAKE)]. In the absence of conflicts of interest and certification effects, and with firewalls binding, this variable should have no significant effect on yield spreads.

4. Empirical Results

4.1 Characteristics

We find that banks are more likely than investment houses to underwrite smaller issues. For example, 31% (25 out of 80 cases) of bank underwritings in our sample were less than $75 million in size, whereas 8% (47 out of 590 cases) of investment house underwritings were less

[9] However, if the firewalls are not breached, discontinuation (or a reduction) of the bank's lending association with a customer may be a potentially negative signal of the firm's prospects such that investors demand higher yields. While there is no evidence on the effect of nonrenewal of lending decisions on stock returns, Lummer and McConnell (1989) find that renewal of loans, even on worse terms, to distressed firms have a positive announcement effect, that is, some loans are better than no loans. James (1987) also finds a significant announcement effect for private placement debt issues used to repay loans.

[10] It might be noted that some investment banks have recently set up wholesale lending units to compete with banks. However, there is currently no publicly available information on the range of these activities.

than \$75 million in size (see Table 1). Using a univariate *t* test, we find that this difference is significant at the 1% level. We also conducted a univariate test of the difference in average issue size of bank and investment house underwritings. The mean issue size of bank underwritings was \$107 million, whereas that of investment houses was \$189 million. The difference is statistically significant at the 1% level. This result is consistent with the view that established investment houses have neglected smaller issuers. While it may be true that Section 20 subsidiaries of the commercial banks were new to underwriting, and may have been forced initially to focus on smaller issues to gain expertise — our sample period starts 4 years after the granting of debt underwriting powers, which presumably would have allowed them sufficient time to establish distributional channels for underwriting all sizes of issues and to gain the necessary expertise to compete with investment banks for larger issues if they so chose. As an additional check, we also examine the trends in average issue size underwritten by banks over time. The average issue size underwritten by banks actually declined over time in absolute terms from \$137.50 million in the first quarter of 1993 to \$54.55 million in the first quarter of 1995 (see Table 2). In relative terms, the average issue size underwritten by banks was 64% of the average issue size underwritten by investment houses in the first quarter of 1993, declining to 23% in the first quarter of 1995. Since small-size issues are usually associated with smaller companies, we find evidence consistent with banks playing a positive role in bringing debt issues of smaller companies to the capital market. That is, there is no evidence that greater universal banking powers of banking organizations has stunted capital market access for such firms.

We also find evidence that banks bring a larger proportion of lower-credit rated (Caa-Ba3) issuers to the market than investment houses, both in terms of number of issues (43% as compared to 38%) and the dollar volume of such issues (52% as compared to 36%), which supports the view that bank underwriting is net beneficial to such firms.

The probit results (see Table 3) provide further corroboration. The probit results suggest that the main factor determining whether a bank underwrites a debt issue is the smallness of issue size. In addition, banks do not have a higher probability of underwriting debt issues whose purpose is to refinance existing bank debt than investment houses.

4.2 Pricing results

We included all the variables discussed in Section 3 in our multivariate linear regression. The results in the following three cases are summarized below: (i) all debt issues, (ii) all debt issues whose purpose is

The Review of Financial Studies / v 10 n 4 1997

Table 1
Descriptive statistics of our sample

Segment	Bank Issues No.	Bank Issues Volume ($m)	Investment House Issues No.	Investment House Issues Volume ($m)	All Issues No.	All Issues Volume ($m)
Issue Size						
Small	25	418.00	47	1,990.00	72	2,408.00
Medium	49	6,410.00	385	50,328.90	434	56,378.90
Large	6	1,725.00	158	58,977.90	164	60,702.90
Maturity						
Low	8	365.00	58	8,046.70	66	8,411.70
Medium	64	7,228.00	403	75,268.40	467	82,496.40
High	8	960.00	129	27,981.70	137	28,941.70
Exchange-listed						
Yes	61	5,665.00	423	77,427.80	484	83,092.80
No	19	2,888.00	167	33,869.00	186	36,757.00
Credit Rating						
Caa-Ba3	34	4,435.00	221	40,351.10	225	44,786.10
Baa1-Aaa	46	4,118.00	369	70,945.70	415	75,063.70
Secured						
Yes	13	1,980.00	94	14,751.30	107	16,731.30
No	67	6,573.00	496	96,545.50	563	103,118.50
New Debt Issues						
Yes	28	3,646.00	199	32,739.10	227	36,385.10
No	52	4,907.00	391	78,557.70	443	83,464.70
Reputation						
Low	5	435.00	10	1,190.00	15	1,625.00
Medium	46	4,168.00	23	3,350.00	69	7,518.00
High	29	3,950.00	557	106,756.80	586	110,706.80
Total	80	8,553.00	590	111,296.80	670	119,849.80

This table classifies our sample based on (1) issue size into small (less than $75 million), medium (between $75 million and $150 million) and large (greater than $150 million) segments, (2) maturity into low (less than 5 years), medium (between 5 and 15 years), and high (greater than 15 years) segments, (3) whether the firm is listed on an exchange, (4) based on Moody's credit rating into lower-credit rated (Caa-Ba3) and higher-credit rated (Baa1-Aaa) categories, (5) whether secured, (6) whether a new debt issue, and (6) a reputation measure determined by the market share rank of the dollar volume of underwriting into low (ranked between 16 and 20), medium (ranked between 11 and 15), and high (ranked between 1 and 10). In addition, within each of these segments, the issues are classified as bank (Section 20) underwritings and investment house underwritings.

to refinance existing bank debt, and (iii) all debt issues whose purpose is not to refinance existing bank debt. As stated above, potential conflicts of interest should be most prominent in the group (ii) issues.

4.2.1 All debt issues. Specifically, we run the regression

$$\begin{aligned} \text{BPS} = {} & \beta_0 + \beta_1\,\text{LN(STAKE)} + \beta_2\,\text{EXCHANGE} + \beta_3\,\text{LN(AMOUNT)} \\ & + \beta_4\,\text{REF BK DEBT} + \beta_5\,\text{SECURED} + \beta_6\,\text{NEW ISSUE} \\ & + \beta_{\text{ind}}\,\text{INDUSTRY} + \beta_{\text{cr}}\,\text{CREDIT RATING} \\ & + \beta_{\text{rep}}\,\text{REPUTATION} + \beta_{\text{mat}}\,\text{MATURITY}. \end{aligned} \tag{1}$$

Table 2
Average issue size over time and by underwriter type

Year: Quarter	Bank Issues (average issue size, $m)	Investment House Issues (average issue size, $m)
1993:Q1	137.50	215.78
1993:Q2	149.80	193.17
1993:Q3	133.50	173.60
1993:Q4	89.46	193.70
1994:Q1	108.00	172.94
1994:Q2	125.70	168.35
1994:Q3	86.00	162.62
1994:Q4	59.17	166.81
1995:Q1	54.55	232.81
1993–1995(Q1)	106.91	188.64

This table presents the average issue size (in millions of dollars) of debt securities underwritten by banks and investment houses for each quarter for our sample period.

The regression results[11] are presented in Table 4. We find that controlling for the underlying lending relationship, there is no statistically significant difference between the yield spreads on similar debt issues underwritten by banks and investment houses [i.e., the coefficient on the variable LN(STAKE) is not statistically significant]. As hypothesized in Section 4.3, we find that higher-credit rated issues lead to lower yield spreads — the coefficient on the credit rating dummies are positive and decline for higher-credit rating dummies. The coefficients on other independent variables have the expected signs (see Section 4.3) and are statistically significant or marginally significant in most cases.

When we divided the sample by credit ratings, bank underwritings relative to investment house underwritings reduce yield spreads by 27 basis points for lower-credit rated (Caa-Ba3) issues (see Table 5) for a one-unit increase of LN(STAKE). Based on the definition of LN(STAKE), and since one unit of LN(STAKE) translates to $1.7183 million of lending exposure, bank underwritings reduce yield spreads by 16 basis points per $1 million of lending exposure to the issuer (through its commercial banking affiliate). This finding is consistent with the view that bank association is valuable for lower-credit rated issues due to a net certification effect that dominates any potential conflict of interest effect. We also used another measure of outstanding lending exposure, as a proportion of the issue size, PROP(STAKE) = (STAKE/AMOUNT). The results are qualitatively similar.

[11] We have seven credit ratings, only six of which can be included to avoid linear dependence. We exclude the Aaa dummy in this regression. For the same reason, we exclude LOWREP, MEDMAT, and the industry dummy corresponding to the one-digit SIC code 9 in all the linear regressions.

Table 3
Probit estimations — bank versus investment house underwritings

Variable	Coefficient		T ratio
INTERCEPT	−1.24		−0.01
LN(STAKE)	2.58		0.07
EXCHANGE	−0.32		−1.54
LN(AMOUNT)	−0.70		−5.93[a]
SECURED	−0.09		−0.44
REF BK DEBT	0.17		1.05
NEW ISSUE	0.12		0.07
LOWMAT	−0.89		−2.19[c]
HIMAT	−0.19		−0.84
p-value		0.0000	
Observations		670	
Pseudo R^2		0.3840	

This table presents results of the probit regression. The dependent variable is a dummy variable, BANK, assigned the value 1 if the lead underwriter is a Section 20 subsidiary. The independent variables used in this table are LN(STAKE) is the natural log of 1 plus STAKE, the outstanding lending exposure by the commercial banking affiliate of the bank underwriter (Section 20 subsidiary) to the issuer at the time of issuance of the debt issue. EXCHANGE is a dummy variable which is 1 if the firm is listed on an exchange. LN(AMOUNT) is the natural logarithm of the offered dollar amount of the issue (in millions of dollars). SECURED is a dummy variable which is 1 if the issue is secured. REF BK DEBT is a dummy variable which is 1 if the purpose of the issue is to refinance existing bank debt. NEW ISSUE is a dummy variable which is 1 if the issue is a first time issue. INDUSTRY is a the set of industry dummy variables constructed based on one digit SIC codes. MATURITY stands for three dummy variables based on maturity of the security. LOWMAT is 1 if the issue matures in less than 5 years, MEDMAT is 1 for 5 to 15 years, and HIMAT is 1 if the maturity is greater than 15 years. All dummy variables are 0 otherwise. Pseudo R^2 is the likelihood ratio computed as $R^2 = 1 - \log L/\log L_0$ where $\log L$ is the maximized value of the log-likelihood function, $\log L_0$ is the log-likelihood computed only with a constant term. The point estimates and T ratios for the industry dummys are not reported though they are included in the regressions. The estimation was also conducted with the full set of independent variables. The results are qualitatively similar. a, b, and c stand for significant at 0.01, 0.025, and 0.05 level using a two-tailed test.

We next looked at whether this holds true across different credit rating classes, when the purpose of the issue is (i) to refinance existing bank debt, and (ii) not to refinance existing bank debt.

4.2.2 Debt issues whose purpose is to refinance existing bank debt. As hypothesized earlier, if conflicts of interest are present, they are most likely to be found in cases where the purpose of an issue is to refinance existing bank debt. Specifically, we run the following regression across each credit rating category (Caa-Ba3 versus Baa1-Aaa) for those debt issues whose purpose is to refinance existing bank debt:

$$\text{BPS} = \beta_0 + \beta_1\,\text{LN(STAKE)} + \beta_2\,\text{EXCHANGE} + \beta_3\,\text{LN(AMOUNT)}$$

Table 4
Multivariate tests for bank versus investment house underwritings

Variable	Coefficient	*T* ratio
INTERCEPT	68.73	1.44
LN(STAKE)	−5.28	−1.51
EXCHANGE	−22.05	−2.86[a]
LN(AMOUNT)	−5.39	−1.47
REF BK DEBT	14.33	2.49[b]
SECURED	21.69	2.74[a]
NEW ISSUE	19.41	2.87[a]
Ca-C	522.21	12.77[a]
B1-B3	395.76	13.36[a]
Ba1-Ba3	247.15	8.15[a]
Baa1-Baa3	67.84	2.32[b]
A1-A3	31.83	1.10
Aa1-Aa3	18.72	0.62
LOWREP	−10.05	−0.50
HIREP	−23.38	−2.26[b]
LOWMAT	−20.75	−1.92
HIMAT	25.75	3.32[a]
Observations	670	
Adjusted R^2 = 0.8669		

This table gives the OLS estimates of the following equation:

$$\begin{aligned} BPS = {} & \beta_0 + \beta_1\,\text{LN(STAKE)} + \beta_2\,\text{EXCHANGE} + \beta_3\,\text{LN(AMOUNT)} + \beta_4\,\text{REF BK DEBT} \\ & + \beta_5\,\text{SECURED} + \beta_6\,\text{NEW ISSUE} + \beta_{ind}\,\text{INDUSTRY} + \beta_{cr}\,\text{CREDIT RATING} \\ & + \beta_{rep}\,\text{REPUTATION} + \beta_{mat}\,\text{MATURITY}. \end{aligned}$$

The dependent variable BPS is the premium of the ex ante yield of a security over the ex ante yield of a Treasury of comparable maturity in basis points. The independent variables are LN(STAKE) is the natural log of 1 plus STAKE, the outstanding lending exposure by the commercial banking affiliate of the bank underwriter (Section 20 subsidiary) to the issuer at the time of issuance of the debt issue. EXCHANGE is a dummy variable which is 1 if the firm is listed on an exchange. LN(AMOUNT) is the natural logarithm of the offered dollar amount of the issue (in millions of dollars). REF BK DEBT is a dummy variable which is 1 if the purpose of the issue is to refinance existing bank debt. SECURED is a dummy variable which is 1 if the issue is secured. NEW ISSUE is a dummy variable which is 1 if the issue is a first-time issue. INDUSTRY is a set of industry dummy variables constructed based on one digit SIC codes. CREDIT RATING is a set of credit rating dummy variables. For example, B1–B3 is a dummy variable which is 1 if Moody's credit rating for the issue is B1, B2, or B3. REPUTATION stands for three dummy variables based on market share rank of dollar volume of underwritings of debt issues in our sample. We consider the issues underwritten by the top 20 underwriters in this study. LOWREP is 1 if the rank based on market share is between 16 and 20. MEDREP is 1 if the rank is between 11 and 15. HIREP is 1 if the rank is between 1 and 10. MATURITY stands for three dummy variables based on maturity of the security. LOWMAT is 1 if the issue matures in less than 5 years, MEDMAT is 1 for 5 to 15 years, and HIMAT is 1 if the maturity is greater than 15 years. All dummy variables are 0 otherwise. The point estimates and *T* ratios for the industry dummys are not reported though they are included in the regressions. a, b, and c stand for significant at 0.01, 0.025 and 0.05 level using a two-tailed test.

$$\begin{aligned} & + \beta_4\,\text{SECURED} + \beta_5\,\text{NEW ISSUE} + \beta_{ind}\,\text{INDUSTRY} \\ & + \beta_{rep}\,\text{REPUTATION} + \beta_{mat}\,\text{MATURITY}. \qquad (2) \end{aligned}$$

We find the LN(STAKE) is economically and statistically insignificant (see Table 6) at any meaningful level of significance. This is consistent with investors perceiving either an absence of conflicts of

Table 5
Multivariate tests for bank versus investment house underwritings of debt issues segmented by credit rating category

	Caa-Ba3		Baa1-Aaa	
Variable	Coeff	T ratio	Coeff	T ratio
INTERCEPT	591.54	5.36[a]	56.27	4.37[a]
LN(STAKE)	−27.21	−2.93[a]	0.63	0.28
EXCHANGE	−63.85	−3.72[a]	−17.98	−2.95[a]
LN(AMOUNT)	−32.63	−2.35[b]	−1.16	−0.53
REF BK DEBT	32.41	2.09[c]	13.23	3.64[a]
SECURED	28.10	1.60	15.42	2.32[b]
NEW ISSUE	28.53	1.67	14.61	3.19[a]
LOWREP	−41.94	−0.91	−20.53	−1.38
HIREP	−46.47	−2.09[c]	0.11	0.01
LOWMAT	*	*	−21.67	−4.07[a]
HIMAT	−98.72	−1.11	18.59	4.92[a]
Observations	255		415	
Adjusted R^2	0.2099		0.2689	

This table gives the OLS estimates of the following equation:

$$\begin{aligned} \text{BPS} = {} & \beta_0 + \beta_1 \text{ LN(STAKE)} + \beta_2 \text{ EXCHANGE} + \beta_3 \text{ LN(AMOUNT)} + \beta_4 \text{ REF BK DEBT} \\ & + \beta_5 \text{SECURED} + \beta_6 \text{ NEW ISSUE} + \beta_{\text{ind}} \text{ INDUSTRY} + \beta_{\text{rep}} \text{ REPUTATION} \\ & + \beta_{\text{mat}} \text{ MATURITY} \end{aligned}$$

The dependent variable BPS is the premium of the ex ante yield of a security over the ex ante yield of a treasury of comparable maturity in basis points. The independent variables are LN(STAKE) is the natural log of 1 plus STAKE, the outstanding lending exposure by the commercial banking affiliate of the bank underwriter (Section 20 subsidiary) to the issuer at the time of issuance of the debt issue. EXCHANGE is a dummy variable which is 1 if the firm is listed on an exchange. LN(AMOUNT) is the natural logarithm of the offered dollar amount of the issue (in millions of dollars). SECURED is a dummy variable which is 1 if the issue is secured. NEW ISSUE is a dummy variable which is 1 if the issue is a first time issue. INDUSTRY is a the set of industry dummy variables constructed based on one digit SIC codes. REPUTATION stands for three dummy variables based on market share rank of dollar volume of underwritings of debt issues in our sample. We consider the issues underwritten by the top 20 underwriters in this study. LOWREP is 1 if the rank based on market share is between 16 and 20. MEDREP is 1 if the rank is between 11 and 15. HIREP is 1 if the rank is between 1 and 10. MATURITY stands for three dummy variables based on maturity of the security. LOWMAT is 1 if the issue matures in less than 5 years, MEDMAT is 1 for 5 to 15 years, and HIMAT is 1 if the maturity is greater than 15 years. All dummy variables are 0 otherwise. The point estimates and T ratios for the industry dummys are not reported though they are included in the regressions. The asterisk (*) indicates that none of the issues are of low maturity. a, b, and c stand for significant at 0.01, 0.025, and 0.05 level using a two-tailed test.

interest or that the firewalls were effective in containing the conflict of interest.

4.2.3 Debt issues whose purpose is to not to refinance existing bank debt. Interestingly, in the case when debt proceeds are to be used for purposes other than refinancing bank debt, the effect of bank underwritings (controlling for underlying lending relationship) is to lower yield spreads by 42 basis points — statistically significant at the 1% level (t statistic 2.63) for the lowest credit quality (Caa-Ba3) issues (see Table 7). These results also hold when we employ

Table 6
Multivariate tests for bank versus investment house underwritings of debt issues which are used for refinancing existing bank debt segmented by credit rating category

	Caa-Ba3		Baa1-Aaa	
Variable	Coeff	T ratio	Coeff	T ratio
INTERCEPT	751.17	6.82[a]	100.39	2.23[c]
LN(STAKE)	−16.09	−1.34	−1.81	−0.43
EXCHANGE	−90.51	−4.09[a]	−25.76	−2.10[c]
LN(AMOUNT)	−48.03	−2.36[b]	−3.35	−0.54
SECURED	−5.05	−0.22	0.52	0.02
NEW ISSUE	15.19	0.67	13.64	1.60
LOWREP	−36.72	−0.68	−14.51	−0.42
HIREP	−73.36	−2.49[b]	1.90	0.08
LOWMAT	*	*	−34.33	−2.59[a]
HIMAT	*	*	18.83	2.55[b]
Observations	144		148	
Adjusted R^2	0.1794		0.0679	

This table gives the OLS estimates of the following equation:

$$\begin{aligned}\text{BPS} = {} & \beta_0 + \beta_1\,\text{LN(STAKE)} + \beta_2\,\text{EXCHANGE} + \beta_3\,\text{LN(AMOUNT)} + \beta_4\,\text{SECURED} \\ & + \beta_5\,\text{NEW ISSUE} + \beta_{\text{ind}}\,\text{INDUSTRY} + \beta_{\text{rep}}\,\text{REPUTATION} \\ & + \beta_{\text{mat}}\,\text{MATURITY}\end{aligned}$$

The dependent variable BPS is the premium of the ex ante yield of a security over the ex ante yield of a treasury of comparable maturity in basis points. The independent variables are LN(STAKE) is the natural log of 1 plus STAKE, the outstanding lending exposure by the commercial banking affiliate of the bank underwriter (Section 20 subsidiary) to the issuer at the time of issuance of the debt issue. EXCHANGE is a dummy variable which is 1 if the firm is listed on an exchange. LN(AMOUNT) is the natural logarithm of the offered dollar amount of the issue (in millions of dollars). SECURED is a dummy variable which is 1 if the issue is secured. NEW ISSUE is a dummy variable which is 1 if the issue is a first time issue. INDUSTRY is a set of industry dummy variables constructed based on one-digit SIC codes. REPUTATION stands for three dummy variables based on market share rank of dollar volume of underwritings of debt issues in our sample. We consider the issues underwritten by the top 20 underwriters in this study. LOWREP is 1 if the rank based on market share is between 16 and 20. MEDREP is 1 if the rank is between 11 and 15. HIREP is 1 if the rank is between 1 and 10. MATURITY stands for three dummy variables based on maturity of the security. LOWMAT is 1 if the issue matures in less than 5 years, MEDMAT is 1 for 5 to 15 years, and HIMAT is 1 if the maturity is greater than 15 years. All dummy variables are 0 otherwise. The point estimates and T ratios for the industry dummys are not reported though they are included in the regressions. The asterisk (*) indicates that all issues are of medium maturity. a, b, and c stand for significant at 0.01, 0.025, and 0.05 level using a two-tailed test.

the second (alternative) measure of outstanding lending exposure, PROP(STAKE), as can be seen in Table 8. This yield spread lowering supports a certification effect of banks' underwriting debt issues of relatively risky firms while a lending relationship with the issuer exists (through its commercial banking affiliate).[12] For higher-credit rated

[12] Our conclusion that there is a dominant certification effect in commercial bank underwritings is similar to that of Puri (1996a), but differs from that of subsequent work by Kroszner and Rajan (1997). Puri analyzes, in the pre-Glass-Steagall period, pricing differentials of securities underwritten by commercial banks and investment houses, including those by departments and affiliates

(Baa1-Aaa) issues, we find LN(STAKE) is statistically insignificant.

We also conducted several robustness checks. The first deals with the maturity of issues. We included a continuous variable equal to the maturity of an issue instead of our dummy variables based on short-term and long-term maturity of the debt issue. We also reestimated the regressions using the natural log of maturity. In both cases the results are qualitatively similar. Second, since our definition of reputation might be proxying for the new issue distribution network, and the distribution network might differ between banks and investment houses (as suggested by a referee), we interacted the reputation dummy variables with underwriter type. Our results again are qualitatively similar to those reported earlier. Third, differences in call provisions of bonds underwritten by banks and investment houses may also bias our results. While there are no easy ways to control for call provisions, we perform the following checks: (i) We checked if the presence of call provisions depended on the underwriter type (i.e., whether the underwriter is a bank or an investment house). In our sample, 43% of bank underwritings are callable, whereas 44% of investment house underwritings are callable. The chi-square test fails to reject the null that presence of call provisions is independent of the underwriter type — suggesting that on average, the call provisions of bonds underwritten by banks and investment houses were similar. (ii) We examined the extent of call protection of bonds underwritten by banks and investment houses. The call protection of callable bonds underwritten by banks was 5.27 years as compared to 5.64 years of callable bonds underwritten by investment houses, a difference not statistically significant at the 5% level. (iii) The average call premium on callable bonds underwritten by banks was 4%, marginally higher than the 3.7% premium on callable bonds underwritten by investment houses; however, this difference was also not statistically significant at the 5% level. Thus the evidence shows call provisions were, on average, similar for bank and investment house underwritings. Fourth,

of commercial banks whereas Kroszner and Rajan (KR) focus solely on the latter dichotomy. KR conclude that conflicts of interest led commercial banks to evolve to an affiliate structure to underwrite securities. However, this interpretation is questionable for the following reasons: First, regulations favored an affiliate structure. Only after the 1927 McFadden Act were national banks explicitly allowed to underwrite securities. Additionally, affiliates could be chartered under state laws as limited liability corporations; could help evade interstate branching restrictions; had no minimal capital requirements; and could do almost anything "except solemnize marriages and perform religious ceremonies" (U.S. Senate, 1934, p. 4776). Finally, KR had no access to direct lending data. Since both departments and affiliates could lend to firms, better prices for affiliate underwritings might simply reflect that affiliates lent more than departments to issuers in their sample. This would support a certification rather than a conflict of interest effect. In contrast, since only banks can lend, it is easier to interpret which effect dominates by comparing bank and investment house underwritings, as in Puri (1996a), or by gathering direct lending data, as done here; both approaches indicate a dominant certification effect.

Table 7
Multivariate tests for bank versus investment house underwritings of debt issues which are not used for refinancing existing bank debt segmented by credit rating category

	Caa-Ba3		Baa1-Aaa	
Variable	Coeff	T ratio	Coeff	T ratio
INTERCEPT	530.91	3.82[a]	39.59	3.04[a]
LN(STAKE)	−41.63	−2.63[a]	3.17	1.20
EXCHANGE	−36.56	−1.23	−14.15	−1.98[c]
LN(AMOUNT)	−29.12	−1.41	−0.32	−0.14
SECURED	47.13	1.52	16.44	2.49[b]
NEW ISSUE	46.99	1.63	17.99	3.29[a]
LOWREP	−138.62	−1.47	−15.98	−0.95
HIREP	−25.86	−0.71	3.54	0.38
LOWMAT	*	*	−15.55	−2.81[a]
HIMAT	−109.92	−1.12	17.55	4.14[a]
Observations	111		267	
Adjusted R^2	0.2219		0.3789	

This table gives the OLS estimates of the following equation:

$$\begin{aligned}\text{BPS} = {} & \beta_0 + \beta_1\,\text{LN(STAKE)} + \beta_2\,\text{EXCHANGE} + \beta_3\,\text{LN(AMOUNT)} + \beta_4\,\text{SECURED} \\ & + \beta_5\,\text{NEW ISSUE} + \beta_{\text{ind}}\,\text{INDUSTRY} + \beta_{\text{rep}}\,\text{REPUTATION} + \beta_{\text{mat}}\,\text{MATURITY}\end{aligned}$$

The dependent variable BPS is the premium of the ex ante yield of a security over the ex ante yield of a treasury of comparable maturity in basis points. The independent variables are LN(STAKE) is the natural log of 1 plus STAKE, the outstanding lending exposure by the commercial banking affiliate of the bank underwriter (Section 20 subsidiary) to the issuer at the time of issuance of the debt issue. EXCHANGE is a dummy variable which is 1 if the firm is listed on an exchange. LN(AMOUNT) is the natural logarithm of the offered dollar amount of the issue (in millions of dollars). SECURED is a dummy variable which is 1 if the issue is secured. NEW ISSUE is a dummy variable which is 1 if the issue is a first time issue. INDUSTRY is a set of industry dummy variables constructed based on one-digit SIC codes. REPUTATION stands for three dummy variables based on market share rank of dollar volume of underwritings of debt issues in our sample. We consider the issues underwritten by the top 20 underwriters in this study. LOWREP is 1 if the rank based on market share is between 16 and 20. MEDREP is 1 if the rank is between 11 and 15. HIREP is 1 if the rank is between 1 and 10. MATURITY stands for three dummy variables based on maturity of the security. LOWMAT is 1 if the issue matures in less than 5 years, MEDMAT is 1 for 5 to 15 years, and HIMAT is 1 if the maturity is greater than 15 years. All dummy variables are 0 otherwise. The point estimates and T ratios for the industry dummys are not reported though they are included in the regressions. The asterisk (*) indicates that none of the issues are of low maturity. a, b, and c stand for significant at 0.01, 0.025, and 0.05 level using a two-tailed test.

another important issue that may affect the difference in yield spreads between bank and investment house underwritings is whether banks bring proportionally more (or fewer) issues to the market during periods of high-yield term spreads and high credit spreads, such as during the first year of our sample. We find that while banks brought 53.75% (43 out of 80) to the market, investment houses brought 60.68% (358 out of 590) of their issues during 1993 (of the initial year of our sample). However, this difference is not statistically significant at the 5% level. The chi-square test fails to reject the null that the timing aspect of the issues is independent of the underwriter type — as a result, we do not expect our results to be affected in any meaningful manner.

The Review of Financial Studies / v 10 n 4 1997

Table 8
Multivariate tests for bank versus investment house underwritings of debt issues which are not used for refinancing existing bank debt segmented by credit rating category

	Caa-Ba3		Baa1-Aaa	
Variable	Coeff	T ratio	Coeff	T ratio
INTERCEPT	577.86	4.15[a]	38.65	2.99[a]
PROP(STAKE)	−16.22	−3.21[a]	1.43	1.45
EXCHANGE	−26.47	−0.91	−14.09	−1.97[c]
LN(AMOUNT)	−42.47	−1.97[c]	−0.12	−0.05
SECURED	49.18	1.62	16.21	2.46[b]
NEW ISSUE	53.27	1.92	18.53	3.37[a]
LOWREP	−130.16	−1.41	−16.09	−0.97
HIREP	−15.78	−0.46	3.37	0.38
LOWMAT	*	*	−15.36	−2.78[a]
HIMAT	−96.94	−1.00	17.61	4.16[a]
Observations	111		267	
Adjusted R^2	0.2465		0.3805	

This table gives the OLS estimates of the following equation:

$$\begin{aligned} \text{BPS} = {} & \beta_0 + \beta_1 \text{ PROP(STAKE)} + \beta_2 \text{ EXCHANGE} + \beta_3 \text{ LN(AMOUNT)} + \beta_4 \text{ SECURED} \\ & + \beta_5 \text{ NEW ISSUE} + \beta_{\text{ind}} \text{ INDUSTRY} + \beta_{\text{rep}} \text{ REPUTATION} + \beta_{\text{mat}} \text{ MATURITY} \end{aligned}$$

The dependent variable BPS is the premium of the ex ante yield of a security over the ex ante yield of a treasury of comparable maturity in basis points. The independent variables are PROP(STAKE) is STAKE/AMOUNT, the outstanding lending exposure by the commercial banking affiliate of the bank underwriter (Section 20 subsidiary) to the issuer at the time of issuance of the debt issue as a proportion of the issue size. EXCHANGE is a dummy variable which is 1 if the firm is listed on an exchange. LN(AMOUNT) is the natural logarithm of the offered dollar amount of the issue (in millions of dollars). SECURED is a dummy variable which is 1 if the issue is secured. NEW ISSUE is a dummy variable which is 1 if the issue is a first-time issue. INDUSTRY is a set of industry dummy variables constructed based on one-digit SIC codes. REPUTATION stands for three dummy variables based on market share rank of dollar volume of underwritings of debt issues in our sample. We consider the issues underwritten by the top 20 underwriters in this study. LOWREP is 1 if the rank based on market share is between 16 and 20. MEDREP is 1 if the rank is between 11 and 15. HIREP is 1 if the rank is between 1 and 10. MATURITY stands for three dummy variables based on maturity of the security. LOWMAT is 1 if the issue matures in less than 5 years, MEDMAT is 1 for 5 to 15 years, and HIMAT is 1 if the maturity is greater than 15 years. All dummy variables are 0 otherwise. The point estimates and T ratios for the industry dummys are not reported though they are included in the regressions. The asterisk (*) indicates that none of the issues are of low maturity. a, b, and c stand for significant at 0.01, 0.025, and 0.05 level using a two-tailed test.

These results are consistent with an implicit breach of firewalls in which bank underwritings have a net certification effect for investors.[13] Alternatively, it could be argued that this result comes from investment bank underwriters serving different markets from commercial bank underwriters, with prices reflecting different degrees of market power. If this alternate explanation holds then it should be the case

[13] The bank could also use information acquired from loan monitoring to help firms that are solvent but seemingly in financial distress. Insofar as this is also an outcome of the bank's private information of the true value of the firm, it can be broadly classified as a net certification effect of the bank.

that we would find a reduction in yield spreads for all bank underwritings, rather than the source of the reduction being the bank's lending relationship with the issuer. To test this alternative explanation we replaced the LN(STAKE) variable with a BANK dummy variable, which is 1 if the underwriter is a Section 20 subsidiary and 0 otherwise, in our regressions. We find that the coefficient on the BANK dummy for both the Caa-Ba3 issues as well as the Baa1-Aaa issues was not statistically significant. Based on this, we conclude that as far as the reduction in yield spreads due to the net certification effect is concerned, it is the extent of the bank's underlying lending relationship with the borrower (whose magnitude is captured by the volume of outstanding loans) that matters rather than underwriter type. Further, since higher-credit rated borrowers, such as AAA rated borrowers, have more choices than lower-credit rated borrowers, banks should be able to extract more rents from the latter group. In other words, if banks have a monopolistic power, one would expect the bias to be against finding a net certification effect for low quality issuers. Finally, to examine further the question that segmentation in bank underwritings drives pricing differentials we use the selectivity methods described below.

4.3 Selectivity bias adjustments

In the multivariate linear regressions reported in this article, we have by implication assumed that LN(STAKE) is an exogenous variable. However, such an assumption may be problematic for the following reasons: (i) the decision to underwrite a particular debt issue is endogenous, inducing a selection bias, and (ii) the decision to lend and the magnitude of lending is also an endogenous decision which also induces a selection bias. When a selection bias caused by an endogenous independent variable exists, the coefficient estimators in a linear regression model with the endogenous variable [such as LN(STAKE)] may be inconsistent [see Maddala (1983)]. In other words, the bank's decision to underwrite and its decision to lend (through its commercial banking affiliate) are endogenous and are based on some information set that it has. However, the market cannot observe the information set that the bank has, but can only partially extract such information.

Our results are robust to a two-step selectivity adjustment (see Appendix A.2 for details). The results using this selectivity adjustment for debt issues segmented by credit rating category (see Table 5) are reported in Table 9. In other words, we find that conditioning for the apparent selection bias in LN(STAKE), our results are qualitatively unchanged.

Table 9
Selectivity bias adjustments — bank versus investment house underwritings of debt issues segmented by credit rating category

	Caa-Ba3		Baa1-Aaa	
Variable	Coeff	*T* ratio	Coeff	*T* ratio
INTERCEPT	590.71	5.36[a]	56.32	4.41[a]
RESIDUAL	−27.12	−2.91[a]	0.65	0.29
EXCHANGE	−63.88	−3.73[a]	−17.99	−2.95[a]
LN(AMOUNT)	−32.50	−2.34[b]	−1.17	−0.53
REF BK DEBT	32.45	2.09[c]	13.23	3.64[a]
SECURED	28.11	1.60	15.41	2.32[b]
NEW ISSUE	28.61	1.68	14.62	3.19[a]
LOWREP	−41.85	−0.91	−20.54	−1.38
HIREP	−46.32	−2.09[c]	0.09	0.01
LOWMAT	*	*	−21.67	−4.07[a]
HIMAT	−98.92	−1.11	18.60	4.92[a]
Observations	255		415	
Adjusted R^2	0.2096		0.2689	

This table gives the OLS estimates of the following equation:

$$\begin{aligned} \text{BPS} = {} & \beta_0 + \beta_1 \text{ RESIDUAL} + \beta_2 \text{ EXCHANGE} + \beta_3 \text{ LN(AMOUNT)} + \beta_4 \text{ REF BK DEBT} \\ & + \beta_5 \text{ SECURED} + \beta_6 \text{ NEW ISSUE} + \beta_{\text{ind}} \text{ INDUSTRY} + \beta_{\text{rep}} \text{ REPUTATION} \\ & + \beta_{\text{mat}} \text{ MATURITY} \end{aligned}$$

The dependent variable BPS is the premium of the ex ante yield of a security over the ex ante yield of a treasury of comparable maturity in basis points. The independent variables are RESIDUAL is the residuals from the first pass regression of LN(STAKE) on a set of explanatory variables (see Appendix A.2 for details) — where LN(STAKE) is the natural log of 1 plus STAKE, the outstanding lending exposure by the commercial banking affiliate of the bank underwriter (Section 20 subsidiary) to the issuer at the time of issuance of the debt issue. EXCHANGE is a dummy variable which is 1 if the firm is listed on an exchange. LN(AMOUNT) is the natural logarithm of the offered dollar amount of the issue (in millions of dollars). SECURED is a dummy variable which is 1 if the issue is secured. NEW ISSUE is a dummy variable which is 1 if the issue is a first-time issue. INDUSTRY is a set of industry dummy variables constructed based on one-digit SIC codes. REPUTATION stands for three dummy variables based on market share rank of dollar volume of underwritings of debt issues in our sample. We consider the issues underwritten by the top 20 underwriters in this study. LOWREP is 1 if the rank based on market share is between 16 and 20. MEDREP is 1 if the rank is between 11 and 15. HIREP is 1 if the rank is between 1 and 10. MATURITY stands for three dummy variables based on maturity of the security. LOWMAT is 1 if the issue matures in less than 5 years, MEDMAT is 1 for 5 to 15 years, and HIMAT is 1 if the maturity is greater than 15 years. All dummy variables are 0 otherwise. The point estimates and *T* ratios for the industry dummys are not reported though they are included in the regressions. The asterisk (*) indicates that none of the issues are of low maturity. a, b, and c stand for significant at 0.01, 0.025, and 0.05 level using a two-tailed test.

5. Conclusions

This article examines recent evidence on the characteristics and pricing of debt securities of firms underwritten by two types of financial intermediaries: Section 20 subsidiaries of bank holding companies and investment houses. We find bank underwriting of lower-credit rated issues, where the bank retains a significant stake (through its commercial banking affiliate), results in lower yields (higher prices) consistent with a net certification role of banks through their lending activities.

Interestingly, even in circumstances where a potential conflict of interest is high, that is, where the stated purpose of an issue is to refinance existing bank debt and the bank has a lending stake (through its commercial banking affiliate), we find no evidence of conflict of interest since there is no significant difference between yield spreads on similar debt issues underwritten by banks and investment houses.

The results are consistent with the view that when banks lend to firms (through their commercial banking affiliate) there is a dominant net certification effect present — especially for lower-credit rated issues. These results are obtained in the presence of firewalls and suggest an implicit breach of the firewalls. While we cannot directly extend these results to suggest what would happen in the absence of firewalls in today's market, previous research on similar issues in the pre-Glass–Steagall period by Puri (1996a) also suggests a net certification effect by banks. Together these results suggest that banks have a net certification effect on yield spreads of debt issuers as compared to investment houses that is largely independent of the organizational form within which the bank undertakes such underwritings (i.e., whether there are firewalls, as in the post-Section 20 era, or there are no firewalls, as in the pre-Glass–Steagall period).

We also find that banks bring a relatively larger proportion of smaller-size issues to the market. Over time, as banks have gained underwriting experience, this trend toward underwriting smaller issues, both in absolute terms, and as compared to issue sizes underwritten by investment houses has been increasing. This evidence is contrary to the contention that greater universal banking powers, and larger-size banks, will stunt capital market access for smaller firms.

Our article investigates bank corporate debt underwriting in the first few years (1993–1995) of their having received permission to pursue such activity. The results raise a number of interesting issues. Will the trend toward banks underwriting smaller issues persist in the future? If banks other than money center banks enter the underwriting arena in any scale, would we see differences between the underwriting behavior of different kinds of banks, for example, money center banks and superregionals? What is the long-term default performance of bank underwritten issues? Now that some of the firewalls are being eliminated, what will the impact on future bank underwritings be? We leave these questions to future research when a longer time series of bank underwriting performance will be available.

The Review of Financial Studies / v 10 n 4 1997

Appendix

A.1 Description of the data

The sample consists of fixed-rate U.S. nonconvertible debt issues of nonfinancial, nonregulated firms underwritten by the top 20 underwriters. The ranking of the underwriters is based on the total dollar volume of such underwritings during the sample period — January 1, 1993–March 31, 1995. The sample consists of 670 debt issues for which all the required data was available, for example, no missing price information, no missing information on yield of comparable treasury, etc. In this study we exclude all the financial firms (one-digit SIC code 6) since the nature of conflicts of interest is significantly different from those associated with lending to nonfinancial firms. We also exclude all firms in regulated industries (one-digit SIC code 4) since the absence of regulation contrasts the firms in the nonregulated industries from those in the regulated industries. The construction of the dependent and independent variables from the relevant SDC data variable(s) and from Dealscan is explained below. The value of dummy variables is 0 otherwise.

BPS: Same as SDC variable BPS.

LN(STAKE): The natural log of 1 plus STAKE. We need to add 1 to the variable STAKE since the natural log of 0 (the value STAKE takes for all investment house underwritings) is not defined. STAKE is the outstanding lending exposure to the issuer (in millions of dollars) by the commercial banking affiliate of the Section 20 subsidiary. By definition, STAKE is 0 for investment house underwritings (since they have no lending relationship). For all bank underwritings, the issuer name from SDC data is matched with the issuer name in Dealscan. If there is no match then STAKE is 0 and LN(STAKE) is 0 also. If there is a match, we extract all facilities where the commercial banking affiliate of the Section 20 subsidiary which underwrote the debt issue is the lender. STAKE is then obtained by aggregating the dollar value of only those loans by the commercial banking affiliate of the Section 20 underwriter that are outstanding at the time of debt issue. In case a loan is offered by multiple lenders where each of them lend a fraction of the total loan, the dollar value is obtained by multiplying the fraction of the loan and the total value of the loan. Where information on the fraction of the loan is not available, we assume it to be 0. Such an assumption is conservative as it biases against finding any net certification effect.

EXCHANGE: A dummy variable that takes the value 1 if the firm is listed on an exchange and 0 otherwise.

LN(AMOUNT): The natural log of the SDC data variable AMT.

REF BK DEBT: 1 if SDC variable UOPCODE has a value 10.

SECURED: Information from SDC variable SECURL is the primary source. We look for the words *collateralized, mortgage, guaranteed, secured* to mean a value of 1 for this dummy variable. Besides we cross-reference the description with Fabozzi and Fabozzi (1995) to infer if a particular issue can be classified as secured. For example, Equipment Trust Certificates are considered as secured. The secondary sources are the SDC variables GTDC and ENH. For example, a C for ENH indicates collateralized credit enhancement and we upgrade such a debt issue to being secured.

NEW ISSUE: The construction of this variable is done in the following manner: We search to see if the company had a similar debt issue in the last 20 years. If yes, it is taken to be a seasoned issue and this dummy variable takes a value of 0. If not, it is assumed to be a first-time issue (debt IPO) and this dummy variable takes a value of 1.

CREDIT RATING: A set of credit rating dummys (Caa-C, B1-B3, Ba1-Ba3, Baa1-Baa3, A1-A3, Aa1-Aa3, Aaa) are constructed from the SDC variable MDY. For example, B1-B3 is 1 if MDY is B1, B2, or B3.

REPUTATION: Three dummy variables based on market share rank of dollar volume (by aggregating the SDC variable AMT) of underwritings of debt issues in our sample. We consider the issues underwritten by top 20 underwriters in this study. LOWREP is 1 if the rank based on market share is between 16 and 20. MEDREP is 1 if the rank is between 11 and 15. HIREP is 1 if the rank is between 1 and 10.

MATURITY: Three dummy variables are constructed based on YTOFM, the maturity of a debt issue. LOWMAT is 1 if YTOFM is less than 5 years. MEDMAT is 1 if YTOFM is between (and including) 5 and 15 years. HIMAT is 1 if YTOFM is greater than 5 years.

INDUSTRY: Ten industry dummy variables constructed based on one-digit primary SIC codes. For example, if the primary SIC code is 861, the one-digit primary SIC code is 8 and the corresponding dummy variable is 1 and all other dummy variables are 0.

A.2 Selectivity bias adjustments

The multivariate linear regression model used in our article is of the following form:

$$BPS_i = X_i'\beta + \gamma LN(STAKE)_i + u_i$$

where BPS_i is the ex ante yield premium of the debt issue, i, X_i is the vector of factors considered significant in determining ex ante yield

The Review of Financial Studies / v 10 n 4 1997

premium, and $LN(STAKE)_i$ is the natural log of one plus STAKE, the outstanding lending exposure by the commercial banking affiliate of the bank underwriter (Section 20 subsidiary) to the issuer at the time of issuance of the debt issue. Our inferences in this article are based on the significance of γ, the coefficient of LN(STAKE).

It can be easily seen that $LN(STAKE)_i$ is a tobit variable: positive if the bank has an underlying lending relationship through its commercial banking affiliate, and underwrites the debt issue; 0 otherwise. From the general formulation of a tobit variable, we have:

$$LN(STAKE)_i^* = Z_i'\delta + \epsilon_i$$

$$LN(STAKE)_i = \begin{cases} LN(STAKE)_i^* & \text{when } LN(STAKE)_i^* > 0 \\ 0 & \text{when } LN(STAKE)_i^* \leq 0 \end{cases}$$

where $LN(STAKE)_i^*$ is the latent variable which is observed when positive as $LN(STAKE)_i$. The error term ϵ_i is normally distributed with mean 0 and a finite variance, and Z_i is the vector of publicly available factors considered significant in determining $LN(STAKE)_i^*$. Z_i consists of the following variables, described in detail in Appendix A.1, namely, EXCHANGE, LN(AMOUNT), SECURED, NEW ISSUE, REF BK DEBT, MATURITY, and INDUSTRY.

Note that while the above formulation examines the bank underwriting decision, we could reinterpret the above model in terms of the issuers' decision to go to a commercial bank or an investment house to get their securities underwritten. Thus issuers with particular kinds of characteristics take loans (of certain magnitudes) from banks who have underwriting affiliates. The market observes this and updates its expectations of the private information about the firm, which is now in the bank's possession.

In either case, we need to account for the selection bias induced by tobit variable $LN(STAKE)$. To do this we need to estimate the above equation as a tobit regression and then use the residuals in place of the tobit variable in the linear regression.

Greene (1991) suggests that a practical approach to estimating the tobit regression is to reformulate the tobit model as a probit model. This method of estimation is easy to implement and there is no loss in efficiency in finite samples. In other words we recode the dependent variable as 0 for existing zero observations and 1 for the existing nonzero observations and estimate it as a probit model.

Accordingly, we use the following two-stage method: (i) Estimate the probit likelihood function of the recoded probit model. We use the estimates to construct the residuals, $RESIDUAL_i$ for the tobit model using the parameter estimates of the recoded probit model. (ii) We use $RESIDUAL_i$ in place of $LN(STAKE)_i$ in Equation (1) and estimate the equation with simple OLS.

Inference can now be made on the basis of the coefficient on $RESIDUAL_i$ which accounts for the selection bias in the tobit variable $LN(STAKE)_i$.

References

Ang, J. S., and T. Richardson, 1994, "The Underwriting Experiences of Commercial Bank Affiliates Prior to the Glass-Steagall Act: A Re-examination of Evidence for Passage of the Act," *Journal of Banking and Finance*, 18, 351–395.

Beatty, R. P., and J. R. Ritter, 1986, "Investment Banking, Reputation, and the Underpricing of Initial Public Offerings," *Journal of Financial Economics*, 15, 213–232.

Benston, G. J., 1990, *The Separation of Commercial and Investment Banking*, Oxford University Press, New York.

Berger, A., and G. F. Udell, 1990, "Collateral, Loan Quality, and Bank Risk," *Journal of Monetary Economics*, 25, 21–42.

Fabozzi, F. J., and T. D. Fabozzi, 1995, *The Handbook of Fixed Income Securities*, Irwin Professional Publishing, Homewood, Ill.

Fama, E., 1985, "What's Different about Banks?," *Journal of Monetary Economics*, 15, 5–29.

Flannery, M. J., 1986, "Asymmetric Information and Risky Debt Maturity Choice," *Journal of Finance*, 41, 19–38.

GAO, 1990, *Bank Powers: Activities of Securities Subsidiaries of Bank Holding Companies*, United States General Accounting Office, Washington, D.C.

Greene, W., 1991, *LIMDEP version 6.0 User's Manual and Reference Guide*, Econometric Software, Inc., New York.

James, C., 1987, "Some Evidence on the Uniqueness of Bank Loans," *Journal of Financial Economics*, 19, 217–236.

Kroszner, R. S., and R. G. Rajan, 1994, "Is the Glass-Steagall Act Justified? A Study of the U.S. Experience with Universal Banking Before 1933," *American Economic Review*, 84, 810–832.

Kroszner, R. S., and R. G. Rajan, 1997, "Organization Structure and Credibility: Evidence from Commercial Bank Securities Activities before the Glass-Steagall Act," working paper, University of Chicago.

Lummer, S. L., and J. J. McConnell, 1989, "Further Evidence on the Bank Lending Process and the Capital-Market Response to Bank Loan Agreements," *Journal of Financial Economics*, 25, 99–122.

Maddala, G. S., 1983, *Limited Dependent and Qualitative Variables in Econometrics*, Econometrics Society Monographs No. 3, Cambridge University Press, Cambridge.

New York Times, 1994, *U.S. proposes letting banks enter new fields*, November 29, 1994, D1, D5.

Puri, M., 1994, "The Long Term Default Performance of Bank Underwritten Security Issues," *Journal of Banking and Finance*, 18, 397–418.

Puri, M., 1996a, "Commercial Banks in Investment Banking: Conflict of Interest or Certification Role?" *Journal of Financial Economics*, 40, 373–401.

Puri, M., 1996b, "Conflicts of Interest, Intermediation, and the Pricing of Underwritten Securities," working paper, Stanford University.

Saunders, A., 1985, "Conflicts of Interest: An Economic View," in I. Walter (ed.), *Deregulating Wall Street*, John Wiley and Sons, New York.

Saunders, A., and I. Walter, 1994, *Universal Banking in the U.S.*, Oxford University Press, New York.

Wall Street Journal, 1996, *Fed set to ease bank underwriting curbs*, August 1, 1996, A2.

Walter, I. (ed.), 1985, *Deregulating Wall Street*, John Wiley and Sons, New York.

ELSEVIER Journal of Financial Economics 54 (1999) 165–195

JOURNAL OF Financial ECONOMICS

www.elsevier.com/locate/econbase

Bank entry, competition, and the market for corporate securities underwriting☆

Amar Gande[a], Manju Puri[b,*], Anthony Saunders[c]

[a]*Owen Graduate School of Management, Vanderbilt University, Nashville, TN 37203-9726, USA*
[b]*Graduate School of Business, Stanford University, Stanford, CA 94305-5015, USA*
[c]*Stern School of Business, New York University, New York, NY 10012-1126, USA*

Received 15 July 1998; received in revised form 30 October 1998

Abstract

This paper examines the competitive effects of commercial bank entry into the corporate debt underwriting market, particularly with respect to underwriter spreads, ex-ante yields, and market concentration. We find that underwriter spreads and ex-ante yields have declined significantly with bank entry, consistent with the market becoming more competitive. This effect is strongest among the lower-rated and smaller debt issues of which banks have underwritten a relatively greater share. The early evidence also indicates that bank entry has tended to decrease market concentration. Overall, our results suggest that bank entry has had a pro-competitive effect. © 1999 Elsevier Science S.A. All rights reserved.

JEL classification: G21; G24; N22

Keywords: Commercial banks; Underwriters; Certification; Spreads; Yields; Glass–Steagall

* Corresponding author. Tel.: + 1-650-723-3402; fax: + 1-650-725-6152.

E-mail address: mpuri@gsb.stanford.edu (M. Puri)

☆We thank Christopher James (the referee), Jay Ritter, G. William Schwert (the editor), Larry Wall and the seminar participants at the Financial Economics and Accounting conference in New York, Bank structure conference of the Federal Reserve Bank of Chicago for helpful comments. Puri thanks the National Science Foundation for financial support.

PII: S0304-405X(99)00035-5

1. Introduction

The corporate bond market is a major source of financing for companies. During 1996–1997, more than $1970 billion was raised by way of public debt, generating underwriting fees of $4.6 billion. Despite the size and importance of the corporate bond market, the competitive structure of this market has been inadequately investigated.[1] Perhaps one reason for the paucity of studies on the competitive structure of the corporate debt underwriting market is the fact that for many years the investment banking industry has been protected by the 1933 Glass–Steagall Act (and in particular Section 20 of the Act) which for all intents and purposes prevents commercial banks from underwriting corporate bonds and equities.

Although Glass–Steagall remains on the books, regulators have reinterpreted Section 20 of the Act to allow banks to expand their underwriting activities. Specifically, in 1987, the Federal Reserve permitted banks, on a case-by-case basis, to establish special Section 20 investment banking subsidiaries engaged in certain "ineligible" securities activities. Section 20 subsidiaries (referred to as *banks* in this paper) are subject to a substantial set of *firewalls* limiting information, resource, and financial linkages between them and their respective parent holding companies as well as with their commercial banking affiliates. They are also subject to a limit (or cap) on revenue generation from their "ineligible" securities activities.

At the end of 1996, however, the Federal Reserve raised the limit on revenue generation from "ineligible" securities activities of commercial bank holding companies from 10% to 25% of total Section 20 revenues (it had initially been set at 5% in 1987); it also dropped some of the most restrictive firewalls. These relaxations made it feasible for banks to acquire investment banking firms, a phenomenon which we have witnessed from 1997 onwards. It seems likely that banks will be allowed to expand their securities underwriting activities even further in the future, raising questions regarding the public benefits and costs of relaxing the Glass–Steagall provisions (and other regulations limiting the ability of U.S. banking organizations to expand their nonbank activities).

This paper contributes to the debate by examining the competitive effect of commercial bank entry into the market for corporate debt underwriting. We take advantage of the unique conditions created by deregulation to evaluate the

---

[1] Indeed, one has to go back to the 1970s and early 1980s to find relevant research on this issue. For example, Ederington (1976) finds that, in general, competitive bidding by securities firms to underwrite a particular issue results in lower underwriting costs for the issuer than when a single underwriter is chosen under a negotiated underwriting. Similarly, Sorensen (1979) finds that the larger the number of bidders in a competitive underwriting, the smaller the underwriter spread, the interest cost, and the yield of the issue.

net benefits of Section 20 subsidiaries' entry into investment banking. Specifically, our paper addresses the following issues: (i) the effect of bank entry on corporate debt underwriting spreads and ex-ante yield spreads, (ii) which segments of the market these effects are most pronounced, (iii) the extent to which commercial bank and investment house corporate debt underwriting spreads differ, and (iv) the effect of commercial bank entry on concentration in the market for corporate debt underwriting. To the best of our knowledge, ours is the first paper to address these issues.

Underwriter spread is defined as the difference between the offered amount and the proceeds to the issuer, expressed as a percentage of the offered amount. A recent article in the *Economist* (June 27, 1998, pp. 73–74) argues that equity underwriting spreads in the U.K. and the U.S. have not budged for a decade and claims that underwriting spreads are "excessive". This raises the question of how these spreads are determined. In general, underwriter spreads are determined by two major factors. The first factor relates to distribution costs, information production costs, and other costs including compensation for the risk carried in underwriting a security issue. The second factor is the competitive element in the market, i.e., whether markets are fully competitive or whether there are some "monopoly" rents to underwriters. On the one hand, bank entry can make markets more competitive, leading to reduced underwriter spreads. On the other hand, large, well-capitalized banks could monopolize the debt underwriting market, especially in the long run, leading to increased underwriter spreads. This is the subject of our first test. We find that bank entry has significantly reduced underwriter spreads in the corporate debt market. This finding could, however, arise from changes in debt issue characteristics over the pre- and post-Section 20 periods. We control for issue characteristics and find our results are robust to such changes.

Further, we find that the reduction in underwriter spreads is strongest among lower-rated and smaller debt issues, with banks underwriting a relatively larger proportion of such issues. To further ensure that other factors are not contributing to these declines in underwriter spreads, such as greater ease of distribution, lower information production costs, etc., we compare and contrast the trends in the corporate bond market, where banks now have a significant market share, to that in equity markets, where banks have not yet made major inroads. We examine the trends in both the initial public offerings (IPOs) of equities and the seasoned equity offerings (SEOs) markets. Interestingly, we find that while Section 20 deregulation appears to have resulted in a significant decline in underwriting spreads in the corporate bond market, similar declines are not apparent in equity markets.

A related issue is the impact of bank entry on ex-ante yield spreads of corporate bond issues, where, ex-ante yield spread is defined as the ex-ante yield of a debt security minus the ex-ante yield of a U.S. Treasury security of comparable maturity. While underwriter spreads have decreased, underwriters might have sought to offset this effect on their expected profits by raising yields (and lowering the prices paid to the issuer) at the time of a firm-commitment offering. Lowering the bid (and offer) price lowers the proceeds to the issuer, but increases the probability that the underwriter will sell out an issue, albeit at a lower spread. This issue is also important from another perspective. Banks differ from investment houses in that they can obtain private information about a firm through their loan monitoring activities. If banks are more credible certifiers than investment houses, e.g., because of better information at their disposal, then bank-underwritten securities will have better prices (lower yields) than will securities underwritten by investment houses, as long as bank entry does not increase the degree of market concentration and banks' power over issuers. Bank entry can therefore force investment houses to expend more resources and produce more information about issuing firms. An important reason for better prices (and lower yields) for the market as a whole is the improved information flow. We test whether bank entry affects ex-ante yield spreads of corporate bond issues. We find that ex-ante yield spreads have declined (rather than increased) with bank entry, and this decline is most apparent in the smaller issues.

There is also the question of whether banks and investment houses have similar or different underwriter spreads at any moment in time. For example, banks might charge lower spreads to obtain market share on entry. Alternatively, if banks can secure better prices for firms through their underwriting activities, these benefits can be offset through higher underwriter spreads. We test if banks and investment houses have had significantly different underwriting spreads post-bank entry and find no significant differences in spreads. This evidence suggests that any differences in underwriter spreads on bank versus investment house underwritings (due to banks undercutting investment houses' spreads) have not persisted over time, perhaps due to investment houses' matching bank spreads on an immediate basis.

Finally, there is the question of the impact of bank entry on the competitive structure of the market, particularly on market concentration. Opponents of universal banking have argued that banks, with their superior information about firms, will monopolize the market (e.g., Benston, 1994). We find that bank entry into the corporate debt underwriting market has lowered market concentration. However, we must be cautious in interpreting this result since it is somewhat early to assess the long-term impact of bank underwriting on market concentration. Our sample ends in 1996, prior to the relaxation of the revenue cap (from 10% to 25%) which made it feasible for banks to acquire investment banks since 1997. Whether bank entry will have an anticompetitive long-term effect, pushing traditional investment banking firms out of the market, poses an interesting issue for future research.

Overall, our results suggest that bank entry into the corporate debt underwriting market has had a pro-competitive effect in reducing underwriter spreads, yield spreads, and market concentration. The reduction in underwriter spreads and yield spreads has been greatest in the smaller and lower-rated issues, where bank underwritings have been most concentrated. This evidence tends to refute the contention that bank entry into the market for underwriting of corporate securities would result in banks monopolizing the market, adversely affecting the availability of finance to smaller and lower-rated firms.

The remainder of the paper is organized as follows. Section 2 describes the regulatory changes that allowed bank entry into the corporate securities underwriting market. We describe the data and our sample selection process in Section 3. Section 4 develops the testable hypotheses. Section 5 explains the test methodology and presents the major empirical results. Section 6 concludes.

2. Regulatory changes and bank entry into the corporate securities underwriting market

The Glass–Steagall Act of 1933, particularly Section 20 of the Act, effectively prohibits commercial banks from underwriting corporate securities. There have been many attempts to get Congress to amend or remove the Act. However, these attempts have, by and large, been unsuccessful. While the Glass–Steagall Act remains on the books, regulators and banks have effectively bypassed many provisions of the Act by reinterpreting Section 20 of the Act. In 1987, the Federal Reserve permitted banks to set up special Section 20 investment banking subsidiaries. Not all banks can establish Section 20 affiliates, and special permission must be received from the Federal Reserve. These Section 20 subsidiaries are allowed to engage in certain "ineligible" securities activities. In 1987, the Federal Reserve gave the first permission to a bank to underwrite commercial paper, municipal revenue bonds, and securitization issues. In 1989, corporate bond underwriting was permitted for the first time as was corporate equity underwriting in 1990.

The Federal Reserve initially posted a gross revenue cap of 5% on the ineligible securities activities. The spirit of a revenue cap is to avoid violation of the Section 20 of the Act. By keeping the revenue cap below 50%, a majority of the subsidiaries' revenues are generated from eligible securities activities such as government bond underwriting, swaps origination, etc. The gross revenue cap limit was subsequently raised to 10% and then to 25% at the end of 1996.

The number of Section 20 affiliates has expanded from five in the late 1980s to over 40 today, representing the largest U.S. and international banks. Table 1 gives a list of Section 20 subsidiaries and their related debt and equity underwriting powers. Until recently, these Section 20 subsidiaries, and their bank holding company parents, were subject to a substantial set of firewalls limiting information, resource, and financial linkages between the subsidiaries and their

Table 1
Section 20 subsidiaries[a] (as of May 31, 1997)

This table presents the Section 20 subsidiaries as of May 31, 1997.

	Initial order
Boston District	
Fleet Financial Group	10/88
Bank of Boston Corporation[b]	11/96
New York District	
Banco Santander, S.A.[b]	3/95
The Bank of New York Company, Inc.[b]	6/96
The Bank of Nova Scotia[b]	4/90
Bankers Trust N.Y. Corp.[b]	4/87
Barclays Bank PLC[c]	1/90
Canadian Imperial Bank of Commerce[b]	1/90
Chase Manhattan Corp.[b]	5/87
Citicorp[b]	4/87
Deutsche Bank AG[b]	12/92
Dresdner Bank AG[b]	7/96
HSBC Holdings PLC[b]	2/96
J.P. Morgan & Co.[b]	4/87
National Westminster Bank Plc	9/96
The Royal Bank of Canada[b]	1/90
Saban/Republic New York Corp.[b]	1/94
Swiss Bank Corporation[b]	12/94
The Toronto-Dominion Bank[b]	5/90
Philadelphia District	
Dauphin Deposit Corp.[b,d]	6/91
Cleveland District	
Banc One Corp.[b]	7/90
Huntington Bancshares, Inc.	12/92
KeyCorp	2/96
Mellon Bank Corporation	4/95
National City Corporation[b]	2/94
PNC Bank Corp.	7/87
Richmond District	
Crestar Financial Corporation	4/97
First Union Corp.[b]	8/89
NationsBank Corp.[b]	5/89
Atlanta District	
Barnett Banks, Inc.[e]	1/89
SouthTrust Corp.[b]	7/89
SunTrust Banks, Inc.	8/94
Synovus Financial Corp.	9/91

Table 1 (*continued*)

	Initial order
Chicago District	
ABN AMRO Bank N.V.[b]	6/90
The Bank of Montreal[b,f]	5/88
First of America Bank Corp.[c]	10/94
First Chicago NBD Corp.[c]	8/88
Minneapolis District	
Norwest Corp.[b]	12/89
Kansas City District	
BOK Financial Corporation	4/97
San Francisco District	
Bank America Corp.[b]	3/92
Dai-Ichi Kangyo Bank Ltd.	1/91
The Sanwa Bank, Ltd.	5/90

[a] Authorized to underwrite and deal in certain municipal revenue bonds, mortgage related securities, commercial paper and asset-backed securities (Tier I authority).
[b] Also has corporate debt and equity underwriting and dealing powers (Tier II authority).
[c] Also has corporate debt securities powers.
[d] By Order dated May 19, 1997, the Board approved the applications and notices submitted by Allied Irish Banks plc and First Maryland Bancorp to acquire Dauphin Deposit Corporation, and thereby all of its banking and nonbanking subsidiaries.
[e] As of June 30, 1995, the Section 20 subsidiary of this organization was dormant.
[f] Currently has two Section 20 subsidiaries.
Source: Board of Governors of the Federal Reserve System, Washington, D.C.

respective parent holding companies as well as with their commercial banking affiliates. GAO (1990) provides a complete discussion of the scope and limitations of firewalls on activities of Section 20 subsidiaries. The Federal Reserve has dropped some of the most restrictive firewalls (*Wall Street Journal*, August 1, 1996, p. A2), and all indications point to the likelihood of further relaxations, allowing banks to expand their securities underwriting activities in the future.

Table 2 shows the percent of dollar volume and percent of issues underwritten by Section 20 subsidiaries of commercial bank holding companies on a year-by-year basis. The proportion of corporate debt issues underwritten has risen to over 20% (as of 1996) while the proportion of corporate equity has risen to approximately 2%. Thus, given their traditional role as credit or loan monitors and certification agents (e.g., James, 1987; Puri, 1996) the Section 20 subsidiaries of commercial banks have largely specialized in competing with traditional investment banks in the market for underwriting corporate debt issues. To

Table 2
Market share of bank underwritings

This table presents the bank share (in percentage terms) of the annual dollar volume and number of issues of corporate debt underwritings in the following segments: (1) nonfinancial and nonregulated fixed-rate U.S. debt issues and (2) nonfinancial and nonregulated U.S. equity issues.

Year	Debt		Equity	
	$ Volume	# Issues	$ Volume	# Issues
1985	0.00	0.00	0.00	0.00
1986	0.00	0.00	0.00	0.00
1987	0.00	0.00	0.00	0.00
1988	0.00	0.00	0.00	0.00
1989	0.00	0.00	0.00	0.00
1990	0.00	0.00	0.00	0.00
1991	4.40	5.78	0.00	0.00
1992	6.44	8.47	0.37	0.14
1993	6.76	9.41	1.13	0.44
1994	7.29	8.65	1.32	0.58
1995	10.15	21.13	1.18	0.96
1996	16.28	20.42	2.15	1.88
Overall	5.36	7.25	0.93	0.51

date, commercial banks have made little inroads into the equity underwriting market.

3. Data and sample selection

We employed the following criteria in the selection of the sample period. First, the sample period must include underwritings of corporate securities in a time prior to bank entry. Second, to ensure that the test results of the competitive effect of commercial bank entry are representative, the sample must have a nontrivial number of issues underwritten by banks. Third, in devising econometric tests examining the effect of bank entry on underwriter spreads and yield spreads, it is necessary to control for other factors such as the issuer's credit rating, size of the issue, industry, and maturity. Data on these variables must also be available for the entire sample period.

Based on these considerations, we define our sample period as the 12 years from January 1, 1985 to December 31, 1996. Thus, our sample period ends just prior to the Fed's raising of the Section 20 revenue cap from 10% to 25% and the concurrent lowering of firewalls. We exclude financial firms (one-digit SIC code 6) and firms in regulated industries (one-digit SIC code 4) from our study. The absence of regulation contrasts firms in nonregulated industries from those in regulated industries, and many regulated firms, such as public utilities, have historically relied on negotiated rather than competitive underwritings. Additionally, we focus on U.S. fixed-rate nonconvertible debt. Our sample consists of 2992 fixed-rate U.S. nonconvertible debt issues for which all the required data was available, e.g., no missing information on gross spread, issue size, credit rating, maturity, etc. Approximately 7% of the debt issues in our sample are underwritten by Section 20 subsidiaries.

We obtain information about these issues, such as date of issuance, the yield to maturity, credit rating, industry, the size of the issue, the maturity of the debt, etc., from the Securities Data Company, Inc. (SDC). The sample is constructed from the U.S. domestic public new-issues database of SDC. The SDC database is compiled from regulatory filings, news sources, company press releases, and prospectuses.

3.1. Variables

The principal dependent variable is GROSS SPREAD, the underwriting spread of a debt issue measured as the difference between the offered amount and the proceeds to the issuer, expressed as a percentage of the offered amount (issue size). The other dependent variable is YIELD SPREAD, the ex-ante yield of the debt security minus the ex-ante yield of a U.S. Treasury security of comparable maturity. The independent variables are as follows:

BANK ENTRY: A dummy variable that equals one in 1989 and succeeding years (based on the year of the debt issue) and zero otherwise.

LN(MKT SHARE): The natural log of bank share (in percentage terms) of the annual dollar volume of corporate debt underwritings.

TIME: This variable is based on the year of the debt issue. For example, if the issue date is September 12, 1986, TIME takes the value 86.

LN(AMOUNT): The natural log of the size of the issue (in millions of dollars).

NEW ISSUE: A dummy variable that is one if the issue is a first-time issue by the firm (a debt IPO). If the company did not have a debt issue during the 15 years prior to the sample period, the issue is assumed to be a first-time issue.

INDUSTRY: Stands for a set of industry dummy variables based on one-digit primary SIC codes. For example, if the primary SIC code is 861, the one-digit primary SIC code is 8. The corresponding dummy variable is one and all other industry dummy variables are zero.

INVGRADE: A dummy variable that is one if the debt issue is an investment grade issue, i.e., has a Moody's debt rating in the range Baa1–Aaa.

CREDIT RATING: Stands for a set of seven credit rating dummy variables (Caa–C, B1–B3, Ba1–Ba3, Baa1–Baa3, A1–A3, Aa1–Aa3, Aaa) based on Moody's credit rating for the debt issue. For example, B1–B3 is a dummy

variable which is one if Moody's credit rating for the issue is B1, B2, or B3. The dummy variable is zero otherwise.
MATURITY: Stands for three dummy variables based on the maturity of the debt security. LOWMAT is one if the security matures in less than five years. MEDMAT is one if it matures in five to 15 years. HIMAT is one if the maturity is greater than 15 years. The dummy variables are zero otherwise.

3.2. Discussion of variables

The relevant competitive variable is BANK ENTRY or, as we discuss below, LN(MKT SHARE). Because 1989 marks the year in which the first approval was given to a bank (J.P. Morgan) to undertake corporate debt underwriting activities through its Section 20 subsidiary, BANK ENTRY has a value of one in 1989 and succeeding years and zero otherwise. The credit rating of a debt issue reflects the greater cost and difficulty underwriters have in placing non-investment-grade issues (e.g., Sorensen, 1979). Thus, the lower the credit rating, the larger should be the underwriter spread. Lower-credit rated issues should also have higher yield spreads over U.S. Treasury securities. The log of issue size is included to measure potential economies of scale to the underwriter in placing larger issues. That is, the larger the issue size, the smaller should be the underwriter spread. In addition, as larger offerings are likely to be associated with less uncertainty than smaller offerings, be more liquid, and have more public information associated with them, one would also expect larger issues to have lower yields. A new (debt IPO) issue is potentially associated with greater uncertainty than a seasoned issue and should result in relatively higher underwriter spreads and yield spreads. Maturity is another variable potentially affecting underwriter spreads and yield spreads, which we address via two maturity dummies: LOWMAT (reflecting issues with less than five years to maturity) and HIMAT (reflecting issue with maturity of 15 years or over). We have three maturity dummies, but only two can be included to avoid linear dependence. We exclude the MEDMAT dummy in this regression (similarly, of the seven credit rating dummies, we exclude the Aaa dummy, and, of the eight industry dummies, we exclude the industry dummy variable corresponding to the one-digit SIC code 9 in all our linear regressions). Longer-maturity debt issues are potentially subject to greater interest-rate risk exposure over the offer period and can have a higher default risk (Flannery, 1986). This may be reflected in higher spreads being demanded by underwriters as well as investors on longer-maturity issues. Finally, the effect of bank entry on the underwriter spreads is measured by the magnitude and the significance of the coefficient on the BANK ENTRY or, alternatively, the LN(MKT SHARE) variable. In the absence of any effect of bank entry on underwriter spreads and yield spreads, this variable should be statistically insignificant.

4. Test hypotheses

In this section, we develop test hypotheses pertaining to the impact of bank entry into the corporate debt underwriting market on underwriter spreads, yield spreads, differences in underwriter spreads between banks and investment houses, and on market concentration.

4.1. Underwriter spreads

Given banks' entry and their substantial market share in the corporate debt market, bank competition, to the extent that such competition is material, should have a direct effect on the underwriter spreads. Specifically, the underwriter spread has two components. One component covers the marketing, distributional, financing, and other operating costs involved in a firm-commitment underwriting. The second component is a function of the competitive structure of the market. To the extent that the market for underwriting services is less than fully competitive, the underwriter spread could well reflect economic rents in addition to the distributional and other costs related to the issue.

We hypothesize that to the extent that competition, as a result of bank entry into the corporate debt underwriting market (in 1989) is material, underwriter spreads should have declined in the post-1989 period. We also hypothesize that this decline in spreads is positively related to the market share of the banks in the corporate debt underwriting market. In other words, the decline in underwriter spreads should be most significant in those segments of the corporate debt underwriting market in which banks have made the most significant strides in gaining market share.

4.2. Yield spreads

The ex-ante yield spread over a U.S. Treasury security of comparable maturity reflects the market's assessment of the risk of the security. If the underwriter produces accurate and credible information about a security, then for the same observable characteristics, investors will be willing to pay higher prices (earn lower yields) for the security. For firms to which banks lend, banks potentially have better information about the firm than investment houses because banks have access to private information obtained from the loan monitoring and customer relationship process. Prior empirical evidence by Gande et al. (1997) finds that corporate securities underwritten by Section 20 subsidiaries have lower yields (higher prices) than comparable securities underwritten by investment houses, and that this differential is higher for the non-investment-grade segment in which bank underwritings are concentrated. Puri (1996) finds similar evidence from pre-Glass–Steagall bank and investment house underwritings. A potential implication of this evidence is that the presence of banks can force investment houses to expend more resources and produce better information about firms. Consequently, as long as bank entry is pro-competitive, the net result should be a decline in yield spreads for debt securities, post-bank entry, after taking credit ratings and other observables into account. Again, the decline in yield spreads should be most significant in those segments of the corporate debt market in which banks have made the most significant strides in gaining market share.

4.3. Differences in underwriter spreads between banks and investment houses

To obtain market share, banks may undercut investment houses' underwriting spreads and charge lower fees. Such undercutting of the market can help improve penetration in new markets and increase long-run market share and power. On the other hand, the theoretical literature (see Puri, 1999) suggests that if banks are able to secure better prices for underwritten securities, then banks might try to extract rents from firms and charge higher underwriter spreads. Given that prior empirical literature documents banks' success in getting lower yields (higher prices), particularly for some segments such as non-investment-grade firms (Gande et al., 1997; Puri, 1996), the question arises as to whether the gains to the firms from higher security prices at issuance are offset by higher underwriter spreads. An interesting and important question is whether commercial banks and investment houses differ significantly in the gross spread that they charge to firms at any moment in time.

4.4. Market concentration

Opponents of universal banking have long argued that banks, with prior access to superior information about the quality of issuing firms through their loan monitoring activities, will force specialized investment houses out of the market. However, it is possible that bank entry into corporate debt market has a pro-competitive effect. Accordingly, we hypothesize that bank entry into corporate debt markets reduces market concentration, especially in segments in which banks have made the most significant strides in gaining market share.

5. Methodology and results

Since our hypotheses relating to the effect of bank entry on underwriter spreads and yield spreads suggest that the effects will be more pronounced in those segments of the market in which banks have underwritten relatively more issues, we need to identify those segments. We find that banks are more likely than investment houses to underwrite smaller issues. For example, 21% (46 out of 217 cases) of bank underwritings in our sample are less than $75 million in size, whereas only 11% (301 out of 2775 cases) of investment house underwritings are less than $75 million in size. We also find evidence that banks bring a larger proportion of lower-rated (Caa–Ba3) issuers to the market than do investment houses (38% of issues as compared to 30%). Univariate chi-square tests confirm the significance of these differences, i.e., banks underwrite a relatively larger proportion of lower-rated issues and smaller issues than do investment houses. For example, banks underwrite 82 lower-rated issues, significantly more than the expected 62 issues (based on probabilities in a 2×2 χ^2 test of independence of underwriter type and credit rating). Similarly, banks underwrite 46 smaller issues, significantly more than the expected 25 issues (based on probabilities in a 2×2 χ^2 test of independence of underwriter type and issue size).

The probit results in Table 3 supplement the univariate chi-square tests. The dependent variable for the probit regression is BANK, a dummy variable that takes the value of one if the lead underwriter is a bank (Section 20 subsidiary) and zero otherwise (an investment house). The independent variables for the probit regression are as described earlier. The probit tests show that the

Table 3
Probit estimations – bank versus investment house underwritings

This table presents results of the probit regression. The dependent variable is a dummy variable, BANK, assigned the value one if the lead underwriter is a Section 20 subsidiary. The independent variables are: LN(AMOUNT) is the natural logarithm of the offered dollar amount of the issue (in millions of dollars). NEW ISSUE is a dummy variable which is one if the issue is a first-time issue (debt IPO). INDUSTRY is a set of industry dummy variables constructed based on one-digit SIC codes. INVGRADE is a dummy variable if the debt issue is rated in the range Baa1–Aaa (i.e., investment-grade debt). MATURITY stands for dummy variables based on the maturity of the security. LOWMAT is one if the issue matures in less than five years, and HIMAT is one if the maturity is greater than 15 years. All dummy variables are zero otherwise. Pseudo R^2 is the likelihood ratio computed as $R^2 = 1 - \log L/\log L_0$ where $\log L$ is the maximized value of the log-likelihood function, $\log L_0$ is the log-likelihood computed only with a constant term. The point estimates and T ratios for the industry dummy variables are not reported though they are included in the regressions (a, b, and c stand for significance at the 1%, 5%, and 10% levels using a two-tailed test).

Variable	Coeff.		T ratio
INTERCEPT	0.31		0.75
INVGRADE	− 0.18		− 2.00[b]
LN(AMOUNT)	− 0.34		− 7.49[a]
LOWMAT	− 0.12		− 0.83
HIMAT	− 0.21		− 2.06[b]
NEW ISSUE	− 0.12		− 1.36
p-value		0.0000	
Observations		2992	
Pseudo R^2		0.0561	

probability that a bank is the underwriter varies inversely with both issue size (at the 1% level) and credit quality (at the 5% level). Overall, our univariate and probit results suggest that, to date, bank underwritings have been most concentrated in smaller and lower-rated issues.

5.1. Underwriter spreads

We examine the variable GROSS SPREAD, the underwriting spread of a debt issue measured as the difference between the offered amount and the proceeds to the issuer, expressed as a percentage of the offered amount [see Lee et al. (1996) for average underwriter spreads for debt and equity issues of U.S. corporations]. Preliminary evidence that commercial bank entry into the corporate bond underwriting market has reduced spreads can be seen from Table 4, which plots the trends in average underwriting spreads for investment and non-investment-grade securities over the sample period. Corporate debt underwriting spreads fall 25% from 2.99% to 2.24% for non-investment-grade debt and from 0.77% to 0.66% or 14% for investment-grade debt over the 12-year period.

Univariate tests for differences in underwriter spreads between the pre-1989 and post-1989 periods in corporate debt markets show that underwriter spreads have declined significantly from an average of 1.61% in the pre-1989 period to 1.19% in the post-1989 period. The decline in underwriter spreads is higher for non-investment-grade corporate debt securities, for which underwriter spreads were 3.28% in the pre-1989 period as compared to 2.47% in the post-1989 period. Both these declines are statistically significant at the 1% level.

We also run the following regression to examine the effect of bank entry on underwriter spreads:

$$\begin{aligned}\text{GROSS SPREAD} = \beta_0 &+ \beta_{cr}\,\text{CREDIT RATING}\\ &+ \beta_{mat}\,\text{MATURITY} + \beta_{ind}\,\text{INDUSTRY}\\ &+ \beta_1\,\text{LN(AMOUNT)} + \beta_2\,\text{NEW ISSUE}\\ &+ \beta_3\,\text{BANK ENTRY}. \end{aligned} \tag{1}$$

The regression results are presented in Table 5. For the overall sample, the control variables have the expected signs, i.e., larger issues generally have lower underwriter spreads, new (debt IPO) issues have larger underwriter spreads, and longer-maturity issues have higher underwriter spreads. For our purposes, the important coefficient is that of the BANK ENTRY variable which is negative (− 24 basis points) and statistically significant at the 1% level. As a measure of economic significance, the effect of the BANK ENTRY variable is three times that of the A1–A3 rating. The results are consistent with bank entry into corporate debt markets significantly reducing underwriter spreads.

Table 4
Average gross spread

This table presents the average gross spread, measured as a percentage of the issue size. Panel A classifies the sample of nonfinancial and nonregulated fixed-rate U.S. debt issues based on credit rating into two segments (Caa–Ba3, Baa1–Aaa). Panel B presents the average gross spread for nonfinancial nonregulated U.S. equity issues into two segments: initial public offerings (IPOs) and seasoned equity offerings (SEOs).

Panel A: Debt issues

Year	All issues		Caa–Ba3		Baa1–Aaa	
	# Issues	Spread (%)	# Issues	Spread (%)	# Issues	Spread (%)
1985	198	1.51	66	2.99	132	0.77
1986	348	1.62	114	3.34	234	0.78
1987	235	1.65	83	3.34	152	0.73
1988	183	1.64	65	3.37	118	0.68
1989	166	1.44	53	3.26	113	0.59
1990	103	0.67	3	2.38	100	0.62
1991	225	0.83	27	2.11	198	0.65
1992	354	1.25	130	2.31	224	0.63
1993	404	1.45	166	2.56	238	0.68
1994	208	1.44	88	2.63	120	0.56
1995	284	0.98	64	2.15	220	0.64
1996	284	1.08	76	2.24	208	0.66
Overall	2992	1.32	935	2.76	2057	0.67

Panel B: Equity issues

Year	All issues		IPOs		SEOs	
	# Issues	Spread (%)	# Issues	Spread (%)	# Issues	Spread (%)
1985	457	7.41	236	8.40	221	6.36
1986	721	7.32	453	8.29	268	5.69
1987	555	7.46	360	8.30	195	5.91
1988	227	7.52	143	8.37	84	6.08
1989	290	7.41	151	8.42	139	6.30
1990	260	7.07	131	8.11	129	6.00
1991	626	6.61	304	7.56	322	5.71
1992	702	6.88	387	7.60	315	6.00
1993	903	6.78	480	7.65	423	5.80
1994	692	6.97	423	7.85	269	5.58
1995	835	6.62	442	7.66	393	5.43
1996	1116	6.71	640	7.59	476	5.52
Overall	7384	6.96	4150	7.89	3234	5.78

Table 5
Multivariate regressions of gross spread of debt issues

This table gives the OLS estimates of the following equation:

$$\text{GROSS SPREAD} = \beta_0 + \beta_{cr}\ \text{CREDIT RATING} + \beta_{mat}\ \text{MATURITY} + \beta_{ind}\ \text{INDUSTRY} + \beta_1\ \text{LN(AMOUNT)} + \beta_2\ \text{NEW ISSUE} + \beta_3\ \text{BANK ENTRY}.$$

The dependent variable GROSS SPREAD is the gross spread of a debt issue measured as a percentage of the issue size. The independent variables are: CREDIT RATING is a set of credit rating dummy variables. For example, B1–B3 is a dummy variable which is one if Moody's credit rating for the issue is B1, B2, or B3. MATURITY stands for dummy variables based on maturity of the security. LOWMAT is one if the issue matures in less than five years, and HIMAT is one if the maturity is greater than 15 years. INDUSTRY is a set of industry dummy variables constructed based on one-digit SIC codes. LN(AMOUNT) is the natural logarithm of the offered dollar amount of the issue (in millions of dollars). NEW ISSUE is a dummy variable which is one if the issue is a first-time issue (debt IPO). BANK ENTRY is a dummy variable which is one in 1989 and succeeding years (based on the year of the debt issue) and zero otherwise. All dummy variables are zero otherwise. The *T* ratios are adjusted for heteroskedasticity using White's (1980) variance–covariance matrix. The point estimates and *T* ratios for the industry dummy variables are not reported though they are included in the regressions. The sample is also classified into small (less than \$75 million) and others (not less than \$75 million) segments based on the issue size (a, b, and c stand for significance at the 1%, 5%, and 10% levels using a two-tailed test).

Variable	All issues		Credit rating				Issue size			
	Coeff.	*T* ratio	Caa-Ba3		Baa1-Aaa		Small		Others	
			Coeff.	*T* ratio	Coeff.	*T* ratio	Coeff.	*T* ratio	Coeff.	*T* ratio
INTERCEPT	0.86	11.40^{a}	2.83	13.92^{a}	0.64	9.06^{a}	1.54	5.63^{a}	0.50	5.69^{a}
Caa–C	2.52	21.28^{a}	0.95	7.73^{a}			2.59	13.68^{a}	2.53	16.97^{a}
B1–B3	2.37	59.30^{a}	0.86	16.74^{a}			2.33	13.11^{a}	2.39	69.74^{a}
Ba1–Ba3	1.40	24.03^{a}					1.31	5.50^{b}	1.44	25.50^{a}
Baa1–Baa3	0.13	3.95^{a}			0.11	3.76^{a}	– 0.02	– 0.14	0.18	6.79^{a}
A1–A3	0.08	2.35^{b}			0.06	1.93^{c}	– 0.04	– 0.20	0.11	4.47^{a}
Aa1–Aa3	0.07	2.05^{b}			0.06	1.97^{b}	– 0.07	– 0.41	0.10	4.05^{a}
LOWMAT	– 0.26	– 11.12^{a}	– 0.48	– 1.43	– 0.26	– 17.68^{a}	– 0.33	– 3.79^{a}	– 0.23	– 11.78^{a}
HIMAT	0.24	16.10^{a}	– 0.07	– 0.50	0.24	21.54^{a}	0.20	1.73^{b}	0.23	19.58^{a}
LN(AMOUNT)	– 0.04	– 3.50^{a}	– 0.05	– 1.82^{c}	– 0.03	– 2.34^{b}	– 0.18	– 3.89^{a}	0.01	0.88
NEW ISSUE	0.18	8.22^{a}	0.32	7.62^{a}	0.05	2.69^{a}	0.22	2.50^{b}	0.17	8.00^{a}
BANK ENTRY	– 0.24	– 15.50^{a}	– 0.58	– 15.49^{a}	– 0.08	– 7.05^{a}	– 0.40	– 4.97^{a}	– 0.20	– 13.64^{a}
Observations	2992		935		2057		347		2645	
Adjusted R^2	0.8782		0.5233		0.4237		0.8587		0.8886	

5.1.1. Trends in non-investment-grade and smaller issues

Table 5 also examines investment-grade and non-investment-grade issues separately to assess the impact of bank entry in these segments. For both the investment-grade and non-investment-grade issues, the coefficient on the BANK ENTRY variable is significantly negative, although its size (in absolute value) is much larger for the non-investment-grade issues (i.e., − 0.58 versus − 0.08). The difference is statistically significant at the 1% level.

Table 5 further divides the sample into small and other issues, with small issues consisting of those under $75 million. From Table 5 it can be seen that the largest decline in underwriter spreads is for small issues (− 0.40 versus − 0.20). Again, this difference is statistically significant at the 1% level. The results of Table 5 support that bank entry into corporate debt markets has resulted in a reduction of underwriter spreads in those segments in which bank underwriting is most concentrated.

While the first bank permission to underwrite corporate debt was given in 1989, banks started to underwrite corporate debt only in 1991 (see Table 2). Hence one could argue that actual bank competition only started in 1991. To address this concern we rerun the regression in Table 5 with the BANK ENTRY variable defined as one in 1991 and succeeding years (based on the year of debt issue) and zero otherwise. The results are qualitatively unchanged.

We also use LN(MKT SHARE), the natural log of the market share of bank underwritings based on the annual dollar volume of corporate debt underwritings, as an alternative measure of the effect of bank entry on corporate debt underwriting. Additionally, we need to control for any time trend in the data. For example, information-gathering costs might have declined over time because of technology advances and greater access to public information. To control for any such time trends, we employ the TIME variable, which represents the year of the debt issue in question.

Specifically, we run the following regression:

$$\begin{aligned}\text{GROSS SPREAD} = \beta_0 &+ \beta_{cr}\,\text{CREDIT RATING} \\ &+ \beta_{mat}\,\text{MATURITY} + \beta_{ind}\,\text{INDUSTRY} \\ &+ \beta_1\,\text{LN(AMOUNT)} + \beta_2\,\text{NEW ISSUE} \\ &+ \beta_3\text{TIME} + \beta_4\,\text{LN(MKT SHARE)}. \qquad (2)\end{aligned}$$

The regression results are presented in Table 6. The coefficient on the LN(MKT SHARE) variable is negative and statistically significant at the 1% level. The (other) control variables also have the expected signs. In addition, the coefficient on LN(MKT SHARE) is significantly negative for non-investment-grade issues and larger (in absolute terms) than for the investment-grade issues (i.e., − 0.38 versus 0.01), with the difference significant at the 1% level. Finally, the decline in underwriter spreads is larger for the smaller issues (i.e., − 0.18

versus − 0.12), with the difference significant at the 1% level. Overall, the results are qualitatively similar to the univariate results and the regression results in Table 5.

5.1.2. Robustness checks

We conducted the following robustness checks. First, the nominal issue size may have grown over time due to inflation. To account for this, we adjust the issue size for inflation using the average Consumer Price Index (CPI) for each year and run the regressions in this paper with LN(AMOUNT) measured in real terms. The results are qualitatively unchanged. Second, Table 4 of our paper suggests that proportionately more higher-rated bonds came to the market during 1990 and 1991, coinciding with the collapse of Drexel and the subsequent credit crunch. We examine whether the events in 1990–1991 explain the lowering of underwriter spreads in two ways. First, we augment our regression in Table 6 with a dummy variable, YRDUM9091, which takes a value of one if a debt security is issued in 1990 or 1991 and zero otherwise. The results are qualitatively similar. The YRDUM9091 variable is generally negative, although statistically significant only for small issues. Second, we run the regression in Table 6 after excluding debt issues underwritten during 1990 and 1991. Again, the results are qualitatively similar. Finally, it is possible that initial engagement discounting could lead to lower spreads when banks enter a market (James, 1992). That is, banks charge a lower spread the first time that they underwrite and then subsequently increase their spreads. We test for this by examining all issuers with multiple debt issues underwritten by the same bank. We found 25 such issuers. Clearly, the sample is small and hence the results must be interpreted with caution. The mean underwriter spread for initial issues is 0.83% as compared to 0.73% for subsequent issues, although this difference is not statistically significant at any meaningful level. Since new issues are likely to have larger spreads than seasoned issues, we remove all debt IPOs leaving 18 issuers with multiple seasoned debt issues underwritten by the same bank. The initial average underwriter spread for the seasoned debt issuers is 0.65% versus 0.59% for subsequent issues. Again, this difference is not statistically significant at any meaningful level.

5.1.3. Equity markets as a control group

We next compare and contrast the markets for equity underwritings, in which banks have not yet made major inroads, with the corporate debt markets. While the trends in Table 4 suggest that underwriter spreads in both the IPO and seasoned equity markets have declined significantly over time, similar to debt issues, it is important to control for changes in issue characteristics over time. Hence we run multivariate regressions for our control sample of 7384 non-regulated, nonfinancial equity issues during 1985–1996, similar to those run for debt. The dependent and independent variables in our regressions are defined

Table 6
Multivariate regressions of gross spread of debt issues

This table gives the OLS estimates of the following equation:

$$\text{GROSS SPREAD} = \beta_0 + \beta_{cr}\,\text{CREDIT RATING} + \beta_{mat}\,\text{MATURITY} + \beta_{ind}\,\text{INDUSTRY} + \beta_1\,\text{LN(AMOUNT)} + \beta_2\,\text{NEW ISSUE} + \beta_3\,\text{TIME} + \beta_4\,\text{LN(MKT SHARE)}.$$

The dependent variable GROSS SPREAD is the gross spread of a debt issue measured as a percentage of the issue size. The independent variables are: CREDIT RATING is a set of credit rating dummy variables. For example, B1–B3 is a dummy variable which is one if Moody's credit rating for the issue is B1, B2, or B3. MATURITY stands for dummy variables based on maturity of the security. LOWMAT is one if the issue matures in less than five years, and HIMAT is one if the maturity is greater than 15 years. INDUSTRY is a set of industry dummy variables constructed based on one-digit SIC codes. LN(AMOUNT) is the natural logarithm of the offered dollar amount of the issue (in millions of dollars). NEW ISSUE is a dummy variable which is one if the issue is a first-time issue (debt IPO). TIME is based on the year of the debt issue, e.g., if the issue date is September 12, 1986, TIME takes the value 86. LN(MKT SHARE) is the natural log of the bank share (in percentage terms) of the annual dollar volume of corporate debt underwritings. All dummy variables are zero otherwise. The *T* ratios are adjusted for heteroskedasticity using White's (1980) variance–covariance matrix. The point estimates and *T* ratios for the industry dummy variables are not reported though they are included in the regressions. The sample is also classified into small (less than $75 million) and others (not less than $75 million) segments based on the issue size (a, b, and c stand for significance at the 1%, 5%, and 10% levels using a two-tailed test).

Variable	All Issues		Credit rating				Issue size			
			Caa–Ba3		Baa1–Aaa		Small		Others	
	Coeff.	*T* ratio	Coeff.	*T* ratio	Coeff.	*T* ratio	Coeff.	*T* ratio	Coeff.	*T* ratio
INTERCEPT	0.83	1.62	– 1.45	– 0.98	1.74	4.39[a]	0.52	0.26	– 0.13	– 0.28
Caa-C	2.54	21.03[a]	0.95	7.47[a]			2.55	14.17[a]	2.55	16.83[a]
B1-B3	2.37	59.68[a]	0.81	15.92[a]			2.32	14.08[a]	2.38	69.80[a]
Ba1-Ba3	1.41	24.52[a]					1.30	5.79[a]	1.45	25.90[a]
Baa1-Baa3	0.13	3.95[a]			0.11	3.75[a]	– 0.05	– 0.33	0.18	6.66[a]
A1-A3	0.06	1.98[b]			0.05	1.86[c]	– 0.09	– 0.56	0.10	3.99[a]
Aa1-Aa3	0.05	1.56			0.05	1.82[c]	– 0.13	– 0.77	0.09	3.48[a]
LOWMAT	– 0.28	– 11.64[a]	– 0.40	– 1.26	– 0.26	– 17.66[a]	– 0.33	– 4.02[a]	– 0.26	– 12.04[a]
HIMAT	0.25	17.13[a]	– 0.04	– 0.30	0.24	21.81[a]	0.25	2.15[b]	0.25	20.48[a]
LN(AMOUNT)	– 0.05	– 4.22[a]	– 0.07	– 2.49[b]	– 0.03	– 2.59[a]	– 0.24	– 4.52[a]	0.01	0.87
NEW ISSUE	0.19	8.59[a]	0.31	7.72[a]	0.05	2.84[a]	0.23	2.57[a]	0.18	8.45[a]
TIME	0.00	0.09	0.05	2.96[a]	– 0.01	– 2.91[a]	0.01	0.63	0.01	1.31
LN(MKT SHARE)	– 0.11	– 6.35[a]	– 0.38	– 8.43[a]	0.01	0.69	– 0.18	– 3.25[a]	– 0.12	– 7.10[a]
Observations	2992		935		2057		347		2645	
Adjusted R^2	0.8803		0.5658		0.4245		0.8617		0.8910	

similarly to those defined for our sample of debt issues. First, we regress GROSS SPREAD on LN(AMOUNT), NEW ISSUE, INDUSTRY, TIME, and LN(MKT SHARE). As can be seen from Table 7, for the overall sample, the coefficient on LN(MKT SHARE) is − 0.05 and is not statistically significant ($t = -0.69$). Also, for seasoned issues, we include an additional variable STOCKVOL, defined as the volatility of daily stock returns for the issuing firm in the year prior to the offer date. We compute this variable as the standard deviation of daily stock returns for seasoned issues for those firms in our sample with daily stock return data available through the Center for Research in Security Prices (CRSP).[2] The coefficient on LN(MKT SHARE) for seasoned issues is 0.05 and is not statistically significant ($t = 0.64$). Second, we replace the LN(MKT SHARE) variable in the above regression with a BANK ENTRY variable. For equity issues, as suggested by the referee, we define BANK ENTRY as a dummy variable which takes a value one during the period 1991–1996 and zero otherwise. For the overall sample, the coefficient on BANK ENTRY is − 0.04 and is not statistically significant ($t = -0.63$). Similarly, the coefficient on BANK ENTRY for seasoned issues is − 0.07 and is also not statistically significant ($t = -0.83$). As a robustness check, we also run the above regressions with YRDUM9091 as an additional independent variable. The results are qualitatively similar. Thus, in equity market underwritings (where banks have made little headway to date), we find no evidence that bank participation has been associated with a significant decline in equity market underwriting spreads. In a related paper, Chen and Ritter (1999) present evidence that at least 90% of the IPO deals raising between \$20 and \$80 million during 1985–1997 have gross spreads of exactly 7% and attribute this finding to 'strategic pricing' by investment bankers. Viewed as a backdrop to our results, this lack of variation is consistent with the view that commercial banks have not yet made significant inroads into this market segment.

5.2. *Yield spreads*

We run the following regression to examine the effects of bank entry on ex-ante yield spreads:

$$\text{YIELD SPREAD} = \beta_0 + \beta_{cr}\,\text{CREDIT RATING} + \beta_{mat}\,\text{MATURITY} + \beta_{ind}\,\text{INDUSTRY}$$

[2] The rationale for including the STOCKVOL variable in the regression for seasoned issues is that the underwriter spread is analogous to a put premium. That is, a firm-commitment underwriting is analytically equivalent to writing a put option on the firm's assets, and an increase in the volatility of assets (proxied by the stock volatility) increases the required put premium (spread). As can be seen from Table 7, the coefficient on STOCKVOL variable has the correct (positive) sign and is statistically significant at the 1% level. We thank the referee for this suggestion.

Table 7
Multivariate regressions of gross spread of equity issues

This table give the OLS estimates of the following equation:

$$\text{GROSS SPREAD} = \beta_0 + \beta_{ind}\,\text{INDUSTRY} + \beta_1\,\text{LN(AMOUNT)} + \beta_2\,\text{NEW ISSUE} + \beta_3\,\text{TIME} + \beta_4\,\text{LN(MKT SHARE)}.$$

The dependent variable GROSS SPREAD is the gross spread of a equity issue measured as a percentage of the issue size. The independent variables are: INDUSTRY is a set of industry dummy variables constructed based on one-digit SIC codes. LN(AMOUNT) is the natural logarithm of the offered dollar amount of the issue (in millions of dollars). NEW ISSUE is a dummy variable which is one if the issue is a first-time issue (IPO). TIME is based on the year of the equity issue, e.g., if the issue date is September 12, 1986, TIME takes the value 86. LN(MKT SHARE) is the natural log of the bank share (in percentage terms) of the annual dollar volume of corporate equity underwritings. All dummy variables are zero otherwise. The T ratios are adjusted for heteroskedasticity using White's (1980) variance–covariance matrix. The point estimates and T ratios for the industry dummy variables are not reported though they are included in the regressions. The sample is classified into initial public offerings (IPOs) and seasoned equity offerings (SEOs) based on the issue type. In addition, for SEOs, we include an additional variable STOCKVOL, defined as the volatility of daily stock returns during the year prior to the offer date. We compute this variable as the standard deviation of daily stock returns for seasoned issues for those firms in our sample that have daily stock returns data available on CRSP. The sample is also classified into small (less than $25 million) and others (not less than $25 million) segments based on the issue size (a, b, and c stand for significance at the 1%, 5%, and 10% levels using a two-tailed test).

Variable	All issues		Issue type				Issue size			
	Coeff.	*T* ratio	IPOs		SEOs		Small		Others	
			Coeff.	*T* ratio	Coeff.	*T* ratio	Coeff.	*T* ratio	Coeff.	*T* ratio
INTERCEPT	3.96	4.94[a]	6.70	12.03[a]	4.40	4.04[a]	3.17	3.90[a]	2.63	3.08[a]
LN(AMOUNT)	− 1.19	− 78.60[a]	− 1.08	− 64.15[a]	− 1.08	− 35.70[a]	− 1.63	− 51.70[a]	− 0.77	− 38.63[a]
NEW ISSUE	1.36	47.42[a]					1.01	21.03[a]	1.77	88.61[a]
TIME	0.06	7.38[a]	0.05	7.74[a]	0.05	4.14[a]	0.08	9.76[a]	0.06	6.61[a]
STOCKVOL					0.23	12.54[a]				
LN(MKT SHARE)	− 0.05	− 0.69	− 0.03	− 0.65	0.05	0.64	− 0.21	− 1.40	− 0.02	− 0.31
Observations	7384		4150		2788		3925		3459	
Adjusted R^2	0.7036		0.5797		0.6175		0.5169		0.7678	

$$+ \beta_1 \text{ LN(AMOUNT)} + \beta_2 \text{ NEW ISSUE}$$

$$+ \beta_3 \text{ TIME} + \beta_4 \text{ LN(MKT SHARE)}. \qquad (3)$$

The regression results are presented in Table 8. The LN(MKT SHARE) variable has a negative coefficient of − 0.18, significant at the 1% level. This is also economically significant as measured by the coefficient of Baa1–Baa3 (which is 0.06). This suggests that the increasing market share of banks in the corporate debt market has led to a reduction in yield spreads over time. The data for the yield on comparable U.S. Treasury issues is not available for 64 issues in our sampe and hence we can not compute the ex-ante yield spread for those 64 issues. As a robustness check, we run the regressions in this paper using the observations for which the data on both the gross spread and ex-ante yield spreads are available (2928 observations). The results are qualitatively similar.

We next test if this reduction in yield spreads has taken place in the segments in which bank underwritings are concentrated, that is, in non-investment-grade and small issues. Table 8 suggests that the increasing bank market share in debt underwritings has had a greater impact on lowering the yield spreads of smaller issues than of larger issues (and the difference is statistically significant at the 1% level).

5.3. Impact of competition on investment house underwritings

To further test for the source of reduction in underwriter spreads and yield spreads over time, we first examine if investment houses lowered their underwriter spreads over time in response to competition from commercial banks. We run the multivariate regression in Table 6 using only investment house underwritten securities, and examine if the increasing market share of banks results in lower underwriter spreads over time. Interestingly, we find this to be the case and the effect is strongest in segments in which bank underwriting is most pronounced, i.e., smaller and lower-rated issues (see Table 9). Second, while bank underwritings are known to reduce yield spreads in some segments (Gande et al., 1997; Puri, 1996), we examine whether competition from banks forced investment houses to lower yields (have higher offering prices) over time. We run the multivariate regression in Table 8 using only investment house underwritten securities, and examine if the growing market share of banks results in lower yields over time. As before, banks' increasing market share significantly reduces offering yields for investment house underwritten securities. This effect is strongest in segments in which bank underwriting is most prevalent, i.e., smaller and lower-rated issues (see Table 10).

Collectively, the results so far are consistent with commercial bank affiliates having a pro-competitive impact on underwriter spreads and yield spreads. This

Table 8
Multivariate regressions of yield spread of debt issues

This table gives the OLS estimates of the following equation:

$$\text{YIELD SPREAD} = \beta_0 + \beta_{cr}\,\text{CREDIT RATING} + \beta_{mat}\,\text{MATURITY} + \beta_{ind}\,\text{INDUSTRY} + \beta_1\,\text{LN(AMOUNT)} + \beta_2\,\text{NEW ISSUE} + \beta_3\,\text{TIME} + \beta_4\,\text{LN(MKT SHARE)}.$$

The dependent variable YIELD SPREAD is the ex-ante yield spread (in percentage terms) of a debt issue, i.e., ex-ante yield of debt security minus the ex-ante yield of a U.S. Treasury security of comparable maturity. The independent variables are: CREDIT RATING is a set of credit rating dummy variables. For example, B1–B3 is a dummy variable which is one if Moody's credit rating for the issue is B1, B2, or B3. MATURITY stands for dummy variables based on maturity of the security. LOWMAT is one if the issue matures in less than five years, and HIMAT is one if the maturity is greater than 15 years. INDUSTRY is a set of industry dummy variables constructed based on one-digit SIC codes. LN(AMOUNT) is the natural logarithm of the offered dollar amount of the issue (in millions of dollars). NEW ISSUE is a dummy variable which is one if the issue is a first-time issue (debt IPO). TIME is based on the year of the debt issue, e.g., if the issue date is September 12, 1986, TIME takes the value 86. LN(MKT SHARE) is the natural log of the bank share (in percentage terms) of the annual dollar volume of corporate debt underwritings. All dummy variables are zero otherwise. The T ratios are adjusted for heteroskedasticity using White's (1980) variance–covariance matrix. The point estimates and T ratios for the industry dummy variables are not reported though they are included in the regressions. The sample is also classified into small (less than \$75 m) and others (not less than \$75 million) segments based on the issue size (a, b, and c stand for significance at the 1%, 5%, and 10% levels using a two-tailed test).

Variable	All issues		Credit rating				Issue size			
	Coeff.	T ratio	Caa–Ba3		Baa1–Aaa		Small		Others	
			Coeff.	T ratio	Coeff.	T ratio	Coeff.	T ratio	Coeff.	T ratio
INTERCEPT	1.20	1.12	1.86	0.64	2.44	2.20[b]	– 4.02	– 0.92	1.92	2.00[b]
Caa–C	4.35	10.43[a]	2.39	11.28[a]			– 0.20	– 0.14	4.82	14.04[a]
B1–B3	3.43	9.88[a]	1.54	17.65[a]			– 1.13	– 0.84	3.98	19.86[a]
Ba1–Ba3	1.80	5.15[a]					– 3.02	– 2.23[b]	2.37	11.34[a]
Baa1–Baa3	0.06	0.17			0.21	0.72	– 4.54	3.41[a]	0.63	3.19[a]
A1–A3	– 0.38	– 1.09			– 0.28	– 0.93	– 4.80	3.59[a]	0.19	0.95
Aa1–Aa3	– 0.47	– 1.29			– 0.39	– 1.25	– 3.82	– 2.58[a]	0.01	0.06
LOWMAT	0.55	3.65[a]	1.11	2.18[b]	0.54	3.47[a]	2.42	5.08[a]	0.06	0.66
HIMAT	0.26	11.42[a]	– 0.23	– 1.14	0.27	13.86[a]	– 0.05	– 0.25	0.27	12.42[a]
LN(AMOUNT)	– 0.07	– 2.80[a]	– 0.09	– 1.84[c]	– 0.05	– 1.65	0.62	3.69[a]	– 0.05	– 1.58
NEW ISSUE	0.23	5.11[a]	0.56	7.25[a]	– 0.04	– 0.91	0.20	1.07	0.22	5.20[a]
TIME	– 0.00	– 0.29	0.02	0.44	– 0.02	– 1.45	0.00	0.03	– 0.01	– 1.14
LN(MKT SHARE)	– 0.18	– 4.96[a]	– 0.17	– 1.91[c]	– 0.17	– 4.82[a]	– 0.29	– 2.33[b]	– 0.12	– 3.72[a]
Observations	2928		912		2016		321		2607	
Adjusted R^2	0.7510		0.4123		0.1477		0.6689		0.8257	

Table 9
Multivariate regressions of gross spread of debt issues underwritten by investment banks

This table gives the OLS estimates of the following equation:

$$\text{GROSS SPREAD} = \beta_0 + \beta_{cr}\ \text{CREDIT RATING} + \beta_{mat}\ \text{MATURITY} + \beta_{ind}\ \text{INDUSTRY} + \beta_1\ \text{LN(AMOUNT)} + \beta_2\ \text{NEW ISSUE} + \beta_3\ \text{TIME} + \beta_4\ \text{LN(MKT SHARE)}.$$

The dependent variable GROSS SPREAD is the gross spread of a debt issue measured as a percentage of the issue size. The independent variables are: CREDIT RATING is a set of credit rating dummy variables. For example, B1–B3 is a dummy variable which is one if Moody's credit rating for the issue is B1, B2, or B3. MATURITY stands for dummy variables based on maturity of the security. LOWMAT is one if the issue matures in less than five years, and HIMAT is one if the maturity is greater than 15 years. INDUSTRY is a set of industry dummy variables constructed based on one-digit SIC codes. LN(AMOUNT) is the natural logarithm of the offered dollar amount of the issue (in millions of dollars). NEW ISSUE is a dummy variable which is one if the issue is a first-time issue (debt IPO). TIME is based on the year of the debt issue, e.g., if the issue date is September 12, 1986, TIME takes the value 86. LN(MKT SHARE) is the natural log of the bank share (in percentage terms) of the annual dollar volume of corporate debt underwritings. All dummy variables are zero otherwise. The *T* ratios are adjusted for heteroskedasticity using White's (1980) variance–covariance matrix. The point estimates and *T* ratios for the industry dummy variables are not reported though they are included in the regressions. The sample is also classified into small (less than \$75 million) and others (not less than \$75 million) segments based on the issue size (a, b, and c stand for significance at the 1%, 5%, and 10% levels using a two-tailed test).

Variable	All issues		Credit rating				Issue size			
	Coeff.	*T* ratio	Caa–Ba3		Baa1–Aaa		Small		Others	
			Coeff.	*T* ratio	Coeff.	*T* ratio	Coeff.	*T* ratio	Coeff.	*T* ratio
INTERCEPT	0.79	1.53	− 1.91	− 1.24	1.71	4.30[a]	− 0.46	− 0.23	− 0.09	− 0.20
Caa–C	2.54	21.05[a]	0.97	7.55[a]			2.59	14.58[a]	2.55	16.92[a]
B1–B3	2.38	59.06[a]	0.82	15.54[a]			2.32	13.41[a]	2.40	68.65[a]
Ba1–Ba3	1.41	23.98[a]					1.43	6.32[a]	1.44	24.88[a]
Baa1–Baa3	0.12	3.70[a]			0.11	3.57[a]	− 0.07	− 0.45	0.17	6.41[a]
A1–A3	0.06	1.72[c]			0.05	1.71[c]	− 0.08	− 0.50	0.09	3.67[a]
Aa1–Aa3	0.04	1.34			0.05	1.69[c]	− 0.13	− 0.79	0.08	3.17[a]
LOWMAT	− 0.27	− 11.03[a]	− 0.28	− 0.85	− 0.27	− 16.84[a]	− 0.36	− 3.53[a]	− 0.26	− 11.73[a]
HIMAT	0.25	16.61[a]	− 0.04	− 0.27	0.24	20.91[a]	0.22	1.70[c]	0.25	19.98[a]
LN(AMOUNT)	− 0.06	− 4.18[a]	− 0.09	− 3.06[a]	− 0.04	− 2.75[a]	− 0.30	− 4.73[a]	0.01	0.66
NEW ISSUE	0.18	7.73[a]	0.29	6.91[a]	0.04	2.43[b]	0.21	2.16[b]	0.17	7.76[a]
TIME	0.02	0.26	0.06	3.22[a]	− 0.01	− 2.67[a]	0.03	1.25	0.01	1.27
LN(MKT SHARE)	− 0.11	− 6.34[a]	− 0.40	− 8.68[a]	0.01	0.67	− 0.21	− 3.60[a]	− 0.12	− 7.04[a]
Observations	2775		853		1922		301		2474	
Adjusted R^2	0.8820		0.5779		0.4183		0.8560		0.8935	

Table 10
Multivariate regressions of yield spread of debt issues underwritten by investment banks

This table gives the OLS estimates of the following equation:

$$\text{YIELD SPREAD} = \beta_0 + \beta_{cr}\,\text{CREDIT RATING} + \beta_{mat}\,\text{MATURITY} + \beta_{ind}\,\text{INDUSTRY} + \beta_1\,\text{LN(AMOUNT)} + \beta_2\,\text{NEW ISSUE} + \beta_3\,\text{TIME} + \beta_4\,\text{LN(MKT SHARE)}.$$

The dependent variable YIELD SPREAD is the ex-ante yield spread (in percentage terms) of a debt issue, i.e., ex-ante yield of debt security minus the ex-ante yield of a U.S. Treasury security of comparable maturity. The independent variables are: CREDIT RATING is a set of credit rating dummy variables. For example, B1–B3 is a dummy variable which is one if Moody's credit rating for the issue is B1, B2, or B3. MATURITY stands for dummy variables based on maturity of the security. LOWMAT is one if the issue matures in less than five years, and HIMAT is one if the maturity is greater than 15 years. INDUSTRY is a set of industry dummy variables constructed based on one-digit SIC codes. LN(AMOUNT) is the natural logarithm of the offered dollar amount of the issue (in millions of dollars). NEW ISSUE is a dummy variable which is one if the issue is a first-time issue (debt IPO). TIME is based on the year of the debt issue, e.g., if the issue date is September 12, 1986, TIME takes the value 86. LN(MKT SHARE) is the natural log of the bank share (in percentage terms) of the annual dollar volume of corporate debt underwritings. All dummy variables are zero otherwise. The T ratios are adjusted for heteroskedasticity using White's (1980) variance–covariance matrix. The point estimates and T ratios for the industry dummy variables are not reported though they are included in the regressions. The sample is also classified into small (less than \$75 million) and others (not less than \$75 million) segments based on the issue size (a, b, and c stand for significance at the 1%, 5%, and 10% levels using a two-tailed test).

Variable	All issues		Credit rating				Issue size			
	Coeff.	*T* ratio	Caa–Ba3		Baa1–Aaa		Small		Others	
			Coeff.	*T* ratio	Coeff.	*T* ratio	Coeff.	*T* ratio	Coeff.	*T* ratio
INTERCEPT	0.66	0.60	– 0.33	– 0.11	2.39	2.09[b]	– 7.68	– 1.67[c]	1.31	1.36
Caa–C	4.36	10.55[a]	2.43	11.27[a]			0.42	0.33	4.85	14.07[a]
B1–B3	3.42	9.96[a]	1.53	16.89[a]			– 0.43	– 0.36	3.97	19.79[a]
Ba1–Ba3	1.79	5.20[a]					– 2.23	– 1.82[c]	2.34	11.20[a]
Baa1–Baa3	0.08	0.24			0.21	0.71	– 3.83	– 3.17[a]	0.65	3.26[a]
A1–A3	– 0.39	– 1.12			– 0.30	– 1.00	– 4.37	– 3.66[a]	0.19	0.94
Aa1–Aa3	– 0.46	– 1.28			– 0.40	– 1.26	– 3.25	– 2.41[b]	0.01	0.05
LOWMAT	0.63	3.80[a]	1.60	5.20[a]	0.59	3.52[a]	3.44	5.63[a]	0.07	0.70
HIMAT	0.26	11.19[a]	– 0.22	– 1.09	0.27	13.33[a]	0.02	0.10	0.26	12.04[a]
LN(AMOUNT)	– 0.11	– 3.55[a]	– 0.11	– 2.27[b]	– 0.09	– 2.42[b]	0.88	4.02[a]	– 0.04	– 1.21
NEW ISSUE	0.19	4.16[a]	0.52	6.49[a]	– 0.06	– 1.25	0.31	1.59	0.20	4.55[a]
TIME	0.01	0.38	0.04	1.23	– 0.01	– 1.18	0.02	0.39	– 0.01	– 0.56
LN(MKT SHARE)	– 0.20	– 5.34[a]	– 0.25	– 2.79[a]	– 0.17	– 4.54[a]	– 0.36	– 2.45[b]	– 0.14	– 4.32[a]
Observations	2719		832		1887		281		2438	
Adjusted R^2	0.7449		0.4244		0.1480		0.6748		0.8239	

impact is greatest for the smaller and lower-quality end of the corporate debt new issue market.

Our findings of the effect on underwriter spreads and yields in the corporate debt securities market is similar in spirit to those obtained in the literature on the municipal revenue bond market in the 1970s, when banks were allowed to underwrite certain types of these bonds for the first time. In an excellent survey of the studies of that time, Silber (1979) summarized the empirical evidence concerning the effects of bank underwriting in the municipal revenue bond market and cites '... overwhelming evidence that number of bids affects borrowing costs and that bank eligibility affects borrowing costs either directly or indirectly through the number of bids. The impact on borrowing costs stems from reductions in both reoffering yields and underwriting spreads. All of these impacts are statistically significant ... (p. 29)'. Silber concludes that 'The weight of the evidence clearly rejects the position that expected savings from permitting banks to underwrite is trivial (p. 8)'.[3]

5.4. Differences in underwriting spreads post-1989

An important issue is the effect of bank entry on the comparative realized underwriting spreads of banks and investment houses in the post-1989 period. There are two distinct possibilities. First, banks (to gain long-term market share) undercut investment houses' spreads and charge lower spreads than investment houses at any moment in time. Alternatively, banks as better and more credible certifiers are able to help obtain higher prices (lower yields) than investment houses and take advantage of this to charge higher underwriter spreads. We test which (if any) of these phenomenon has occurred.

We run a regression of post-1989 underwriter spreads on characteristics of the issue such as issue size, whether a new issue, time (year), industry dummies, credit rating, and maturity. We also include a dummy variable, BANKUND, which equals one if a bank underwrites the issue and zero otherwise. Specifically, we run the following regression:

$$\text{GROSS SPREAD} = X_i'\beta + \gamma\,\text{BANKUND}_i + u_i \tag{4}$$

[3] Related studies in this municipal bond literature, (e.g., Hopewell and Kaufman, 1977; Frankle, 1979) find that reoffering yields and/or net interest costs are significantly reduced by an increase in the number of bids. Kessel (1971) presents evidence that bank eligibility increases the number of bids and that the number of bids is inversely related to the underwriter spread. Rogowski (1980) establishes more directly that bank eligibility results in a significant reduction in municipal bond underwriting spreads. In other related work exploring the effects of global competition on equity underwriter spreads, consistent with our paper, Beatty et al. (1998) find that foreign issuers, who face a more competitive underwriting market than US issuers, have significantly lower underwriting costs.

where X_i is the vector of factors considered significant in determining gross spread, such as LN(AMOUNT), CREDIT RATING dummies, MATURITY dummies, the NEW ISSUE variable and the TIME variable.

We find that BANKUND is not a significant determinant of post-1989 underwriter spreads. We also examine the more recent subperiod 1993–1996 (about four years after the granting of debt underwriting powers, giving Section 20 subsidiaries sufficient time to establish distributional channels for underwriting new issues by themselves) and the results are qualitatively unchanged (see Table 11). The result suggest that any differences in underwriter spreads (or rents) on bank versus investment house underwritings due to banks undercutting investment houses have not persisted over time, perhaps because investment houses match bank spreads on an immediate basis. In fact, there have been no significant underwriter spread differentials in recent years (see Table 11). We further test if any differentials exist in the smaller and lower-rated segments in which bank underwriting has been most concentrated, and find no evidence of spread differentials in bank versus investment house underwritten issues.

In the multivariate regressions in Eq. (4), we have implicitly assumed that BANKUND is exogenous. However, the decision to underwrite a particular issue can be endogenous, based on the information the bank has. The bank's private information is $z_i'b + \eta_i$, where z_i is the vector of factors considered significant in determining the bank's underwriting decision. The bank will underwrite ($\text{BANKUND}_i = 1$) if $z_i'b + \eta_i \geqslant 0$. The market cannot observe the bank's latent information but can partially extract this information. In particular, the market uses the bank's underwriting decision to update its expectations of the bank's private information. This endogeneity of the bank underwriting decision induces a correlation between u_i and η_i. The coefficient estimates in the linear regression in Eq. (4) are inconsistent (Maddala, 1983). Under the assumption that η_i is distributed normally $N(0, \sigma^2)$, Eq. (4) now becomes

$$\text{GROSS SPREAD} = X_i'\beta + \phi\lambda_{\text{B}}\text{BANKUND}_i + \phi\lambda_{\text{NB}}(1 - \text{BANKUND}_i) + v_i, \tag{5}$$

where $\lambda_{\text{B}} = n(z_i'b|\sigma)/N(z_i'b|\sigma)$; $\lambda_{\text{NB}} = -n(z_i'b|\sigma)/(1 - N(z_i'b|\sigma))$, $\lambda \in \{\lambda_{\text{B}}, \lambda_{\text{NB}}\}$ is the Inverse-Mills Ratio and represents the private information revealed by the bank underwriting decision $\phi = \pi\sigma$, where $\pi = \text{cov}(u_i, \eta_i)/\text{var}(\eta_i)$. The significance and sign of the coefficient of λ tell us whether the information revealed by the bank underwriting significantly affects gross spreads.

We use a two-stage methodology advocated by Heckman (1979) to obtain consistent estimates. The first step is to estimate a probit of the likelihood of the bank underwriting, and from this step we obtain estimates of λ. The second step involves plugging the estimates of λ into Eq. (5), which can now be estimated by ordinary least squares. The standard errors are corrected for heteroskedasticity and for the errors-in-variables problem caused by using estimates of λ rather

Table 11
Multivariate regressions of gross spread of debt issues with Heckman's correction

This table give the OLS estimates of the following equation:

$$\text{GROSS SPREAD} = \beta_0 + \beta_{cr}\,\text{CREDIT RATING} + \beta_{mat}\,\text{MATURITY} + \beta_{ind}\,\text{INDUSTRY} + \beta_1\,\text{LN(AMOUNT)} + \beta_2\,\text{NEW ISSUE} + \beta_3\,\text{TIME} + \beta_4\,\text{BANKUND}.$$

The dependent variable GROSS SPREAD is the gross spread of a debt issue measured as a percentage of the issue size for debt issues during the years 1993–96 in our sample. The independent variables are: CREDIT RATING is a set of credit rating dummy variables. For example, B1–B3 is a dummy variable which is one if Moody's credit rating for the issue is B1, B2, or B3. MATURITY stands for dummy variables based on the maturity of the security. LOWMAT is one if the issue matures in less than five years, and HIMAT is one if the maturity is greater than 15 years. INDUSTRY is a set of industry dummy variables constructed based on one-digit SIC codes. LN(AMOUNT) is the natural logarithm of the offered dollar amount of the issue (in millions of dollars). NEW ISSUE is a dummy variable which is one if the issue is a first-time issue (debt IPO). TIME is based on the year of the debt issue, e.g., if the issue date is September 12, 1986, TIME takes the value 86. BANKUND takes the value one if the lead underwriter is a Section 20 subsidiary. All dummy variables are zero otherwise. The *T* ratios are adjusted for heteroskedasticity using White's (1980) variance–covariance matrix. The point estimates and *T* ratios for the industry dummy variables are not reported though they are included in the regressions. The second-step regression of the Heckman's two-step estimation procedure involves using estimates of the inverse-mills ratio LAMBDA from the first-step (probit regression — not shown here) instead of BANKUND (a, b, and c stand for significance at the 1%, 5%, and 10% levels using a two-tailed test), as in Eq. (5).

Variable	OLS		Heckman's correction	
	Coeff.	*T* ratio	Coeff.	*T* ratio
INTERCEPT	1.94	2.15[b]	2.06	2.48[b]
Caa–C	2.32	14.10[a]	2.33	13.37[a]
B1–B3	2.13	30.84[a]	2.13	18.45[a]
Ba1–Ba3	1.09	11.26[a]	1.09	9.32[a]
Baa1–Baa3	0.07	1.08	0.07	0.58
A1–A3	0.05	0.80	0.05	0.43
Aa1–Aa3	0.08	1.31	0.08	0.69
LOWMAT	− 0.29	− 6.26[a]	− 0.29	− 6.50[a]
HIMAT	0.23	11.11[a]	0.23	8.69[a]
LN(AMOUNT)	− 0.03	− 1.95[c]	− 0.02	− 1.81[c]
NEW ISSUE	0.17	5.57[a]	0.17	6.87[a]
TIME	− 0.02	− 1.59	− 0.02	− 1.90[c]
BANKUND	− 0.04	− 1.15		
LAMBDA			− 0.02	− 0.93
Observations	1180		1180	
Adjusted R^2	0.8725		0.8725	

than true values by using an appropriate asymptotic covariance matrix developed in Heckman (1979) and Greene (1981). Based on this estimation, we find that the coefficient of λ is insignificant (see Table 11). A similar result obtains when we run the regressions for the smaller and lower-rated subsamples in which bank underwritings are concentrated. These results suggest that differences in underwriter spreads on bank versus investment house underwritings (due to banks undercutting investment houses' by charging lower underwriter spreads) have not persisted over time, perhaps because investment houses' match the bank spreads on an immediate basis. In other words, increased market competition appears to have resulted in a similar lowering of spreads among banks and investment houses.

5.5. *Market concentration*

Given that banks have been acquiring investment banks since 1997, it is somewhat early to assess the long-term impact of bank entry on market concentration. However, it is interesting to assess the short-term impact of bank entry on market concentration. For this purpose we use two measures of concentration: a five-firm concentration index and a Herfindahl index [see Tirole (1990) for an explanation of these indices]. Table 12 presents these measures for our sample of debt issues. In Table 12 we also break down these measures to look at concentration in different segments of the corporate debt market reflected by credit rating.

Both measures show that the market for corporate debt securities is less concentrated post-1989 (see Table 12). In addition, for our sample, the share of the top five underwriters declines from 72.45% in the pre-1989 period to 69.25% in the post-1989 period, statistically significant at the 10% level. Similarly, the Herfindahl index also declines from 1217.82 in the pre-1989 period to 1179.57 in the post-1989 period for our sample. The decline is particularly pronounced for non-investment-grade debt, where the share of the top five underwriters declines from 81.07% in the pre-1989 period to 59.21% in the post-1989 period. This decline is statistically significant at the 1% level. Similarly, the Herfindahl index declines from 2626.86 in the pre-1989 period to about a third of its magnitude (910.10) in the post-1989 period for non-investment-grade debt. Both these measures suggest that the decline in market concentration, in the short-run, has been particularly pronounced in the lower-rated corporate debt issues market.

6. Conclusions

The results of our paper are consistent with the post-1989 entry of Section 20 commercial banking subsidiaries into corporate debt underwriting having a favorable (pro-competitive) effect on corporate debt underwriting costs to

Table 12
Measures of concentration of underwritings of debt issues

This table presents two measures of concentration of underwriters, namely a five-firm concentration index (in percentage terms) and a Herfindahl index (in squared-percentage terms) in our sample of nonfinancial and nonregulated fixed-rate U.S. debt issues. Further, this table also classifies the sample of nonfinancial and nonregulated fixed-rate U.S. debt issues based on credit rating into two segments (Caa–Ba3, Baa1–Aaa).

Year	All issues		Caa–Ba3		Baa1–Aaa	
	Five-firm	Herfindahl	Five-firm	Herfindahl	Five-firm	Herfindahl
1985	75.62	1506.38	86.40	3786.98	82.89	1879.03
1986	73.44	1297.52	83.25	3306.14	74.85	1366.86
1987	73.05	1271.88	87.24	2316.27	80.20	1418.88
1988	68.02	1130.30	80.37	2148.46	70.55	1213.66
1989	75.84	1338.89	84.23	2061.29	83.08	1547.66
1990	94.30	1999.83	100.00	5061.73	94.17	1971.49
1991	79.25	1631.36	80.68	2595.55	80.52	1685.06
1992	72.51	1325.09	63.49	1035.62	80.18	1557.92
1993	67.52	1120.86	68.51	1202.02	81.49	1480.60
1994	65.63	1087.08	68.33	1103.41	83.54	1551.86
1995	64.63	1170.84	65.13	1223.82	74.13	1399.27
1996	61.69	1175.43	47.88	754.71	71.93	1588.80
Overall	67.72	1102.92	60.42	940.50	76.55	1390.15

issuers. Specifically, bank entry appears to have resulted in reduced underwriter spreads and yields. Our results are also consistent with bank entry resulting in lower market concentration in the market for corporate debt underwriting. Interestingly, the results of our paper also suggest that the pro-competitive effect of declining underwriting spreads, yield spreads, and market concentration has been strongest in the smaller, lower-quality end of the corporate debt market where banks do a relatively larger proportion of their underwriting. Thus the main beneficiaries of the passage of the Section 20 Act and the subsequent modifications have been relatively smaller issuers of below-investment-grade quality.

References

Beatty, R.P., Thompson, R.W., Vetsuypens, M.R., 1998. Issuance costs and regulatory changes in the investment banking industry. Unpublished working paper. Southern Methodist University, Dallas.

Benston, G.J., 1994. Universal banking. Journal of Economic Perspectives 8, 205–225.

Chen, Hsuan-Chi, Ritter, J.R., 1999. The seven percent solution. Journal of Finance, forthcoming.

Ederington, L.H., 1976. Competitive versus negotiated underwriting of public utility debt. Journal of Finance 31, 17–28.
Flannery, M.J., 1986. Asymmetric information and risky debt maturity choice. Journal of Finance 41, 19–38.
Frankle, A.W., 1979. Effects of bank underwriting on competition and interest costs for tax-exempt revenue bonds. Mimeo, State University of New York at Albany, NY.
Gande, A., Puri, M., Saunders, A., Walter, I., 1997. Bank underwriting of debt securities: modern evidence. Review of Financial Studies 10, 1175–1202.
GAO, 1990. Bank Powers: Activities of Securities Subsidiaries of Bank Holding Companies. United States General Accounting Office, Washington, DC.
Greene, W., 1981. Sample selection bias as a specification error: comment. Econometrica 47, 795–798.
Heckman, J.J., 1979. Sample selection bias as a specification error. Econometrica 47, 153–161.
Hopewell, M.H., Kaufman, G.G., 1977. Commercial bank bidding on municipal revenue bonds: new evidence. Journal of Finance 32, 1647–1656.
James, C., 1987. Some evidence on the uniqueness of bank loans. Journal of Financial Economics 19, 217–236.
James, C., 1992. Relationship-specific assets and the pricing of underwriter services. Journal of Finance 47, 1865–1885.
Kessel, R., 1971. A study of the effects of competition in the tax-exempt bond market. Journal of Political Economy 79, 706–738.
Lee, I., Lochhead, S., Ritter, J., Zhao, Q., 1996. The costs of raising capital. Journal of Financial Research 19, 59–74.
Maddala, G.S., 1983. Limited dependent and qualitative variables in econometrics. In: Econometric Society monograph. Cambridge University Press, Cambridge, MA.
Puri, M., 1996. Commercial banks in investment banking: conflict of interest or certification role? Journal of Financial Economics 40, 373–401.
Puri, M., 1999. Commercial banks as underwriters: implications for the going public process. Journal of Financial Economics 54, 133–163.
Rogowski, R.J., 1980. Underwriting, competition and issuer borrowing costs in the municipal revenue bonds. Journal of Bank Research 10, 212–220.
Silber, W.H., 1979. Municipal revenue bond costs and bank underwriting: a survey of the evidence. In: Monograph Series in Finance and Economics, Salomon Brothers Center for the Study of Financial Institutions. New York University, New York.
Sorensen, E.H., 1979. The impact of underwriting method and bidder competition upon corporate bond interest cost. Journal of Finance 34, 863–870.
Tirole, J., 1990. The Theory of Industrial Organization. MIT Press, Cambridge, MA.
White, H., 1980. A heteroskedasticity-consistent covariance matrix estimator and a direct test for heteroskedasticity. Econometrica 48, 817–838.

II. Regulation: Mergers and Acquisitions

ELSEVIER Journal of Financial Economics 50 (1998) 187–229

JOURNAL OF Financial ECONOMICS

The effects of bank mergers and acquisitions on small business lending[1]

Allen N. Berger[a,b,*], Anthony Saunders[c], Joseph M. Scalise[d], Gregory F. Udell[e]

[a] *Board of Governors of the Federal Reserve System, Washington, DC 20551, USA*
[b] *Wharton Financial Institutions Center, Philadelphia, PA 19104, USA*
[c] *Stern School of Business, New York University, New York, NY 10012, USA*
[d] *Wharton School of Business, University of Pennsylvania, Philadelphia, PA 19104, USA*
[e] *Kelley School of Business, Indiana University, Bloomington, IN 47405, USA*

Received 31 March 1997; received in revised form 18 November 1997

Abstract

We examine the effects of bank M&As on small business lending using data on over 6000 recent U.S. bank M&As. We are the first to decompose the impact of M&As into the static effects from simply melding the antecedent institutions and the dynamic effects associated with post-M&A refocusing of the consolidated institution. We are also the first to estimate the dynamic reactions of other local banks. We find that the static effects of consolidation reduce small business lending, but are mostly offset by the reactions of other banks, and in some cases also by refocusing efforts of the consolidating institutions themselves. © 1998 Elsevier Science S.A. All rights reserved.

JEL classification: E58; G21; G28; G34; L89

Keywords: Bank; Mergers; Small business

* Corresponding author. Tel.: 202/452-2903; fax: 202/452-5295; e-mail: aberger@frb.gov.

[1] The opinions expressed do not necessarily reflect those of the Board of Governors or its staff. The authors thank an anonymous referee and Bill Schwert (the editor) for valuable guidance and suggestions, Gary Gorton, Randy Kroszner, and Raghu Rajan for very useful discussants' comments, Jim Burke, Ed Ettin, Jim Kolari, Myron Kwast, Steve Pilloff, Steve Rhoades, Phil Strahan, and participants at the ASSA meetings, Federal Reserve Bank of Chicago Bank Structure and Competition conference, SBA conference on bank consolidation, and Federal Reserve Bank of New York seminar series for their useful insights, and Seth Bonime and Margaret Kyle for their valuable research assistance.

PII: S0304-405X(98)00036-1

1. Introduction

The liberalization of geographic restrictions on U.S. banking institutions beginning in the late 1970s has produced a rapid consolidation of the banking industry. Since that time, banking has been in a state of continuous transition, with mergers and acquisitions averaging over 600 per year. During the first half of the 1990s, banks with more than 20% of the industry's assets were involved in M&As each year. Given the magnitude of this consolidation and the importance of this industry, it is not surprising that bank M&A activity has garnered much attention from researchers, policy analysts, and the press.

There are a number of potential benefits from the lifting of geographic barriers to competition in banking and the associated wave of M&A activity, including increased geographic diversification, improved competition, and the elimination of entrenched inefficient or self-serving bank managers. What is less clear is the effect of consolidation on the supply of credit to businesses, particularly small businesses that depend on banks for external credit. Cole et al. (1996) find that commercial banks are the single most important source of credit to small firms using the National Survey of Small Business Finance. Prior research has established a strong link between banking institution size and the supply of small business credit, with larger institutions devoting lesser proportions of their assets to small business lending than smaller institutions (see, e.g., Berger et al., 1995; Keeton, 1995; Levonian and Soller, 1995; Berger and Udell, 1996; Peek and Rosengren, 1996; Strahan and Weston, 1996).

To illustrate, banks with less than $100 million in assets devoted about 9% of their portfolios to small business lending (i.e., loans to business borrowers with bank credit less than $1 million) based on the June 1997 Call Report, whereas banks with over $10 billion in assets invested about 2% of their assets in these loans. On the surface, this finding would seem to suggest that as bank assets are shifted from smaller to larger institutions through M&As, the overall supply of bank credit to small businesses may fall substantially. As an upper bound, if the industry were to become so consolidated that all banks were larger than $10 billion and if the propensities to lend to small business were to remain constant, small business lending would fall by more than half.

However, this simplistic analysis assumes that lending propensities are static and are determined solely by size of bank. It neglects the fundamental nature of M&As as dynamic events that may involve significant changes in organizational focus. Such conclusions also ignore the reactions of other lenders in the same local markets who might pick up any profitable loans that are no longer supplied by the consolidated institutions, or react with other dynamic changes in behavior.

This research departs from most of the extant literature by examining the dynamic impact of M&As, rather than drawing conclusions from a static comparison. We also depart from the entire extant literature – including the other dynamic studies of bank M&As on lending – by modeling the net impact of an M&A on small business lending as a combination of static and dynamic effects, and by measuring the effects of M&As on lending by other banks in the same local markets.

We measure four effects of M&As on small business lending. The *static effect* is the change in lending propensities that results from simply combining the balance sheets of the participating banks into a larger pro forma institution, much like our simple example above. The remaining effects are dynamic. The *restructuring effect* identifies the change in lending that follows from any restructuring of the institution in terms of its size, financial characteristics, and local market competitive position. For example, the consolidated institution may divest some of the combined assets to reduce excess capacity in its market, and this reduction in size after the M&A may alter its lending propensities. The *direct effect* captures the change in lending by the consolidated institution attributable to a direct change in lending focus above and beyond the changes associated with the transformations of institution size and other characteristics created by the static and restructuring effects. The direct effect captures the difference in lending between the new 'restructured' institution and the lending of an otherwise similar institution that has not undergone a recent M&A. Finally, the *external effect* captures the dynamic responses to M&As of other lenders in the same local markets. The external effect incorporates the possibility that some loans that are dropped by the consolidating institutions may represent valuable business opportunities for other nearby banks or nonbank lenders. Thus, even if merging institutions reduce their small business lending substantially, the total supply of these loans need not change substantially because some or all of these loans could be picked up by other institutions.

We measure the static, restructuring, direct, and external effects of the great majority of U.S. bank M&As from the late 1970s to the early 1990s, a total of over 6,000 M&As. Because a number of research and policy issues turn on the type of M&A, we allow for the possibility that these loan supply effects differ for bank mergers versus bank holding company (BHC) acquisitions, for 'mergers of equals' versus other M&As, for out-of-state acquisitions, etc. We also examine whether the effects of M&As differ by the relative and absolute sizes of the participants. Importantly, using a data set with a relatively long time series allows us to examine a large number of M&As and leaves enough time for most of the dynamic effects to occur and be measured.

We find that the static effect tends to substantially reduce small business lending, consistent with prior research. However, this effect is largely if not fully offset by the dynamic effects. For bank mergers (consolidations of two or more bank charters), the external effect suggests a strong positive reaction by other banks in the same local markets. For BHC acquisitions (the banks retain their separate charters), the direct and external effects are each large enough to offset the static effect. These results strongly suggest that a dynamic approach is needed and that inclusion of external effects of M&As on other local banks may be particularly important. We also find important differences by type of M&A and by size of participant.

The remainder of the paper is organized as follows. Section 2 reviews the literature. Section 3 motivates each of the effects of M&As on the supply of small business lending, and Section 4 econometrically models these effects. Section 5 presents our empirical analysis, and Section 6 concludes.

2. Previous research

The bank M&A literature can be categorized into five main topics: (1) event studies of the ex ante evaluation of the M&As by capital market participants (see, e.g., Houston and Ryngaert, 1994; Palia, 1994; Cornett et al., 1998); (2) the relationship of these returns to ex post measures of performance (see, e.g., Cornett and Tehranian, 1992; Pilloff, 1996); (3) the determinants of the premium paid for the target (see, e.g., Palia, 1993); (4) the cost and profit efficiency consequences of M&As (see, e.g., Berger and Humphrey, 1992, Akhavein et al., 1997); and (5) the topic of this paper – the effects of bank M&As on the supply of credit to small business borrowers – a topic that has only been studied quite recently despite its important policy and research implications.

Theory suggests that the larger, more organizationally complex institutions that are created by M&As may be less inclined than smaller, less complex institutions to lend to small, informationally opaque borrowers – the borrowers who are most dependent on banks for credit and for whom the bank-borrower relationship is most important. Large institutions may be less inclined to extend loans that demand intimate knowledge of the small business, its owner, and its local market because of Williamson (1967, 1988) type organizational diseconomies associated with producing such loans along with other financial service products. These diseconomies might arise because lending to small, informationally opaque borrowers and lending to large, informationally transparent borrowers may be distinctly different activities that require the use of different technologies and entirely different credit cultures. That is, the policies and procedures associated with screening and monitoring small, informationally opaque borrowers and transmitting the relevant information within the banking institution may be very different from those associated with providing transaction-driven loans to large, informationally transparent borrowers.[2] In addition to a financial institution's size, its organizational complexity may also

[2] See Ang (1992), Petersen and Rajan (1994, 1995), Berger and Udell (1995), Houston and James (1995, 1998), Blackwell and Winters (1997), Angelini et al. (1998), Berlin and Mester (1998), and Cole (1998) for more evidence regarding relationship lending to small businesses.

affect its small business lending. Greater organizational complexity – such as having multiple layers of management or operating in multiple states or nations – may make it more difficult to provide locally-based small business services. Together, these arguments suggest that large, complex banking institutions – whose core business is the provision of capital market financial services – may have difficulty competing against small, less complex banking institutions in the provision of the latter group's core business product – loans to small, informationally opaque borrowers.[3]

Other factors associated with M&As, such as changes in market competitiveness or changes in the degree of ownership control, may affect small business lending either positively or negatively. For example, prior to M&As, some banks may have made non-value maximizing choices with respect to small business lending because of a lack of competitive pressure to optimize and/or agency problems in which bank owners had difficulty controlling inefficient or self-serving managers. These difficulties may be more severe in banking than in other industries because geographic limits on competition and other regulatory restrictions may have resulted in deviations from value maximization. Bank M&As that occur in reaction to the lifting of some of these restrictions may improve value maximizing behavior and economic efficiency. This may reduce small business lending to the extent that some negative net present value loans that were formerly made are not renewed, or may increase small business lending to the extent that some positive net present value loans that were formerly neglected are made.[4]

The relatively recent empirical research on the effects of bank M&As on small business lending has employed two main data sources. The Federal Reserve's Survey of the Terms of Bank Lending to Businesses (STBL) contains detailed contract information on a sample of loans made by about 300 banks per quarter since the late 1970s, and includes virtually all large banks. The second source is a new section on the June Call Reports on quantities of lending to small borrowers. Because it began in June 1993, very few time periods are available. Both data sources have sufficient information to estimate the proportions of loans to small business borrowers, defined here and in other studies as

[3] Consistent with these arguments, the corporate finance literature has found that large conglomerate nonfinancial firms often engage in asset sales which allow the firms to focus better on their core businesses or specialize in fewer product areas. Such improvements in focus tend to be associated with better operating performance over the three years following the asset sales as well as improvements in stock returns (see John and Ofek, 1995).

[4] Alternatively, increased competition may eliminate some positive net present value small business loans to relationship borrowers as greater competition makes it more difficult to enforce long-term implicit contracts in which the borrower receives a subsidized interest rate in the short term and then compensates the bank by paying a higher rate in a later period (see Petersen and Rajan, 1995).

borrowers with bank credit of less than $1 million. The STBL has the advantage of covering many more years of data, but it includes only some of the banks. The small business lending section of the Call Report has the advantage of including all banks, but it is available for only a few years, making it difficult to use for studying the dynamic effects of M&As. Despite the differences, however, the two data sources virtually always yield the same qualitative conclusions.

Several studies focus on the association between small business lending and banking institution size and organizational complexity. Berger et al. (1995) and Berger and Udell (1996) using the STBL data, and Keeton (1995), Levonian and Soller (1995), Berger and Udell (1996), Peek and Rosengren (1996), and Strahan and Weston (1996) using the recent June Call Reports all find that small banking institutions tend to invest much higher proportions of their assets in small business loans than large institutions. In contrast, the empirical evidence on the effects of organizational complexity on the supply of small business credit are more mixed (see, e.g., Keeton, 1995; Whalen, 1995; Berger and Udell, 1996). Other studies concentrate on the liberalization of state geographic banking restrictions, which allows banking institutions to increase in both size and organizational complexity. Berger et al. (1995), using the STBL data, find that past relaxation of geographic restrictions is associated with a reduction in the supply of bank loans to small businesses.

More in line with the analysis in this paper, Peek and Rosengren (1996, 1998), Strahan and Weston (1996, 1998), Craig and Santos (1997), Kolari and Zardkoohi (1997a,b), Zardkoohi and Kolari (1997), and Walraven (1997) pursue dynamic approaches. These studies all use the recent June Call Report information on small business lending to compare lending before and after M&As. Peek and Rosengren and Strahan and Weston generally find that M&As between small banking institutions increase small business lending. Strahan and Weston also find that M&As between large institutions and small institutions or between two large institutions yield no clear effect on small business lending. In contrast, Peek and Rosengren find decreases in small business lending associated with M&As between large institutions, although their results depend on the small business lending propensity of the acquiring bank prior to consolidation. Craig and Santos find no clear effect of M&As of either type, with the results depending crucially on the econometric method employed. Kolari and Zardkoohi and Zardkoohi and Kolari also find mixed results – larger institutions generally reducing small business lending after acquisition, mergers reducing small business lending more than acquisitions, and more complex organizations often increasing small business lending after consolidation. Walraven finds that merging banks tend to revert to the small business lending propensity of the surviving bank. Keeton (1996, 1997) does not use the new small business lending section of the Call Report, but is able to isolate small business lending by looking at small banks, which typically cannot make large loans because of legal lending limits and problems of diversification.

Keeton finds that certain types of acquisitions of these small banks, particularly purchases by out-of-state institutions, are associated with reductions in small business lending.

Thus, the literature gives a very mixed picture of the effects of bank M&As on the supply of small business credit, depending upon whether a static versus dynamic approach is pursued, the type of econometric procedure employed, whether bank mergers versus BHC acquisitions are analyzed, whether the consolidating institutions are small versus large, and whether they are in the same versus different states. This literature also does not reveal *how* M&As change the supply of credit, i.e., the extent to which various static and dynamic effects may interact to reach a new equilibrium. Importantly, this literature also does not address whether any reduction in supply of small business credit by consolidating institutions may be offset by the reactions of other lenders in the same local market.

Our analysis extends the dynamic approach to answer these difficult questions. A structural model decomposes the effects of M&As on small business lending into several static and dynamic effects to improve accuracy and to identify how M&As affect the credit supply process. We are also the first to examine the impact of M&As on lending by other banks in the same local market to estimate the total effect of bank M&As on the supply of credit to small businesses. In addition, we distinguish between the effects of bank mergers and BHC acquisitions, as well as among several types of each, to account for the possibility that different categories of M&As may have very different effects on the supply of small business credit. Finally, our use of the long data series from the STBL allows us to analyze a much greater number of M&A observations than prior studies that use the small business lending section of the Call Report, and allows for a fuller treatment of the dynamic effects of M&As by using data from a three-year gestation period following the M&As.

3. The four effects of M&As on bank lending

Our analysis suggests that the impact of M&As on bank lending behavior is quite complex, with one static effect and three types of dynamic effects. Disentangling these four effects allows us to identify more precisely than the extant literature how M&As affect small business lending. The static effect is simply the result of the banking institutions combining their pre-M&A assets into a larger institution with a combined balance sheet and competitive position. The static effect might be expected to result in a decreased supply of small business loans, since (as discussed above) larger banking institutions tend to make fewer small business loans per dollar of assets. For example, if a bank with $600 million in assets merges with a $400 million bank, the static effect on small business lending captures the predicted difference in lending between a typical

$1 billion bank and the two smaller banks. The $1 billion bank that results from simply adding together the pre-M&A balance sheets of the merging parties is referred to as the pro forma bank. The static effect also incorporates any impact from combining the financial conditions and other exogenous variables of the two smaller institutions.

The restructuring effect is a dynamic effect of the M&A due to a change in focus in which the institution changes its size, financial condition, or competitive position from their pro forma values after consummating an M&A. In our simple example, the merger of the $600 million bank and the $400 million bank might eventually result in a consolidated bank of only $800 million after the merger, rather than $1 billion. This could occur, for example, if the purpose of the merger was to reduce excess banking capacity in the local market. This reduction in bank size from the $1 billion pro forma bank to the $800 million actual bank would likely increase its proportion of assets devoted to small business lending since smaller institutions tend to have higher proportions of these loans.

The consolidated institution's new focus may also be associated with changes in portfolio composition and financial ratios after consolidation because of the inherent diversification benefits of the M&A, the implementation of new risk-management techniques, changes in operating efficiency, or changes in risk preferences. The change in focus of the consolidated institution may also affect its local market competitive position if, for example, the consolidated institution chooses to shrink after the M&A and have a smaller market share. Thus, the new institution may restructure itself over time in ways that alter its size, financial condition, or local market competitive position. In turn, these post-consolidation changes may affect the institution's propensity to make small business loans.

In some cases, the restructuring might occur not by choice, but rather because antitrust authorities require divestiture of some banking operations in overlapping local markets pursuant to an M&A to keep market concentration from rising excessively. The deposits in some branches and the loans associated with these deposits or branches may be sold to another bank as a condition for M&A approval, although required divestitures are relatively rare and they typically involve only a small percentage of the pro forma institution's assets or deposits when they do occur. Over the decade 1982–91 (which covers most of our sample period), divestitures were required in only 35 of 4515 M&A approvals, or about 0.78% of all M&A approvals.[5] Within these 35 required divestitures, a weighted average of only 1.59% of the deposits of the pro forma institution were divested.

[5] The number of M&A approvals reported here differs from the number of M&As used elsewhere in the paper. This is because an M&A approval often involves a consolidation of holding companies involving many banks. In our empirical analysis, each bank that is acquired is counted as a separate acquisition. This enables us to examine lending at the level of the individual bank.

The third potentially important factor affecting the merged or acquired bank's supply of business lending is the direct effect. This is the change in lending attributable to a direct refocussing of attention toward or away from small business lending, net of any of the static and restructuring effects already discussed. That is, the direct effect of an M&A is the difference between a bank's lending after consolidation and the lending of another institution of the same size, financial condition, local market competitive position, and economic environment as the restructured bank that has not undergone a recent M&A. In terms of our simple example in which the $600 million and $400 million banks merge and become an $800 million bank after restructuring, the direct effect is how this bank's lending differs from that of another $800 million bank that is the same in every respect as the restructured bank except that it did not engage in a recent M&A.

One type of direct effect would be a change in the institution's lending policies and procedures to bring the acquired part of the institution into accord with the acquirer's lending focus on either small or large borrowers. Consolidated institutions could also choose to become more or less aggressive in reissuing loans to past customers than other institutions, all else equal, because of the management's philosophy for improving the institution. The institutions that survive mergers may also be more efficient or better diversified than other institutions, and therefore better equipped to extend more loans.[6]

It may be argued that the restructuring and direct effects of M&As on lending are not necessarily independent, but rather may be part of the same dynamic refocusing of the consolidated institution. That is, the decision to change institution size, financial condition, and competitive position, and the decision to lend to small businesses at a different rate than other institutions with similar characteristics as the restructured institution may be part of the same managerial plan. For example, an institution may restructure to grow larger after a merger because it wishes to switch into larger loans that only more sizable institutions can extend. Nonetheless, we estimate these effects separately, primarily because the evidence cited above suggests that banking institution size is very important in determining the propensity to make small business loans. In estimation, we control for institution size to allow it to have an effect on lending that is independent of the direct effect of M&As. This in turn necessitates estimating a separate restructuring effect of M&As that operates through size and similar factors. In any event, the total effect on the lending of consolidating

[6] Empirical studies, for example Berger and Humphrey (1992), generally do not find that M&As improve cost efficiency. However, Hawawini and Swary (1990), Benston et al. (1995), Hughes et al. (1996), Akhavein et al. (1997), and Demsetz and Strahan (1997) find evidence suggesting that M&As improve profit efficiency and other measures of performance through enhanced loan diversification.

banks from their dynamic refocusing may be determined simply as the sum of the restructuring and direct effects.

The final dynamic effect of M&As, the external effect, captures the reactions of other lenders in the local market to the change in competitive conditions created by the M&A. For example, if a consolidated institution reduces its small business lending, this may create opportunities for other local banks to pick up loans with positive net present values. In some cases, loan officers that leave the consolidated institution may take some of their relationship-based loan portfolios with them and start a de novo bank or join other local competitors. Consistent with this possibility, Goldberg and White (1998) and DeYoung (1998) find that de novo banks tend to lend a greater percentage of their assets to small businesses than do other small banks of comparable size. The magnitude and direction of the external effect cannot be determined ex ante. The external effect could partially offset, fully offset, or even more than offset the change in lending by consolidating banks, depending upon the dynamics of the change in competitive conditions in the market. Alternatively, the external effect could move in the same direction as these other effects if for example, an acquirer increases the supply of small business loans and local banks respond to the more aggressive competitor by also increasing their supplies. Inclusion of the external effect is critical to any analysis of the impact of M&As on the total supply of small business lending.

Our empirical analysis below measures the external effects of M&As on banks in the same local market. Although we exclude nonbank lenders and banks in other local markets from the external effect (because of data and computational limitations), Kwast et al. (1997) find that 84.9% of small businesses use the services of a commercial bank within 30 miles, suggesting that we are likely to capture most of the external effect with our measure.

The measurement of the four effects of M&As on small business lending requires consideration of the time dimension of the effects. The static effect ends at the time of the M&A with the combination of the participants into the pro forma institution. In contrast, the dynamic restructuring, direct, and external effects begin after the M&A and may take several years to complete. For example, it may take time to restructure the consolidated institution's portfolio by divesting assets, or to change its lending focus by promulgating revised lending policies and procedures. There may also be temporary disequilibrium due to downsizing, meshing of corporate cultures, or turf battles that draw managerial attention away from the refocusing efforts. Bank managers and consultants often mention three years as the gestation period needed to restructure the institution and change its focus after an M&A. Toevs (1992) finds performance changes as long as five years after M&As. Cornett and Tehranian (1992) and other researchers use a three-year interval to measure other performance effects of bank M&As. The external effect on other banks in the local market is likely to take at least as long as the effects on the institutions involved in the M&As, implying that a minimum of three years is appropriate for measuring the external effect.[7]

The previous empirical literature that uses the small business lending section of the Call Report has generally been limited to examining only one or two years after the M&As because these data have only recently been collected (since June 1993). It seems likely that these studies may have missed some of the dynamic effects that take longer to complete. This study uses the longer time series available from the STBL data to estimate the three types of dynamic effects over a three year horizon. For comparison purposes, we also estimate the dynamic effects for a single year after an M&A.

4. An econometric model of lending and the potential effects of M&As

This section presents the econometric framework. We refer to a union in which two or more banks with separate charters are consolidated under a single bank charter as a 'merger', and denote the remaining bank as the 'survivor' and the bank or banks whose charter(s) disappear as 'targets'. We refer to a union in which a bank retains its charter but obtains a different top-tier holding company as an 'acquisition', where a top-tier holding company is a BHC that is not owned by any higher-tier BHC. The surviving top-tier BHC is referred to as the 'acquirer', and the banks that are directly purchased or are in holding companies that were purchased as the 'acquired'. Whether lending is affected more by mergers or acquisitions depends in large part upon whether effective control of lending decisions most often resides at the bank or holding company level, which is an interesting empirical question on its own.

The lending equations specify the proportions of a bank's gross total assets (GTA) that are allocated to domestic commercial and industrial (C&I) loans to different borrower size categories. We analyze lending in terms of GTA, which includes loan loss reserves, rather than (net) total assets because the value of loans is inclusive of loan loss reserves and because GTA is a superior measure of the size of the bank.

Following prior research, we proxy for the size of the borrower by the maximum of (1) the size of the loan from the bank, (2) the total commitment under which the loan was drawn from the bank (if any), and (3) the total size of the participation by all banks in a loan participation (if any). This measure is an estimate of the total bank credit available to the borrower. Also consistent with prior research, small business borrowers are defined as those with bank credit below \$1 million, medium-sized borrowers as those with credit between \$1

[7] For example, Epstein (1996) reports that it often takes one to three years after an M&A for the departing loan officers to start a rival de novo bank.

million and \$25 million, and large borrowers as those with access to more than \$25 million in bank credit.

The equations are specified in log-odds logit form, so that the dependent variables are $\ln(P_i/(1-P_i))$, $i = 1, 2, 3$, where ln indicates natural log, P_i is the proportion of the bank's GTA invested in loans to domestic borrowers in credit category i ($i = 1$ indicates small borrowers, etc.). This is consistent with the banking institution choosing how to allocate its assets among loans to three categories of domestic C&I borrowers and to other assets. The log-odds ratios are specified as functions of the size, financial condition, and competitive position of both the bank and its total organization (including assets of other banks held by the top-tier BHC if any), recent past M&A activity, and other bank-specific and environmental factors that might affect lending decisions. The main equations of the model are of the form:

$$\begin{aligned}
&\ln(P_{it}/(1-P_{it}))\\
&\quad = f_i(\text{BANK AND ORG SIZE}_{t-1}, \text{BANK AND ORG FINANCIAL}_{t-1},\\
&\qquad \text{BANK AND ORG COMP POSITION}_{t-1}, \text{ORG COMPLEXITY}_{t-1},\\
&\qquad \text{PAST M\&A}_{t-1,t-2,t-3}, \text{MARKET PAST M\&A}_{t-1,t-2,t-3}, \text{TIME}_{t-1},\\
&\qquad \text{ENVIRONMENT}_{t-1}) + \varepsilon_{it}, \quad i = 1, 2, 3. \qquad (1)
\end{aligned}$$

The definitions and sample means of all the variables in Eq. (1) are given in Table 1. The data are annual and all of the right-hand-side variables are lagged at least one year relative to the lending proportions on the left-hand-side to eliminate endogenous feedback effects (except for the time and environmental variables). Thus, lending decisions in one year are functions of the bank and organization size, financial condition, M&A activity, etc. in the previous year or years. All of the right-hand-side variables except for the M&A variables are stock figures as of year-end $t-1$ and occur before the lending on the left-hand side, which is a flow that occurs throughout year t.

Eq. (1) is estimated for all banks in the STBL. The STBL contains data on the characteristics of individual loans, allowing us to categorize whether the borrower is small, medium, or large.[8] The estimation of the effects of M&As below uses predicted values from this equation for essentially all banks involved in M&As. This is feasible because the right-hand-side variables are observable for all commercial banks over time from the main body of the Call Report and other regulatory reports.

[8] An exception is that we do not include observations if an M&A occurs in year t because some of the lending in year t is made by the consolidated firms and some by the unconsolidated firms. The lending by these banks is re-included in year $t+1$ if no M&A occurs in that year.

The BANK SIZE variables include first- and second-order terms in the log of gross total assets, LNGTA and $\frac{1}{2}$LNGTA^2, as well as dummies for bank size class measured in real 1994 dollars. The size classes are SMALLBANK (GTA $<$ \$100 million), MEDBANK (\$100 million–\$1 billion), LARGEBANK (\$1 billion–\$10 billion), and HUGEBANK ($\geqslant$ \$10 billion). The dummy for the smallest size class is excluded from the regression specification as the base case. The inclusion of bank size as a continuous variable and as size class dummies allows for both small effects and large changes at the size class level.

The ORG SIZE variables replicate the BANK SIZE variables, except that they are based on ORGGTA, which includes all the banking assets in the organization. For banks in BHCs, ORG SIZE is based on all the assets in the banks directly controlled by the top-tier holding company or indirectly controlled through the ownership of lower-tier BHCs. For independent banks or banks in one-bank holding companies, ORG SIZE and BANK SIZE are identical. The inclusion of ORG SIZE allows for the possibility that at least partial control of lending procedures is exercised at the centralized level of the organization.

The BANK AND ORG FINANCIAL variables measure the equity position and condition of the loan portfolio at the bank and organization levels. These variables include the equity/GTA ratio, loan loss reserves/total loans, other real estate owned/total loans, nonperforming loans/total loans, and second-order terms in these ratios (i.e., $\frac{1}{2}X^2$) to allow for nonlinearities. Banks with higher capital ratios and lower problem loan ratios should have a greater supply of credit, all else equal, because of fewer market and regulatory constraints.

The COMP POSITION variables – the Herfindahl index and market shares of the bank and organization – control for the competitive conditions in the local banking markets in which the institution competes (Metropolitan Statistical Area (MSA) or non-MSA county). These variables are measured as weighted averages over all the local markets in which the institution has offices with deposits.

The ORG COMPLEXITY variables control for the organizational structure of the institution, which may affect small business lending. We measure whether the bank is owned by a BHC, whether there are multiple layers of BHCs over the bank, and whether the bank's top-tier BHC is registered with the SEC for public trading. We also include OUT-OF-STATE, an indicator of whether the bank's top-tier BHC is located in another state. This allows for the possibility that interstate ownership makes it more difficult to make small relationship loans or makes it easier to extend some large business loans.

The PAST M&A variables account for the bank's M&A activity in the past three years and are used for measuring the direct effect of M&As. We measure the effects of several different types of M&As because they may have different potential impacts on small business lending policies and procedures. The variables MERGEDk, $k = 1, 2, 3$ indicate whether the bank is a survivor of one or more bank mergers k years ago. The variables MERGEDk-EQ designate

Table 1
Definitions and sample means of variables employed in the analysis (All financial values are in thousands of 1994 dollars)

Variable	Definition	Sample means	
		STBL banks	All banks
A. Loan proportions			
P_1	Proportion of gross total assets (GTA) lent to small businesses, i.e., those with less than \$1 million in bank credit.	0.075	–
P_2	Proportion of GTA lent to medium businesses, i.e., between \$1 million and \$25 million in bank credit.	0.060	–
P_3	Proportion of GTA lent to large businesses, i.e., more than \$25 million in bank credit.	0.018	–
B. Bank and organization size variables (BANK AND ORG SIZE)			
LNGTA	Log of bank GTA.	13.528	10.958
SMALLBANK	Dummy, equal to one if bank has GTA < \$100 million.	0.250	0.741
MEDBANK	Dummy, equal to one if \$100 million $\leqslant$ GTA < \$1 billion.	0.281	0.230
LARGEBANK	Dummy, equal to one if \$1 billion $\leqslant$ GTA < \$10 billion.	0.353	0.025
HUGEBANK	Dummy, equal to one if GTA $\geqslant$ \$10 billion.	0.116	0.004
LNORGGTA, SMALLORG, MEDORG, LARGEORG, HUGEORG	Same as BANK SIZE variables, except defined over all the banking assets in the organization (independent bank or top-tier holding company).		
C. Bank and organization financial variables (BANK AND ORG FINANCIAL)			
EQRAT	Bank equity to GTA ratio.	0.071	0.087
LLRRAT	Bank loan loss reserve to total loan ratio.	0.018	0.015
OREORAT	Bank Other Real Estate Owned to total loan ratio.	0.008	0.009
NPFRAT	Bank nonperforming loans to total loan ratio.	0.030	0.029
PFRAT	Purchased funds to GTA ratio.	0.251	0.136
ORGEQRAT, ORGLLRRAT, ORGOREORAT, ORGNPFRAT, ORGPFRAT	Same as BANK FINANCIAL variables, except defined for the organization.		

D. Local market competitive position variables (COMP POSITION)			
BANKHERF	Herfindahl index for local market (MSA or non-MSA county).	0.204	0.234
BANKSHARE	Bank's share of market deposits.	0.194	0.154
ORGHERF, ORGSHARE	Same as BANK COMP POSITION variables, except over the organization.		
E. Organizational complexity variables (ORG COMPLEXITY)			
BHCOWNED	Dummy, equal to one if bank is in a bank holding company (BHC).	0.831	0.593
MULTILEVELBHC	Dummy, equal to one if there are multiple levels of BHC.	0.141	0.057
PUBLICLYTRADED	Dummy, equal to one if top-tier BHC is SEC-registered.	0.606	0.222
OUT-OF-STATE	Dummy, equal to one if top-tier BHC is in another state.	0.136	0.045
F. Market past merger and acquisition variables (PAST M&A) (Means shown only for the first lag)			
MERGEDk	Dummy, equal to one if bank survived one or more mergers k years ago, $k = 1, 2, 3$.	0.100	0.017
MERGEDk-EQ	Dummy, equal to one if bank survived merger of equals k years ago, $k = 1, 2, 3$.	0.012	0.005
MERGEDk-FAM	Dummy, equal to one if bank survived family merger k years ago, $k = 1, 2, 3$.	0.045	0.007
ACQUIREDk	Dummy, equal to one if bank was acquired (i.e., changed top-tier BHC) k years ago, $k = 1, 2, 3$.	0.038	0.028
ACQUIREDk-EQ	Dummy, equal to one if bank acquired by an equal k years ago, k years ago, $k = 1, 2, 3$.	0.012	0.006
ACQUIREDk-OUT	Dummy, equal to one if bank acquired by an out-of-state BHC k years ago, $k = 1, 2, 3$.	0.017	0.007
PURCHk	Dummy, equal to one if bank's top-tier BHC acquired other banks k years ago, $k = 1, 2, 3$.	0.169	0.070
G. Market past merger and acquisition variables (MARKET PAST M&A)			
MAR-MERGEDk, MAR-MERGEDk-EQ, MAR-MERGEDk-FAM, MAR-ACQUIREDk, MAR-ACQUIREDk-EQ, MAR-ACQUIREDk-OUT, MAR-PURCHk	Weighted average proportions of PAST M&A variables of all the banks in the same local markets		
H. Time variables (TIME)			
YEARt	Dummies, equal to one if the lending takes place in year t. All year dummies (1980–95) are included, and no intercept is specified.		

Table 1. Continued

Variable	Definition	Sample means	
		STBL banks	All banks
I. Environmental variables (ENVIRONMENT)			
INMSA	Dummy, equal to one if the bank is in an MSA	0.698	0.433
STATEs	Dummy equal to one if the bank is in State s, for all U.S. states and D.C. except the base case of California.		
FED, FDIC, OCC	Dummies for primary federal regulator (OCC excluded as base case).		
Number of observations		5,351	206,203

Data sources:
Federal Reserve Survey of Terms of Bank Lending to Business (STBL)
Consolidated Report of Condition and Income for Banks (Schedule RC)
Consolidated Report of Condition and Income for Bank Holding Companies (Schedule Y9-C)
FDIC Summary of Deposits
National Information Center Entity Structure Data File

Our STBL sample contains 5351 annual bank observations from 1980 to 1995 on lending from the Survey of Terms of Bank Lending, which contains detailed contract information on a sample of loans made by about 300 banks per quarter. The All Banks sample contains 206 203 annual bank observations, most of which are lagged at least one year relative to 1980 to 1995 to eliminate endogenous feedback effects from lending (except for the t ime and environmental variables).

The lending by borrower size category can only be observed over time for STBL banks, and so only these banks were included in the estimation of Eq. (1) (although the other equations use all banks). The flows of loan originations reported in the STBL were converted into estimates of the stocks of loans used in the P_1, P_2, and P_3 proportions by weighting the flows throughout the year by the size and duration of the loans (see Berger et al., 1995, pp. 193–195 for more details). Of the 5351 annual bank observations available, 851 were not used in equation (1) because of M&A activity in the same year. The remaining 4500 were used in the P_1 and P_2 versions of Eq. (1). The P_3 version eliminated observations in which either the bank or organization had less than $100 million in GTA, leaving 3,232 observations. For this regression we also deleted the MEDBANK and MEDORG variables and treated medium size as the base case in place of small size. The reason for this treatment is that small banks almost all have either zero or very small proportions of loans to borrowers with credit over $25 million, which would make the intercept in this equation (for small banks in small organizations being the base case) essentially equal to minus infinity, which would create obvious estimation problems.

See Berger et al. (1997) for more details.

whether these were mergers of equals, defined here as when the surviving bank (whose charter is retained) had between one-third and two-thirds of the pro forma bank's GTA before the merger. The variables MERGED*k*-FAM denote whether the MERGED*k* were 'family mergers' of banks that were already in the same top-tier BHC. The ACQUIRED*k*, $k = 1, 2, 3$ variables indicate whether the bank was acquired *k* years ago, i.e., switched to the control of a different top-tier BHC. Similarly, ACQUIRED*k*-EQ shows whether the change in control was an 'acquisition of equals' in which the acquiring BHC's GTA before the merger was between one-third and two-thirds of the pro forma holding company's GTA. The variables ACQUIRED*k*-OUT designate whether the bank was purchased by an out-of-state BHC. These variables should be distinguished from the OUT-OF-STATE variable above, which measures the steady-state effect of interstate ownership. Finally, the variables PURCH*k* denote whether the bank's top-tier BHC purchased other banks, incorporating the effects of any drain of managerial attention from the existing affiliates.

The MARKET PAST M&A variables are the weighted averages of the PAST M&A variables of all the banks and BHCs in the same local markets (MSA or non-MSA county). For example, MAR-MERGED*k* measures the weighted average proportion of deposits in the bank's local market that were in banks that survived mergers *k* years ago. These variables are used to measure the external effect, the impact of M&As on lending by other banks in the same local market.

The PAST M&A variables and the MARKET PAST M&A variables are both also interacted with the BANK SIZE and ORG SIZE variables. Specifically, we interact all past bank merger variables with the log of bank size, LNGTA, and interact all past acquisition variables with the log of BHC size, LNORGGTA. These variables allow the effects of M&As to depend on the size of the institution.

The remaining variables control for differences in the time period and economic environment of the bank. The TIME dummies for every year control for changes in macroeconomic conditions, regulations, and technology over time. The ENVIRONMENT variables include dummies for every state (except the base case of California) to control for differences in demand and supply conditions and state banking regulations. We also specify dummies for the bank's primary federal regulator, FED, FDIC or OCC, to control for differences in regulatory treatment (OCC is excluded as the base case). Finally, INMSA is a dummy for whether the bank is headquartered in an MSA, since metropolitan and rural markets differ so greatly.

4.1. Measurement of the static effect

To measure the static effect, we simply take the lending predicted by Eq. (1) for the pro forma bank less the lending predicted by Eq. (1) for the pre-M&A

banks. This gives the effects of increasing the size of the institution (bank, organization, or both), any change in organizational complexity, local market share or concentration, and any effects of combining the financial ratios and other conditioning variables of the consolidating parties.

Consider again the simple example of the \$600 million and \$400 million banks merging, denoted as Banks A and B, respectively. Assume that neither bank is in a BHC, so that organization size equals bank size here. The pro forma bank has: bank and organization size of \$1 billion; financial ratios, past M&A and market M&A activity numbers that are weighted averages of the year-end $t-1$ figures for A (weight = 0.6) and B (weight = 0.4); and competitive position, organizational complexity, and environmental variables that depict the consolidated institution. These values are substituted into equation Eq. (1) to yield the proportion of assets predicted to be invested in loans to borrower size category i during year t for the pro forma bank, P_{it}^{PF}. To measure the static effect, we subtract the weighted average of the predicted values of proportions of GTA that Banks A and B would lend to borrower category i during year t if they had not been merged, i.e.,

$$\text{Static Effect} = P_{it}^{\mathrm{PF}} - 0.6 \cdot P_{it}^{\mathrm{A}} - 0.4 \cdot P_{it}^{\mathrm{B}} \quad i = 1, 2, 3. \tag{2}$$

4.2. Measurement of the restructuring effect

The restructuring effect measures the change in lending associated with the changes in the institution's size, financial condition, and competitive position that occur after consummating an M&A. This is somewhat complicated by the secular change in these variables over time due to changes in macroeconomic conditions, regulations, and technology. Essentially the same two-step procedure is used to estimate both secular change and the restructuring effect. We estimate the changes in size, condition, and competitive position that are expected to occur over time after the M&A, and then we plug these changes into Eq. (1) to obtain the predicted effects of these changes on bank lending.

To estimate the expected changes over time in size, condition, and competitive position, we estimate regression equations with the changes in these factors as the dependent variables. We illustrate this procedure for the change in the log of bank GTA over the j years after $t-1$. The regression for the change in LNGTA from period $t-1$ to $t+j-1$, $j \geqslant 1$, is given by

$$\begin{aligned}\Delta\mathrm{LNGTA}_{t+j-1} = g^{j}(&\text{BANK AND ORG SIZE}_{t-1},\\ &\text{BANK AND ORG FINANCIAL}_{t-1},\\ &\text{BANK AND ORG COMP POSITION}_{t-1},\\ &\text{ORG COMPLEXITY}_{t-1}, \text{PAST M\&A}_{t-1,t-2,t-3},\end{aligned}$$

$$\text{MARKET PAST M\&A}_{t-1,t-2,t-3}, \text{TIME}_{t-1},$$
$$\text{ENVIRONMENT}_{t-1}, \text{CURRENT M\&A}_t,$$
$$\text{MARKET CURRENT M\&A}_t) + \eta^j_{t+j-1}, \quad j \geqslant 1, \qquad (3)$$

where $\Delta\text{LNGTA}_{t+j-1} \equiv \text{LNGTA}_{t+j-1} - \text{LNGTA}_{t-1}$. Similar equations are run for changes in the LNORGGTA, BANK AND ORG FINANCIAL, and COMP POSITION variables. The right-hand side of these equations includes all the variables from Eq. (1) plus variables for CURRENT M&A and MARKET CURRENT M&A for year t. These M&A variables do not create a problem of endogeneity, since the current M&As occur during year t and the dependent variables are measured at the end of year t or later.

Eq. (3) is estimated for virtually all observations using Call Report data, since data on loan size, etc. from the STBL are not needed. For banks involved in M&As, the data on the right-hand side of Eq. (3) and the LNGTA_{t-1} on the left-hand side are based on the pro forma bank, so that we may measure the changes in size, condition, and competitive position relative to the pro forma bank. As discussed above, our main estimates of the dynamic effects of mergers allow for three years of changes after the M&A, so we set $j = 3$ and estimate lending in year $t + 3$. Since the size, condition, and competitive position variables are all lagged one year in the lending equation, Eq. (1), we estimate in Eq. (3) the three-year changes in these variables from year $t - 1$ to year $t + 2$. To estimate the dynamic effects one year after M&A for comparison, we also set $j = 1$ and estimate Eq. (3) for the change in variables from years $t - 1$ to t.

The secular change in LNGTA is measured by the predicted value of Eq. (3), setting all the $t - 1$ values and the PAST M&A values to those of pro forma bank, and setting the CURRENT M&A values to zero (as if the bank was not in a current M&A). Thus, the secular change reflects how the pro forma bank's LNGTA would be expected to evolve from period $t - 1$ to $t + j - 1$, leaving out any effects of the current M&A other than the static effect that created the pro forma bank. Put another way, the secular change is identical for all banks of a given size, financial condition, etc., whether or not they underwent a current M&A, although we only measure it for the consolidating institutions. This procedure is repeated for the changes in organization size, and the bank and organization financial and competitive position variables. The predicted lending proportions inclusive of secular change as well as the static effect are obtained by plugging the changed values for size, condition, and competitive position into the estimates of Eq. (1).

To estimate the restructuring effect, we repeat this process, except using the appropriate values of MERGED*k*, MERGED*k*-EQ, etc. in the CURRENT M&A vector, instead of all zeroes as in the secular change prediction model. Thus, the restructuring effect of M&As on lending is given by the predicted lending proportions in Eq. (1) based on the institution's size, financial condition, and competitive position that embody the effect of the current M&A less the predicted value after the static effect and secular change.

4.3. Measurement of the direct effect

The direct effect is the additional effect of M&As on lending after taking into account the restructuring of the bank from the other effects. It is calculated from the parameters of Eq. (1), using as a starting point the simulated changes in the right-hand side variables from the static effect, secular change, and restructuring effects. That is, it is the effect of 'turning on' the PAST M&A variables to include the effect of the current M&A being analyzed by putting ones in the PAST M&A vector the appropriate number of years back. Thus, the dynamic direct effect of a merger of equals three years after it occurred is taken from the predicted value of Eq. (1) setting MERGED3 and MERGED3-EQ equal to one, less the predicted value of Eq. (1) with these variables set to zero, and with all other right-hand-side variables inclusive of the other M&A and secular changes.

4.4. Measurement of the external effect

To measure the external effect, we use the MARKET PAST M&A variables, which to this point have been treated as control variables. For every bank, we measure the external effect as the impact on their lending of M&As in their local markets over the past 3 years. If there had been no M&As in their local markets, the predicted proportion lent to borrowers in size category i would be given by the predicted value from Eq. (1) with the MARKET PAST M&A variables set to zero. The external effect is incorporated by setting the MARKET PAST M&A variables to their actual values. The estimate of the external effect equals the difference between the predicted value of Eq. (1) when these variables are set to their actual values and the predicted value when these variables are set to zero.

The external effect is likely to be less accurately measured than the other effects, and so should be looked upon primarily as a qualitative measure of how other banks in the market tend to react to M&As. This is because it would be intractable to form a structural econometric model to measure the external effect like that used to measure the static, restructuring, and direct effects. Such a model would require tracing the effect of each individual M&A to every one of the other banks in the local market, and then mapping out how each of these other banks might change their size, financial ratios, and competitive positions in response to each M&A event. Instead, we measure the simple reduced form response of every bank in the nation to the percentage of bank assets in its local market(s) that were involved in M&As, recognizing the limitations of this measure. The external effect is useful for determining generally whether other local banks pick up substantial proportions of small business loans that might be dropped by banks involved in M&As or otherwise react to local M&As, and whether these effects are large in magnitude, but should not be viewed as a precise measure of these reactions. This measure also excludes the reactions of nonbanks and nonlocal lenders, but as discussed above, these other sources are much less important than local banks in servicing small business borrowers.

5. Empirical results

We estimated Eq. (1) – which predicts the proportions of assets invested in loans to domestic borrowers in different credit size categories – using data on banks in the STBL sample over the period 1980 through 1995. Recall that we are able to predict lending for all banks from this sample because all the regressors are available from the Call Report and other sources. These log-odds equations were estimated by weighted least squares in order to avoid heteroskedasticity problems and the adjusted R^2's were corrected, as in prior research (see, e.g., Berger and Udell, 1996).[9] We estimated Eq. (3) by OLS for the one-year and three-year changes in the bank and organization size, financial condition, and competitive position variables using all the banks over the periods such that $t+j-1$ was in 1979–94, the years just before lending is analyzed.

5.1. The static, restructuring, and direct effects

The top panel of Table 2 shows our analysis of the static, restructuring, and direct effects for M&As three years after the events, and the bottom panel gives the corresponding information for acquisitions. Although we believe that allowing three years for the dynamic effects is the best approach, Table 3 shows the corresponding results from a single year after an M&A. Tables 2 and 3 show the effects of M&As on small, medium, and large business lending, i.e., to domestic business borrowers with bank credit below $1 million, $1 million to $25 million, and over $25 million. However, we will concentrate on the consequences for small business lending, where most of the important policy and research questions reside.

All results represent the effects of M&As on lending during the years 1980–95, i.e., period $t+j$ after the M&A ranges from 1980–95. For the main results shown in Table 2, $j=3$, so that the M&As range from 1977–92, three years

[9] The parameter estimates for Eq. (1) are shown in Berger et al. (1997).

Table 2
Decomposition of the effects of merger and acquisition activity on aggregate domestic commercial and industrial (C&I) lending 1980–1995[a]
Three years after an M&A

	Pre-M&A	Static effect	Secular change	Restructuring effect	Direct effect	Post-M&A	Total static, restructuring plus direct effects[b]
	All mergers						
Number of banks	6,369	– 3,861	n.a.	n.a	n.a.	2,508	
Gross total assets (billions)	4852.4	n.a.	365.5	31.1	n.a.	5249.0	
Lending proportions to borrowers with bank credit:							
Less than $1 million	0.03702	– 0.00533**	– 0.00879**	0.00067**	0.00049*	0.02416	– 0.00416**
$1 million–$25 million	0.08641	0.00337**	0.00160**	– 0.00205**	– 0.00097**	0.08856	0.00035
Greater than $25 million	0.05918	0.01442**	0.00709**	– 0.00153**	– 0.01006**	0.06857	0.00283*
Total	0.18261	0.01246**	– 0.00010	– 0.00291**	– 0.01054**	0.18129	– 0.00098
	All acquisitions						
Number of banks	4,146	n.a.	n.a.	n.a.	n.a.	4,146	
Gross total assets (billions)	1100.0	n.a.	106.0	52.9	n.a.	1258.9	

Lending proportions to borrowers with bank credit:							
Less than $1 million	0.06054	– 0.00638**	– 0.01396**	0.00032**	0.00616**	0.04659	0.00011
$1 million–$25 million	0.08565	0.00267**	0.00236**	0.00004	0.00579**	0.09631	0.00851**
Greater than $25 million	0.05229	0.02660**	– 0.00088	– 0.00276**	– 0.01343**	0.06199	0.01041**
Total	0.19848	0.02289**	– 0.01248**	– 0.00240**	– 0.00147	0.20488	0.01902**

[a]Financial values are expressed in 1994 dollars using the GDP implicit price deflator.

[b]Total is the sum of the weighted averages specified. This total does not take into account the slight changes in GTA across columns. We correct for these differences in Table 7.

n.a. Not all of the effects change the number of banks or their gross total assets.

*Significantly different from zero at 5% level, two-tailed.

**Significantly different from zero at the 1% level, two-tailed.

The mergers and acquisitions occurred between 1977 and 1992, and the effects on lending are measured three years after the event, i.e., between 1980 and 1995. A union in which two or more banks with separate charters are consolidated under a single charter is called a merger. A union in which a bank retains its charter but obtains a different top-tier holding company is called an acquisition. The static effect is the change in lending propensities that results from simply combining the balance sheets of the participating banks into a larger pro forma institution with a combined balance sheet and competitive position. Secular change captures changes in bank lending over time that are independent of bank M&As. The restructuring effect is the change in lending owing to changes in focus in which the institution changes its size, financial condition, or competitive position from their pro forma values after consummating the M&A. The direct effect is the change in lending attributable to a direct refocusing of attention toward or away from types of lending, net of any static and restructuring effects. All effects are measured as a percent of bank GTA.

Table 3
Decomposition of the effects of merger and acquisition activity on aggregate domestic C&I lending 1980–1995[a]
One year after an M&A

	Pre-M&A	Static effect	Secular change	Restructuring effect	Direct effect	Post-M&A	Total static, restructuring plus direct effects[b]
	All mergers						
Number of banks	7,916	– 4,810	n.a.	n.a	n.a.	3,106	
Gross total assets (billions)	6253.1	n.a.	321.7	– 117.2	n.a.	6457.6	
Lending proportions to borrowers with bank credit:							
Less than $1 million	0.03324	– 0.00417**	– 0.00398**	0.00066**	0.00271**	0.02879	– 0.00081*
$1 million–$25 million	0.08738	0.00509**	– 0.00134**	– 0.00014**	0.01261**	0.10401	0.01756**
Greater than $25 million	0.05691	0.01165**	0.01063**	– 0.00085**	– 0.01035**	0.06829	0.00045
Total	0.17753	0.01257**	0.00531**	– 0.00033**	0.00497	0.20109	0.01720**
	All acquisitions						
Number of banks	4714	n.a.	n.a.	n.a.	n.a.	4714	
Gross total assets (billions)	1276.5	n.a.	57.4	25.2	n.a.	1359.1	

Lending proportions to borrowers with bank credit:							
Less than $1 million	0.05723	– 0.00614**	– 0.00694**	– 0.00005	0.00715**	0.05117	0.00096*
$1 million–$25 million	0.08686	0.00052	0.00040	– 0.00082**	– 0.00284**	0.08390	– 0.00314**
Greater than $25 million	0.05621	0.03135**	0.00467**	0.00258**	– 0.02769**	0.06747	0.00624**
Total	0.20031	0.02574**	– 0.00186*	0.00171**	– 0.02338**	0.20254	0.00407**

[a]Financial values are expressed in 1994 dollars using the GDP implicit price deflator.
[b]Total is the sum of the weighted averages specified. This total does not take into account the slight changes in GTA across columns. We correct for these differences in Table 7.
n.a. Not all of the effects change the number of banks or their gross total assets.
*Significantly different from zero at 5% level, two-tailed.
**Significantly different from zero at the 1% level, two-tailed.

The mergers and acquisitions occurred between 1979 and 1994, and the effects on lending are measured one year after the event, i.e., between 1980 and 1995. A union in which two or more banks with separate charters are consolidated under a single charter is called a merger. A union in which a bank retains its charter but obtains a different top-tier holding company is called an acquisition. The static effect is the change in lending propensities that results from simply combining the balance sheets of the participating banks into a larger pro forma institution with a combined balance sheet and competitive position. Secular change captures changes in bank lending over time that are independent of bank M&As. The restructuring effect is the change in lending owing to changes in focus in which the institution changes its size, financial condition, or competitive position from their pro forma values after consummating the M&A. The direct effect is the change in lending attributable to a direct refocusing of attention toward or away from types of lending, net of any static and restructuring effects. All effects are measured as a percent of bank GTA.

before the lending data.[10] Note that the 'All mergers' and 'All acquisitions' results shown in Tables 2 and 3 do not force all types of mergers or acquisitions, respectively, to have the same effects on lending. Recall that the model has dummy variables for mergers of equals, family mergers, etc., as well as interactions of these dummies with the size of the institution. Thus, these different types of M&As and M&As of different sized institutions are allowed have different effects on lending. Subsequent tables investigate some of these differences. The results in Tables 2 and 3 should be viewed as weighted average effects over the different types of mergers and acquisitions.

Looking first at the merger results, the first column of the top panel of Table 2 shows that the 6369 merging banks invested 3.702% of their gross total assets in small business loans the year before the merger. The static effect combines the balance sheets of these banks, reducing their number by 3641 to 2508 surviving pro forma banks. More than half of the bank charters disappear because there were multiple targets in the same year for some survivor banks. The static effect reduces the small business lending proportion of the pro forma banks by 53.3 basis points, using predicted values from the lending equation, Eq. (1). This decline of about one-half of one percentage point amounts to about $25.8 billion less of small business lending in real 1994 dollars ($-$ 0.00533 · $4,852.4 billion in GTA), which is about 16% of total small business lending as of 1995. This substantial reduction of small business lending confirms the main result of the static literature on the relationship between bank size and small business lending, but does so in a model that takes into account many more factors than are typically employed in these studies.

The secular change shows that the pro forma banks would be predicted to grow in assets and change their small business lending proportions in the absence of the dynamic effects of mergers. The data suggest that these banks would have reduced their proportion of small business lending by 87.9 basis points of GTA. Since secular change applies equally to banks that were involved in M&As and those that were not, these data suggest a strong overall decline in small business lending over time that is independent of bank M&As, consistent with the results of Berger et al. (1995).

The restructuring effect slightly increases the proportion of GTA invested in small business lending by 6.7 basis points and slightly increases the assets of the merged banks by about $31 billion. These data suggest that any restructuring of the participating banks after M&As is not very important.

The direct effect also appears to increase the proportion of assets invested in small business loans by a very small amount, 4.9 basis points of GTA. Thus, by

[10] We include all M&As except those involving failed banks and those with incomplete data, which would make our results less accurate depictions of typical M&As. The excluded banks account for only a small proportion of the bank assets involved in M&As and so likely do not substantially affect the results shown in the tables.

the end of our three-year dynamic period after mergers, the negative static effect of mergers on small business lending is only slightly offset by the positive restructuring and direct effects. This is illustrated in the final column of Table 2. The sum of static, restructuring, and direct effects of mergers is -41.6 basis points, almost as large as the static effect alone. As a caveat, note that the individual static and dynamic effects are subject to measurement error and that some part of each effect may potentially be attributed to another effect. Nevertheless, the sum of these effects is negative, large in magnitude, and statistically significant, giving us confidence that the overall effect of mergers on the small business lending of the merging banks is negative.

The merger results generally show positive effects on lending to medium and large borrowers, especially to large borrowers with bank credit exceeding $25 million. The positive static effects for these borrowers are consistent with the previous literature that found that larger banks tend to lend more to larger borrowers. These positive static effects are offset in part by negative restructuring and direct effects.

The bottom panel of Table 2, shows the lending effects for 4146 acquisitions in which a bank has a new top-tier holding company but retains its charter. In many cases, these acquisitions occur simultaneously as one holding company buys another holding company that owns a number of banks. The results of the acquisitions are similar in a number of ways to the merger results, but there are some key differences. For small business lending, the static effects on lending are negative, the restructuring effects are very small, and the direct effects are positive. A key difference from the merger results is that the direct effect for acquisitions is relatively large and essentially offsets all of the static effect, so total effects of acquisitions on small business lending are approximately zero.

This result – that holding company acquisitions do not appear to reduce small business lending by the acquired bank – suggests that acquisitions may be associated with keeping mostly the same lending policies and procedures and loan officers within the bank. The acquired bank's loan officers may have strong ties to the local community that enable them to continue extending relationship-based loans to small, informationally opaque borrowers, minimizing the impact of the consolidation on small business lending. The choice of a merger, on the other hand, may more often be associated with a strategic decision to integrate the acquired bank more fully into the acquiring organization, rather than maintaining its local identity, making it less inclined or less able to extend relationship-based small business loans.

Acquisitions may still have important effects on small business lending in the long run, however, if these acquisitions are preludes to family mergers over the next few years. In some cases, an acquired bank is merged with an existing BHC affiliate some time after the acquisition, which then yields a reduction in small business lending. These family mergers are analyzed separately below. In our data, 41.3% of the mergers from 1977 through 1992 (1036/2508) are family mergers, and nearly a quarter (23.7%) of newly acquired banks engage in family mergers in the three years after acquisition. Importantly, family mergers are likely to increase dramatically in the near future, as relaxation of interstate banking rules under the Riegle-Neal Act of 1994 removed most of the restrictions on family mergers across state lines as of June 1, 1997.

The acquisitions information also suggests more of a shift into medium and large business lending than was the case for mergers. For large loans, the increase in lending is driven by a large positive static effect, suggesting that larger BHCs may improve diversification and allow the acquired banks to initiate more large loans, consistent with the literature cited above.

To check the main results and give some insights on how well the parameters of Eq. (1) are working to produce the direct effects of M&As on small business lending, we also compute several marginal effects of the PAST M&A variables on small business lending and calculate several F-tests on the PAST M&A coefficients. We compute derivatives of the small business lending proportion with respect to six categories of M&As: mergers ($\partial P_1/\partial$MERGEDk), mergers of equals ($\partial P_1/\partial$MERGEDk + $\partial P_1/\partial$MERGEDk-EQ), family mergers ($\partial P_1/\partial$MERGEDk + $\partial P_1/\partial$MERGEDk-FAM), and similarly for acquisitions, acquisitions of equals, and out-of-state acquisitions. For each of the six main types of M&As, we calculate the derivatives for the three lags, i.e., for $k = 1, 2, 3$. The results are heterogenous, and depend on the size of the bank or organization because of the interaction terms. At the mean values for LNGTA and LNORGGTA, only 6 of the 18 derivatives are positive, but at the maximum values for institution size, 11 of 18 are positive. These results suggest that the positive direct effects shown in Table 2 primarily reflect the large institutions (which receive the greatest weights in the weighted averages shown), and that the type of merger or acquisition might also matter. We will investigate this heterogeneity further below when we break out the results by institution size and by type of M&A. The PAST M&A variables are also generally statistically significant when evaluated in logical groupings. Specifically, we conduct F-tests of the PAST M&A variables and their interaction terms for each of the six main types of M&As, of all the merger parameters jointly, of all the acquisition parameters jointly, and of all the PAST M&A variables jointly. The parameters were jointly significant at the 1% level in seven of nine cases.

Table 3 shows the results for one year after M&As (i.e., $j = 1$) for comparison purposes. The analysis includes mergers that combine 7916 banks, reducing them by 4810 into 3106 surviving banks, and 4714 acquisitions of banks that occur over 1979–94. The available set of M&As is slightly different from that used for three years after an M&A because we hold the lending years constant at 1980–95 in order to control for the substantial changes in lending behavior over time. We concentrate on the dynamic effects, as the static effects reflect only the differences in sample. The one-year restructuring and direct effects of all mergers on small business lending were 6.6 basis points and 27.1 basis points, respectively. Thus, the short-term restructuring effect is small (similar to the longer term effect), but the short-term direct effect is quite large and offsets most of the static effect. This suggests that immediately after merging, banks may look more favorably on small business lending than other banks of the same size and other characteristics, or at least are reluctant to cut much of this lending quickly. However, the direct effect becomes much smaller by three years after the merger, so a substantial reduction in this lending by merged banks eventually occurs. The effects of acquisitions on small business lending, as well as the effects of both mergers and acquisitions on other types of lending also show considerable differences from the three-year effects shown above in Table 2.

This pattern in which most of the changes in lending take place more than a year after merger, supports the prevailing views of bank managers, consultants, researchers, and the press that a three-year gestation period is needed to complete the transition to a new equilibrium after an M&A. This finding also raises questions about recent applications that employed the small business lending section of the Call Report. Data from this new source simply may not have been available long enough to measure much of the dynamic effects of M&As. From this point forward, all reported results allow three years after M&As for the dynamic effects to be completed.

5.2. The effects by type of M&A

Table 4 summarizes the static, restructuring, and direct effects on small business lending by type of M&A. This table shows the total of these three effects on small business lending for mergers of equals, family mergers, acquisitions of equals, and out-of-state acquisitions, plus the All mergers and All acquisitions categories from Table 2 for comparison. These results may give insights as to which types of consolidation are likely to produce the most change in lending. As noted above, family mergers and out-of-state acquisitions are of particular interest because they bear on the likely future effects of interstate banking.

The findings shown in Table 4 suggest that all categories of mergers tend to reduce small business lending by comparable amounts. However, for acquisitions there appears to be considerable heterogeneity. Results suggest considerable positive effects on lending for acquisitions of equals and for out-of-state acquisitions, in contrast to the essentially zero effect overall. The excluded categories (acquisitions of unequals, in-state acquisitions) yield negative effects on small business lending (− 6.1 basis points, − 61.0 basis points, respectively). The finding for out-of-state acquisitions runs contrary to some of the results in

Table 4
Effects of merger and acquisition activity on domestic C&I lending < $1 million by type of M&A[a]
Three years after an M&A

	All mergers	Mergers of equals	Family mergers	All acquisitions	Acquisitions of equals	Out-of-state acquisitions
Number of pro forma banks	2,508	615	1,036	4,146	938	796
Gross total assets (billions)	4852.4	1027.4	1910.2	1100.0	375.3	554.5
Total static, restructuring, plus direct effects on lending proportions	– 0.00416**	– 0.00288*	– 0.00405**	0.00011	0.00150**	0.00622**

[a]Financial values are expressed in 1994 dollars using the GDP implicit price deflator.

The mergers and acquisitions occurred between 1977 and 1992, and the effects on lending are measured three years after the event, i.e., between 1980 and 1995. A union in which two or more banks with separate charters are consolidated under a single charter is called a merger. A union in which a bank retains its charter but obtains a different top-tier holding company is called an acquisition. Mergers of equals are mergers in which the surviving bank (whose charter is retained) had between one-third and two-thirds of the pro forma bank's gross total assets (GTA) before the merger. Family mergers are mergers in which both banks were already in the same top-tier bank holding company of equals are acquisitions in which the acquiring bank holding company's GTA before the merger was between one-thirds of the pro forma holding company's GTA. An out-of-state acquisition is an acquisition in which the bank was purchased by an out-of-state holding company. Static, restructuring and direct effects are measured as a percent of bank GTA and are defined in Table 2.

the literature cited in Section 2 and goes against the conventional wisdom that out-of-state acquirers impose non-local policies and procedures that inhibit relationship-driven small business lending. However, as discussed above, such policies may eventually be imposed if these acquisitions are preludes to family mergers with other banks within the BHC, which are found here to decrease small business lending.

5.3. The effects by absolute and relative size of M&A participants

Table 5 summarizes the total static, restructuring, and direct effects segmented by the absolute and relative sizes of the M&A participants. Absolute size may matter, for example, because small and large institutions start from such different small business lending proportions. Relative size may matter, among other reasons, because banks of differing sizes may have more divergent lending focuses.

The top panel of Table 5 suggests that the impact of mergers on small business lending is positive when small and medium size banks (GTA $<$ \$1 billion) merge with each other, consistent with Peek and Rosengren (1996, 1998) and Strahan and Weston (1996, 1998). This may be because these mergers allow small and medium sized banks to increase their business lending as a whole, most of which is restricted to small business lending because of legal lending limits and limited diversification. For example, a bank with \$50 million in assets and a 6% equity capital ratio has a legal lending limit to a single borrower of \$450,000 (15% of equity). A merger with a similar bank would double the size of loans and commitments that are permitted, but any extra lending would still generally count as small business lending.

The negative effect on small business lending generally occurs when large survivor banks (GTA $\geqslant$ \$1 billion) merge with either large or medium sized target banks. These two large bank merger categories represent about two-thirds of the dollar value of assets merged. The negative effect on small business lending for the larger merger combinations is also consistent with Peek and Rosengren, although Strahan and Weston find no significant effect of large mergers. However, comparisons with prior studies are difficult to make because of our longer sample period, our use of data three years after the mergers, and our structural model that takes into account the separate static, restructuring, and direct effects of M&As.

The bottom panel of Table 5 suggests that acquisitions of large banking organizations by other large organizations (about two-thirds of assets involved in acquisitions) tends to increase small business lending, but the acquisitions of smaller organizations tends to decrease this type of lending. Thus, our earlier result of essentially no change related to acquisitions masks some significant effects that depend on the sizes of the organizations involved. One potential explanation of this heterogeneity is that the purposes of these acquisitions differ.

Table 5
Effect of merger and acquisition activity on domestic C&I lending < \$1 million by absolute and relative size of participants[a]
Three years after an M&A

Size of survivor	Mergers		
	Small (GTA < \$100M)	Medium (GTA \$100M–\$1B)	Large (GTA ⩾ \$1B)
Small (GTA < \$100M)			
Number of pro forma banks	689		
Gross total assets (billions)	55.6		
Total static, restructuring, plus direct effects on lending proportions	0.06210**		
Medium (GTA \$100M–\$1B)			
Number of pro forma banks	589	293	
Gross total assets (billions)	185.6	180.8	
Total static, restructuring, plus direct effects on lending proportions	0.01318**	0.01286**	
Large (GTA ⩾ \$1B)			
Number of pro forma banks	122	192	83
Gross total assets (billions)	579.9	932.7	1147.8
Total static, restructuring, plus direct effects on lending proportions	0.00139	– 0.00449	– 0.01046**

Size of acquirer organization	Acquisitions Size of acquired organization Small (ORGGTA < \$100M)	Medium (ORGGTA \$100M–\$1B)	Large (ORGGTA ⩾ \$1B)
Small (ORGGTA < \$100M)			
Number of acquired banks	721		
Gross total assets (billions)	21.7		
Total static, restructuring, plus direct effects on lending proportions	– 0.01149**		
Medium (ORGGTA \$100M–\$1B)			
Number of acquired banks	948	398	
Gross total assets (billions)	44.4	66.2	
Total static, restructuring, plus direct effects on lending proportions	– 0.00242*	– 0.00946**	
Large (ORGGTA ⩾ \$1B)			
Number of acquired banks	472	711	634
Gross total assets (billions)	28.9	152.3	603.4
Total static, restructuring, plus direct effects on lending proportions	0.00155	– 0.00619**	0.00233*

[a]Financial values are expressed in 1994 dollars using the GDP implicit price deflator.

Mergers are categorized by size of target and size of survivor, where each is defined according to gross total assets (GTA). Acquisitions are similarly categorized by size of acquired organization and size of acquirer organization, where each is defined according to organization GTA (ORGGTA). The mergers and acquisitions occurred between 1977 and 1992, and the effects on lending are measured three years after the event, i.e., between 1980 and 1995. Static, restructuring and direct effects are measured as a percent of bank GTA and are defined in Table 2.

For instance, the very largest acquisitions may often be for the purpose of market expansion by aggressive acquirers who wish to expand all types of lending.[11]

5.4. The external effect of M&As

Table 6 shows the external effect of M&As on the lending of all banks in the local market in response to the changes in business conditions created by the M&As. As discussed above, even if institutions engaging in M&As reduce their small business lending substantially, the total local supply of these loans need not decrease substantially if there is a strong external effect in which other local banks or nonbanks pick up many of these loans. This external effect is not likely to capture the bulk of the external market for loans to larger business borrowers, because these borrowers typically have access to credit on a regional or nationwide basis. As discussed above, small businesses tend to rely on nearby banks for financial services, so our analysis of the external effect centers on these local market banks. The external effect has been neglected in prior empirical analyses of the effects of bank consolidation on small business lending.

The first column of Table 6 shows the proportions of GTA devoted to the loan categories assuming no M&As in the local market, i.e., by taking the predicted values from Eq. (1) setting all the MARKET PAST M&A variables to zero. The remaining columns reflect the effects of setting some of these variables to their actual proportions of local market assets involved in M&As. The merger results suggest that other banks in the local market tend to increase their small business lending by 8.5 basis points of their assets, which tends to offset the decline in small business lending by merging banks themselves. The results tend to differ, depending upon the type of merger involved. Similarly, acquisitions

[11] We also conduct a robustness check using the small business lending sections of the June 1993, 1994, and 1995 Call Reports, that are used by some of the other studies. We re-estimate the small business lending proportion equation, Eq. (1), using the data for all banks for these three years and then analyze the findings for the year after the M&As for the 309 mergers and 293 acquisitions with complete data for 1994. These findings are compared with our one-year-after M&A results which used STBL data in the estimation. The comparison is imperfect because the STBL results are based on a much longer period of estimation (16 years versus 3 years) and because we can only replicate our one-year dynamic analysis, in which we have much less confidence than our three-year analysis. The merger results came out quite similar, with the STBL and Call predicting 0.0250% and 0.0358% increases in small business loans from 1994 mergers, respectively. This positive finding is consistent between the two data sets for 1994 mergers, but differs from our finding of a negative effect from mergers over the much longer 1979–1994 period, possibly suggesting a change over time. The estimates for 1994 acquisitions differ, with the STBL yielding a positive estimate and the Call yielding a negative estimate. This may reflect the heterogeneity in the acquisition results overall, which yield essentially a zero effect overall, but strong negative and positive effects for different groups.

Table 6
External effect of M&A activity in local market on aggregate domestic C&I lending[a]
Three years after an M&A

	Lending proportions assuming no M&As	All mergers	Mergers of equals	Family mergers	All acquisitions	Acquisitions of equals	Out-of-state acquisitions	Other BHC purchases
Lending proportions to borrowers with bank credit:								
Less than $1 million	0.03473	0.00085**	0.00021**	0.00010**	0.00039**	– 0.00037**	– 0.00052**	0.00035**
$1 million–$25 million	0.07212	0.00121**	0.00174**	0.00182**	– 0.00082**	0.00061**	0.00168**	0.00282**
Greater than $25 million	0.05399	0.00138**	– 0.00077**	– 0.00027**	0.00097**	– 0.00083**	0.00069**	0.00375**
Total	0.16084	0.00344**	0.00118**	0.00165**	0.00054**	– 0.00059**	0.00185**	0.00691**

[a]Financial values are expressed in 1994 dollars using the GDP implicit price deflator.
*Significantly different from zero at the 5% level, two-tailed.
**Significantly different from zero at the 1% level, two-tailed.

The first column is the estimated lending distribution, as a percent of bank GTA, for every bank, across all years, as if there were no M&A activity in the bank's market. The remaining columns are the estimated changes in the lending distribution for every bank in the market due to the M&A activity of all market banks, for example due to all mergers, due to mergers of equals, etc. The external effect captures the dynamic responses to M&As of other lenders in the same local market to the change in competitive conditions created by the M&A. Mergers, acquisitions, and the specific types of mergers and acquisitions are defined in previous tables. The mergers and acquisitions occurred between 1977 and 1992, and the effects on lending are measured three years after the event, i.e., between 1980 and 1995.

tend to increase small business lending by other local banks by 3.9 basis points of GTA, and this effect differs by type of acquisition, with some types having a negative effect on lending by other local banks. The general finding of positive, statistically significant effects of both mergers and acquisitions on small business lending by other local banks suggests that any conclusions about the impact of banking consolidation that fail to take into account the reactions of other banks may be misleading.[12]

5.5. The total effects of M&As on small business lending

The external effect measured in Table 6 raises the issue of the extent to which the estimated reductions in small business lending reported above for merging banks may be offset by increases in small business lending by other local banks. That is, the total supply of small business loans depends on all the banks in the local market (as well as nonbanks which are not included here). The results given thus far are difficult to compare because the static, restructuring, and direct effects of M&As are expressed in terms of the assets of the consolidating institutions, whereas the external effect is expressed in terms of the assets of all the banks in the nation.

Table 7 puts these effects in comparable terms by multiplying by the appropriate assets and adding up the estimated real dollar magnitudes. The static effect of mergers is shown to reduce small business lending by an estimated $25.8 billion, which as noted above represents about 16% of total small business loans. The positive restructuring and direct effects tend to offset the negative static effect by increasing small business lending by $3.5 billion and $2.6 billion, respectively, but these effects are relatively weak in economic significance. The estimated external effect of $48.6 billion, however, more than offsets the reduction in lending by the merging banks. As noted earlier, the external effect is not measured as accurately as the three effects of M&As on the participating banks, and we view it primarily as a qualitative indicator of the direction and general magnitude of the reaction of other banks. Despite this acknowledged imprecision, the strong, positive external effect supports the notion that other banks in the local market may respond positively to the change in competitive conditions brought about by a local merger, and offset much if not all of the reduction in supply of these loans by merging banks. For acquisitions, the external effect

[12] We also check the derivatives and perform F-tests on the parameters involving the MARKET PAST M&A variables, analogous to our checks of the PAST M&A variables. Again, there is some heterogeneity in the results, and this heterogeneity is reflected in some of the differing signs of the results shown in Table 6. At the mean values for LNGTA and LNORGGTA, 11 of the 18 derivatives are positive, and 9 are positive at the maximum values for institution size. Of the nine F-tests of the sets of parameters, seven show joint significance at the 1% level, and one shows significance at the 5% level.

Table 7
Total magnitudes of the effects of M&A activity on aggregate domestic C&I lending
Three years after an M&A

	All mergers					All acquisitions				
	Static	Restructuring	Direct	External	Total	Static	Restructuring	Direct	External	Total
Billions of dollars of lending to borrowers with bank credit:										
Less than $1 million	– 25.8	3.5	2.6	48.6	28.9	– 7.0	0.4	7.8	22.6	23.7
$1 million–$25 million	16.3	– 10.8	– 5.1	69.6	70.1	2.9	0.1	7.3	– 47.1	– 36.8
Greater than $25 million	70.0	– 8.0	– 52.8	79.5	88.6	29.3	– 3.5	– 16.9	55.7	64.6
Total	60.5	– 15.3	– 55.3	91.4	81.3	25.2	– 3.0	– 1.8	– 6.9	13.4

The mergers and acquisitions occurred between 1977 and 1992, and the effects on lending are measured three years after the event, i.e., between 1980 and 1995. The static, restructuring, direct, external, and total effects are measured in billions of 1994 dollars using the GDP deflator and represent the estimated changes in the lending distribution for every bank in the country, not just those engaging in M&A activity. The purpose of this table is to show general magnitudes. Statistical significance can not be computed because the static, restructuring, and direct effects of M&As are based upon the projected effects of mergers assuming no confounding effects from interceding M&As, whereas the external effect is based upon actual data for all banks inclusive of interceding M&As. Although the magnitudes are not strictly additive, they should nevertheless give good rough estimates of the general magnitudes. The static, restructuring, direct, and external effects are defined in previous tables.

tends to operate in the same way by increasing small business lending. However, in this case, there is no reduction in lending by acquired banks to offset, since the positive direct effect alone appears to offset the negative static effect. Thus, overall, we cannot reject the notion that the total supply of small business credit associated with M&As is either unchanged or perhaps positive, despite the finding that mergers tend to reduce such loans by the merging banks.

As a caveat, we measure only quantities of credit, and not the other terms of the loan. Some of the research on relationship lending finds that as a bank-small business borrower relationship matures, the interest rates charged and collateral requirements tend to decline as the bank gains information on the borrower (see, e.g., Berger and Udell, 1995), although other research finds no significant change in rates charged (see, e.g., Petersen and Rajan, 1994). This suggests that some borrowers who are dropped by consolidating banks and picked up by other banks through the external effect may have to pay higher rates, pledge more collateral, or be subject to stricter covenants or other lending terms in the short run until their new banking relationship matures. In addition, some of the small business borrowers who continue to receive credit from the consolidated institutions may pay higher rates or otherwise be subject to stiffer contract terms.

As an additional caveat, consolidating banks may change their mix of borrowers in ways that we do not measure. For example, the Williamson-based theory discussed above suggests that larger, more organizationally complex institutions that are created by M&As may reduce their supplies of credit to informationally opaque, relationship borrowers, and perhaps increase their supplies to informationally transparent transactions borrowers (see Hubbard et al., 1998). Although borrower size may be highly correlated with informational opacity and other borrower characteristics, we can only measure how M&As affect different sizes of borrowers, and we cannot directly measure the effect of M&As on information-problematic relationship borrowers versus transparent transactions borrowers.

6. Conclusions

This study addresses an issue that is currently the subject of considerable debate and concern – Is the consolidation of the U.S. banking industry substantially reducing the supply of credit to small businesses? Much has been made of the static cross-sectional relationship between banking institution size and the proportion of assets devoted to small business lending. However, such analysis ignores the basic nature of M&As as dynamic events that take place for the purpose of changing the focus of the participants, as well as to increase size. It also neglects the reaction of other potential lenders that could offset any reduction in the supply of small business loans by M&A participants.

While several recent papers have viewed this issue in a dynamic context, this study departs significantly from these papers and the rest of the extant literature in a number of ways. We examine three distinct effects of M&As on the small business lending of the participants. The static effect captures the melding of the balance sheets of the consolidating banks into a larger institution, and the restructuring and direct effects capture two sources of change in the strategic focus of the consolidating institutions after their M&As are completed. Unlike the existing literature, we also follow the effects of M&As three years after the M&A event to capture more of the dynamic effects. We are also the first to examine the external effect, the impact of M&As on small business lending by other banks in the same local market. Without taking into account the reaction of other banks, it is impossible to draw conclusions about the overall impact of consolidation on the supply of small business credit. Finally, to the best of our knowledge, this is the most exhaustive analysis of the impact of mergers and acquisitions on bank lending behavior. Our data and methodology permit us to analyze the effects of over 6,000 M&As over a variety of economic conditions from the late 1970s through the early 1990s on the lending of virtually all U.S. banks.

Results indicate that the effects of M&As may be more complex than previous analyses would suggest. While the static aggregation of banking institutions is associated with a considerable negative impact on small business lending, there are significant offsetting effects. In the case of mergers (consolidations of bank charters), the external reaction of other banks in the same local markets appears to offset much if not all of the negative static effect, whereas the dynamic restructuring and direct effects on lending by the consolidating banks themselves appear to be relatively minor. In the case of acquisitions (changes of the top-tier BHC with charter retained), the negative static effect is offset by both the direct effect of the acquisition and by the external effect. Contrary to conventional wisdom and to some prior research results, acquisitions by out-of-state banking organizations do not appear here to be associated with a reduction in small business lending by the participating banks.

The absolute and relative sizes of the participating banks also appear to matter. Consistent with earlier work, we find that small and medium size bank mergers are associated with an increase in small business lending. However, larger bank mergers are in general associated with a decrease in small business lending. For acquisitions the opposite result obtains – large holding company acquisitions appear to increase small business lending, whereas smaller acquisitions may tend to decrease small business lending. However, acquisitions are often preludes to family mergers among banks in the same holding company in the following few years, that tend to decrease small business lending. Such family mergers are likely to increase dramatically in the near future, given the relaxation of interstate branching rules.

On the whole, these findings are consistent with a reasonably well-functioning dynamic marketplace in which some relationship-based small business loans may be dropped because consolidated institutions no longer have a comparative advantage in making this type of loan, but other local lenders step forward and extend these loans if they are positive net present value investments. Nevertheless, several important caveats are in order. Our analysis concentrates only on credit quantities and not on prices or other contract terms. It is quite possible that as a result of banking industry consolidation, small business borrowers are paying higher rates or otherwise dealing with harsher contract terms in ways that we do not measure. This is most likely to be case for borrowers that are dropped by consolidating banks and are picked up by other lenders via our external effect. Such borrowers may suffer temporary disruptions in credit availability, and may have to pay higher rates, pledge more collateral, or face more restrictive loan covenants or other lending terms in the short run until their new banking relationships mature.

We also note that our data set does not contain borrower characteristics other than our measure of the size of their bank credit. It is quite possible that consolidating banking institutions change their mixes of borrowers in ways not detected here. For example, consolidating institutions may substitute transactions-based loans to relatively informationally transparent small businesses in place of some relationship-based loans to relatively informationally opaque small borrowers.

We also caution that results on past M&As may not accurately predict the effects of future M&As. In the last few years, there has been heightened legislative, regulatory, and public concern over the issue of credit availability for small businesses. The small business lending section of the June Call Reports published since 1993, itself a byproduct of this heightened concern, makes available to all interested parties information on the small business lending behavior of every U.S. bank on an annual basis. Perhaps in part in reaction to the heightened awareness and scrutiny, some banking institutions seeking to participate in M&As have made commitments to continue or increase small business lending after consolidation. For example, Wells Fargo pledged to make $25 billion in small business loans in the ten years following its consolidation with First Interstate.

Recent changes in the regulatory environment could also change the focus of financial institutions regarding small business lending. For example, family mergers of cross-state affiliates of the same BHC that are now allowed may or may not yield the same effects as past family mergers of within-state affiliates. Technological changes may affect small business lending in the future as well. As analytical and information technologies such as credit scoring decrease the costs of lending to small businesses, the organizational issues that may have discouraged small business lending by larger banking institutions may diminish.

Despite these caveats, it seems likely that whatever changes occur in the supply of small business credit by banks participating in M&As, there will be a significant external effect that will offset much of this change in supply. Most observers project that thousands of small, community banks – which tend to specialize in small business lending – will survive consolidation of the banking industry. Nonbank lenders, such as commercial finance companies, are also available to supply credit to small businesses. To the extent that profitable small business lending opportunities continue to exist, and many small banks and nonbank lenders continue to exist, it seems likely that the total supply of small business credit will not change drastically in response to the consolidation of the banking industry.

References

Akhavein, J., Berger, A., Humphrey, D., 1997. The effects of bank megamergers on efficiency and prices: evidence from the profit function. Review of Industrial Organization 12, 95–139.

Ang, J., 1992. On the theory of finance for privately held firms. Journal of Small Business Finance 1, 185–203.

Angelini, P., DiSalvo, R., Ferri, G., 1998. Availability and cost for small businesses: customer relationships and credit cooperatives. Journal of Banking and Finance 22.

Benston, G., Hunter, W., Wall, L., 1995. Motivations for bank mergers and acquisitions: enhancing the deposit insurance put option versus earnings diversification. Journal of Money, Credit, and Banking 27, 777–788.

Berger, A., Humphrey, D., 1992. Megamergers in banking and the use of cost efficiency as an antitrust defense. Antitrust Bulletin 37, 541–600.

Berger, A., Kashyap, A., Scalise, J., 1995. The transformation of the U.S. banking industry: what a long, strange trip it's been. Brookings Papers on Economic Activity 2, 55–218.

Berger, A., Saunders, A., Scalise, J., Udell, G., 1997. The effects of bank mergers and acquisitions on small business lending. Finance and Economics Discussion Series 97-28. Board of Governors of the Federal Reserve.

Berger, A., Udell, G., 1995. Relationship lending and lines of credit in small firm finance. Journal of Business 68, 351–382.

Berger, A., Udell, G., 1996. Universal banking and the future of small business lending. In: Saunders, A., Walter, I. (Eds.), Financial System Design: The Case for Universal Banking. Irwin, Burr Ridge, IL, pp. 559–627.

Berlin, M., Mester, L., 1998. On the profitability and cost of relationship lending. Journal of Banking and Finance 22.

Blackwell, D., Winters, D., 1997. Banking relationships and the effect of monitoring on loan pricing. Journal of Financial Research 20, 275–289.

Cole, R., 1998. The importance of relationships to the availability of credit. Journal of Banking and Finance 22.

Cole, R., Wolken, J., Woodburn, L., 1996. Bank and nonbank competition for small business credit: evidence from the 1987 and 1993 National Surveys of Small Business Finances. Federal Reserve Bulletin 82, 983–995.

Cornett, M., Hovakimian, G., Palia, D., Tehranian, H., 1998. The impact of the manager-shareholder conflict on acquiring bank returns. Unpublished working paper, Boston College.

Cornett, M., Tehranian, H., 1992. Changes in corporate performance associated with bank acquisitions. Journal of Financial Economics 31, 211–234.

Craig, B., dos Santos, J., 1997. Banking consolidation: impact on small business lending. Working paper, Federal Reserve Bank of Cleveland.

Demsetz, R., Strahan, P., 1997. Diversification, size, and risk at bank holding companies. Journal of Money, Credit, and Banking 29, 300–313.

DeYoung, R., 1998. Comments on de novo banks and lending to small businesses. Journal of Banking and Finance 22.

Epstein, J., 1996. Years of bank mergers trigger a rise in start-ups looking for their niche. American Banker 1, 6.

Goldberg, L., White, L. 1998. De novo banks and lending to small businesses. Journal of Banking and Finance 22.

Hawawini, G., Swary, I., 1990. Mergers and Acquisitions in the U.S. Banking Industry: Evidence from the Capital Markets. North-Holland, Amsterdam.

Houston, J., James, C., 1995. Banking relationships, financial constraints and investment: are bank dependent borrowers more financially constrained? University of Florida working paper.

Houston, J., James, C., 1998. Do bank internal capital markets promote lending? Journal of Banking and Finance 22.

Houston, J., Ryngaert, M., 1994. The overall gains from large bank mergers. Journal of Banking and Finance 18, 1155–1176.

Hubbard, R., Kuttner, K, Palia, D., 1998. Are there bank effects in borrowers' costs of funds?: evidence from a matched sample of borrowers and banks. Unpublished working paper, Columbia University.

Hughes, J., Lang, W., Mester, L., Moon, C., 1996. Efficient banking under interstate branching. Journal of Money, Credit and Banking 28, 1045–1071.

John, K., Ofek, E., 1995. Asset sales and increase in focus. Journal of Financial Economics 37, 105–126.

Keeton, W., 1995. Multi-office bank lending to small businesses: some new evidence. Federal Reserve Bank of Kansas City Economic Review 80 (2), 45–57.

Keeton, W., 1996. Do bank mergers reduce lending to businesses and farmers? new evidence from Tenth District States. Federal Reserve Bank of Kansas City Economic Review 81 (3), 63–75.

Keeton, W., 1997. The effects of mergers on farm and business lending at small banks: new evidence from Tenth District States. Working paper, Federal Reserve Bank of Kansas City.

Kolari, J., Zardkoohi, A., 1997a. The impact of structural change in the banking industry on small business lending. Report to the Small Business Administration (a).

Kolari, J., Zardkoohi, A., 1997b. Bank acquisitions and small business lending. Working paper, Texas A&M University (b).

Kwast, M., Starr-McCluer, M., Wolken, J., 1997. Market definition and the analysis of antitrust in banking. Antitrust Bulletin 42, 973–995.

Levonian, M., Soller, J., 1995. Small banks, small loans, small business. Federal Reserve Bank of San Francisco working paper.

Palia, D., 1993. The managerial, regulatory, and financial determinants of bank merger premiums. Journal of Industrial Economics 41, 91–102.

Palia, D., 1994. Recent evidence on bank mergers. Financial Markets, Institutions, & Instruments 3, 36–59.

Peek, J., Rosengren, E., 1996. Small business credit availability: how important is size of lender? In: Saunders, A., Walter, I. (Eds.), Financial System Design: The Case for Universal Banking. Irwin, Burr Ridge, IL, pp. 628–655.

Peek, J., Rosengren, E., 1998. Bank consolidation and small business lending: it's not just bank size that matters. Journal of Banking and Finance 22.

Petersen, M., Rajan, R., 1994. The benefits of firm-creditor relationships: evidence from small business data. Journal of Finance 49, 3–37.

Petersen, M., Rajan, R., 1995. The effect of credit market competition on lending relationships. Quarterly Journal of Economics 110, 407–443.

Pilloff, S., 1996. Performance changes and shareholder wealth creation associated with mergers of publicly traded banking institutions. Journal of Money, Credit, and Banking 28, 294–310.

Strahan, P., Weston, J., 1996. Small business lending and bank consolidation: is there cause for concern? Current Issues in Economics and Finance 2. Federal Reserve Bank of New York.

Strahan, P., Weston, J., 1998. Small business lending and the changing structure of the banking industry. Journal of Banking and Finance 22.

Toevs, A., 1992. Under what circumstances do bank mergers improve efficiency? Proceedings of a Conference on Bank Structure and Competition. Federal Reserve Bank of Chicago, Chicago, IL, pp. 602–628.

Walraven, N., 1997. Small business lending by banks involved in mergers. Finance and Economics Discussion Series 97-25, Board of Governors of the Federal Reserve.

Whalen, G., 1995. Out-of-state holding company affiliation and small business lending, Office of the Comptroller of the Currency. Economic and Policy Analysis working paper 95–4.

Williamson, O., 1967. The economics of defense contracting: incentives and performance. In: McKean, R. (Ed.), Issues in Defense Economics. Columbia University Press, New York.

Williamson, O., 1988. Corporate Finance and Corporate Governance. Journal of Finance 43, 567–591.

Zardkoohi, A., Kolari, J., 1997. The effect of structural changes in the U.S. banking industry on small business lending. Working paper, Texas A&M University.

ELSEVIER

Journal of International Money and Finance
21 (2002) 857–877

Journal of International Money and Finance

www.elsevier.com/locate/econbase

The effects of cross-border bank mergers on bank risk and value

Yakov Amihud [a], Gayle L. DeLong [b,*], Anthony Saunders [c]

[a] *Ira L. Rennert Professor of Entrepreneurial Finance, Stern School of Business, New York University, 44 West 4th Street, Suite 9-190, New York, NY 10012, USA*

[b] *Assistant Professor of Finance, Zicklin School of Business, Baruch College, One Bernard Baruch Way, Box B10-225, New York, NY 10010, USA*

[c] *John M. Schiff Professor of Finance, Stern School of Business, New York University, 44 West 4th Street, Suite 9-190, New York, NY 10012, USA*

Abstract

This paper examines the effects of cross-border bank mergers on the risk and (abnormal) returns of acquiring banks. We find that, overall, the acquirers' risk neither increases nor decreases. In particular, on average, neither their total risk nor their systematic risk falls relative to banks in their home banking market. The abnormal returns to acquirers are negative and significant, but are somewhat higher when risk increases relative to banks in the acquirer's home country.

JEL classification: G14; G21; G34; F23

Keywords: Banks; Mergers; Market reaction; International business

1. Introduction

A common argument in banking is that cross-border (geographic) mergers have the potential to reduce bank (and thus regulators') risk of insolvency (Segal, 1974; Vander Vennet, 1996; Berger, 2000). This conventional wisdom is based on the traditional notion that it is better for a bank not to put all of its "eggs in one basket"

* Corresponding author. Tel: +1-646-312-3493; fax: +1-646-312-3451.
E-mail address: Gayle_DeLong@baruch.cuny.edu. (G.L. DeLong).

0261-5606/02/$ - see front matter.
PII: S0261-5606(02)00026-8

and thus geographic diversification is a naturally risk reducing activity. However, offsetting these perceived benefits are at least two potential costs that may well enhance the risk of bank insolvency and ultimately the risk exposure of bank regulators.[1]

The first risk increasing effect comes from the incentives banks have to risk shift when the regulatory "safety net" and its associated implicit and explicit guarantees are underpriced. As discussed by John et al. (1991, 2000), banks have incentives to increase their risk exposure beyond the level that would be privately optimal in a world in which there were no safety net guarantees or the safety net—deposit insurance, capital requirements, and implicitly, bank closure—is fairly priced. One way in which the safety net might be exploited is for a bank to acquire other (risky) banks by cross-border expansion. If the risky investment pays off, then the acquiring bank has the potential to keep any upside returns. If the acquisition of the foreign target fails and the domestic bank's (acquirer's) solvency is threatened, then the acquiring bank may be bailed out either by its own home or domestic regulator or perhaps by the host regulator (the regulator of the target bank). As a result, cross-border mergers may increase the insolvency risk exposure of either one or both the domestic (acquirer) and host (target) bank regulators. Repullo (2001) pointed out that while cross-border bank acquisitions may reduce risk due to diversification, they also shift responsibility to the domestic regulatory agency for supervision of the foreign bank and the insurance of its deposits.

A second reason why cross-border acquisitions may increase an acquirer's risk concerns "who is watching the eggs in the basket" (Winton, 1999). Specifically, by extending its operations into new overseas markets, the (domestic) bank is confronted with potentially new and risk increasing monitoring problems related to the loan customer base, the operating cost structure, etc. of the target bank. If monitoring costs are high, these problems may also increase the insolvency risk of the domestic acquiring bank and implicitly the risk of domestic (and foreign) regulators.

The overall question as to whether cross-border mergers are net beneficial and to whom they are net beneficial (i.e., bank owners, bank regulators, etc.) remains an open question. For example, if cross-border mergers do not raise the risk of acquiring banks relative to other domestic (home country) banks, or indeed, reduces their risk, then domestic regulators may encourage domestic banks to expand abroad. By contrast, if cross-border mergers increase the relative domestic riskiness of the acquiring bank, then domestic regulators may wish to scrutinize such mergers more carefully and may even seek to restrict them in an effort to reduce safety net subsidies and to reduce risk-shifting behavior.

Similarly, with respect to the target (host) country, if the (foreign) acquiring bank's risk rises relative to the risk of host country banks, then foreign acquisitions may be viewed as undesirable in that they increase the insolvency risk of that host country's banking system.

[1] Cross-border bank mergers have been on the rise for over a decade. In 1985, Thomson Financial Securities Data reports 28 cross-border bank mergers. By 2000, this number had climbed to 527.

To gain insight into these issues, we examine cross-border bank mergers from three perspectives. First, we analyze the change in *total* risk of an acquiring bank as a result of a cross-border banking merger. It is the acquiring bank's total risk relative to the risk of home banks that is of greatest concern to bank regulators (such as the Federal Deposit Insurance Corporation and Federal Reserve) in the acquirer's home country, because of the regulators' undiversified exposure to domestic bank risk. Second, we examine the changes in the *systematic* risk of acquiring banks relative to three bank indexes: the world bank index, the domestic bank index and the bank index of the host country (i.e. the country where the target is located). Third, we study the reaction of stock prices to news about the acquisition and examine the relationship between this stock price reaction and changes in risk brought about by cross-border bank mergers.

The main finding of our paper is that, on average, cross-border bank mergers do not change the risk of acquiring banks in any significant way. This finding has important regulatory policy implications in that the effect of an overseas acquisition is highly bank dependent or idiosyncratic. In particular, there are no general or average increases or decreases in either systematic or total risk. That is, on average, the risk decreasing effects of cross-border bank mergers are offset by risk increasing effects, and the nature of the merging partners' operation changes in a way so as to leave the acquirer's risk unchanged. Thus, based on the historical sample analyzed in this paper, there is no overall need for regulators to be concerned with a rise in risk following cross-border mergers and there is no need to restrict them.

The paper proceeds as follows. Section 2 discusses the methodology used to measure geographic acquisition risk. Section 3 discusses the data used. Section 4 details the tests and their results, and Section 5 concludes.

2. Methodology

We analyze the changes in the acquiring bank's risk after the cross-border acquisition is completed compared to its risk prior to the acquisition, relative to an index of all banks in three domiciles: the world, the home country and the host country (i.e., the country where the target is located). We also analyze the value (abnormal return) effects of these acquisitions. For the analysis of risk, we compare the acquirer's risk 1 year after the acquisition with its risk 1 year prior to the acquisition announcement. Specifically, we analyze data from 10 to 260 days after an acquisition is completed and compare the results with data from 10 to 260 days before an acquisition is announced. Since we analyze the acquirer's stock return, we convert the world and host country indexes to the currency of the acquirer's home country. For example, for a British acquirer of a German bank, we multiply the daily host country index (the German index) by the daily exchange rate for £/DM, and for the world index we multiply the world index, which is given in terms of US dollars, by the daily exchange rate for £/$. Returns are calculated from these converted indexes.[2]

[2] Exchange rates before 1986 come from the New York Fed. For exchange rate data starting in 1986, we use Datastream.

2.1. Risk

We measure the change in risk in two ways and compare its magnitude after the acquisition to that before the acquisition was announced.

2.1.1. Total relative risk

We calculate the ratio of the variance of the acquirer's daily stock returns to the variance of each of three bank index return series: world, home country and host country.

2.1.2. Systematic risk

We calculate the change in the *beta* coefficient of the acquiring bank's stock return relative to the returns on three bank indexes: the world bank index and the bank indexes of the home and host countries, controlling for the effects of the world bank index.

2.2. Abnormal returns

We measure abnormal returns to bank equity investors using the world, home, and host bank indexes as benchmarks. The event window that we consider is the 12-day period surrounding the announcement of the merger, from 10 days before the merger announcement to 1 day after it was announced (days −10 to +1). The event window of 12 days captures possible leakages of information before the merger is announced.[3] We then analyze investor reaction to changes in total risk as well as to changes in systematic risk.

3. Data

We examine mergers where at least one partner is a commercial bank and the partners are headquartered in different countries. The acquirer owns at least 51% of the target after the acquisition, the acquisition must be completed by December 1999, and the acquirer must be traded on a major exchange. The Thomson Financial Securities Data Merger and Acquisition Database lists 507 such mergers announced between 1985 and 1998. We use only those mergers where the acquirer's stock is publicly traded and daily stock return data are available in addition to the acquirer's country's bank and market indexes, and the target country's bank and market indexes. The data source for the individual banks' returns as well as the world, home, and host indexes is DataStream. Our final sample consists of 214 mergers.

[3] For example, Cybo-Ottone and Murgia (2000) find significant leakage effects for cross-border mergers in the days just prior to announcements of European bank mergers.

Table 1, Panel A shows the national identities of acquirers and targets (source: Thomson Financial Securities Data). While banks in countries such as Australia and the UK are active both in acquiring and being the targets of acquisitions, other countries such as Canada, France, Germany, Japan and the Netherlands have at least 50% more cross-border acquisitions than targets. Countries that have targets but no acquirers are usually smaller or less developed. The US has the largest number of target banks, and it has by far the largest number of banks of any sample country.

Table 1
Cross-border bank mergers and acquisitions, 1985–1998[a]

Panel A: National identities[a]

Country	Acquirers	Targets
Argentina	0	2
Austria	0	4
Australia	17	13
Belgium	6	2
Brazil	0	6
Canada	13	3
Denmark	3	1
Finland	0	1
France	28	12
Germany	26	7
Hong Kong	5	5
Ireland	3	1
Italy	4	8
Japan	14	1
Luxembourg	0	3
Malaysia	2	0
Mexico	0	3
Netherlands	18	6
New Zealand	0	7
Norway	0	1
Philippines	0	2
Poland	0	4
Portugal	0	3
Singapore	4	3
South Africa	1	3
South Korea	2	0
Spain	8	8
Sweden	3	3
Switzerland	10	5
Thailand	0	1
United Kingdom	28	32
United States	19	63
Venezuela	0	1
Total	**214**	**214**

(continued on next page)

Table 1 (*continued*)

Panel B: Number of mergers announced per year[b] Year	Number of mergers
1985	5
1986	8
1987	8
1988	12
1989	17
1990	16
1991	13
1992	15
1993	11
1994	14
1995	16
1996	24
1997	26
1998	29
Total	**214**

[a] The sample consists of mergers where at least one partner is a commercial bank and the partners are headquartered in different countries. The acquirer owns at least 51% of the target after the acquisition, and trades on a major exchange for which daily return data are available. The merger is announced between 1985 and 1998 and completed by December 1999.

[b] Data sources: Thomson Financial Securities Data Merger and Acquisition Database and Datastream.

Until 1997, US banks were restricted from pursuing full nationwide branch banking.[4] This restriction, along with bank holding company legislation restraining domestic mergers, kept US banks small relative to banks outside the US. Since targets tend to be smaller banks, US banks were attractive takeover targets.[5]

Table 1, Panel B shows the year each merger was announced from Thomson Financial Securities Data. The table reflects the steady growth in cross-border mergers that include a bank as at least one of the partners. We are able to find data for five mergers announced in 1985. By 1998, this number rises to 29.

In nearly all acquisitions, the target was not a public company. Only 30 targets were publicly-traded, and for 12 of them we were able to find stock market information. For this subset, we calculated the weighted-average return on the portfolio of the acquirer and the target, the weights being the market capitalization of the target and acquirer ten days before the merger was announced. As with the world and host indexes, we convert the stock prices of the target into the acquirer's currency.

[4] Until the final repeal of the McFadden Act in 1997 (phased in starting 1994), US banks were not permitted to engage in interstate banking except under restricted circumstances.

[5] Buch and DeLong (2002) explore the determinants of cross-border bank mergers.

4. Tests

4.1. Total risk

A common measure of total risk is the variance of a firm's (bank's) stock return. We examine first the return variance of he acquiring bank relative to the variance of three bank return indexes. Denote TRR_j = total relative risk of acquirer j,

$$TRR_{j,k} = \frac{\mathrm{Var}(R_j)}{\mathrm{Var}(RB_k)}, \tag{1}$$

R_j is the daily return on acquirer j and RB_k is the return on bank index k, where k = world, home or host. We then calculate the change in the total relative risk, $\Delta TRR_{j,k}$,

$$\Delta TRR_{j,k} = TRR_{j,k}(\text{after}) - TRR_{j,k}(\text{before}), \tag{2}$$

where "after" refers to days +10 to +260 after the acquisition is consummated, and "before" refers to days −260 to −10 before the announcement. In addition to examining the results for the entire sample, we divide the sample into subgroups according to the locations of the acquirers and targets. The subgroups are mergers involving:

1. US acquirers,
2. UK acquirers,
3. European acquirers with European targets,
4. European acquirers with non-European targets,
5. Acquirers from the rest of the world, mainly Australia, Canada, and Japan.

Table 2, Panel A presents the results of the tests that compare the acquirer's (relative) risk before and after the acquisition. Neither the net risk increasing nor the net risk decreasing hypothesis is supported by the data. In particular, ΔTRR_{home} and ΔTRR_{host} are not significantly different from zero, using a Z-test. However, there is a weak indication of a decline in the acquirer's risk relative to its home bank index. That is, in most mergers, 56.07% of them, $\Delta TRR_{\text{home}}<0$ and all five median values of ΔTRR_{home} are negative.

It is instructive to compare the two groups of European bank acquisitions. The first group (60) has European targets, the second group (49) has non-European targets. Potentially, the two groups have two conflicting effects on the acquirer's risk. On the one hand, non-European targets may be more risky—partly because of exchange rate risk—than European targets and therefore contribute more to the acquirer's total risk. On the other hand, the non-European targets may provide greater diversification benefits because the business of a European acquirer may be less correlated with the business of a non-European target than with that of a European target. Overall, the evidence is that cross-border mergers between two European banks contribute less to the acquirer's risk than mergers between European and non-European banks. Notably, however, in both cases, the acquirer's risk does not rise relative to the home

Table 2
Changes in total risk[a]

	ΔTRR_{world}			ΔTRR_{home}			ΔTRR_{host}		
	Mean (*t*-statistic)	Median	% positive (Z-statistic)	Mean (*t*-statistic)	Median	% positive (Z-statistic)	Mean (*t*-statistic)	Median	% positive (Z-statistic)
Panel A: Acquirer's stock[b]									
Acquirer's country (cases)									
Entire sample (214)	−0.0701	0.1757	53.74%	−0.0193	−0.0580	43.93%**c**	−0.0983	0.0820	54.21%
	(−0.20)		(1.09)	(−0.18)		(−1.78)	(−0.59)		(1.23)
US (19)	0.5346	−0.2390	47.37%	0.0566	−0.3836	47.37%	0.3770	−0.0532	47.37%
	(0.93)		(−0.23)	(0.09)		(−0.23)	(0.87)		(−0.23)
UK (28)	0.2240	0.1455	57.14%	−0.0150	−0.0649	32.14%**c**	−0.2275	−0.1349	42.86%
	(0.66)		(0.76)	(−0.13)		(−1.89)	(−1.28)		(−0.16)
European acquirers of European targets (60)	−0.8856	−0.1455	48.33%	−0.0944	−0.0286	46.67%	−0.1689	0.0950	51.67%
	(−1.01)		(−0.25)	(−0.33)		(−0.52)	(−0.40)		(0.26)
European acquirers of non-European targets (49)	0.3688**c**	0.5544	61.22%	−0.0129	−0.0074	48.98%	0.4318**b**	0.2778	71.43%**a**
	(1.68)		(1.57)	(−0.12)		(−0.14)	(2.08)		(3.00)
Rest of the world (58)	0.0624	0.3421	53.45%	0.0260	−0.0910	41.38%	−0.5664	−0.0366	50.00%
	(0.07)		(0.53)	(0.20)		(−1.31)	(−1.62)		(0.00)
Panel B: A portfolio of 12 acquirers and targets, value weighted (both publicly traded)[c]									
	1.1259**b**	0.8054	66.67%	0.3629**b**	0.1302	66.67%	0.5202**b**	0.2598	75.00%**b**
	(2.42)		(1.15)	(2.28)		(1.15)	(2.23)		(1.73)

[a] **a**, **b**, **c**=statistically significant at the 1, 5, and 10% level, respectively.

[b] Panel A: change in the acquiring bank's variance of daily stock return relative to the variance of three bank return indexes. $TRR_{k,j}$ = total relative risk of acquirer $j = \frac{\mathrm{Var}(R_j)}{\mathrm{Var}(RB_k)}$. R_j is the daily return on acquirer j and RB_k is the return on bank index k, k = world, home and host (the last two are the acquirer's home country and the target's country). $\Delta TRR_{k,j} = TRR_{k,j}(\text{after}) - TRR_{k,j}(\text{before})$, where "before" is days −260 to −10 before the announcement, and "after" is days +10 to +260 after the consummation of the merger. The *t*-statistics test the hypothesis that $\Delta TRR_{k,j} = 0$. The *Z*-statistics test the hypothesis that the proportion of $\Delta TRR_{k,j} > 0$ is 0.5.

[c] Panel B: tests for the 12 cases with public targets. The pre-merger returns are the weighted average of the partners, based on the market capitalization of the partners 10 days before the merger is announced.

bank's risk (see ΔTRR_{home} column in Table 2, Panel A). Thus, the results show that while the acquirer's risk does not decline after cross-border bank merger, as would be expected from the simple diversification story, it does not rise either.

The results in Table 2 Panel A imply that in general, cross-border mergers do not lead acquirers to engage in post-merger risk shifting or risk increasing behavior. This result has important regulatory implications. Bank regulators that are concerned with the insolvency (total) risk of their domestic banking institutions need not be overly concerned that cross-border acquisition strategies pose a threat to domestic bank system stability. Neither is there an increase in total risk with respect to the bank index of the host country, where the target is located. Thus regulators in host countries may be less concerned about imposing barriers to foreign acquisitions.

In Table 2, Panel B, we examine whether the risk of the two merged banks *put together* changed after the merger. To that end, we calculate the return on a value-weighted portfolio of pairs of acquirer and target firms using their market values ten days before the announcement (see Eun et al., 1996). If the operational characteristics of the banks have not changed, there should be no change in the risk of this portfolio return relative to the benchmark indexes. The results in Table 2, Panel B show, however, that relative to the risk of a portfolio of the acquirer and target before the merger, the risk of the acquiring bank after the merger increases relative to all three benchmarks. Interestingly, before the merger, the correlation between the returns of the two banks, acquirer and target, was extremely small (0.0227 on average). This low correlation suggests a significant degree of potential diversification benefits impacting the total risk of a portfolio of the acquirer and target at the time of acquisition. After the acquisition, the operations of the acquirer and target became more integrated, which in turn is likely to have increased the correlation between their returns and thus increased their risk, compared to total risk prior to acquisition.

4.2. Systematic risk

After a domestic bank acquires a foreign bank, there is a rise in the share of its income that is derived from foreign markets and a decline in the share of its income that is derived from the domestic market. It is thus expected that after the merger, the acquirer's return will show a weaker covariance with the home market banking index and a stronger covariance with foreign market banking indexes—the world as a whole and in particular the country where the target bank is located. Agmon and Lessard (1977) showed, for US multinational corporations, that the *beta* of their return with respect to the home market is lower and the *beta* on the world index is higher when the proportion of sales outside the US is higher. We examine this issue here. We expect that a cross-border merger would reduce the acquirer's *beta* with respect to the home bank portfolio and raise its *beta* with respect to the world and host bank portfolios. While regulators are principally concerned about the total risk of a bank from engaging in cross-border mergers, they might want to observe whether the cross-border merger affects the extent to which the acquirer's return moves with the rest of the banks under its regulatory supervision. If, for example, the acquiring bank's *beta* with respect to the home market *rises*, it means that the cross-border merger augments the risk of banks in the home country rather than reduces it.

Specifically, we measure the acquiring bank's systematic risk—its β coefficient—relative to three bank indexes: world, home and host. To do this, we use the world bank index return, RB_{world}, and then include the home and host bank return indexes after having removed the effect of the world market index. This is obtained by regressing the home and host bank return indexes on the world market return index and then using the respective residuals, denoted RB^*_{home} and RB^*_{host}. The estimated model for the return of stock j on day t, $R_{j,t}$, is

$$R_{j,t} = \alpha_j + \alpha_{1j}D_t + \beta_{\text{world},j}RB_{\text{world},t} + \gamma_{\text{world},j}RB_{\text{world},t}D_t + \beta_{\text{home},j}RB^*_{\text{home},t} + \gamma_{\text{home},j}RB^*_{\text{home},t}D_t + \beta_{\text{host},j}RB^*_{\text{host},t} + \gamma_{\text{host},j}RB^*_{\text{host},t}D_t + u_{j,t}. \quad (3)$$

D_t is a dummy variable, $D_t = 0$ for days -260 to day -10 before the merger announcement, and $D_t = 1$ for days +10 to +260 after the consummation of the merger. We can directly obtain the change in *beta*, $\Delta\beta_{k,j}$, defined as follows:

$$\Delta\beta_{kj} = \beta_{kj}(\text{after}) - \beta_{kj}(\text{before}) = \gamma_{kj}, \quad (4)$$

where k = world, home or host.

Our hypotheses are as follows:

(H1): β_{home} should decline after cross-border mergers, since part of the acquirer's return is generated by banking activity abroad which is not perfectly correlated with banking activity in the home market.

(H2): β_{world} and especially $\Delta\beta_{\text{host}}$ should rise since the acquirer's return in part reflects the return on banks (and their activities) in the countries where the target bank is doing business.

Surprisingly, neither hypothesis is supported by the data. The results, presented in Table 3, Panel A, show that $\Delta\beta_{k,j}$ is not significantly different from zero for all three indexes. Again, this result should assuage both domestic and host country regulator concerns regarding the effects of cross-border bank acquisitions on the solvency of their banking systems.

Table 3, Panel B analyzes the change in *betas* for the small subset of merger partners where we can find daily stock market return information for the target. Here, we compare the weighted-average *betas* of the merged partners before the merger is announced with the *beta* of the merged entity, where the weighting uses the acquirer's and target's market capitalization 10 days before the merger is announced. We do find a significant increase in the beta for the world bank index of the acquirer (as expected) but no significant change in either home or host country betas.

As a further check on the results in Table 3, Panel A, we examine the changes in the betas in a 2×2 matrix, where $\Delta\beta_{\text{home}}$ is tabulated against $\Delta\beta_{\text{host}}$ (Table 4, Panel A) and $\Delta\beta_{\text{world}}$ (Table 4, Panel B). In Table 4, Panel A we expect the observations to more likely fall into the quadrants (cells) where $\Delta\beta_{\text{home}}<0$ and $\beta_{\text{host}}>0$. However, we find that only 28% of our sample adheres to this expectation. Indeed, the outcomes in the four cells are largely random (with randomness not being rejected by a χ^2 test). In Table 4, Panel B, we expect most cases to fall into the quadrant where

Table 3
Changes in systematic risk[a]

	$\Delta\beta_{world}$			$\Delta\beta_{home}$			$\Delta\beta_{host}$		
	Mean (*t*-statistic)	Median	% positive (Z-statistic)	Mean (*t*-statistic)	Median	% positive (Z-statistic)	Mean (t-statistic)	Median	% positive (Z-statistic)
Panel A: Acquirer's stock									
Acquirer's country (cases)[b]									
Entire sample (214)	0.0032	0.0022	51.40%	0.0159	0.0015	51.40%	−0.0017	−0.0009	49.53%
	(0.26)		(0.41)	(0.95)		(0.41)	(−0.18)		(−0.14)
US (19)	−0.0033	0.0258	63.16	0.0245	−0.0313	47.37	−0.0445	−0.0287	36.84
	(−0.06)		(1.15)	(0.28)		(−0.23)	(−1.29)		(−1.15)
UK (28)	−0.0523	−0.0482	39.29	−0.0306	−0.0131	46.43	−0.0149	−0.0088	46.43
	(−1.39)		(−1.13)	(−0.85)		(−0.38)	(−0.63)		(−0.38)
European acquirers of	0.0199	0.0097	55.00	0.0318	0.0210	60.00	0.0055	0.0006	51.67
European targets (60)	(0.94)		(0.77)	(1.21)		(1.55)	(0.21)		(0.26)
European acquirers of	−0.0178	−0.0209	40.82	0.0102	0.0129	48.98	−0.0078	−0.0037	46.94
non-European targets (49)	(−1.00)		(−1.29)	(0.31)		(−0.14)	(−0.57)		(−0.43)
Rest of the world (58)	0.0327	0.0234	58.62	0.0237	−0.0081	48.28	0.0163	0.0146	55.17
	(1.28)		(1.31)	(0.67)		(−0.26)	(0.92)		(0.79)
Panel B: A portfolio of 12 acquirers and targets, value weighted (both publicly traded)[c]									
	0.0431	0.0568	75.00**b**	0.0697	0.1309	58.33	−0.0040	0.0009	50.00
	(1.37)		(1.73)	(1.58)		(0.58)	(−0.10)		(0.00)

[a] **b**=statistically significant at the 5% level.

[b] Panel A reports the change in *beta* coefficient of the acquirer's return after the cross-border merger compared to beforehand. $R_{j,t} = \alpha_j + d_j + \beta_{world,j}\, RB_{world,t} + \gamma_{world,j}\, RB_{world,t} D_t + \beta_{home,j} RB^*_{home,t} + \gamma_{home,j} RB^*_{home,t} D_t + \beta_{host,j} RB^*_{host,t} + \gamma_{host,j} RB^*_{host,t} D_t + u_{j,t}$. $R_{j,t}$ is the return on acquirer j on day t, $RB_{k,t}$ is the bank index on day t, where k = world, home or host. RB^*_{home} and RB^*_{host} are the residuals from a regression of the respective bank index return on RB_{world}, and D is a dummy variable that is zero for days −260 to day −10 before the merger announcement, and one for days +10 to +260 after the consummation of the merger. $\Delta\beta_{k,j} = \gamma_{k,j}$.

[c] Panel B reports the 12 cases or subset of mergers with public targets. The pre-merger returns are the weighted average of the partners, based on the market capitalization of the partners ten days before the merger is announced.

Table 4
Matrices of changes in betas on home and host bank return indexes and on home and world bank return indexes as a result of a cross-border bank merger[a]

		β_{home}		Total
		Decreases	Increases	
Panel A: Home and host bank indexes[b]				
β_{host}	Decreases	22.4%	26.2%	48.6%
	Increases	28.0	23.4	51.4
Total		50.4	49.6	100
Panel B: Home and world bank indexes[c]				
β_{world}	Decreases	24.8%	23.8%	48.6%
	Increases	23.8	27.6	51.4
Total		48.6	51.4	100

[a] The table reports the change in systematic risk before and after a cross-border merger. Systematic risk is measured as the *beta* resulting from a regression of the acquiring bank's return on the world, home, and host bank return indexes. See Table 3 for details.
[b] H_0: 25% of observations in each cell; $\chi^2 = 1.70$, df = 1, $p = 0.1922$.
[c] H_0: 25% of observations in each cell $\chi^2 = 0.80$, df = 1, $p = 0.3700$.

$\Delta\beta_{world}>0$ and $\Delta\beta_{home}<0$. However, only 23.8% of the cases fall into this quadrant, with the rest being distributed randomly among the remaining three quadrants (randomness is not rejected by a χ^2 test).

These results further confirm that cross-border bank related mergers do not significantly shift the acquirer's (systematic) risk away from the home market, as might be expected a priori.

So far, our analysis has been carried out using *bank* return indexes as the benchmark return indexes against which to measure relative risk changes, since we wish to compare the risk effects of banks that engage in cross-border merger activity versus those that do not. The effect of cross-border bank mergers on bank systematic risk could alternatively be examined using *market* indexes instead of bank indexes. However, doing this poses a problem since there are potentially factors that affect bank industry performance that are not captured by the market indexes. Specifically, our estimation of *beta* changes covers a relatively long period of time, 250 days before and after the bank merger. If, during that period, the performance of banking as an industry changes relative to the market as a whole—for example, due to a regulatory change that impacts all banks in a given country—then the *betas* of the merging banks would change although this change has nothing to do with the merger being analyzed. Thus, using the market index as a benchmark for our analysis would likely confound two effects: (1) the change in the acquirer's risk after the merger relative to the risk of all other banks; and (2) the change in the risk of the banking industry relative to the market as a whole.

To test for this possible confounding, we estimate two alternative equations (models):

$$\begin{aligned} R_{j,t} &= \alpha_j + \alpha_{1j}D_t + \beta_{\text{world},j}RM_{\text{world},t} + \gamma_{\text{world},j}RM_{\text{world},t}D_t \\ &+ \beta_{\text{home},j}RM^*_{\text{home},t} + \gamma_{\text{home},j}RM^*_{\text{home},t}D_t + \beta_{\text{host},j}RM^*_{\text{host},t} + \gamma_{\text{host},j}RM^*_{\text{host},t}D_t \\ &+ u_{j,t}. \end{aligned} \tag{5}$$

$$\begin{aligned} RB_{j,t} &= \alpha_j + \alpha_{1j}D_t + \beta_{\text{world},j}RM_{\text{world},t} + \gamma_{\text{world},j}RM_{\text{world},t}D_t \\ &+ \beta_{\text{home},j}RM^*_{\text{home},t} + \gamma_{\text{home},j}RM^*_{\text{home},t}D_t + \beta_{\text{host},j}RM^*_{\text{host},t} + \gamma_{\text{host},j}RM^*_{\text{host},t}D_t \\ &+ u_{j,t}. \end{aligned} \tag{6}$$

Model (5) is identical to our original model (3), except that it replaces the bank index RB_k by the market index RM_k. In model (6), the dependent variable $RB_{j,t}$ is the bank index in the home country of acquirer j.

The estimation results of these two models are presented in Table 5. For reasons of parsimony, we present only the results for the entire sample. The results for the first equation show increases in the market *beta* coefficients of acquirers after cross-border mergers against all three market indexes (only the increase in the world beta and home beta are significant). The estimation results of the second equation show that banks' systematic risk has risen over time relative to the market. That is, the *beta* coefficients of banks—irrespective of their involvement in cross-border mergers—increased during the period under study. The reasons for this increase in bank systematic risk is an interesting question in itself and is not analyzed here. However, these results support our use of bank industry indexes rather than market indexes as benchmarks in our study of cross-border bank acquisitions.

4.3. Abnormal return effects

This sub-section examines two questions:

1. Do cross-border bank mergers benefit the acquirer's stockholders relative to those of other banks not involved in cross-border mergers?
2. Is the return on the acquirer's stock related to changes in its risk?

To answer these questions, we proceed as follows. We first estimate cumulative abnormal returns (*CAR*s) for the acquirer, using the following model

$$R_{j,t} = \alpha_j + \beta_{\text{world},j}RB_{\text{world},t} + \beta_{\text{home},j}RB^*_{\text{home},t} + \beta_{\text{host},j}RB^*_{\text{host},t} + \varepsilon_{j,t}. \tag{7}$$

The model is estimated over days −260 to −10 before the announcement day. Then, we calculate the abnormal return for stock j on day t, $AR_{j,t}$, as

$$AR_{j,t} = R_{j,t} - (\alpha_j + \beta_{\text{world},j}RB_{\text{world},t} + \beta_{\text{home},j}RB^*_{\text{home},t} + \beta_{\text{host},j}RB^*_{\text{host},t}), \tag{8}$$

where the parameters in the parentheses in Eq. (8) are estimated from model (7). Finally, the cumulative 12-day abnormal return, CAR_j, is calculated starting 10 days before the announcement, (day 0), to account for possible leakages of information, to one day after the announcement:

Table 5
Changes in systematic risk using market indexes as benchmarks[a,b]

Model	$\Delta\beta_{world}$			$\Delta\beta_{home}$			$\Delta\beta_{host}$		
	Mean (t-statistic)	Median	% positive (Z-statistic)	Mean (t-statistic)	Median	% positive (Z-statistic)	Mean (t-statistic)	Median	% positive (Z-statistic)
1	0.0493**b**	0.0343	57.94%**b**	0.0503**b**	0.0214	52.34%	0.0214	0.0131	51.87%
	(2.67)		(2.32)	(2.22)		(0.68)	(1.43)		(0.55)
2	0.0510**a**	0.0711	61.22%**a**	0.0257	0.0306	50.47%	0.0149**b**	0.0130	54.21
	(3.88)		(3.28)	(1.51)		(0.14)	(2.04)		(1.23)

[a] **a**,**b** = statistically significant at the 1 and 5% levels, respectively.

[b] The table reports the change in the *beta* coefficient of the acquirer's return after cross-border merger compared to beforehand.

Model 1: $R_{j,t} = \alpha_j + \alpha_{1j}D_t + \beta_{world,j}RM_{world,t} + \gamma_{world,j}RM_{world,t}D_t + \beta_{home,j}RM^*_{home,t} + \gamma_{home,j}RM^*_{home,t}D_t + \beta_{host,j}RM^*_{host,t} + \gamma_{host,j}RM^*_{host,t}D_t + u_{j,t}$,

Model 2: $RB_{j,t} = \alpha_j + \alpha_{1j}D_t + \beta_{world,j}RM_{world,t} + \gamma_{world,j}RM_{world,t}D_t + \beta_{home,j}RM^*_{home,t} + \gamma_{home,j}RM^*_{home,t}D_t + \beta_{host,j}RM^*_{host,t} + \gamma_{host,j}RM^*_{host,t}D_t + u_{j,t}$.

$R_{j,t}$ is the return on acquirer j on day t, and $RB_{j,t}$ is the bank index of the home country of acquirer j, $RM_{k,t}$ is the market index where k = world, home or host. RM^*_{home} and RM^*_{host} are the residuals from a regression of the respective market index return on RM_{world}, and D is a dummy variable that is zero for days −260 to day −10 before the merger announcement and one for days +10 to +260 after the consummation of the merger. $\Delta\beta_k = \gamma_{k,j}$.

$$CAR_j = \sum_{t=-10}^{+1} AR_{j,t}. \tag{9}$$

In general, we expect that banks only engage in acquisitions that are ex-ante value increasing. Moreover, in the case of banks, investors will rationally assign value to any mis- (under-) priced safety net guarantees (see Kane, 2000). These guarantees will potentially make bank acquisitions even more valuable to stockholders.

Table 6, Panel A presents the results. The average *CAR* is negative, approximately -1%, and is statistically significant. This result is consistent with acquirers over-paying for targets even in the presence of safety net subsidies. In nearly 63% of all cross-border mergers the acquirer had negative *CAR*s (significantly different from a chance result of 50%). Moreover, the average *CAR* is negative for *all* five geographic groups. This means that cross-border acquisitions on their announcement were not perceived as beneficial to the acquiring bank stockholders relative to benchmark banks. Since British acquirers experienced a relatively large and negative 2.4% *CAR*, the results for the overall sample could be driven by mergers with UK acquirers. We check the robustness of the result by removing the mergers with UK acquirers and find that overall, the average loss is about 0.8% and is statistically significant ($t = -2.24$).

Our results of negative acquirer's return resulting from cross-border acquisitions contrast with those of Doukas and Travlos (1988) for multinational firms. They found that for US multinational acquirers who were not operating in the target's country, the acquisition announcement was associated with a significant positive excess returns, whereas for MNCs that were already operating in the target's country, the acquisition generated a small negative and insignificant excess returns. Eun et al. (1996) analyzed acquisitions of US targets by foreign acquirers. On average, acquirers experienced negative abnormal returns, although the negative abnormal returns were insignificant.

Our results are consistent with the results of a number of studies on domestic bank acquisitions.[6] Hawawini and Swary (1990) found, for 126 bank acquisitions between 1968 and 1987, that the bidders' abnormal returns were negative and significant. Houston and Ryngaert (1994) also found negative abnormal returns for 153 bidding US banks between 1985 and 1991. Cybo-Ottone and Murgia (2000) found that for 54 European bank mergers between 1988 and 1997, the acquirers' abnormal returns were insignificantly different from zero.

Examining the effects of cross-border acquisitions on the acquirer alone may overlook synergistic gains from cross-border mergers (see Eun et al., 1996). These synergistic gains are likely to be divided between the acquirer and its target. Following Eun et al. (1996), we examine where possible (given the data constraints), the *total* value creation in cross-border mergers to both acquirer and target. To do this, we examine the *CAR*s on the weighted *pairs* of acquirers and targets for the 12 cases where these stock return data are available on both banks. The weights are the rela-

[6] For a comprehensive revise, see Piloff and Santomero (1998).

Table 6
Market reaction to changes in systematic risk[a,b]

Acquirer's country (cases)	Mean (t-statistic)	Median	% positive (Z-statistic)	Minimum	Maximum
Panel A: Acquirer's stock					
Entire sample (214)	−0.0098**a**	−0.0091	37.38%**a**	−0.1498	0.2013
	(−3.08)		(−3.69)		
US (19)	−0.0053	0.0008	52.64	−0.0792	0.1089
	(−0.52)		(0.23)		
UK (28)	−0.0238**a**	−0.0285	28.57**b**	−0.1013	0.0896
	(−2.93)		(−2.27)		
European acquirers of European targets (60)	−0.0016	−0.0033	43.33	−0.1015	0.2013
	(−0.27)		(−1.03)		
European acquirers of non-European targets (49)	−0.0129**c**	−0.0133	32.65**b**	−0.1498	0.1360
	(−1.79)		(−2.43)		
Rest of the world (58)	−0.0103**c**	−0.0123	34.48**b**	−0.1373	0.1450
	(−1.73)		(−2.36)		
Panel B: A portfolio of 12 acquirers and targets, market value weighted (both publicly traded)					
	−0.0127	−0.0094	25.00**b**	−0.0837	0.0248
	(−1.68)		(−1.73)		

[a] **a**, **b**, **c**=statistically significant at the 1, 5, and 10% level, respectively.
[b] The table measures the abnormal returns for stock j on day t, $AR_{j,t}$ estimated using a three factor market model:

$$AR_{j,t} = R_{j,t} - (\alpha_j + \beta_{\text{world},j} RB_{\text{world},t} + \beta_{\text{home},j} RB^*_{\text{home},t} + \beta_{\text{host},j} RB^*_{\text{host},t}).$$

The model is estimated over days −260 to −10 before the announcement. The cumulative twelve-day abnormal return, CAR_j, is $CAR_j = \sum_{t=-10}^{+1} AR_{j,t}$.

tive equity market values of the acquirer and target 10 days before the acquisition announcement.

As can be seen from Table 6, Panel B, the average *CAR* on the portfolio of the acquirer and target is negative, 1.27%, with 75% of the sub-sample having negative abnormal returns. While the statistical significance is low, because of the very small sample size, this evidence is consistent with the results of DeLong (2001) who found negative abnormal returns on average for US domestic bank mergers that are geographically diversifying. However, the results are different from the results of Eun et al. (1996) on foreign acquisitions of US target companies. The difference may reflect the difference in industry—we examine only bank acquisitions—and target country. Overall, our results suggest that the market value effect of cross-border mergers for bank stockholders is negative, notwithstanding possibly synergistic gains and the underpricing of bank safety nets.

We examine next whether the change in the acquirer value is related to changes in its risk. There are two opposing hypotheses.

(Ha): An increase in risk, particularly *beta* risk, raises the company's expected rate of return and thereby reduces its value if its cash flows remain unchanged. Thus, *CAR*s should decline when *beta* risk increases.

(Hb): In a highly levered company such as bank, an increase in risk induces a transfer of wealth from debt holders (and regulators/taxpayers) to stockholders. In the presence of wealth transfers, *CARs* should increase as risk increases.

We test these hypotheses in two ways. First, we estimate the effect on *CAR*s of changes in beta coefficients:

$$CAR_j = \gamma_0 + \gamma_1\Delta\beta_{\mathrm{world},j} + \gamma_2\Delta\beta_{\mathrm{home},j} + \gamma_3\Delta\beta_{\mathrm{host},j}. \tag{10}$$

Hypothesis **(Ha)** implies $\gamma_k < 0$ for $k = 1$, 2 and 3, while hypothesis **(Hb)** implies $\gamma_k > 0$. In estimating the model, we eliminated from each variable $\Delta\beta$ extreme outliers, i.e., the upper and lower 1% of the distribution of the respective variable leaving 203 merger cases in the sample to be estimated.

The results are presented in Table 7. The evidence appears to support neither hypothesis **(Ha)** nor **(Hb)**. That is, acquirer's *CAR*s appear to be unrelated to changes in *beta* risk.

As was discussed earlier, because of the relatively undiversified or industry specific exposure, domestic regulators are concerned with the *total* risk of the bank. Thus, from their viewpoint the proper benchmark is the home bank index. Consequently, we also estimate the model:

$$CAR_j = \gamma_0 + \gamma_1\Delta TRR_{j,\mathrm{home}}, \tag{11}$$

$\Delta TRR_{\mathrm{j,home}}$ is the change in total relative risk, as defined in (1), using the *home* banking index as benchmark. Again, we drop the extreme 1% of observations in each tail of the distribution of $\Delta TRR_{\mathrm{j,home}}$ from the sample.

The results, presented in Table 8, give weak support to hypothesis **(Hb)**. The change in the acquirer's value as a result of cross-border acquisition is higher when the acquirer's risk rises relative to other home banks. We reestimated this model as follows:

Table 7
Regression results of *CAR* on changes in *betas*[ab]

Acquirer's country (cases)	Constant (*t*-statistic)	$\Delta\beta_{world}$ (*t*-statistic)	$\Delta\beta_{home}$ (*t*-statistic)	$\Delta\beta_{host}$ (*t*-statistic)	Adjusted-R^2
Panel A: Acquirer's stock					
Entire sample (203)	−0.0108**a**	0.0218	0.0109	−0.0362	0.39%
	(−3.31)	(0.79)	(0.75)	(−1.17)	
US (18)	−0.0129	0.0153	0.0476**c**	0.0076	4.82
	(−1.53)	(0.24)	(1.81)	(0.0810)	
UK (28)	−0.0218**b**	0.0573	−0.0025	−0.0627	−0.02
	(−2.13)	(0.85)	(−0.08)	(−0.71)	
European acquirers of European	−0.0005	−0.0686	−0.0242	−0.0409	−0.91
targets (57)	(−0.08)	(−0.69)	(−0.90)	(−0.89)	
European acquirers of non-European	−0.0140**c**	0.0660	0.0494	−0.0853	3.69
targets (48)	(−1.95)	(0.70)	(1.47)	(−0.88)	
Rest of the world (53)	−0.0095	0.0101	−0.0268	−0.0090	−0.04
	(−1.32)	(0.30)	(−0.97)	(−0.11)	
Panel B: A portfolio of 12 acquirers and targets, value weighted (both publicly traded)					
	−0.0068	−0.0151	−0.0808	−0.0747	24.338
	(−1.33)	(−0.24)	(−1.44)	(−0.93)	

[a] **a**, **b**, **c**=statistically significant at the 1, 5, and 10% level, respectively.
[b] The table measures the effects of changes in systematic risk on *CAR*, using the model:

$$CAR_j = \gamma_0 + \gamma_1\Delta\beta_{world,j} + \gamma_2\Delta\beta_{home,j} + \gamma_3\Delta\beta_{host,j}.$$

In this regression, outliers that are at the top and bottom 1% of the distribution of each RHS variable are removed.

Table 8
Regression results of *CAR* on changes in total relative to the acquirer's home bank index[ab]

Acquirer's country (cases)	Constant (*t*-statistic)	ΔTRR_{home} (*t*-statistic)	Adjusted-R^2
Panel A: Acquirer's stock			
Entire sample (209)	−0.0095**a**	0.0045**c**	0.50%
	(−2.98)	(1.71)	
US (17)	−0.0023	0.0057**c**	−0.58
	(−0.21)	(2.05)	
UK (28)	−0.0236**a**	0.0155**c**	0.01
	(−3.01)	(1.77)	
European acquirers of European targets (57)	−0.0005	0.0016	−0.02
	(−0.08)	(0.28)	
European acquirers of non-European targets (49)	−0.0127**c**	0.0175**c**	4.68
	(−1.79)	(1.81)	
Rest of the world (58)	−0.0103**c**	−0.0027	−0.01
	(−1.72)	(−0.63)	
Panel B: A portfolio of 12 acquirers and targets, value weighted (both publicly traded)			
	−0.0108	−0.0052	−0.09
	(−1.72)	(−0.47)	

[a] **a**, **b**, **c**=statistically significant at the 1, 5, and 10% level, respectively.
[b] Estimates of the effect of changes in total relative risk on *CAR*, using the model:

$$CAR_j = \gamma_0 + \gamma_1 \Delta TRR_{j,home}.$$

In this regression, outliers that are at the top and bottom 1% of the distribution of each RHS variable are removed.

$$\begin{array}{llll} CAR_j & = & -0.015 & + \ 0.012 DUMPOS_j \\ (t \text{ stat.}) & & (3.69) & \quad (1.85) \end{array}$$

where $DUMPOS_j$=1 if $\Delta TRR_{j,home}$>0 and zero otherwise. The results show that in cross-border mergers where there was a decline in total risk relative to the acquirer's home bank index, there was a significant decline in value of 1.5% (the value of the intercept coefficient). However, in mergers where the total risk increased, there was practically no decline in value—the positive slope coefficient almost offsets the negative intercept. (In this regression, the slope coefficient was positive for all five geographical subgroups.) That is, investors were better off ex ante when the acquirer's risk increased after the merger. If acquirers overpaid for targets, a decrease in risk would exacerbate any loss of value by inducing a transfer of wealth from stockholders to creditors, depositors and regulators. However, an increase in risk offsets any overpayment by transferring wealth from regulators and creditors to stockholders. Apparently investors believe that regulators, directly or indirectly, will support (with guarantees and other mechanisms) the acquisition activities of large banks, even if they are ex-ante risk increasing.

5. Summary and conclusions

The growth of cross-border banking, largely driven by mergers and acquisitions, has raised concerns among regulators that the insolvency risk of banking systems will rise. Specifically, home country regulators are concerned that an acquirer's risk will rise relative to its domestic competitors, while host country regulators are concerned that the foreign acquirer may be more risky than the target it acquires. These concerns are heightened by the incentives banks have to increase risk in the presence of under-priced safety net guarantees and the difficulties that acquirers often have in monitoring and controlling the activities of their foreign acquisitions. Indeed, such effects may well offset any potential diversification gains that arise from geographic diversification.

Our main findings are interesting in that they suggest that whether an acquirer's risk rises or falls, following a cross-border acquisition, is highly idiosyncratic. On average, there is no evidence that cross-border merging banks add to the risk exposure of either domestic or host country regulators, whether looking at the total risk of the acquirer or its systematic risk relative to various banking industry indexes (home, host, world). These results hold for cross-border mergers in general and for various sub-samples of interregional cross-border mergers.

The policy implications of these results are clear, in that they do not support a systematic policy being adopted by regulators to limit cross-border acquisitions. Rather, they suggest (at least as far as risk is concerned) that a case by case approach should be adopted by both home and host country regulators.

In addition to our main findings, we examined the announcement effects of cross-border mergers on acquirer's abnormal returns. The *CAR*s of acquiring banks were significantly negative (approximately 1%). This result is consistent with acquiring banks overpaying for targets even in the presence of potential safety-net subsidies. Regressions linking acquirer *CAR*s to either the systematic risk of the acquirer were generally insignificant, while the results show a weak positive effect of increase in the total risk (relative to the home bank index) on *CAR*s. Again suggesting that even if significant risk shifting opportunities exist, via cross-border mergers, stockholders do not expect acquiring banks to exploit them, or that such risk shifting opportunities are limited.

In sum, the growth of cross-border banking appears to pose limited systemic risk dangers to the stability and solvency of the international banking system.

Acknowledgements

We thank the referee, Eun Cheol, for comments and suggestions that helped to improve the paper.

References

Agmon, T., Lessard, D., 1977. Investor recognition of corporate international diversification. Journal of Finance 32 (4), 1049–1055.

Berger, A., 2000. The big picture of bank diversification. Proceedings, Federal Reserve of Chicago, May, pp. 162-174.

Buch, C., DeLong, G., 2002. Cross-border bank mergers: What lures the rare animal? Working paper, Baruch College, NY.

Cybo-Ottone, A., Murgia, M., 2000. Mergers and shareholder wealth in European banking. Journal of Banking and Finance 24 (6), 831–859.

DeLong, G.L., 2001. Stockholder gains from focusing versus diversifying bank mergers. Journal of Financial Economics 59 (2), 221–252.

Doukas, J., Travlos, N.G., 1988. The effect of corporate multinationalism on shareholders' wealth: evidence from international acquisitions. Journal of Finance 43 (5), 1161–1175.

Eun, C.S., Kolodny, R., Scheraga, C., 1996. Cross-border acquisitions and the shareholder wealth: tests of the synergy and internalization hypothesis. Journal of Banking and Finance 20 (9), 1559–1582.

Hawawini, G., Swary, I., 1990. Mergers and Acquisitions in the US Banking Industry. North Holland, Amsterdam.

Houston, J.F., Ryngaert, M.D., 1994. The overall gains from large bank mergers. Journal of Banking and Finance 18 (6), 1155–1176.

John, K., John, T., Senbet, L., 1991. Risk shifting incentives of depository institutions: a new perspective on Federal Deposit Insurance reform. Journal of Banking and Finance 15 (4-5), 895–915.

John, K., Saunders, A., Senbet, L., 2000. A theory of bank compensation and management regulation. Review of Financial Studies 3 (1), 95–126.

Kane, E., 2000. Incentives for banking megamergers: what motives might regulators infer from event-study evidence? Journal of Money, Credit and Banking 32 (3), 671–699.

Piloff, S.J., Santomero, A.M., 1998. The value effects of bank mergers and acquisitions. In: Amihud, Y., Miller, G. (Eds.), Bank Mergers and Acquisitions. Kluwer Academic Publishing, Boston.

Repullo, R., 2001. A model of takeover of foreign banks. Spanish Economic Review 3 (1), 1–21.

Segal, Z., 1974. Market and Industry Factors Affecting Commercial Bank Stocks: An Analysis of the Price Behavior of Bank Stock Prices. Unpublished doctoral dissertation. New York University, NY.

Vander Vennet, R., 1996. The effect of mergers and acquisitions on the efficiency and profitability of EC credit institutions. Journal of Banking and Finance 20 (9), 1531–1558.

Winton, A., 1999. Don't put all your eggs in one basket? Diversification and specialization in lending. Working paper. University of Minnesota, MN.

III. Regulation: Deposit Insurance

JOURNAL OF FINANCIAL INTERMEDIATION 5, 409–423 (1996)
ARTICLE NO. 0022

Contagious Bank Runs: Evidence from the 1929–1933 Period

ANTHONY SAUNDERS*

Stern School of Business, New York University

AND

BERRY WILSON

Federal Communications Commission

Received October 5, 1994

This paper empirically examines contagion effects of bank failures by analyzing the behavior of deposit flows in a sample of failed and healthy banks over the 1929–1933 period. We find evidence of contagion for 1930–1932, while none seems to have existed in 1929 or 1933. In addition, the pace of contagion accelerated over 1930–1932. We find that even during 1930–1932, failing-bank deposit outflows exceeded those at a matched control sample of nonfailing banks. This finding is consistent with the presence of a significant number of informed depositors who distinguished among ex ante failing and nonfailing banks. *Journal of Economic Literature* Classification Number: G21.

1. INTRODUCTION

Recently, much theoretical interest has focused on the roles of contagion and information in bank runs. In a noncontagious run, informed depositors switch deposits (often locally) from banks they perceive as insolvent to

*The authors thank George G. Kaufman, Richard Sylla, Gregory Udell, David Walker, an anonymous referee, the editors, and participants at the 1995 Western Economic Association conference for helpful comments. Saunders also thanks the Downing Fellowship at the University of Melbourne, where part of this paper was completed, and a visiting fellowship at the Federal Reserve Board, where the project was conceived.

1042-9573/96 $18.00

those they perceive as solvent. In contrast, in a contagious run or "panic," uninformed depositors withdraw indiscriminately from both solvent and insolvent banks. Diamond and Dybvig (1983), Waldo (1985), and Postlewaite and Vives (1987) show that a contagious run can develop as a "bubble," i.e., a run that occurs in anticipation of a run. Calomiris and Kahn (1991), Gorton (1985), Chari and Jaganathan (1988), and Park (1991) emphasize the informational role of bank runs in which uninformed depositors initiate runs against solvent banks when they observe noisy indicators of bank solvency.

However, little bank-level evidence has been presented to test the importance of contagion and information effects in explaining bank runs. Indeed, most empirical studies to date (e.g., Friedman and Schwartz, 1963; Gorton, 1988; Calomiris and Gorton, 1991; and Donaldson, 1992) focus on the time-series behavior of monetary aggregates. However, aggregate data are unlikely to reveal whether a monetary contraction was a consequence of informed or uninformed depositor behavior.

One possible rationale for using aggregate data is that a run on a representative bank is equivalent to a run on the system as a whole (see Diamond and Dybvig, 1983, for example). Yet, Kaufman (1993) argues that the social cost of an informed bank run may be much less than a bank panic. In a panic, there may be a flight from bank deposits to assets such as currency and Treasury securities. As a result, solvent banks may be forced into costly balance-sheet adjustments, and perhaps into insolvency. As a result, panics can lead to both regional and national contractions in the deposit/lending base of banks.

This paper examines bank-level informed and uninformed depositor behavior over the 1929–1933 period. To illuminate contagion effects, we identify if and when depositors switched from selective to contagious runs. Our analysis sheds light on appropriate regulatory responses to panics. If significant contagion is found, then, as Diamond and Dybvig (1983) argue, "Government deposit insurance can improve on the best allocations that private markets provide." In contrast, if we find significant evidence of informed withdrawals in bank runs, then greater bank solvency information might deter contagious runs without requiring deposit insurance. Our results are intended to inform the debate over restructuring deposit insurance, depositor discipline, and market-value accounting (see, for example, White, 1990).

This paper is organized as follows. In Section 2 we discuss depositor withdrawal behavior during 1929–1933. Section 3 presents the data and Section 4 the empirical results. Section 5 presents a regression analysis of bank deposit flows. Section 6 considers the impact of contagion on correspondent banks. Section 7 concludes.

2. METHODOLOGY

We perform a matched-pair analysis of deposit withdrawals for the 3 years preceding a bank failure. For example, deposit withdrawals at banks that failed in 1929 are examined for 1926–1928 as well as for 1929. We compare withdrawals to those of a matched sample of banks that survived beyond 1929.

In a nonpanic situation, we would expect to find depositors withdrawing funds from failing banks and redepositing them in solvent banks. There should be little contraction in either the local or national deposit aggregates. In a panic, we would expect increased withdrawals at both solvent and insolvent banks in the same locality.

We repeat this withdrawal analysis for each year in the 1929–1933 period. We use an analysis of variance (ANOVA) to examine the impact of the year of failure, years prior to failure, and bank type (control versus failed) on deposit flows. We also test whether less-informed depositors increased withdrawals over 1929–1932, which would be indicative of spreading contagion. Finally, we test whether federal actions, such as the 1933 national suspension of convertibility (the so-called "bank holiday"), the announcement of federal deposit insurance, and the creation of the Federal Reconstruction Corporation deterred contagious bank runs.

Our methodology is similar to Sinkey (1975), Kurtz and Sinkey (1973), and Swary (1986).

3. DATA

Failed national banks were drawn from the 1936–1938 *Annual Report of the Comptroller of the Currency.* These reports list failed national banks that completed liquidation in a particular year of the report, and list their deposits at time of closure, starting in 1936. In particular, the 1936 annual report lists 214 previously closed national banks whose liquidations were completed in 1936. Of these 214 liquidations, we selected those banks that failed during 1929–1933 as the study's failed-bank sample. However, this sample contained too few 1929 bank failures. Therefore, to extend the sample, we used all 1929 failed national banks reported in the 1937–1938 Comptroller reports. This resulted in a total of 163 failed national banks. Sample sizes by year of closure are listed in Table I (year 0 column).

We obtained annual deposit and other accounting data from the "Rand McNally Bankers Directory," which was also used to select a matched sample of nonfailing banks. We required control banks to have survived for at least 2 years after the last full year of operation of the failed bank. In addition, we chose banks either from the same town, if available (50%

TABLE I
MEAN DEPOSIT FLOW RATES (%)

Year of failure	Sample	Year relative to failure year						Aggregate national rate
		−3	−2	−1	0	0[a]	1	
1929	Fail	−2.8	−9.5	−5.5	−18.5	−46.0		
		(9.1)	(6.6)	(6.2)	(5.8)	(5.8)		
		(11)	(21)	(24)	(27)	(27)		
	Control	1.9	−6.4	15.8**	5.4**		−3.4	5.1
		(5.6)	(5.7)	(5.5)	(5.3)		(6.3)	
		(29)	(28)	(30)	(32)		(32)	
1930	Fail	−0.5	10.5	1.4	−38.5	−52.4		
		(6.0)	(6.0)	(6.0)	(6.2)	(5.3)		
		(25)	(25)	(25)	(24)	(24)		
	Control	11.1	7.2	3.7	−10.1**		−4.8	−0.6
		(4.3)	(4.7)	(4.6)	(4.6)		(5.6)	
		(48)	(41)	(42)	(43)		(40)	
1931	Fail	2.6	−2.0	−11.5	−33.2	−46.9		
		(3.9)	(3.8)	(3.8)	(3.9)	(3.3)		
		(61)	(63)	(64)	(59)	(59)		
	Control	7.9	2.3	4.3**	− 4.7**		−12.4	−2.7
		(3.2)	(3.2)	(3.1)	(3.1)		(3.9)	
		(88)	(91)	(93)	(92)		(83)	
1932	Fail	−0.2	−7.7	−16.7	−37.8	−51.8		
		(5.2)	(5.4)	(5.7)	(5.9)	(4.4)		
		(34)	(31)	(28)	(26)	(26)		
	Control	1.2	−2.8	−13.6	−19.3*		9.9	−15.2
		(5.1)	(5.0)	(5.0)	(5.0)		(5.9)	
		(35)	(36)	(36)	(37)		(36)	
1933	Fail	−0.1	−13.1	−34.8	−6.8	−7.2		
		(5.3)	(5.7)	(5.7)	(5.8)	(2.3)		
		(32)	(28)	(28)	(27)	(27)		
	Control	−6.0	−15.8	−11.3**	−12.9*		28.6	−8.7
		(6.0)	(6.0)	(6.0)	(6.0)		(7.1)	
		(25)	(25)	(25)	(25)		(25)	

Note. Mean deposit flow rates are given for failing (Fail) and matched nonfailing (Control) banks, for failure years 1929–1933, for 3 years prior (−3, −2, −1), the failure year (0), and the year post-failure for control banks (1). We used Proc GLM of SAS to perform analysis of variance tests between Fail and Control groups, with significance level denoted as *(**) for differences at $p \leq 0.05$ ($p \leq 0.01$). Standard errors and sample size are listed parenthetically, respectively. Deposit data source: "Rand McNally Bankers Directory."

[a] These rates are annualized to account for the day and month of failure within the failure year.

of cases), or from a comparably sized town within 30 miles of the failed bank. In cases where several control banks met both criteria, we included all such banks, thus capturing as much deposit substitution as possible. This resulted in a total of 229 control banks.

Mean deposit levels were similar for the 1929 control ($934,057) and failed ($998,898) banks. Standard deviation of deposits were $841,789 and $758,143, respectively. Not surprisingly, over the period 1930–1933, control banks tended to increase and failed banks to decrease in mean deposit size.

We also collected regional economic data. We obtained bank failures per state from the *Federal Reserve Bulletin* (September, 1937). The data on business failures per state were taken from the *Statistical Abstract of the United States* (various years). In addition, we obtained state-level personal income data from the U.S. Department of Commerce (DOC) Regional Economic Information System (1993). The DOC data are available only post-1929.

4. DEPOSIT FLOWS AT FAILED VERSUS CONTROL SAMPLE BANKS

This section presents evidence of deposit substitution in 1929, contagion and informational effects over 1930–1932, and an end to contagion and return to deposit substitution in 1933.

4.1. *Evidence of Deposit Susbstitution: 1929*

The last column of Table I indicates that large contractions in the national deposit base occurred only in 1932 (−15.2%) and 1933 (−8.7%). In 1929, the national deposit base was still growing (+5.1%), implying an absence of panic. This expansion also reflected Federal Reserve actions after the October 1929 market crash, when it loaned freely through its discount window, purchasing about $160 million of government securities (Friedman and Schwartz, 1963). Federal Reserve action after 1929 was hampered by member disagreements over appropriate policy (see Friedman and Schwartz, 1963).

The bank-specific results in Table I support this interpretation. From 1926–1928, average net withdrawals increased at banks that failed in 1929. However, except for 1927, deposits increased on average at control banks. In the year of failure itself, 1929, failing banks realized mean net outflows of 18.5%, while control banks had mean net inflows of 5.4% (the difference is statistically significant at the 0.01 level.) This evidence argues against regional or national contagion in 1929.

4.2. *Evidence Consistent with Contagion Effects: 1930–1932*

The 1930–1932 results in Table I are consistent with significant contagion effects over this period, in that deposit withdrawals occurred at both failing and control banks. We examine alternative explanations for the systematic deposit decline in Section 5, including deteriorating local economic conditions (e.g., declining personal income) and declining bank solvency.

Failing banks show a pattern of heightened year-of-failure average withdrawals during 1930–1932, with outflow rates increasing from 18.5% in 1929 to 38.5, 33.2, and 37.8% in 1930–1932, respectively. Consistent with contagion, control banks suffered corresponding average net deposit withdrawals of 10.1, 4.7, and 19.3% from 1930–1932, respectively. Control banks also suffered increased deposit withdrawals in years prior to their matched-bank failure. Comparing 1932 with 1931, the control bank average deposit flow rates were greater in each year prior to failure, i.e., 1.2% compared to 7.9%, −2.8% compared to 2.3%, −13.6% compared to 4.3%, and −19.3% compared to −4.7% over year −3 to year 0. The latter two differences are statistically significant at the 1 and 5% levels, respectively. These results are consistent with an acceleration of contagion effects over the 1930–1932 period.

The distribution of deposit flows for 1929–1932 are summarized in Figs. 1–4, respectively. In Fig. 1, control banks show a positive median flow rate, while failing banks show mostly deposit outflows in 1929. Over the period 1930–1932, both the control-bank and failing-bank distributions are skewed left of zero. Indeed, by 1932 all but a few control banks faced net withdrawals.

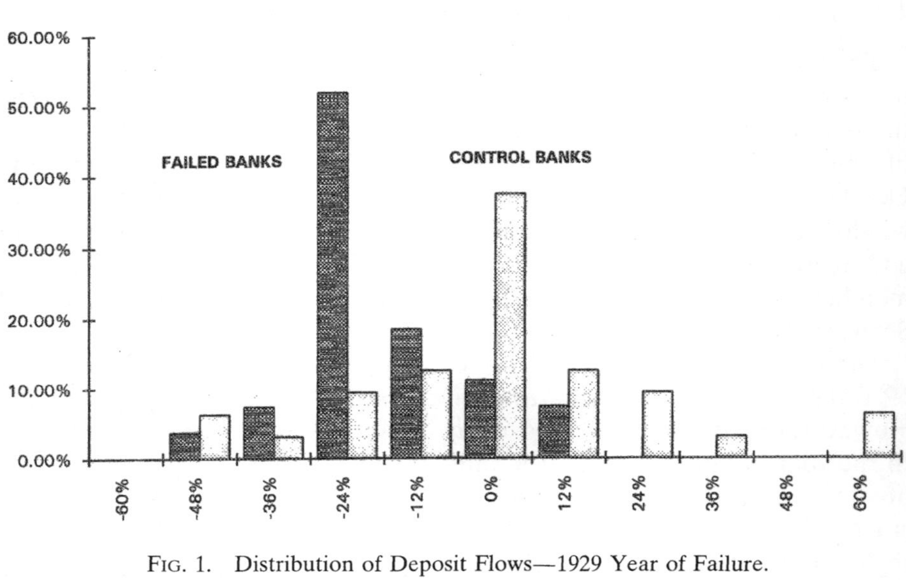

FIG. 1. Distribution of Deposit Flows—1929 Year of Failure.

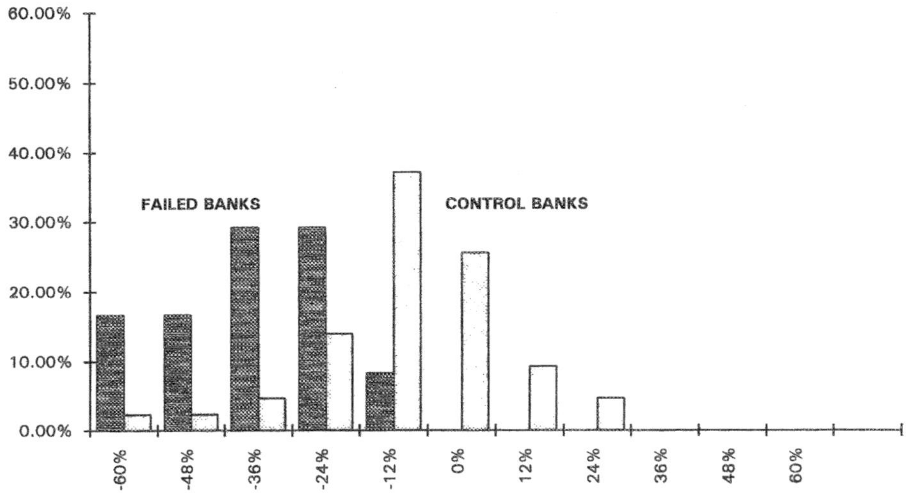

FIG. 2. Distribution of deposit flows—1930 year of failure.

4.3. *Evidence of an Informational Role In Deposit Withdrawals*

The Table I results, while supporting contagion over 1930–1932, also provide evidence on informational effects. A "pure" contagion implies that withdrawals occur indiscriminately against all banks. In contrast, "informed" withdrawals (potentially redeposited locally) imply that failing-bank withdrawal rates should exceed control-bank withdrawal rates.

Consistent with an information effect, the failed-bank mean withdrawal rates exceeded those of control banks by 28.4% (taken as 38.5% versus 10.1%) in 1930, and by 28.5 and 18.5% in 1931–1932, respectively. The 1930–1931 and 1932 differences are significant at the 1 and 5% levels, respectively. The rates one year prior to failure are also consistent with an information effect, with failing-bank rates exceeding control-bank rates by 15.8 and 23.5% in 1931 and 1933, respectively, both significant at the 1% level.

Table I also suggests that informed-depositor withdrawals approximated or exceeded uninformed-depositor withdrawals over 1930–1932. We measure uninformed withdrawals as the mean control-bank withdrawal rate, and the informed rate as the failing-bank minus the control-bank withdrawal rate. Using this approach, the uninformed rates were 10.1, 4.7, and 19.3% compared to informed rates of 28.4, 28.5, and 18.5%, respectively, for 1930–1932. This analysis assumes that informed depositor withdrawals were not redeposited at matched control banks, which is consistent with Table I results [e.g., control-bank withdrawal rates in the failure year (year 0) are comparable in magnitude to withdrawal rates at control banks whose matched banks did not fail that year].

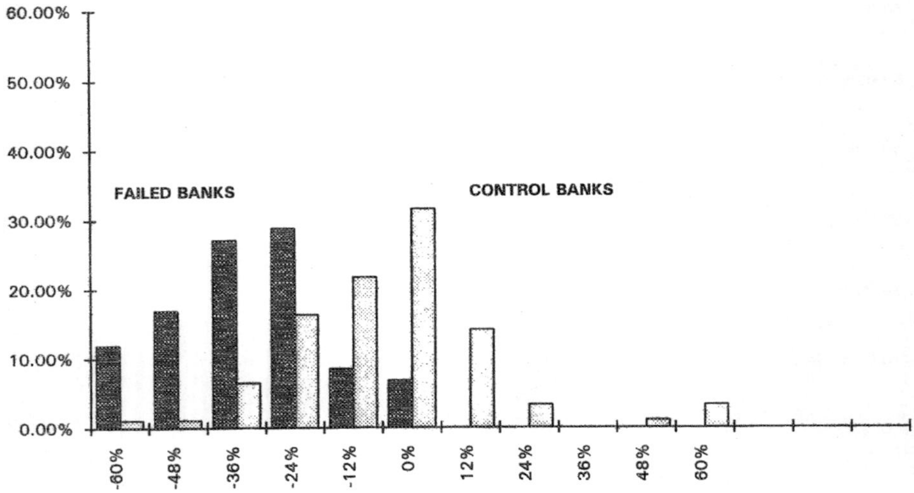

FIG. 3. Distribution of deposit flows—1931 year of failure.

4.4. *Recovery Period: 1933*

Finally, we analyze 1933, the year of the national bank holiday, the announcement of deposit insurance, and other federal interventions. Figure 5 charts the 1933 deposit-flow distribution. While it is difficult to disentangle the deposit insurance announcement and bank holiday effects, the decrease

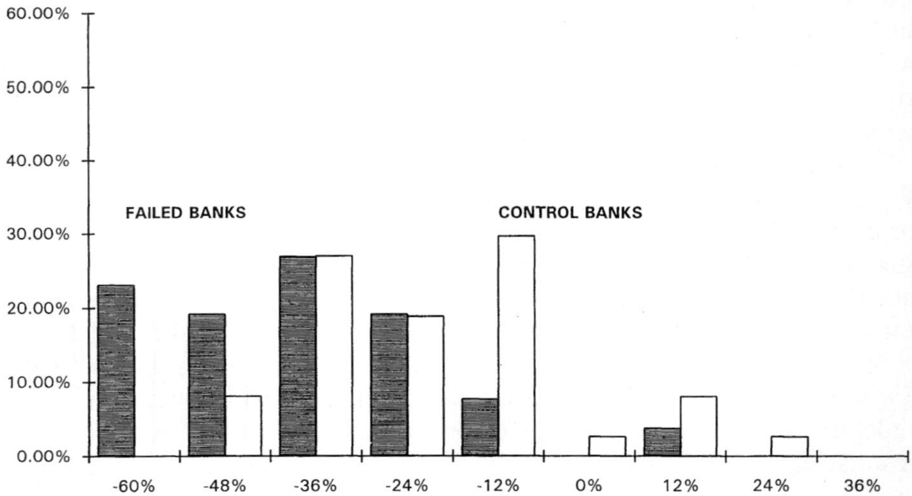

FIG. 4. Distribution of deposit flows—1932 bank failure.

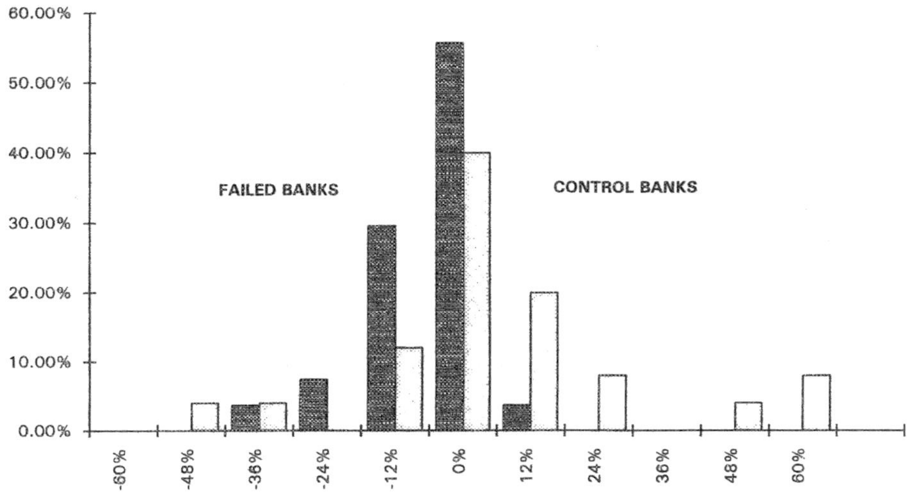

FIG. 5. Distribution of deposit flows—1933 bank failures.

in 1933 withdrawal rates is quite dramatic. Specifically, in Table I, banks that failed in 1933 suffered "only" a 6.8% withdrawal rate, compared to 34.8% one year earlier. In contrast, control banks showed average deposit inflows of 12.9% in 1933, compared to 11.3% outflows one year earlier. Both differences are significant at the 0.01 level. In addition, the control-bank results are consistent with a return to deposit substitution in 1933 as opposed to the apparent contagion found in the 1930–1932 period.

5. REGRESSION ANALYSIS OF BANK DEPOSIT FLOWS

The evidence presented in Section 4.2 is consistent with contagion effects over the 1930–1932 period. It is also consistent with systematic economic, or "flight to quality" effect, interpretations. This section discusses whether observed deposit withdrawals in this period reflected changed economic conditions, declining bank solvency positions, or the effects of contagion per se.

We use a panel regression approach to analyze the deposit-flow data of the previous section. We use several state-level economic variables—e.g., annual change in nonfarm personal income (DNFPI), bank failure rate (BFAIL), and annual change in the bank failure rate (DBFAIL)—in the analysis.[1] The three data sources used, as detailed in Section 3, exhaust

[1]State-level personal income data from the U.S. Department of Commerce's Regional Economic Information System (1993) are not available pre-1930. Also, the personal income data from the Regional Economic Information System include a number of subcategories, e.g., "wages and salaries," of which "nonfarm personal income" proved most significant.

most local data available for the period. Even though state-level data was the best available for the period, the failed-bank sample was geographically dispersed enough to warrant its use.

We also include bank-specific measures: book-capital-to-asset (BCAP) and cash-to-deposit (CDEP) ratios in the panel regressions, which we derived from published balance sheet data. Finally, to test for local "spill-over" effects, we added the failing-bank deposit-flow rate as a covariate for each matched-control bank.

Table II presents the deposit-flow regression results. We segment the analysis into three periods: the baseline year 1929, the 1930–1932 contagion period, and the transition year 1933. Table II lists the sample size (N), R^2, and regression intercept (constant) separately by period and for control-versus-failing banks, with standard errors listed parenthetically where appropriate. BCAP and CDEP are beginning-of-period values and represent information available to depositors prior to the observed deposit flows.

The 1929 regression results are listed in the top panel (A) of Table II. Consistent with an information effect,[2] the bank-specific variables BCAP and CDEP had a significant impact on deposit flows, particularly with failing banks. Consistent with the lack of contagion, the local contagion variable, DDEP_FB, measured as the deposit flow rate at the matched failed bank, does not show a significant impact on control-bank deposit flows. Finally, the regional economic variables are insignificant, although, as discussed in Section 3, state income data were not available in 1929.

Regression results for 1930–1932 are given in the middle panel (B) of Table II. Aggregation tests supported combining these 3 years in a single regression. The bank-specific factors, BCAP and CDEP, are again significant, which is consistent with an informational effect on bank withdrawal rates. The negative coefficient of CDEP for failing-banks could indicate a liquidity crisis among distressed banks during this period. Regional economic variables are also highly significant during 1930–1932. These results indicate that a 10% decline in nonfarm personal income (DNFPI) resulted in deposit declines of 8 and 9.52% for control and failing banks, respectively.[3]

Consistent with state-level contagion, both the bank failure rate (BFAIL) and change in annual bank failure rate (DBFAIL) had an inverse impact on deposit flows at control and failing banks during 1930–1932. The results are consistent with depositors using state-level bank failure information in making deposit–withdrawal decisions. In addition, evidence of a local contagion effect is supported by the significant positive coefficient on

[2]However, the regression analysis may understate the potential informational effect, since included variables may not fully capture all publicly available information, e.g., information leaked from bank insiders to depositors.

[3]The state-level commercial failure rate was insignificant and is not listed in Table II for brevity.

DDEP_FB (the matched-failing bank's deposit-flow rate). As constructed, this variable captures potential spillover effects of depositor withdrawal runs on failing banks to matched-control banks.

We found the relative explanatory power of the regression effects for 1930–1932 particularly interesting. If the variables are ranked as listed in

TABLE II
DEPOSIT-FLOW REGRESSION RESULTS

	Control Banks		Failed Banks	
Term	Value	SE	Value	SE
	A. Baseline period: 1929			
Constant	−.253	0.09	−.457	0.08
BCAP	0.885	0.29***	1.463	0.34***
CDEP	0.067	0.18	0.887	0.11***
DDEP_FB	0.002	0.07	—	—
GLAK	−.082	0.05	−.046	0.05
N	206		179	—
R^2	0.094	—	0.477	
	B. Recessionary period: 1930–1932			
Constant	−.149	0.05***	−.002	0.04
BCAP	0.478	0.20**	0.144	0.18
CDEP	0.761	0.11***	−.207	0.09**
DNFPI	0.800	0.26***	0.952	0.22***
BFAIL	−.459	0.30	−1.15	0.27***
DBFAIL	−.442	0.27*	−0.40	0.22*
DDEP_FB	0.162	0.07**	—	—
GLAK	0.060	0.03*	0.092	0.03***
RKMT	0.087	0.06	−.086	0.05*
N	594		326	
R^2	0.122	—	0.240	—
	C. Recovery period: 1933			
Constant	−.204	0.15	−.271	0.20
BCAP	3.04	0.49***	0.756	0.76
CDEP	0.552	0.26**	−.865	0.54
DDEP_FB	−1.44	0.54***	—	—
GLAK	−.183	0.10*	0.009	0.09
N	65		23	—
R^2	0.488	—	0.194	

Note. Regression analysis of the deposit flow data. Factors include book capital ratio (BCAP), cash-to-deposit ratio (CDEP), change in nonfarm personal income (DNFPI), state-level bank failure rate (BFAIL), change in bank failure rate (DBFAIL), and deposit flow at the matched failing bank (DDEP_FB). Listed are the sample size (*N*), percentage variation explained (R^2), intercept (Constant), estimated coefficient (Value), and standard error (SE). GLAK and RKMT are regional dummies indicating the Great Lakes and Rocky Mountain regions. *, **, *** give significance levels of 10, 5, and 1%, respectively.

Table II, then bank-specific variables BCAP and CDEP jointly explain the first 7.7 (2.4)%, the change in nonfarm personal income (DNFPI) variable explains the next 2.1 (12.4)%, and the bank-failure variables BFAIL and DBFAIL jointly explain the next 0.8 (5.3)% of total variation for control (failing) banks. The local-contagion variable, DDEP_FB, explains an additional 0.9% for control banks. Therefore, the contagion variables explain much less variation than the information variables, confirming the results of Section 4.3. However, the economic significance of the contagion variables is difficult to assess relative to their statistical significance.

Finally, the Table II results for 1933 can be compared with those for 1930–1932. First, the bank-specific factors, BCAP and CDEP, are still significant determinants of deposit withdrawals (particularly for control banks), while regional economic factors are no longer significant. Second, the coefficient on the contagion variable, DDEP_FB, is significant and negative (−1.44), consistent with a return to deposit substitution from failing to control banks, as we reported in Section 4.4.

Overall, the regression results indicate significant information effects on bank deposit withdrawal rates, with both bank-specific and local economic effects as important factors. In addition, the significant spillover variable, DDEP_FB, provides evidence consistent with contagion during 1930–1932. While these contagion effects may proxy for local conditions not fully captured by state-level data, the reversal of the DDEP_FB variable's sign in 1933 (i.e., to a sign consistent with deposit substitution among failing and control banks) gives corroborative evidence in favor of a contagion effect for 1930–1932.

6. IMPACT ON CORRESPONDENT BANKS AND NEW YORK CITY BANKS

A positive relationship between local and correspondent deposit runs would support the view that correspondent relationships may have transmitted local shocks regionally and nationally.

Table III lists deposit flows for each failed bank's two primary correspondent banks. We defined these as the first two correspondents listed for that bank in the 1929 "Rand McNally Bankers Directory." Of the resulting 83 correspondent banks, 14 were from the northeast, 25 from the southeast, 30 from the midwest, and 14 from the west. In addition, 85.5% of correspondents were national banks. Finally, of these 83 correspondents, 47 survived, 19 were merged, 13 closed, and 4 had unknown endpoints over 1927–1932. Table III also includes deposit flows for a sample of New York City banks (including the major money center banks). The New York City sample is split between state and national banks.

TABLE III
MEAN DEPOSIT FLOW RATES (%): CORRESPONDENT AND NEW YORK CITY BANKS

	1927	1928	1929	1930	1931	1932	1933
			Correspondent banks				
Mean	5.4%	8.1%	2.4%	2.3%	−12.1%	−5.1%	14.0%
SE	1.4%	2.4%	2.3%	2.3%	1.7%	1.7%	3.6%
N	83	78	64	55	50	47	41
			New York City state banks				
Mean	14.8%	112.1%	2.3%	−13.1%	−15.2%	−6.4%	2.3%
SE	23.8%	75.2%	5.1%	11.2%	9.0%	6.4%	5.9%
N	6	6	6	6	10	10	8
			New York City national banks				
Mean	−0.4%	15.6%	308.0%	−0.3%	6.8%	−1.4%	9.9%
SE	3.3%	16.1%	297.0%	7.4%	28.1%	3.3%	8.0%
N	8	9	10	11	16	16	10
			Aggregate New York City banks				
Mean	6.1%	54.2%	193.4%	−4.8%	−1.6%	−3.3%	6.5%
SE	10.1%	32.5%	185.8%	6.2%	17.6%	3.2%	5.1%
N	14	15	16	17	26	26	18

Note. Deposit flow data is for the two primary correspondent banks of each failed bank. Of 83, 14 correspondents were from the northeast, 25 from the southeast, 30 from the midwest, and 14 from the west. Forty-seven survived, 19 merged, 13 closed, and 4 had unknown endpoints over 1927–1932. Finally, 85.5% of the correspondents were national banks, and 7 correspondents overlap with the New York City bank sample. SE is the standard error of the mean and *N* is the sample size. Source of deposit data: "Rand McNally Bankers Directory."

Table III indicates positive deposit growth over the 1927–1929 period for both correspondent and New York City banks. Moreover, correspondent banks' net deposit withdrawals did not start until 1931 and 1932. New York City national banks were also largely insulated from contagion during 1930–1931, while state banks located in New York City suffered net deposit withdrawals during 1930–1932 similar in magnitude to those in Table I. However, while the New York City national banks showed the smallest withdrawal rates of all banks for 1932, these rates are still consistent with even the largest banks being affected through correspondent relationships.

7. SUMMARY AND CONCLUSIONS

During the 1930–1933 period, the national deposit base declined sharply, while currency held by the public increased. This pattern is consistent with a flight-to-currency by depositors. However, past studies of this period have not established the role played by information and contagion in deposit withdrawals. This paper addresses this issue by analyzing bank-level data on a group of failed and control banks during 1929–1933. Particularly interesting is the relative impact of local economic conditions, bank-specific solvency, and contagion effects on deposit flow rates at failing and control banks.

We found evidence consistent with failing-bank deposit withdrawals being redeposited locally in nonfailing banks for both 1929 and 1933. The implication is that depositors distinguished between insolvent and solvent banks. In contrast, during 1930–1932, we found evidence consistent with contagion, with deposit withdrawals occurring at both nonfailing and failing banks. Further, we found support consistent with Gorton (1985) and other studies for informed-depositor withdrawals, even during the 1930–1932 contagion period. Specifically, failing-bank deposit withdrawals significantly exceeded control-bank withdrawals, indicating that some depositors were more informed than others about individual bank solvency positions.

These results are further supported by a deposit-flow regression analysis. During 1930–1932, bank-specific solvency measures significantly impacted withdrawals at failing and control banks, consistent with the information hypothesis. Significant contagion effects occurred both in terms of spillovers from failing to control banks and panic-induced deposit outflows affected by regional bank failure rates. Moreover, economic and informational effects outweighed pure contagion effects in terms of importance.

REFERENCES

Calomiris, C., and Gorton, G. (1991). The origins of banking panics: models, facts and regulation, *in* "Financial Markets and Financial Crises" (G. Hubbard, Ed.), pp. 109–174. Univ. of Chicago Press, Chicago.

Calomiris, C., and Kahn, C. (1991). The role of demandable debt in structuring optimal banking arrangements, *Amer. Econ. Rev.* **81,** 497–513.

Chari, V. V., and Jagannathan, R. (1988). Banking panics, information, and rational expectations equilibrium, *J. Finance* **43,** 749–761.

Diamond, D. W., and Dybvig, P. H. (1983). Bank runs, deposit insurance, and liquidity, *J. Polit. Econ.* **91,** 401–419.

Donaldson, R. G., (1992). Sources of panics: Evidence from the weekly data, *J. Monet. Econ.* **30,** 277–305.

Federal Reserve Bulletin (Sept. 1937). "Bank Suspensions, 1921–1936," pp. 866–910. Board of Governors of the Federal Reserve System.

Friedman, M., and Schwartz, A. J. (1963). "A Monetary History of the United States: 1867–1960." Princeton Univ. Press, Princeton.

Gorton, G. (1985). Bank suspension of convertibility, *J. Monet. Econ.* **15,** 177–193.

Gorton, G. (1988). Banking panics and business cycles, *Oxford Econ. Papers* **40,** 751–781.

KAUFMAN, G. G. (1993). Bank contagion: Theory and evidence, Working Paper 93-1. Loyola University, Chicago.

KURTZ, R. D., AND SINKEY, J. F. (1973). Bank disclosure policy and procedures, adverse publicity, and bank deposit flows, *J. Bank Res.* 177–184.

PARK, S. (1991). Bank failure contagion in historical perspective, *J. Monet. Econ.* **28,** 271–286.

POSTLEWAITE, A., AND VIVES, X. (1987). Bank runs as an equilibrium phenomenon, *J. Polit. Econ.* **95,** 485–491.

"Rand McNally Bankers Directory, The Bankers Blue Book" (various editions), Rand McNally, New York.

SINKEY, J. F. (1975). Adverse publicity and bank deposit flows: The cases of Franklin National Bank of New York and United States National Bank of San Diego, *J. Bank Res.* 109–112.

STATISTICAL ABSTRACT OF THE UNITED STATES (various years, 1927–1934). Bureau of the Census, U.S. Department of Commerce.

SWARY, I. (1986). Stock market reaction to regulatory action in the Continental Illinois Crisis, *J. Business* **59,** 451–473.

U.S. Department of Commerce. (1993). "Total Personal Income By Major Source & Earnings By Industry," Regional Economic Information System. Economics And Statistics Administration, Bureau of Economic Analysis.

WALDO, D. G. (1985). Bank runs, the deposit–currency ratio and the interest rate, *J. Monet. Econ.* **15,** 269–277.

WHITE, L. (1990). "The S&L Debacle: Public Policy Lessons for Bank and Thrift Regulation." *Oxford Univ. Press*, New York.

JOURNAL OF FINANCIAL INTERMEDIATION **4**, 396–413 (1995)

If History Could Be Rerun: The Provision and Pricing of Deposit Insurance in 1933

ANTHONY SAUNDERS*

Stern School of Business, New York University, New York, New York 10012

AND

BERRY WILSON*

Federal Communications Commission, Washington, DC 20554

Received December 1, 1993

This paper examines cross-subsidy, moral hazard, and bank liability issues related to the provision of federal deposit insurance by "rerunning" its implementation, i.e., determining fair premium values, over the period 1927–1932. The pre-1933 period was characterized by historically high asset-price volatility, a large number of bank failures, and a weak federal safety net. In this economic context, we find a high degree of self-insurance on the part of the banks in our sample, both in terms of higher overall capital levels and a strong correlation between capital levels and asset volatility. Potentially large, regional cross-subsidies among banks were also found. *Journal of Economic Literature* Classification Number: G21.

1. INTRODUCTION

The passage of the Federal Deposit Insurance Corporation Improvement Act (FDICIA) of 1991 focused renewed attention on deposit insurance provision and its pricing. Specifically, the "risk-based" deposit insurance premium system, implemented in 1993, is the first major deviation from the

* We thank Mitch Berlin, Charles Calomiris, Brian Gendreau, Charles Jacklin, George Kaufman, Randall Kroszner, George Pennacchi, Richard Sylla, and two anonymous referees and the editors of *JFI* for their comments on earlier drafts. We also thank the Salomon Center at NYU and the Center For Business Government Relations at Georgetown University for financial support.

1042-9573/95 $12.00

flat premium schedule since the introduction of federal deposit insurance.[1] Further, the prompt corrective action (PCA) program is a modification of the limited liability rule for banks introduced in 1933 and 1935.[2] These FDICIA initiatives were in response to concerns regarding bank cross-subsidies and moral hazards thought to inhere in fixed-rate deposit insurance.

Similar cross-subsidy, moral hazard, and bank liability issues were actively debated in 1933. At that time, large money-center and Eastern U.S. banks opposed federal deposit insurance on the grounds that stronger banks would be forced to subsidize poorly managed and weaker ones. However, the final legislative outcome was the flat-rate premium schedule that existed until 1993.[3] At the same time, limited liability of bank stockholders replaced the double liability prevalent since the end of the Civil War.[4]

This study examines bank-specific fair premium values as if federal deposit insurance had been in place during the 1927–1932 period. This period, just prior to the passage of deposit insurance legislation in 1933, is of particular interest for two reasons. First, a relatively clean assessment of fair-pricing and cross-subsidy issues can be made at this time, since the confounding effects of mispriced federal deposit insurance were not present. Second, given that the FDIC was established in the aftermath of the banking panic of 1931–1933, our analysis can examine the subsidy and pricing issues from the perspective of the 1933 legislative debate.

To value the deposit insurance contract, the study employs the limited-term option-pricing approach of Marcus and Shaked (1984, hereafter MS) and Ronn and Verma (1986, hereafter RV) and for comparison a modified unlimited-term approach following Merton (1978) and Pennacchi (1987). A correction is made to the original RV formulation so that "put–call parity" is satisfied. In addition, Merton's (1978) unlimited-term model is extended to account for dividend payments.

[1] Under the 1993 risk-based scheme, deposit insurance premia range from 23 bp (basis points) to 32 bp. However, Chan *et al.* (1992) cast doubt on whether a truly fair-priced deposit insurance scheme is possible.

[2] Under PCA, a bank may be closed when its book capital falls below 2% of its assets (with residual capital used to settle postclosure claims). Under pre-1933 double liability rules, bank stockholders also suffered potential postclosure losses. Limited liability was introduced and double liability phased-out starting in the early 1930s. See Macey and Miller (1992) for the legislative history of double liability in banking.

[3] Section 8 of the Banking Act of 1933 created the Federal Deposit Insurance Corporation through an amendment to the Federal Reserve Act. A temporary plan went into effect on January 1, 1934. Initial coverage was limited to $2500, but increased to $5000 on July 1, 1934. The initial assessment rate was 50 bp of insurable deposits. The temporary plan remained in effect until 1935 when the premium was fixed at one-twelfth of 1% (or 8.33 cents per $100 of deposits).

[4] Under double liability, bank stockholders not only lost the value of their common equity invested in the bank, but were additionally (doubly) liable up to the par value of shares held.

Section 2 of the paper briefly discusses the regulatory setting prior to 1933 and the 1933 legislative debate regarding deposit insurance. Section 3 describes the methodology for estimating bank-specific deposit-insurance premia. Section 4 describes data and Section 5 presents the empirical results. A summary and conclusion follows in Section 6.

2. REGULATORY BACKGROUND AND 1933 LEGISLATIVE DEBATE

Prior to federal deposit insurance three "safety nets" protected banks, each with major defects that became apparent in the 1920s. State-sponsored deposit insurance was available in eight states in the 1920s, but these programs were poorly funded and administered (Calomiris, 1992). All collapsed by the end of the 1920s (FDIC, 1984).

Local clearinghouses were a second line of defense. During the panics of 1857 and 1907, these organizations provided liquidity and liability guarantees to troubled member banks (Gorton, 1985a, 1985b). However, clearinghouse guarantees were deployed selectively (Kennedy, 1973).

The third safety net was the lender-of-last-resort facilities of the Federal Reserve System. However, as discussed in Friedman and Schwartz (1963), the Federal Reserve's failure to expand the money base sufficiently and restrictions on its lender-of-last-resort policies contributed to the economic contraction during this period.

In this environment of weak safety nets, bank owners chose to self-insure by operating with less financial leverage. For example, Calomiris (1992) shows that in June 1928 book capital plus surplus of Federal Reserve member banks was 19% of their total assets. This compares to 6% for all U.S. banks in 1990.

Double liability of stockholders, together with the weakness of the safety net, motivated greater monitoring by stockholders. Double liability was legislated in the National Bank Act of 1863 for national banks, and was adopted in some form by all but 10 states. Under double liability, each shareholder could be additionally assessed up to the par value of shares he (or she) held, so as to satisfy postclosure creditor claims. This extended liability gave bank stockholders greater incentives to control risk.[5]

While federal deposit insurance had been included in the Senate version of the Federal Reserve Act of 1914, it was eventually eliminated in a joint House and Senate conference. The idea resurfaced during the banking panic of the early 1930s, but the cross-subsidy concerns of large banks

[5] Winton (1993) observes that double liability can introduce adverse selection effects as well as costs associated with monitoring other stockholders' personal wealth.

impeded its serious consideration until the national "bank holiday" in March 1933.[6]

The cost of providing deposit insurance was an additional concern. Historically, depositor losses at national banks had averaged 14 bp (basis points) since the passage of the National Banking Act, 19 bp since the passage of the Federal Reserve Act, and 70 bp in 1931, all as a percentage of deposits (Congressional Record, p. 3839). The 8.33 bp flat premium eventually adopted reflected regulators' expectations of increased banking stability with federal deposit insurance.

Finally, the advent of federal deposit insurance signaled the end of double liability. Congressional disenchantment with double liability was threefold. First, it had failed to bolster public confidence and thereby prevent bank panics. Second, those left holding bank stock in failed banks were often the most unsophisticated investors. Finally, double liability hampered bank recapitalizations.

3. DEPOSIT INSURANCE PRICING METHODOLOGY

To value deposit insurance, we utilize both the limited-term put–option model, developed in Merton (1977), MS (1984), and RV (1986), and the unlimited-term put-option model developed by Merton (1978), Pennacchi (1987), and Cooperstein *et al.* (1995).[7] As a special case, we extend the limited-term model to account for double liability.

The limited-term model is appealing as a model of the initial federal deposit insurance contract, since considerable controversy accompanied its introduction. Indeed, deposit insurance legislated in the Banking Act of 1933 was temporary, pending permanent legislation in the Banking Act of 1935. However, the 8.33 bp assessment established in 1935 did remain in effect without revision until 1950 when rebates were introduced.[8] Thus, post-1935 federal deposit insurance behaved more like an unlimited-term contract.

Details of the limited-term model are given in Appendix A. Appendix

[6] Eastern bankers fears of cross-subsidies to weaker banking regions were reinforced by the Michigan banking crisis. The Michigan bank holiday, declared on February 14, 1933, has been credited as the regional crisis that helped to precipitate the national banking collapse in March 1933 (Colt and Keith, 1933).

[7] Under a limited-term contract, the deposit insurer resets premia at the start of each contract period (or forces an equivalent change in a bank's capital ratio). In contrast, with an unlimited-term contract the deposit insurer charges a single, time-invariant deposit insurance rate over the life of the contract.

[8] Further, capital ratios were largely unregulated during this period. However, to qualify for a charter, national banks were required to have at least $50,000 in paid-up capital. State bank capital requirements differed, but $15,000 and $20,000 minimums were typical.

B extends Merton's (1978) unlimited-term approach to allow for dividend payments.

4. DATA

Weekly bank stock data for New York City banks were obtained from the *Commercial and Financial Chronicle.* Cash dividend, stock dividend and stock split data are from *Moody's Manual of Investments.* Using the average of the reported bid and ask prices, a weekly stock return series for each bank, adjusted for dividends and stock splits, was compiled. Estimates of σ, the annualized standard deviations of return on bank equity, was obtained from these time series.

To analyze the cross-subsidy issue, the monthly stock price series, reported in the *Bank and Quotation Record*, was used. This sample included major banks from each banking region in the country. These data covered some 1900 banks, but lack of monthly trading for many banks reduced the usable sample to 550 banks. Bank stock returns were then calculated for each year, 1927–1932, and the final sample of banks was selected under a criterion that their stock had traded for at least 8 months in each year considered for inclusion in the data set.

Annual data on bank deposits and other bank liabilities were collected from various issues of *Rand McNally Bankers Directory.* Par values and the number of shares outstanding were also obtained from *Moody's Manual of Investments.*

5. RESULTS

5.1. *Summary Statistics*

Table I shows the sample size of banks (N), total deposits (D), deposit-weighted average equity volatility (σ_E), deposit-weighted average implied asset volatility (σ_v) and deposit-weighted average market equity-to-asset ratio (κ). The sample size varied from 303 banks in 1929 to 122 banks to 1932. Variations in sample size are due to changes in trading activity, mergers, closures, and voluntary liquidations.

Total deposits for the sample of banks varied across regions from the relatively large New York City (NYC) banks, with total deposits of \$6.4 billion in 1929 to the District of Columbia (DC) with total deposits of \$0.20 billion. The sample deposit total for 1929 was \$17.5 billion, representing 28.8% of total national deposits.[9]

[9] The national deposit base, as given in *Rand McNally Bankers Directory* (1927–1932), was 45.7, 58.1, 61.0, 60.7, 59.0, and 50.1 (billions of dollars) in the years 1927 to 1932, respectively.

TABLE I
SUMMARY STATISTICS AGGREGATED BY REGION AND TOTAL SAMPLE

	NYC[a]	PHIL	CHI	GNY	INE	IMW	OMW	DC	SE	WC	TOTAL
						1927					
N	47	8	33	20	11	20	10	12	30	18	209
D	5.3	0.29	1.59	0.77	1.04	1.04	0.33	0.17	0.56	0.90	12.0
σ_E	22.8	14.7	20.5	21.8	17.0	20.2	8.59	11.2	13.0	15.7	20.0
σ_V	3.9	4.40	5.05	5.66	3.70	3.64	1.74	2.79	2.45	2.76	3.92
κ	18.1	30.3	24.3	24.5	20.4	17.5	20.3	24.0	18.3	16.6	19.8
						1928					
N	45	15	17	25	16	26	10	12	44	19	229
D	5.4	0.44	0.94	0.55	1.51	1.58	0.28	0.19	0.95	0.65	12.5
σ_E	33.8	21.1	31.2	17.3	18.3	16.8	13.3	7.03	14.5	22.1	25.4
σ_V	8.1	7.05	10.4	4.91	3.90	3.49	3.62	1.75	2.74	3.96	6.20
κ	24.7	31.5	32.8	29.8	21.6	20.1	27.8	24.4	19.4	17.1	24.1
						1929					
N	34	28	48	45	22	24	18	14	46	24	303
D	6.4	1.16	2.26	1.07	1.84	1.40	0.34	0.20	1.00	1.80	17.5
σ_E	48.6	31.0	31.8	22.4	61.0	61.3	13.5	9.95	39.0	27.4	42.1
σ_V	15.5	8.93	9.77	5.88	13.4	13.2	4.20	2.42	8.66	5.84	11.6
κ	31.4	28.0	30.3	25.3	22.9	24.4	27.6	23.8	18.2	20.0	27.1
						1930					
N	29	32	29	21	17	12	10	11	36	23	220
D	5.6	1.37	2.22	0.69	1.51	0.72	0.33	0.20	0.82	1.89	15.4
σ_E	31.4	20.4	25.2	15.6	29.9	19.6	14.5	21.7	35.0	15.4	25.8
σ_V	10.6	4.20	5.02	3.36	4.90	3.27	3.09	4.55	5.35	2.18	6.43
κ	34.0	20.9	20.3	20.5	16.6	17.2	20.3	20.6	14.2	14.3	23.8
						1931					
N	34	20	20	18	19	14	2	8	21	17	173
D	5.6	1.01	1.56	0.59	1.45	0.48	0.04	0.16	0.61	1.66	13.8
σ_E	35.9	38.7	46.7	33.5	47.5	30.6	23.0	12.2	30.7	24.7	36.1
σ_V	8.0	5.09	4.83	4.10	4.74	1.70	3.08	2.28	3.20	2.82	5.49
κ	22.5	14.1	10.4	12.9	9.95	6.98	12.9	18.6	11.2	11.4	15.6

5.2. *Equity and Asset Volatilities*

One measure of bank risk-taking is given by the estimated equity volatilities and implied asset volatilities derived from the RV equity formula (Appendix A). Deposit-weighted average volatility estimates are shown in Table I by banking region. For 1929, the highest regional weighted-average equity and asset volatilities were found in the industrial midwest banks (IMW) (61.3 and 13.2%), the industrial northeast banks (INE) (61.0 and

TABLE I—*Continued*

	NYC[a]	PHIL	CHI	GNY	INE	IMW	OMW	DC	SE	WC	TOTAL
						1932					
N	19	23	10	15	19	2	2	—	14	18	122
D	4.1	1.06	1.43	0.61	1.40	0.45	0.06	—	0.32	1.61	11.0
σ_E	40.0	62.2	61.7	48.2	64.6	103	11.6	—	53.5	46.0	51.8
σ_V	5.6	8.85	5.33	5.51	4.52	0.99	0.87	—	3.85	4.51	5.37
κ	14.0	15.1	8.63	11.4	8.64	1.27	7.51	—	8.06	9.70	11.2

Note. The data sample includes monthly stock price and annual accounting data on 303 banks (in 1929), covering the period 1927–1939 and aggregated by region. Sample statistics are denoted as follows. N is the sample size and D is total deposits (billions of dollars); σ_E and σ_V are deposit-weighted average estimated equity and (option-implied) asset volatilities (percent); κ is the deposit-weighted average (option-implied) market equity-to-asset ratio (percent).

[a] The cities included in each region are as follows: GNY included Bayonne, Brooklyn, Elizabeth, Hartford, Hoboken, Jamestown, Jersey City, Newark, New Brunswick, New Rochelle, Port Chester, Providence, Union City, Wilmington, and Yonkers; INE included banks in Binghamton, Boston, Buffalo, Rochester, and Syracuse; IMW included Cleveland, Detroit, Grand Rapids, Milwaukee, Minneapolis, and Scranton; OMW included Allentown, Columbus, Cincinnati, Erie, Indianapolis, Pittsburgh, Wiles-Barre, and Youngstown; SE included Atlanta, Baltimore, Birmingham, Charleston, Greenville, Knoxville, Louisville, Lynchburg, Memphis, Montgomery, Nashville, New Orleans, Norfolk, Richmond, Shreveport, Spartanburg, Wilmington, and Winston–Salem; WC included Dallas, Houston, Los Angeles, Oakland, Omaha, Portland, Salt Lake City, San Francisco, Seattle, Spokane, and St. Louis.

13.4%), the New York City (NYC) banks (48.6 and 15.5%), and the southeast (SE) region banks (39.0 and 8.66%). Low-volatility regions included west coast (WC) banks (27.4 and 5.84%) District of Columbia banks (DC) (9.95 and 2.42%), and other midwest (OMW) banks (13.5 and 4.20%). Intermediate volatility regions in 1929 included Philadelphia (PHIL) (31.0 and 8.93%), Chicago (CHI) (31.8 and 9.77%), and banks in the greater New York region (GNY, not including New York City banks) (22.4 and 5.88%). The dispersion in regional volatility lends support to a potential cross-subsidy effect among banking regions.

Table I results also indicate that average equity and asset volatilities rose from 1927 to 1929 and then abated until 1932. This pattern is consistent with that found for stocks in general over this period (Wilson *et al.* 1990). Furthermore, our estimates for σ_E in the noncrisis years of 1927 and 1928 are on a similar order of magnitude to those found by RV for 1983. Finally, note that the largest increases in asset volatility from 1927 to 1929 were with the New York City (NYC), industrial northeast (INE), industrial midwest (IMW), and southeast (SE) banks.

5.3. *Bank Capital Ratios*

Table I gives deposit-weighted average market capital-to-asset ratios (κ), derived from observed market equity values and option-implied bank asset values. In 1929, the highest average capital ratios were those of New York City (31.4%), Chicago (30.3%), and Philadelphia (28.0%) banks. The lowest capital-to-asset ratios were among west coast (20.0%) and southeast (18.2%) banks. Not only are these ratios high by current standards, the averages indicate a tendency for banks in higher asset risk regions to hold more capital.

Average capital ratios peaked in 1928 and 1929 and declined sharply thereafter. Cross-regional differences in capital ratios were still apparent in 1932, with average capital ratios for New York City, greater New York City, and Philadelphia banks still in excess of 11%. In contrast, capital ratios of Chicago and industrial midwest banks had declined to 8.6 and 1.3%, respectively. Clearly, the midwest, industrial northeast, and southeast banks were in the weakest capital positions by the end of 1932.

5.4. *Bank Capital Ratio/Asset Volatility Correlations*

Table II shows contemporaneous correlations among individual bank asset volatilities and capital ratios by region. Correlations are positive and significant in most regions and sample years, suggesting that the best capitalized banks were exposed to the most asset risk. This is consistent with the general absence of moral-hazard-type risk-taking by banks. Arguably, excessive risk-taking was discouraged by the double liability rules.

5.5. *Insurance Premium Estimates—Limited Liability*

Table III displays deposit-weighted average insurance premia calculated from the limited-term (RV) model.

Focusing on 1929, the potential cross-subsidy effects between regions become readily apparent. The highest average premia would have been generated by banks in the southeast (SE), industrial midwest (IMW), and industrial northeast (INE), with average premia of 103, 44.5, and 25.9 bp, respectively. In contrast, low average premia were associated with other midwest (OMW) banks, District of Columbia (DC) banks, Greater New York (GNY, outside New York City) banks, and west coast (WC) banks, with premia of 0.0, 0.0, 0.36, and 0.45 bp, respectively. Chicago (CHI) and Philadelphia (Phil) banks were associated with average premia of approximately 1.5 bp. Finally, New York City (NYC) banks would have had an average premium value of 9.96 bp. These results accord with the cross-subsidy concerns of the money-center and large Eastern banks. The cumulative distribution of deposit premia for the sample banks in 1929 are graphed

TABLE II

CORRELATIONS BETWEEN RV OPTION-IMPLIED ASSET VOLATILITY AND CAPITAL RATIOS

	1927	1928	1929	1930	1931	1932
NYC	0.46	0.33	0.85**	0.63**	0.33	0.52**
PHIL	0.63	0.68**	0.67**	0.72**	0.91**	0.87**
CHI	0.66**	0.61**	0.68**	0.24	0.64**	0.95**
GNY	0.34	0.56**	0.56**	0.67**	0.38	0.78**
INE	0.98**	0.49	0.83**	0.24	0.63**	0.62**
IMW	0.24	0.70**	0.58**	0.91**	0.87**	—
OMW	0.73*	0.39	0.82**	0.97**	0.88	—
DC	0.74**	0.63*	0.78**	0.24	0.77*	—
SE	0.36*	0.39**	0.56**	0.55**	0.63**	0.77**
WC	0.72**	0.61**	0.85**	0.26	0.79**	0.34
All banks						
	0.55**	0.52**	0.57**	0.63**	0.53**	0.75**

Note. Bank asset volatilities and (option-implied) market equity-to-asset ratios are derived using the RV limited-term equity model, modified to account for double liability with national banks and those state banks with mandated double liability. Otherwise, limited liability is used. Model formulation is discussed in Appendix A. Results are presented by banking region and for the total sample.

* Significant at the 5% level.

** Significant at the 1% level.

TABLE III

RV FAIR-VALUE DEPOSIT INSURANCE PREMIA UNDER LIMITED LIABILITY OF BANK STOCKHOLDERS

	1927	1928	1929	1930	1931	1932
NYC	0.57	3.48	9.96	0.15	3.84	2.13
PHIL	0.45	0.17	1.85	0.04	1.71	22.6
CHI	0.18	5.80	1.42	0.61	3.77	11.6
GNY	0.94	0.30	0.36	0.00	0.66	7.31
INE	0.00	0.04	25.9	0.07	4.69	11.8
IMW	0.05	0.11	44.5	0.00	0.17	7.41
OMW	0.00	0.00	0.00	0.00	0.05	0.00
DC	0.00	0.00	0.00	4.68	0.00	—
SE	0.15	0.15	103	23.2	1.49	7.69
WC	0.08	1.70	0.45	0.34	0.00	9.70
All banks						
	0.37	2.06	16.2	1.49	2.71	8.24

Note. DI premia are calculated from the RV limited-term model, assuming limited liability of bank stockholders. Details of the model formulation are discussed in Appendix A. Bank-specific premium values are weighted by each bank's deposit proportion of aggregate sample deposits, and the resulting deposit-weighted average premia are expressed in basis points (bp).

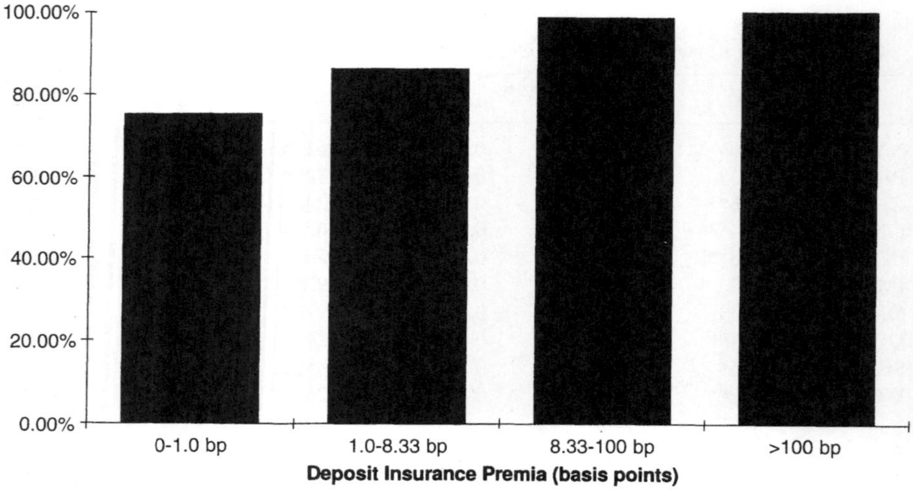

FIG. 1 Cumulative premia, 1929.

in Fig. 1. As can be seen, 13.6% of the sample banks in 1929 had fair premia in excess of the 8.33 bp rate legislated in 1935.

In contrast to 1929, the deposit insurance premia in 1927 and 1928 were mostly small and reveal only small cross-regional differences. By 1929, the increased stock market volatility and the developing economic crisis had the greatest adverse impact on those regions that were the least diversified, i.e., the highly specialized economies of the industrial midwest and northeast, as well as the agricultural southeast. These regions experienced large increases in asset volatility in 1929 without compensating increases in bank capital. Asset volatilities for New York City banks increased in 1929 as well, but were offset to a greater extent by capital increases (see Table I, column 1).

Cross-regional differences in deposit insurance premia appeared to ameliorate post-1929 for three reasons. First, the largest number of bank closures and mergers occurred in 1930 and 1931, removing weaker banks from the sample.[10] In addition, many of the more volatile stocks in 1929 were infrequently traded after the sharp decline in stock prices post-1929.[11] Third, stock market volatility declined after 1929.

[10] For our sample of banks, bank failures numbered 3, 5, 18, and 9 and bank mergers numbered 1, 29, 18, and 5, respectively, in the years 1929 to 1932.

[11] Comparing banks that failed with those that did not fail over the 1929–1931 period, failed banks traded less frequently (with stock price changes in 6.3 versus 7.2 months each year), had lower market capital ratios (13.6 versus 18.0%) and lower asset volatilities (2.9 versus 4.4%) in the year before failure, all significant at the 1% level. Therefore, distressed banks were less likely to be included in the data sample, under the sampling criterion employed. For the baseline years, 1927 and 1928, few banks were closed.

Of additional interest is how national deposit-weighted insurance premia (TOTAL) for these banks compares with the 8.33 bp premium introduced in 1935. Table III shows that except for 1929 and 1932, average deposit insurance premium values were well below the 8.33 bp standard. One reason for these low average premia was the relatively high capital ratios in these years. Specifically, even in 1932 the sample average market capital-to-assets ratio remained above 10.0%.

Whereas the 1932 estimates might be viewed as tainted by survivorship bias, 1927 can be viewed as a baseline in terms of asset and equity volatilities. Moreover, equity volatility in 1927 was on a similar order of magnitude to that found in RV for banks in 1983. The average premium for 1927 was 0.37 bp, with only 7 of the 209 banks displaying premia exceeding 8.33 bp.[12]

5.6. *Insurance Premium Estimates—Double Liability*

The deposit insurance premia reported in the previous section are calculated assuming limited liability. These would be appropriate if the likelihood of collecting assessments against stockholders were essentially zero, or with the anticipation that double liability provisions would be repealed with the advent of deposit insurance.

For completeness, we computed fair-value premiums assuming: (i) double liability with fully-enforced assessments against stockholders, and (ii) double liability with partial (51%) assessments against stockholders in failed banks. The 51% assessment rate represents the historic percentage of assessments actually collected from stockholders during the double liability period (Macey and Miller, 1992). The results under the 100 and 51% assessment rates are shown in Table IV.

Not surprisingly, these premia are well below those obtained under limited liability. Indeed, even in 1929, the year with the highest asset return volatility, the weighted-average premia were 9.84 bp (100% assessment) and 12.4 bp (51% assessment). For 1927, the weighted-average deposit premia were 0.16 and 0.23 bp, respectively.

5.7. *Unlimited-Term Contract Results*

For comparison, fair premia were also calculated under the dividend-extended, Merton–Pennacchi unlimited-term model discussed in Section 3. For brevity, attention is restricted to the sample of New York City banks. The resulting annualized fair-value premiums are shown in Table V.

As expected, the baseline 8.33 bp rate appears underpriced relative to

[12] RV found that 15 of 43 banks had fair premia exceeding 8.33 bp, and Marcus and Shaked (1984) found that 35 and 30% of banks in their sample of 40 bank-holding companies had fair premia exceeding 8.33 bp in 1979 and 1980, respectively.

TABLE IV
RV Fair-Value Deposit Insurance Premium under 100 and 51% Double Liability Assessments of Bank Stockholders

	1927	1928	1929	1930	1931	1932
NYC	0.30/0.40	1.74/2.42	5.73/7.51	0.01/0.04	0.05/0.21	0.04/0.25
PHIL	0.00/0.02	0.00/0.04	0.83/1.21	1.74/0.21	0.04/0.07	0.86/0.9
CHI	0.03/0.08	3.45/4.46	0.56/0.88	1.74/0.21	0.04/0.07	0.86/0.9
GNY	0.29/0.52	0.03/0.10	0.06/0.14	0.00/0.00	0.00/0.00	0.36/0.58
INE	0.00/00.0	0.00/0.01	10.4/15.3	0.00/0.00	0.03/0.14	1.80/0.58
IMW	0.00/0.01	0.02/0.05	25.8/34.0	0.00/0.00	0.00/0.00	0.00/0.00
OMW	0.00/0.00	0.00/0.00	0.00/0.00	0.00/0.00	0.00/0.00	0.00/0.00
DC	0.00/0.00	0.00/0.00	0.00/0.00	3.05/1.11	0.00/0.00	—/—
SE	0.01/0.04	0.03/0.07	77.7/88.6	9.53/10.1	0.19/0.09	0.06/0.13
WC	0.00/0.01	0.64/1.05	0.03/0.12	0.88/14.3	0.00/0.00	1.38/1.00
All banks	0.16/0.23	1.04/1.44	9.84/12.4	0.60/0.91	0.05/0.28	1.04/2.40

Note. DI premia are calculated using the RV limited-term model, under alternative assumptions of (i) 100% double liability, and (ii) 51% double liability. The latter (51%) assumption is the average percent of assessments collected historically from bank owners. The resulting deposit-weighted average premium results are expressed in basis points (bp).

the limited-term contract results in Table V. The resulting deposit-weighted average fair premia range from 11.41 bp in 1927 to 37.12 bp in 1929 and 14.50 bp in 1932. Also listed in Table V, for comparison, are the deposit-weighted average deposit insurance premia from Table III adjusted for auditing costs.

TABLE V
Unlimited-Term Fair-Value Deposit Insurance Premium

1927	1928	1929	1930	1931	1932
Average (deposit-weighted) unlimited-term premia					
11.41	21.85	37.12	26.68	25.80	14.50
Average (deposit-weighted) limited-term premia plus auditing costs					
1.91	4.82	11.30	1.49	5.18	3.47

Note. Deposit-weighted average premia are calculated using a dividend-extended, Merton–Pennacchi unlimited-term model, as formulated in Appendix B. The resulting premia are then taken as lump-sum perpetuities and multiplied by the Treasury bond yield to derive equivalent annual premia. For comparison, the deposit-weighted average premia in Table III are restated with 1.34 bp in auditing costs, calculated as the ratio of 1935 FDIC administrative expenses ($2.7 million) to 1935 FDIC-insured deposits ($20,158 million). All results are expressed in basis points (bp).

6. SUMMARY AND CONCLUSIONS

During the early 1930s, large Eastern and money-center banks lobbied strongly against federal deposit insurance legislation on the grounds that better-capitalized banks would be forced to subsidize the poorly managed and weaker ones. Cross-subsidy and related moral hazard issues also attracted considerable interest as a result of the deposit insurance crises of the 1980s. These renewed concerns were addressed, in part, by the FDICIA of 1991, which led to the introduction of risk-based deposit insurance premiums and implementation of the PCA program. The initiatives taken under FDICIA were the first significant departures from the original flat-rate premium and limited liability rules legislated in the Banking Acts of 1933 and 1935.

This paper examined these cross-subsidy, fair pricing, and bank liability issues through an analysis of fair-value deposit insurance premia during 1927–1932 period, just prior to the introduction of federal deposit insurance. This period is of particular interest since the confounding effects of mispriced federal deposit insurance system were absent.

Our results indicate large cross-subsidies in the period just prior to the inception of deposit insurance. Sharp regional differences in asset volatilities were found over this period, particularly in 1929. In addition, capital ratios declined to historically low levels, particularly at banks outside of the large Eastern and money-center bank regions. These results are especially striking given that our sample consisted primarily of large banks with actively traded stocks. Even greater cross-subsidies might be expected among smaller local banks, since these failed in greater numbers in the 1930–1932 period.

Specifically, using the limited-term European put–option valuation model, our results show that the initial 8.33 bp rate for federal deposit insurance was overpriced on average, relative to fair-value premia estimated over the pre-FDIC period 1927–1932, with the possible exception of 1929 and 1932. Using 1927 as a benchmark, the weighted-average, fair-value premium for that year was 0.37 bp. These findings of over-pricing parallel those of MS (1984) and RV (1986), in their estimation of fair deposit insurance premium values during the late 1970s and early 1980s.

The double liability of bank stockholders in this period also allows an assessment of the effects of relaxing limited liability rules, both in terms of stockholder discipline and regulator (FDIC) exposure. Double liability in conjunction with deposit insurance is shown to significantly reduce resulting fair value deposit insurance premia.

Finally, relaxing the limited-term assumption for the deposit insurance contract reverses the findings of overpricing, despite the high capital ratios and double liability of the period. Thus, whether the contact was overpriced or underpriced at its inception depends crucially on whether regulators, depositors, and stockholders rationally expected at the time of the contract's introduction (i) a limited-term contract with frequent premium adjustments or (ii) an unlimited contract with fixed premia.

APPENDIX A: LIMITED-TERM DEPOSIT INSURANCE PRICING

Following Merton (1977), MS and RV, deposit insurance is assumed to be isomorphic to a one-period European put option.[13] Let

V = the unobserved value of bank assets,

B_1 = the face value of insured bank deposits,

B_2 = the face value of other bank liabilities,

$B = B_1 + B_2$ = the face value of total debt liabilities,

E = bank equity value,

σ_E = the instantaneous standard deviation of the return on bank equity,

σ_V = the instantaneous standard deviation of the return on bank assets,

δ = dividends per dollar of bank assets, paid n times per year,

T = time until the next bank audit,

$N(\cdot)$ = the standard normal distribution, and

d = the insurance premium per dollar of insured deposits.

The fair-value premium, d, under limited liability is then given as

$$d = N(y + \sigma_V\sqrt{T}) - (1 - \delta)^n (V/B) N(y) \tag{A1}$$

and

$$y = \{\ln[B/V(1 - \delta)^n] - \sigma_V^2 T/2\}/\sigma_V\sqrt{T}. \tag{A2}$$

The bank's equity value, E, is modeled as a European call option, which must satisfy the "put–call parity" condition, $E = V - B + dB_1$. Substituting from (A1) yields

[13] As in RV, bank audits are assumed to be annual. Klebaner (1990) indicates that national, and most state, bank examinations were annual until the Federal Reserve Act of 1913, when biennial examinations were instituted for national banks.

$$
\begin{aligned}
E &= V - B + B_1 N(y + \sigma_V\sqrt{T}) - (1-\delta)^n V(B_1/B)N(y) \\
&= V[1 - (1-\delta)^n (B_1/B)N(y)] - B_2 N(y + \sigma_V\sqrt{T}) \\
&\quad - B[1 - N(y + \sigma_V\sqrt{T})] \qquad \text{(A3)} \\
&= [1 - (1-\delta)^n (B_1/B)]VN(y) - B_2 N(y + \sigma_V\sqrt{T}) + VN(-y) \\
&\quad - BN(-y - \sigma_V\sqrt{T})
\end{aligned}
$$

and

$$\sigma_V = \sigma_E E/V(\partial E/\partial V). \qquad \text{(A4)}$$

(A4) differs from RV, which does not satisfy the put–call parity condition, by the first two terms given in (A4).[14]

Deposit Insurance and Equity Value under Double Liability

Under double liability, bank owners bear a residual (postbank closure) liability, equal to the total par value (Par) of equity outstanding. The deposit insurance liability is then defined as

$$\max\{0, \mathrm{FV}(B_1) - (V_T + \mathrm{Par})B_1/(B_1 + B_2)\}. \qquad \text{(A5)}$$

Let $f^*B_1 = [1 - \mathrm{PV}(\mathrm{Par})/B]B_1$, where PV (FV) denotes present (future) value. Then

$$d = N(y + \sigma_V\sqrt{T})f^* - (1-\delta)^n (V/B)N(y) \qquad \text{(A6)}$$

and

$$y = \{\ln[f^*B/V(1-\delta)^n] - \sigma_V^2 T/2\}/\sigma_V\sqrt{T}. \qquad \text{(A7)}$$

As expected, double liability reduces the cost of deposit insurance provision. Derivation of E follows from the put–call parity condition, $E = V - B + dB_1$:

$$
\begin{aligned}
E &= V - B + B_1 f^* N(y + \sigma_V\sqrt{T}) - (1-\delta)^n V(B_1/B)N(y) \\
&= [1 - (1-\delta)^n (B_1/B)]VN(y) - B_2 f^* N(y + \sigma_V\sqrt{T}) \qquad \text{(A8)} \\
&\quad + VN(-y) - Bf^* N(-y - \sigma_V\sqrt{T}) - B(1 - f^*)
\end{aligned}
$$

[14] The Solver Routine of Microsoft Excel was used to solve for implied asset value, V, and asset volatility, σ_V. The Solver routine uses standard Gauss–Newton procedures. No convergence problems were encountered with the routine.

and

$$\sigma_V = \sigma_E E/V(\partial E/\partial V). \tag{A9}$$

APPENDIX B: THE MERTON/PENNACCHI UNLIMITED-TERM MODEL

Merton's (1978) unlimited-term model, extended by Pennacchi (1987) to endogenize mispriced deposit insurance, is extended to include dividend payments, since these are included in RV. Let the premium value, p, satisfy the following set of differential equations:

$$\tfrac{1}{2}\sigma_V^2 x^2 p_1'' + (r - g - \theta)xp_1' - (r - g)p_1 + \lambda c = 0, \qquad x \geq 1$$

$$\tfrac{1}{2}\sigma_V^2 x^2 p_2'' + (r - g - \theta)xp_2' - (r - g + \lambda)p_2 + \lambda[c + 1 - x] = 0, \qquad x \leq 1. \tag{B1}$$

The following boundary conditions must be satisfied:

$$p_1(1) = p_2(1), p_1'(1) = p_2'(1), p_2(0) = \lambda[1 + c]/(r + \lambda - g)$$

and

$$p_1(x) \text{ is bounded as } x \to \infty.$$

The resulting solutions are given as

$$p_1(x) = \lambda c/\mu + a_2 x^{r12}, \qquad x \geq 1$$

$$p_2(x) = \lambda(c + 1)/(\mu + \lambda) - (\lambda/(\theta + \lambda))x + b_1 x^{r21}, \qquad x \leq 1, \tag{B2}$$

where

$$a_2 = [\lambda/(r_{21} - r_{12})][(1 - r_{21})/(\lambda + \theta) + r_{21}[(1 + c)/(\mu + \lambda) - c/\mu]]$$

$$b_1 = [\lambda/(r_{21} - r_{12})][(1 - r_{12})/(\lambda + \theta) + r_{12}[(1 + c)/(\mu + \lambda) - c/\mu]]$$

$$r_{21} = [-\Phi + (\Phi^2 + 2(\mu + \lambda)\sigma_V^2)^{1/2}]/\sigma_V^2,$$

$$r_{12} = -[\Phi + (\Phi^2 + 2\mu\sigma_V^2)^{1/2}]/\sigma_V^2,$$

$$\mu = r - g,$$

and

$$\Phi = r - \theta - g - \tfrac{1}{2}\sigma_V^2,$$

With free entry into banking, $\mu = \lambda c$, it then follows that

$$p_1^*(x) = 1 + \lambda(1 - r_{21})x^{r_{12}}/(\theta + \lambda)(r_{21} - r_{12}), \tag{B3}$$

where

$$x = V/D,$$
$$r_{21} = [-\Phi + (\Phi^2 + 2(\mu + \lambda)\sigma_V^2)^{1/2}]/\sigma_V^2,$$
$$r_{12} = -[\Phi + (\Phi^2 + 2\mu\sigma_V^2)^{1/2}]/\sigma_V^2,$$

and

$$\Phi = r - \theta - g - \tfrac{1}{2}\sigma_V^2.$$

In addition, c are audit costs, λdt is the probability of an audit over the next instant, θ is the dividend payout rate, and $\mu = r - g$ is the interest rate minus the deposit growth rate.

Merton (1978) results if θ equals zero. Audit costs, c, are set to 0.000134, which is the 1935 FDIC administrative expenses ($2.7 million) divided by 1935 total insured deposits ($20,158 million). Auditing frequency, λ, is set equal to 1.0. The resulting premium values are treated as lump-sum perpetuities and multiplied by the Treasury bond yield[15] of the period to derive an equivalent annual payment amount.

REFERENCES

"Bank and Quotation Record." (1927–1932). William B. Dana Co., New York.

CALOMIRIS, C. W. (1992). Regulation, industrial structure, and instability in U.S. banking: An historical perspective, *in* "Structural Change in Banking" (M. Klausner and L. J. White, Eds.), pp. 19–116, Dow Jones-Irwin, Homewood, IL.

CHAN, Y., GREENBAUM, S. I., AND THAKOR, A. V. (1992). Is fairly priced deposit insurance possible?, *J. Finance* **47,** 227–246.

COLT, C. C., AND KEITH, N. S. (1933). "28 Days: A History of the Banking Crisis." Greenberg, New York.

"Commercial and Financial Chronicle." (1927–1932). William B. Dana Co., New York.

[15] Long-term government bond yields were taken from Ibbotson Associates (1991), Exhibit A-9, p. 154. Corresponding yields for corporate bonds are not available for comparison.

"Congressional Record, Volume 3." (1993). Debates, Legislative History, Public Law 73-66, Banking Act of 1933. U.S. Congress, Washington, DC.

COOPERSTEIN, R. L., PENNACCHI, G., AND REDBURN, F. S. (1995). The aggregate cost of deposit insurance: A multi-period analysis, *J. Finan. Intermed.* in press.

FDIC. (1984). "Federal Deposit Insurance Corporation: The First Fifty Years, A History of the FDIC 1933–1983." Federal Deposit Insurance Corporation, Washington, DC.

FRIEDMAN, M., AND SCHWARTZ, A. J. (1963). "A Monetary History of the United States, 1867–1960," Princeton Univ. Press, Princeton, NJ.

GORTON, G. (1985a). Bank suspension of convertibility. *J. Monet. Econ.* **15,** 177–193.

GORTON, G. (1985b). Clearinghouses and the origin of central banking in the United States, *J. Econ. Hist.* **45,** 277–283.

IBBOTSON ASSOCIATES. (1991). "Stocks, Bonds, Bills, and Inflation: 1991 Yearbook," Ibbotson Associates, Chicago.

KENNEDY, S. E. (1973). "The Banking Crisis of 1933." Univ. of Kentucky Press, Lexington, KY.

KLEBANER, B. J. (1990). "American Commercial Banking: A History." Twayne, Boston.

MACEY, J. R., AND MILLER, G. P. (1992). Double liability of bank shareholders: History and implications, *Wake Forest Law Rev.* **27,** 31–62.

MARCUS, A. J., AND SHAKED, I. (1984). The valuation of FDIC deposit insurance using options-pricing estimates, *J. Money, Credit, Banking* **16,** 446–460.

MERTON, R. C. (1977). An analytic derivation of the cost of deposit insurance and loan guarantees: An application of modern option pricing theory, *J. Banking Finance* **1,** 3–11.

MERTON, R. C. (1978). On the cost of deposit insurance when there are surveillance costs, *J. Bus.* **51,** 439–452.

"Moody's Manual of Investments." (1928–1933). Moody's Investors Service, New York.

PENNACCHI, G G. (1987). A reexamination of the over- (or under-) pricing of deposit insurance, *J. Money, Credit, Banking* **19,** 340–360.

"Rand McNally Bankers Directory, The Bankers Blue Book." (1927–1933). Rand McNally, New York.

RONN, E. I., AND VERMA A. K. (1986). Pricing risk-adjusted deposit insurance: An option-based model, *J. Finance* **41,** 871–895.

WILSON, J. W., SYLLA, R. E., AND JONES, C. P. (1990). Financial market panics and volatility in the long run, 1830–1988, *in* "Crashes and Panics: The Lessons from History" (E. N. White, Ed.), pp. 85–125, Dow Jones-Irwin, Homewood, IL.

WINTON, A. (1993). Limitation of liability and the ownership structure of the firm, *J. Finance* **48,** 487–512.

JEAN-FRANCOIS DREYFUS
ANTHONY SAUNDERS
LINDA ALLEN

Deposit Insurance and Regulatory Forbearance: Are Caps on Insured Deposits Optimal?

CONSIDERABLE ACADEMIC AND PUBLIC POLICY attention has been focused on the deposit insurance contract and, in particular, its mispriced deposit insurance premium. This has resulted in a burgeoning literature on the optimal pricing of deposit insurance guarantees [see Merton (1977, 1978), Pyle (1983), Ronn and Verma (1986), Acharya and Dreyfus (1989), and Allen and Saunders (1993) for examples]. In addition, other authors have studied the ability of uninsured depositors, or debtholders, to provide market discipline in the form of market-based risk premia in the absence of explicit risk-based insurance premia [see, for example, Ellis and Flannery (1989) and Avery, Belton and Goldberg (1988)].

However, a third control instrument, namely the setting of ceilings or caps on the amount of deposit insurance coverage, has not been subject to rigorous investigation. In particular, while the FDIC (1989) and others have considered the general pros and cons of limiting the scope of deposit insurance, for instance, by lowering the $100,000 ceiling on the amount of insurance per account or by restricting the brokering in of deposits,[1] no formal analysis of the role of coverage caps can be

1. A deposit broker is hired by large investors to parcel out investment funds into $100,000 lots which are then invested in a variety of insured institutions. In 1984, the FDIC and FSLIC introduced a joint resolution intended to deny insurance coverage to funds invested via deposit brokers. This resolution was subject to extensive Congressional hearings and was ultimately rejected. However, the Financial Institutions Reform, Recovery and Enforcement Act (FIRREA) passed by Congress in 1989 specified that insured financial institutions failing to meet capital standards would be prohibited from accepting brokered deposits as well as from soliciting deposits by offering interest rates that were "significantly higher than prevailing rates." These restrictions, formalized in the FDIC Improvement Act (FDICIA) of 1991, may be waived by the FDIC as long as so doing is not deemed to violate safety and soundness practices.

JEAN-FRANCOIS DREYFUS *is assistant professor of finance at the Stern School of Business, New York University.* ANTHONY SAUNDERS *is John M. Schiff Professor of Finance, also at the Stern School of Business.* LINDA ALLEN *is associate professor of finance at Baruch College, City University of New York.*

Journal of Money, Credit, and Banking, Vol. 26, No. 3 (August 1994, Part 1)

APPENDIX TABLE A1

MAXIMUM LIKELIHOOD ESTIMATES AND TESTS OF COINTEGRATION IN THE COMPLETE MONETARY MODEL WITH INTEREST RATES

Row	(Lags) Money	IP	Inflation	U.S.-Money	U.S.-IP	U.S.-Interest	L_1(0 vs. 1)	L_2(0 vs. 1)	L_1(1 vs. 2)	L_2(0 vs. 2)
	Israel									
1a	(10) (*M*1)	12.43	0.18	−2.64(M1)	−3.44	0.07	82.9***	273.9***	71.2***	191.0***
1b	(10) (*M*1)	−22.07	0.48	6.10(M1)	29.38	1.15				
2a	(8) (*M*1)	−9.78	0.17	5.48(M2)	−12.86	−0.11	49.9***	140.2***	41.0***	90.3***
2b	(8) (*M*1)	−22.06	0.002	11.78(M2)	−5.83	0.37				
3a	(6) (*M*2)	2.32	−0.01	−3.33(M1)	2.35	−0.05	52.2***	118.9***	29.1	66.8*
3b	(6) (*M*2)	1.01	−.001	6.05(M1)	−40.70	−0.98				
4a	(6) (*M*2)	2.84	−0.01	4.81(M2)	4.16	−0.12	46.5***	114.0***	32.8*	67.6*
4b	(6) (*M*2)	0.05	0.0004	−0.68(M2)	−3.88	−0.94				
	Argentina									
5a	(6) (*M*1)	0.97	0.002	1.02(M1)	−4.02	−0.12	53.85***	153.75***	33.87**	99.89***
5b	(6) (*M*1)	40.27	−0.02	70.71(M1)	−139.50	−3.67				
6a	(6) (*M*1)	0.75	0.003	1.21(M2)	−5.75	−0.10	51.29***	146.84***	39.96***	95.55***
6b	(6) (*M*1)	−15.35	−.008	−46.35(M2)	127.17	0.64				
7a	(6) (*M*2)	3.82	0.001	−1.67(M1)	1.82	−0.16	48.53***	148.32***	33.62**	99.79***
7b	(6) (*M*2)	−2.23	0.003	−1.90(M1)	0.65	0.03				
8a	(6) (*M*2)	14.84	−0.003	−2.809(M2)	9.90	−0.44	40.44**	140.25***	39.23***	99.81***
8b	(6) (*M*2)	−0.35	0.002	−0.46(M2)	−2.19	−0.10				

found in the literature. Consequently, there is a clear need to outline conditions under which the imposition of limits or caps on the scope of insured deposit coverage increases or decreases the expected liabilities of the FDIC, and to analyze the role of such caps in reducing the FDIC's failure resolution costs.[2]

We show in this paper that allowing additional access to insured deposits, even in a world of fixed (mispriced) deposit insurance premia, can under certain conditions reduce the FDIC's costs or expected liabilities. In other words, allowing a bank to collect additional insured deposits (for example, raising the cap on insurance coverage) and thus allowing the bank to continue in business for an additional period (or periods), may actually serve to lower FDIC failure resolution costs. This result obtains in the presence of either early resolution costs (associated with a "fire-sale of assets"), moral hazard (asset substitutability), or imperfectly competitive deposit markets. To the best of our knowledge, this is the first attempt to rigorously analyze the important policy question regarding the optimality of caps on the coverage of insured deposits.[3]

In this paper, we study the optimality of establishing caps on the scope of insured deposits *given* the existence of a flat ("mispriced") premium schedule for deposit insurance.[4] If the premium income generated by a deposit insurer, using a flat premium schedule, is less than the insurer's actuarially calculated liability (so that the insurance is underpriced), it is intuitively clear that a cost-minimizing insurer would prefer to limit the insurance coverage as much as possible, ceteris paribus.[5] However, the existence of a flat premium schedule raises the possibility that deposit insurance might actually become overpriced if a bank is low risk. Since the extent of over- or underpricing of deposit insurance depends on the scale of the coverage of insured deposits, that is, on the ratio of insured deposits to the bank's total liabilities, the choice of a cap on insured deposits by the FDIC need not be trivial. Further, unlike early papers on deposit insurance pricing that assumed the bank to be closed according to a fixed rule (the bank being closed when the value of its deposits fell below the value of its assets or a fixed percentage thereof), this paper takes into

2. The FDIC requires all banks to file a "Notification of Planned Rapid Growth" if the bank intends to increase its assets by more than 7.5 percent over the following quarter through the solicitation of brokered deposits or other forms of insured borrowings (for example, secured repurchase agreements).

3. Since brokered deposits allow banks to increase their insured/uninsured deposit ratio when they otherwise would be restricted regionally to a local insured deposit base, we model caps on insured deposits as being isomorphic to caps on the ratio of insured to uninsured deposits. That is, caps are bank-size independent. This conforms with actual practice, for example, the FDIC's concern with rapid growth (see footnote 2) as a percentage of asset size, not an absolute dollar amount. However, if larger banks are covered by a "too big to fail" policy, then for these banks only, all deposits are insured and insured deposit caps have no meaning. Thus, the setting of optimal insured/uninsured deposit ratios is relevant either for small banks or for large banks in the eventuality that the Federal insurer abandons the "too big to fail" policy.

4. The FIRREA legislation continued to specify "flat" insurance premia for commercial banks and thrifts now set at a rate of .23 percent of total domestic deposits. However, the FDICIA of November 1991 specified implementation of risk-based deposit insurance premia by January 1, 1994.

5. Of course, the creation of deposit insurance was motivated by a number of social welfare considerations. The formal model in this paper does not account for such considerations (a trait common to the extant literature on deposit insurance pricing) and while we formally allow the insurer to reduce the amount of insured deposits to zero, the level of insured deposits is always initially set to be positive so as to reflect potential social welfare benefits.

account the fact that, in a multiperiod setting, the insurer (the FDIC) need not abide by an exogenous closure rule and may instead be assumed to follow an endogenously determined optimal closure policy. Indeed, the FDIC and FSLIC have been observed, on numerous occasions, to exercise their forbearance option and to delay the closure of banks known to be insolvent in a market value sense.[6] In turn, the relative size of insured versus uninsured deposits will affect the probability with which the bank will be (optimally) closed by the insurer.

Finally, and importantly, it should be noted that the insurer's premium policy, the imposition of caps on insured deposit coverage, and bank closure decisions are not mutually independent. Indeed, the market discipline implied by "fair" pricing of deposits by large uninsured depositors, and hence the imposition of competitively priced interest rate risk premia on uninsured deposits, also impacts the insurer's liabilities. The imposition of a very low cap or ceiling on insured deposits also impacts the insurer's liabilities. Indeed, it might be expected that imposition of a low cap would always minimize the insurer's liabilities. However, the imposition of a very low ceiling on insured deposits would require the bank to rely extensively on uninsured deposits. For this to be feasible, the value of the bank's assets has to be high enough for the bank to be able to offer a competitive expected rate of return to uninsured depositors, for any chosen risk exposure. If the insured deposit coverage ceiling is set "too low," the bank may be unable to pay the interest rate or risk premium required by uninsured depositors. As a result, such a bank will have to be closed, unless the insurer increases the bank's value by injecting additional funds, which is analytically equivalent to charging a net deposit insurance premium below the maximum flat premium schedule.[7] Therefore, imposition of a lower insured deposit cap increases the likelihood that either the bank will have to be closed prematurely (that is, the insurer incurs early liquidation costs) or, given forbearance, the bank's shareholders will engage in value reducing asset substitution (that is, the insurer incurs moral hazard costs).

Specifically, we show that it may be optimal for the insurer to allow a bank to attract insured deposits beyond the minimum level consistent with the existence of a feasible financing structure, especially when "early" liquidation of a bank's assets via either a "payoff" or a "purchase and assumption"[8] results in realized asset values

6. Acharya and Dreyfus (1989) were among the first to recognize that the deposit insurance pricing problem could be usefully recast in a setting where the insurer dynamically and optimally adjusts the insurance premium and endogenously selects optimal stopping (closure) times. Their analysis was conducted under the assumptions that the insurer would charge actuarially fair premia whenever feasible and that all bank deposits were insured.

7. The net premium paid by the bank can be viewed as being equal to the required flat insurance premium minus any premium rebates and/or direct cash subsidies from the FDIC to the bank. Alternatively, one can view Federal Reserve discount window borrowings as an alternate form of subsidy if the rate charged on such borrowings is less than "competitive" rates.

8. In the absence of bid premia reflecting the value to a sound bank of assuming a failed bank's charter, the Purchase and Assumption cost is no less than the FDIC's expected cost of keeping the bank open via direct cash subsidies from the insurer to the insured (Open Bank Assistance). The cost to the insurer of paying off insured depositors only can never exceed the cost to the insurer of either a Purchase and Assumption or Open Bank Assistance. An examination of past practices shows that the majority of bank failures have been resolved via Purchase and Assumption, rather than the payoff method, with 175 of the

that are less than competitive market values. Indeed, (more) stringent caps on insured deposits are shown to increase the probability of bank liquidation since the higher interest rate required by uninsured depositors increases the probability that a bank will eventually be insolvent.

Section 1 defines the underlying assumptions and basic structure of our model. Section 2 provides an analysis of the insurer's optimal premium/subsidy, closure, and insured cap policies in a dynamic setting with perfectly competitive capital markets. In section 3, the assumption of perfect competition is relaxed to consecutively consider the impact of either moral hazard (asset substitutability) or imperfectly competitive deposit markets. Section 4 concludes the paper.

1. THE MODEL

We consider the following three-date model of a representative bank, operating in an economy populated by risk-neutral investors. The equilibrium riskfree rate of interest r is taken to be equal to zero.[9] At time 0, the bank invests in a homogeneous technology (portfolio) yielding a cash flow of $\tilde{X}$ at time 2.[10] For simplicity, we assume that the bank does not engage in any further investments at time 1, that no cash flows accrue at time 1, and that the time 2 cash flow on the initial portfolio has the following two-point distribution:

$$\begin{aligned} \tilde{X} &= H \qquad \text{with probability } q \\ &= 0 \qquad \text{with probability } 1 - q \end{aligned}$$

The probability q of the "high state," H, is unknown to all agents as of time 0. Let F(.) denote the cumulative distribution of q as of time 0. This c.d.f. is assumed to be common knowledge to all agents.

At time 1, all market participants receive new, public information, regarding the market value of the bank's assets. Given the assumed two-point distribution of $\tilde{X}$, we may assume, without loss of generality, that all agents (depositors, the FDIC, etc.) learn at time 1 the probability q of the "high" state (H) arising.

In order to focus on the impact of coverage caps, we abstract from the setting of

207 bank failures in 1989 (accounting for 92.5 percent of all failed bank assets) resolved using the Purchase and Assumption method. The less costly failure resolution methods, insured deposit transfers and insured deposit payoffs, accounted for 31 of the 207 bank failures in 1989 and 7.4 percent of all failed bank assets. However, the FDICIA sharply limits the FDIC's ability to reimburse uninsured depositors for failed bank resolutions after 1994. Thus, insured deposit payout or transfer may be expected to be more important failure resolution methods in the future.

9. Given risk neutrality, this assumption entails no loss of generality. The positive promised rate of interest required by uninsured depositors (see below) can be interpreted as a default risk premium. (The expected rate of return to uninsured depositors is of course zero.)

10. In section 3A, this assumption is relaxed to allow the bank to choose among assets of varying risk. This introduces the possibility of moral hazard since (insolvent) banks have the incentive to liquidate less risky assets and replace them with riskier assets so as to increase the value of the bank's deposit insurance put option.

capital or net worth requirements and take the initial equity contribution by the bank's stockholders to be fixed. Alternatively, the model is consistent with the assumption that the bank starts (at time 0) with zero net worth. This has the advantage of focusing attention on the role of insured deposit caps for "failing" banks, that is, banks bordering on insolvency. Let A_0 denote the market value of the bank's assets as of time 0, or equivalently the original dollar amount to be financed by insured and uninsured deposits.[11]

To investigate the effect of restricting a bank's access to insured deposits, we assume that regulators set a cap on the level of a bank's insured deposits. That is, in selecting the division of its liabilities between insured and uninsured deposits at time 0, and again at time 1, the bank is constrained by an upper (dollar) limit $\bar{D}_{it}$, $t = 0,1$, set by regulators on the use of insured deposits.[12] All deposits are assumed to have a one-period maturity. Deposits maturing at time 1 may be rolled over until time 2 at the new competitive one-period interest rate, or may equivalently be replaced by new one-period deposits.[13]

1A. Closure Assumptions

The bank operates under the auspices of a regulator (the FDIC) offering deposit insurance covering some but not all deposits. Specifically, we assume that the bank offers two distinct products, insured and uninsured deposits.[14] In the event of a bank insolvency, Federal deposit insurers can choose either to keep the bank open (thereby granting forbearance through Open Bank Assistance) or to immediately close the bank. In the event of bank closure, the insurer can choose among a variety of failure resolution methods—deposit payoff, Purchase and Assumption, or creation of a bridge bank. When there is no bid premium (reflecting the perceived franchise value of the failed bank), then the cost to the insurer of a whole bank Purchase and Assumption is the same as that of Open Bank Assistance since both insured and uninsured depositors are fully covered. These methods of failure resolution are more costly to the insurer than an insured deposit payoff, which only covers insured depositors. Since the FIRREA legislation mandates that the deposit insurer choose the lowest cost failure resolution method, we focus on the cheaper payoff method. The payoff method is equivalent, in terms of insurer cost, to the insured deposit transfer or "clean bank" Purchase and Assumption. Moreover, the FDIC Improvement Act mandates that the FDIC limit its policy of reimbursement of uninsured depositors suggesting that the insured deposit payoff or insured deposit transfer will be a more important bank failure resolution method in the future. Thus, we focus on the case of insured deposit payoff to model bank liquidations.

11. Flannery (1989), for instance, provides a cogent analysis of the impact of regulatory capital standards on the choice of portfolio risk by a bank. See also Kim and Santomero (1988), among others.

12. Note that this upper limit could be stated as a percentage of total deposits, as we allow the regulatory constraint to be state- and time dependent.

13. The assumption in this section that the bank is a price taker is relaxed in section 3B.

14. The exact nature of the distinction between the products (for example, whether all depositors are specified to be insured up to $100,000) is immaterial here.

1B. "Early" Closure versus Forbearance

Given the information received at time 1, that is, given the probability q of the "high" state H, the insurer must decide whether (i) to close the bank and liquidate its assets or (ii) to keep the bank open, adjusting the insured deposit cap and/or providing the bank with a subsidy (or cash infusion), which can be modeled as a rebate to the flat insurance premium levied by the FDIC.

Specifically, if the bank is kept open, we assume that the insurer's premium assessment is constrained by law to a "flat fee" schedule $\bar{P}(D_1)$, which specifies the *maximum* premium which may be charged by the insurer on the total level of insured and uninsured deposits at time 1, denoted by $D_1 = D_{i1} + D_{u1}$.[15] Note that, unlike most of the literature on deposit insurance, this paper does *not* focus on the pricing of "fair" risk-adjusted insurance premia. Instead, we wish to investigate the costs and benefits of caps on insured deposit coverage, given the current use of flat premium schedules and given dynamically optimal FDIC bailout (or forbearance) policies. Indeed, the insurer would be indifferent to the use of one means of bank financing relative to any other if insurance premia could be accessed to reflect the actuarially fair value of the insurance provision. Importantly, the schedule $\bar{P}(.)$ only represents the maximum premium level that the FDIC may charge a bank. In particular, this model allows for FDIC cash infusions (or other regulator-provided subsidies) that reduce the net premium paid by the bank below the maximum level $\bar{P}(.)$. Indeed, negative net premia are possible and can be interpreted as an injection of cash funds (in excess of the explicit deposit insurance premium) by the FDIC, into the bank, so as to avoid liquidating the bank's portfolio at that time. In what follows it is shown that subsidizing the continued operation of the bank (that is, exercising its forbearance option at time 1) may indeed be an optimal policy for the FDIC in some states of the world.

The need for such subsidies, and hence the choice between closure and forbearance, will be affected by the interest rate risk premia demanded by the bank's uninsured depositors, which in turn will depend on the level of the insured deposit coverage cap. Indeed, since the time 2 payoff to uninsured depositors is contingent upon the uncertain time 2 realized value of the bank's assets, uninsured depositors will in general require a positive risk premium on their deposits between $t = 1$ and $t = 2$, such that the equilibrium expected rate of return (the riskfree rate) equals zero. If the expected value of the bank's assets at time 2, conditional on time 1 information, is low enough, the bank may find itself unable to pay the risk premia required by uninsured depositors. In this case, the bank will be unable to refinance its uninsured deposits maturing at time 1. As a result, for the bank to be kept in operation until asset maturity at time 2, the insurer would have to provide the bank with additional cash funds (used to repay maturing uninsured deposits) or the insurer would have to allow the bank to refinance its uninsured liabilities with additional insured deposits (that is, would have to relax any existing cap on insured deposits). *It is shown below that allowing a bank to refinance its liabilities through additional*

15. The current premium system may be described as $\bar{P}(D_i + D_u) = .0023(D_i + D_u)$.

insured deposits at the riskfree rate, as opposed to closing the bank, may be an optimal (least-cost) policy for the FDIC. In other words, raising the insurance coverage cap may minimize the FDIC's failure resolution costs.

Specifically, if the bank is closed (that is, if no extension of insured deposit coverage is granted), then the "early" liquidation or transfer of the bank's assets may be costly. First, the premature or "fire-sale" liquidation of the bank's assets, at time 1, may prevent the insurer from immediately realizing the full market value of the bank's assets.[16] Secondly, even a simple transfer of assets (in a purchase and assumption) may result in some loss of value linked to the dissipation of specialized information (such as a detailed knowledge of local market conditions) or to transaction and reorganization costs.[17] Finally, timely closure may be exceptionally costly because of insurer budget constraints.[18] The existence of "fire-sale" liquidation costs, transaction and reorganization costs, and political costs could all be considered "early" liquidation costs.

We therefore assume that the early liquidation of the bank's assets would lead the FDIC to realize only a fraction $(1 - \gamma)$ of the value of the failing bank's assets in the absence of closure, which, conditional on time 1 information, would have an expected value equal to qH. γ reflects the cost of the insurer of conducting a "fire-sale" of the bank's assets at time period 1.[19]

Let D_{i1} and D_{u1} denote the amount of insured and uninsured deposits outstanding at time 1 (including any accrued interest) and let $D_1 = D_{i1} + D_{u1}$. If the FDIC elects to close the bank at time 1 using the payoff (or insured deposit transfer) method, its costs equal

$$Q_c \equiv max\left[\, 0, D_{i1} - \frac{D_{i1}}{D_1}(1 - \gamma)qH \,\right]. \tag{1}$$

16. See Kane (1985) for example. Also, for documentation of the costs and problems involved in bank asset liquidations, see General Accounting Office, *Failed Banks: FDIC's Asset Liquidation Operations*.

17. It was to avoid these early liquidation costs that Congress granted the FDIC "bridge bank authority" in the Competitive Equality Banking Act of 1987. The bridge bank failure resolution method allows the FDIC to operate a failing institution as a bridge bank for up to two years, with the option of three additional one-year extensions. An advantage of the bridge bank method is avoidance of early liquidation costs. "[I]t may be worthwhile to keep an insolvent bank operating [as a bridge bank] for a brief period until prospective acquirers can assess the institution's condition in order to make a reasonable offer for the bank. If it continues to function, the bank can retain much of its value . . ." (Bovenzi and Muldoon (1990), p. 3–4.

18. If the government's closure policy is determined by elected officials and/or civil servants with finite time horizons of public service, the imputed cost of liquidation may be disproportionately high in the short run if there is a personal cost to acknowledging bank failures. This would induce the decision-making agent to discount future liquidation costs at a rate higher than simply the time value. [See Kane [1985] for a discussion of the principal-agent problem.]

19. In the model, γ is assumed to fall to zero at time period 2. Conceivably, however, there could be liquidation costs at each time period (even extending to an infinite maturity model). This could be incorporated into the model as $\gamma_2 > 0$ at time period 2. Our results obtain as long as $\gamma_1 > \gamma_2 > 0$, a plausible assertion. That is, $\gamma_1 > \gamma_2$ if the more rapidly the insurer attempts to dispose of the bank's assets, the greater their price write-down and therefore the lower the early liquidation value of the bank's assets to the insurer. The bridge bank authority (see footnote 17) and the gradual liquidation policies followed by the Resolution Trust Corporation in liquidating the assets of failed thrifts is consistent with such a time path of γ values.

The existence of liquidation costs (γqH) will be shown to have important implications for our model—especially in regard to the optimality of deposit insurance caps. Specifically, immediate closure will prove to be the least costly policy whenever the bank is insolvent at time 1 ($qH < D_1$) in the absence of early liquidation costs ($\gamma = 0$). However, in the presence of early liquidation costs ($\gamma > 0$), the presumption in favor of closure versus forbearance, financed either through increased access to insured deposits or through cash subsidies, will be weakened. This is because, ceteris paribus, closure becomes more costly to the insurer when early liquidation costs are present. Allowing banks greater access to insured deposits may then lower the FDIC's overall failure resolution costs. Thus, in the presence of liquidation costs, regulators might find it optimal to allow weak banks to increase the scope of their insured deposit coverage (for example, through greater access to brokered deposits) rather than closing them immediately. More generally, since access to (cheaper) insured deposits reduces the likelihood of bank insolvency, the insurer's costs may be reduced in the presence of deadweight insolvency costs (for example, early liquidation costs, moral hazard costs, and/or costs resulting from an imperfectly elastic supply of deposits).

1C. Model Summary

The timing of the FDIC's decision process is assumed to be as follows (see Table 1).

Time 0: The insurer sets an initial coverage cap $\bar{D}_{i0}$, on the use of insured deposits.

Time 1: (i) All agents (insured and uninsured depositors, the FDIC, . . .) receive new information on the value of the bank's assets at time 2.

(ii) The insurer decides whether to allow the bank to operate until time 2. If optimal, the insurer can reset the coverage cap on the use of insured deposits, or provide the bank with a cash infusion or subsidy.

TABLE 1

FDIC'S DECISION PROCESS

Time 0		Time 1		Time 2	
FDIC sets a cap $\bar{D}_{i0}$ on insured deposits	Bank selects insured/uninsured mix (D_{i0}, D_{u0}); $D_{i0} \leq \bar{D}_{i0}$	Probability q of high state is revealed publicly	Closure decision by the FDIC. If no closure, the FDIC resets $\bar{D}_{i1}$ and (if necessary) injects a cash subsidy into the bank	Bank selects a new deposit mix (asset mix for section 3A) subject to cap on insured deposits (Section 3A: Asset substitution for insolvent banks)	Assets mature

(iii) Given insured deposit caps and net insurance premia, and given the interest rate (risk premia) required by uninsured depositors, the bank selects an optimal mix of insured versus uninsured deposits (selling assets if necessary) in order to maximize the value of its equity (net worth) at time 1.

Time 2: Assets mature and depositors are paid from asset proceeds. Shareholders receive any residual asset value.

We now turn to the determination of the deposit insurer's optimal dynamic regulatory policies at times 0 and 1. These policies are determined by standard backward dynamic programming. Note that, in the finite-horizon setting of our model, an important economic difference exists in the model between "time 0" and "time 1," which in turn is related to the difference between the nature of the FDIC's closure policies and available options at times 1 and 2. At time 2 (the "end of the world"), the insurer has no choice but to close the bank and to cover the insured deposits if the bank is insolvent. At time 1, however, the insurer has a choice, in that his closure policy is *endogenously* determined (jointly) with the setting of his optimal regulatory controls on (i) insured deposit caps and (ii) cash subsidies. Thus, the insurer at time 1 makes a closure choice facing a fixed closure rule at time 2, while at time 0 the closure choice is made given a dynamically optimal, endogenous closure policy at time 1.

2. COST-MINIMIZING PREMIUM AND CLOSURE POLICIES, AND OPTIMAL INSURED DEPOSITS CAPS

Given the above model structure, we solve successively for the time-1 and time-0 optimal subsidy, closure, and insured deposit cap policies of a cost-minimizing deposit insurer.

2A. *Optimal Time-1 Policies*

Suppose that instead of closing the bank the insurer decides to let the bank continue to operate until time 2. Let P denote the *net* insurance premium charged at time 1 by the insurer, that is, the flat premium $\bar{P}(D_1)$ minus any cash subsidies paid by the insurer to the bank, and let $A_1 = D_{i1} + D_{u1} + P$ denote the total liabilities of the bank at time 1. These liabilities may be financed by either insured or by uninsured deposits.[20] Let D_{i1} and D_{u1} respectively denote the amounts of insured and unin-

20. Of course, the bank could also engage in loan sales, that is, could repay some maturing deposits with funds generated by the liquidation at time 1 of a fraction of the bank's asset portfolio. This option need not be explicitly considered, however. Indeed, it is easy to check that loan sales are financially fully equivalent to refinancing maturing deposits through new *uninsured* deposits, if the early liquidation of the bank's assets (or part thereof) entail no loss of value. That is, if $\gamma = 0$, the value of the bank's equity and the value of the insurer's expected liability are both independent of the chosen mode of financing. Further, if early liquidation costs are positive, repaying maturing deposits through loan sales is easily seen to be dominated by the option of refinancing these deposits through new competitively priced uninsured deposits. Pennacchi (1988), for instance, provides an analysis of the role of loan sales when banks have superior information on the quality of the loans in their portfolios.

sured deposits where D_{i1} and D_{u1} denote the chosen time-1 levels of insured and uninsured deposits.

Given any financing scheme (D_{i1}, D_{u1}) chosen by the bank at time 1, and given the revealed probability (q) of the high state (H) for bank assets at time 2, uninsured depositors will require a promised interest rate risk premium between $t = 1$ and $t = 2$, which produces a competitive expected return. This required rate, r_1, satisfies[21]

$$E\left[\min\left[D_{u1}(1+r_1), \tilde{X}\frac{D_{u1}(1+r_1)}{D_{i1}+D_{u1}(1+r_1)}\right]\right] = D_{u1}. \tag{2}$$

We define a financing scheme (D_{i1}, D_{u1}) to be *feasible* if $D_{i1} + D_{u1} = A_1$ and there exists an interest rate r_1 such that (2) is satisfied when $D_{u1} > 0$.

Since, in the event of insolvency at time 2, uninsured depositors receive a share of the bank's assets proportional to their time-2 claim, which is itself a function of the *promised* rate of interest (r_1) on uninsured deposits, the uninsureds' share of the bank's assets at time 2 will be close to one if the promised rate of interest is "very high." Consequently,[22]

LEMMA 1: *There exists a feasible financing plan at time 1 if and only if the cap* $\bar{D}_{i1}$ *on insured deposits imposed by the FDIC is such that* $\bar{D}_{i1} \geq D_1 + P - qH$.

A cap set below this lower bound would require the bank to raise uninsured deposits in excess of the amount for which the bank is able to offer a competitive (expected) return to uninsured depositors. Note that the existence of a feasible financing plan for the bank is dependent on the insurer's control variables, and not on the expected value of the bank's assets at time 1, that is, not solely on whether $qH > D_{i1} + D_{u1}$. In particular, FDIC cash infusions and the insurer's ceiling on the use of insured deposits at time 1 are policies that are constrained by a requirement that a feasible financing plan must exist if the bank is to continue in operation until time 2. *That is, forbearance (backed by cash infusions) and insured deposit caps are alternative regulatory policy instruments that can be manipulated to keep failing banks open if desired (that is, to allow "troubled" banks to meet their financing constraints).*

2B. Deposit Caps and Cash Subsidies as Policy Instruments

Once q is revealed at time 1, and assuming for now that the bank is kept in operation until time 2, let the insurer inject a cash subsidy (if required) into the bank resulting in a net insurance premium $P \leq \bar{P}(.)$ and a set cap $\bar{D}_{i1}$ on the use of insured deposits consistent with the existence of a feasible financing scheme for the bank. As might be expected, given the use of a flat explicit insurance premium schedule

21. The expected future payoff to uninsured depositors must equal the current value of their deposits. Recall that the riskfree rate is assumed to be zero. Equation (1) reflects the fact that, under current regulations, the relative share of the uninsured depositors is based on the value of their deposits at the time of closure *including accrued interest*.

22. All proofs omitted from the main text are provided in the appendix.

levied on the bank's total deposit base,[23] the value of the bank equity at time 1 (that is, the market value of the residual claim held by the bank's shareholders) is an increasing function of the level of insured deposits D_{i1}. Indeed, the time-1 value of the bank's equity (net worth) is given by

$$E_1 = q \max[0, H - D_{i1} - D_{u1}/q] = \max[0, qH + (1 - q)D_{i1} - A_1] \ . \quad (3)$$

Equation (3) reflects the value of the FDIC's "mispriced" deposit insurance to the bank's shareholders, since $(1 - q) = q(1/q - 1)$ may be interpreted as the expected value of the difference (per dollar of insured deposits) between the return paid by shareholders to uninsured depositors $(1/q)$ and the lower return required by insured depositors (who demand no risk premium).

Consequently, the bank will elect to use insured deposit financing up to the cap set by the FDIC, that is, $D_{i1} = \bar{D}_{i1}$. If $\bar{D}_{i1} < A_1$, the remaining liabilities, $A_1 - \bar{D}_{i1}$, are refinanced through the collection of additional uninsured deposits. Since uninsured deposits are priced at time 1 for depositors to receive a payoff of D_{u1}/q at time 2 in state H, the insurer's expected time-2 liability may be calculated as

$$(1 - q)\bar{D}_{i1} + q \max\left[0, \bar{D}_{i1} - \left[H - \frac{D_{u1}}{q}\right]\right] =$$

$$(1 - q)\bar{D}_{i1} + \max[0, A_1 - \bar{D}_{i1}(1 - q) - qH] \ . \quad (4)$$

Consequently:

LEMMA 2: *The optimal (cost-minimizing) settings of insured deposit caps and cash subsidies (or, equivalently, net insurance premia) at time 1, and the resulting expected net cost* Q_{NC} *to the insurer if the bank is kept* open *at time 1 are given by*

$$Q_{NC} = \max[-\bar{P}(D_1), D_1 - qH] \ , \quad (5)$$

and

$$P = \min[\bar{P}(D_1), qH - D_1], \bar{D}_{i1} = 0 \qquad \text{if } qH \geq D_1 \quad (6a)$$

$$P \in [0, \bar{P}(D_1)], \bar{D}_{i1} \in \left[D_1 + P - qH, \frac{D_1 + P - qH}{1 - q}\right], \qquad \text{if } qH < D_1. \quad (6b)$$

Since uninsured deposits are competitively priced, it is clear that the settings of regulatory control variables simply result in a transfer of value between the insurer's expected liability on one hand, and the value of the bank shareholders' equity on the other. Hence, if the bank is *solvent* at time 1, that is, if $qH \geq D_1$ (so that the stockholders' equity stake is positive prior to the payment of insurance premia), the insur-

23. Here we assume for convenience that all deposits are domestic deposits.

er would optimally desire to restrict the value of insurance subsidies to bank stockholders—given its control over the size of any cash subsidy infusions and the insured deposit cap. While for simplicity we formally allow the insurer to set a zero cap on insured deposits ($\bar{D}_{i0} = 0$) and thus to effectively eliminate insurance coverage, this policy may more realistically be interpreted as one in which the insurer finds it undesirable to allow a *solvent* bank to collect more than a "normal" level of insured deposits and, in particular, wishes to restrict bank access to the brokered deposit market.

If the bank is technically insolvent, that is, $qH < D_1$, cash subsidies (which reduce the net insurance premium (P) levied by the insurer) and increases in the insured deposit cap are perfect-substitute policy instruments, as can be seen from equation (6b). *That is, allowing a failing bank to extend its insured deposit base may be used, by the deposit insurer, in place of cash subsidies to minimize the cost of forbearance.*

In order to ascertain whether such a policy is in fact optimal, we must of course first examine the optimality of granting forbearance. Recall that the FDIC can choose to either (i) close the bank using an insured deposit payoff (thereby incurring early liquidation costs) or (ii) keep the bank open using an optimal combination of cash subsidies and insured deposit cap (thereby granting forbearance to the bank). Comparing the cost of closure to that of forbearance yields

COROLLARY 1: *The bank is optimally closed at time 1 (by the payoff method) if and only if*[24]

$$q \leq \underline{q} = \frac{D_{u1}[D_{u1} + D_{i1}]}{H[D_{u1} + \gamma D_{i1}]}. \tag{7}$$

If $\gamma = 0$, $\underline{q} = (D_{i1} + D_{u1})/H$. Thus, directly closing the bank at time 1 and paying off depositors is superior to forbearance with optimal caps and subsidies. In the absence of early liquidation costs, payoff or liquidation of an insolvent bank's assets *strictly* dominates forbearance at time 1.

If, however, liquidation costs are positive, that is, $\gamma > 0$, it can be directly seen from equation (7) that $\underline{q}$ is a *decreasing* function of γ, and in particular that $\underline{q}$ is strictly less than D_1/H, the threshold closure point in the absence of early liquidation costs. That is, as might be expected, the existence of asset liquidation costs leads the insurer to optimally close the bank "less frequently" at time 1, and in particular, leads the FDIC to exercise its forbearance option with positive probability. (Forbearance is granted in the event that $\underline{q} < q \leq D_1/H$.) In such a case, Lemma 2 shows that the *optimal cost-minimizing policy for the FDIC is to allow a failing*

24. The bank is closed iff $Q_{NC} = \max[-\bar{P}(.), D_1 - qH] > Q_C = \max\left[0, D_{i1} - \frac{D_{i1}}{D_1}(1-\gamma)qH\right]$. Closure will therefore be optimal if and only if $Q_{NC} = D_1 - qH > \max\left[0, D_{i1} - \frac{D_{i1}}{D_1}(1-\gamma)qH\right] = Q_C$, that is, iff $q \leq D_1/H$ and $q \leq \underline{q}$ where $\underline{q}$ is defined in (7). Since $\underline{q} \leq D_1/H$, the result follows.

bank to expand its coverage cap on insured deposits.[25] We now turn to the analysis of optimal regulatory policies at time 0.

2C. Optimal Time-0 Policies

Let D_{i0} and D_{u0} denote, respectively, insured and uninsured deposits at time 0. Let r_0 and r_{i0} denote the interest promised to uninsured and insured depositors, respectively, between $t = 0$ and $t = 1$. Since the equilibrium (riskfree) rate of interest is assumed to be zero, it is clear that $r_{i0} = 0$. However, the time-1 payoff of uninsured depositors is contingent upon the information received at time 1 regarding the quality of the bank's assets (the revealed value of q) and the resulting probability of bank closure at that time. Since under optimal regulatory policies, closure of the bank and payoff by the insurer result in some potential loss of principal by uninsured depositors at time 1, these depositors will require a positive promised risk premium r_0 that satisfies equation (8):[26]

$$D_{u0} = (1 - F(\underline{q}))D_{u0}(1 + r_0) + \frac{D_{u0}(1 + r_0)}{D_{i0} + D_{u0}(1 + r_0)} \int_0^{\underline{q}} (1 - \gamma)qH \, dF(q) \quad (8)$$

where $\underline{q}$ is defined as in Corollary 1 and where $D_{u1} = D_{u0}(1 + r_0)$ denotes the level of uninsured deposits at time 1 inclusive of accrued intrest.[27] Let $\hat{D}_{u0}$ denote the maximum level of uninsured deposits at time 0 for which equation (8) admits a solution $r_0 > 0$. Correspondingly, let $\hat{D}_{i0} = A_0 - \hat{D}_{u0}$ denote the minimum level of insured deposits consistent with the existence of a feasible financing plan at time 0.[28] From (8), it can be shown that

LEMMA 3: *The probability of closure at time 1,* (that is, $F(\underline{q})$), *is a* non-decreasing *function of the level of uninsured deposits at time 0.*

Intuitively, higher levels of uninsured deposits imply a higher probability of insolvency for a bank at time 1, since uninsured depositors require a positive risk premium on their deposits. Given $D_{u0} \leq \hat{D}_{u0}$, let $Q_1(.) = \min[Q_{NC}(.), Q_C(.)]$ denote the insurer's expected cost at time 1, given an optimal closure decision, FDIC cash sub-

25. Recall, however, that this analysis is conducted in a world of symmetric information and in the absence of moral hazard. The existence of moral hazard costs will be examined in section 3A.

26. Since, for simplicity, investors are assumed to be risk neutral, the expected return on uninsured deposits equals the riskfree rate. Risk-averse investors would demand a higher risk premium, thereby increasing r_0 and increasing the insurer's costs of capping access to insured deposits. That is, risk-averse investors requiring a higher return on uninsured deposits increase the cost to the deposit insurer of a more stringent cap on insured deposits since the likelihood of bank insolvency increases.

27. This assumes that the bank does not seek additional deposits between time 0 and time 1. But recall that the nominal size of the bank's investment portfolio is assumed to remain constant between time 0 and time 2, absent partial liquidation at time 1.

28. Given D_{i1}, $\underline{q}$ is monotonically increasing in $D_{u1} = D_{u0}(1 + r_0)$. Thus, letting $E(\pi_u)$ denote the expected time-1 payoff to uninsured depositors, given by the right-hand side of (8), $\lim E(\pi_u) = (1 - \gamma)H\,E(q)$ as $D_{u1} \to +\infty$. It may, however, be checked that $E(\pi_u)$ need not be monotonically increasing in D_{u1}. Thus, $\hat{D}_{u0}$ may strictly exceed $(1 - \gamma)H\,E(q)$. Of course, $\hat{D}_{u0} \leq H\,E(q)$. Hence, $\hat{D}_{u0} = H\,E(q)$ if $\gamma = 0$.

sidy (net premium assessment) and insured deposit cap at that time. Let $Q_0 = E[Q_1(.)]$ denote the resulting expected cost to the insurer at time 0 if the bank is kept open until time 1. Further, letting $\bar{q} = [D_{i1} + D_{u1} + \bar{P}(D_1)]/H$, we have[29]

$$Q_0 = \int_0^{\underline{q}} \left[D_{i1} - \frac{D_{i1}}{D_{i1} + D_{u1}} q(1 - \gamma)H \right] dF(q)$$

$$+ \int_{\underline{q}}^{\bar{q}} (D_{i1} + D_{u1} - qH)dF(q) - \bar{P}(D_1)(1 - F(\bar{q})) . \qquad (9)$$

PROPOSITION 1: (i) *If asset liquidation costs on closure are zero* ($\gamma = 0$), *the insurer's expected cost at time 0 if the bank is kept open until time 1 is a* non-decreasing *function of the level of insured deposits at time 0,* D_{i0}. *Hence, it is optimal for the FDIC to set the insured deposit coverage cap equal to* $\hat{D}_{i0}$, *that is, equal to the minimum level of insured deposits consistent with the existence of a feasible financing plan at time 0.*

(ii) *If closure and liquidation of the bank's assets at time 1 entails positive liquidation costs* ($\gamma > 0$), *it may be optimal for the insurer to set an insured deposit cap which exceeds the minimum level consistent with the existence of a feasible financing plan for the bank.*[30]

Proposition 1 results from the fact that the level of uninsured deposits has two conflicting effects on the FDIC's expected costs of keeping the bank open until time 1. First, the more uninsured deposits a bank has (that is, the stricter the insured deposit cap), the lower the FDIC's liability in the event of closure, as the bank has fewer deposits with insurance coverage. However, secondly, high levels of uninsured deposits increase the interest burden on the bank and increase the probability of its failure at time 1.

In the absence of early liquidation costs, Proposition 1(i) shows that, for the FDIC, the benefits of stringent caps, that is, reduced insurance coverage, more than offset the costs from an increased probability of future insolvency by the bank. If, however, $\gamma > 0$, Proposition 1(ii) shows that the FDIC's costs are not necessarily minimized by reducing insured deposits to their lowest possible level consistent with keeping the bank open (that is, fully financed). This is because low levels of insured deposits imply high levels of high interest-bearing uninsured deposits, a higher probability of early liquidation of a bank's assets, and hence higher expected closure costs.

Proposition 1(ii) may be proved through the provision of an example, which we

29. Note that $\bar{q}$ may be simply viewed as a function of D_{u0}, or alternatively of D_{i0}, since $D_{i1} = D_{i0} = F_0 - D_{u0}$.

30. That is, there exist probability distributions $F(.)$ such that the insurer's *expected* costs at time 0, viewed as a function of insured deposits at time 0, D_{i0}, are locally increasing at $\bar{D}_{i0}$. Intuitively, the insurer's cost curve may be U-shaped in the interval $[0, \bar{D}_{i0}]$.

do below. However, it can be shown that such an example is in no way "patholog-ical." Indeed, substituting (8) into (9) yields

$$Q_0 = \int_{\bar{q}}^{1} (qH - D_1 - \bar{P})dF(q) + \gamma \text{H} \int_{0}^{\underline{q}} qdF(q) - HE(q) + A_0 \,.$$

(1)	(2)	(3)
value of bank equity's residual claim	expected loss of value upon closure (transaction costs)	NPV of the bank's asset portfolio

Taking the derivative of this expression yields

$$\frac{\partial Q_0}{\partial D_{u0}} = -(1 - F(\bar{q}))\left[\frac{\partial [Du_0 r_0(D_{u0})]}{\partial D_{u0}} + \frac{\partial \bar{P}(D_1)}{\partial D_{u0}} \right] + \gamma H \frac{\partial \underline{q}}{\partial D_{u0}} \underline{q} f(\underline{q}) \,. \tag{10}$$

If $\gamma = 0$, $\frac{\partial Q_0}{\partial D_{u0}} \leq 0$, providing Proposition 1(i). However, when $\gamma > 0$, the last (positive) term on the right-hand side of (10) reflects the fact that an increase in D_{u0} raises the threshold closure point $\underline{q}$ and increases the probability of early clo-sure. Thus, stringent restrictions on insured deposits may potentially increase the FDIC's closure costs when $\gamma > 0$. The presence of asset liquidation costs, in the event of bank failure, therefore favors policies aimed at allowing (some) additional access to insured deposits (such as "brokered" insured deposits) as part of a fore-bearance strategy. Alternatively said, high bank liquidation costs favor high insured deposit coverage caps.

To illustrate this fact more clearly, we undertake some simulations evaluating the optimal time-0 ratio of insured to uninsured deposits, from the perspective of a cost-minimizing insurer, in the presence of liquidation costs ($\gamma > 0$).

It is assumed for simplicity that q itself has a two-point distribution

$$q = \begin{cases} q_2 \text{ with probability } \phi \\ q_1 \text{ with probability } 1 - \phi. \end{cases} \qquad 0 < q_1 < q_2 < 1$$

Figure 1 depicts the behavior of the FDIC's expected failure resolution costs at time 0, $Q_0(.)$, as a function of the ratio of insured deposits to total time-0 deposits, $D_{i0}/A_0 \in [0, 1]$, given the following assumptions: $H = 1400$, $A_0 = 700$, $q_1 = 0.45$, $q_2 = 0.51$, $\phi = .8333$, $\gamma = 0.01$. Note that $A_0 = E(q)H$, that is, the bank's asset portfolio is assumed to have zero NPV for the purpose of this simulation.

As can be seen from Figure 1, in the presence of liquidation costs the relationship between the FDIC's expected failure resolution costs at time 0, $Q_0(.)$, and the ratio

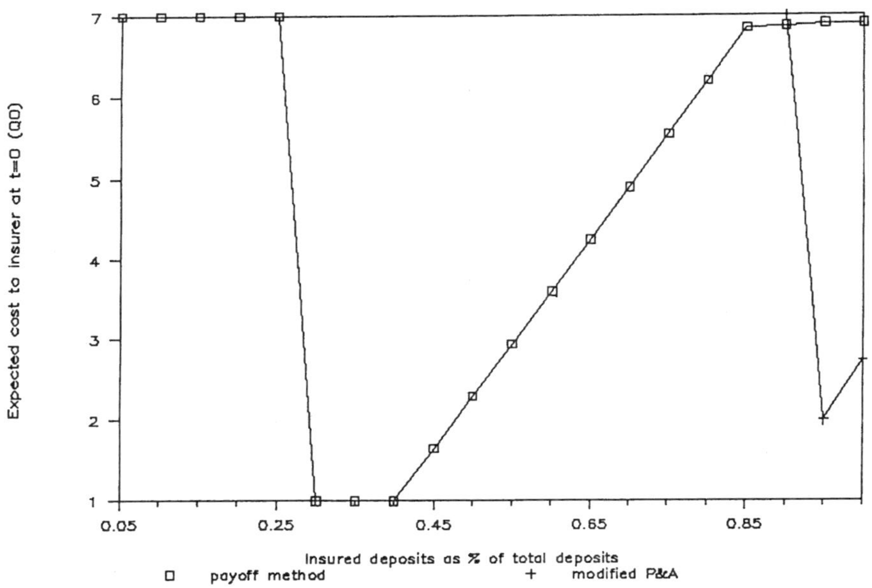

Fig. 1. Expected Cost to the FDIC at Time 0 under Optimal Policies at Time 1 If Closure at Time 1 Is Effected by (i) Payoff and (ii) Modified Purchase and Assumption, in the Presence of Early Liquidation Costs (γ = 1%)

of insured to total deposits (D_{i0}/D_0) is U-shaped. Given the assumed parameter values, the insurer's cost is minimized for a cap on insured deposits in the 30–40 percent range relative to total deposits. A more restrictive cap increases the FDIC's expected costs, since a higher risk premium is demanded by uninsured depositors to reflect the larger quantity of uninsured deposits, which in turn implies a higher probability of bank failure at time 1. Moreover, a higher probability of insolvency implies higher expected liquidation costs for the FDIC, given that $\gamma > 0$. On the other hand, a less stringent cap would also lead to higher costs for the FDIC, due to the increased proportion of the deposit base covered by (fixed premium) insurance guarantees.

3A. INCORPORATING MORAL HAZARD

As is well known, levered equityholders can potentially increase the value of their call option on a firm's assets by substituting assets with a high variance of returns. This agency problem is particularly acute for banks with high leverage and low equity capital levels. Indeed, shareholders of technically insolvent banks would have the greatest incentive to engage in this form of asset substitution. In the basic model, in sections 1 and 2, the probability q of the "high state" is fully revealed to both the bank and the insurer. Moral hazard may result if the bank can take actions to affect the return distribution of assets in ways that are contrary to the interests of the insurer. In this specification of moral hazard behavior, the bank is able, at time period 1, to substitute a higher asset risk portfolio for a lower asset risk portfolio without the approval of the insurer. This can be viewed as a relaxation of the assumption that the bank cannot make any further investments at time 1. However, the asset switch does not generate any cash flows at time 1.[31] Thus, under this specification of moral hazard, the size of the bank is assumed fixed, but managers have discretion to change the risk composition of the asset portfolio.

This type of moral hazard behavior is incorporated into the basic model by introducing another (riskier) asset into the bank's period-1 choice set. At period 1, the bank may switch from the original investment yielding cash flow $\tilde{X}$ to an investment yielding cash flow $\tilde{Y}$, where time-2 cash flow has the following two point distribution:

$$\begin{aligned} \tilde{Y} &= H_1 \quad \text{with probability } q_1 \\ &= 0 \quad \text{with probability } 1 - q_1 \end{aligned}$$

such that $H_1 > H$, $q_1 < q$, and $q_1 H_1 < qH$. Since $q_1 H_1 < qH$ only insolvent banks will have any incentive to engage in asset substitution to the detriment of the insurer. The cost to the (risk neutral) insurer of the bank's moral hazard behavior is $qH - q_1 H_1$.[32]

In the absence of either early liquidation costs ($\gamma = 0$) or a merger premium, the insurer always closes insolvent banks at time period 1. We assume that if the insurer closes the bank at time 1, the bank will be unable to substitute assets and moral hazard will not result. If the insurer elects to close the bank at time 1 (before an insolvent bank's asset substitution) and pays off its depositors, its costs (with no early liquidation costs) are

$$Q_C = \max\left[0, D_{i1} - \frac{D_{i1}}{D_1} qH\right].$$

This expression is the same as in the basic model without moral hazard. However, if the insurer allows the bank to remain open during period 1, the insolvent bank will have an opportunity to substitute assets. In this case, the expected loss to the FDIC of keeping the bank open until period 2 is

31. The nominal size of the bank's investment portfolio is still assumed to remain constant between time 0 and time 2. Thus, for instance, as loans are repaid the bank can be viewed as replacing liquidated loans with riskier loans (of equal nominal value).

32. In general, an insurer may be uninformed about the asset substitution and would therefore not know the cost of moral hazard, $qH - q_1 H_1$. However, the insurer would know that insolvent banks have incentives to engage in costly moral hazard. It is assumed that the insurer will set the insured deposit cap, the deposit insurance premium, and closure policy in anticipation of such behavior, prior to the bank's selection of a new asset mix at the end of time period 1. (See Table 1 for the chronology of events.) This costly moral hazard behavior cannot be circumvented by the insurer because the insurer does not set policy instruments continuously, but instead at discrete time intervals.

$$Q'_{NC} = max[-\bar{P}(D_1), D_1 - q_1H_1] \tag{11}$$

in contrast to the FDIC's expected losses, without moral hazard, of

$$Q_{NC} = max[-\bar{P}(D_1), D_1 - qH]$$

where since $q_1H_1 < qH$, $Q'_{NC} > Q_{NC}$. That is, the existence of moral hazard increases the cost to the insurer of forbearance.

In determining whether to close the bank, the insurer must weigh the costs of early liquidation (if $\gamma > 0$) against the moral hazard costs of asset substitution. That is, the introduction of moral hazard increases the cost to the insurer of offering regulatory forbearance (delaying the closure decision), at all levels of early liquidation costs. Comparing the cost of paying off depositors (thereby preventing the bank from switching to riskier assets) against the cost of early closure (thereby incurring early liquidation costs), yields

COROLLARY 2: *The bank is optimally closed at time 1 (therefore avoiding the costs of moral hazard) if and only if*

$$q_1 \leq \underline{q}' = \frac{D_{u1}[D_{u1} + D_{i1}]}{H_1[D_{u1} + \gamma D_{i1}]}.$$

If $\gamma = 0$ $\underline{q}' = D_1/H_1$. If $\gamma = 1$ $\underline{q}' = D_{u1}/H_1$. Since $q_1 < q$, this condition is more likely to hold and therefore the insurer more likely to close the bank at time 1 in the model with moral hazard than in the basic model, for all levels of γ.

LEMMA 4: *If banks can substitute riskier assets for less risky assets, the cost to the insurer of delaying bank closure increases and the insurer's optimal period 1 closure point increases, making early closure more likely.*

In the presence of early liquidation costs it is in the interests of the insurer to keep the bank open for a longer period of time. However, with moral hazard, the insurer optimally closes the bank "sooner" to prevent the bank's shareholders from substituting assets. We now examine the optimal period-1 insured deposit cap and insurance premium pricing policies. The presence of moral hazard leads the insurer to set *higher* insured deposit caps and *lower* deposit insurance premiums at all levels of deposits. That is, with moral hazard, Lemma 2 becomes Lemma 5.

LEMMA 5: *In the presence of both moral hazard and early liquidation costs, the optimal (cost minimizing) settings of insured deposit caps and cash subsidies (or equivalently, net insurance premia) at time 1, are given by*

$$P' = \min[\bar{P}(D_1), q_1H_1 - D_1], \bar{D}'_{i1} = 0, \text{ if } qH \geq D_1; \tag{12a}$$

$$P' \in [0, \bar{P}(D_1)], \bar{D}'_{i1} \in \left[D_1 + P - q_1 H_1, \frac{D_1 + P - q_1 H_1}{1 - q_1} \right] \text{ if } qH < D_1 \, . \tag{12b}$$

The presence of moral hazard induces the insurer to set a lower deposit insurance premium ($P' \leq P$ for all values of D_1). Moreover, if the bank can substitute riskier assets for less risky assets, it is optimal for the insurer to set the insured deposit cap higher than in the basic model ($\bar{D}'_{i1} \geq \bar{D}_{i1}$).

Optimal Time-0 Policies

The insurer will optimally set time-0 policy parameters with the expectation that any insolvent bank will engage in asset substitution at time 1. The deposit insurer may minimize resolution costs and avoid the costs of bank asset substitution by setting a more lenient cap (thereby, expanding insurance coverage) to reduce the likelihood of bank insolvency by lowering the bank's financing costs (that is, limiting the bank's reliance on (costly) uninsured deposits).

PROPOSITION 2: (i) *In the presence of moral hazard with no early liquidation costs* ($\gamma = 0$), *it may be optimal for the insurer to set an insured deposit cap which exceeds the minimum level consistent with the existence of a feasible financing plan for the bank.*

(ii) *In the presence of moral hazard with early liquidation costs* ($\gamma > 0$), *it may be optimal for the insurer to set an insured deposit cap which exceeds the minimum level consistent with the existence of a feasible financing plan for the bank. Indeed, the optimal insured deposit cap will be the highest for this case.*

Intuitively, Proposition 2 results from the fact that insolvent banks have the greatest incentives to exploit asset substitution to the detriment of the insurer. The higher the level of uninsured deposits, ceteris paribus, the greater the probability of bank insolvency, and therefore the greater the likelihood of the insurer's incurring moral hazard costs (as well as early liquidation costs). Consequently, the insurer chooses the least restrictive insured deposit cap when there are both early liquidation costs and moral hazard "costs" present. That is, the presence of moral hazard reinforces the central result of the paper, that is, that imposition of the strictest possible insured deposit cap may increase, rather than decrease, costs to the deposit insurer.

3B. DEPOSIT MARKET STRUCTURE CONSIDERATIONS

In sections 1 and 2, all banks were assumed to be price takers in the markets for insured and uninsured deposits. However, suppose banks compete with nonbank intermediaries for uninsured deposit funds; then banks may face an upward-sloping supply of deposits function. The supply of insured deposits can be assumed to be perfectly elastic at the riskfree rate (assumed to be zero here). If the uninsured deposit supply function is less than perfectly elastic, the cost to the insurer of pursuing a policy that lowers the insured deposit cap increases. That is, it is more costly, ceteris paribus, for the insurer to lower the ceiling on insured deposits since this will induce banks to rely more heavily on relatively costly uninsured deposits, given the bank's size.[33] As the bank's access to the insured deposit pool decreases (the cap is lowered), the promised rate on uninsured deposits must increase to elicit a larger quantity of uninsured deposits to satisfy the financing constraint, thereby increasing the likelihood of bank insolvency. This will increase overall insurer costs in the presence of either early liquidation costs and/or moral hazard costs as discussed above.

If all banks face the same upward-sloping deposit supply function, then the insurer's optimization problem for the entire banking industry would be identical to the individual bank solution. That is, the insurer could minimize total costs by minimizing marginal costs of resolution for each bank, determining an optimal closure role, insured deposit cap, and deposit insurance premium as in section 2 with $r_{ut} = r_{ut}(D_{ut})$ where $\frac{\partial r_{ut}}{\partial D_{ut}} > 0$ for $t = 0, 1$.

Consider a linear form of an uninsured deposit supply function, $r_{u0} = r_0 + \alpha D_{u0}$, where $\alpha > 0$ and r_0 is the risk-adjusted, uninsured deposit rate under the assumption of perfectly elastic uninsured deposit supply. (See the solution to equation (8) in section 2C.) If $\dot{D}_{ut}$ is the time-t ($t = 0, 1$) level of uninsured deposits with perfectly elastic supply, with an upward-sloping supply of uninsured deposits we have $D_{u1} = \dot{D}_{u1} + \alpha D_{u0}^2$.[34]

As in the case of moral hazard, the insurer sets the optimal bank closure point, $\underline{q}$, at a *higher* level. That is, the insurer is less willing to grant forbearance because the FDIC's costs increase, in the event of insolvency, as the uninsured deposit share increases. However, since with inelastic uninsured deposit supply, bank dependence on uninsured deposits will be more likely to induce bank insolvency, the insurer sets the insured deposit cap at a higher level and insurance premiums at a lower level than is the case when banks are faced with a perfectly elastic uninsured deposit supply schedule. Therefore,

PROPOSITION 3: (i) *In the presence of an inelastic supply of uninsured deposits with no early liquidation costs* ($\gamma = 0$), *it may be optimal for the insurer to set an insured deposit cap that exceeds the minimum level consistent with the existence of a feasible financing plan for the bank.*

(ii) *In the presence of an inelastic supply of uninsured deposits with early liquidation costs* ($\gamma > 0$), *it may be optimal for the insurer to set an insured deposit cap which exceeds the minimum level consistent with the existence of a feasible financing plan for the bank. Indeed, the optimal insured deposit cap will be the highest for this case.*

33. Winton (1993) models the loss of risk diversification benefits resulting from the bank's self-imposed restriction on bank size as deposit rates increase.

34. Recall that $\dot{D}_{u1} = \dot{D}_{u0}(1 + r_0)$. Since, $D_{u1} = D_{u0}(1 + r_{u0})$, and $r_{u0} = r_0 + \alpha D_{u0}$, the result follows. We use a linear supply function for simplicity of exposition only, with no loss of generality.

This result parallels the moral hazard result of Proposition 2. Since the deposit insurer's claim on the banking system's assets is a pro rata (equal seniority) share related to uninsured depositors' claims (face value including accrued interest), a relative increase in the uninsured depositors' claims decreases the insurer's proportion and increases the FDIC's failure resolution costs. In the case of moral hazard, the value of uninsured depositors' claims increases because of the higher risk premium required to compensate uninsured depositors for the costs imposed by asset substitution. In the case of imperfectly competitive deposit markets, the increase in the value of uninsured depositors' claims depends on the elasticity of supply of uninsured deposits. In both cases, the insurer can reduce resolution costs by minimizing bank dependence upon uninsured deposits by raising insured deposit caps.

The model can be extended to consider segmented banking markets, that is, all banking firms need not be identical. For instance, the elasticity of supply of uninsured deposits may differ across banks in different market segments. Gennotte (1990) considers the impact of differential bank ability in the management of the bank's loan portfolio. He finds that since inefficient banks outbid efficient banks for deposits, the banking industry will overinvest in risky projects, thereby increasing deposit insurer costs. Indeed, we can relax the restriction of identical banks of fixed size and solve for optimal policies for a total cost-minimizing deposit insurer. When done, the result is to reinforce Propositions 1, 2, and 3. That is, reducing the insured deposit cap may actually increase the insurer's total costs since, to maintain a feasible financing plan, banks in less competitive markets (less elastic supply of deposit functions) must increase their promised uninsured deposit rates by more than banks in more competitive markets. Since insolvent institutions will make up a greater proportion of the banking population, as the rate on uninsured deposits is bid up, the total cost to the insurer increases more rapidly under imperfectly competitive deposit markets than in the perfectly competitive case. Therefore, the cost to the insurer of restrictive caps on insured deposits will be greater under such conditions. Since information is symmetric, the insurer would set the most restrictive insured deposit caps for those banks in the most competitive uninsured deposit markets, thereby exploiting these banks' comparative advantage in acquiring uninsured deposits and lowering overall resolution costs for the entire banking system.[35]

4. CONCLUSION

This paper is among the first to analyze the optimality of imposing caps on the scope of coverage for insured deposits. We show that the optimal setting of caps on insured deposit coverage cannot be analyzed independently from either the FDIC's bank closure policy or the nature of the deposit insurance premium. Specifically, while the existence of flat (non-actuarially fair) premium schedules might seem, at

35. This assumes that the deposit insurer can impose a discriminatory policy in such a way that banks in the most competitive uninsured deposit markets have the lowest insured deposit caps and vice versa. If this policy mix is not feasible, perhaps because of political considerations, then the insurer's optimal policy parameters would be determined by the mix of banks in different markets over the entire banking industry.

first glance, to imply that the expected liability of the insurer is an increasing function of the size of a bank's insured deposits, we show this need *not* be the case when the insurer follows dynamically optimal closure policies and when the early liquidation of a bank's assets entails positive transaction costs. Indeed, under certain conditions, the FDIC's failure resolution cost will be minimized by allowing the bank to collect insured deposits in an amount exceeding the minimum level consistent with the existence of a feasible financing plan for the bank. Moreover, the optimal (cost-minimizing) insured deposit cap or ceiling was found to be even higher in the presence of either moral hazard or an inelastic supply of deposits. That is, reliance on uninsured deposits increases the likelihood of bank insolvency, thereby imposing early liquidation costs and/or asset substitution moral hazard costs on the insurer. Our results suggest that, given the potential ease with which regulators could, at a policy level, implement and monitor caps on insured deposits, such a policy measure could prove to be a useful weapon in restructuring the insurance deposit contract toward reducing the FDIC's expected failure resolution costs. However, caps on insured deposit coverage cannot be evaluated separately from the broader context of the insurer's optimal cash subsidy, premium setting, forbearance, and closure policies.

APPENDIX

PROOF OF LEMMA 1: For uninsured depositors to earn a competitive expected return, their time-2 payoff in the "high state" must be equal to D_{u1}/q. This payoff is equal to $D_{u1}(1 + r_1)$ if $H \geq D_{i1} + D_{u1}(1 + r_1)$ and to $\dfrac{HD_{u1}(1 + r_1)}{D_{i1} + D_{u1}(1 + r_1)}$ otherwise. Thus,[36] (2) has a solution r_1 if and only if $D_{u1} < qH$, where

$$1 + r_1 = \frac{1}{q} \qquad \text{if } D_{u1} \leq q[H - D_{i1}];$$

$$1 + r_1 = \frac{D_{i1}}{qH - D_{u1}} \qquad \text{if } qH > D_{u1} \geq q[H - D_{i1}] \,.$$

The result stated in the lemma follows trivially. QED.

PROOF OF LEMMA 2: Given the premium P assessed at time 1, the insurer's cost is a nondecreasing function of $\bar{D}_{i1}$. See equation (4). Indeed,

$$\bar{D}_{i1} < \frac{A_1 - qH}{1 - q} \Rightarrow Q_{NC} = D_1 - qH \,;$$

$$\bar{D}_{i1} \geq \frac{A_1 - qH}{1 - q} \Rightarrow Q_{NC} = -P + (1 - q)\bar{D}_{i1} \,.$$

36. If $D_{u1} \leq q((1 - \gamma)H - D_{i1})$, $1 + r_1 = 1/q$, trivially. If $D_{u1} > q((1 - \gamma)H - D_{i1})$, for all r_1, the payoff to uninsured depositors in the high state is equal to $\dfrac{(1 - \gamma)HD_{u1}(1 + r_1)}{D_{i1} + D_{u1}(1 + r_1)}$. Setting this payoff equal to D_{u1}/q yields the desired result.

The insurer's expected cost net of the time-1 premium is in fact independent of the insured deposit cap for $\bar{D}_{i1} < (A_1 - qH)/(1 - q)$. Given a net insurance premium equal to P, the optimal setting of the deposit cap $\bar{D}_{i1}$ and the resulting net expected cost Q_{NC} to the insurer if the bank is kept in operation at time 1 are given by

$$\bar{D}_{i1} = 0, \qquad Q_{NC} = -P \text{ if } D_1 + P - qH \leq 0\,;$$

$$\bar{D}_{i1} \in \left[D_1 + P - qH, \frac{D_1 + p - qH}{1 - q}\right], Q_{NC} = D_1 - qH, \text{ otherwise.}$$

The resulting cost function is also a nonincreasing function of P. The optimal value of the premium and the insurer's net cost are thus given by

$$P = \bar{P}(D_1), \qquad Q_{NC} = -\bar{P}(D_1) \qquad \textit{if } \bar{P}(D - 1) \leq qH - D_1\,;$$

$$P \in [qH - D_1, \bar{P}(D_1)], \qquad Q_{NC} = D_1 - qH, \textit{ otherwise.}$$

Substituting this optimal premium policy into the optimal deposit constraint policy yields Lemma 2. QED.

PROOF OF LEMMA 3:

LEMMA: $\dfrac{\partial[r_0 D_{u0}]}{\partial D_{u0}} \geq 0, > 0$ IF $\underline{q} > \inf(\text{support of } F)$.

PROOF: If $\underline{q} \leq$ inf (support of F), $r_0 = 0$. Suppose now that $\underline{q} >$ inf (support of F). Then $X \equiv D_{u0} r_0$ satisfies

$$G(D_{u0}, X) \equiv -D_{u0} + (1 - F(\underline{q})(D_{u0} + X) + H\,\frac{D_{u0} + X}{A_0 + X}\int_0^{\underline{q}} q dF(q) \equiv 0$$

where $\underline{q} \equiv [A_0 + X]/H$. We have

$$\frac{\partial G}{\partial D_{u0}} \equiv -1 + (1 - F(\underline{q})) + \frac{H}{A_0 + X}\int_0^{\underline{q}} q dF(q) < -F(\underline{q}) + F(\underline{q}) = 0$$

and

$$\frac{\partial G}{\partial X} = 1 - F(\underline{q}) - f(\underline{q})\,\frac{D_{u0} + X}{H} + H\,\frac{A_0 - D_{u0}}{[A_0 + X]^2}\int_0^{\underline{q}} \mathrm{q dF}(q)$$

$$+ H\,\frac{D_{u0} + X}{A_0 + X}\,\underline{q} f(\underline{q})\,\frac{1}{H}$$

$$= 1 - F(\underline{q}) + H\,\frac{A_0 - D_{u0}}{[A_0 + X]^2}\int_0^{\underline{q}} q dF(q) > 0\,.$$

The result thus follows from the Implicit Function Theorem.

PROOF OF LEMMA 3: For $D_{u0} \leq \hat{D}_{u0}$, letting $X \equiv D_{u0}r_0$ as above, $\frac{\partial q}{\partial D_{u0}}$ is equal to

$$H^{-1}[D_{u0}(1 + r_0) + \gamma(A_0 - D_{u0})]^{-2}$$

times

$$\left(\left[1 + \frac{\partial X}{\partial D_{u0}}\right][A_0 + X] + (D_{u0} + X)\frac{\partial X}{\partial D_{u0}}\right)[D_{u0}(1 - \gamma) + X + \gamma A_0]$$

$$-\left[1 - \gamma + \frac{\partial X}{\partial D_{u0}}\right](A_0 + X)(D_{u0} + X) =$$

$$\left[1 - \gamma + \frac{\partial X}{\partial D_{u0}}\right](A_0 + X)\gamma(A_0 - D_{u0})$$

$$+\left[\gamma(A_0 + X) + (D_{u0} + X)\frac{\partial X}{\partial D_{u0}}\right][D_{u0} + X + \gamma(A_0 - D_{u0})] .$$

Hence $\partial q/\partial D_{u0} > 0$. QED.

PROOF OF LEMMA 4: $q' > q$ for all levels of γ since $Q'_{NC} > Q_{NC}$. QED

PROOF OF LEMMA 5: If $D_1 \leq q_1H_1 < qH$, then with asset substitution,

$$P' = min[\bar{P}(D_1), q_1H_1 - D_1]$$

is less than $P = \min[\bar{P}(D_1), qH - D_1]$, without moral hazard. Moreover, $\bar{D}'_{i1} = 0$.

If $qH \geq D_1 > q_1H_1$, then with asset substitution,

$$P' \in [0, \bar{P}(D_1)]$$

is less than $P = \min[\bar{P}(D_1), qH - D_1]$, without moral hazard. Moreover,

$$\bar{D}'_{i1} \in \left[D_1 + P - q_1H_1, \frac{D_1 + P - q_1H_1}{1 - q_1}\right]$$

is greater than $\bar{D}_{i1} = 0$, without moral hazard.

If $q_1H_1 < qH < D_1$, then in both models (with and without asset substitution),

$$P = P' \in [0, \bar{P}(D_1)],$$

and

$$\bar{D}'_{i1} \in \left[D_1 + P - q_1H_1, \frac{D_1 + P - q_1H_1}{1 - q_1}\right]$$

exceeds $\bar{D}_{i1} \in \left[D_1 + P - qH, \frac{D_1 + P - qH}{1 - Q} \right]$ without moral hazard. Thus, for all values of q, D, H, $P' \leq P$ and $\bar{D}'_{i1} \geq \bar{D}_{i1}$. QED.

PROOF OF PROPOSITION 2: Using Lemma 4, $\underline{q}' > \underline{q}$. That is, for all values of γ, the insurer is "more likely" to close the bank if moral hazard is present. Thus, the insurer's expected cost, with asset substitutability and early liquidation costs, is

$$Q'_0 = \int_{\underline{q}}^{1} (q_1 H_1 - D_1 - \bar{P}) dF_1(q_1) + \gamma H \int_0^{\underline{q}'} q dF(q) - H_1 E(q_1) + A_0 \, .$$

The first term is the value of equity's residual claim on the bank's assets, if the bank remains solvent. With asset substitutability, this term is reduced since $q_1 H_1 < qH$ and $\underline{q}' > \underline{q}$. The second term is the insurer's expected loss upon closure given F_1, the probability distribution of returns on $\tilde{Y}$. This is the same as in the basic model without moral hazard since if the bank is closed at time period 1, there is no opportunity for the bank's shareholders to substitute assets. However, time-1 closure is more likely to take place when moral hazard is present. The last term, ($A_0 - HE(q_1)$ equal to the net present value of the bank's asset portfolio), is reduced by the presence of moral hazard since $E_1(q_1) < E(q)$. Thus, the insurer's costs are minimized if it speeds up the bank closure decision.

Differentiating yields

$$\frac{\partial Q'_0}{\partial D_{u0}} = -(1 - F_1(\bar{q}_1)) \left[\frac{\partial [D_{u0} r_0(D_{u0})]}{\partial D_{u0}} + \frac{\partial \bar{P}'(D_1)}{\partial D_{u0}} \right] + \gamma H \frac{\partial \underline{q}'}{\partial D_{u0}} \underline{q}' f(\underline{q}') \, . \tag{10'}$$

Since the first term in equation (10′) measures the direct effect of increases in uninsured deposits, D_{u0}, on insurer resolution costs, it is always negative. That is, increases in insured deposits (decreases in uninsured deposits) directly increase insurer resolution costs. Since $F_1(\bar{q}_1) > F(\bar{q})$ the absolute size of the direct effect (first term) increases with the introduction of moral hazard.

The second term in equation (10′) measures the indirect effect of increases in uninsured deposits on insurer resolution costs, that is, the impact on bank solvency. Since uninsured deposits are more costly than are insured deposits, an increase in uninsured deposits (lowering of the insured deposit cap) increases the probability of bank insolvency resulting in moral hazard behavior that is costly to the deposit insurer. With the presence of moral hazard, this term increases ($\underline{q}' > \underline{q}$). The increase in the (positive) second term makes it more likely for $\frac{\partial Q'_0}{\partial D_{u0}}$ to be locally positive, for any value of γ, when moral hazard is introduced. QED.

PROOF OF PROPOSITION 3: The proof parallels that of Proposition 2 where the lower the insured deposit cap, the greater the likelihood of bank insolvency ($F(\bar{q})$ increases) as the cost of bank financing increases. With an inelastic supply of uninsured deposits, the absolute value of the first term in equation (10), $(1 - F(\bar{q}))$ $\frac{\partial D_{u0} r_0(D_{u0})}{\partial D_{u0}}$ increases. Using the example of the linear supply function, $\frac{\partial D_{u0} r_{u0}}{\partial D_{u0}}$ $= r_0 + \alpha > \frac{\partial \dot{D}_{u0} \dot{r}_0}{\partial \dot{D}_{u0}} = r_0 \geq 0$, for the perfectly elastic demand in Lemma 3. However, since the introduction of an inelastic uninsured deposit supply increases $\underline{q}$, the (positive) second term in equation (10) increases, thereby making it more likely for $\frac{\partial Q_0}{\partial D_{u0}}$ to be locally positive, for any value of γ, when uninsured deposits are inelastically supplied. QED

LITERATURE CITED

Acharya, Sankar, and Jean-Francois Dreyfus. "Optimal Bank Reorganization Policies and the Pricing of Federal Deposit Insurance." *Journal of Finance* 34 (1989), 1313–33.

Allen, Linda, and Anthony Saunders. "Forbearance and Valuation of Deposit Insurance as a Callable Put." *Journal of Banking and Finance* 17 (1993), 629–43.

Avery, Robert, Timothy Belton, and Michael Goldberg. "Market Discipline in Regulating Bank Risk: New Evidence from Capital Markets." *Journal of Money, Credit, and Banking* 20 (1988), 597–610.

Bovenzi, John, and Maureen Muldoon. "Failure-Resolution Methods and Policy Considerations." *FDIC Banking Review* 3 (Fall 1990), 1–11.

Diamond, Douglas, and Paul Dybvig. "Bank Runs, Deposit Insurance, and Liquidity." *Journal of Political Economy* 91 (1983), 401–19.

Ellis, D. M., and Mark Flannery. "Does the Debt Market Assess Large Banks' Risk? Time Series Evidence from Money Center CDs." University of North Carolina and University of Florida Working Papers, 1989.

Federal Deposit Insurance Corporation. "Deposit Insurance for the Nineties: Meeting the Challenge." 1989.

Flannery, Mark. "Capital Regulation and Insured Banks' Choice of Individual Loan Default Risks." *Journal of Monetary Economics* 24 (1989), 235–58.

Fraust, B. "Broker Convicted in Linked-Finance Scheme." *American Banker* (February 18, 1987), 14.

Furlong, Frederick. "A View on Deposit Insurance Coverage." *Federal Reserve Bank of San Francisco Economic Review* 2 (Spring 1984), 31–38.

General Accounting Office. *Failed Banks: FDIC's Asset Liquidation Operations.* Washington, D.C. (September 1988), Doc. #GAO/GGD-88-132.

Gennotte, Gerard. "Deposit Insurance and Bank Competition." University of California at Berkeley Working Paper, August 1990.

Kane, Edward. *The Gathering Crisis in Federal Deposit Insurance.* Cambridge: MIT Press, 1985.

Kim, Daesik, and Anthony Santomero. "Risk in Banking and Capital Regulation." *Journal of Finance* 43 (1988), 1219–33.

Merton, Robert. "An Analytic Derivation of the Cost of Deposit Insurance and Loan Guarantees." *Journal of Banking and Finance* 1 (1977), 3–11.

______. "On the Cost of Deposit Insurance When There Are Surveillance Costs." *Journal of Business* 51 (1978), 439–52.

Pennacchi, George. "Loan Sales and the Cost of Bank Capital." *Journal of Finance* 43 (1988), 375–96.

Pyle, David. "Pricing Deposit Insurance: The Effects of Mismeasurement." University of California Berkeley Working Paper, 1983.

Ronn, Ehud, and Avinash Verma. "Pricing Risk-Adjusted Deposit Insurance: An Option-Based Model." *Journal of Finance* 41 (September 1986), 871–95.

Winton, A. "Banks as Delegated Monitors: Industrial Structure in a Finite Economy." Department of Finance Working paper no. 124, Northwestern University, January 1993.

A Theory of Bank Regulation and Management Compensation

Kose John
New York University

Anthony Saunders
New York University

Lemma W. Senbet
University of Maryland

We show that concentrating bank regulation on bank capital ratios may be ineffective in controlling risk taking. We propose, instead, a more direct mechanism of influencing bank risk-taking incentives, in which the FDIC insurance premium scheme incorporates incentive features of top-management compensation. With this scheme, we show that bank owners choose an optimal management compensation structure that induces first-best value-maximizing investment choices by a bank's management. We explicitly characterize the parameters of the optimal management compensation structure and the fairly priced FDIC insurance premium in the presence of a single or multiple sources of agency problems.

Capital requirements and mandatory restrictions on asset choice have been central features of recent U.S. bank regulation. For example, a central feature of the FDIC Improvement Act (FDICIA), passed in 1991, is a system of capital-based regulations based on prompt corrective action (PCA). In this regulatory framework five capital zones for banks are specified ranging from well capitalized to critically undercapitalized. Of importance, as a bank's capital adequacy ratio declines—moving from well capitalized to undercapitalized—regulators are required to take (or consider) a number of *mandatory* and *discretionary* actions restricting the asset and liability activities of weakly capitalized banks as well as imposing constraints on their payment of fees, dividends, and management compensation.

Kose John acknowledges support from a Bank and Financial Analysts Faculty Fellowship. We are grateful for helpful comments from David Beim, Allen Berger, Rebecca Demsetz, Jaime Dermody, Jean Helwege, Robert Hauswald, Teresa John, Ed Kane, Rita Maldonado-Bear, Marti Subrahmanyam, David Yermack and participants in the Wharton Financial Institutions Center Conference, and seminars at Columbia University, Federal Reserve Bank of New York, Georgetown University, International Monetary Fund, ESSEC, New York University, Rutgers University, University of Utah, Kansas State University, and the London School of Economics. We are also grateful to Ravi Jaganathan (the editor) and anonymous referees of this journal. An earlier version of this article was presented at the American Finance Association meetings.
Address correspondence to Kose John, Stern School of Business, New York University, Finance Department, 44 West 4th St. Suite 9-190, New York, NY 10012, or e-mail: kjohn@stern.nyu.edu.

The Review of Financial Studies Spring 2000 Vol. 13, No. 1, pp. 95–125

The Review of Financial Studies / v 13 n 1 2000

In this article we examine the incentive structure underlying the existing PCA regime—especially the potential role of capital rules, asset restrictions, and mandatory interventions by regulators in controlling the risk-shifting incentives of banks. We argue that bank regulation, through capital requirements and asset restrictions, has limited effectiveness, given the high leverage ratios of banks. Instead, we propose a more direct and effective mechanism for curbing risk-shifting incentives through exploiting the incentive features inherent in bank management compensation structures. Specifically we propose an actuarially fair, revenue-neutral scheme for pricing FDIC insurance by explicitly incorporating features of a bank's management compensation schedule in the risk-based pricing of deposit insurance. Such a pricing scheme is shown to provide bank owners with appropriate incentives to put in place optimal management compensation structures which induce the first-best, or most efficient, bank investment policies. In fact, for any level of deposit financing (or leverage) for a bank, we can characterize the optimal management compensation structure that bank owners will choose (in their own self-interest) as well as the appropriate actuarially fair revenue-neutral FDIC insurance premium. In particular, the investment policy implemented by a bank is shown to be Pareto optimal.

As is well known, stockholders of limited-liability banks financed by deposits (whether insured or uninsured) have incentives to take risk beyond that which is optimal for an "all equity" bank [see, e.g., John, John, and Senbet (1991)]. This risk-shifting behavior by banks has been widely viewed as a major culprit in the recent S & L crisis. Capital regulation, prompt corrective action, asset restrictions, and FDIC premiums—based on the level of capitalization and supervisory characterization (CAMEL) of bank risk—have been major policy initiatives by regulators since the 1991 passage of the FDICIA. In the first part of the article we examine the risk-shifting incentives of banks in a simple model of asset choice in the presence of moral hazard and incomplete contracting. We then analyze the effectiveness of FDICIA-type capital regulations and asset choice restrictions in that framework.

Our analysis shows several limitations of capital and asset choice regulation. First, capital regulation still leaves a high degree of risk-shifting incentives even for the best-capitalized banks (given the high leverage of banking firms). Second, for any level of bank capitalization, the degree of risk-shifting incentives critically depends on the characteristics of its investment opportunity set (i.e., the asset technology for risk taking available to the bank). Third, mandatory asset restrictions can result in a significant degree of investment inefficiency.

Our analysis also has good news and bad news for the FDICIA provisions regarding the risk-based pricing or premium setting of FDIC insurance. The good news is that there is a qualitative parallel between

A Theory of Bank Regulation and Management Compensation

the 1993 implementation of FDIC insurance premia that utilizes a bank's capital ratio and supervisory classifications, on the one hand,[1] and our theoretical result which links fair insurance premia to leverage and the observable parameters of a bank's asset investment schedule. The bad news is that mandatory restrictions on asset choice, which induce a common type of risk taking for banks, are distortionary from an investment efficiency point of view. Further, we show that capital regulation may only have limited effectiveness in curbing risk-shifting incentives. Indeed, it is particularly ineffective for certain types of investment schedules (and wholesale loan markets) facing the largest banks.

The principal message of our paper is to argue for a prominent role for managerial compensation structures in bank regulation.[2] Unlike capital and asset regulations, which have at best *indirect* effects on managerial incentives and thus on managerial decisions, altering top-management compensation is a direct and effective way of influencing managerial return and risk-taking incentives. Indeed, not only is management compensation readily observable by regulators, but recent empirical studies by Houston and James (1993) and Saunders, Strock, and Travlos (SST) (1990), Evans, Noe, and Thorton (1997), and Knopf and Teall (1996) have found that managerial compensation—salary and bonus in the case of Houston and James and managerial equity stakes in the case of SST—are significantly correlated with bank returns and risk.

Further, Esty (1998) analyzes how liability rules and, therefore, the shape of the equity holders' payoff function affects incentives for risk-taking among banks. Studying a sample of national and state banks from 1863 to 1935 operating under a range of differing liability rules, Esty documents that risk taking is negatively correlated with the severity of stockholders' liability (i.e., bank stockholders subject to stricter liability exhibit less risk). There is also evidence consistent with managerial contracts in place influencing bank managerial behavior toward risk taking in the 1980s [see Barth, Bartholomew, and Labich (1990), and Cole, McKenzie, and White (1990)].

[1] The FDICIA required risk-based premiums to be fully implemented by 1994. The 1993–1995 premium structure allowed for a 9 basis point spread in premiums between the best and worst banks. The premiums were set according to a bank's capital ratio and supervisory rating. Since 1996, the premiums for the best banks have been reduced to zero in response to falling bank failure rates and the build up of reserves at the FDIC to over 1.25% of bank deposits.

[2] The FDICIA of 1991 required regulators to restrict the compensation of managers in significantly undercapitalized banks. This implied a systematic regulation of compensation structures in undercapitalized banks. In 1992 Congress amended this regulation, allowing bankers to determine their own compensation structures, but giving regulators the *discretion* to impose restrictions on undercapitalized banks on a bank-by-bank basis [see Kane (1986)].

In an environment of moral hazard, investment-risk choices made by management are not readily observable by depositors and regulators, and hence are not contractible. However, for a given compensation structure in place, the risk choices which will be made by managers, in their own "self-interest," can be correctly anticipated by outsiders, such as depositors and regulators. This anticipated risk taking could be incorporated in pricing all claims issued by the bank, including the pricing of deposit insurance. Therefore, for any level of bank capitalization, the incentive features in a bank's top-management compensation structure should be crucial inputs into deposit insurance pricing and other aspects of bank regulation. Thus even though the setting may be one of moral hazard, and investment choices are unobservable, stockholders can be viewed as effectively precommitting to specific risk choices through the observable parameters of the compensation structure they put in place. Thus incorporating the parameters of the compensation structure, as a determinant of FDIC insurance premia, prices the risk choices that will optimally be made by bank management.

Given such an FDIC pricing mechanism, which we characterize explicitly as a function of incentive parameters in the management compensation structure, we show that bank insiders (acting on behalf of the stockholders) would directly choose—and put in place—an optimal management compensation structure. The compensation structure is optimal in that it would induce management to undertake Pareto-optimal (value-maximizing) investment policies, *with no risk shifting.* That is, stockholders use the management's compensation structure to precommit to the implementation of an optimal investment policy.[3] We show that for any level of deposits (or debt) such an optimal compensation scheme can be structured, and the associated FDIC premium can be characterized, in terms of the level of bank capitalization and the features of the bank's compensation structure. Moreover, the resulting investment policy is shown to be socially optimal. It should also be pointed out that the proposed scheme not only achieves an optimal bank investment policy and fair (revenue-neutral) pricing of FDIC insurance, but does so for any level of depository financing. This feature of the proposed scheme is important in that a socially optimal investment policy can be induced while simultaneously maintaining leverage

[3] It would be in the best interest of the stockholders to adopt *ex ante* compensation contracts which will induce the self-interested manager to implement *ex post* the value maximizing investment policy. Given that all other claims, such as deposits and insurance guarantees, are properly priced, fully anticipating this induced investment policy, equity holders cannot do better choosing any other compensation contract. The value decline resulting from the investment policy induced by any alternative (suboptimal) contract would thus be reflected in lower equity value and thus be borne by the equity holders. Hence the equity holders (the residual claim holders) will find it in their best interest to put in place contracts which provide incentives for managers to implement the investment policy which maximizes firm value [see, e.g., Barnea, Haugen, and Senbet (1985)].

levels which optimize an alternative objective that the social planner may have (e.g., provision of liquidity in the economy).

The rest of the article is organized as follows: Section 1 characterizes a bank's risk-shifting incentives and examines the efficiency of capital requirements and mandatory restrictions on asset choice. Section 2 provides a generalized analysis which incorporates the crucial role of a bank's management compensation structure on its asset choice and risk taking. Section 3 is a summary and conclusions.

1. Capital Regulation and Risk-Shifting Incentives

In this section we study the effectiveness of capital adequacy requirements and the risk-shifting incentives of a bank as a function of its asset or investment opportunity set. The model developed in this section also provides the setting for an analysis of the potential role of bank management compensation structures in bank regulation (and the setting of FDIC insurance premia) in Section 2.

We show that the effectiveness of capital regulation depends on the shape of the investment schedule facing a bank. Different investment schedules imply different optimal levels of bank risk taking, in the sense of the efficient allocation of bank funds. Mandatory provisions that attempt to force banks into adopting a common pool or level of risk induce allocational inefficiencies. Likewise, deposit insurance premia should, at a minimum, recognize differences in bank investment schedules as well as bank leverage.

In a market with a large supply of risky (near) zero net present value (NPV) investments (such as those in the capital markets or wholesale loan markets), the investment schedule is such that even at high levels of capitalization there are incentives for a high degree of risk shifting. The current, post-FDICIA, risk-based FDIC deposit insurance premium schedule does not seem to reflect the existence of such an investment opportunity set. Even for high degrees of capitalization, large premiums may be required for some banks (e.g., wholesale money center banks) to take into account risk shifting to very high levels under such investment opportunity sets.[4]

1.1 An analytical framework

A detailed model of the asset-risk choices made by a bank under moral hazard and incomplete contracting is developed here.[5] The model is

[4] It is not unreasonable to expect that different banks face different investment opportunity sets. For example, JP Morgan as a wholesale bank will tend to face a different investment opportunity set than more retail-oriented banks such as BankAmerica and Citigroup.

[5] In the structure of its basic setup, the model is similar to that in Section 2 of John, John, and Senbet (1991). The reader may refer to that article for additional details.

designed to capture the key regulatory issues in a simple framework. This model serves as the analytical framework to study the relative effectiveness of capital regulation and for the development of the deposit insurance pricing mechanism based on management incentive structures proposed in Section 3.

We begin with a representative depository institution (bank) under moral hazard and incomplete contracting. Consider a three-date, two-period model. At $t = 0$, the bank collects deposits and engages in residual financing through equity subject to existing regulatory constraints. Deposits are insured by a government agency (the FDIC) and the bank pays the relevant insurance premium π. All associated contracts are written and "priced" at $t = 0$, given the information available at $t = 0$ and admissible contracting opportunities. The prices of the bank's financial claims (interest rates on deposits and the price of equity) are determined in a rational expectations manner.

At $t = 1$, investment opportunities appear. This represents the possible loans (asset choices) that the bank can make. For simplicity we assume that these investment opportunities are of two types: (1) safe investments which are loan opportunities (to which the bank has monopoly access) with zero risk and nonnegative NPV, and (2) a choice from a menu of possible risky investments (loans) which are indexed by a parameter q. The investment required at $t = 1$ is an amount I. The returns from the risky loan-backed projects are high or low (H dollars or L dollars, respectively), with $H > I > L > 0$, where q is the probability of the high outcome H, and $(1 - q)$ the probability of the low outcome, L. The bank's insiders observe the parameter q at $t = 1$ before they choose between the riskless loan and risky loans. The value of the parameter q is not observed by outsiders—that is, by either depositors or regulators (government). This precludes any contracting contingent on the value of the parameter q. However, all the relevant parties know that q is distributed uniformly over the interval [0,1]. This modeling device captures the intuition that, given the level of monitoring undertaken by regulators and outside investors, the managers/owners of the bank have additional (inside) information about the prospects of the loan (captured in q).[6] Therefore bank insiders have discretion in their choice of investment risk.

The amount $(I + \pi)$ needed by the bank for investment and payment of the FDIC premium is raised at $t = 0$, in the form of deposits (debt) and equity. For simplicity, we assume that the deposits are in the form of pure discount debt of promised payment F due at $t = 2$. The

[6] This informational friction gives rise to noncontractability of specific levels of q, hence of investment risk choices. This results in the well-know risk-shifting incentives in the presence of risky debt. This modeling device is consistent with the literature on agency costs of debt.

depositors pay an amount B at $t = 0$ into the bank, where B represents the rational expectations price of the guaranteed promised payment F, incorporating the rationally anticipated loan choices to be made by the bank. In our framework, π can also be determined in a rational expectations manner as the actuarially fair value of the deposit insurance premium for the bank. However, the regulator may choose to charge an insurance premium that is less than actuarially fair (e.g., fixed) as a means of inducing a bank to expand its deposit base. This may serve the regulator's social objectives better (e.g., achieve a greater supply of liquidity to the economy).

At $t = 2$, loans mature and the proceeds are collected. Let T denote this terminal cash flow, which is equal to I if the riskless investment was chosen at $t = 1$, or equal to H or L depending on the outcome from the risky investment if that choice was made at $t = 1$. The firm pays the depositors $min(F, T)$ and the deposit insurance agency (FDIC) honors its guarantee by paying the depositors $max(0, F - T)$. Depositors are thus paid off fully if their deposits are fully insured for failure. We assume that all deposits are insured.

In this section, we assume that management's compensation in place completely aligns their incentives with those of the shareholders. In Section 3 we will consider the choice of managerial compensation structures and their effect on risk choices and risk-shifting incentives, and how they should affect FDIC insurance premiums and regulatory actions. We do this through the following full-fledged, more elaborate, regulatory game: at $t = 0$ the regulator announces the "rules of the game" for the pricing of deposit insurance premium, π, and the bank stockholders optimally choose the structure of the management compensation scheme to be put in place also at $t = 0$. (Two classes of regulatory regimes for determining π, differentiated by whether or not the parameters of managerial compensation are incorporated in determining π, are studied along with the corresponding choice of managerial compensation structures). At $t = 1$, given the compensation structure in place, the manager observes the parameter q and chooses between safe loans and the risky loans. As in the model of Section 2, all claims and contracts are settled at $t = 2$.

We abstract from discounting in all time periods by assuming that the riskless rate of interest is zero and we assume universal risk-neutrality.

1.2 Bank's optimal investment policy

Definition 1. *For a given cutoff value of $q^c, 0 \leq q^c \leq 1$, an investment policy of investing in the risky asset (loan) for $q \geq q^c$ and in the riskless asset (loan) for $q < q^c$ will be denoted as an investment policy $[q^c]$.*

The Review of Financial Studies / v 13 n 1 2000

Lemma 1. *Given that q is uniformly distributed over* [0,1], *an investment policy* $[\tilde{q}]$ *produces the distribution of terminal cash flow as follows: H with a probability* $\frac{1}{2}[1-\tilde{q}^2]$, *I with a probability* $\tilde{q}$, *and L with a probability* $\frac{1}{2}[1-\tilde{q}]^2$.

Proof. Straightforward computation yields the probabilities of the outcomes L, H, and I as stated. ■

The value of the terminal cash flows resulting from an investment policy $[\tilde{q}]$ denoted $V(\tilde{q})$ can easily be specified:

$$V(\tilde{q}) = \tilde{q}I + \frac{L}{2}[1-\tilde{q}]^2 + \frac{H}{2}[1-\tilde{q}^2]. \tag{1}$$

The standard deviation (risk) of the terminal cash flows, $\sigma(\tilde{q})$ can also be specified in the obvious manner. It is easily seen that as $\tilde{q}$ varies from 1 to 0, $\sigma(\tilde{q})$ varies from 0 to $\left(\frac{H-L}{2}\right)^2$. This relationship between $\tilde{q}$ and $\sigma(\tilde{q})$ is strictly monotonic (decreasing), and hence one-to-one. $V(\tilde{q})$ also varies with $\tilde{q} \in [0,1]$. The Pareto-optimal investment policy $[\hat{q}]$ which maximizes $V(\tilde{q})$ is given by

$$\hat{q} = \frac{I-L}{H-L}, \tag{2}$$

and the resulting value $V(\hat{q})$ can be specified as follows:

$$V(\hat{q}) = \hat{q}I + \frac{L}{2}[1-\hat{q}]^2 + \frac{H}{2}[1-\hat{q}^2]. \tag{3}$$

When $\tilde{q}$ is varied from 1 to 0, the value of terminal cash flows increases from I to $V(\hat{q})$ and then decreases to $(H+L)/2$. We can now combine the behavior of the standard deviation $\sigma(\tilde{q})$ and mean $V(\tilde{q})$ achievable under different investment policies $[\tilde{q}]$ to obtain the following pattern: as $\tilde{q}$ varies from 1 to 0, the investment policy becomes increasingly riskier [i.e., $\sigma(\tilde{q})$ increases monotonically], but the mean value first increases [from I to $V(\hat{q})$], attains a maximum at $\hat{q}$, and then decreases to $(H+L)/2$. As risk $\sigma(\tilde{q})$ increases from 0 to $\sigma(\hat{q})$, the mean increases first from I to $V(\hat{q})$, and then for further increases in risk [from $\sigma(\hat{q})$ to $\left(\frac{H-L}{2}\right)^2$], the value declines from $V(\hat{q})$ to $\frac{(H+L)}{2}$.

Equation (3) characterizes $V(\hat{q})$, the value which could have been achieved if q were perfectly observed by all parties (including investors and regulators) and if a complete set of enforceable contracts specifying the bank's investment policy could have been written. In other words, $V(\hat{q})$ is the highest value achievable in a full-information scenario with complete contracting. Thus the investment policy $[\hat{q}]$ and the resulting

A Theory of Bank Regulation and Management Compensation

value, $V(\hat{q})$, from useful benchmarks to measure the distortions caused by risk-shifting incentives due to financing with deposits (debt).[7]

1.3 An analysis of capital regulation

We now consider the incentive effects of a bank's financial structure on its investment incentives. Consider a bank with an arbitrary level of equity capitalization and corresponding level of deposit claims of promised payment F. Clearly F and a bank's equity capital ratio are inversely related. That is, as F increases the proportion of funds provided by equity holders decreases. Henceforth, high levels of F parametrize correspondingly low levels of bank capital adequacy (i.e., low capital-asset ratios).

When the level of depository financing is high enough, such that the bank's cash flows from investment are insufficient to repay the depositors in some state of the world (i.e., $L < F$), then bank management (acting on behalf of shareholders) will implement an investment policy riskier than $[\hat{q}]$. These risk-shifting incentives, induced by outstanding debt, are well known. For completeness we will characterize these incentives explicitly in Proposition 1 as a basis for capital regulation.

Proposition 1 (Risk Shifting). *For a level of deposits of promised payment* $F \geq 0$, *the bank manager will implement an investment policy* $[q(F)]$ *where* $q(F)$ *is given in Equation* (4):

$$\begin{aligned} q(F) &= \hat{q} \quad when \quad F \leq L \\ &= \frac{(I-F)}{(H-F)} \quad when \quad L < F < I \\ &= 0 \quad when \quad F \geq I. \end{aligned} \tag{4}$$

Proof. Follows from John, John, and Senbet (1991), Proposition 1.

[7] The investment technology used in this article is commonly used to study risk shifting in agency models. Here increases in risk are accompanied by declines in NPV. Under an alternative technology of mean (value) preserving spread, there is no decline in value as risk increases. In our technology, risk-shifting incentives induced by risky debt lead to agency costs in the form of value loss, whereas in the alternative technology, risky debt induces risk-shifting incentives which are not accompanied by value loss, and hence no agency costs obtain. We argue that the technology of this article is appropriate for modeling risk shifting in the banking context. Even when banks appear to have access to a menu of investment opportunities, which may allow for increases in risk without declines in value, our technology recognizes the incentive that bank managers have to continue to move into high-risk projects despite their negative NPVs. Our characterization is also supported by some recently documented evidence. Money center and wholesale banks may face a linear gross revenue function (i.e., they can lend at rates close to LIBOR) but their cost functions appear to be nonlinear. Specifically, the empirical evidence suggests that there are "diseconomies of superscale" beyond $25 billion in assets [see, e.g., Allen and Rai (1993) and Berger and Mester (1997)]. This is consistent with the nonlinear investment opportunity set, and with decreasing returns to scale considered in this article. There is also evidence that real estate investments by both Japanese and U.S. banks in the late 1980s and early 1990s were characterized by negative returns [see, e.g., Mei and Saunders (1997)].

The Review of Financial Studies/v 13 n 1 2000

Remark. For any value of deposits such that $F > L$ (i.e., in some states the bank cannot honor the promise to depositors from the cash flows of its investments), the bank manager implements an investment policy $[q(F)]$ which is suboptimal [i.e., $V(q(F)) < V(\hat{q})$] and riskier than the Pareto-optimal one, $[\hat{q}]$, that is, $\sigma(q(F)) > \sigma(\hat{q})$.

Using the risk-shifting incentives of depository financing characterized in Proposition 1, we formalize the motivation for capital regulation in the following corollary.

Corollary (Capital Regulation). *In the range of depository financing F, $L < F < I$, higher levels of required equity capital (and correspondingly lower levels of F) lead to lower risk in the investment policy $[q(F)]$ implemented by the manager and a higher value $V[q(F)]$ of the firm, that is,*

$$\frac{\partial\sigma(q(F))}{\partial F} > 0 \quad \textit{and} \quad \frac{\partial V(q(F))}{\partial F} < 0.$$

Proof. From Equation (4), for $L < F < I$,

$$\frac{\partial q(F)}{\partial F} < 0$$

is readily verified. From the remarks below Equation (3), it follows that

$$\frac{\partial\sigma}{\partial F} > 0 \quad \text{and} \quad \frac{\partial V}{\partial F} < 0, \quad \text{for } L < F < I. \qquad \blacksquare$$

As shown in the corollary, the extent of risk undertaken beyond the optimal level, $\Delta\sigma(F) \equiv \sigma(q(F)) - \sigma(\hat{q})$, as well as the value lost due to risk shifting, $\Delta V(F) \equiv V(\hat{q}) - V(q(F))$, are both functions of the bank's equity capital. With a higher capital ratio (i.e., lower F), $\Delta\sigma$ is lower and ΔV is higher. Regulating the bank's incentives, via capital requirements, leaves the bank enough freedom to pursue activities which are unique to its investment opportunity set with attendant risk $\sigma(\hat{q})$. Of importance, regulations mandating the risk level of bank activities (loans extended) may push it to levels below $\sigma(\hat{q})$. That is, while capital regulation does allow the bank to go to a risk level of $\sigma(\hat{q})$ or beyond, the bank's own incentives would limit the risk shifting to a total risk of $\sigma(\hat{q}) + \Delta\sigma(F)$. From a regulatory perspective, since banks have different investment opportunities with different maximal $\sigma(\hat{q})$, direct intervention by regulators to push *all banks to some common* (low) level of risk will not be optimal.

Since $\Delta\sigma(F)$ is increasing in F, it is clear that the total risk taken by the bank $\sigma(\hat{q}) + \Delta\sigma(F)$ is increasing in its leverage ratio or decreasing in its capital adequacy ratio. This implies that with lower and lower levels of capitalization, bank asset risk shifting will be more and more severe. As the bank's degree of capitalization falls from well capitalized to critically undercapitalized, the degree of bank risk shifting, $\Delta\sigma(F)$, may increase dramatically. In the current regulatory case of prompt corrective action (PCA) zones 3 to 5, when the bank is undercapitalized (or worse, significantly or critically undercapitalized), $\Delta\sigma(F)$ could be at unacceptable levels. Here regulators may require insiders to recapitalize the bank so as to move it to a higher capital zone. Moreover, the regulator may have incentives to restrict asset choice—especially for poorly capitalized banks. That is, the regulator may directly restrict the asset activities of the bank such that for any given level of F, its risk-shifting incentives are low.

Proposition 2 (pricing of FDIC premium under capital regulation). *Given a level of capitalization corresponding to F, $F < H$, a fairly priced, revenue-neutral FDIC premium is specified as follows:*

$$\pi(F) = q(F)(F - I)^{+} + (1/2)(1 - q(F))^{2}(F - L)^{+}, \quad (5)$$

where $q(F)$ is specified in Equation (4) of Proposition 1 and a quantity y^{+} denotes max $\{0, y\}$.

Proof. Given a level of capitalization corresponding to F, the investment policy implemented is $[q(F)]$, see Definition 1. By Lemma 1, this investment policy produces payouts from the guarantor to the depositors of 0 with probability $\frac{1}{2}\{1 - (q(F))^2\}$, $(F - I)^+$ with probability $q(F)$, and $(F - L)^+$ with probability $\frac{1}{2}(1 - q(F))^2$, respectively. The expected value yields $\pi(F)$ as in Equation (5). ■

It should be noted that even though we have assumed moral hazard (and incomplete contracting vis-*a*-vis risk choices), an appropriate FDIC insurance premium can still be specified. This premium can be tied to the capital ratio maintained by the bank as well as observable parameters of its investment opportunity set. In our framework, the FDIC premium could be tied to F (the capital ratio) and $\{I, H, L\}$, the parameters of a bank's investment technology. Even though the details of the bank's risk choice (the realized level of q) are not observed by the regulator and are not contractable, the investment policy which will be implemented is $[q(F)]$, as specified in Proposition 1. Hence the appropriate fair, revenue-neutral FDIC premium π is given by Proposition 2. For any level of debt $F > L$, Equation (5) specifies the fair pricing of FDIC insurance incorporating the investment policy $q(F)$ that would be induced. However, $q(F) \neq \hat{q}$ which follows from Proposition 1.

Note that $\pi(F)$ is completely specified in terms of the bank's capitalization level and the observable parameters $\{I, H, L\}$ of its investment opportunity set. In spite of moral hazard, the level of bank capitalization fixes the investment policy $[q(F)]$ that a bank's management will pursue in their own best interest (in this case, also the best interest of the stockholders). If the regulator further restricts the bank's activities directly, so as to alter the bank's investment parameters $\{I, H, L\}$, this will also be reflected in the premium $\pi(F)$ specified in Equation (5). The implementation of the post-1993 FDIC risk-based premium based on capital zone rating and supervisory ratings (i.e., CAMEL or Capital, Asset Quality, Management Quality, Earnings, and Liquidity) does have its parallels to our specification where the premium depends on capital and observable asset or investment technology parameters. However, the following limitations of capital regulation are immediate:

(i) For any level of risky debt, that is, $F > L$, Proposition 1 tells us that $q(F) < \hat{q}$ and there is risk shifting (i.e., $\Delta\sigma(F) > 0$) even if the FDIC premium is priced fairly [as given in Equation (5)]. This is because risk-shifting incentives remain, since banks typically have high leverage levels even in the high capitalization zones of the FDICIA's PCA provisions [see, e.g., John, John, and Senbet (1991) and Chan, Greenbaum, and Thakor (1992)].

(ii) Given that the FDIC premium is priced as in Equation (5), and all other claims are fairly priced, the stockholders of the bank still suffer the costs of risk shifting given by $\Delta V(F) \equiv V(\hat{q}) - V(q(F))$.[8] Since this value loss is minimized at $F = L$, stockholders would want to limit deposit (debt) financing. However, low levels of debt in the bank's capital structure may be inconsistent with the regulator's social objective regarding bank's provision of liquidity services to the economy. At high levels of leverage, the bank's risk-shifting problems get aggravated. In this context, it would be useful to have a solution to the risk-shifting problem that can be implemented at any level of leverage (bank deposits) and which would also be acceptable to a social planner (regulator). It can be seen that the mechanisms of bank regulation that we propose in Section 2 can be implemented at *any level* of deposits (debt) for the banking sector.

[8] As in the established agency tradition, the agency costs of risk shifting here are measured as the loss in firm value resulting from distorted investment compared to the first-best investment [e.g., Jensen and Meckling (1976), Green (1984)]. Note that the equity holders bear the entire agency costs, given that all external claims would be priced ex ante, anticipating the distorted investment policy which would result from the equity holders ex post incentives to maximize equity value. Since the equity holders bear all agency costs, they would find it in their best interest to adopt mechanisms that minimize agency costs.

A Theory of Bank Regulation and Management Compensation

(iii) According to the provisions of the FDICIA, for poorly capitalized banks, certain mandatory restrictions may be imposed on the bank's asset choice. While the rationale for asset regulation involving restrictions on the menu of risky investment opportunities available to the bank is clear, it can potentially lead to investment inefficiencies since the restrictions imposed by the regulator may also remove some positive-NPV projects from the bank's menu of investment opportunities.[9]

2. Bank Management Compensation

In this section we will explore the role of management compensation contracts in bank regulation. This is done by realistically allowing for different incentives among bank managers and bank owners, that is, explicitly recognizing agency conflicts between bank owners and managers as well as between bank insiders and outsiders. A general way of looking at bank regulation and the fair pricing of FDIC insurance is as follows: given the lack of contracting opportunities on specific risk choices to be made by the bank manager, the ability to precommit to specific risk choices is lost—giving way to risk-shifting incentives and the possibility of mispriced FDIC insurance. The level of bank capitalization can provide some indirect precommitment. The level of bank capitalization is generally observable and it can be used to precommit to an investment policy, $[q(F)]$ in Equation (4), which in turn can be used to arrive at the FDIC premium $\pi(F)$ in Equation (5). However, as Proposition 1 shows, some risk-shifting incentives will still remain.

In many ways, the incentives of a bank manager are most directly influenced through his or her compensation structure. In other words, bank owners can precommit to specific investment choices by revealing to regulators (outsiders) the observable details of the compensation mechanism they use to influence the incentives of the decision maker (i.e., the manager).[10] By revealing the parameters of top-management's

[9] Although we do not model asset regulation explicitly, the best way to do so within our framework would be for the regulator to restrict the menu of investments available to the bank by narrowing the admissible parameters $\{L, H\}$ of the risky technology to be such that $L \geq \underline{L}$ and $H \leq \underline{H}$. Such restrictions may represent moving away from universal banking activities to more narrowly focused activities, say toward narrow banking. These restrictions do reduce risk-shifting incentives for any level of deposits F. However, except in the limiting case when $\underline{L} = I = \underline{H}$ (and both projects are identical and riskless), the moral hazard problem of asset substitution still remains. This is because (as discussed earlier) specific asset risk choices are still private actions even if the asset menu is restricted. In our framework the private choice from the menu is parametrized by q which is observed only by bank insiders and is not contractible. The values of L and H are observed by the regulator such that the constraints $L \geq \underline{L}$ and $H \leq \underline{H}$ can be enforced.

[10] It is assumed here that bank corporate insiders (such as the board of directors) establish management compensation schedules.

compensation structure, owners can precommit to an investment policy, which will be freely chosen by the manager given the compensation structure (and associated incentives) put in place by bank owners. Consequently, bank regulation and the pricing of FDIC insurance should take into account the parameters of top-management's compensation. If regulators price FDIC insurance correctly (incorporating parameters of the bank's compensation structure), but otherwise leave the choice of the compensation structure itself entirely to the bank's owners, it can be shown that bank owners will choose, *on their own*, the compensation structure that will induce a Pareto-optimal investment policy, $[\hat{q}]$. Moreover, to the extent that this can be accomplished, for any level of bank capital or deposits F, we obtain an additional degree of freedom such that the regulator can optimally choose bank leverage F^*.

The analysis in Section 1 dealt with the risk-shifting incentives of managers who fully act in the best interests of equity holders. In other words, the compensation structure in place was assumed to perfectly align management's interests with those of equity holders. In this section we study the full-fledged regulatory game which proceeds as follows: at $t = 0$, the regulator announces the determinants of π, the FDIC premium (in particular, whether π will incorporate the parameters of the management compensation or not). At $t = 0$, given the announced regulatory scheme for the determination of π, the bank owners freely choose the optimal compensation structure to put in place. Given the compensation structure chosen at $t = 0$, the manager makes an asset choice at $t = 1$ (in his or her best interest) after observing the realized value of q (the probability of the high outcome H for the risky asset). As in Section 1, all claims and contracts are settled at $t = 2$.

The augmentation of the regulatory game in this section, allowing for the bank owners to choose management compensation structures optimally in response to the "rules of the game" for determining π, is a significant change from the model analyzed in Section 1. The announced determinants of π will affect the optimal choice of management compensation structures in important ways. In particular, unlike in Section 1, the endogenously chosen management compensation scheme may or may not align management interests with those of shareholders. The structure of management compensation in place most directly affects the riskiness of the investment policy implemented by management, when moral hazard and incomplete contracting provide some degree of managerial discretion over investment policy. In Section 2.1 we examine how the incentive features of management compensation structures, together with a bank's capital ratio, determine the investment policy (and risk) implemented by the bank's management in its own interest. In Section 2.2 we examine the optimal choice of management compensation structures by bank shareholders for different regulatory regimes for determining π. These results provide the rationale for linking features of management compensation, along with the level of capital, to FDIC insurance pricing. This is particularly important in light of the fact that capital requirements and asset restrictions have been the primary focus for U.S. bank regulation to date (including post-FDICIA), while managerial compensation has, at best, played a subsidiary role in regulatory design.

2.1 Incentive features of management compensation

Although a large variety of compensation structures can be considered as candidates for bank management compensation contracts, we will consider a simple family of contracts with some important incentive features. This family is closely related to the structures observed in practice and includes among its members an optimal contract. In this sense, we believe that a restriction of the compensation structure to this piecewise linear family is without too much loss of generality.

The generic compensation structure is characterized as follows: The manager gets a fixed cash salary, $S \geq 0$, and a fraction α of the equity of the bank. In addition to the salary he (or she) gets a bonus which is increasing in the degree of capitalization of the bank (or equivalently in the terminal cash flows realized).[11] If the bank is insolvent, or severely undercapitalized, the bonus is zero.[12] When the terminal cash flow T is such that $T - F > 0$, the first λ dollars of $T - F$ is paid to the manager as a bonus. The total payout to equity holders is max $\{0, T - F - \lambda\}$, and the manager gets a fraction α of the payoff to equity holders. Such a compensation contract will be called the contract $\{S, \lambda, \alpha\}$. For convenience, we will assume that the fixed salary component is paid out of the bank's operating cash flow such that the terminal cash flow $T = \{I, H, L\}$ is residual to the fixed payments, S, to the manager (see Figure 1).

The manager will implement an investment policy, $[q^m]$, which is optimal for him, given his compensation contract $\{S, \lambda, \alpha\}$. It is clear that the investments undertaken (e.g., loans made) will depend on the

[11] See Houston and James (1993) for a discussion of the greater relative empirical importance of cash compensation salary plus bonus—in banks relative to nonbank firms.

[12] This is intended to capture the adverse impact of financial distress on management such that management incentives are partially aligned with depositors. This is consistent with the empirical evidence on increased management turnover in financial distress [e.g., Gilson (1989)] and reduced management compensation in financial distress [e.g., Gilson and Vetsuypens (1993)].

The Review of Financial Studies / v 13 n 1 2000

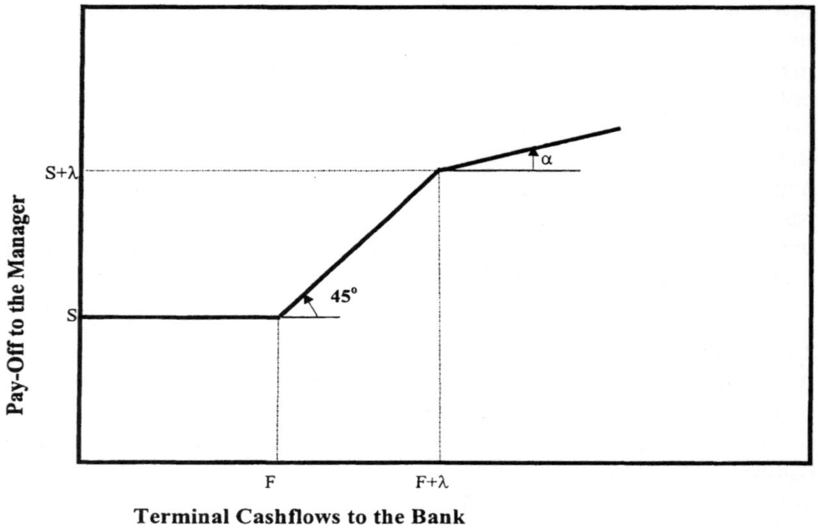

Figure 1
The generic form of the management compensation contract $\{S, \lambda, \alpha\}$.
The generic compensation structure is characterized as follows: The manager gets a fixed cash salary, $S \geq 0$, and a fraction α of the equity of the bank. In addition to the salary he (or she) gets a bonus which is increasing in the degree of capitalization of the bank (or equivalently in the terminal cash flows realized). If the bank is insolvent, or severely undercapitalized, the bonus is zero. When the terminal cash flow T is such that $T - F > 0$, the first λ dollars of $T - F$ is paid to the manager as a bonus. The total payout to equity holders is max $\{0, T - F - \lambda\}$, and the manager gets a fraction α of the payoff to equity holders. Such a compensation contract will be called the contract $\{S, \lambda, \alpha\}$.

parameters λ and α of the management compensation structure as well as the level of bank capitalization implied by F.[13]

In the next proposition, we assume that $I - F - \lambda \geq 0$, for expositional convenience. That is, equity has some payout even when the riskless asset is chosen. We will now characterize the investment policy $[q^m]$ and some of its properties.

Proposition 3 (incentive effects of compensation features). *Given the management contract $\{S, \lambda, \alpha\}$ and a capitalization level corresponding to $F > L$,*

[13] There is now growing attention to the interaction between managerial compensation and capital structure in corporate finance. The relationship between investment policy and managerial compensation, given an existing capital structure, has been studied in John and John (1993). Also, Madan, Senbet, and Soubra (1993) study the relationship between compensation structure and capital structure in the context of a three-party conflict between management, shareholders, and debt-holders.

A Theory of Bank Regulation and Management Compensation

(i) *The investment policy* $[q^m]$ *implemented is given by Equation* (6):

$$q^m = \frac{(1-\alpha)\lambda + \alpha(I-F)}{(1-\alpha)\lambda + \alpha(H-F)} \tag{6}$$

(ii) *For any* $\lambda > 0$ *and* $\alpha < 1$, $q^m > q(F)$, *that is, the investment policy is less risky than when manager's interests are fully aligned with equity interests.*

(iii) $q^m(\lambda)$ *is increasing in* λ, *that is, the larger the bonus, the more conservative the investment policy.*

(iv) $q^m(\alpha)$ *is decreasing in* α, *that is, the larger the equity share of the manager, the riskier the investment policy.*

Proof. [14]

(i) Given a management compensation schedule $\{S, \lambda, \alpha\}$ and $I - F - \lambda \geq 0$, the manager undertakes the risky project only when q is such that

$$q[\lambda + \alpha(H - F - \lambda)] \geq [\lambda + \alpha(I - F - \lambda)].$$

Equivalently, when $q \geq q^m$, where q^m is given by Equation (6), the investment policy implemented is $[q^m]$.

(ii) Since $(H-F) > (I-F) \geq \lambda$, we have from Equation (6),

$$q^m > q(F) = \frac{\alpha(I-F)}{\alpha(H-F)}, \text{ from Equation (4).}$$

(iii) Given $H > I$, and $0 < \alpha < 1$, we have $\dfrac{\partial q^m}{\partial \lambda} > 0$, for $\lambda \leq (I - F)$.

(iv) For $(I-F) > \lambda > 0$, $\alpha > 0$ and $H > I$, we have $\dfrac{\partial q^m}{\partial \alpha} < 0$. ■

The intuition of Proposition 3 is straightforward. For $\lambda > 0$, and $\alpha = 0$, the manager implements the very conservative investment policy [1] of investing in the riskless project for all values of q. He is only worried about protecting his bonus λ and implements an investment policy which turns out to be in the interest of depositors. Of course, such an investment policy is suboptimal from an efficiency point of view and results in loss of bank value $V(\hat{q}) - I$. As managerial equity share α

[14] As mentioned above, the restriction that $\lambda \leq (I-F)$ in Proposition 3 is mainly for expositional convenience. Although the expression for q^m in Equation (6) changes slightly, result (ii) holds for all values of $\lambda < (H-F)$ and $q^m = q(F)$ for $\lambda \geq (H-F)$. $(H-F)$ is a natural upper bound for λ. Of interest, q^m is increasing in λ for $\lambda \leq (I-F)$ and then decreases toward $q(F)$ in the range $(I-F) \leq \lambda \leq (H-F)$. Note that $q(F)$ is the lower bound for q^m for all values of λ. Indeed, our focus on the restricted case $\lambda \leq (I-F)$ is without loss of generality. In Proposition 6, we show that an optimal compensation contract $\{S, \hat{\lambda}, \hat{\alpha}\}$ exists such that $\hat{\lambda} \leq (I-F)$.

is increased from 0, the manager acts more and more like an equity holder, implementing riskier and riskier investment policies. However, for any $\alpha < 1$, protecting the bonus makes him act in a more conservative fashion than the $q(F)$ of Proposition 1, where his interests were fully aligned with those of equity holders. As λ gets larger, the bonus is more important and he becomes more conservative, that is, q^m is larger. Thus, in general, α and λ have offsetting effects on managerial risk-taking incentives.

Corollary (management incentives and FDIC premia). *For any capital level corresponding to F, where $I > F > L$, and management compensation structure $\{S, \lambda, \alpha\}$:*

(i) *when $\lambda = 0$ and $0 < \alpha \leq 1$, the manager is fully aligned with equity holders and implements the investment policy $q^m = q(F)$. The corresponding, fairly priced, revenue-neutral FDIC premium is $\pi(F)$, as specified in Equation (5).*

(ii) *when $(I - F) > \lambda > 0$ and $\alpha = 0$ the manager is fully aligned with the depositors and implements the investment policy [1], that is, for all $q \in [0, 1]$, he invests in the riskless loan. The corresponding, fairly priced, revenue-neutral FDIC premium is zero.*

Proof.

(i) Substitute $\lambda = 0$ in Equation (6) to obtain $q^m = \frac{\alpha(I - F)}{\alpha(H - F)} = q(F)$ from Equation (4). Here the manager is fully aligned with equity holders and the investment policy $q(F)$ and the corresponding FDIC risk premium, $\pi(F)$ are as in Propositions 1 and 2, respectively.

(ii) Substitute $\alpha = 0$ in Equation (6) to obtain $q^m = 1$. The investment policy [1] involves investing in the riskless loan for all $q \in [0, 1]$. The resulting output I is always sufficient to pay back the depositors, given $F < I$. The guarantor's liability is always zero, and the fairly priced, revenue-neutral FDIC premium equals zero. ■

Two insights follow from the above discussion for FDIC regulation. First, it is clear that the structure of management compensation, for example, size of bonus (λ) relative to managerial equity share (α), may affect the riskiness of the bank's asset portfolio in a manner analogous to the level of capital (leverage) maintained. The corresponding FDIC premium can vary from 0 to $\pi(F)$. Hence regulatory policy, and FDIC premiums, should potentially take into account the incentive features of management compensation. Second, since managerial bonus and the equity fraction have offsetting effects on a manager's risk-shifting incentives, a bank may be able to fine tune these two incentive features so as to precommit to implementing a Pareto-optimal investment policy. We will discuss these two insights further below.

For any level of debt F, Proposition 3 implies that investment policy $[q^m]$ is safer than $[q(F)]$, for $\lambda > 0$. How much more conservative $[q^m]$ is in relation to $[q(F)]$ is determined by the management's compensation structure; specifically, by the relative importance of λ and α. Larger α's bring q^m closer to $q(F)$ and larger λ's take it closer to 1. By implication, regulatory actions in each of PCA's five zones of capitalization should take into account the incentive features of the management compensation schedule used by the bank. For example, a bonus that is lower for inadequate levels of bank earnings and by implication inadequate levels of bank capital will induce *less* risk-shifting incentives by management.

Discretionary regulatory restrictions on the salary of officers (top management) in significantly and critically undercapitalized banks—included in the PCA provisions of FDICIA—seem to be somewhat similar in spirit to the results we have derived here, although our results suggest that such regulatory restrictions should be *bank specific*. We can also argue that the incentive features of the compensation structure in place should be considered more directly in setting appropriate FDIC insurance premia.

2.2 Pricing of deposit insurance and management compensation

In this section we will consider the effect of the pricing of deposit insurance on the optimal choice of management compensation structures by bank stockholders. We will consider two classes of deposit insurance pricing schemes. The first class of schemes do not explicitly incorporate incentive features of management compensation structures in the pricing of deposit insurance. As examples of this class of pricing schemes we will consider fixed premium deposit insurance pricing and a risk-based scheme based on a bank's capital adequacy. Together these two schemes are stylistic representations of the pre-1993 and post-1993 FDIC insurance pricing schemes.[15]

The second class of schemes proposed here will incorporate explicitly the observable features of management compensation structures in the setting of the deposit insurance premiums. The results below will show that when the regulator is using compensation-based deposit insurance pricing, it would be in the best interest of stockholders to select and

[15] It might be noted, though, that the post-1993 pricing scheme also takes into account the bank's CAMEL supervisory rating. However, CAMEL ratings do not explicitly incorporate incentive features of management compensation.

implement a compensation structure for the bank manager that eliminates risk shifting. On the other hand, deposit insurance pricing schemes of the first class, which do not incorporate the management's compensation features explicitly in deposit insurance pricing, will induce the bank stockholders to pick management compensation structures that align management's interests with shareholders and leave risk-shifting incentives intact.

Proposition 4 (FDIC premium schemes and managerial compensation structures). *Consider a deposit insurance pricing regime where*

(i) *the premium π is fixed,*
(ii) *the premium $\pi(F)$ is capital based, that is, $\pi(F) = kF$, where $0 \leq k \leq 1$, and F = the level of deposits.*

Given the above pricing schemes, (i) or (ii), the bank's stockholders will optimally choose a compensation structure (S, λ, α) where $\lambda = 0$, $\alpha > 0$, which preserves management's risk-shifting incentives.

Proof.

(i) *The premium π is fixed.* Given that π is independent of $F > 0$, and $\{S, \lambda, \alpha\}$, the bank stockholders will find it optimal to choose a compensation structure that will induce an investment policy that maximizes equity value. The investment policy which maximizes the value of equity is to invest in the risky project when q satisfies

$$q[H - F]^{+} + (1 - q)[L - F]^{+} \geq [I - F]^{+}$$

(where a quantity y^{+} denotes max $\{0, y\}$). The corresponding investment policy is $[q(F)]$, where

$$q(F) = \frac{(I - F)}{(H - F)}.$$

This investment policy will be induced by stockholders through choosing, for the management, a compensation contract $\{S, \lambda, \alpha\}$, with $\alpha > 0$, $\lambda = 0$, as shown in (i) of the corollary of Proposition 3. By the corollary, the chosen compensation structure will preserve the management's risk-shifting incentives. ■

(ii) *The premium $\pi(F)$ is capital based.* Given that the deposit insurance regime $\pi(F)$ is independent of the compensation structure $\{S, \lambda, \alpha\}$, the bank stockholders will pick the parameters of compensation structure to induce an investment policy $[q(F)]$ that is equity-value maximizing. As in (i), this can be accomplished by setting $\alpha > 0$ and $\lambda = 0$ in the chosen compensation contract, which again preserves management's risk-shifting incentives. ■

Both of the above FDIC pricing schemes, which do not incorporate management compensation features into FDIC pricing, lead to compensation choices by bank stockholders that induce an investment policy $[q(F)]$ involving risk shifting.

In Proposition 5, we characterize an FDIC insurance pricing scheme that incorporates the incentive features of bank management compensation for any given compensation structure $\{S, \lambda, \alpha\}$. In Proposition 6, we show that a compensation-based deposit insurance pricing scheme will lead bank stockholders to choose compensation structures that induce management to choose the optimal investment policy, that is, $q^m = \hat{q}$.

In Proposition 5, we derive the appropriate FDIC insurance premium, π^m, where the incentive effects of management compensation on asset risk choice are directly considered.

Proposition 5 (pricing FDIC premia by incorporating managerial compensation features). *Given a level of bank capital corresponding to F, $F < H$, and a management compensation contract $\{S, \lambda, \alpha\}$ in place, a fairly priced, revenue-neutral FDIC premium is specified as follows:*

$$\pi^m = q^m(F - I)^+ + \tfrac{1}{2}(1 - q^m)^2(F - L)^+ \tag{7}$$

where q^m is specified in Equation (6) *of Proposition* 3 (*and a quantity y^+ denotes max* $\{0, y\}$).

Proof. From Proposition 3 (i), given the managerial compensation contract $\{S, \lambda, \alpha\}$, the manager implements an investment policy $[q^m]$, where q^m is as in Equation (6). By Lemma 1, such an investment policy produces the cash flow distribution L with probability $\frac{1}{2}(1 - q^m)^2$, I with probability q^m, and H with probability $\frac{1}{2}\{1 - (q^m)^2\}$, with corresponding payoffs from the guarantor to the depositors of $(F - L)^+$, $(F - I)^+$, and 0, respectively. The expected value of these payoffs, π^m in Equation (7), is therefore a fairly priced, revenue-neutral FDIC premium. ■

Note that π^m is specified in terms of F, the observable parameters of the management compensation structure, λ, and α, and, as before, parameters of the bank's investment opportunity set $\{I, H, L\}$. In spite of moral hazard and incomplete contracting, we know that $[q^m]$ in Equation (6) is the investment policy that bank managers will pursue in their own best interest, given the bank's capital and management compensation structure in place. Linking FDIC premia to the capital and compensation parameters enables the regulator to get at the correct risk choices that would be implemented by investment policy $[q^m]$.

2.3 An optimal management compensation structure

For any given level of F, and management compensation $\{S, \lambda, \alpha\}$ in place, the investment policy implemented will be $[q^m]$, where q^m is specified in Equation (6). If the insurance premium π^m is correctly priced as in Equation (7) (and correspondingly, depositors' claims are correctly priced), anticipating rationally the investment policy $[q^m]$, then the bank's equity holders suffer the loss in value, $V(\hat{q}) - V(q^m)$, due to the distorted investment policy $[q^m]$. This makes it in the best interest of the equity holders to choose, at $t = 0$, capital and compensation structures that will induce managers to pick (at $t = 1$) an investment policy $[q^m]$, where $q^m = \hat{q}$, the Pareto-optimal investment policy.

Given the level of F, the management compensation parameters λ and α can be chosen by the equity holders to induce the investment policy $[\hat{q}]$. In fact, for any level of F, an optimal compensation structure can be chosen by owners such that the Pareto-optimal investment policy is implemented.

Proposition 6 (optimal compensation features).

(i) *Under the deposit insurance pricing scheme given in Proposition 5, the bank stockholders will optimally choose a compensation structure that induces an investment policy $[\hat{q}]$.*
(ii) *A compensation structure $\{S, \hat{\lambda}, \hat{\alpha}\}$ that induces the investment policy $[\hat{q}]$ has its parameters satisfying the relation*

$$\hat{\lambda} = \frac{\hat{\alpha}}{(1 - \hat{\alpha})}(F - L). \tag{8}$$

Proof.

(i) For any compensation structure (S, λ, α), the investment policy picked by the management satisfies $[q^m]$ in Equation (6) and the resulting total value is $V(q^m)$ as specified in Equation (1), but substituting $q = q^m$. If the deposits and deposit insurance (and any other outstanding claims) are priced correctly (as zero NPV transactions), the residual claimants' wealth equals $V(q^m)$. Any deviations $q^m \neq \hat{q}$ from the optimal investment $\hat{q}$ in Equation (2) results in a wealth loss $V(\hat{q}) - V(q^m)$ to the bank's stock owners. The stock owners will optimally pick a compensation structure that will induce the management to pursue an investment policy $[\hat{q}]$, which minimizes $V(\hat{q}) - V(q^m)$.

(ii) Substitute Equation (8) in the expression for q^m in Equation (6) and simplify to obtain $q^m = \hat{q}$. This implies that a compensation structure $\{S, \hat{\lambda}, \hat{\alpha}\}$ satisfying Equation (8) is an optimal one. ■

Although the optimal pair $(\hat{\lambda}, \hat{\alpha})$ are not uniquely specified, the relationships in Equation (8), which imply larger $\hat{\alpha}$'s with larger $\hat{\lambda}$'s, are intuitive. For a large value of the bonus λ and a small value of equity ownership α, the manager will invest too conservatively, that is, $q^m > \hat{q}$. On the other hand, if λ is small and α is large, then the manager engages in risk shifting, that is, $q^m < \hat{q}$. The trade-off between λ and α produces the "middle-ground" optimal values given by Equation (8).

Remark. It is useful to contrast Proposition 6 with Proposition 4. As we know from Equation (6), a given set of compensation parameters can be uniquely mapped into the investment policy $[q^m]$, hence an insurance premium specifying the parameters of the compensation structure is tantamount to contracting on a specific investment policy $[q^m]$. In such a setting, it is optimal for the stockholders to pick the optimal compensation structure $\{S, \hat{\lambda}, \hat{\alpha}\}$ and equivalently precommit to implementing the value-maximizing investment policy $[\hat{q}]$. On the other hand, in Proposition 4, since regulators currently use a deposit insurance pricing scheme that is insensitive to the compensation parameters $\{S, \lambda, \alpha\}$ it is tantamount to making $[q^m]$ noncontractible. As is well-known, in such a setting, the choice of compensation structure (and equivalently the subsequent choice of the corresponding investment policy $[q^m]$) is made to maximize the value of equity. Even when the resulting investment policy $[q(F)]$ is anticipated in the pricing of deposit insurance [as in Equation (5)], the risk-shifting incentives remain as $q(F) < \hat{q}$.

The role of management compensation in controlling investment distortions has been previously considered in the literature. In particular, Dybvig and Zender (1991) show how the underinvestment problem à la Myers and Majluf (1984) can be solved by using optimal managerial compensation contracts. There are, however, important differences between our article and Dybvig and Zender (1991). We model the incentive problems in a banking system with deposit insurance in place. In our article the rules of the game used by the regulator in pricing deposit insurance determine the choice of management compensation structures by the bank's stockholders. Whether or not the optimal compensation structure would be chosen by the bank's stockholders depends on the determinants of the deposit insurance pricing schedule set by the regulator, as we show in Propositions 4, 5, and 6. This additional stage of interaction, between the deposit-insurance pricing scheme used by the regulator and the bank stockholders' choice of management compensation scheme, which is absent in Dybvig and Zender, plays a central role in our analysis.[16] We show that the correct pricing of deposit insurance premiums, based on compensation features in place, is crucial to providing the bank owners incentives to choose optimal compensation structures for its top management, which in turn induces the optimal investment policy by the bank's management.

Another interesting observation is that in a regime where FDIC premiums are fairly priced, by linking premiums to both capitalization (i.e., F) and management compensation parameters (i.e., λ and α), equity holders are induced to pick the optimal compensation structure $\{S, \hat{\lambda}, \hat{\alpha}\}$ at $t = 0$ as a means of *precommitting* to the depositors and regulators that the optimal investment policy $[\hat{q}]$ will be implemented. Consequently, banks need only be charged the insurance premium $\pi^m(\hat{q})$ specified in Equation (7). That is, the regulator does not have to *mandate* the exact details of the bank's managerial compensation as was initially implied under the original FDICIA proposal for poorly capitalized banks. Instead, equity holders will, in their own self-interest, put in place an optimal compensation structure at $t = 0$. Since the effectiveness of the precommitment depends on the observability of the parameters of the compensation scheme, such as λ and α, the appropriate audit and regulatory processes must play a role in facilitating the precommitment aspect of the compensation structure. Moreover, recent SEC regulation, which requires mandatory disclosure of the details of management compensation structures, should be helpful in achieving the degree of transparency required. Finally, the disclosure costs for banks should also be quite small. That is, requiring (and monitoring) disclosure of bank compensation schemes should be a relatively low-cost form of regulation, especially compared to seeking to monitor and control the asset/investment technologies of banks, as is current practice.

2.4 Additional agency problems

In the main model of this article we have considered the risk-shifting incentive as the central source of agency problems. In the context of regulation of banks with more than 90% leverage in their capital structures, this has been viewed as the primary agency problem. In this section we show that the basic approach that we have suggested in the article is robust to the introduction of additional agency problems.

[16] Other differences include the specific nature of information problem and the priority structure of the manager's claim. The investment distortion in Dybvig and Zender (1991) arises from asymmetric information, while in our framework, moral hazard and incomplete contracting induce risk-shifting incentives. Moreover, the explicit form of the optimal compensation differs from Dybvig and Zender. We adopt a priority structure for manager's claims consistent with current legal and regulatory policy (e.g., Depositor Preference Legislation, 1993).

Before we present the model with additional sources of agency problems, two remarks are in order. First, given a set of agency problems and an admissible set of compensation contracts, it is quite possible that the optimally chosen compensation contract does not lead to the first-best investment policy (as is the case in the model of Section 2). However, in a regime where the FDIC insurance premium takes into account the parameters of the compensation contract, the insiders of the bank would have incentives to put in place the optimal compensation contract that minimizes agency costs arising from multiple agency problems. Second, such an approach provides the correct, revenue-neutral pricing of FDIC insurance which incorporates the fair price of the liability of the insurer, anticipating the investment choices to be made by the manager given the compensation structure in place.[17]

In the finance literature, two broad classes of agency problems have been considered. One set of agency problems arises from the fact that the agent controlling the investment decisions (say, corporate insiders or the management) holds only a small subset of claims issued by the firm. Agency costs of debt of highly levered institutions belong to this category. Another class of agency problems arises, because decision-making agents may be motivated by benefits other than the value of cash flow claims. Private benefits of control, managerial perks, human capital concerns, and effort aversion are examples that have been studied in the literature.[18]

In this section we present a simple extension of our basic model to include managerial private benefits as the source of additional agency problems. A simple way to introduce a representation of these agency costs into our framework would be to use the following device. The manager derives benefits of control equal to r from implementing the risky project, and s from implementing the safe project, where both r and s are positive.[19] Let us denote as δ, the differential benefits of control, that is, $\delta = r - s$.

[17] In the model with multiple agency problems presented here and the model of Section 2, the agency problems are completely eliminated by the optimal compensation contract. However, in general the optimal compensation contract chosen from a given admissible class will only minimize the total agency costs arising from the multiple agency problems.

[18] For example, Jensen and Meckling (1976), Jensen (1986), and Harris and Raviv (1988a, b) study different versions of managerial benefits of control as a source of agency problems. Examples of such control benefits are management perquisites, synergy with other projects run by the same management, returns to firm-specific investments in human capital, reputation effects arising from successfully managing the project, etc. Harris and Raviv (1979) and Holmstrom (1979) exemplify the principal-agent literature where managerial effort aversion is another source of agency problems.

[19] Examples of such project (loan)-specific benefits of control are easy to motivate. When r is large, it may correspond to a bank manager who has a special affinity to make risky real estate loans because he is building influence among real estate developers. On the other hand, when s is large compared to r, the manager derives utility from implementing the safe project (even when its NPV is lower). This scenario can be considered similar to a setting where the manager is motivated by risk aversion or human capital concerns to implement risk choices in investment that are suboptimal from the perspective of diversified shareholders.

The Review of Financial Studies / v 13 n 1 2000

The existence of differential private benefits of control will affect the investment choice as follows. In the benchmark case, with no risky debt, when the management is compensated through equity participation only, the investment policy $[q^a]$ chosen by the manager [see Equation (9) of the appendix] deviates from the investment policy $[\hat{q}]$ [see Equation (2)] with no risky debt. Depending on the sign of δ, the relative magnitude of the differential private benefits between the two projects, the managerial bias would result in investment choices that are more aggressive or more conservative than the investment policy $[\hat{q}]$. Similarly, in the presence of risky debt, the risk-shifting incentives characterized in Proposition 1 could be aggravated or mitigated by the nature of the additional agency costs parametrized by δ. If $\delta > 0$, the risk-shifting incentives of debt are aggravated by the other agency costs and when $\delta > 0$, it is mitigated.

Now consider the effect of the compensation-based deposit insurance scheme as analyzed in the Sections 2.1–2.4. The investment risk choice by management will be influenced not only by the differential private benefits of control, as reflected in δ, but also by the incentive features of management compensation (S, λ, α). This is formally shown in the appendix, but the intuition is straightforward. The managerial bias toward riskier projects $(\delta > 0)$ can be controlled by making the bonus (λ) portion of the compensation structure larger, and when the bias is toward the less risky project $(\delta < 0)$, a higher equity participation (α) can be used to control the bias. Again, as shown in the appendix, the procedure for the design of optimal management compensation and the resulting optimal regulation are analogous to the case of a single agency problem. The presence of such a scheme is shown in the appendix to provide the bank insiders incentives to put in place, optimal compensation structures [characterized in Equation (11)]. This is turn induces the investment policy $[\hat{q}]$. We show in the appendix that a fairly priced FDIC premium is also feasible in this case, as in the case of a single agency problem (Propostion 5).

2.5 Implementation issues: compensation versus capital regulation

There are some additional issues related to implementation. First, what happens if bank owners shift the compensation schedule after the insurance premium is set? It should be noted that this is no different from banks' reducing their capital-asset ratios after premiums are set. In both cases this can be addressed by either (i) a more frequent adjustment of insurance premiums, and/or (ii) a back-evaluation approach whereby banks are penalized by an additional (back-end) premium at the end of each premium-setting period, should actual compensation (capital) structures differ significantly from initial compensation (capital) structures.[20] If penalties are sufficiently high, there is no incentive for bank owners to distort compensation (capital) structures in this fashion.

The second issue relates to the view that bank capital is potentially more observable (measurable) than bank compensation structures. However, as is well known, measuring the economic (market) rather than the book value of bank capital can be extremely difficult, involving among other things, the valuation of nontraded assets and liabilities (e.g., demand deposits) as well as valuing contingent (off balance sheet) assets and liabilities. By contrast, as noted above, bank compensation contracts may be relatively more transparent, especially in view of recent changes by the SEC requiring greater disclosure of managerial compensation.

A third issue in implementation relates to the level of management whose compensation parameters should enter the regulatory process, since banks have multiple layers of management with possibly differing compensation structures. In our framework, the primary focus should be on the incentives of the top-management team or the CEO in linking compensation schedules to regulatory policy. The CEO (or the top-management team) sets the guidelines for the bank and monitors other bank executives. That is, outsiders need to monitor only the top-management team or design their incentive compensation schemes to elicit the desired outcomes when monitoring is difficult and costly. There is some empirical evidence supporting this point of view. Ang, Lauterbach, and Schreiber (1997) provide evidence that there is little differentiation in compensation schemes among top bank executives, except for the CEO. Specifically, there appears to be a two-tier compensation scheme in most banks they studied—one for the CEO and the other for the other top executives—in the form of incentive compensation scaled by total compensation. They argue that the reason for the minimal variation in non-CEO top-executive compensation results from the ability of the CEO to monitor those executives below him. In contrast, the CEO receives more incentive compensation due to the greater potential agency conflict between him and the stockholders.

3. Conclusions

We have examined the incentive structure of the post-FDICIA regulation of U.S. banks, and particularly the efficacy of bank capital requirements and restrictions on asset risk choice in controlling banks' risk-shifting incentives. While demonstrating the limitations of capital and

[20] This type of "back-end" penalty scheme has been implemented to support capital requirements for market risk that came into effect in January 1998.

asset regulation, we argue for a more prominent role for management compensation structures in bank regulation and specifically in the pricing of FDIC insurance. We show that the effectiveness of capital regulation hinges on the characteristics of the underlying asset investment opportunity set facing a depository institution.

A principal aspect of our analysis is to consider not only agency conflicts between the regulator and a bank, but also between a bank's management and the owners of the bank. This is particularly important because investment risk choices are generally controlled by management, whose risk-taking behavior depends on the structure of their compensation schedules specified by stockholders. In particular, we show how managerial compensation serves as a direct regulatory mechanism that induces optimal investment risk choice from the standpoint of the regulator.

Of importance, we show that Pareto-optimal investment risk choices by banks can be achieved without direct regulation of managerial compensation and/or equity capitalization. More specifically, when a fairly priced insurance premium reflects the structure of managerial compensation, along with the level of bank capitalization, it pays bank equity holders to pick optimal managerial compensation contracts that ensure first-best investment risk choices. That is, there is no need to regulate the details of managerial compensation contracts, so long as they are observable, since picking an optimal compensation scheme precommits equity holders to value-maximizing investment choices. The regulatory role of bank management compensation is particularly significant, given the limitations of capital and asset regulation.

Analogous to our results on capital regulation, there is a practical regulatory parallel regarding the role of bank management compensation. In particular, it is clear that regulatory action in the five zones of the PCA program should actively take account of the incentive effects of managerial compensation on bank risk taking. While discretionary bank-specific restrictions on the pay of officers of critically undercapitalized banks, as suggested in the PCA provisions of FDICIA, seem desirable in the context of our analysis, our results suggest that *no direct or mandatory regulation* of management compensation is required as long as the insurance premium incorporates parameters of the compensation structure in place, as well as the level of bank capitalization.

Appendix: Analysis of Multiple Agency Problems

In this appendix we characterize the investment policy, FDIC pricing scheme, and managerial compensation structure in the presence of an additional agency problem arising from managerial benefits of control beyond the risk-shifting incentive considered in the article. This managerial bias is intended to capture the private benefits of control, as studied in the literature. Examples include managerial perks, effort aversion, risk aversion, etc. As detailed in the text (Section 3.4), the manager derives benefits of control equal to $r > 0$ and $s > 0$ from extending the risky loan and the safe loan, respectively. Let $\delta = r - s$. The analysis presented below contains results parallel to all the crucial results obtained for the main model with the single agency problem arising from risk-shifting incentives.

First, we will examine the distortionary effect of the managerial benefits of control in the benchmark case of a bank with no risky debt. We can characterize the investment policy where the manager is compensated with only equity. The investment policy to be denoted $[q^a]$ will be

$$q^a = \frac{(I - L) - \delta}{(H - L)}. \tag{9}$$

We see that the investment policy $[q^a]$ in Equation (9) will deviate from the Pareto-optimal investment policy $[\hat{q}]$, where $[\hat{q}]$ is given in Equation (2) as long as $\delta \neq 0$ (i.e., when there are differential private benefits from the risky investment and the safe investment). If $\delta > 0$, then $q^a < \hat{q}$ and the manager pursues an investment policy that involves overinvestment in the risky project. Intuitively the higher control benefits from the riskier project induces this overinvestment (compared to $[\hat{q}]$). If $\delta < 0$, the investment policy $[q^a]$ is safer than $[\hat{q}]$, induced by the higher private benefits in the safer project. In both cases, the agency costs resulting from the distorted investment policy $[q^a]$ is given by $V(\hat{q}) - V(q^a)$ as before (see the text).

With the introduction of risky debt of promised payment $F > L$, the risk-shifting incentives interact with the investment distortions caused by benefits of control. Whether the investment distortions from risk-shifting incentives are aggravated or mitigated by those induced by the benefits of control depends on the relative values of r and s, or equivalently the sign of $\delta = r - s$. If $\delta > 0$, risk-shifting incentives of debt are aggravated by the other agency costs and when $\delta < 0$, it is mitigated. The investment policy implemented by a manager who is compensated only by equity (levered equity) can be characterized as in Proposition 1. Our results on the effects of capital regulation (in the corollary to Proposition 1) and the pricing of FDIC insurance premium under capital regulation (Proposition 2) continue to hold where the straightforward modification of the appropriate investment policy $[q^a(F)]$ is used instead of $[q(F)]$, where

$$q^a(F) = \frac{I - F - \delta}{H - F} \text{ for } L < F < I.$$

Now we consider the same class of bank management compensation structures $\{S, \lambda, \alpha\}$ as in Section 2 (and introduced in Section 2.1). The resulting investment policy $[q^{ma}]$ can be characterized in a manner analogous to that in Equation (6):

$$q^{ma} = \frac{(1 - \alpha)\lambda + \alpha(I - F) - \delta}{(1 - \alpha)\lambda + \alpha(H - F)}. \tag{10}$$

All the results of Section 2 (Propositions 3, 4, and 5) continue to hold with q^{ma} substituting for q^m.

To derive the optimal compensation structure in the presence of both agency costs we proceed as follows: Recall $\hat{q}$ in Equation (2), which characterizes the cutoff level for value-maximizing investment policy $[\hat{q}]$. The parameters λ^a and α^a of an optimal compensation structure $\{S^a, \lambda^a, \alpha^a\}$ can be chosen as follows:

$$\lambda^a = \frac{1}{(1 - \alpha^a)}\left[\alpha^a(F - L) + \frac{\delta}{(1 - \hat{q})}\right]. \tag{11}$$

The Review of Financial Studies/v 13 n 1 2000

Comparing Equation (11) with Equation (8) in the text, which characterizes the optimal contract with the risk-shifting incentives as the only agency cost, the following observations are immediate. When $\delta > 0$, (i.e., a managerial bias exists for the risky project), the level of bonus λ^a has to be larger to induce some conservatism. On the other hand, $\delta < 0$ implies that the bonus λ^a can be smaller. For a given level of λ^a and $(F - L)$, the optimal proportion of managerial equity ownership α^a can be larger when $\delta < 0$ and smaller when $\delta > 0$ to offset the managerial bias induced by private benefits of control. Substituting Equation (11) into Equation (10) it can be seen that $[q^{ma}]$ reduces to $[\hat{q}]$, proving that the compensation contract $\{S^a, \lambda^a, \alpha\}$, where λ^a and α^a are characterized by Equation (11) is optimal, and induces the value-maximizing investment policy $[\hat{q}]$. Remarks similar to those following Proposition 6 also apply to the optimal combinations λ^a, α^a characterized by Equation (11) regarding their nonuniqueness and the intuition of balancing conservatism of the bonus (λ^a) and of ownership (α^a) to achieve optimality.

In conclusion, the approach of this article can be implemented in the presence of multiple agency problems. An FDIC pricing regime which incorporates observable features of managerial compensation provides incentives for bank insiders to put in place an optimal compensation structure for its management. Such a compensation contract induces optimal investment policy.

References

Allen, L. and A. Rai, 1993, "Economies of Scale and Scope in International Banking," *Journal of International Financial Markets, Institutions, and Money*, 3(2), 1–31.

Ang, J., B. Lauterbach, and B. Z. Schreiber, 1997, "Pay at the Executive Suite: How Do U.S. Banks Compensate the Five Most Senior Executives in Each Bank?," working paper, Florida State University, December.

Barnea, A., R. A. Haugen, and W. L. Senbet, 1985, *Agency Problems and Financial Contracting*, Prentice-Hall, Englewood Cliffs, N. J.

Barth, J. R., P. F. Bartholomew, and C. J. Labich, 1990, "Moral Hazard and the Thrift Crisis: An Empirical Analysis," *Consumer Finance Law: Quarterly Report*, 9, 22–34.

Berger, A., and L. J. Mester, 1997, "Inside the Black Box: What Explains Differences in the Efficiencies of Financial Institutions," *Journal of Banking and Finance*, 21, 895–947.

Chan, Y., S. I. Greenbaum, and A. V. Thakor, 1992, "Is Fairly Priced Deposit Insurance Possible?," *Journal of Finance*, 47, 227–246.

Cole, R. A., J. McKenzie, and L. White, 1990, "Deregulation Gone Awry: Moral Hazard in the Thrift Industry," working paper, Stern School of Business, New York University, December.

Dybvig, P. H., and J. F. Zender, 1991, "Capital Structure and Dividend Irrelevance with Asymmetric Information," *Review of Financial Studies*, 4, 201–219.

Esty, B. C., 1998, "The Impact of Contingent Liability on Commercial Bank Risk Taking," *Journal of Financial Economics*, 47, 189–212.

Evans, J., T. H. Noe, and J. H. Thorton, Jr., 1997, "Regulatory Distortion of Management Compensation: The Case of Golden Parachutes for Bank Managers," *Journal of Banking and Finance*, 21, 825–848.

Flannery, M. J., 1989, "Capital Regulation and Insured Bank's Choice of Individual Loan Default Risks," *Journal of Monetary Economics*, 24, 235–258.

Gilson, S. C., 1989, "Management Turnover and Financial Distress," *Journal of Financial Economics*, 25, 241–262.

Gilson, S. C., and M. R. Vetsuypens. 1993, "CEO Compensation in Financially Distressed Firms: An Empirical Analysis," *Journal of Finance*, 48, 425–458.

Green, R. C., 1984, "Investment Incentives, Debt and Warrants," *Journal of Financial Economics*, 13, 115–136.

Harris, M., and A. Raviv, 1979, "Optimal Incentive Contracts with Imperfect Information," *Journal of Economic Theory*, 20, 231–259.

Harris, M., and A. Raviv, 1988a, "Corporate Control Contests and Capital Structure," *Journal of Financial Economics*, 20, 55–86.

Harris, M., and A. Raviv, 1988b, "Corporate Governance: Voting Rights and Majority Rules," *Journal of Financial Economics*, 20, 203–235.

Holmstrom, B., 1979, "Moral Hazard and Observability," *Bell Journal of Economics*, 10, 74–91.

Houston, J., and C. James, 1993, "Management and Organizational Changes in Banking: A Comparison of Regulatory Intervention with Private Creditor Actions in Nonbank Firms," *Carnegie-Rochester Conference Series on Public Policy*, 38, 143–178.

Jensen, M., 1986, "Agency Costs of Free Cash Flow, Corporate Finance and Takeovers," *American Economic Review*, 76, 323–329.

Jensen, M., and W. Meckling, 1976, "Theory of the Firm: Managerial Behavior, Agency Costs and Ownership Structure," *Journal of Financial Economics*, 3, 305–360.

John, T. A., and K. John, 1993, "Top-Management Compensation and Capital Structure," *Journal of Finance*, 48, 949–974.

John, K., T. A. John, and L. W. Senbet, 1991, "Risk-Shifting Incentives of Depository Institutions: A New Perspective on Federal Deposit Insurance Reform," *Journal of Banking and Finance*, 15, 895–915.

Kane, E. J., 1986, "Appearance and Reality in Deposit Insurance: The Case for Reform," *Journal of Banking and Finance*, 10, 175–188.

Knopf, J. D., and J. L. Teall, 1996, "Risk-Taking Behavior in the U.S. Thrift Industry: Ownership Structure and Regulation Changes," *Journal of Banking and Finance*, 20, 1329–1350.

Madan, D. B., L. W. Senbet, and B. Soubra, 1993, "Capital Structure and the Design of Managerial Compensation," working paper, University of Maryland, December.

Mei, J., and A. Saunders, 1997, "Have U.S. Financial Institutions' Real Estate Investments Exhibited "Trend-Chasing" Behavior?," *Review of Economics and Statistics*, 79 (2), 248–258.

Myers, S. C., and N. S. Majluf, 1984, "Corporate Financing and Investment Decisions When Firms Have Information That Investors Do Not Have," *Journal of Financial Economics*, 13, 187–221.

Saunders, A., E. Strock, and N. Travlos, 1990, "Ownership Structure, Deregulation and Bank Risk-Taking," *Journal of Finance*, 45, 643–654.

IV. Banks and Corporate Governance

Bank Debt and Corporate Governance

Victoria Ivashina
Harvard University

Vinay B. Nair
Wharton School, University of Pennsylvania

Anthony Saunders
Leonard N. Stern School of Business, New York University

Nadia Massoud
Schulich School of Business, York University

Roger Stover
Iowa State University

In this paper, we investigate the disciplining role of banks and bank debt in the market for corporate control. We find that relationship bank lending intensity and bank client network have positive effects on the probability of a borrowing firm becoming a target. This effect is enhanced in cases where the target and acquirer have a relationship with the same bank. Moreover, we utilize an experiment to show that the effects of relationship bank lending intensity on takeover probability are not driven by endogeneity. Finally, we also investigate reasons motivating a bank's informational role in the market for corporate control. (*JEL* G10, G20, G21, G34)

As is well known, there is a long literature dating back to Fama (1985) and James (1987) that views banks as "insiders" to a firm. Specifically, in their role as suppliers of private debt (bank loans), they gather information that may well be unavailable to outside investors. Such information collection places them in the position of acting as firm monitors.[1] Banks, however, not only gather information but may also facilitate the transmission of this private information to potential acquirers. An example of such a private information transfer can

The authors would like to thank an anonymous referee, the editors, Yakov Amihud, Allen Berger, Andrew Metrick, and Randall Morck as well as seminar participants at the Australasian Conference of Banking and Finance, the European Financial Association Meeting in Maastricht, for helpful comments. Guo Hou, Rahul Ravi, Igor Semenenko, and Federica Pazzaglia provided excellent research assistance. Massoud would like to acknowledge financial support from the Social Sciences and Humanities Research Council of Canada. Send correspondence to Victoria Ivashina, Harvard Business School, Baker Library 233, Boston, MA 02116; telephone: (617)-495-8018; fax: (617)-495-6198; E-mail: vivashina@hbs.edu.

[1] Thus, a large number of studies have shown that bank loan announcements of loan renewals are taken as positive signals by investors in the capital markets and *vice versa* for loan sales (see, e.g., Dahiya, Puri, and Saunders, 2003).

doi:10.1093/rfs/hhn063 Advance Access publication June 19, 2008

The Review of Financial Studies / v 22 n 1 2009

be found in the litigation between Dana Corporation and its lender UBS. In the course of Dana's banking relationship, UBS was given "substantial amounts of confidential information about Dana, its financial condition, its business plan and prospects, its competitive posture, its trade secrets, and its potential liabilities."[2] Dana claimed that UBS passed this information to a potential acquirer (Arvin Meritor Inc.) to facilitate a takeover attempt.

In this paper, we investigate whether the information transmission role of banks has an important effect in the market for corporate control.[3] Unlike most of the recent corporate governance literature that views governance emanating from equity holders such as institutional investors, we examine the corporate governance role of private debt (in this case, bank debt). In particular, we examine the role of bank loans and their associated information production role in impacting the takeover probability of firms.[4] In using a sample of merger targets over the 1992–2005 period, we document several findings consistent with a positive information-based corporate governance role of banks in impacting the probability of corporate takeovers.

First, we find that greater bank lending intensity to a firm results in a higher likelihood that it will receive a takeover bid. Second, we find that those (target) firms having lending relationships with banks that have more clients in the same industry are more likely to be subject to a takeover attempt.[5] Third, we find that the role of bank lending intensity in predicting takeover attempts is stronger for those takeovers in which the target and acquirer have a relationship *with the same bank*. These results are robust to the inclusion of several controls shown to be important in predicting takeover targets (see, e.g., Palepu, 1986; Mikkelson and Partch, 1989; and Ambrose and Megginson, 1992 among others). Fourth, we conduct an experiment that is likely to be free of endogeneity problems; specifically, we analyze the bidding behavior of potential acquirers that switch relationship banks. Since switching is likely to be for reasons other than targeting a particular firm, it allows us to examine whether postswitching a potential acquirer has a higher probability of bidding for a client (target) of its new relationship bank. Evidence supporting this effect will be consistent with an

---

2 *Dana Corporation v. UBS Securities LLC, SEC file 5-10058.*

3 Easterbrook and Fischel (1991) and Jensen (1993) argue that takeovers constitute the critical mechanism in the United States and the U.K. without which managerial discretion cannot be controlled. Gompers, Ishii, and Metrick (2003) and Cremers, Nair, and John (2005) show a significant link between firm value, equity returns, and takeover vulnerability. The information we have in mind not only reflects the soft information that comes from close banking relationships (e.g., Stein, 2002; and Kano et al., 2006) but also private and early access to information that will eventually become public (e.g., banks often have access to firm cash-flow data on an interim period) (see Udell, 2004), as well as on business plans. Further, banks gain access to valuable information in their ability to monitor the size and variability of a firm's transaction accounts held at the bank (see Mester, Nakumura, and Renault, 2007).

4 In a recent paper, Santos and Rumble (2006) look at the role banks play via trust department equity holdings to gain access to corporate boards of directors (after controlling for the importance of bank lending). The role of banks in the collection and transfer of information in the context of small business is discussed in Berger, Klapper, and Udell (2001) among others.

5 We focus on clients in the same industry since it is in these cases where relationships that generate potential acquirers are most likely to be important.

informational role played by banks in the market for corporate control. Importantly, we find that firms with the characteristics of potential acquirers who switch to a new relationship bank are more likely to enter a bid for the clients of that new relationship bank.

Overall, our evidence is consistent with a role for banks in facilitating takeovers through information production via bank lending and the transmission of generated information to potential acquirers.[6] A question naturally arises as to why banks would actively engage in the transmission of information regarding client targets to potential acquirers. There are at least three plausible reasons. The first is to generate takeover advisory fees. The second is to generate additional loan and relationship-based revenues through a financing role in the takeover. The third is to reduce the bank's exposure to default risk by transferring debt from *ex ante* weak borrowers to *ex ante* strong borrowers.[7] These alternative motivational factors are analyzed in the final section of the paper. While we do not find evidence supporting the first two motives, it does appear that banks seek to transfer debt from *ex ante* weak borrowers to *ex ante* strong borrowers.

This documented "information intermediary" role of banks is not without controversy. Indeed, as noted above in the Dana example, there have been recent lawsuits in which target firms (or potential target firms) have sued their own bank over the transfer of "private" information regarding the firm to an outside acquirer. Since regulation does not prohibit commercial banks from providing M&A advisory services, nor is there a law against a bank "switching sides" and acting against its client in the role of advisor to a bidder, the courts have tended to look at case law to assess the merits of such complaints. The case filed by security systems company ADT Ltd against its long-time lender Chase Manhattan Corp in February 1997 received particular attention. ADT claimed Chase's managing directors repeatedly promised not to assist in any attempt to takeover the company. In that sense, this legal case was expected to set a precedent on lenders "duty of loyalty" to their borrowers.[8] At the time of the filing of the complaint, ADT had $1.1 billion in debt outstanding that it would have been forced to repay immediately if it lost the case. This included a repayment of its loans to Chase. Four months after the case filing, the court dismissed most of ADT's claims ruling that "a bank has no per se

[6] Our findings add to the literature on predicting takeover targets following Palepu (1986); Stulz (1988); Mikkelson and Partch (1989); and Ambrose and Meggison (1992). We find that in addition to factors such as leverage, industry, asset structure, and firm value, bank lending intensity as well as the presence of external blockholders is important in predicting takeover targets.

[7] Note that the motive is to transfer debt from a bad debtor to a good debtor and not simply to transfer bad debt. In the former case, debt improves in quality simply because of the transfer (e.g., due to better management) while the latter view considers debt quality fixed. If the quality of debt cannot be changed, then it is not clear why an acquirer would be willing to purchase a firm with troubled debt.

[8] *The Wall Street Journal*, February 11, 1997, "ADT sues Chase for aiding bidder seeking takeover"; *Bank Loan Report*, February 24, 1997, "ADT sues Chase over Western Resources Financing."

obligation to refrain from such participation, and that plaintiff has not pleaded the existence of a fiduciary relationship which might give rise to such an obligation."[9]

Even though the ADT ruling has reduced the number of similar pleadings, there are other cases relating to similar issues involving banks both in the United States and abroad. Most of this centers on the supposed disclosure of confidential loan information. For example, in 1999, Mannesmann, the German telecommunications company, which was the target of an unsolicited takeover bid by Vodafone, sued Vodafone's adviser Goldman Sachs arguing that Goldman used private information generated through a prior lending relationship without Mannesmann's consent. A British court later dismissed the case calling it "hopeless." For similar reasons, in 2000, Dime Bancorp sued Salomon Smith Barney on the grounds that it acted as an adviser to North Fork Bancorp in its unsolicited takeover attempt; this case was also dismissed. More recently, in August 2003, auto-parts maker Dana Corporation argued that UBS, which had a prior lending relationship with the company, used confidential information to help its rival Arvin Meritor Inc. to launch a $2.2 billion unsolicited bid.[10] This last case is still undetermined. The question thus arises as to whether these complaints are founded or are they just part of a target's effort to thwart a takeover? Overall, it appears that the courts are seeking to make a legal distinction between the use of information generated in the course of a banking relationship and the use of information disclosed under a confidentiality agreement, the breach of which, if proven in Court, would be considered a breach of fiduciary duty. Clearly, where the line is drawn is fuzzy and the courts have so far appeared to side with the first view.[11]

We proceed by outlining a simple framework to specify our hypotheses in Section 1. In Section 2, we discuss the data sources for our study, in particular the source of our takeover and loan data and the measurement of key variables. Using a sample of Compustat companies, Section 3 examines the impact of bank lending intensity and bank client networks on the probability of a takeover attempt occurring, using control variables from the existing literature on takeover activity in general. In that section, we also present a variety of robustness checks including controlling for equity-side corporate governance mechanisms and an experiment that looks at how the effect of a potential acquirer switching its relationship bank affects the probability of targeting a client of its new relationship bank. Section 4 looks at the motives for banks playing an informational role in the takeover market. Finally, Section 5 concludes.

---

[9] *ADT Operations, Inc. v. Chase Manhattan Bank*, N.A. 662 N.Y.S. 2d 190 (1997).

[10] *The New York Times*, August 5, 2003, "Auto part manufacturer sues banker of an unwanted suitor."

[11] We thank William Allen, former Chancellor of the Delaware Court, for discussions and insights relating to the legal issues involved.

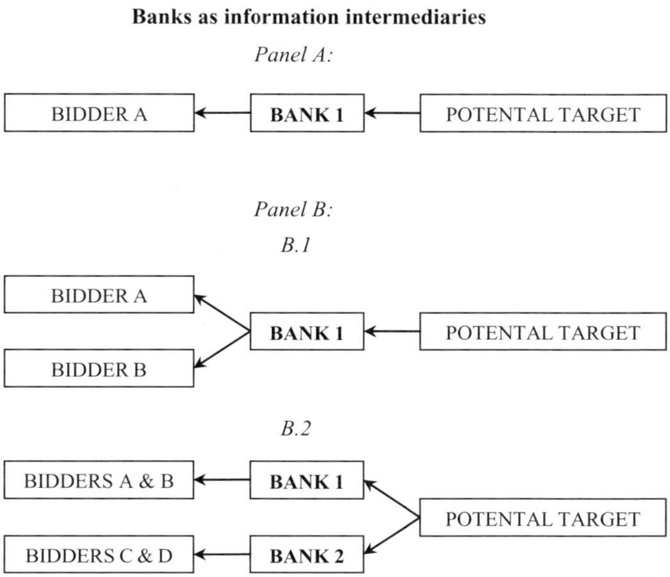

Figure 1
Banks as information intermediaries

1. Banks as Information Intermediaries

In this section, we specify our hypotheses that, if supported, would be consistent with the view that banks act not only as information collectors and monitors but also as information transmitters in the market for corporate control. If these hypotheses are left unsupported, then this latter role of information transmission is unlikely to be important in affecting the takeover mechanism.

Figure 1 (panel A) depicts the information intermediary role that a main or relationship bank plays among firms in the takeover market. The bank shown (Bank 1) has one borrower and can transfer information about one firm (potential target) to another (Bidder A); the motivations for this, such as credit risk reduction, merger fee generation, and finance fee generation are analyzed later in the paper. More generally, since a bank has lending relationships with many firms, it can transfer information about any borrowing firm to a number of potential acquirers. Importantly, the more intensive the bank-borrower relationship, the more information about the borrower that can be generated and transferred to potential acquirers, that is, the more extensive a bank's information set is, the greater is the likelihood that an acquirer will appear. Our first hypothesis is then

Hypothesis 1. *Greater lending intensity by its relationship bank increases the probability of a borrower being a takeover target.*

If banks' act as information intermediaries and actively transfer information to potential acquirers, then a firm is more likely to be a target if it deals with a relationship bank that has many borrowing clients and hence many lending relationships. In Figure 1 (panel B.1), for example, if the relationship bank deals with both firms A and B, there is an additional potential acquirer and hence a greater likelihood of being taken over. This is particularly so if firms A and B are in the same industry as the potential target. Similarly (panel B.2), the pool of potential acquirers is likely to be greater when the target firm deals with more than one relationship bank (Banks 1 and 2 in Figure 1), each with its own client base. Since a greater pool of potential acquirers is likely to increase the chance of a bid, we hypothesize that

Hypothesis 2. *The larger the number of firms (client base) that the target relationship bank(s) deals with, the greater is the associated probability of being a takeover target.*

If a bank acts as an information intermediary, it is also more likely that the acquirer will appear from among the bank's own clients. Thus, we would expect to see a higher takeover probability when the acquirer and the target have a relationship with *the same relationship bank.* More importantly, in such takeovers, the predictive role of bank lending intensity would also be expected to be stronger, which leads us to our third hypothesis:

Hypothesis 3. *The importance of relationship bank lending intensity in predicting takeovers is higher for takeovers where the acquirer and the target share a relationship with the same bank.*

While confirming Hypotheses 1, 2, and 3 would provide evidence consistent with a bank's informational role in takeovers, they do not establish a clear *causal* relationship or link between bank information and the probability of an acquirer pursuing a particular target. In Hypothesis 4, we explore further banks' informational role in takeovers by constructing an experiment in which a potential acquirer (a firm matched by size and industry) switches its relationship bank and test whether *following the switch*, a potential acquirer is more likely to bid on a target that is a client of the new relationship bank (see Figure 2).[12] Since acquirers that switch banks are likely to do so for reasons *other than acquisition of a particular target*, we can view the decision (by a potential acquirer) to switch as *independent* of the decision to bid on a particular target. A switch represents an exogenous shift in the private information about a potential target that an acquirer could receive from its relationship bank. Thus, a finding that a potential acquirer, after switching to a new relationship bank, has a higher probability of acquiring potential client firms of its new relationship bank would be consistent with a causal link between bank

[12] A number of issues arise as to the degree to which this test of Hypothesis 4 is a "natural experiment." We examine this when we discuss our results of Hypothesis 4 later in the paper in Section 3.4.

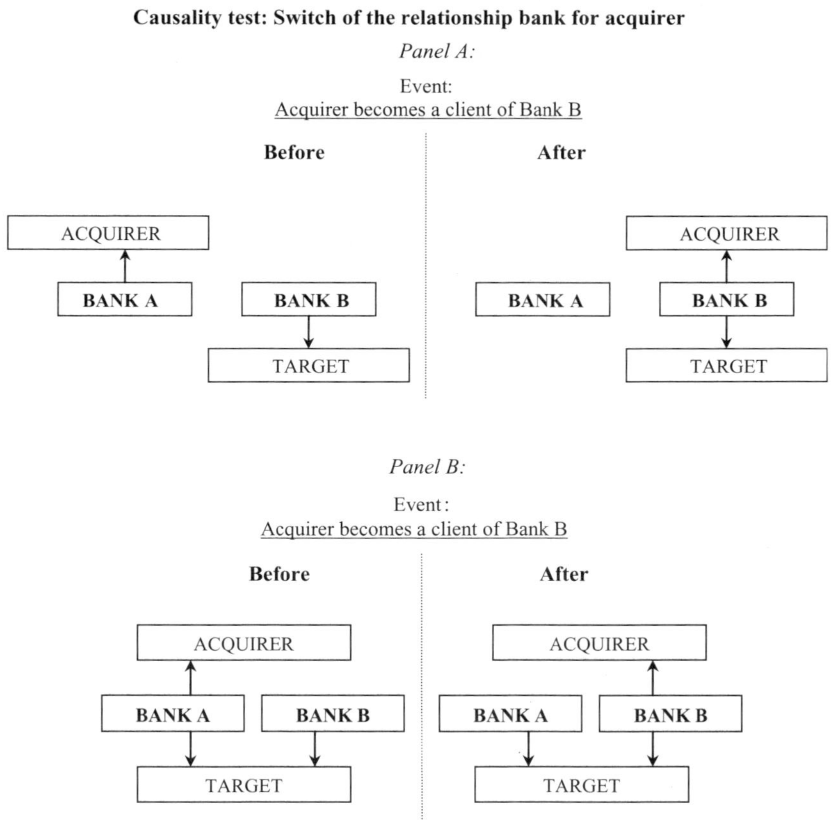

Figure 2
Causality test: switch of the relationship bank for acquirer

information production and the probability of a takeover. This leads to our fourth hypothesis:

Hypothesis 4. *A firm that switches relationship banks is more likely to acquire a client firm of its new relationship bank.*

2. Data and Methodology

2.1 Takeovers

A crucial issue is defining the set of takeovers relevant to our tests. In particular, hostile takeovers are most likely to reflect the type of information transfers that are of interest here. However, linking theory to the data is a little more difficult; specifically, in defining our sample of hostile takeovers, we use the SDC definition and data. In using SDC, we felt that there might be a "gray" area

The Review of Financial Studies / v 22 n 1 2009

that was worth exploring given our hypotheses that relate to private information transfers from a bank to potential acquirers. The gray area arises because of the difference between deal attitudes when initiated and when announced; SDC codes deal with attitude based on the *announcement* of the deal while we are interested in the *initiation*. There is a mismatch between these two because, in general, the deal could be initiated by the acquirer, the target, or the bank. Ideally, we would be interested in deals initiated by the bank and the acquirer; however, the "deal attitude" identified by the SDC often does not allow us to detect these deals in a precise manner. It is true that if the deal is initiated by the target, it is unambiguously classified as friendly. Yet if initiated by the acquirer, the deal could be classified as hostile (where the target resists), unsolicited, or even friendly since the first approach might then lead to friendly negotiations (this is consistent with Boone and Mulherin's (2006) description of how deal activity evolves preannouncement).[13] Similar possibilities exist for deals where the bank acts as the matchmaker. Further, based on our hypotheses, we might expect lesser resistance from weaker targets to acquirers (due to bank pressure) making the "deal attitude" variable in SDC somewhat noisy for our purposes. Thus, in our tables and hypothesis tests, we report the results for *both* the total and hostile takeover samples.[14]

To examine the impact of bank information transmission on takeovers, we employ a number of datasets, specifically focusing our tests on the acquisition activity of firms in the Compustat database over the 1992–2005 period. A full description of our data can be found in the Appendix, where the key variables employed in our (logit) tests are fully described. In addition, in Table 1 we present descriptive statistics and correlations for each explanatory variable.

2.2 Bank loans

To generate data on bank lenders and loans, we use the Loan Pricing Corporation's (LPC) DealScan database for individual bank loans. These data track large loan originations made by banks to generally large companies from 1987 to the present. Currently, over 150,000 loans have been included in the LPC database, with U.S. loans accounting for 60% of these loans. LPC collects data from SEC filings, industry contacts, and directly from lenders. As LPC has established a reputation for tracking loans and publishing league tables that rate bankers, e.g., in syndications, banks have an incentive to voluntarily report their loans.[15] These loans tend to be the largest and most important loans made by any bank.[16]

---

13 Boone and Mulherin (2006) also raise issues concerning gray areas in SDC's definition of takeover terminations.

14 We exclude from the sample financial companies with two-digit SIC Codes 60 through 64. Between 1992 and 2005, our sample identifies 1,454 takeover attempts of which 330 are classified as hostile.

15 Note that even smaller banks have an incentive to report their large syndicated loans, as these ratings are important in syndications where smaller banks are often participants.

16 We looked at a sample of 10-K reports of one hundred randomly selected firms with zero loan intensity based on LPC's DealScan and found that in 70% of the cases companies in fact don't report having any loans outstanding,

Table 1
Descriptive statistics of the sample

Panel A: Sample characteristics

Compustat sample (number of observations = 28,234)

Variable	Median	Mean	Standard error
Industry M&A intensity	1	0.819	0.002
ROA (adj.)	0.010	−0.103	0.005
Sales growth (adj.)	0.003	0.176	0.005
Market/Book assets (adj.)	−0.022	0.703	0.027
Ln (Assets)	4.566	4.794	0.013
Asset structure (PPE)	0.180	0.276	0.001
Cash	0.149	0.242	0.001
Leverage	0.432	0.500	0.003
Institutional blockholder	0	0.471	0.003
Rated	0	0.142	0.002
High yield	0	0.070	0.002
Bad z-score	0	0.342	0.003
Bank dependence	0	0.131	0.002
Short maturity	0	0.121	0.002
Loan intensity (Exposure)	0	0.419	0.055
Loan intensity (N)	0	0.553	0.006
Relation intensity (Exposure)	0	0.165	0.030
Relation intensity (N)	0	0.405	0.004
Bank net (log)	−2.303	−1.262	0.011

Table 1
Continued

Panel B: Correlation coefficients

		1	2	3	4	5	6	7	8	9
1	*Industry M&A intensity*									
2	*ROA (adj.)*	0.005								
3	*Sales growth (adj.)*	−0.003	0.022***							
4	*Market/Book assets (adj.)*	0.012**	−0.189***	0.120***						
5	*Ln(Assets)*	−0.002	0.241***	0.001	−0.113***					
6	*Asset structure (PPE)*	0.009	0.025***	−0.044***	−0.063***	0.274***				
7	*Cash*	0.070***	−0.039***	0.124***	0.137***	−0.241***	−0.488***			
8	*Leverage*	−0.022***	−0.452***	−0.074***	0.161***	−0.052***	0.103***	−0.237***		
9	*Institutional blockholder*	−0.007	0.104***	−0.016***	−0.055***	0.224***	−0.022***	0.037***	−0.099***	
10	*Rated*	−0.016***	0.069***	−0.035***	−0.035***	0.523***	0.250***	−0.228***	0.083***	0.056***
11	*High yield*	−0.028***	0.032***	−0.005	−0.037***	0.239***	0.138***	−0.129***	0.090***	0.080***
12	*Bad z-score*	−0.017***	−0.247***	−0.047***	−0.066***	−0.067***	0.200***	−0.148***	0.380***	−0.132***
13	*Bank dependence*	−0.007	0.024***	−0.012	−0.018***	−0.053***	−0.001	−0.052***	−0.008	0.091***
14	*Short maturity*	−0.002	0.029***	−0.013**	−0.013**	0.054***	0.018***	−0.073***	0.006	0.093***
15	*Loan intensity (Exposure)*	0.010	−0.029***	−0.005	0.009	−0.030***	0.001	−0.013**	0.039***	0.000
16	*Loan intensity (N)*	−0.027***	0.061***	−0.024***	−0.051***	0.331***	0.161***	−0.254***	0.082***	0.206***
17	*Relation intensity (Exposure)*	0.008	−0.021***	0.000	0.006	−0.023***	−0.002	−0.006	0.017***	0.002
18	*Relation intensity (N)*	−0.024***	0.067***	−0.027***	−0.051***	0.324***	0.151***	−0.254***	0.062***	0.226***
19	*Bank net*	0.001	0.060***	−0.039***	−0.050***	0.228***	0.099***	−0.208***	0.047***	0.221***

Bank Debt and Corporate Governance

		10	11	12	13	14	15	16	17	18
10	*Rated*									
11	*High yield*	0.675***								
12	*Bad z-score*	0.042***	0.084***							
13	*Bank dependence*	−0.063***	−0.024***	−0.022***						
14	*Short maturity*	0.030***	−0.001	−0.027***	0.549***					
15	*Loan intensity (Exposure)*	0.006	0.000	0.027***	0.023***	0.025***				
16	*Loan intensity (N)*	0.277***	0.210***	0.041***	0.295***	0.337***	0.075***			
17	*Relation intensity (Exposure)*	0.005	−0.003	0.012**	0.026***	0.025***	0.861***	0.045***		
18	*Relation intensity (N)*	0.264***	0.179***	0.005	0.379***	0.412***	0.059***	0.887***	0.043***	
19	*Bank net*	0.165***	0.136***	−0.001	0.462***	0.443***	0.066***	0.649***	0.049***	0.712***

Panel A presents descriptive statistics for the all Compustat-based samples for 1992–2005. *Industry M&A intensity* is equal to 1 if there was an M&A in a firm's four-digit SIC industry in the year prior to the year of observation. *ROA (adj.)* is the industry-median-adjusted return on assets. *Sales growth (adj.)* is the industry-median-adjusted annual rate of change in the firm's net sales. *Market/Book assets (adj.)* is the industry-median-adjusted ratio of market-to-book value of assets, where market assets are defined as total assets plus market value of common stock minus book common equity and deferred taxes. Firm size is proxied by the natural logarithm of *a firm's assets*. *PPE* is property, plant, and equipment-to-assets ratio. *Cash* is cash and short-term investments-to-assets ratio. *Leverage* is book debt-to-assets ratio. *Institutional blockholder* is a dummy variable assigned the value 1 if at least one institutional investor holds more than 5% of the firm's stock and 0 otherwise. *Rated* is a dummy equal to 1 if the company has a debt rating. *High yield* is a dummy equal to 1 if the debt rating is below investment grade. *Bad z-score* is a dummy equal to 1 if the z-score is below 1.81. *Bank dependence*, *Short maturity*, *Bank net*, *Loan*, and *Relation intensity* are all defined in the Appendix. The sample includes firms that were targets of an M&A and the control sample is matched by industry and asset size, with valid accounting information in the event year excluding financial firms identified with two-digit SIC Codes 60 through 64.

***, **, and* stand for significance at the 1%, 5%, and 10% levels, respectively.

The Review of Financial Studies / v 22 n 1 2009

Since bank information is likely to be related to its lending intensity to a particular firm, we begin by assuming that LPC loan activity (normalized by the borrowing firm's assets) is an appropriate proxy or indicator of a bank's incentive to gather information. Greater loan activity, all else equal, implies greater credit risk exposure and greater potential relationship banking activity.[17]

To measure lending intensity, we examine two key aspects of a lending relationship that are related to the amount of *private* information in the hands of a bank: (1) its dollar lending exposure to a borrower (*Loan intensity* (*Exposure*)) and (2) the frequency of its lending interaction with a borrower (*Loan intensity* (*N*)). The first measure, dollar exposure, reflects that the incentives banks have to collect information in the face of enhanced credit exposure. Using lending facility level data, we collect the amount and maturities of loans so as to calculate a measure of the maximum bank *exposure* (*stock* of loans) to a given company prior to the event (takeover). Thus, this measure reflects loans made in the prior year plus older loans that are still outstanding in the year prior to a takeover bid.[18]

The second measure reflects the frequency of a lender-borrower interaction and thus the flow of (new) private information in the hands of a bank generated as the result of each new loan. We use deal level information to compute the number of loans originated by the bank in the three years prior to a takeover attempt on a target firm. A three-year period was chosen for two reasons: (1) the period is sufficiently long enough to establish banking relationships that produce a flow of valuable private information to potential acquirers and (2) the mean maturity of a loan in the LPC database is approximately three years.[19]

While we utilize both measures for completeness, we recognize that the exposure variable may have some measurement problems. First, we are trying to proxy for a stock of loans' exposure using flow data from DealScan, which only allows us to observe new loan data at the time of origination. Second, some of these loans may be lines of credit (LCs) that are undrawn (although we deal with this issue later in the case of commercial paper backed LCs). Third, not all loans in DealScan may be new; in fact, some may be renegotiations of old loans. Fourth, some of the loans in the database are to finance prior loans, and to avoid double-counting, they cannot be added to new loans. While we are able to track loan renegotiations on DealScan, and there is no

including *credit lines* and term loan. Thus our search of the 10-Ks included LCs, as well as term loans. For those cases where companies report having some loans, but are not reflected in DealScan (30% of the cases), we found the amount of loans outstanding was economically very small. In fact, the median stock loan/assets ratio was close to 0% and the mean close to 9%. In the DealScan sample for companies with loans reported, the median loan exposure/assets ratio corresponds to nearly 100%.

17 In fact, banks commonly take a portfolio view (based on the law of large numbers) for small and medium enterprise loans. To ensure that our results are not driven by any omitted loan information, we use a narrower control for the target sample in Section 3 that is matched by propensity scores.

18 We tested the robustness of this result using various maturity limits.

19 The LPC database starts from 1987. We choose to focus on targets from 1992 to avoid the potential impact of Drexel Burnham on the takeover market.

double-counting there, it is not possible to identify refinancings, although a bank can be viewed as updating its information when it engages in a refinancing. As will be discussed below, it is the *Loan intensity* (*N*) variable (which reflects information updating) rather than *Loan intensity* (*Exposure*) variable that has the greatest impact on takeover probability and is the major focus of our tests.

The dollar amount of loans (*Loan intensity* (*Exposure*)) and frequency of lending (*Loan intensity* (*N*)) may reflect positions taken by all banks in the lending syndicate, including active relationship-based roles and passive or transactional roles. Hence, we use information on the role of the bank in the syndicate and the actual amount of the loan retained by the bank as the result of the syndication to distinguish between loan intensity and relationship intensity. Specifically, to define a relationship bank, we exclude all the syndicate members that act as "participants" and we look at the amount of the loan retained by each remaining bank to identify the banks with the largest exposures.[20] Because the lead bank might just play an administrative or underwriting role in the lending syndicate, an exposure-based variable is a better way to identify the relationship bank. Using this criterion, we identify a relationship bank for a borrower (loan) and use it to define *Relation intensity* (*Exposure*) and *Relation intensity (N)*. It is important to note, in passing, that the correlations of the loan intensity variables with firm overall leverage measures are very small (see Table 1, panel B), thus reducing concerns of multicollinearity in tests that involve both firm leverage and loan intensity.

A final key lending variable, in measuring the impact of bank-related information transmission effects on the probability of takeovers, is a measure of the target's relationship banks' links with their own clients who fit the characteristics of potential acquirers (*Bank net*). This is calculated by summing the number of potential acquirers that share a lending relationship with the *same* relationship bank as the potential target, where potential acquirers are selected

[20] To measure a relationship bank or banks to a particular firm, we need to designate a cutoff point to distinguish relationship banks from nonrelationship banks. To do this we first look at each firm's syndicated loans over a three-year window. For each of these loans, we exclude banks designated as participants by DealScan and retain those lenders designated as either an arranger or coarranger. We then add the dollar amounts of loans made to that borrower by each arranger or coarranger bank during the three-year period. Second, we designate the largest dollar lender to the firm as having a scale of 100 (or 100%). The next largest lender is scaled to be a percentage of the largest lender (e.g., 80% as large, 70% as large, etc.). Third, this exercise is repeated for every borrower in our sample. We then aggregate the lender-scaled shares (below 100%) across all borrowing firms. This produces a distribution of scaled shares below the largest relationship bank (i.e., the 100% scaled bank). Examining this distribution, we find that the top decile of this empirical distribution has shares exceeding 80% of the largest relationship bank share. We then designate 80% as the cutoff point to identify the identity of relationship banks for each borrower. The characteristics of this variable are perhaps best explained by a simple example. If over the past three years there are two loans made to the same borrower, say, \$180 million and \$200 million, then in the first case Chase is the lead bank and it retains 50% of the loan (\$90 million); in the second case, Citi is the lead and it retains 50% of the loan (\$100 million). Under our criteria, both banks will be defined as relationship banks because Chase's \$90 million retained is 90% as large as the \$100 million retained by Citi. While Chase's exposure is smaller than Citi's, it is sufficiently large to be viewed as a relationship bank along with Citi using the 80% cutoff point. However, if it retained \$70 million, it would not be a relationship bank because it does not correspond to the top decile of the empirical distribution of bank syndicate exposures (i.e., it doesn't exceed the 80% cutoff relative to the largest bank's lending exposure).

The Review of Financial Studies / v 22 n 1 2009

based on the commonality of their two-digit SIC Code and asset size to the target, over a three-year window prior to a takeover attempt.

While this variable measures both the extensive nature of the relationship bank's network of potential acquirers (and thus the takeover threat to the target), it is possible that the target's managers might seek to avoid a takeover by switching from a high "net" relationship bank to a low "net" relationship bank. If such switching is complete and includes both new loans and the refinancing of all old loans, then the value of the *Bank net* variable could fall. However, if switching is incomplete, e.g., some older loans remain with the original relationship bank, then both the old and new relationship banks will have incentives to disseminate information and *Bank net* would increase. Importantly, the *Bank net* variable is inclusive of old and new banks.[21]

2.3 Other loan-related control variables

In addition to our lending intensity and relationship variables, we also introduce *Short maturity*, dummy equal to 1 if the borrowing firm receives loans of a shorter maturity than the industry median and 0 otherwise. This controls for the fact the frequency of loan issues (*N*) is also likely to be related to the choice of maturity. In addition, a positive coefficient on this variable would be consistent with riskier borrowers being more likely to be the subject of a takeover bid since banks tend to lend shorter term to riskier borrowers. Secondly, we control for relationship bank dependence (*Bank dependence*) with a dummy equal to 1 if the borrower had only one relationship bank over the three years prior to a takeover attempt and 0 otherwise. The relationship bank dependence dummy is 1, if no other bank had an exposure (dollar amount) to the borrower within 80% of the dollar exposure of the main relationship bank.[22] If other banks are above the 80% threshold, the borrowing firm is viewed as having multiple relationship banks (dummy is 0). An alternative measure of exclusivity or dependence would be one where the target had an exclusive relationship with its lead syndicate bank, i.e., lead bank exclusivity, as will be discussed later, the major results of the paper are unchanged whether we use relationship bank exclusivity or lead bank exclusivity to measure bank dependence.

2.4 Shareholder control

While our focus is on governance effects emanating from bank lending activity, we also collected data on shareholder (equity) control. It has been argued that takeovers are more likely to occur as shareholder control increases (Shleifer and Vishny, 1986). Cremers, Nair, and John (2005) also document supporting evidence that firms with a large external blockholder are more

[21] As we show later in the paper, the role of banks in facilitating takeovers is more important for underperforming borrowers. In that sense, if managers use switching to prevent takeovers, this will create a large adverse selection cost.

[22] See the earlier discussion on measuring the relationship bank, as well as the example provided justifying the 80% cutoff in Footnote 20.

likely to be takeover targets. Thus, we control for a large shareholder corporate governance effect by using a dummy for the existence of an institutional blockholder, denoted by *Institutional blockholder* = 1, if such an institutional blockholder is present and 0 otherwise. We define blockholders to be those institutional shareholders that have more than a 5% ownership stake in the firm's outstanding shares. To construct this measure, we use data on institutional share holdings from Thompson/CDA Spectrum, which collects quarterly information from SEC 13f filings.[23] By using institutional blockholdings rather than simply institutional ownership, we mitigate the problem that institutions with small equity stakes have little incentive to be involved in firm-specific decisions. Furthermore, Shleifer and Vishny (1986) argue that blockholders often have substantial voting control, thereby enabling them to pressure a firm's management. Such control rights can be especially valuable in a proxy fight.

2.5 Other control variables

In addition to the bank-side information production and equity-side corporate governance variables, we utilize a number of other control variables that have been used in the prior literature seeking to explain the probability of takeovers in general; these variables might thus also be expected to impact the probability of a takeover bid occurring (see, for example, Hasbrouck, 1985; Palepu, 1986; Mikkelson and Partch, 1989; and Ambrose and Megginson, 1992, among others). The additional variables introduced, based on the existing takeover literature, are a takeover intensity dummy that measures whether a takeover attempt occurred in the same four-digit SIC industry in the year prior to the takeover event, the return on assets (ROA) of the firm (adjusted for the industry median), annual sales growth (adjusted for the industry median), firm leverage (measured by the book debt-to-assets ratio), cash (the cash and short-term investments-to-assets ratio), firm size (measured by the log of assets), the ratio of market-to-book value of assets (industry-median-adjusted), asset structure (measured by the property, plant, and equipment-to-assets ratio), and sales growth (industry-median-adjusted). Finally, we introduce a number of controls for the credit quality of the borrower including a dummy of 1 if its rated, and a credit-quality-related variable based on the Altman (1968) z-score model, which is *Bad z-score*, a dummy of 1, if the z-score falls below the Altman threshold value of $z = 1.81$, denoting that the firm is in the bad creditworthiness (high default probability) region. We also introduce a high-yield dummy that is 1 if the target is rated below investment grade. Table 1A provides the mean, median, and standard error of the Compustat sample variables used in our tests, as well as the correlations among these variables (Table 1B).

[23] The 1978 amendment to the Security and Exchange Act of 1934 requires all institutional investors with more than $100 million under management to report their shareholdings to the SEC.

The Review of Financial Studies / v 22 n 1 2009

2.6 Logit methodology

To analyze the impact of a banking relationship on the probability of becoming a target, we use a logit methodology. Two methods of selecting the control sample were employed. In the first method, we select companies that were not a target of a takeover attempt in the entire sample period, starting with all the companies reported in Compustat that are not included in the takeover target sample. To ensure that the control sample contains similar companies to the targets, we identify control firms with the same four-digit SIC Code as the target in the same event year.[24] Thus, we use SIC Code (four-digit) and year as matching variables to generate 26,780 such control firms; based on this sample, each firm has approximately a 0.5% average probability of being a target each year. The cumulative probability of becoming a target between 1992 and 2005 is much higher and equal to 51%. In the second method, we utilize a logit analysis as a first step in *propensity score* matching, where matching occurs over an array of financial characteristics of target and matching firms.

An issue of concern is that certain industries have more control firms than others, thus leading to a different number of matches for different targets. To deal with this issue, we use industry dummies (not reported in the tables) that control for differences in the number of firms across industries and other industry-specific effects.[25]

3. Results

3.1 Relationship bank lending intensity and the likelihood of becoming a target (Hypothesis 1)

Our first set of tests focus on bank lending intensity and the probability of an acquisition occurring over the 1992–2005 period. A logit model is used to detect the probability of a firm being the target of a bid, where a target firm receiving a bid has a dummy of 1 and 0 otherwise; the target dummy is the dependent variable in the logit model.[26] The probability of becoming a target in year *t* is estimated annually. Table 2 shows the logit test results for the total sample of 1,454 targets and 28,234 firm observations.

The first column of coefficients in Table 2 reports the results without bank lending intensity variables. The statistically significant variable coefficients in column 1 are ROA, market-to-book ratio, asset size, cash, the presence of a large institutional blockholder, existence of a debt rating, and a dummy of 1 if the target's debt is below investment grade quality (high yield). These results indicate that firms that are profitable (high industry-adjusted ROA) with cash

[24] Targets for which we are unable to find at least one matching control company with valid accounting information are dropped.

[25] Using a one-to-one matching technique, utilizing a Barber-Lyon (1996) matching methodology, also produced similar results. These results are available from the authors on request.

[26] We used the four-digit SIC match to construct a control sample. This is because we want the control sample (companies that don't become targets) to be very similar to the cases where they are targets.

Table 2
Bank lending intensity and takeover probability

	1		2		3		4		5		6	
Variable	Coefficient	Wald	Coefficient	Wald	Coefficient	Wald	Coefficient	Wald	Coefficient	Wald	Coefficient	Wald
Industry M&A intensity	0.06	0.1	0.04	0.0	0.03	0.0	0.03	0.0	0.03	0.0	−0.57	6.6***
ROA (adj.)	0.20	4.1**	0.19	3.7*	0.20	3.9**	0.20	3.9**	0.20	3.9**	0.33	1.6
Sales growth (adj.)	0.00	0.0	0.00	0.0	0.00	0.0	0.00	0.0	0.00	0.0	−0.12	1.2
Market/Book assets (adj.)	−0.06	12.0***	−0.06	12.5***	−0.06	12.5***	−0.06	12.5***	−0.06	12.5***	−0.23	15.0***
Ln(Assets)	0.04	3.5*	0.02	0.9	0.01	0.5	0.02	0.7	0.02	0.5	−0.01	0.0
Asset structure (PPE)	−0.16	0.5	−0.12	0.3	−0.12	0.3	−0.12	0.3	−0.12	0.3	−0.05	0.0
Cash	0.34	4.5**	0.46	7.8***	0.49	8.8***	0.49	8.8***	0.49	8.8***	−0.58	2.3
Leverage	−0.09	0.8	−0.12	1.2	−0.12	1.2	−0.13	1.3	−0.12	1.2	0.24	1.2
Institutional blockholder	0.83	175.4***	0.78	152.4***	0.77	147.0***	0.77	147.0***	0.77	147.0***	0.72	31.0***
Rated	−1.01	39.9***	−1.03	41.6***	−1.05	43.0***	−1.05	43.1***	−1.05	43.1***	−0.54	4.3**
High yield	0.60	10.4***	0.58	9.7***	0.60	10.3***	0.60	10.5***	0.60	10.5***	0.53	3.3*
Bad z-score	0.07	0.8	0.06	0.6	0.07	0.7	0.07	0.8	0.07	0.7	−0.16	1.1
Bank dependence			0.10	1.3	0.06	0.4	0.06	0.4	0.06	0.4	−0.14	0.6
Short maturity			0.19	4.2**	0.16	3.0*	0.16	3.0*	0.16	2.9***	0.18	1.0
Loan intensity (Exposure)			−0.02	0.6	0.00	0.0						
Loan intensity (N)			0.12	16.9***	0.02	0.1						
Relation intensity (Exposure)					−0.05	0.5			−0.06	0.9	−0.12	0.3
Relation intensity (N)					0.19	6.2***	0.20	21.9***	0.21	23.2***	0.33	15.8***
Observations		28,234		28,234		28,234		28,234		28,234		11,355
Targets		1,454		1,454		1,454		1,454		1,454		330
Pseudo R^2		0.64		0.64		0.64		0.64		0.64		0.68
Max.-rescaled R^2		0.85		0.85		0.85		0.85		0.85		0.91

This table presents results of the maximum likelihood estimates of the logit model for the sample of takeovers that occurred between 1992 and 2005 excluding financial firms identified with two-digit SIC Codes 60 through 64. The dependent variable is a dummy (*Target*) equal to 1 if the company is target of an attempted takeover or merger. The sample includes firms that were targets of a takeover or merger and the control sample is matched by industry and size with valid accounting information in the event year. Columns 1–5 test the robustness of alternative measures of lending intensity for all takeovers. Column 6 examines the case of unsolicited takeovers only. The point estimates and Wald chi-square statistics for industry effects are not reported, although they are included in the logit tests and they are jointly significant at the 1% level. Year effects are jointly insignificant and not included in the logit tests. ***, **, and * indicate p-values of 1%, 5%, and 10%, respectively.

but have low valuations (market-to-book) and a large external shareholder are more likely to become targets. Further, the *lack* of access to bond markets as indicated by the absence of a debt rating is also associated with a higher probability of becoming a target, while of those who are rated, lower rated quality issuers (high yield) have the highest probability of becoming targets.

The second column of Table 2 includes four additional variables that are related to bank lending intensity and hence a bank's information generation about a borrower. A bank's information about a borrower is likely to be a function of the amount of loans outstanding to that borrower (*Loan intensity* (*Exposure*)). Further, new information is collected at loan origination. Thus, lending frequency (*Loan intensity* (*N*)) captures the flow of new private information to the bank.

Specifically, as discussed above, *Loan intensity* (*Exposure*) is the maximum loan amount (estimated stock of loans) available to the borrower one year prior to the takeover date divided by the firm's assets. This reflects both loan transactions occurring within that (prior) year and loans made earlier to that year, where their maturities extend beyond the year of the proposed takeover. *Loan intensity* (*N*) is the number of loans issued by a bank to a borrower over a three-year window prior to the year of the takeover. Furthermore, we add two lending control variables: a *Short maturity* dummy, which equals 1 if the maturity of the loans made to the target are shorter than the industry median and a *Bank dependence* dummy, which equals 1 if the target had only one relationship bank in the three years prior to the takeover attempt. The *Bank dependence* variable reflects the target's reliance on a single relationship bank and controls for the potential effect of pressure being applied by the main relationship bank on the target to engage in a takeover deal.[27]

As can be seen in column 2 of Table 2, it is the frequency (*N*) with which new loans are made to the target, rather than the dollar amount outstanding that is important in explaining the probability of a borrowing firm becoming a target. This is consistent with the argument made above regarding the link between informational disclosure at the time a loan is made and the probability that the bank will utilize that information to promote future takeover deals. Since banks are more likely to collect new and additional information at the time of loan origination, this finding is consistent with the presence of a bank-lending-related informational channel in the market for corporate control.

Since our focus is on the bank information channel, we refine our tests by focusing next on the intensity of a potential target's borrowing relationship with its *main* or *relationship* bank. We define a relationship bank, or banks, using actual exposure (dollar amount) loaned to the target as a syndicate lead arranger, measured over a three-year window (see Footnote 20).[28] Because

[27] This is the mirror image of the type of holdup problems considered by Rajan (1992).

[28] We use loan syndicate structure to calculate the actual exposure to the target. Multiple relationship banks are possible if there are other banks with exposure no less than 80% of the top relationship bank (see Footnote 20).

relationship banks are expected to generate more information about a borrower than other banks, we would expect the intensity with which a firm borrows from a relationship bank to be a superior indicator of bank information production than a general or transactional banking relationship (e.g., a syndicate participant or a bank with a small syndicate share). In column 3 of Table 2, we use variables capturing loan exposure and loan frequency but focus only on the lending by main or relationship banks. The results, reported in column 3 of Table 2, show that a higher frequency of borrowing from a relationship bank is associated with a greater likelihood of a target receiving a takeover bid. This can be seen by the large and highly significant positive sign of the *Relation intensity* (*N*) variable. Interestingly, the other measures of lending intensity—including the general measures of lending intensity, *Loan intensity* (*Exposure*), and *Loan intensity* (*N*)—are now insignificantly different from zero. This suggests that the dominant factor underlying *Loan intensity* (*N*)'s earlier significance was emanating from lending interactions between the main relationship bank and the borrowing firm rather than from general bank lending activity.

Given the results in column 3 in Table 2, we next use a "baseline" model that focuses only on lending intensity by relationship banks (i.e., *Relation intensity* (*Exposure*) and *Relation intensity* (*N*)). The results of the baseline model are shown in column 4 of Table 2, which confirms the highly significant nature of the *Relationship intensity* (*N*) variable found in column 3. Column 5 further confirms the importance of the relation intensity (*N*) measure compared to the relation intensity (exposure) measure, by showing the statistical insignificance of the latter in the presence of the former. In column 6 of Table 2, we consider only unsolicited takeover bids. As noted earlier, unsolicited or hostile takeovers are the subsamples where one would expect the impact of bank lending intensity and relationships to be the strongest. Indeed, we find that the coefficient on *Relation intensity* (*N*) is larger than that for the total takeover sample as a whole such that a firm with just one loan over three years has a 4.1% probability of becoming an unsolicited target each year, while a firm with no bank loans has a 3.3% probability of becoming a target each year.[29] This represents a 6.2% increase in the cumulative probability of becoming a target over the entire 1992–2005 sample period.

There are four potential concerns regarding our "baseline" model in column 4 of Table 2. The first concern is that our matching criteria used in the logit tests may be too general to pick up the true underlying relationship between loan intensity and takeover probability. Accordingly, we use a propensity-score-matching procedure that matches firms with targets along a number of financial characteristic dimensions (see Leuven and Sianesi, 2003; Drucker and Puri, 2005; and Aggarwal et al., 2007, among others). The propensity score tests involve three steps. We first run a logit test for all potentially matching firms (restricting these firms to the same four-digit SIC Code and year). We

[29] We use average variable values to calculate probabilities.

run the logit model based on *ROA* (*adj.*), *Sales growth* (*adj.*), *Market/Book assets* (*adj.*), *Ln*(*Assets*), *Asset structure* (*PPE*), *Cash*, *Leverage*, and with and without *Bad z-score*. Second, in order to implement propensity matching, we calculate each firm's propensity score. This is computed based on the probability (p) that a firm with given characteristics is a target of an attempted takeover computed using the firm's financial characteristics denoted above. The propensity score is computed as $ln((1-p)/p)$. Firms are then matched again using Leuven and Sianesi's (2003) propensity-score-matching procedure (at the nearest neighborhood caliper of 0.1), again restricting by year and two-digit SIC Code.[30] Then, we compare the average difference between the sample target firms and their matches for the variables that we did not use in the computation of the propensity score itself (i.e., the loan intensity variables). We report the result in Table 3, where we present a paired mean comparison between the sample of takeovers and their propensity score matches with respect to bank lending intensity. Panel 1 of Table 3 shows the matched results for unsolicited takeovers, while panel 2 shows results for all takeovers. As can be seen, there is a significant difference between the loan intensity variables for the target firms compared to the propensity-score-matched sample of nontarget firms. Specifically, for both the unsolicited and all takeover samples, both *Loan intensity* (*N*) and *Relationship intensity* (*N*) are significantly larger for target firms than for matched firms, consistent with our results in Table 2.

A second concern relates to possible missing governance-related control variables in Tables 2 and 3. While we have used an equity-related blockholder dummy, one equity-related governance variable possibly missing from our logit model is that of managerial ownership. We now include variables relating to managerial ownership but note that theoretically, the impact of managerial ownership on takeover probability is ambiguous. On the one hand, a higher ownership stake allows a manager to gain from a takeover since the individual now receives an equity-related payoff share of any takeover premium. On the other hand, since takeovers might be accompanied by the loss of private benefits for the manager, the individual may use voting power to thwart any takeover attempt.

Using the Compustat Executive Compensation (Execucomp) dataset, we measured managerial ownership in two ways: percentage of shares owned by top management (results reported in column 2 of Table 4) and percentage of shares owned by the CEO (results reported in column 3 of Table 4). Column 1 shows the results without the management ownership variables. While the signs on both of these managerial ownership variables are negative, they are statistically insignificant. Moreover, including these variables radically lowers the sample size (to only 5,314) since we are now constrained by the Execucomp dataset, which is limited to firms in S&P's large-cap, mid-cap, and

[30] A caliper is a tolerance level for acceptable matches defined in terms of the empirical variance of the propensity score. In the second step, we also restrict the propensity score matching to two-digit SIC Codes.

Table 3
Bank lending intensity and takeover probability: alternative construction of the control sample

	1		2		3		4	
Variable	Difference	Standard error	Difference	Standard error	Difference	Standard error	Difference	Standard error
Industry M&A intensity	0.03	0.01**	0.00	0.01	−0.04	0.03*	−0.06	0.03**
Institutional blockholder	0.15	0.01***	0.17	0.02***	0.12	0.03***	0.15	0.03***
Rated	−0.03	0.01***	−0.04	0.01***	−0.01	0.02	−0.03	0.03
High yield	−0.01	0.01	−0.01	0.01	0.00	0.02	−0.01	0.02
Bad z-score	−0.02	0.02	–	–	0.01	0.03	–	–
Bank dependence	0.02	0.01*	0.03	0.01***	0.02	0.02	0.03	0.02
Short maturity	0.03	0.01***	0.05	0.01***	0.02	0.03	0.05	0.03**
Loan intensity (Exposure)	0.03	0.01**	0.00	0.05	0.03	0.04	0.09	0.04**
Loan intensity (N)	0.13	0.03***	0.18	0.04***	0.22	0.08***	0.34	0.08***
Relation intensity (Exposure)	0.01	0.01**	−0.03	0.04	−0.01	0.03	0.03	0.02**
Relation intensity (N)	0.10	0.02***	0.15	0.03***	0.12	0.05**	0.20	0.05***
Paired observations		2,113		1,496		426		340

The table presents a paired mean comparison between the sample of takeovers that occurred between 1992 and 2005 and their propensity-score-matching firms with respect to bank lending intensity governance variables and loan-related measures. We excluded financial firms identified with two-digit SIC Codes 60 through 64. Columns 1 and 2 present the results for all takeovers and columns 3 and 4 present the result only for unsolicited takeovers. We consider two different models for the *p*-score. Model 1 (columns 1 and 3) includes only financial characteristics variables (*ROA (adj.)*, *Sales growth (adj.)*, *Market/Book assets (adj.)*, *Ln(Assets)*, *Asset structure (PPE)*, *Cash*, and *Leverage*). Model 2 (columns 2 and 4) includes, in addition to the variables in model 1, *Bad z-score* variable. In all models, controls are also matched by the two-digit SIC Code and year. The matching is within the nearest neighborhood of 0.1 caliper. ***, **, and * indicate *p*-values of 1%, 5%, and 10%, respectively.

Table 4
Bank lending intensity, managerial ownership and takeover probability

	1		2		3		4		5		6	
Variable	Coefficient	Wald	Coefficient	Wald	Coefficient	Wald	Coefficient	Wald	Coefficient	Wald	Coefficient	Wald
Industry M&A intensity	−0.33	4.3**	−0.33	4.3**	−0.33	4.3**	−0.45	0.6	−0.44	0.5	−0.45	0.6
ROA (adj.)	0.10	0.1	0.10	0.1	0.10	0.1	−0.52	1.5	−0.52	1.4	−0.52	1.5
Sales growth (adj.)	−0.08	0.3	−0.07	0.3	−0.07	0.3	−0.11	0.1	−0.09	0.1	−0.11	0.1
Market/Book assets (adj.)	−0.08	3.5*	−0.08	3.5*	−0.08	3.4**	−0.21	2.8*	−0.21	2.8*	−0.21	2.8*
Ln (Assets)	0.00	0.0	0.00	0.0	0.00	0.0	−0.03	0.1	−0.04	0.1	−0.03	0.1
Asset structure (PPE)	−0.28	0.4	−0.27	0.3	−0.27	0.3	0.23	0.1	0.25	0.1	0.24	0.1
Cash	−0.42	1.0	−0.43	1.1	−0.43	1.1	−1.66	2.6	−1.67	2.6	−1.67	2.6
Leverage	0.58	3.8*	0.57	3.8**	0.57	3.7**	0.92	2.9*	0.91	2.8*	0.91	2.8*
Institutional blockholder	0.84	27.2***	0.84	26.7***	0.84	26.6***	1.28	14.9***	1.27	14.7***	1.27	14.9***
Managerial ownership (total)			−0.25	0.1					−0.85	0.3		
Managerial ownership (CEO)					−0.49	0.3					−0.17	0.0
Rated	−0.82	18.3***	−0.83	18.4***	−0.83	18.5***	−0.31	0.9	−0.33	1.0	−0.31	0.9
High yield	0.42	3.1*	0.43	3.1*	0.43	3.1*	0.28	0.5	0.28	0.5	0.28	0.5
Bad z-score	−0.11	0.4	−0.12	0.4	−0.12	0.4	−0.14	0.2	−0.14	0.2	−0.14	0.2
Bank dependence	−0.21	1.2	−0.21	1.2	−0.21	1.2	−0.16	0.2	−0.16	0.2	−0.16	0.2
Short maturity	0.13	0.6	0.13	0.6	0.13	0.6	−0.10	0.1	−0.09	0.1	−0.10	0.1
Relation intensity (Exposure)	−0.05	0.1	−0.05	0.1	−0.05	0.1	−0.36	0.2	−0.35	0.2	−0.36	0.2
Relation intensity (N)	0.12	2.7*	0.12	2.8*	0.12	2.8*	0.16	1.2	0.16	1.1	0.16	1.2
Observations		5,314		5,314		5,314		1,038		1,038		1,038
Targets		337		337		337		103		103		103
Pseudo R^2		0.61		0.61		0.61		0.56		0.56		0.56
Max.-rescaled R^2		0.82		0.82		0.82		0.75		0.75		0.75

This table analyzes robustness of the results in Table 2 to the presence of *Managerial ownership*. The sample is based on Compustat for the M&A period 1992–2005. *Managerial ownership* is computed using Compustat Executive Compensation (Execucomp) and corresponds to shares owned by executives (excluding stock options) as a fraction of total shares outstanding. *Managerial ownership* (total) corresponds to the total shares held by executives. *Managerial ownership* (CEO) corresponds to the fraction of shares held by CEO. All other variables are the same as in Table 2. The sample includes firms that were targets of a takeover and the control sample is matched by industry and size, with valid accounting information in the event year, excluding financial firms identified with two-digit SIC Codes 60 through 64. The point estimates and Wald chi-square statistics for the industry effects are not reported although they are included in the logit tests and are jointly significant at the 1% level. Year effects are jointly insignificant and not included in the logit tests. ***, **, and * indicate *p*-values of 1%, 5%, and 10%, respectively.

small-cap indices. Despite the significant reduction in sample size, the *Relationship intensity* (*N*) variable remains positive and significant at the 10% level whether these management variables are included or excluded (see column 1, Table 4). We also reran these results for the unsolicited takeover subsample. Column 4 of Table 4 shows the results without the managerial ownership variables, while columns 5 and 6 include them. As can be seen, the results for the managerial ownership variable are qualitatively similar to all takeover samples (i.e., they are statistically significant). Although the *Relationship intensity* (*N*) variable has the expected positive sign, it loses statistical significance due to the small sample size (103 observations).

A third concern is that there may in part be an investment banking explanation here, along with a commercial banking explanation. That is, there may be a difference in the type of information flows provided by larger universal banks through their M&A activity and/or underwriting activity compared to the information flows produced by commercial banks through their loan activity alone.

To examine this concern, we reran our tests of Table 2 in Table 5 excluding target deals linked to the top ten M&A banks in each year as defined by *Mergers and Acquisitions* magazine (column 1) and excluding the top ten securities underwriters in each year as measured by the amount of debt and equity underwritten by these banks in the SDC database (column 2). The *Relation intensity* (*N*) variable remains positive and statistically significant. We also reran similar tests focusing on the subsample of unsolicited targets (columns 3 and 4) and found the *Relation intensity* (*N*) variable result to be robust.[31]

A fourth concern relates to the possibility that some of these loans may be to back up commercial paper issues that never get drawn down. To examine whether these type of loans affect our results, in Table 6 we exclude all commercial paper backup loans identified in DealScan, as well as look at the impact of a variable that measures the interaction between loan intensity and a dummy variable as to whether a target has a commercial paper rating or not.

As can be seen, the strong results found for the *Relation intensity* (*N*) variable in the sample that included CP-related loans hold up in column 1 of Table 6 when these loans are excluded. In addition, we find that interacting our relation intensity measures with a dummy that is 1 if there is a CP rating and 0 otherwise is statistically insignificant.[32] Conducting similar tests for the unsolicited hostile subsample produced qualitatively similar results. Overall, our results are consistent with Hypothesis 1, i.e., greater lending intensity by

[31] The hypotheses discussed below are also robust to the exclusion of the top ten M&A and investment banks. We do not include these results for reasons of space, but they are available from the authors on request.

[32] We also experimented with splitting the sample into different firm-size-based groups. We did not find any qualitative difference of the impact of the loan intensity variables on takeover probability according to these size splits. This may be because the smallest firms that utilize syndicated loans and are on DealScan are large compared to the type of small business loans analyzed in the small business finance literature.

The Review of Financial Studies / v 22 n 1 2009

Table 5
Bank lending intensity, M&A, and investment banking expertise

	1		2		3		4	
Variable	Coefficient	Wald	Coefficient	Wald	Coefficient	Wald	Coefficient	Wald
Industry M&A intensity	0.06	0.1	0.08	0.1	−0.62	7.2***	−0.61	6.7***
ROA (adj.)	0.20	4.1**	0.22	4.4**	0.30	1.4	0.35	1.6
Sales growth (adj.)	0.00	0.0	0.00	0.0	−0.08	0.5	−0.06	0.3
Market/Book assets (adj.)	−0.06	11.6***	−0.05	10.5***	−0.25	16.2***	−0.23	14.0***
Ln (Assets)	0.01	0.3	0.02	0.7	−0.02	0.1	−0.01	0.1
Asset structure (PPE)	−0.21	0.8	−0.11	0.2	−0.20	0.2	−0.08	0.0
Cash	0.45	7.1***	0.48	7.8***	−0.62	2.5	−0.63	2.5
Leverage	−0.12	1.0	−0.16	1.7	0.26	1.3	0.16	0.5
Institutional blockholder	0.81	152.6***	0.79	141.9***	0.74	29.6***	0.71	26.4***
Rated	−0.97	26.2***	−1.05	26.3***	−0.35	1.4	−0.50	2.4
High yield	0.56	6.6***	0.67	8.4***	0.52	2.5	0.76	4.5**
Bad z-score	0.07	0.7	0.11	1.7	−0.20	1.4	−0.15	0.7
Bank dependence	0.07	0.6	0.06	0.4	−0.08	0.2	−0.15	0.5
Short maturity	0.10	1.0	0.16	2.4	0.04	0.0	0.17	0.7
Relation intensity (Exposure)	−0.05	0.9	−0.05	0.7	−0.09	0.2	−0.11	0.2
Relation intensity (N)	0.22	20.5***	0.22	18.4***	0.32	12.9***	0.33	11.9***
Observations		25,818		25,020		10,164		9,756
Targets		1,344		1,301		298		281
Pseudo R^2		0.64		0.64		0.68		0.68
Max.-rescaled R^2		0.85		0.85		0.91		0.91

This table analyzes robustness of the results in Table 2 to the exclusion of the top ten M&A banks (columns 1 and 3) and exclusion of the top ten investment banks (columns 2 and 4) each year. The sample is based on Compustat for the M&A period 1992–2005. Columns 1 and 2 look at the sample of all takeovers. Columns 3 and 4 look at the subsample of hostile takeovers. All variables are the same as in Table 2. The sample includes firms that were targets of a takeover and the control sample is matched by industry and size, with valid accounting information in the event year, excluding financial firms identified with two-digit SIC Codes 60 through 64. The point estimates and Wald chi-square statistics for the industry effects are not reported although they are included in the logit tests and are jointly significant at the 1% level. Year effects are jointly insignificant and not included in the logit tests. ***, **, and * indicate p-values of 1%, 5%, and 10%, respectively.

Table 6
Bank lending intensity and commercial paper

	1		2		3		4		5		6	
Variable	Coefficient	Wald	Coefficient	Wald	Coefficient	Wald	Coefficient	Wald	Coefficient	Wald	Coefficient	Wald
Industry M&A intensity	0.02	0.0	0.03	0.0	0.03	0.0	−0.57	6.7***	−0.56	6.5***	−0.57	6.5***
ROA (adj.)	0.20	3.9**	0.20	4.1**	0.20	4.0**	0.32	1.5	0.34	1.7	0.34	1.7
Sales growth (adj.)	0.00	0.0	0.00	0.0	0.00	0.0	−0.12	1.2	−0.11	1.1	−0.11	1.1
Market/Book assets (adj.)	−0.06	12.4***	−0.06	12.5***	−0.06	12.6***	−0.22	14.8***	−0.23	15.2***	−0.23	15.3***
Ln (Assets)	0.02	0.9	0.01	0.3	0.01	0.2	0.01	0.1	−0.01	0.1	−0.02	0.2
Asset structure (PPE)	−0.12	0.3	−0.13	0.3	−0.13	0.3	−0.05	0.0	−0.04	0.0	−0.04	0.0
Cash	0.46	7.9***	0.49	8.9***	0.49	8.9***	−0.60	2.5	−0.58	2.3	−0.58	2.3
Leverage	−0.12	1.2	−0.13	1.4	−0.13	1.3	0.25	1.3	0.23	1.2	0.24	1.2
Institutional blockholder	0.78	149.2***	0.77	147.7***	0.77	147.7***	0.73	31.5***	0.73	31.6***	0.73	31.5***
Rated	−1.02	41.1***	−1.12	42.6***	−1.12	42.6***	−0.50	3.6*	−0.69	5.8**	−0.69	5.7**
High yield	0.57	9.4***	0.68	11.6***	0.68	11.6***	0.50	2.9*	0.70	4.7**	0.70	4.7**
Bad z-score	0.07	0.7	0.07	0.8	0.07	0.8	−0.17	1.1	−0.17	1.1	−0.17	1.1
Bank dependence	−0.13	1.8	0.06	0.4	0.06	0.4	−0.08	0.2	−0.12	0.5	−0.12	0.4
Short maturity	0.24	8.6***	0.15	2.8*	0.15	2.7*	0.18	1.3	0.17	0.9	0.17	0.9
CP rating			0.32	1.9	0.33	2.1			0.25	0.4	0.26	0.4
Relation intensity (Exposure)	−0.05	0.8			−0.06	0.8	−0.12	0.2			−0.13	0.2
Relation intensity (N)	0.21	18.7***	0.21	19.2***	0.22	20.4***	0.29	9.6***	0.29	10.9***	0.31	10.9***
*CP rating *Relation intensity (Exposure)*					−0.01	0.0					0.07	0.0
*CP rating *Relation intensity (N)*			−0.09	0.5	−0.09	0.6			0.07	0.1	0.06	0.1
Observations		28,234		28,234		28,234		11,355		11,355		11,355
Targets		1,454		1,454		1,454		330		330		330
Pseudo R^2		0.64		0.64		0.64		0.68		0.68		0.68
Max.-rescaled R^2		0.85		0.85		0.85		0.91		0.91		0.91

This table analyzes robustness of the results in Table 2. Column 1 excludes all loans used as commercial paper backup. Columns 2 and 3 add an interaction term between relationship intensity variables and commercial paper rating to the test presented in Table 2 (columns 4 and 5, respectively). The sample is based on Compustat for the M&A period 1992–2005. All variables are the same as in Table 2. The sample includes firms that were targets of a takeover and the control sample is matched by industry and size, with valid accounting information in the event year, excluding financial firms identified with two-digit SIC Codes 60 through 64. The point estimates and Wald chi-square statistics for the industry effects are not reported, although they are included in the logit tests and are jointly significant at the 1% level. Year effects are jointly insignificant and not included in the logit tests. ***, **, and * indicate p-values of 1%, 5%, and 10%, respectively.

The Review of Financial Studies / v 22 n 1 2009

a relationship bank increases the probability of a borrower being a takeover target.

3.2 The number of potential acquirers (Hypothesis 2)

While Hypothesis 1 examines the linkage between a target and its relationship bank(s), we next analyze the extent to which a relationship bank client network—the number of target bank clients that *have the characteristics to become a potential acquirer*—affect the probability of a takeover. Controlling for *bank size*, we expect that the greater the relationship bank's client base, the greater the probability of a borrowing firm receiving a takeover bid. Accordingly, Hypothesis 2 states that the larger the client base the relationship bank has, the greater is the associated probability of a borrowing firm becoming a takeover target. To examine Hypothesis 2, we need a measure of the number of client firms dealing with the target's relationship bank that have the characteristics to become an acquirer of the target. We call this measure *Bank net*, which is equal to the log of the number of potential acquirers that exclusively borrow from the same relationship bank as a potential target over a three-year window. Potential acquirers are selected based on the two-digit SIC Code and asset size.[33] Since a bank's information about a target is more valuable to an acquirer in the same industry, we look at the number of the target's relationship bank clients in the same industry as the target firm, *controlling for bank size.* Since a larger number of lending relationships increases the number of potential acquirers to whom the target's bank (or banks) can transfer private information, we expect the *Bank net* variable to have a positive effect on the probability of becoming a takeover candidate.

Table 7 presents the results for Hypothesis 2. As can be seen in Table 7, columns 1 and 3, we find a positive and statistically significant coefficient on the probability of being acquired resulting from the size of the target relationship bank's client network (i.e., *Bank net*) for both the all-takeover and hostile takeover samples. Furthermore, the *Relationship intensity* (*N*) variable remains statistically significant for both the hostile and all-takeover samples. One concern might be that larger banks, which are prominent in the takeover market, simply have larger client networks and consequently are more likely to be involved in acquisition activity. To address this issue, we add a variable that controls for the size of the relationship bank as measured by a bank's market share in the takeover market based on the number of deals it engaged in during the takeover year.[34] As can be seen in Table 7, column 2, the likelihood of a takeover is negatively related to bank size. In other words, firms that deal with

[33] We allow the potential acquirer to be in the same two-digit SIC Code as the target. This criterion is based on observable data. According to SDC, close to 60% of hostile takeover and M&A activity in general happens between a target and an acquirer with the same two-digit SIC Code and only 30% corresponds to targets and acquirers with the same four-digit SIC Code.

[34] We also controlled for bank asset size (as an alternative measure). This variable was found to be statistically insignificant.

Bank Debt and Corporate Governance

Table 7
Bank client network and takeover probability

	1		2		3	
Variable	Coefficient	Wald	Coefficient	Wald	Coefficient	Wald
Industry M&A intensity	0.02	0.0	0.02	0.0	−0.57	6.6***
ROA (adj.)	0.20	3.9**	0.19	3.7**	0.32	1.5
Sales growth (adj.)	0.00	0.0	0.00	0.0	−0.11	1.1
Market/Book assets (adj.)	−0.06	12.4***	−0.06	12.2***	−0.23	15.2***
Ln (Assets)	0.01	0.4	0.02	0.8	−0.01	0.1
Asset structure (PPE)	−0.12	0.3	−0.13	0.4	−0.04	0.0
Cash	0.51	9.6***	0.50	9.1***	−0.50	1.7
Leverage	−0.13	1.4	−0.14	1.5	0.21	0.9
Institutional blockholder	0.76	141.5***	0.76	141.2***	0.69	27.9***
Rated	−1.04	41.8***	−1.02	40.3***	−0.51	3.8**
High yield	0.58	9.7***	0.57	9.2***	0.49	2.7*
Bad z-score	0.07	0.8	0.07	0.8	−0.15	0.9
Bank dependence	0.01	0.0	−0.01	0.0	−0.23	1.5
Short maturity	0.13	1.9	0.12	1.7	0.11	0.4
Relation intensity (Exposure)	−0.06	1.0	−0.07	1.1	−0.14	0.3
Relation intensity (N)	0.15	8.4***	0.16	8.8***	0.21	4.9**
Bank net	0.05	4.9**	0.08	9.5***	0.09	3.5*
Bank size			−1.75	5.0**	0.34	0.1
Observations		28,234		28,234		11,355
Targets		1,454		1,454		330
Pseudo R^2		0.64		0.64		0.68
Max.-rescaled R^2		0.85		0.85		0.91

The focus of this table is the *Bank net* variable. *Bank net* is computed separately for each observation in the sample and is the logarithm of the number of potential acquirers that share the same relationship bank with the potential target. Potential acquirers are selected based on the two-digit SIC Code and asset size. *Bank net* is measured over a three-year window. *Bank size* is the relationship bank's market share based on number of deals in the year of the takeover event. All other variables are the same as in Table 2. Columns 1 and 2 look at the sample of all takeovers. Column 3 looks at the subsample of hostile takeovers. The point estimates and Wald chi-square statistics for the industry effects are not reported, although they are included in the logit tests and they are jointly significant at the 1% level. Year effects are jointly insignificant and not included in the logit tests. ***, **, and * indicate p-values of 1%, 5%, and 10%, respectively.

a smaller bank (in a takeover market share sense) with a relatively large client network are more likely to be acquired.

Looking at economic significance, we find that the impact of a bank's network is economically important in explaining the probability of a takeover bid in general. Conditional on *Loan intensity* being equal to 1 (number of loans (*N*) received in the past three years is equal to 1), a company is exposed to approximately three potential acquirers through its relationship bank. For this average relationship bank client network, a firm faces a 4.8% annual average probability of becoming a target. If the firm were to deal with an additional relationship bank with a similar number of clients in its network, the probability of facing a takeover increases by 1.0% per annum.

Given these results, and their support for Hypothesis 2, comparing the economic impact in Table 7 with the economic impact when we consider acquisitions *where both the acquirer and the target deal with the same bank* (i.e., have a shared lending relationship) will provide more concrete evidence of the importance of the bank information channel in effecting takeover bids.

The Review of Financial Studies / v 22 n 1 2009

3.3 Shared lending relationships (Hypothesis 3)

In focusing on Hypothesis 3, we test whether a bank's transmission of information about one client to another client is enhanced by the presence of a (shared) bank lending relationship with both the target and acquirer. If this hypothesis is to be supported, we should expect the bank lending relationship intensity (*N*) variable to be more important in takeovers where the acquirer has a lending relationship with the *same bank* as the target. To test Hypothesis 3, we analyze those takeover bids where the bidder and the target have established a prior lending relationship with the same bank over a three-year window prior to the takeover bid.

For the 1,454 acquisition bids in the Compustat sample, we identified the acquirer in each case and checked if the acquirer's main bank was the same as the target's main bank and found 107 such cases (of which 26 cases were for unsolicited (hostile) takeovers). In all other cases, the target and acquirer did not share a relationship with the target's bank. The results are shown in Table 8.

Column 1 of Table 8 looks at the 107 takeovers in which the target firm had a lending relationship with a bank that also had a lending relationship with the acquirer.[35] Firms were matched to these 107 cases based on event year and four-digit SIC Codes to get 3,699 control firms that did not face any takeover attempt. The dependent variable is *Bank link*, which has a value of 1 if the target and acquirer have a common banking relationship and 0 otherwise. To see the economic importance of relationship intensity (*N*), in the case of shared target-acquirer lending relationships, note that a firm with a single loan issued has an annual average probability of 5.3% of facing a takeover attempt by an acquirer who deals with the target's relationship bank.[36] That is, *Bank link* is both statistically and economically important.

We also examine the impact of a shared lending relationship in the case of the unsolicited takeover subsample. As can be seen in column 2 of Table 8, the results for relation intensity are very similar for those 26 out of 107 cases that are defined as hostile by SDC.

3.4 New relationships, new targets?

While the panel-based logit analysis presented above is instructive, it is also susceptible to criticisms of *endogeneity*. To mitigate this concern, we now take a different approach to check whether bank relationship intensity (and the related transmission of information) affects takeover vulnerability. Hypothesis 4 examines whether a potential acquiring firm that *switches* to a new relationship bank has a higher probability of entering a takeover bid for a target that transacts with its new relationship bank after the new lending relationship is

[35] We do not use a dummy for a common target and acquirer bank as an independent variable since this information is not known at time "$t-1$" for takeovers that happen at time "t". Thus, such a dummy cannot be used in these predictive logit regressions as an independent variable or to interact with other independent variables.

[36] All other variables are at the average levels.

Table 8
The probability of a takeover when the acquirer and target share the same relationship bank

	1		2		3	
Variable	Coefficient	Wald	Coefficient	Wald	Coefficient	Wald
Industry M&A intensity	−0.59	3.0*	0.37	0.1	−0.57	2.7*
ROA (adj.)	0.88	1.2	2.75	0.9	0.81	0.8
Sales growth (adj.)	−0.21	0.6	−0.10	0.0	−0.19	0.4
Market/Book assets (adj.)	−0.14	1.4	0.04	0.0	−0.13	1.1
Ln (Assets)	0.18	5.6**	0.36	3.8**	0.27	9.8***
Asset structure (PPE)	0.60	0.6	0.26	0.0	0.64	0.6
Cash	−2.70	6.7***	−2.05	0.7	−2.17	4.1**
Leverage	−0.41	0.6	0.18	0.0	−0.52	0.9
Institutional blockholder	0.66	6.6***	0.91	2.1	0.48	3.4*
Rated	−1.37	12.1***	−3.03	7.1***	−1.17	8.9***
High yield	1.42	10.2***	2.73	4.8**	1.14	6.5***
Bad z-score	0.40	1.8	0.57	0.8	0.39	1.6
Bank dependence	0.50	2.7*	0.33	0.3	0.28	0.8
Short maturity	0.45	2.9*	0.09	0.0	0.24	0.8
Relation intensity (Exposure)	−0.01	0.1	−1.14	0.5	−0.01	0.0
Relation intensity (N)	0.78	42.8***	0.98	9.1***	0.44	10.2***
Bank net					0.44	26.2***
Bank size					−2.99	2.7*
Observations		3,806		769		3,806
Targets		107		26		107
Pseudo R^2		0.70		0.69		0.70
Max.-rescaled R^2		0.93		0.92		0.93

This table presents results of the maximum likelihood estimates of the logit model for the 1992–2005 subsample, where the acquirer and target share the same relationship bank, excluding financial firms identified with two-digit SIC Codes 60 through 65. The subsample includes 107 takeovers in which the target firm had a lending relationship with a bank that also had a lending relationship with the acquirer. Firms were matched to these 107 cases based on event year and industry and size to get 3,699 control firms that did not face any takeover attempt. The dependent variable is *Bank link*, which has a value of 1 if the target and acquirer have a common banking relationship and 0 otherwise. Column 1 looks at the sample of all takeovers. Column 2 looks at the subsample of hostile takeovers. This point estimates and Wald chi-square statistics for the industry effects are not reported, although they are included in the logit tests and are jointly significant at the 1% level. Year effects are jointly insignificant and not included in the logit tests. Model 2 looks at hostile takeovers only. ***, **, and * indicate *p*-values of 1%, 5%, and 10%, respectively.

established. The basic structure of the test is illustrated in Figure 2, panel A. As discussed, the decision of the acquirer to switch its relationship bank is likely to be independent (exogenous) of any particular decision to acquire a client of its new relationship bank.

In order to conduct this switching experiment, we first identify events where a firm switches its relationship bank. To identify the time of the firm's switch, we look at all companies that have lending relationships and pick the dates when companies switch relationship banks. We then identify all takeovers in a three-year window before and after the switching event date and exclude switching events linked to bank mergers. We ensure that the switcher is a potential acquirer for a specific firm by matching by industry (two-digit SIC Code) and size to the target. Thus, this test is conditional on a takeover taking place and each observation in the sample (of which there are 649) is a takeover of a client of the new (switched-to) bank. We estimate the probability that the

Table 9
The effect of an acquirer switching relationship banks on the probability of a takeover

	1		2	
Variable	Coefficient	Wald	Coefficient	Wald
Industry M&A intensity	−1.96	114.0***	−12.57	0.0
After switch	1.82	43.9***	0.89	3.9**
Observations		649		54
Cases		39		7
Pseudo R^2		0.56		0.34
Max.-rescaled R^2		0.74		0.45

This table tests how a potential acquirer switching to a new relationship bank affects the probability of it bidding for a client target of the new relationship bank. The dependent variable equals 1 if the bidder is the switching firm and 0 otherwise. Of particular interest is the dummy variable *After switch*, which identifies the period after the switch has occurred. This variable takes the value 1 if the takeover occurs in the three years after the switching event and 0 otherwise. We identify all takeovers in a three-year window before and after companies switch relationship banks. Each observation in the sample is a takeover of a client of the new/switched to bank. We ensure that the switcher is a potential acquirer for a specific firm by matching by industry (the two-digit SIC Code) and size to the target. Column 1 corresponds to all takeovers and column 2 corresponds to hostile takeovers. The table presents results of the maximum likelihood estimates of the logit model for the 1992–2005 sample, excluding financial firms identified with two-digit SIC Codes 60 through 64. Each observation in the sample is the takeover of a client of the switched-to bank. ***, **, and * indicate p-values of 1%, 5%, and 10%, respectively.

bidder is the switching firm. Accordingly, the dependent variable is equal to 1 if the bidder is the switching firm (thirty-nine observations) and 0 otherwise. We hypothesize that the probability of bidding on a client of a certain bank increases when the potential bidder establishes a relationship with the new bank. To test this, we focus on the dummy variable *After switch*, which is equal to 1 for the three years following the bank switch, and 0 before that. In addition, we control for industry takeover activity.

We ensure that targets are not connected by any other banking relationship (arranging bank or participant) to the acquirer. As illustrated in panel B of Figure 2, if the switching firm and the target shared any relationship bank before the switch, this takeover is excluded from the sample. Only takeovers of the firms that were in no way connected to the potential acquirer before the switch and became connected *as a consequence* of the switch of relationship bank by the potential acquirer are included in the sample.

The results of the logit test are presented in Table 9. As can be seen, conditional on an acquirer switching to a new relationship bank, we find that the coefficient on the *After switch* variable is significant and positive. This implies that the probability that the acquirer firm will target one of its new bank's clients is enhanced as the result of the new information regarding the target acquired postswitching.

It may reasonably be argued that there are caveats to the results in Table 9. First, it might be argued that thirty-nine switching observations for all takeovers and seven observations for hostile takeovers are small. We agree that the sample is limited due to the highly restrictive criteria we impose: (1) the target and potential acquirer must be borrowing from the same bank, (2) the potential acquirer must be the switcher, and (3) the target and potential acquirer cannot be linked through any other banking relationship. Also, we note that our earlier tests are consistent with bank information dissemination for both the total sample and the hostile subsample.

Second, there might be an unobservable characteristic (e.g., "good" companies) that correlates with both bank switching and the probability of extending a takeover bid. However, such a characteristic does not explain why the acquirer is bidding on a particular target client of the new bank rather than targets in general. Also, switching might be induced by sweetened loan terms offered by the new bank that is eager to attract "good" companies. To examine this, we investigated the all-in-spread drawn (AISD) on the first loan offered by the new bank relative to the last loan offered by the old bank to the switching firm. After controlling for the main determinants of the loan spread (i.e., (log) loan amount, maturity, and leverage, as well as year-fixed effects), we found that a dummy that was 1 for a new loan spread and 0 otherwise was insignificantly different from 0.[37] That is, there is no evidence of a lower loan spread being offered by the new bank as a sweetener for the borrower to switch.

3.5 Summary of logit tests

Overall we find evidence consistent with an informational role of banks in the market for corporate control. In particular, we find the probability of a target being subject to a takeover bid to be increasing (1) in the degree of lending intensity by its relationship bank, (2) in the size of the target bank's client network, (3) when the acquirer and target have the same (linked) relationship bank, and (4) when a potential acquiring firm switches to a new relationship bank of which the target is a client.

4. Bank Motives

While the above tests are consistent with an informational role for banks in the market for corporate control, they do not explain the underlying motives for banks to engage in such information transmission.

4.1 Default risk motive

We next attempt to shed more light on a bank's motives for transferring information about the target. In particular, a bank might transmit information about one client to another so as to increase the probability of transferring loans from

[37] We tested the following regression equation controlling for year-fixed effects where the dependent variable is AISD (over LIBOR):

Variable	Coeff.	t-stat	
New/switched load (dummy)	11.28	0.9	
Ln (Loan amount)	−35.11	−9.8	***
Maturity	0.52	2.5	**
Leverage	1.37	2.2	**

The Review of Financial Studies / v 22 n 1 2009

Table 10
Bank's motives for informational transfer: multivariate analysis

	1		2	
Variable	Coefficient	Wald	Coefficient	Wald
Industry M&A intensity	0.02	0.0	−0.57	6.6***
ROA (adj.)	0.17	3.1*	0.30	1.3
Sales growth (adj.)	0.00	0.0	−0.12	1.2
Market/Book assets (adj.)	−0.06	12.9***	−0.23	15.1***
Ln (Assets)	0.02	0.6	−0.01	0.0
Asset structure (PPE)	−0.12	0.3	−0.03	0.0
Cash	0.46	7.9***	−0.62	2.6*
Leverage	−0.11	1.1	0.25	1.3
Institutional blockholder	0.77	145.0***	0.72	30.6***
Rated	−1.04	42.3***	−0.52	3.9**
High yield	0.57	9.4***	0.48	2.6*
Bad z-score	−0.05	0.2	−0.33	3.0*
Short maturity	0.07	0.5	−0.13	0.5
Bank dependence	0.17	3.3*	0.19	1.1
Relation intensity (Exposure)	−0.06	1.0	−0.11	0.3
Relation intensity (N)	0.15	7.7***	0.24	5.9**
*Relation intensity (N) *Bad z-score*	0.18	6.3**	0.23	2.8*
Observations		28,234		11,355
Targets		1,454		330
Pseudo R^2		0.64		0.68
Max.-rescaled R^2		0.85		0.91

This table presents the results of maximum likelihood estimates of a logit model that reestimates our benchmark model (Table 2, column 5) with the addition of the interaction variable *Relation intensity (N)* * *Bad z-score*. Column 1 corresponds to all takeovers and column 2 corresponds to hostile takeovers. ***, **, and * indicate *p*-values of 1%, 5%, and 10%, respectively.

an *ex ante* bad borrower to an *ex ante* good borrower so as to reduce its overall credit risk. It is worth noting that this possibility assumes that the nature of the debt can be changed by the transfer (e.g., by better management), or else the acquirer will not be willing to take on unchangeable bad debt.

We first check whether the link between relationship loan intensity and takeover probability is stronger for firms that have performed poorly. To do so, in the logit specification, we use an interaction term between the loan relationship intensity (*N*) variable and a "bad" Altman *z*-score dummy that reflects a high probability of a target firm defaulting. The results are shown in Table 10. In column 1, we show the results for all takeovers and in column 2 for the subsample of unsolicited takeovers. We focus on the *interaction term* between *Relationship intensity* and the *Bad z-score dummy*. While the *Bad z-score* variable on its own is insignificant in explaining takeovers in column 1, it can also be seen from column 1 that the interaction between this variable and *Relationship intensity* (*N*) is positive and significant. This suggests that in cases where a target firm's credit quality is low, a relationship bank has a greater incentive to transfer information to a potential acquirer and thus increase the probability of a target firm's takeover, a result that is consistent with the relationship bank seeking to preserve the credit quality of its overall loan portfolio. A similar, but less significant relationship effect appears to hold

Table 11
Bank's motives for informational transfer: comparison of acquirer and target

	Target		Acquirer			
	Mean	*t*-ratio	Mean	*t*-ratio	Difference	*t*-ratio
		Panel A: Credit quality				
z-score	2.95	13.4***	3.69	13.2***	−0.75	−2.1**
S&P senior debt rating	11.18	20.0***	9.54	13.3***	1.64	1.8*
		Panel B: Performance				
ROA (adj.)	0.025	2.8***	0.044	4.4***	−0.020	−1.5
ROE (adj.)	−0.011	−0.7	0.042	3.6***	−0.053	−2.6***
Net profit margin (adj.)	−0.043	−0.9	0.066	1.8*	−0.110	−1.8*
Market/Book (adj.)	−0.058	−0.8	0.281	2.9***	−0.339	−2.7***
Observations	107		98			
	Advisor = 1		Advisor = 0			
	Mean	*t*-ratio	Mean	*t*-ratio	Difference	*t*-ratio
		Panel C: The impact of advising				
ROA (adj.)	0.021	1.2	0.021	1.6	−0.000	−0.0
ROE (adj.)	−0.050	−1.0	0.014	0.6	−0.064	−1.2
Net profit margin (adj.)	−0.043	−0.6	−0.011	−0.3	−0.032	−0.4
Market/Book (adj.)	−0.274	1.8*	0.065	0.7	−0.339	−1.8*
Observations	14		69			

This table uses a *t*-ratio difference in means tests to compare the credit quality of targets and acquirers for those cases where the target and potential acquirer share the same relationship bank (panels A and B). Panel C analyzes the credit quality of targets when the relationship bank is the merger advisor to the acquirer (bidder) versus where it is not. There are 98 acquirers with valid accounting information corresponding to the 107 targets. Only 83 cases (out of 107) had financial advisor information. ***, **, and * indicate *p*-values of 1%, 5%, and 10%, respectively.

for unsolicited takeovers in column 2 of Table 10. Finally, excluding the top ten M&A banks described earlier did not impact the positive and significant relationship of the relationship intensity-*z*-score interaction variable.[38]

This raises an interesting question: Why do acquirers takeover poorly performing targets as Table 10 suggests? While we cannot address this question directly, we find evidence that acquiring firms may have an incentive to participate in this bad "debt transfer" if based on their performance (Table 11) they *ex ante* believe that they can improve the performance of the target (and by implication the credit quality of the bank's debt).

Table 11 compares the relative performance of target and acquiring firms in the subsample where the acquirer and target have the same relationship bank (i.e., they are "linked") using a variety of metrics. From Table 11, it can be seen, consistent with the notion that acquirers tend to be better "performers" than targets, that acquirers have a higher ROA, return on equity (ROE), net profit margins, and market-to-book ratios than targets (Table 11, panel B). In addition acquirers have higher (better) Altman *z*-scores and S&P senior debt ratings (see Table 11, panel A). This suggests that bank debt does get transferred from *ex ante* weaker clients of the bank to *ex ante* stronger clients.

[38] Results not shown for reasons of space, but available from the authors on request.

4.2 Financing and fee motives

In addition to the credit quality motive, a bank's incentive to facilitate a takeover of its client through the transfer of information to a potential acquirer may be due to two other reasons. First, a bank can transfer information to the acquirer because it benefits from financing a takeover and/or second, a bank may transfer information to an acquirer because it benefits from the fees resulting from its advisory role in the transaction.

To examine the potential impact of the financing motive among cases where the acquirer and the target had a lending relationship with the same bank, we first collected data on whether the acquirer received a new loan from the bank *in the same year* as a takeover bid was announced. We further checked the purpose of each loan to see whether a loan was issued for the purpose of financing a takeover. Among the seventy-five cases for which we were able to obtain these data, there were only eighteen such cases where the stated purpose of loans was to finance a takeover. Thus, the limited amount of data that is available suggests that the financing motive may not be a key motive in determining a bank's decision to channel information to a potential acquirer.

With respect to merger advisory fees, we could find only fourteen cases where the relationship bank was also serving as an advisor to the bidder (panel C, Table 11). This suggests that bidders frequently seek outside merger advice from banks other than their main or relationship bank and that any potential conflict of interest in this area is likely to be low. Moreover, as panel C of Table 11 shows, the financial conditions of targets, where the relationship bank acted as advisor to the acquirer (Acquirer 1) as opposed to where it did not (Acquirer 0), were not significantly different from each other at the 5% level.

Thus, the results for the linked bank sample are consistent with *ex ante* default risk motives largely driving the informational transfer from a relationship bank to a potential acquirer. Indeed, the fact that relationship banks do not act extensively as advisors or financers to a particular takeover attempt is consistent with them seeking to avoid the type of lawsuit prevalent in a Dana Corp-like situation.

5. Conclusions

This paper is the first to establish the role of a private debt, or a bank lending channel, in the market for corporate control. We show that (1) bank lending intensity has a significant and positive effect on the probability of a firm becoming a target, (2) the number of same-industry client firms that a bank deals with is positively and significantly related to the takeover probability of a borrowing firm, (3) the importance of bank lending intensity in predicting a takeover is higher for those takeovers where the acquirer and the target share a lending relationship with the same bank, and (4) firms that switch relationship banks are more likely to acquire a client of its new bank as a target.

These results are consistent with banks impacting the probability of takeovers via a lending-related information channel. In addition, while the equity channel, operating through blockholder equity stakes, is found to be important, the bank lending channel effects are robust to the inclusion of equity channel variables, management control variables, and many other control variables.

From a policy perspective, the growing penetration of banks into the merger and investment banking arena in the United States since the passage of the Financial Services Modernization Act of 1999, along with a recent surge in takeovers, implies that the disciplining (or governance) role of banks and bank debt is likely to become even more prominent and controversial in the future.

Appendix

Variable	Source	Description
Relationship bank	LPC: DealScan	We define relationship bank based on syndicate role and actual exposure (dollar amount) to the target, measured over a three-year window. We exclude all participants. However, we allow for banks with secondary roles, such as coarranger to be a relationship bank. We define relationship banks based on actual dollar exposure. Multiple relationship banks are possible if there are other banks with exposure no less than 80% of the top relationship bank
Bank dependence	LPC: DealScan	Dummy, equals 1 if the target has one relationship bank over three years prior to a takeover attempt and 0 otherwise
Bank link	LPC: DealScan	Dummy, equal to 1 if the target and acquirer share the same relationship bank and 0 otherwise
Short maturity	LPC: DealScan	Dummy, equal to 1 if a target receives loans of a shorter maturity than the industry median and 0 otherwise
Loan intensity (*Exposure*)	LPC: DealScan	Measures maximum bank dollar exposure within one year prior to the takeover event. Counts all the loans outstanding (a proxy for dollar the stock of loans)
Relation intensity (*Exposure*)	LPC: DealScan	Measures maximum dollar exposure of the relationship bank available under commitment within one year prior to the takeover event. Only relationship bank share is counted. Counts all the loans outstanding
Loan intensity (*N*)	LPC: DealScan	Total number of loans issued over a three-year window prior to the takeover event
Relation intensity (*N*)	LPC: DealScan	Total number of loans over a three-year window prior to the takeover event issued by the relationship bank
Bank net	LPC: DealScan	*Bank net* is computed separately for each observation in the sample and is the logarithm of the number of potential acquirers that share the same relationship bank with the potential target. Potential acquirer's are selected based on the two-digit SIC Code and asset size. *Bank net* is measured over a three-year window.
Bank size	LPC: DealScan	*Bank size* is relationship bank market takeover share based on number of deals in the year of a takeover event
After switch	LPC: DealScan	*After switch* is a dummy variable equal to 1 if the takeover took place in a three-year period following an acquirer's switch of its relationship bank
Industry M&A intensity	SDC	Dummy, equal to 1 if there are takeovers within the same SIC four-digit industry in the year prior to the event. Identifies merger activity
ROA	Compustat	EBITD/Total assets: Data 18/Data 6

continued

Ln (Assets)	Compustat	Ln(Total assets): Ln(Data 6)
Sales growth	Compustat	ΔSales/Sales: ΔData 12/Data 12
Leverage	Compustat	Book debt/Total assets: (Data 6 − (Data 60 + Data 74))/Data 6
ROA	Compustat	EBITD/Total assets: Data 18/Data 6
Ln (Assets)	Compustat	Ln(Total assets): Ln(Data 6)
Sales growth	Compustat	ΔSales/Sales: ΔData 12/Data 12
Leverage	Compustat	Book debt/Total assets: (Data 6 − (Data 60 + Data 74))/Data 6
Cash	Compustat	Cash and Short-term investments/Total assets: Data 1/Data 6
Ln (Equity)	Compustat	Ln(Market equity): Ln(Data 25*Data 199)
Market/book assets	Compustat	Market assets/Book assets: (Data 6 − (Data 60 + Data 74) + Data 25*Data 199)/Data 6
Asset structure (PPE)	Compustat	Property, plant, and equipment/Total assets: Data 7/Data 6
Bad z-score	Compustat	Dummy equal to 1 if $z < 1.81$ and 0 otherwise.
z-score	Compustat	Following the Altman (1968) model, $z = 12$ (Working capital/Total assets) + 1.4 (Retained earnings/Total assets) + 3.3 (EBIT/Total assets) + 0.6 (Market value of equity/Book value of total liabilities) + 1.0 (Sales/Total assets)
Institutional blockholder	Spectrum institutional (13f) holdings	Dummy equal to 1 if there is an institution holding over 5% of the company's shares
Rated	Standard & Poor's	Dummy equals 1 if the target has a bond rating and 0 otherwise
High yield	Standard & Poor's	Dummy equals 1 if the target has issued bonds with a below investment grade rating

References

Aggarwal, R., I. Erel, R. M. Stulz, and R. G. Williamson. 2007. Do U.S. Firms Have the Best Corporate Governance? A Cross-country Examination of the Relation between Corporate Governance and Shareholder Wealth. Working Paper No. 2006-03-006, Fisher College of Business, http://ssrn.com/abstract=954169.

Altman, E. I. 1968. Financial Ratios, Discriminant Analysis and the Prediction of Corporate Bankruptcy. *Journal of Finance* 23(4):589–609.

Ambrose, B. W., and W. L. Meggison. 1992. The Role of Asset Structure, Ownership Structure, and Takeover Defenses in Determining Acquisition Likelihood. *Journal of Financial and Quantitative Analysis* 27(4):575–89.

Barber, B. M., and J. D. Lyon. 1996. Detecting Abnormal Operating Performance: The Empirical Power and Specification of Test Statistics. *Journal of Financial Economics* 41(3):359–99.

Berger, A. N, L. F. Klapper, and G. F. Udell. 2001. The Ability of Banks to Lend to Informationally Opaque Small Businesses. Working Paper, World Bank Policy Research.

Boone, A. L, and J. H. Mulherin. 2006. Do Takeover Provisions Truncate the Takeover Bidding Process. *Review of Financial Studies* 20(2):461–89.

Cremers, M., V. B. Nair, and K. John. 2005. Takeovers and the Cross-section of Returns. Working Paper, Wharton School of Business.

Dahiya, S., M. Puri, and A. Saunders. 2003. Bank Borrowers and Loan Sales: New Evidence on the Uniqueness of Bank Loans. *Journal of Business* 76(4):563–82.

Drucker, S., and M. Puri. 2005. On the Benefits of Concurrent Lending and Underwriting. *Journal of Finance* 60:2763–99.

Easterbrook, F. H., and D. R. Fischel. 1991. *The Economic Structure of Corporate Law*. Cambridge: Harvard University Press.

Fama, E. F. 1985. What's Different about Banks. *Journal of Monetary Economics* 15(11):29–39.

Gompers, P. A., J. L. Ishii, and A. Metrick. 2003. Corporate Governance and Equity Prices. *Quarterly Journal of Economics* 118(1):107–55.

Hasbrouck, J. 1985. The Characteristics of Takeover Targets. *Journal of Banking and Finane* 9:351–62.

James, C. 1987. Some Evidence on the Uniqueness of Bank Loans. *Journal of Financial Economics* 19(2):217–35.

Jensen, M. C. 1993. The Modern Industrial Revolution, Exit, and the Failure of Internal Control Systems. *Journal of Finance* 48(3):831–80.

Kano, M., H. Uchida, G. F. Udell, and W. Watanabe. 2006. Information Verifiability, Bank Organization, Bank Competition and Bank-Borrower Relationships. Working Paper, RIETI.

Leuven, E., and B. Sianesi. 2003. PSMATCH 2: Stata Module to Perform Full Mahalanobis and Propensity Score Matching, Common Support Graphing and Covariate Imbalance Testing. Statistical Software Components S432001, Boston College.

Mester, L. J., L. I. Nakumura, and M. Renault. 2007. Transaction Accounts and Loan Monitoring. *Review of Financial Studies* 20(3):529–56.

Mikkelson, W. H., and M. M. Partch. 1989. Managers Voting Rights and Corporate Control. *Journal of Financial Economics* 25(2):263–90.

Palepu, K. G. 1986. Predicting Takeover Targets. *Journal of Accounting Economics* 8:3–35.

Rajan, R. G. 1992. Insiders and Outsiders: The Choice between Relationship and Arm's Length Debt. *Journal of Finance* 47(4):1367–400.

Santos, J., and A. S. Rumble. 2006. The American Keiretsu and Universal Banks: Investing, Voting and Sitting on Nonfinancials' Corporate Boards. *Journal of Financial Economics* 80(2):419–54.

Shleifer, A., and R. W. Vishny. 1986. Large Shareholders and Corporate Control. *Journal of Political Economy* 94(3):461–88.

Stein, J. C. 2002. Information Production and Capital Allocation: Decentralized versus Hierarchical Firms. *Journal of Finance* 57(5):1891–921.

Stulz, R. M. 1988. Managerial Control of Voting Rights: Financing Policies and the Market for Corporate Control. *Journal of Financial Economics* 20(1–2):25–54.

Udell, G. F. 2004. *Asset Based Finance: Proven Disciplines for Prudent Lending*. New York: Commercial Finance Association.

ELSEVIER

Available online at www.sciencedirect.com

ScienceDirect

Journal of Financial Economics 85 (2007) 368–419

JOURNAL OF Financial ECONOMICS

www.elsevier.com/locate/jfec

So what do I get? The bank's view of lending relationships ☆

Sreedhar Bharath[a], Sandeep Dahiya[b], Anthony Saunders[c,*], Anand Srinivasan[d]

[a] *University of Michigan, Ann Arbor, MI 48109, USA*
[b] *Georgetown University, Washington, DC 20057, USA*
[c] *New York University, New York, NY 10012, USA*
[d] *NUS Business School, 117952, Singapore*

Received 8 September 2004; received in revised form 20 July 2005; accepted 17 August 2005
Available online 20 March 2006

Abstract

While many empirical studies document borrower benefits of lending relationships, less is known about lender benefits. A relationship lender's informational advantage over a non-relationship lender may generate a higher probability of selling information-sensitive products to its borrowers. Our results show that the probability of a relationship lender providing a future loan is 42%, while for a non-relationship lender, this probability is 3%. Consistent with theory, we find that borrowers with greater information asymmetries are significantly likely to obtain future loans from their relationship

☆ Dahiya acknowledges the support of the Lee Higdon, Jr. Faculty Research Fellowship provided by McDonough School of Business. Srinivasan acknowledges the financial support of the Terry-Sanford research grant and the University of Georgia Research Foundation research grant during the course of this project. This is a substantially revised version of an earlier paper of the same title. This paper has benefited from suggestions and comments from the referee and seminar participants at the AFA 2005 meetings, American University, Drexel University, the DIW Berlin Conference on Bank Relationships, Credit Extension and the Macroeconomy, the Federal Reserve Bank of Chicago's Conference on Bank Structure and Competition, the Federal Reserve Bank of New York, Ohio State University and JFE-sponsored Conference on Agency Problems and Conflicts of Interest in Financial Intermediaries, the Federal Reserve Board of Governors in Washington DC, the Federal Deposit Insurance Corporation, the Financial Management Association 2004 meetings, George Mason University, Office of Controller of Currency, University of Michigan, University of Virginia, and Washington University. We thank Chris James, Allen Berger, George Benston, Christa Bouwman, Steven Ongena, Tim Loughran, and Greg Udell for their helpful comments.

*Corresponding author. Tel.: +1 212 998 0711; fax: +1 212 995 4232.
E-mail address: asaunder@stern.nyu.edu (A. Saunders).

doi:10.1016/j.jfineco.2005.08.003

lenders. Relationship lenders are likely to be chosen to provide debt/equity underwriting services, but this effect is economically small.

JEL classification: G21; G24

Keywords: Lending relationships; Bank loans; Information asymmetry; Debt/equity underwriting

1. Introduction

The special nature of lending relationships has been the subject of extensive theoretical and empirical research in finance.[1] While there is no precise definition of "relationship banking," scholars broadly agree that if a financial intermediary's decision to supply various services to a firm is based on borrower-specific information that the intermediary collects over multiple interactions (over time as well as across multiple products), and further, if this information is proprietary (available only to the borrower and the intermediary), the intermediary is engaged in relationship banking (for a detailed discussion, see Berger, 1999; Boot, 2000). Existing theories predict that the establishment of strong lender-borrower relationships can generate significant benefits for the lender.[2]

Empirical evidence on the benefits of banking relationships has largely focused on documenting these benefits to the *borrower*. This literature can be broadly classified into two distinct approaches. The first approach uses indirect tests to establish the value of banking relationships. Specifically, James (1987) and Lummer and McConnell (1989) find a positive stock market reaction to the renewal of lending relationships and thereby establish the value-enhancement role of relationships to borrowers.[3] The second approach attempts to estimate the effects of relationships on borrowers directly by examining the impact that such relationships have on the cost and availability of credit. This approach is best characterized by Petersen and Rajan (1994) and Berger and Udell (1995), who find, among other things, that the stronger (i.e., the longer the duration of) the relationship, the greater the credit availability and the lower the collateral requirements.

In contrast, the focus of our paper is on establishing the existence and the nature of the benefits of relationship banking from the perspective of the *lender*, a subject that has attracted far less attention in the literature. Indeed, relationship studies do not provide any guidance with respect to the sources of these benefits to lenders and how the value created by establishing such relationships is shared between lenders and borrowers.[4] Thus, an

[1]See Boot (2000) and Ongena and Smith (1998) for an extensive survey of this literature.

[2]The benefits could come from multiple sources such as the ability to share sensitive information (Bhattacharya and Chiesa, 1995), more flexible contracts compared to public debt (Berlin and Mester, 1992; Boot et al., 1993), the ability to monitor collateral (Rajan and Winton, 1995), and the ability to smooth out loan pricing over multiple loans (Berlin and Mester, 1999). A relationship lender can also benefit from potential monopoly (holdup) power of the lender (e.g., Sharpe, 1990; Rajan, 1992), which allows the lender to charge its captive borrowers excessive rates for loans. Berlin (1996) provides a good overview of these issues of relationship lending.

[3]Further evidence is provided by Slovin et al. (1993) and Dahiya et al. (2003a), who document a *negative* impact of the potential *termination* of lending relationships on the borrower's market value. Ongena et al. (2003) report similar results for capital-constrained Norwegian borrowers when banks of such borrowers face distress.

[4]One study that attempts to indirectly measure the relationship benefits to the lenders is Dahiya et al. (2003b). They find that a bank's share price drops when its borrower announces default. The stock price decrease is much

important question is: what is the value of establishing a lending relationship to a lender (rather than a borrower)?

Existing theories of financial intermediation (see, e.g., Leland and Pyle, 1977; Diamond, 1984; Ramakrishnan and Thakor, 1984) emphasize the role of banks in generating information, for instance, through screening (Diamond, 1991) and monitoring (Rajan and Winton, 1995). Because relationship lending typically involves repeated interaction between a lender and a borrower over time, such interactions may generate "inside information" for the lender and reduce its cost of providing further loans and other services.[5] To the extent that relationship lending produces reusable and proprietary information about the borrower, a possible benefit for the relationship lender is that it would be better placed to win future loan business and other fee-generating services from its relationship borrower.[6] While the association between past lending relationships and future investment banking business has been examined recently by Drucker and Puri (2005) (for seasoned equity offerings), Yasuda (2005), and Burch et al. (2005) (for public debt underwriting), as far as we are aware, no study has examined the impact of lending relationships on the ability to win future loan business. Our paper provides tests that examine whether establishing a lending relationship translates into a higher probability of winning future lending as well as non lending business for a lender.

The central result of this paper is that strong past lending relationships significantly increase the probability of securing future lending and investment banking business. Holding all else constant, a bank with a prior lending relationship has more than a 40% probability of winning subsequent loan business from its borrower while a bank lacking such a relationship has only a 3% probability of being chosen to provide future loans. Consistent with theory, borrowers that suffer from greater information asymmetry (e.g., small, non rated firms) are more likely to use their relationship lender for future loans. Moreover, on average, a prior lender is almost twice as likely to be retained as the lead debt underwriter by its (loan) borrowers. While the impact of a prior lending relationship has a limited effect on the choice of a seasoned equity offering (SEO) underwriter, the existence of a past lending relationship is associated with almost a four-fold increase in the probability of being retained as a lead initial public offering (IPO) underwriter by a relationship borrower. To the extent that an increase in future lending and underwriting business is profitable, a greater likelihood of winning future business is a significant benefit to a relationship lender.

A number of recent studies examine the effect of past lending relationships on the choice of underwriter. Yasuda (2005) examines the impact of prior lending relationships on the choice of debt underwriter and finds that past lending relationships are associated with

(*footnote continued*)
greater when the borrower has had an ongoing relationship with the bank, signalling that potential termination of the relationship also results in a loss of value to the *bank*.

[5]Petersen and Rajan (1994) provide a succinct description of this argument: "... if scale economies exist in information production, and information is durable and not easily transferable, these theories suggest that a firm with close ties to financial institutions should have a lower cost of capital ... Implicit, therefore, in our analysis is the assumption that reductions in lender's cost are passed on to the borrower in a lower rate."

[6]Petersen and Rajan (1994) discuss reasons as to why a relationship lender would incur lower information production costs. They argue that over time a relationship lender acquires information about its borrower that would be costly for a new lender to acquire, thus giving the relationship lender a cost advantage. Also, if fixed costs of producing information can be spread over multiple products, the marginal cost of providing any individual product would be lower for a relationship lender.

a significantly higher probability of securing the debt underwriting business. Ljungqvist et al. (2006) examine how analyst coverage affects a bank's ability to win both debt and equity underwriting business. While not the focus of their paper, they report that prior lending relationships are associated with a significantly higher probability of winning future investment banking business, especially for debt underwriting. Drucker and Puri (2005) focus exclusively on SEOs and report that "concurrent lending" (a loan six months before or six months after the issue) is associated with a higher likelihood of winning the underwriting business. Our results for underwriter selection are broadly similar to the results of these studies. Similar to Yasuda (2005) and Ljungqvist et al. (2006), we find that prior lending relationships are significantly associated with a higher probability of winning debt underwriting business. While we find that prior lending relationships are associated with a significantly higher probability of winning IPO business, our results for SEOs are not as significant as those reported by Drucker and Puri (2005). This difference in significance could arise in part due to our different methodologies in constructing the relationship measures, as their paper focuses on concurrent lending and underwriting. Also unlike Drucker and Puri, we explicitly control for market shares of potential underwriters in both the lending as well as the underwriting markets. Overall, our results are consistent with the findings of these recent studies, which show that prior lending relationships are associated with a significantly higher likelihood of winning underwriting business.

The remainder of the paper is organized as follows. We describe our main hypotheses in Section 2. Section 3 describes the data and sample selection process. We present the methodology and major results in Section 4. We conclude in Section 5.

2. Theoretical predictions and hypotheses

In this section we discuss testable predictions of existing theories of relationship lending and the main hypotheses that we test in this paper. The hypotheses that we test examine the benefits of relationship lending that accrue from the efficiencies in information production that a relationship lender enjoys. These hypotheses predict that a relationship lender is more likely to secure future business than is a non-relationship lender. We refer to these benefits collectively as *higher business volume benefit*.

As we discuss in the introduction, theoretical models view the economies of scale in information production as the key source of the benefits that arise from strong relationships. If there are fixed costs of information production and if this information is proprietary and reusable, theory suggests that strong relationships would be associated with a lower cost of information production for subsequent lending and service provision decisions (see Greenbaum and Thakor, 1995). A testable implication therefore is that a relationship lender is more likely to capture the future lending business of its borrower.[7] We formalize this implication in Hypothesis 1:

Hypothesis 1 (*H1*). *The stronger the bank-borrower relationship, the greater the probability that a lender attracts future lending business from that borrower.*

[7]A tendency to repeat past relationships is well documented in areas other than the lender-borrower context. For instance, Levinthal and Fichman (1988) report that relationships between auditors and clients are more likely to be renewed as the duration of these relationships increased, and Carlton (1986) reports that the average duration of buyer-supplier relationships in the manufacturing industry typically exceeds five years.

The choice between bank debt and direct public debt has been the focus of a number of studies. Rajan (1992) defines bank financing as "inside" debt due to a bank's enhanced ability to collect information about its borrower. Conceptually, relationship lending can be thought of as repeated extensions of such "informed" debt by the same lender, whereas public debt can be regarded as "arms-length" financing or "outside" debt, as in this case lenders do not engage in proprietary information production. Diamond (1991) argues that the borrowers that suffer from the most severe information asymmetries (e.g., small firms with less established repayment histories and/or borrowers with poor credit ratings) have the most to gain from the monitoring services that banks provide. Such firms would choose bank financing over public debt financing. Also, Berlin and Mester (1992) suggest that borrowers with poor credit would choose bank loans with stringent covenants (because renegotiation of these covenants is easier than that of public debt covenants). In sum, these models predict that informationally opaque borrowers would use relationship loans more frequently than borrowers for whom a substantial amount of information is available publicly. We capture this conjecture in Hypothesis 2:

Hypothesis 2 (*H2*). *The more informationally opaque a borrower, the greater the likelihood it will borrow from its relationship lender.*

Kanatas and Qi (2003) focus on the benefits of "scope economies" that arise when a single institution offers both lending and underwriting services. These scope economies arise in their model, when information costs of learning about their customers in the process of supplying one product, need not be fully incurred again when supplying other products to them.[8] Petersen and Rajan (1994) also discuss the potential benefits to a relationship lender in generating enhanced sales of other non lending products (e.g., investment banking, deposit-related products, etc.). Such future sales may be a source of value creation since cross-selling multiple products gives the bank the ability to spread the fixed costs of information production over multiple products as well as to generate additional revenues.[9] This motivates our Hypothesis 3:

Hypothesis 3 (*H3*). *The stronger the bank-borrower relationship, the greater the probability a lender will attract future investment banking business from that borrower.*

3. Data and sample selection

To gain insights into these hypotheses we construct a unique database using three primary data sources, namely, the Loan Pricing Corporation Dealscan (henceforth, LPC) database,[10] a merged CRSP and COMPUSTAT database, and the Securities Data Corporation (SDC) new securities issues database. As we describe later in the paper, the large number of mergers and acquisitions in the U.S. banking sector over our sample period poses special challenges. To deal with mergers and acquisitions, we manually match

[8]Additionally, these benefits can also arise from "purchasing economies of scope" as outlined in Klemperer and Padilla (1997), who argue that borrowers prefer a single source of multiple products to lower their transaction costs.

[9]That is, the potential for cost and revenue economies of scale.

[10]We discuss the details of data obtained from LPC database in the following sections.

data from the SDC mergers and acquisition database, Lexis-Nexis, and the Hoover's corporate histories database to construct a chronology of banking mergers. Since our hypotheses seek to establish directly measurable benefits of relationships to lenders, the estimation of these benefits requires data on the following four different dimensions: data to construct meaningful relationship variables; characteristics of lenders; characteristics of each loan facility; and, characteristics of the borrowers. We discuss each of these four characteristics next in Sections 3.1–3.4.

3.1. Construction of relationship measures

One of the primary goals of this paper is to examine the existence and extent of the benefits of relationships to lenders. Thus, it is critical to construct meaningful and measurable proxies for bank relationships as well as their associated benefits. There is no uniformly accepted methodology for measuring the presence and strength of banking relationships. In cases in which the precise point of the start of a banking relationship is available, researchers often use the length of a relationship as a proxy for its strength (see, for example, Petersen and Rajan, 1994; Berger and Udell, 1995). In cases in which this information is not available, the existence of a prior lending relationship is used as a proxy (see, for example, Dahiya et al., 2003b; Schenone, 2004). All these relationship measures have a potential drawback, however. If an unobservable characteristic (e.g., physical proximity) causes a borrower and a lender to match up in the first place, and if this factor continues to be present when the borrower seeks subsequent loans or other banking services, our relationship measure would include the effect of this factor. This limitation characterizes all relationship measures that are based on the existence and/or intensity of prior interactions between a borrower and its lender. We try to mitigate this drawback by including a physical proximity measure, LOCATION (described later), that controls for the locational distance between a borrower and its potential lenders.

To construct the relationship measures, we employ the LPC database. This database contains data on loans made to large publicly traded companies.[11] Our sample period extends from 1986 to March 31, 2001. Since coverage of our sample data starts in 1986, our sample period is truncated in the left tail. Thus, a length of relationship measure would be biased because we lack a definitive starting date for any such relationship. Nevertheless, our data set still allows us to construct several other measures that capture the evolution of the bank-borrower relationship over time. We focus on three distinct markets in which a relationship lender can benefit from its close ties with its borrower, specifically, the market for bank loans, the market for public debt underwriting services, and the market for public equity underwriting services. Since we need to take into account the historical relationship at the point in time of a particular transaction, we construct these relationship measures for each of the three markets separately. We describe next our methodology for constructing the measures for each of these markets (Appendix A provides a summary of all the relationship variables and how they are constructed).

[11] Researchers examining bank loans are increasingly employing the LPC database. See, for example, Carey et al. (1998), Strahan (2000), Dahiya et al. (2003b), and Drucker and Puri (2005).

3.1.1. Market for bank loans

For every loan facility, we construct three alternative measures of relationship strength by looking back and searching the past borrowing record of the borrower.[12] Thus, for each loan by borrower i, we look back over a period of five years for any previous loans taken by i.[13] Based on the banks retained for these past loans, we construct various relationship measures as discussed below. For each bank m, we construct the lending relationship measure $\text{LOANREL(M)}_m^{\text{BankLoans}}$, where M indicates one of the three alternative measures.

The process is best illustrated by an example: In May 1997, Texas Instruments Inc. borrowed $600 million from a syndicate led by ABN-AMRO, Citicorp, and NationsBank. To calculate the strength of ABN-AMRO's relationship at the time of this loan we *look back* at the borrowing history of Texas Instruments over the five years preceding this May 1997 loan. In this window, the following records of borrowing activity by Texas Instruments appear in the LPC database. In May 1994, Texas Instruments borrowed $300 million from a syndicate led by JP Morgan. It borrowed another $440 million from ABN-AMRO, Citicorp, Fuji Bank, and NationsBank in May 1995. Then in May 1996, it borrowed $600 million from ABN-AMRO, Citicorp, Fuji Bank, and NationsBank. Thus, looking back from the point of the May 1997 loan, Texas Instruments contracted loans of $1340 million (300 + 440 + 600) prior to the May 1997 loan of $600 Million. Of the $1340, ABN-AMRO provided $1040 (440 + 600). Thus, in this measure we give full relationship attribution to ABN-AMRO although the loans are syndicated (in constructing the relationship measure for Citicorp or NationsBank, the other lead banks on this loan, we follow the same process). That is, the relationship is established by the granting of the loan rather than the fraction lent by an individual lead bank. Note that in most cases, LPC does not provide details on the shares of individual banks in a syndicated loan. We use this example to illustrate the methodology for constructing various relationship measures.

The first relationship strength variable, $\text{LOANREL(Dummy)}_m^{\text{BankLoans}}$, is a binary measure designed to pick up the *existence* of prior lending by the same lender in the past. In this case, for ABN-AMRO, $\text{LOANREL(Dummy)}_{\text{ABN-AMRO}}^{\text{BankLoans}}$ would equal one, denoting the existence of prior lending to Texas Instruments by ABN-AMRO.

The other two measures of relationship strength are continuous. The first continuous measure of relationship strength, $\text{LOANREL(Amount)}_m^{\text{BankLoans}}$, captures the *size* of past lending by bank m to borrower i. We calculate this variable as

$$\text{LOANREL(Amount)}_m^{\text{BankLoans}} = \frac{\$\text{ Amount of loans to borrower } i \text{ by bank } m \text{ in last 5 years}}{\text{Total \$ amount of loans by borrower } i \text{ in last 5 years}}. \quad (1)$$

---

[12]We focus on the lead bank(s) of a particular loan facility, as the information-intensive role that we test in our hypotheses is most appropriate for the lead bank, which typically holds the largest share of a syndicated loan (see Kroszner and Strahan, 2001), and is frequently the administrative agent that has the fiduciary duty to other syndicate members to provide timely information about the borrower. Dennis and Mullineux (2000) and Madan et al. (1999) list the functions performed exclusively by the administrative agent; these include monitoring the performance of covenants; relationship management; administration of collateral; and, loan workouts in the case of default. Thus, the responsibilities of a lead bank best fit the description of a relationship lender.

[13]We choose the five year window as approximately 75% of the loan facilities in our sample have maturities of less than or equal to five years. Thus, most of the borrowers in our sample would need to refinance their debt within five years.

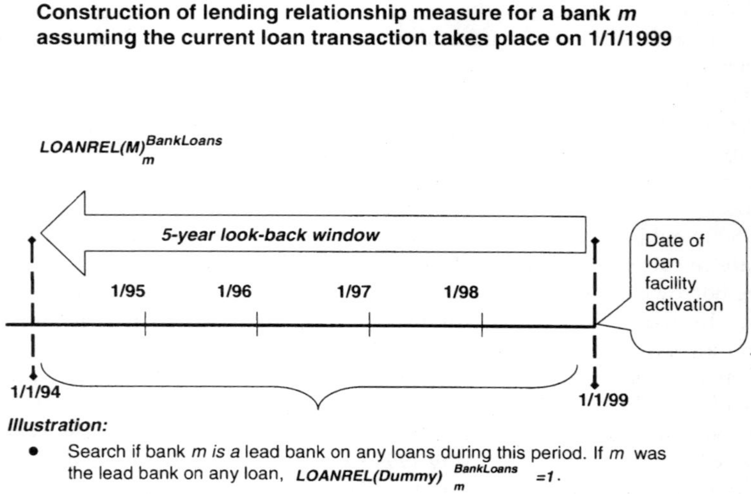

Fig. 1. Construction of relationship measures in bank loan market.

Thus, in the case of the May 1997 loan to Texas Instruments, LOANREL $(\text{Amount})^{\text{BankLoans}}_{\text{ABN-AMRO}}$ for ABN-AMRO is 0.776 (= \$1,040/\$1,340).[14]

The second continuous measure of relationship strength, $\text{LOANREL(Number)}^{\text{BankLoans}}_{m}$, captures the *frequency* of past lending by a bank m to a borrower i. We calculate this variable as

$$\text{LOANREL(Number)}^{\text{BankLoans}}_{m} = \frac{\text{Number of loans to borrower } i \text{ by bank } m \text{ in last 5 years}}{\text{Total Number of loans by borrower } i \text{ in last 5 years}}. \tag{2}$$

Thus, in the case of the May 1997 loan to Texas Instruments, LOANREL $(\text{Number})^{\text{BankLoans}}$ for ABN-AMRO is 0.67 (= 2/3).[15] We depict the construction of $\text{LOANREL(M)}^{\text{BankLoans}}_{m}$ in Fig. 1.

3.1.2. Market for underwriting public debt

To test H3, we focus on two investment banking products that a bank can offer to its relationship borrowers, that is, underwriting services for public debt and for public equity issues. To examine the impact of a prior lending relationship on winning a public debt underwriting mandate for any bank m, we construct a new lending relationship variable, $\text{LOANREL(M)}^{\text{PublicDebt}}_{m}$, in exactly the same way as $\text{LOANREL(M)}^{\text{BankLoans}}_{m}$, the only difference being that for $\text{LOANREL(M)}^{\text{PublicDebt}}_{m}$ the date of the look-back period is the

[14]Because we want to capture relationship strength and because of limited data on syndicate shares, we give full attribution to all lending banks.

[15]For this example $\text{LOANREL(M)}^{\text{BankLoans}}_{\text{Citicorp}}$ and $\text{LOANREL(M)}^{\text{BankLoans}}_{\text{NationsBank}}$ would be the same as those calculated for ABN-AMRO as both these banks were also lead banks on the two past loans on which ABN-AMRO was the lead bank.

date of a public issue of debt while that for LOANREL(M)$_m^{\text{BankLoans}}$ is the loan facility activation date.

Eccles and Crane (1988) argue that prior *investment banking* relationships have a significant impact on winning new investment banking business. Thus, we need to control for the existence of such prior investment banking relationships in identifying the independent effect of lending relationships. To better illustrate how we construct prior investment banking relationships, we use the example of a firm i that issues public debt and for which we wish to calculate the strength of prior investment banking relationships (as we describe in the next section, the process is the same for an equity issuer). There are two types of investment banking relationship that a bank m can have with issuer i. The first type is a *same-market relationship*, i.e., for any bank m and a debt issuer i, we look for previous debt underwriting relationships that m has had with i. The second type is a *cross-market relationship*, i.e., for a debt issuer i, we look to see if i has had a prior *equity* underwriting relationship with bank m. We describe the same-market relationship measures first. For any debt issuer i, we construct Lead-DEBTREL(M)$_m^{\text{PublicDebt}}$ for a bank m in the following way. We take the date of the public issue of debt as the starting point and look back over the preceding five years to determine whether bank m was the "lead underwriter" to any other public issues of debt by this issuer. The variable, Lead-DEBTREL(Dummy)$_m^{\text{PublicDebt}}$, equals one if m was a lead underwriter on any previous debt issue. The variable, Lead-DEBTREL(Amount)$_m^{\text{PublicDebt}}$ for bank m reflects the ratio of public issues of debt underwritten by m (as a lead underwriter) relative to the total number of debt issues of issuer i over the last five years and, is calculated as

$$\text{Lead-DEBTREL(Amount)}_m^{\text{PublicDebt}} = \frac{\text{\$ Amount of } i\text{' s public debt underwritten by bank } m \text{ in last 5 years}}{\text{Total \$ amount of public debt issued by } i \text{ in last 5 years}}. \quad (3)$$

Similarly, we calculate Lead-DEBTREL(Number)$_m^{\text{PublicDebt}}$ for underwriter m and debt issuer i as

$$\text{Lead-DEBTREL(Number)}_m^{\text{PublicDebt}} = \frac{\text{Number of } i\text{' s public debt issues underwritten by bank } m \text{ in last 5 years}}{\text{Total number of public debt issued by } i \text{ in last 5 years}}. \quad (4)$$

While we focus on lead underwriters, we also construct expanded versions of the Lead-DEBTREL(M)$_m^{\text{PublicDebt}}$ variables, denoted by DEBTREL(M)$_m^{\text{PublicDebt}}$, in which we include both lead underwriting and co-manager roles on prior debt issues.

Next, we describe the cross-market relationship measures for a debt issuer i. We take the date of the public issue of debt as the starting point and look back over the preceding five years to determine whether bank m was the lead underwriter to any public issues of *equity* by this issuer. The variable Lead-EQUITYREL(Dummy)$_m^{\text{PublicDebt}}$ equals one if m was a lead underwriter on any previous *equity* issue. The calculations of Lead-EQUITYREL(Amount)$_m^{\text{PublicDebt}}$ and Lead-EQUITYREL(Number)$_m^{\text{PublicDebt}}$ are done in the same way. Again, we construct expanded versions of these cross-market relationship measures (denoted by EQUITYREL(M)$_m^{\text{PublicDebt}}$) by including both the lead underwriting and co-manager roles on previous equity issues. Fig. 2. illustrates the methodology for creating various relationship measures for the public debt underwriting market.

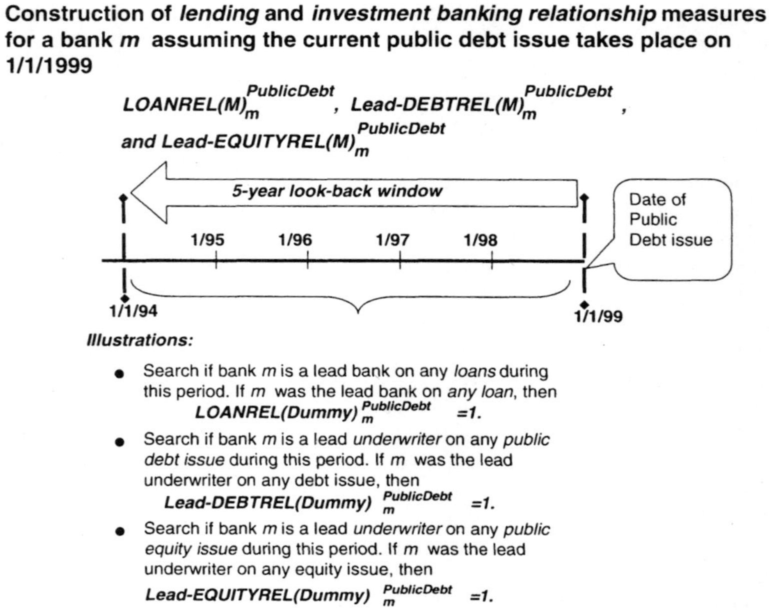

Fig. 2. Construction of relationship measures in public debt underwriting market.

3.1.3. Market for underwriting public equity

The process for constructing relationship measures for the public equity underwriting market is very similar to the one we describe in Section 3.1.2. We separate our equity issuers into IPO and SEO subsamples as the prior investment banking relationships are not meaningful for the IPO sample since the issuer is conducting its first sale of securities in the public market.[16] However, both IPO and SEO issuers can have prior *lending* relationships. We therefore estimate $\text{LOANREL(M)}_m^{\text{PublicEquity}}$ using the date of public issue of equity as the anchor point for the five year look-back window. For SEOs the measure for a same-market investment banking relationship (denoted by $\text{Lead-EQUITYREL(M)}_m^{\text{PublicEquity}}$) and a cross-market relationship (denoted by $\text{Lead-DEBTREL(M)}_m^{\text{PublicEquity}}$) are constructed in a similar fashion. Again we construct expanded versions of $\text{Lead-EQUITYREL(M)}_m^{\text{PublicEquity}}$ and $\text{Lead-DEBTREL(M)}_m^{\text{PublicEquity}}$ variables, denoted by $\text{EQUITYREL(M)}_m^{\text{PublicEquity}}$ and $\text{DEBTREL(M)}_m^{\text{PublicEquity}}$, in which we include both lead underwriting and co-manager roles on the prior equity and debt issues, respectively. Fig. 3 illustrates the construction methodology for all of these relationship measures.

Appendix B provides the correlations among the various relationship measures. Within each market our three relationship measures (Dummy, Number, and Amount)

[16]While an IPO firm cannot have prior equity underwriting relationships, it may still have prior debt underwriting relationships. However, our data show that firms rarely access the debt market if they do not already have publicly traded equity. We therefore assume that prior investment banking relationships are not well defined for IPO issuers.

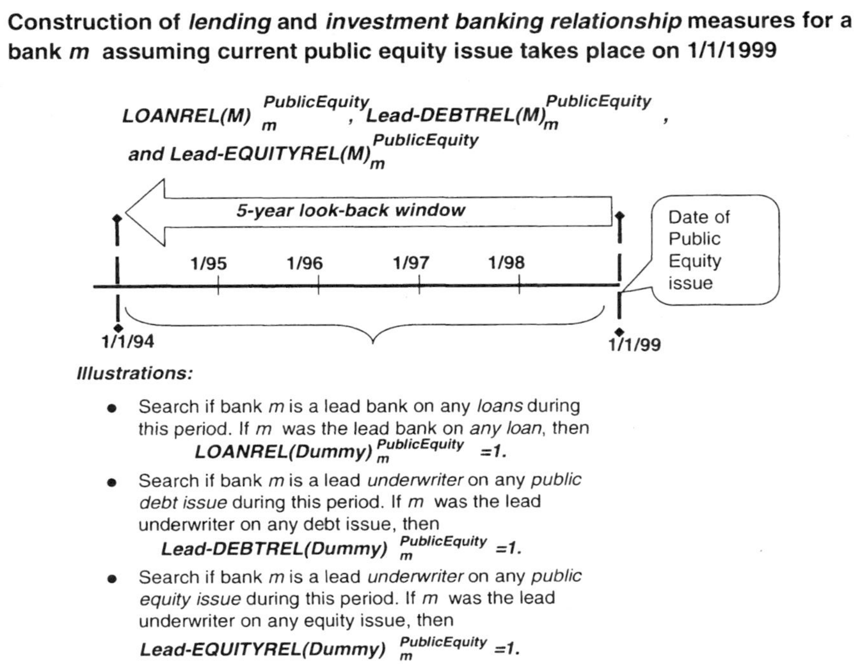

Fig. 3. Construction of relationship measures in public equity underwriting market.

demonstrate a strong positive correlation. Across different markets, however, the relationship measure in one market does not appear to be strongly correlated with relationship measures in other markets.

Table 1 provides descriptive statistics for our data and segregates relationship and non-relationship loans (i.e., loans from a bank that did not have a past relationship with the borrower in the previous five years). Panel A provides the calendar-time distribution of the loan sample. The low number of observations in the early years is driven by two factors. First, LPC database coverage is better in more recent years. Second, our methodology for constructing relationship measures ensures that the very first loan reported for any borrower is excluded, otherwise we would not have a historical starting point with which to classify a loan as either a relationship or a non-relationship loan. To control for this time trend in the sample we include a calendar-year dummy variable in our tests.

We also segregate the samples of public debt issuers and public equity issuers on the basis of prior lending relationships. Panels B and C of Table 1 provide the calendar-time distribution for these issuers.

3.2. Data on lender (bank) characteristics

H1, H2, and H3 hypothesize that the higher volume benefits to lenders manifest as the ability to supply future loans and investment banking services to borrowers. We measure

Table 1
Calendar-time distribution of loan facilities, public debt issues and public equity issues

Panel A below provides the calendar-time distribution for the sample of loan facilities, broken in to loans for which none of the lead banks on the current facility had a prior lead lending relationship in the past five years ($LOANREL(Dummy)^{BankLoans} = 0$) and those for which at least one of the lead banks on the current facility was also the lead lender in the past five years ($LOANREL(Dummy)^{BankLoans} = 1$). Panel B provides similar data for public debt issues segregated by $LOANREL(Dummy)^{PublicDebt}$ (i.e., if one of the lead underwriters had a lead lending relationship in the five years prior to the current debt issue). Panel C provides similar data for public equity issues segregated by $LOANREL(Dummy)^{PublicEquity}$ (i.e., if one of the lead underwriters had a lead lending relationship in the five years prior to the current equity issue).

Year of loan sanction	No relationship $LOANREL(Dummy)^{BankLoans} = 0$	Relationship $LOANREL(Dummy)^{BankLoans} = 1$	Total
Panel A: Calendar time distribution of loans			
1986	1	2	3
1987	67	33	100
1988	222	174	396
1989	237	240	477
1990	212	329	541
1991	222	366	588
1992	373	491	864
1993	404	714	1,118
1994	398	961	1,359
1995	311	1,070	1,381
1996	488	1,207	1,695
1997	543	1,551	2,094
1998	523	1,384	1,907
1999	434	1,293	1,727
2000	348	1,530	1,878
2001Q1	106	464	570
Total	4,889	11,809	16,698

Year of public debt issue	No relationship $LOANREL(Dummy)^{PublicDebt} = 0$	Relationship $LOANREL(Dummy)^{PublicDebt} = 1$	Total
Panel B: Calendar-time distribution of public debt issues			
1989	48	1	49
1990	71	1	72
1991	98	14	112
1992	197	44	241
1993	187	72	259
1994	119	64	183
1995	182	109	291
1996	240	171	411
1997	349	191	540
1998	341	283	624
1999	139	248	387
2000	129	178	307
2001	92	259	351
Total	2,192	1,635	3,827

Table 1 (*continued*)

Year of public equity issue	No relationship $LOANREL(Dummy)^{PublicEquity} = 0$	Relationship $LOANREL(Dummy)^{PublicEquity} = 1$	Total
Panel C: Calendar-time distribution of public equity issues			
1989	1	0	1
1990	1	0	1
1991	24	0	24
1992	45	2	47
1993	70	13	83
1994	43	10	53
1995	58	10	68
1996	147	30	177
1997	154	31	185
1998	125	47	172
1999	128	80	208
2000	94	68	162
2001	85	64	149
Total	975	355	1,330

relationship benefits to the lender in three complementary ways. In particular, a strong relationship implies a higher likelihood of providing future loans to relationship borrowers, a higher probability of winning future debt underwriting from relationship borrowers, and a higher probability of winning future equity underwriting business from relationship borrowers.

However, the choice of lender (see H1) is also be affected by the potential lender's market share or reputation (all else being equal, a top-ranked lender is more likely to be chosen compared to a lower-ranked lender) and the loan's characteristics. Similarly, the probability of winning investment banking business (see H3) would also depend on the lender's reputation in the relevant investment banking product markets.[17] Thus, we need data on lender characteristics. We use the LPC and SDC databases to gather these data.

For the loan market, a key issue is the identification of the "lead" bank (or banks) for a particular loan facility. While the LPC database contains a field that describes the lender's role, it does not have a uniform and consistent methodology to classify which bank is the lead bank. Rather, it includes a number of descriptions such as "arranger," " administrative agent," "agent," or "lead manager" that roughly correspond to the lead bank status of the lender. To ensure that we do not mislabel a lead bank we follow a simple rule. Any bank(s) that is (are) *not* described as a "participant" is (are) treated as a lead bank.[18] This approach ensures that we do not include banks that play a limited information production role. Indeed, Madan et al. (1999) define participant as "the lowest

[17]Krigman et al. (2001), show that issuers often switch underwriters to graduate to a more reputable underwriter.

[18]For example, Walt Disney Co. contracted a $ 1 billion facility on December 19, 1997. Citicorp and Bank of America with the largest share are listed as Administrative Agents, while all others are listed as Participants. We classify Citicorp and Bank of America as the lead banks on this facility.

title given to a bank in a syndication" and describe its role as little more than taking the allocated share of the loan.

Because the borrower's choice of lender bank should also depend on the reputation of the lender, we also need to control for this effect. We measure the reputation of a lender by calculating the market share of that lender, defined as the share of a bank in the loans reported by LPC database in a particular year (market share is a commonly used proxy for reputation; see, e.g., Megginson and Weiss, 1991). Specifically, we calculate market share in the following way: if a bank is a sole lead lender, it gets 100% credit for the loan, and if there are M lead banks, each gets $(1/M)$th share of the loan. As we note earlier the LPC database rarely gives the precise shares of lead and other banks in a loan syndication. To illustrate by an example, if bank m is the sole lead bank on a loan of \$100 Million, the entire loan amount would be used in calculating its market share, whereas if bank m was one of four lead banks, only \$25 Million ((1/4)th of \$100 Million) would be included in its market share calculation.[19] We calculate the market share of bank m in any year t as denoted by $(\text{LOAN MKT SHARE})_{mt}$ as

$$(\text{LOAN MKT SHARE})_{mt} = \frac{(\text{Loan Amount})_{mt}}{\sum_{i=1}^{N} (\text{Loan Amount})_{it}}, \tag{5}$$

where $(\text{Loan Amount})_{mt}$ is the dollar amount of loans in year t for which the bank m was the lead bank and N is the total number of borrowers in the LPC database. Thus, while the numerator captures the lending volume of bank m in year t, the denominator is the "total amount of loans" raised (by all borrowers) in year t. Panel A of Table 2 provides a list of the top 20 lenders over our entire sample period, ranked by their market share. This table shows that while no single bank dominates the sample, the top 20 banks still account for nearly 70% of all loans.

To test H3, we focus on the underwriting business in two distinct markets: issues of public debt and issues of public equity. While debt underwriting is related to commercial banks' historical corporate lending business, e.g., because loan and bond pay-off structures are similar, equity underwriting is a relatively new market for U.S. commercial banks. We use the SDC new issues database to obtain all the public issues of debt and public issues of equity by our sample borrowers. This results in 5,203 distinct issues of debt by 945 firms and 5,219 issues of equity by 3,129 firms. Next we verify whether relationship lenders of these issuers were eligible to underwrite debt (equity) issues at the date of debt (equity) issue.[20] If, at the date of issue, none of the relationship lenders are eligible to underwrite that issue, we exclude that issue from our sample. Our final sample consists of 3,923 distinct issues of debt by 721 firms and 1,358 issues of equity by 895 firms. For this sample we collect data on the amount raised from the debt (equity) issue, the identity of the lead underwriter(s), and the identity of the co-manager(s) of the issue from the SDC database.

[19]For example, Bank of Boston was the sole lender on a June 1997, \$11.9 million facility to GenRad Inc. and thus gets 100% credit for this deal. In contrast, it extended a \$350 million line of credit to Boston Scientific Corp on June 10, 1996 along with Chase Manhattan Bank and Lehman Brothers; for this loan, it gets 1/3rd of the credit in computing market share.

[20]At any given date t, a commercial bank is assumed to be eligible to underwrite a particular class of security if it has underwritten (either as lead or as co-manager) at least one issue of that class of securities in any of the years before t. We could have also used the regulatory approval date as the start of eligibility but in some cases this date is not available. The requirement of having underwritten at least one deal is thus more conservative and ensures that only active participants are included.

Table 2
Market share ranking of major lenders, debt underwriters, and equity underwriters
Panel A describes the top 20 lenders for sample period based on data from the LPC dealscan database. Panel B and Panel C describe the top 20 debt and equity underwriters as reported by the SDC new issues database.

Rank	Bank	Number of Deals	Market share	Amount ($ Million)
Panel A: Top 20 lenders				
1	CITICORP	2,622	9.72%	429,162
2	BANK-AMERICA	4,257	9.44%	416,913
3	CHASE	3,102	7.84%	346,470
4	J-P-MORGAN	1,347	5.76%	254,320
5	CHEMICAL	1,457	5.09%	224,738
6	NATIONS-BANK	2,660	4.54%	200,338
7	FIRST-CHICAGO	1,298	3.04%	134,310
8	BANKERS-TRUST	1,217	2.72%	120,261
9	BANK-NOVA-SCOTIA	1,594	2.58%	113,954
10	BANK-ONE	1,477	2.31%	101,901
11	BANK-NEW-YORK	1,300	2.14%	94,328
12	FIRST-UNION	1,556	2.06%	90,885
13	ABN-AMRO	1,054	1.85%	81,868
14	DEUTSCHE-BANK	767	1.75%	77,314
15	TORONTO-DOMINION-BANK	886	1.66%	73,362
16	CIBC	1,059	1.59%	70,022
17	BANK-BOSTON	1,296	1.44%	63,541
18	CREDIT-LYONNAIS	989	1.38%	60,857
19	SOC-GEN	665	1.20%	53,208
20	WACHOVIA	671	1.20%	53,207
	Overall	24,174	69.29%	4,417,304
Panel B: Top 20 debt underwriters				
1	GOLDMAN-SACHS	640	16.03%	119,331
2	MERRILL	634	14.56%	108,386
3	MORGAN-STANLEY	498	11.38%	84,737
4	CITICORP	319	9.95%	74,119
5	CSFB	371	9.49%	70,660
6	LEHMAN	339	8.81%	65,588
7	SALOMON	310	5.63%	41,895
8	J-P-MORGAN	303	5.28%	39,341
9	BANK-AMERICA	159	4.06%	30,236
10	BEAR-STERNS	109	3.00%	22,309
11	CHASE	132	2.44%	18,167
12	DLJ	89	2.09%	15,544
13	DEUTSCHE-BANK	45	1.04%	7,732
14	UNION-BANK-SWITZERLAND	81	0.97%	7,257
15	SMITH-BARNEY	80	0.89%	6,629
16	BANKERS-TRUST	20	0.46%	3,427
17	NATIONS-BANK	51	0.38%	2,820
18	BANK-ONE	28	0.38%	2,803
19	DILLON-READ	19	0.34%	2,507
20	PAINE-WEBBER	24	0.32%	2,354
	Overall		97.48%	744,643
Panel C: Top 20 equity underwriters				
1	GOLDMAN-SACHS	200	17.05%	47,033
2	MERRILL	236	15.61%	43,082

Table 2 (*continued*)

Rank	Bank	Number of Deals	Market share	Amount ($ Million)
3	MORGAN-STANLEY	180	15.29%	42,195
4	CSFB	131	9.11%	25,129
5	DLJ	98	5.89%	16,247
6	CITICORP	74	5.86%	16,167
7	J-P-MORGAN	40	5.58%	15,397
8	LEHMAN	88	5.09%	14,051
9	SALOMON	76	4.82%	13,301
10	BEAR-STERNS	57	2.95%	8,148
11	BANK-AMERICA	24	1.43%	3,948
12	SMITH-BARNEY	42	1.41%	3,882
13	BANKERS-TRUST	34	1.32%	3,636
14	ALEX-BROWN	21	1.10%	3,044
15	DEUTSCHE-BANK	26	0.97%	2,665
16	UNION-BANK-SWITZERLAND	22	0.65%	1,802
17	MONTGOMERY	19	0.64%	1,773
18	PAINE-WEBBER	26	0.52%	1,438
19	PRUDENTIAL	19	0.42%	1,169
20	ROBERTSON-STEPHENS	9	0.28%	770
	Overall		95.99%	275,927

The sample construction methodology we employ to test H3 ensures that only those debt (equity) issuers who *could* have chosen their relationship lender as an underwriter are included. For example, if an issuer had borrowed exclusively from banks that did not have regulatory approval to underwrite securities then it would not be in our sample. This allows us to test the association between lending relationship and investment banking more precisely. However, this also implies that in the early part of our sample period when fewer issuers meet this criteria (since only a limited number of lenders were eligible to underwrite debt and/or equity issues) our sample size is relatively smaller. By the mid-1990s, a larger number of lenders had received regulatory approval to do such investment banking business and our sample size is relatively larger (Table 1, Panels B and C). We control for this trend by including individual year dummy variables in our tests.

The probability of winning underwriting business in any particular market depends also on the reputation of various players in that market. Again, we use the market share of major underwriters as the proxy for reputation. While we estimate the loan market share for each bank as in Eq. (5), we use the SDC database's league tables to obtain data on the market share for major underwriters. Panel B and Panel C of Table 2 provide the list of top 20 underwriters in debt underwriting and equity underwriting, respectively, and their relative market share. The debt and equity underwriting markets appear to be fairly concentrated, as the top 20 institutions account for over 95% of the market.

Finally, in order to control for physical proximity between a bank and a lender (see discussion in Section 3.1), we construct LOCATION, which is a dummy variable that equals one if both the bank and the borrower have their respective head offices in the same state and zero otherwise. For lenders the head office location is identified by searching Hoover's online company history database and for borrowers the head office state is identified by searching COMPUSTAT. For non-U.S. banks we search for the U.S. headquarters. For a few Japanese banks we are not able to ascertain the exact location of U.S. headquarters; for these, we assume that New York is the U.S. head office (we confirm that all of these banks do have a New York office). For banks that underwent mergers we use the historical head office for the pre-merger period and the head office of the new merged entity in the post-merger period.

3.3. Data on characteristics of loan facilities, debt issues and equity issues

We also need to control for various loan characteristics such as maturity, security, and type of facility. To generate data on loan terms we employ the LPC database. LPC provides data on a facility-level as well as deal-level basis. A given deal may correspond to multiple facilities (i.e., multiple loan contracts) of different types of loans to the same firm by one or more banks. Examples of different types of facilities include term loans, lines of credit, revolvers, etc. In this study, we use each facility as the unit of observation. Panel A of Table 3 provides summary statistics on key loan facility terms.

The key characteristics for the debt and the equity issues are proceeds raised from the issue, date of issuance and identity of lead underwriters and co-managers. Our primary source for these data items, is the SDC new issues database. Panel B of Table 3 reports the summary statistics for debt issues. We segregate the public equity issues into IPOs and SEOs as the fee structure across these two issue classes is different. Panel C of Table 3 provides the summary statistics for equity issues.

3.4. Data on borrower characteristics

Existing theories argue that informational asymmetries between a borrower and potential debt providers are addressed more effectively by relationship lending than by arms-length financing. Because borrowers that suffer from greater information asymmetries should gain more from relationship lending, such borrowers are expected to borrow from their relationship lender more frequently (see H2). We use different proxies for information opacity of a borrower such as borrower size, the loan's credit rating, and the tangibility of borrower's assets. COMPUSTAT is our primary data source for borrower-related variables, since the LPC database does not provide a borrower Cusip that can be used as an identifier to match the borrower to other data sets such as COMPUSTAT or CRSP. We therefore manually match the LPC companies with the merged CRSP/COMPUSTAT database using the name of the company in the LPC database. The matching procedure is conservative in that we assign a match only when we are sure that the company is the same in the two databases. Using this procedure, we obtain a set of 6,322 borrowers in the LPC database for which we can obtain the Cusip of the company from the COMPUSTAT database. Since a number of borrowers merged or were acquired by other borrowers over our sample period, we take this M&A activity into account in constructing our relationship measures. If the post-merger/post-acquisition company retains the Cusip of one of the predecessor firms, we assume that the relationships of the Cusip-retaining firm are inherited by the post-merger/post-acquisition entity while the relationships of the other firm are assumed to be not inherited. Thus, to the extent a post-merger entity also retains the relationships of the target, we underestimate the strength of the relationship variable. If the merger creates an entity with a new Cusip we follow

Table 3
Summary statistics for key loan, debt issue, and equity issue characteristics

The table below provides summary statistics of various loan and borrower characteristics. Panel A reports these for the loan facilities sample. Panel B and Panel C report these for debt issue and equity issue samples respectively. AISD is the "All In Spread-Drawn," which is the all-inclusive cost of a drawn loan to the borrower. This equals the coupon spread over LIBOR on the drawn amount plus the annual fee and is reported in basis points. Loans per borrower is the number of loan facilities for any particular borrower that are included in the LPC Dealscan database. Number of lead banks per loan facility is also from LPC Dealscan database. Number of relationship lead banks are those lead banks that have extended at least one loan to a particular borrower in the five-year period immediately preceding the current loan facility. Loan Facility Size is the dollar amount of the loan facility in millions. Maturity is length in months between facility activation date and maturity date. Syndicate, Secured, and Investment Grade are percent of facility that have the stated attribute. To be classified as Investment Grade the loan has to be rated BBB or above by S&P. Proceeds is the amount of proceeds in USD millions from the debt or the equity issue. Underwriting fee (i.e., gross spread) is the fee charged divided by the proceeds and is reported in basis points. All data are winsorized at the 1st and 99th percentiles.

Variable	*N*	Mean	Std. Dev.	Min	25th Pctile	Median	75th Pctile	Max
Panel A: Loan facilities sample								
AISD	21,843	211.07	129.64	17.5	100.00	200.00	300.00	580.00
Number of loans per borrower	5,687	4.4	4.0	1.0	2.0	3.0	6.0	21.0
Number of lead banks per loan	24,174	2.2	2.8	1.0	1.0	1.0	2.0	18.0
Number of relationship lead banks per loan	15,937	1.4	2.0	0.0	0.0	1.0	1.0	12.0
Loan facility size	25,476	161.51	312.26	0.50	10.78	50.00	151.70	2000.00
Maturity	22,667	44.42	27.51	3.00	18.00	37.00	60.00	120.00
Secured	16,016	0.82	0.38	0.0	1.0	1.0	1.0	1.0
Investment grade	8,484	0.48	0.50	0.0	0.0	0.0	1.0	1.0
Syndicate	25,470	0.77	0.42	0.0	1.0	1.0	1.0	1.0
Panel B: Debt issues sample								
Proceeds	3,923	189.81	249.11	0.20	33.0	124.8	249.3	3237.3
Fee (gross spread)	3,070	88.80	72.33	0.10	55.00	65.00	87.50	465.00
Panel C: Equity issues sample								
Initial public offerings (IPOs):								
Proceeds	283	200.12	536.04	10.80	51.00	96.00	149.80	7322.40
Fee (gross spread)	283	650.96	73.96	250.00	600.00	700.00	700.00	750.00
Seasoned equity offerings (SEOs):								
Proceeds	1,074	204.13	277.05	1.50	63.00	116.50	220.00	2733.70
Fee (gross spread)	1,012	426.73	114.80	24.80	347.55	448.80	500.75	812.50

a conservative approach and consider such an entity as having had no prior relationships. For subsidiaries we follow a similar methodology—if subsidiaries have the same Cusip as the parent company, we assume that subsidiaries have the same relationships as that of the parent company.

We use COMPUSTAT to extract data on accounting variables for the given company. We also extract the primary SIC code for the borrowers from COMPUSTAT and exclude all financial services firms (SIC codes between 6000 and 6999). To ensure that we only use accounting information that is publicly available at the time of a loan, we employ the following procedure: for a loan made in calender year t, we use fiscal year t data only if the loan activation month is at least six months after the fiscal year-ending month. Otherwise, we use fiscal year $t-1$ data.[21] The six-month minimum gap between fiscal year-end and the loan activation date is conservative given the SEC requirement that accounting data be made available within 90 days of the fiscal year-end. However, compliance with this requirement is patchy. Fama and French (1992) state that "on average 19.8% do not comply (with this requirement)."[22]

4. Methodology and empirical results

In this section we describe the tests we employ to estimate the hypothesized (higher volume) benefits of relationships to lenders (Hypotheses H1, H2 and H3).

4.1. Tests of Hypothesis 1

As we discuss in Section 2, existing theories of relationship lending predict that strong relationships should be associated with a lower cost of information production over time, provided this information is proprietary and reusable. A testable implication of these theories is that a relationship lender is more likely to secure the future lending business of its borrower. We formalize this implication in our Hypothesis 1. To test this, for each loan facility we focus on any bank *m's* likelihood of winning the loan business of borrower i at time t.

While the number of lenders that appear in our sample is quite large (see Table 2), a handful of banks account for the bulk of lending. To economize on the size of the data set but still retain most of the large transactions, we choose the following approach. In each year, we keep only those transactions for which one of the lead banks was ranked in the top 40 banks by market share in the prior year. That is, we reduce our sample to those transactions for which the lead bank(s) was among the top 40 in the previous year. This allows us to retain 73% of our original sample as the top 40 banks provide the bulk of all loans.[23] For each loan we create a choice set of 40 potential lenders, thereby creating 40 loan-bank pairs.[24] Since each loan facility generates a cluster of up to 40 loan-bank pair observations, our data set consists of over 400,000 loan-bank pairs, which is the unit of

[21]The following examples illustrate this methodology. Walmart contracted a $1.1 billion loan on October 1, 1999. Walmart's fiscal year ends on January 31 and thus the October loan is more than six months after the month of the fiscal year-end closing. In this case we use the accounting data for fiscal year ending January 31, 1999. On the other hand, Walmart took a $1.25 billion loan on May 29, 1995. Since the May loan was less than six months after the fiscal year-end closing, we use accounting data for the previous fiscal year, i.e., for the year ending January 31, 1994.

[22]Even for those firms that do comply, a large proportion file on the last allowed day. Alford et al. (1992) report that more than 40% of firms with a December fiscal year-end file on March 31, thus, the data becomes available only in April.

[23]Even for the 27% of the original sample that we do not use, a large fraction (20% of the original) is unusable regardless of this requirement because these loans were made in the early years of our sample period and we do not have a long enough history to allow codification of their relationship variables. Thus, we only lose 7% of our sample to the requirement that it must be led by a top 40 bank.

[24]Drucker and Puri (2005) and Ljungqvist et al. (2006) use a similar approach to implement their underwriter selection models.

observation in the following logit model:[25]

$$
\begin{aligned}
(\text{CHOSEN})_m = \beta_0 + \beta_1(\text{LOANREL(M)}_m^{\text{BankLoans}}) + \beta_2(\text{LOAN MKT SHARE})_m \\
+ \beta_3(\text{LOCATION})_m + \sum \beta_k(\text{CONTROL})_k. \qquad (6)
\end{aligned}
$$

The variables are

- $(\text{CHOSEN})_m$: For each loan facility i, we create a dummy variable $(\text{CHOSEN})_m$, which takes the value of one if a bank m was retained as the lead bank for that loan transaction and zero otherwise.[26]
- $\text{LOANREL(M)}_m^{\text{BankLoans}}$: This is the measure of relationship strength constructed by looking back over five years from the date of the loan facility activation and searching whether the bank had a prior lending relationship with this borrower. As we discuss in Section 3.1.1 and Appendix A, we construct three different specifications for this variable to measure the strength of relationship for each of the 40 banks in each loan-bank pair.
- $(\text{LOAN MKT SHARE})_m$: To estimate the probability of winning the loan business by a particular bank, we need to control for the reputation of that bank in the loan market. We use its market share as a proxy for reputation. If the loan facility was activated in the year t, $(\text{LOAN MKT SHARE})_m$ is the market share of bank m in the prior year, $t-1$, calculated as in Eq. (5).
- $(\text{LOCATION})_m$: This variable is a dummy variable that equals one if bank m and the borrower in a loan-bank pair both have their head offices in the same state and zero otherwise. We include this variable to control for the fact that a borrower may be more likely to give repeat business to a particular bank due to its physical proximity. Since our relationship measure is based on existence and intensity of past interactions, it may be biased by a non-relationship factor such as the proximity of a borrower to a particular lender. Including the LOCATION variable controls for the effect of physical proximity between a borrower and a lender and partially mitigates this possible bias in our relationship measures.
- $(\text{CONTROL})_k$: We control for borrower industry (one-digit SIC codes), the stated purpose of the loan facility, and the year of the loan facility activation with dummy variables.

A large number of banking mergers and acquisitions took place during our sample period. We assume that in the case of acquisitions the customer relationships of a bank being acquired are inherited by the acquiring bank.[27] For mergers, the relationships of the merger partners are assumed to be inherited by the new post-merger entity. We also adjust the market shares to reflect the M&A activity. Appendix C describes these issues in more detail and also provides an illustrative example.

[25]Since observations within each cluster may not be independent, we estimate cluster-corrected standard errors using the approach suggested by Williams (2000).

[26]Thus, if a bank was the sole lead bank, only the loan-bank pair for this bank would have CHOSEN equal to one and for the other 39, CHOSEN would be zero. If the loan facility was led by multiple banks, than all the loan-bank pairs corresponding to these banks would have CHOSEN equal one while it would be zero for the rest.

[27]This is one of the objectives of bank mergers and acquisitions.

Table 4
Impact of lending relationships on probability of getting future lending business
Panel A of this table provides the logit regression estimates of the following equation:

$$(\text{CHOSEN})_m = \beta_0 + \beta_1(\text{LOANREL(M)}_m^{\text{BankLoans}}) + \beta_2(\text{LOAN MKT SHARE})_m + \beta_3(\text{LOCATION})_m + \sum \beta_k(\text{CONTROL}_k).$$

For each loan facility i we create a choice set of 40 potential lenders, which creates 40 loan-bank pairs. The top 40 commercial banks in the previous year form the consideration set for each firm in the current year. The dependent variable, $(\text{CHOSEN})_m$, takes a value of one if a bank m was retained as the lead bank for that loan transaction and zero otherwise. We use three proxies for relationship: $\text{LOANREL(Dummy)}_m^{\text{BankLoans}}$ (equals one if there is a relationship with the bank m in the last five years before the current loan and zero otherwise), $\text{LOANREL(Number)}_m^{\text{BankLoans}}$ (ratio of the number of loans with bank m to the total number of loans of the firm in the last five years before the current loan), $\text{LOANREL(Amount)}_m^{\text{BankLoans}}$ (ratio of the dollar value of loans with bank m to the total dollar value of loans of the firm in the last five years before the current loan). $(\text{LOAN MKT SHARE})_m$ is the share of total lending by bank m in the year prior to the year of loan facility i. $(\text{LOCATION})_m$ is a dummy variable that equals one if both bank m and the borrower have their respective head offices in the same state and zero otherwise. In the panel at the bottom we illustrate the economic impact that various variables have on the probability of a bank being chosen as the lead lender. We use the specification estimated in column 1 to estimate the probability of a bank being chosen as the lead lender if all variables except the variable being examined are held equal to their mean. We then estimate the predicted probability as the variable being examined goes from zero to one (except for LOAN MKT SHARE, which is varied from 1% market share (approximately lowest market share of a top 20 lender) to 10% market share (approximately highest market share of a top 20 lender)). For example, the first row reports the predicted probability of a bank being chosen as a lead lender if it did not have a past lending relationship with a borrower ($\text{LOANREL(Dummy)}^{\text{BankLoans}} = 0$) and if all other variables are assumed equal to their means. The next row reports the predicted probability of being chosen if the bank did have a past lending relationship ($\text{LOANREL(Dummy)}^{\text{BankLoans}} = 1$), again holding all else constant at their means. The third row reports the increase in the predicted probability of being chosen as the lead lender for a relationship lender compared to a lender with no prior relationship. Panel B reports the results for a number of alternative specifications of the model estimated in Panel A. Column 1 repeats the analysis in Panel A but uses individual loan deals as the unit of analysis instead of loan facilities. Column 2 provides a control for loan facilities that are renewals of existing facilities-RENEWAL equals one if LPC classifies a facility as a refinancing and zero otherwise. Column 3 uses an alternative measure of lending relationship, MOST RECENT LENDER, which equals one if a bank m was the lead bank on the most recent loan facility preceding the current facility and zero otherwise. Column 4 uses the market share of banks in the borrower's industry, $\text{INDUSTRY LOAN MKT SHARE}_m$, which is the share of loans made to that borrower's industry by bank m in the year preceding the current loan. Finally in Column 5 we control for any pricing effects that could affect the lender selection by imputing the loan spreads that banks that were not chosen may have charged had they been selected. This is denoted by IMPUTED LOAN SPREAD and is estimated using the Expectation-Maximization (EM) algorithm. Numbers in parentheses are standard errors corrected for heteroskedasticity and clustering (*** significant at the 1% level, ** significant at the 5% level, * significant at the 10% level).

	(1)	(2)	(3)
Panel A			
Const.	−3.53***	−2.94***	−3.32***
	(.41)	(0.4)	(0.42)
$\text{LOANREL(Dummy)}_m^{\text{BankLoans}}$	3.27***		
	(0.03)		
$\text{LOANREL(Number)}_m^{\text{BankLoans}}$		4.59***	
		(0.04)	
$\text{LOANREL(Amount)}_m^{\text{BankLoans}}$			4.23***
			(0.04)
$(\text{LOAN MKT SHARE})_m$	12.23***	11.37***	11.32***
	(0.21)	(0.21)	(0.22)
$(\text{LOCATION})_m$	0.38***	0.44***	0.39***
	(0.05)	(0.05)	(0.05)

Table 4 (*continued*)

	(1)	(2)	(3)
Industry dummies	Yes	Yes	Yes
Year dummies	Yes	Yes	Yes
Loan purpose dummies	Yes	Yes	Yes
Number of observations	416,239	416,239	416,239
Pseudo R^2	0.32	0.31	0.32

Impact of past lending relationships on the probability of being chosen as the lead lender using the column 1 specification

	Probability of being chosen (%)
$\text{LOANREL(Dummy)}_m^{\text{BankLoans}} = 0$	2.73
$\text{LOANREL(Dummy)}_m^{\text{BankLoans}} = 1$	42.46
Increase in probability	39.73
$\text{(LOAN MKT SHARE)}_m = 1\%$	3.16
$\text{(LOAN MKT SHARE)}_m = 10\%$	8.93
Increase in probability	5.77
$\text{(LOCATION)}_m = 0$	3.54
$\text{(LOCATION)}_m = 1$	5.08
Increase in probability	1.54

	(1)	(2)	(3)	(4)	(5)
Panel B					
Const.	−4.36***	−3.52***	−3.40***	−3.28***	−2.49***
	(0.39)	(0.41)	(0.43)	(0.65)	(0.41)
$\text{LOANREL(Dummy)}_m^{\text{BankLoans}}$	3.27***	3.23***		3.16***	3.05***
	(0.03)	(0.03)		(0.03)	(0.03)
RENEWAL		−0.10*			
		(0.06)			
$\text{LOANREL(Dummy)}_m^{\text{BankLoans}} \times \text{RENEWAL}$		0.31***			
		(.08)			
$\text{(MOST RECENT LENDER)}_m$			3.41***		
			(0.03)		
$\text{(LOAN MKT SHARE)}_m$	12.56***	12.25***	13.03***		12.92***
	(0.25)	(0.21)	(0.21)		(0.25)
$\text{(INDUSTRY LOAN MKT SHARE)}_m$				5.93***	
				(0.14)	
(LOCATION)_m	0.37***	0.38***	0.52***	0.31***	0.39***
	(.06)	(0.05)	(0.05)	(0.05)	(0.06)
$\text{(IMPUTED LOAN SPREAD)}_m$					−0.001***
					(.0003)
Industry dummies	Yes	Yes	Yes	Yes	Yes
Year dummies	Yes	Yes	Yes	Yes	Yes
Loan purpose dummies	Yes	Yes	Yes	Yes	Yes
Number of observations	288,500	416,239	413,300	230,088	249,440
PseudoR^2	0.32	0.32	0.30	0.31	0.30

Impact of past lending relationships on the probability of being chosen as the lead lender using the column 1 specification (Deal basis)

	Probability of being chosen (%)
$\text{LOANREL(Dummy)}_m^{\text{BankLoans}} = 0$	2.51
$\text{LOANREL(Dummy)}_m^{\text{BankLoans}} = 1$	40.52
Increase in probability	38.01

Panel A of Table 4 reports the results for logit tests of H1. The three columns report the results for different proxies of lending relationship. The coefficient for all specifications of past lending relationships is positive and significant at the 1% level. The panel at the bottom of the table illustrates the economic significance of past lending relationships on the probability of being chosen to provide future loans. We use the model estimated in column (1), where the past lending relationship is captured simply by the existence or lack of prior lending by the same bank in the last five years to calculate these probabilities.[28] The predicted probability of a bank being chosen as the lender for a loan facility if it did not have a past lending relationship (i.e., LOANREL(Dummy)$^{BankLoans} = 0$), holding all other variables constant at their respective means, is 2.73% (bottom panel, first row). When we recalculate the predicted probability keeping all else the same but changing LOANREL(Dummy)$^{BankLoans} = 1$, the predicted probability of being chosen for a relationship lender rises to 42.46%.[29] Thus, holding all else equal, a bank's probability of being chosen to provide a loan is increased by 39.73% if it had a past lending relationship in the prior five years. These results are equally strong if we use continuous measures (specifications in columns 2 and 3) that take into account both the existence and intensity of past lending relationships. For example, changing the LOANREL(Number)^{BankLoans} measure from its minimum value of zero to its maximum value of one increases the probability of being chosen from 3% to 77%, while for LOANREL(Amount)^{BankLoans} this probability is predicted to increase from 3% to 69%.[30]

It is important to highlight that other variables have a predicted and significant impact on the probability of a bank being retained to provide future loans but their economic impact is smaller compared to the existence of prior lending relationships. As expected, past market share is strongly associated with the ability to win a particular loan mandate. The coefficients for LOAN MKT SHARE and LOCATION are positive and significant at the 1% level across all specifications. The bottom panel reports the economic interpretation of these results. As reported in Table 2, the top-ranked lender (Citicorp) had approximately a 10% share of the loan market over our sample period, while the 20th-ranked bank (Wachovia) had approximately a 1% market share. To illustrate the impact of a lender's reputation on its probability of being retained, we calculate predicted probability by first keeping LOAN MKT SHARE equal to 1% and then changing it to 10%, while all other variables are kept constant at their respective means. The effect of this is to increase the probability of being chosen from 3% to 9%. Similar calculations show that the probability of being chosen for a lender that does not have its head office in the same state as the borrower's head office (LOCATION = 0) is 3.54% and increases to 5.08% if both lender and borrower are located in the same state (LOCATION = 1).

[28]To test the power of our specification, we estimate the predicted probabilities for each loan-bank pair observation by fitting our model to the data. If this predicted probability is greater than 0.5, we assign the bank to the chosen group and if it is less than 0.5 we assign it to the not-chosen group. Our model predicts the correct outcome for 93.80% of the observations.

[29]An alternative approach is to interpret the coefficients in terms of an increase in odds ratio. The logit model for a binary dependent variable Y can be written in terms of the odds that Y would equal 1 as $\frac{Prob(Y=1)}{1-Prob(Y=1)} = e^{(\beta' x)}$. Thus, the odds of being chosen as a lender as a function of prior lending relationship is $\frac{Prob((CHOSEN)_m=1)}{1-Prob((CHOSEN)_m=1)} = e^{(\beta_0+\beta_1(\text{LOANREL(Dummy)}^{\text{BankLoans}})+\sum \beta_{\text{other}}(\text{other variables}))}$. The coefficient of 3.27 for LOANREL(Dummy)^{BankLoans} implies that the odds of being chosen as the lender is $e^{3.27}$, or approximately 26 times higher if a lender had a prior relationship compared to if it did not have a prior relationship.

[30]These results are available from the authors on request.

Again, while significant, this is a much smaller economic effect compared to the one associated with having (or not having) a past lending relationship. These results suggest that establishing a lending relationship with a borrower confers significant economic benefits upon a lender in terms of a higher probability of securing the future lending business of that borrower.

4.2. Robustness checks of Hypothesis 1 and other issues

4.2.1. Facilities vs. deals

In Panel B of Table 4 we report results for alternative specifications of lender choice model in Eq. (6) so as to verify the robustness of the results reported above to an alternative definition of "loan business."[31] Specifically, we conduct our analysis on an individual loan facility basis, i.e., we treat each loan facility, including those that are part of the same deal, as new loan business. While this treatment is likely to have a limited effect, since over 70% of the deals in our sample are single loan facility deals, it can still inflate our relationship results since a lender gets multiple "credits" for winning the mandate for a deal that consists of multiple facilities. To examine this issue, we hand-match each loan facility to the original deal and re estimate our relationship measures on a deal-by-deal basis. We report the results in column 1 of Panel B, Table 4. The coefficient for the $\text{LOANREL(Dummy)}^{\text{BankLoans}}$ is essentially unchanged at 3.27 compared to the original facility-basis specification and is significant at the 1% level. The economic significance continues to be high as well: on a deal-by-deal basis, a bank with a prior lending relationship has a 40.52% probability of getting a future loan deal compared to 2.51% for a bank that lacks such past relationships. The results for $\text{LOANREL(Number)}^{\text{BankLoans}}$ and $\text{LOANREL(Amount)}^{\text{BankLoans}}$ are very similar and are omitted to conserve space.

4.2.2. Renewals vs. non-renewals

Another potential issue is whether a loan facility is a new loan or a renewal of an existing facility. For example, a borrower may simply be renewing a revolving line of credit that was part of a deal with a long-maturity loan. In such a case our tests would treat such a renewal as equivalent to winning new loan business. Thus, our test would attribute winning such renewals to a past relationship although it is simply a continuation of a prior loan. To address this concern we check the LPC database to determine whether a particular facility was a renewal. We create the variable RENEWAL, which equals one for a particular facility if the LPC recorded that facility as refinancing, and zero otherwise, and include both RENEWAL and the interaction $\text{RENEWAL} \times \text{LOANREL(Dummy)}^{\text{BankLoans}}$ in our logit model. As expected, the results which we report in column 2, Panel B, show that conditional on a loan being a renewal, past relationships significantly increase the likelihood of winning such a renewal facility (coefficient for the interaction term is positive and significant at the 1% level). Moreover, even after controlling for renewals, the coefficient for $\text{LOANREL(Dummy)}^{\text{BankLoans}}$ remains essentially unchanged and continues to be positive and significant at the 1% level.

[31] We thank the referee for pointing out the issues discussed below and for suggesting the tests to address them.

4.2.3. Syndication among few dominant banks

Given that a limited number of banks dominate the syndicated loan market (a significant proportion of the LPC loan's are syndicated loans), it is possible that borrowers are simply rotating their lending business among relatively few banks. If this is the case, these dominant banks would be classified as relationship banks for most borrowers according to our methodology. The association between past lending and a high probability of winning future business that we report in Panel A of Table 4 would then simply be due to syndicate rotation among banks. To address this issue we construct an alternative measure of lending relationships, MOST RECENT LENDER, which equals one if a particular bank was the lead bank on the most recent loan (prior to the current loan), and zero otherwise. This definition implies that if borrowers are simply rotating their loan business rather than rewarding relationships, MOST RECENT LENDER should have a negative coefficient (since rotation implies switching lenders after each loan). However, if future loan business is associated with strong lending relationships then the MOST RECENT LENDER variable should have a positive coefficient. As we report in column 3, this variable has a coefficient of 3.41 (significant at the 1% level), which is of similar magnitude to the LOANREL(Dummy)^{BankLoans} variable in Panel A. This result is consistent with the argument that lending relationships are associated with a higher likelihood of winning future lending opportunities.

4.2.4. Lender characteristics

A further issue pertains to individual lender characteristics. While we control for the physical proximity and lender reputation of each bank, it is possible that a bank may acquire a very strong reputation for expertise in lending to a certain industry, e.g., chemical industry. In such a case, borrowers in that industry would prefer to borrow from that bank independent of past relationships. To control for "industry lending expertise," we construct lending market shares of each bank for all the major industry sectors of borrowers in our sample (these market shares are constructed for each year for every two-digit industry group for which LPC reports at least 10 loans made in that year). For any bank m this is denoted by INDUSTRY LOAN MKT SHARE$_m$. We reestimate our logit model by using each bank's lagged industry loan market share for that borrower's industry. The results in column 4 show that the coefficient for lagged industry market share is 5.93 and is significant at the 1% level. Thus, having large lending market share to a particular borrower's industry increases the likelihood of winning future loan business. Even after controlling for such industry expertise the coefficient for the LOANREL(Dummy)^{BankLoans} is 3.16 (significant at the 1% level), which is similar to the coefficient we estimate in the original specification.

4.2.5. Loan pricing effects

Finally, we address the issue of controlling for loan pricing effects when a borrower chooses its lender. If the relationship lender also offers the lowest interest rate (measured by all-in-spread drawn or (AISD)), it is even more likely to win lending business.[32] Thus, part of the effect we attribute to relationships may be due in part to a lower price of the relationship loan. However, we cannot directly control for the price charged for a loan in

[32] AISD measures the interest rate spread on a loan (over LIBOR) plus any associated fees in originating the loan.

our logit model since we only observe the actual AISD charged by the bank that was *chosen*, i.e., data are missing for the other "potential" lenders in the choice set that were *not chosen*. We address this issue by imputing the loan price for other banks in the choice set that were *not chosen* using the expectation–maximization (EM) algorithm as suggested by Yasuda (2005).[33]

The EM algorithm is a general technique for finding the maximum-likelihood estimates for parametric models when data are not fully observed. In our context, the principal missing variable of interest is the rate charged (AISD) by the banks that are *not* retained in a given loan facility. We use the observed data on AISD and other borrower- and loan-specific characteristics to construct the following model:

$$\begin{aligned}(\mathrm{AISD})_{im} = {} & \beta_0 + \beta_1 \mathrm{LOANREL(Dummy)}_m + \beta_2 (\mathrm{LOAN\ MKT\ SHARE})_m \\ & + \sum \beta_i (\mathrm{LOAN\_CHARACTERSTICS})_i \\ & + \sum \beta_j (\mathrm{BORROWER\_CHARACTERSTICS})_j \\ & + \sum \beta_k (\mathrm{CONTROL}_k).\end{aligned}$$

Thus, for a loan *i* by borrower *j*, if bank *m* was chosen the AISD_m is the actual observed price charged for the loan, and if bank *m* was not chosen the value for AISD_m is set to missing.

The loan characteristics we use are:

- LN(LOAN SIZE): natural log of loan facility amount.
- MATURITY: maturity of loan facility in months.
- SYNDICATE: equals one if the loan facility was syndicated, and zero otherwise.
- SECURED: equals one if the loan facility was secured, and zero otherwise.

The borrower specific characteristics are:

- LN(ASSET): natural log of the book value of the assets of the borrower.
- LEVERAGE: ratio of the book value of total debt to the book value of assets.
- COVERAGE: natural log of the ratio $\left(1 + \frac{\mathrm{EBITDA}}{\mathrm{Interest\ Expenses}}\right)$.
- PROFITABILITY: ratio of EBITDA to Sales.
- TANGIBILITY: ratio of net property, plant, and equipment (NPPE) to the book value of assets.
- CURRENT RATIO: ratio of current assets to current liabilities.
- MARKET TO BOOK: ratio of (book value of assets − book value of equity + market value of equity) to the book value of assets.
- R&D TO SALES: ratio of research and development expenses to sales.

The other control variables include dummy variables for the year and reported purpose and type of the loan facility, the credit rating of the borrower, and the industry of the borrower (two-digit SIC codes).

Each iteration of the algorithm consists of two steps, an expectation step (E step) and a maximization step (M step). The E step involves finding the conditional expectation of the missing data given the observed data and current estimated parameters (or initial estimated

[33]See Dempster et al. (1977) and McLachlan and Krishan (1997) for good surveys of EM methods.

parameters). Thus, the E step can be thought of as filling in the missing data. The parameter estimates for the complete data set are then computed in the M Step by using maximum likelihood estimation. This process is repeated iteratively until convergence obtains.

This procedure allows us to estimate loan prices that a given bank would have charged if it had been chosen. We call this variable IMPUTED LOAN SPREAD. We then reestimate our original logit model in Eq. (6) including the IMPUTED LOAN SPREAD for each potential lending bank. We present the results of this analysis in the last column of Table 4, Panel B. As expected, the coefficient for IMPUTED LOAN SPREAD is negative and significant, implying higher spreads charged make it less likely that the bank would be chosen to provide the loan. The relationship variable, however, continues to be significant and is essentially unchanged.[34]

4.2.6. Modeling the lender selection process

In our lender choice model we allow up to 40 banks as possible choices to a borrower. This borrower choice set may include a number of banks that potentially did not bid for the business and thus our results may overstate the importance of relationships. To address this concern we carry out a number of robustness checks.[35]

First we model the selection of a particular bank as a two-stage decision. In the first stage the borrower decides whether to use a relationship borrower or not and in the second stage it chooses a *specific* bank conditional on its propensity to choose relationship banks. We construct a binary variable REL for each loan facility; REL equals one if at least one of the lenders chosen had been a lender in the previous five years. We model the choice between a relationship and non-relationship loan as a function of various loan and borrower characteristics. These include loan size, credit rating, borrower size, profitability, leverage, and a specific measure that captures the intensity of using relationship lenders in the past. We estimate this past usage of relationship banks by calculating the fraction of all prior loans in which relationship lenders were used. This model allows us to estimate the predicted probability of using relationship lenders for each loan, which we denote by $\widehat{PROBREL}$. In the second stage we focus on specific *lender* characteristics that determine the choice of a *particular* lender after controlling for the borrower's propensity to choose relationship lenders. Specifically, we estimate a modified version Eq. (6) in which we include $\widehat{PROBREL}$ as another explanatory variable. This second-stage estimation allows us to measure the impact of prior relationships that a *specific* bank *m* has after controlling for that borrower's propensity to use relationship lenders in general. The coefficient for LOANREL(Dummy) in the second-stage regression is 3.09, which is significant at the 1% level and similar to the coefficient of 3.27 as reported in the original specification (column 1 of Panel A, Table 4). Thus, even after controlling for a particular borrower's propensity to use relationship lenders, the prior relationship that a specific lender has is significantly associated with that lender's ability to win future lending business.

[34]We also use an alternative method suggested by Schafer (1997) whereby we simulate 100 random data sets for loan spreads based on the observed distributions of spreads and other independent variables. For each of these samples, we estimate the effect of bank's market share and relationships on loan prices. We use the average estimates from these 100 simulations to calculate imputed fees for a given transaction for each bank-transaction pair. The results from using imputed loan spreads obtained from this simulation- based approach are similar to those estimated by using the EM algorithm.

[35]The results for these tests are not reported but are available from authors on request.

We also reestimate our model with smaller choice set of potential lenders for each loan facility. First we reduce the potential choice of lenders for each loan facility to top 20 banks (as ranked by market share in the previous year). This smaller choice set makes it more likely that all the lenders were potential bidders for the loan. This choice set size is also similar to that used by Drucker and Puri (2005), who use a choice set of 20, and Yasuda (2005), who uses a choice set of 16. The coefficient for LOANREL(Dummy) is 3.17 (significant at the 1% level), which is very similar to that for the original specification. We also rerun our model by restricting the choice set to the top 10 lenders. The coefficient of LOANREL(Dummy) remains essentially unchanged at 3.15, significant at the 1% level. Finally, we restrict the choice set of lenders for each borrower to top 10 lenders in the *borrower's industry* (defined at the two-digit SIC code level). The coefficient for LOANREL(Dummy) is 3.14 and significant at the 1% level. These results imply that our findings of a prior lending relationship having a significant impact on the ability to win future lending business is not driven by the size of the choice set used.

Finally, we construct a subset of borrowers for which key requirements for implementing the nested logit model hold.[36] We construct a subsample of borrowers, which, when faced with a lender selection decision, could have either chosen one of its two relationship borrowers or one of the 37 non-relationship borrowers. These restrictions yield a subsample of 13,416 observations. At the upper level a borrower chooses between the relationship and non-relationship nest. At the lower level it chooses a specific lender. We model the first-stage decision as largely determined by borrower characteristics and the lower-level decision to be based on specific lender characteristics such as market share, location, and whether it was the lead bank for the most recent loan (denoted by MOST RECENT LENDER). We find that the coefficient for MOST RECENT LENDER is positive and significant at the 1% level. Thus, even after conditioning for a borrower choosing a relationship lender, the lender that provided that most recent loan has a significantly higher probability of winning the next loan.

Overall, the robustness tests we employ above suggest that past lending relationships are significantly and positively associated with future lending opportunities.

4.3. Tests for Hypothesis 2

Theoretical models (e.g., Diamond, 1991) predict that relationships are more beneficial for firms that suffer from greater informational asymmetries. This motivates our Hypothesis 2, which conjectures that informationally opaque firms use relationship lenders more frequently. To test this we use different proxies for information "opaqueness," specifically, the borrower's size and the borrower's credit rating (see Sections 4.3.1 and 4.3.2 below). We also report results for alternative proxies for borrower's information opaqueness in Section 4.3.3.

4.3.1. The effect of borrower size and Hypothesis 2

A priori, it is reasonable to argue that smaller-sized firms are less likely to be widely followed by either capital market investors (or credit rating agencies). Stein (2002) argues that small-business lending "relies heavily on information that is *soft*—that is, information

[36]These requirements entail that all borrowers face exactly the same number of choices in both the relationship nest and the non-relationship nests, and that each borrower chooses exactly one lender.

that cannot be verified by anyone other than the agent who produces it." This characterization suggests that smaller borrowers should find strong relationships with their lenders particularly beneficial. Smaller firms are also likely to be relatively more informationally opaque; for example, Petersen and Rajan (1994) state that "... there may be large information asymmetries between these [*small*] firms and potential public investors."[37] Thus, small firms offer the most potential for proprietary information generation by a relationship lender. To the extent that relationships do mitigate the information problems that smaller firms face, we should expect to find a strong association between the size of a borrower and its use of a relationship bank for future loans.

To examine if relationship lending varies across different borrower sizes, we divide our sample into three size terciles based on borrower's book value of assets. Specifically, we add the two dummy variables MIDDLE and BIG to Eq. (6). These variables equal one if the borrower falls in the stated size tercile and zero otherwise. We also add two interaction terms, multiplying the relationship variable with MIDDLE and BIG. The modified logit model is then

$$\begin{aligned}(\text{CHOSEN})_m = \beta_0 &+ \beta_1(\text{LOANREL(M)}_m^{\text{BankLoans}}) + \beta_2(\text{LOAN MKT SHARE})_m \\ &+ \beta_3(\text{LOCATION})_m + \beta_4(\text{MIDDLE}) + \beta_5(\text{BIG}) \\ &+ \beta_6(\text{MIDDLE} * \text{LOANREL(M)}_m^{\text{BankLoans}}) \\ &+ \beta_7(\text{BIG} * \text{LOANREL(M)}_m^{\text{BankLoans}}) + \sum \beta_k(\text{CONTROL}_k). \quad (7)\end{aligned}$$

The results, in Table 5, Panel A, describe how past lending relationships affect the probability of winning future lending business across different-sized borrowers. Since larger borrowers are likely to be informationally more transparent, holding everything else constant the effect of past relationships on the probability of being chosen as a lender should be the weakest for the large borrowers and the strongest for small borrowers. The coefficient of $\text{LOANREL(Dummy)}_m^{\text{BankLoans}}$ is 5.01 if the borrower is in the smallest size tercile, 4.13 for the middle tercile and 3.71 for the largest tercile, even as it continues to be statistically significant across all borrower size terciles (Table 5, column 1). Thus, the effect of past relationships, while significant, declines as one goes from the smallest borrowers to the largest borrowers. This is also captured in the negative coefficient of the size and relationship interaction terms, which are negative and significant at the 1% level across all specifications. In the panel at the bottom of Table 5 we use the specification estimated in column 1 to illustrate the economic significance of past lending relationship benefits across different borrower size terciles. Specifically, we estimate the probability of a bank being chosen as the lead lender if all variables except the relationship variables and the size variables are held equal to their means. The impact of a past relationship on the probability of being chosen as lead lender is measured by setting each specific size variable equal to one while keeping the other size variables equal to zero. The first row reports the predicted probabilities (for borrowers in small, medium, and large terciles) of a bank being chosen as a lead lender if it did not have a past lending relationship with a borrower ($\text{LOANREL(Dummy)}_m^{\text{BankLoans}} = 0$) and if all other variables are assumed to be equal to their means. The next row reports the predicted probability of being chosen if the bank did have a past lending relationship ($\text{LOANREL(Dummy)}_m^{\text{BankLoans}} = 1$). We find that having

[37]A number of empirical studies use smaller borrower size as proxy for higher information asymmetries. See, for example, Blackwell and Kidwell (1988) and Houston and Christopher (1996).

Table 5
Borrower information asymmetries, lending relationships and probability of getting future lending business

Panel A of this table provides the logit regression estimates of the following equation:

$$(\text{CHOSEN})_m = \beta_0 + \beta_1(\text{LOANREL(M)}_m^{\text{BankLoans}}) + \beta_2(\text{LOAN MKT SHARE})_m + \beta_3(\text{LOCATION})_m + \beta_4(\text{MIDDLE}) + \beta_5(\text{BIG}) + \beta_6(\text{MIDDLE} * \text{LOANREL(M)}_m^{\text{BankLoans}}) + \beta_7(\text{BIG} * \text{LOANREL(M)}_m^{\text{BankLoans}}) + \sum \beta_k(\text{CONTROL}_k).$$

The model is the same as one we estimate in Table 4 with except here we include, two dummy variables, MIDDLE and BIG, which take the value one if the borrower falls in the stated size tercile (as measured by the book value of assets) and zero otherwise. We also add two interaction terms, multiplying the relationship variables with MIDDLE and BIG.

Panel B reports the estimates of the following logit regression:

$$(\text{CHOSEN})_m = \beta_0 + \beta_1(\text{LOANREL(M)}_m^{\text{BankLoans}}) + \beta_2(\text{LOAN MKT SHARE})_m + \beta_3(\text{LOCATION})_m + \beta_4(\text{NOT RATED}) + \beta_5(\text{NOT RATED} * \text{LOANREL(M)}_m^{\text{BankLoans}}) + \sum \beta_k(\text{CONTROL}_k).$$

Again, the model is the same as the one we estimate in Table 4 except we add an additional variable NOT RATED (and the interaction with relationship measures), which equals one if the loan is not rated and zero otherwise.

Panel C provides estimates the following logit regression:

$$(\text{CHOSEN})_m = \beta_0 + \beta_1(\text{LOANREL(M)}_m^{\text{BankLoans}}) + \beta_2(\text{LOAN MKT SHARE})_m + \beta_3(\text{LOCATION})_m + \beta_4(\text{INVESTMENT GRADE}) + \beta_5(\text{INVESTMENT GRADE*}(\text{LOANREL(M)}_m^{\text{BankLoans}}) + \sum \beta_k(\text{CONTROL}_k).$$

The model is the same as the one we estimate in Table 4 except we add an additional variable INVESTMENT GRADE (and the interaction with relationship measures), which equals one if the loan is rated BBB or above by S&P and zero otherwise.

At the bottom of each panel we illustrate the economic impact of past lending relationships on the probability of being chosen as the lead lender (across borrowers with different levels of information opacity) using the specification estimated in column 1. Specifically, we estimate the probability of a bank being chosen as the lead lender if all variables except the relationship variables and the information opacity measure (size, credit rating, etc.) are held equal to their means. Then the impact of a past relationship on the probability of being chosen is measured across different information opacity measures for each size tercile (e.g., by setting each size variable equal to one while keeping the other size variables equal to zero). Numbers in parentheses are standard errors corrected for heteroskedasticity and clustering (*** significant at the 1% level, ** significant at the 5% level, * significant at the 10% level).

	(1)	(2)	(3)
Panel A: Borrower size and relationship lending			
Const.	−4.45***	−4.01***	−4.30***
	(0.39)	(0.38)	(0.40)
$\text{LOANREL(Dummy)}_m^{\text{BankLoans}}$	5.01*** (0.09)		
$\text{LOANREL(Number)}_m^{\text{BankLoans}}$		5.88*** (0.13)	
$\text{LOANREL(Amount)}_m^{\text{BankLoans}}$			5.70***
			(0.12)
$(\text{LOAN MKT SHARE})_m$	12.7***	11.97***	11.90***
	(0.21)	(0.22)	(0.22)
$(\text{LOCATION})_m$	0.36***	0.44***	0.38***
	(0.05)	(0.05)	(0.05)
MIDDLE	0.37***	0.41***	0.39***
	(0.05)	(0.05)	(0.05)
BIG	1.26***	1.34***	1.31***
	(0.05)	(0.05)	(0.05)

Table 5 (*continued*)

	(1)	(2)	(3)
MIDDLE × $\text{LOANREL(Dummy)}_m^{\text{BankLoans}}$	−0.88***		
	(0.1)		
BIG × $\text{LOANREL(Dummy)}_m^{\text{BankLoans}}$	−2.30***		
	(0.10)		
MIDDLE × $\text{LOANREL(Number)}_m^{\text{BankLoans}}$		−0.56***	
		(0.15)	
BIG × $\text{LOANREL(Number)}_m^{\text{BankLoans}}$		−1.89***	
		(0.14)	
MIDDLE × $\text{LOANREL(Amount)}_m^{\text{BankLoans}}$			−0.59***
			(0.13)
BIG × $\text{LOANREL(Amount)}_m^{\text{BankLoans}}$			−2.07***
			(0.13)
Industry dummies	Yes	Yes	Yes
Year dummies	Yes	Yes	Yes
Loan purpose dummies	Yes	Yes	Yes
Number of observations	401,699	401,699	401,699
Pseudo R^2	0.33	0.32	0.33

Impact of past lending relationships on the probability of being chosen as the lead lender using the column 1 specification

	Probability of being chosen		
	Small (%)	*Medium* (%)	*Big* (%)
$\text{LOANREL(Dummy)}_m^{\text{BankLoans}} = 0$	1.21	1.74	4.14
$\text{LOANREL(Dummy)}_m^{\text{BankLoans}} = 1$	64.87	52.24	39.28
Increase in probability	63.66	50.50	35.14

Panel B: Availability of borrower credit rating and relationship lending

	(1)	(2)	(3)
Const.	−3.20***	−2.57***	−2.97***
	(0.39)	(0.38)	(0.41)
$\text{LOANREL(Dummy)}_m^{\text{BankLoans}}$	2.87***		
	(0.03)		
$\text{LOANREL(Number)}_m^{\text{BankLoans}}$		4.19***	
		(0.06)	
$\text{LOANREL(Amount)}_m^{\text{BankLoans}}$			3.82***
			(0.05)
$\text{(LOAN MKT SHARE)}_m$	12.41***	11.65***	11.58***
	(.21)	(0.22)	(0.22)
(LOCATION)_m	0.37***	0.45***	0.39***
	(0.05)	(0.05)	(0.05)
NOT RATED	−0.70***	−0.70***	−0.69***
	(0.04)	(0.03)	(0.04)
NOT RATED × $\text{LOANREL(Dummy)}_m^{\text{BankLoans}}$	1.12***		
	(0.06)		
NOT RATED × $\text{LOANREL(Number)}_m^{\text{BankLoans}}$		0.97***	
		(0.09)	
NOT RATED × $\text{LOANREL(Amount)}_m^{\text{BankLoans}}$			1.06***
			(0.08)
Industry dummies	Yes	Yes	Yes

Table 5 (*continued*)

	(1)	(2)	(3)
Year dummies	Yes	Yes	Yes
Loan purpose dummies	Yes	Yes	Yes
Number of observations	416,239	416,239	416,239
Pseudo R^2	0.32	0.32	0.33

Impact of past lending relationships on the probability of being chosen as the lead lender using the column 1 specification

	Probability of being chosen	
	Not rated (%)	*Rated (%)*
$\text{LOANREL(Dummy)}_{m}^{\text{BankLoans}} = 0$	1.84	3.66
$\text{LOANREL(Dummy)}_{m}^{\text{BankLoans}} = 1$	50.31	40.06
Increase in probability	48.47	36.40

Panel C: Borrower credit rating and relationship lending

Const.	−2.98***	−2.34***	−2.70***
	(0.55)	(0.53)	(0.55)
$\text{LOANREL(Dummy)}_{m}^{\text{BankLoans}}$	3.18***		
	(0.05)		
$\text{LOANREL(Number)}_{m}^{\text{BankLoans}}$		4.61***	
		(0.08)	
$\text{LOANREL(Amount)}_{m}^{\text{BankLoans}}$			4.24***
			(0.07)
$\text{(LOAN MKT SHARE)}_{m}$	13.82***	12.55***	12.58***
	(0.27)	(0.29)	(0.29)
(LOCATION)_{m}	0.39***	0.45***	0.39***
	(0.06)	(0.07)	(0.07)
INVESTMENT GRADE	0.52***	0.49***	0.51***
	(.06)	(0.05)	(0.05)
INVESTMENT GRADE × $\text{LOANREL(Dummy)}_{m}^{\text{BankLoans}}$	−0.59***		
	(0.07)		
INVESTMENT GRADE × $\text{LOANREL(Number)}_{m}^{\text{BankLoans}}$		−0.75***	
		(0.11)	
INVESTMENT GRADE × $\text{LOANREL(Amount)}_{m}^{\text{BankLoans}}$			−0.76***
			(0.10)
Industry dummies	Yes	Yes	Yes
Year dummies	Yes	Yes	Yes
Loan purpose dummies	Yes	Yes	Yes
Number of observations	213,420	213,420	213,420
Pseudo R^2	0.30	0.29	0.30

Impact of past lending relationships on the probability of being chosen as the lead lender using the column 1 specification

	Probability of being chosen	
	Non investment grade (%)	*Investment grade (%)*
$\text{LOANREL(Dummy)}_{m}^{\text{BankLoans}} = 0$	2.80	4.64
$\text{LOANREL(Dummy)}_{m}^{\text{BankLoans}} = 1$	40.99	39.08
Increase in probability	38.19	34.44

a past lending relationship increases the probability of being chosen by 63.7% (from 1.2% to 64.9%) for the borrowers in the smallest tercile. The predicted probability increase for borrowers in the middle and the largest size terciles is 50.5% (1.7% to 52.2%) and 35.2% (from 4.1% to 39.3%), respectively. Thus, the probability of a bank being chosen to provide future loans gets smaller as borrower size increases.

4.3.2. The effects of credit rating and Hypothesis 2

An alternative proxy for informational asymmetries is the availability of a credit rating for the borrower. If the borrower is not rated, a debt-holder needs to generate and process a relatively larger amount of information to make its lending decision. Thus, nonrated borrowers are more likely to turn to their relationship lender for their financing needs than to public debt markets. For example, Diamond (1991) argues that a borrower's past repayment reputation would drive its choice of borrowing source. A key prediction of his model is that firms with good reputations (i.e., with high credit ratings) would be able to issue (cheaper) public debt, while firms with lower reputations (as evidenced by lower credit ratings) would use bank financing. It is also frequently argued that the information advantages of an insider lender (scale economies in information production, better ability to renegotiate covenants, etc.) would allow it to adopt a more flexible approach towards debt renegotiations. Thus, a relationship bank is expected to "lean against the wind" when its borrowers face financial difficulties.[38] Consequently, a borrower with a poor credit rating is more likely to use its relationship bank for its borrowing needs.[39] Below, we employ the existence and level a of credit rating for a borrower as a proxy for the information asymmetries that the borrower faces.

To do this we first partition our sample into firms that have a credit rating and those that do not. We use the credit rating of the loan facility being examined (as reported by LPC) as the most timely measure of the borrower's credit worthiness. It is reasonable to assume that, on average, the firms whose loans are not publicly rated, are likely to be less informationally transparent relative to those that have a rating. Thus, we estimate the model

$$\begin{aligned}(\text{CHOSEN})_m = {} & \beta_0 + \beta_1(\text{LOANREL(M)}_m^{\text{BankLoans}}) + \beta_2(\text{LOAN MKT SHARE})_m \\ & + \beta_3(\text{LOCATION})_m + \beta_4(\text{NOT RATED}) \\ & + \beta_5(\text{NOT RATED} * \text{LOANREL(M)}_m^{\text{BankLoans}}) \\ & + \sum \beta_k(\text{CONTROL}_k). \qquad (8)\end{aligned}$$

The model in Eq. (8) includes a dummy variable (NOT RATED), which equals one if the loan is not rated and zero otherwise. We also add an interaction term that interacts the relationship variable with NOT RATED to better isolate the effect of the availability of a credit rating on the use of a relationship banker for future borrowing.

[38]Hoshi et al. (1990) provide evidence in support of this view. They report that among the financially distressed Japanese firms, those with strong banking relationships are better able to maintain their investment programs compared to firms that lacked such banking relationships.

[39]Anecdotal evidence of the limited benefits of relationship lending to the best quality borrowers is highlighted in an Economist article dated February 12, 1998, which states: "... Part of [JP] Morgan's problem is that its customers are simply too good. The trouble with serving only the best firms is that they typically like to maintain relationships with at least three banks and play them off against each other to get prices down."

For the subsample in which the credit rating of the borrower is available, we estimate the model

$$\begin{aligned}(\text{CHOSEN})_m = {} & \beta_0 + \beta_1(\text{LOANREL(M)}_m^{\text{BankLoans}}) + \beta_2(\text{LOAN MKT SHARE})_m \\ & + \beta_3(\text{LOCATION})_m + \beta_4(\text{INVESTMENT GRADE}) \\ & + \beta_5(\text{INVESTMENT GRADE} * \text{LOANREL(M)}_m^{\text{BankLoans}}) \\ & + \sum \beta_k(\text{CONTROL}_k), \qquad (9)\end{aligned}$$

where INVESTMENT GRADE is a dummy variable that equals one if the loan is rated BBB or above by S&P, and zero otherwise. We also add an interaction term that multiplies the relationship variable with INVESTMENT GRADE to better isolate the effect of credit rating on the use of a relationship banker for future borrowing.

Panel B of Table 5 reports the results of Eq. (8). Consistent with our earlier finding, while the existence of a past relationship increases the probability of winning future loans for all borrowers, this increase is significantly higher for borrowers whose loans have not been rated. Specifically, the coefficient of 3.19 for $\text{LOANREL(Amount)}^{\text{BankLoans}}$ if a borrower's loan does not have a rating is higher compared to the coefficient of 2.87 for the borrowers with a rated loan (Table 5, column 1). The impact of credit ratings is also captured by the positive and significant (t-value = 18.7) coefficient of the interaction term (multiplying past relationship by the availability of a borrower's credit rating). The bottom panel provides the economic interpretation of these results. For a nonrated borrower, a relationship lender has a 48% higher probability (50% vs. 2%) of winning future lending business, while for a rated borrower, the existence of past relationships increases the predicted probability of being chosen for future loans by 36% (40% vs. 4%). As a result, while the likelihood of being retained for future loans is fairly low for non-relationship lenders to both nonrated (2%) and rated borrowers (4%), the probability of a relationship lender being retained by a nonrated borrower is 10% higher compared to a rated borrower (50% vs. 40%).

Next, we employ the quality of credit rating as a measure of the informational transparency of a borrower as in Eq. (9). Borrowers with an investment grade rating (BBB or above) are classified as INVESTMENT GRADE. As we discuss earlier, theoretical models predict that high quality borrowers gain relatively less from borrowing from their relationship lender. Thus, we expect the effect of relationships to be weaker for borrowers with a high credit rating. The results we report in Table 5, Panel C provide some weak support for these predictions. The coefficient on the relationship and investment grade rating interaction term is negative and significant at the 1% level across all specifications (t-value range of −6.82 to −8.43). Holding all other variables constant at their means, the existence of a past lending relationship is associated with a 38% increase (3% to 41%) in the probability of being retained for borrowers with loans rated below investment grade. For BBB or above borrowers, past relationships increase the probability of being retained by 34% (5–39%).

4.3.3. Alternative proxies for borrower opaqueness

We also employ some alternative proxies for borrower information transparency to test H2.[40] In particular, we focus on proxies that measure the tangibility of assets owned by

[40]To conserve space these results are not reported but are available from the authors upon request.

a firm so as to capture the information asymmetry faced by its lenders. Firms that have a relatively lower fraction of their asset base in tangible assets, such as plant and machinery, face higher information asymmetries and are more likely to use an informed "insider" lender for their financing needs. For example, Houston and Christopher (1996) note "... smaller firms and firms with higher proportion of intangible assets (and presumably more difficult to value assets) are expected to rely primarily on bank financing."

The first proxy we use is the market-to-book ratio of the borrower, which equals the ratio of the market value of assets to the book value of assets. The market value is calculated as the book value of the assets minus the book value of equity plus the market value of equity. Smith and Watts (1992) and Barclay and Smith (1995a, b) use the market-to-book ratio to proxy for the growth options in a firm's investment opportunity set. Since a firm's balance sheet does not include intangible assets such as growth options but its market value reflects such intangible assets, a high market-to-book ratio can be considered as a firm having a larger fraction of their assets as intangible assets.[41] We also employ the ratio of Research and Development expenses to Sales as another measure of growth options, since a relatively high R&D expenditure could be interpreted as investment in assets that would yield higher future growth. Finally, we also use a "tangibility ratio," calculated as the ratio of net plant, property, and equipment (NPPE) to total assets. A higher fraction of total assets in the form of easier-to-value NPPE implies that such firms face a lower level of informational asymmetry when it comes to raising nonbank debt. This, in turn, implies a lower propensity to use a relationship bank for future financing.

For each of these ratios we partition our sample into three "tangibility" terciles and estimate the impact of lending relationships on these alternative measures of information opacity. We expect firms with a higher market-to-book ratio, a lower NPPE-to-total asset ratio and a higher R&D-to-sales ratio to be more likely to borrow from their relationship lenders. The results for the market-to-book ratio measure are as predicted. Specifically, the coefficient for $\text{LOANREL(Dummy)}_m^{\text{BankLoans}}$ is largest (3.27) for the highest tercile (market-to-book) borrowers and smallest (3.13) for the lowest tercile. When we use the R&D-to-sales ratio as a proxy for the borrower's asset intangibility, we obtain mixed results. The borrowers in the middle tercile have the highest coefficient (3.72) for $\text{LOANREL(Dummy)}_m^{\text{BankLoans}}$, with no statistical difference between the lowest and the highest terciles (3.25 and 3.21, respectively). Using the NPPE-to-total assets ratio as a proxy for the borrower's asset tangibility, we obtain results in the expected direction, i.e., borrowers in the highest tercile (borrower's for which the bulk of their assets are in NPPE), had the lowest coefficient for $\text{LOANREL(Dummy)}_m^{\text{BankLoans}}$ (3.09) while borrowers in the lowest tercile have the highest coefficient (3.39).

Taken together our findings in Section 4.3 provide support for the theoretical predictions underlying H2. That is, informationally opaque firms are more likely to find relationship borrowing beneficial, than are informationally transparent firms.

4.4. Tests for Hypothesis 3

In Hypothesis 3 we conjecture that if there are scope economies in information production, a relationship lender would have a higher probability of supplying future

[41] Houston and Christopher (1996) find that for borrowers with multiple banking relationships, those that have higher market-to-book ratios are more likely to use bank financing.

investment banking and/or underwriting services (i.e., this is the cross-product marketing motivation behind lending relationships—see, for example, Kanatas and Qi, 2003).

4.4.1. Tests of Hypothesis 3 and debt underwriting

For our empirical tests, we concentrate on two specific investment banking products that a relationship lender can potentially sell to its existing borrower. The first is the underwriting of public debt issues and the second is the underwriting of public equity issues (IPOs and SEOs).

From the SDC database we obtain details related to all the debt and equity issues completed by our sample borrowers, that had at least one relationship lender eligible to provide the underwriting service (see Section 3.2 for our sample selection methodology). For each issue of public debt in year t (in what follows, the process for equity markets is exactly the same) we construct a choice set of top 20 financial institutions (ranked by market share of debt underwriting in the year $t-1$). To this set of 20, we add all the commercial banks that are not in the top 20 list that were eligible to underwrite public issues of debt at the date of the debt issue.[42] To test whether prior lending relationships are associated with a higher probability of winning an underwriting mandate for issues of public debt, we estimate the following logit model:

$$\begin{aligned}(\text{RETAIN})_m^{\text{lead-debt}} = {} & \beta_0 + \beta_1(\text{PROCEEDS}) + \beta_2(\text{LOANREL(M)}_m^{\text{PublicDebt}}) \\ & + \beta_3(\text{Lead-DEBTREL(M)}_m^{\text{PublicDebt}}) \\ & + \beta_4(\text{Lead-EQUITYREL(M)}_m^{\text{PublicDebt}}) \\ & + \beta_5(\text{LOAN MKT SHARE})_m + \beta_6(\text{TOP TIER-DEBT})_m \\ & + \beta_7(\text{MID TIER-DEBT})_m + \beta_8(\text{TOP TIER-EQUITY})_m \\ & + \beta_9(\text{MID TIER-EQUITY})_m + \sum \beta_k(\text{CONTROL}_k). \qquad (10)\end{aligned}$$

The variables are:

- $(\text{RETAIN})_m^{\text{lead}}$-debt: For each debt issue, we create a dummy variable $(\text{RETAIN})_m^{\text{lead-debt}}$ that takes a value of one if a bank m was retained as the "*Lead Underwriter*" for that debt issue transaction, and zero otherwise.[43]
- PROCEEDS: The dollar amount of proceeds from the debt issue in USD millions.
- $\text{LOANREL(M)}_m^{\text{PublicDebt}}$: The measure of the lending relationship that m has with the issuer, constructed in exactly the same way as $\text{LOANREL(M)}_m^{\text{BankLoans}}$ except that for $\text{LOANREL(M)}_m^{\text{PublicDebt}}$, the date of the look-back period is the date of a public issue of debt, while for $\text{LOANREL(M)}_m^{\text{BankLoans}}$, the loan facility activation date is used.
- $\text{Lead-DEBTREL(M)}_m^{\text{PublicDebt}}$ and Lead-EQUITYREL $(\text{M})_m^{\text{PublicDebt}}$: The relationship strength measures for debt issue and equity issue markets, respectively. These measure the intensity of past investment banking relationships of a bank m in debt underwriting

[42]That is, if it had underwritten (either as lead or as co-manager) at least one debt issue in the years prior to year t.

[43]Thus, if a bank was the sole underwriter, only the issue-bank pair for this bank would have RETAIN equal to one and for the other members of the choice set RETAIN would be zero. If the issue were led by multiple banks, than all the issue-bank pairs corresponding to these banks would have RETAIN equal one while it would equal zero for the rest.

and equity underwriting markets. The construction of these variables is described in Section 3.1 and Appendix A.

- $(\text{LOAN MKT SHARE})_m$: for each bank m, is calculated for the year prior to the year of the debt issue and is calculated as in Eq. (5).
- $(\text{TOP TIER-DEBT})_m$: a dummy variable equal to one if the bank m is ranked in the top 5 debt underwriters in the previous year, and zero otherwise.
- $(\text{MID TIER-DEBT})_m$: a dummy variable equal to one if the bank m is ranked from 6th to 15th in debt underwriting in the previous year, and zero otherwise.
- $(\text{TOP TIER-EQUITY})_m$: a dummy variable equal to one if the bank m is ranked in the top 5 equity underwriters in the previous year, and zero otherwise.
- $(\text{MID TIER-EQUITY})_m$: a dummy variable equal to one if the bank m is ranked from 6th to 15th in equity underwriting in the previous year, and zero otherwise.

We do not include the LOCATION variable for underwriter selection models as most of the institutions in the choice set of potential underwriters have a New York City head office.

The results, reported in Table 6, provide strong support for H3 in the debt issue underwriting business. In columns 1–3 we report the results for all three alternative measures of prior lending and prior investment banking relationship variables and the controls for underwriter reputation both in the debt and the equity markets (as we describe in Eq. (10)). The coefficient for $\text{LOANREL(M)}^{\text{PublicDebt}}$ is positive and significant at the 1% level for all specifications.[44] Not surprisingly, a prior investment banking relationship in the same market ($\text{Lead-DEBTREL(M)}^{\text{PublicDebt}}$) is a strong determinant of future debt underwriter selection. The bottom panel, in which we use the model specification described in column 1 of Table 6 to explore the impact of prior lending and investment banking relationships, illustrates the economic significance of prior lending relationships and prior debt underwriting relationships. If all variables are held constant at their means and a bank did not have a past lending relationship ($\text{LOANREL(Dummy)}^{\text{PublicDebt}} = 0$) with a debt issuer, its probability of being retained as the lead underwriter of that debt issue is 0.29%. This probability increases to 0.55% if the bank had a prior lending relationship ($\text{LOANREL(Dummy)}^{\text{PublicDebt}} = 1$) with the issuer. While a past lending relationship has a statistically significant impact on the probability of being chosen as the future debt underwriter, the economic significance (0.55% probability) is, nevertheless, relatively small. The economic significance of having a past record of providing (underwriting) the same product is larger but still economically small, as illustrated by the change in probability for a bank with and without a prior debt underwriting with the customer relationship holding all variables constant at their respective means. The existence of a prior debt underwriting relationship increases the probability of winning the lead underwriter role (from 0.28% for banks with no prior debt underwriting relationship to 2.61% for banks with prior debt underwriting relationships). Finally, the existence of a past cross-market investment banking relationship ($\text{Lead-EQUITYREL}^{\text{PublicDebt}} = 1$) is associated with an increase in the probability of being retained as lead debt underwriter (0.31% to 0.79%). A prior investment-banking relationship, even in a different product market (equity underwriting), has a positive relationship with thelikelihood of winning

[44]These results are similar to those reported by Yasuda (2005), who also finds that past lending relationships have a significant impact on winning future debt underwriting mandates.

Table 6
Impact of lending relationships on probability of getting future debt underwriting business
This table provides the logit regression estimates of the following equation:

$$\begin{aligned}(\text{RETAIN})_m^{\text{Lead-debt}} = {} & \beta_0 + \beta_1(\text{PROCEEDS}) + \beta_2(\text{LOANREL(M)}_m^{\text{PublicDebt}}) \\ & + \beta_3(\text{Lead-DEBTREL(M)}_m^{\text{PublicDebt}}) \\ & + \beta_4(\text{Lead-EQUITYREL(M)}_m^{\text{PublicDebt}}) + \beta_5(\text{LOAN MKT SHARE})_m \\ & + \beta_6(\text{TOP TIER-DEBT})_m + \beta_7(\text{MID TIER-DEBT})_m \\ & + \beta_8(\text{TOP TIER-EQUITY})_m + \beta_9(\text{MID TIER-EQUITY})_m + \sum \beta_k(\text{CONTROL}_k).\end{aligned}$$

For each debt issue, we create the dummy variable $\text{RETAIN}_m^{\text{Lead-debt}}$, which takes a value of zero if a bank m was retained as the lead underwriter for that debt issue transaction and zero otherwise. For each debt underwriting deal i we create a choice set of at least 20 potential underwriters, creating at least 20 deal-underwriter pairs. The top 20 debt underwriters (based on market share) from the previous year and all commercial banks eligible to do debt underwriting in the previous year form the consideration set for each issuer in the current year. For each institution in a transaction-bank pair we estimate relationships across three markets: the bank loan market, the debt underwriting market, and the equity underwriting market. Within each market we use three different proxies of relationship strength for any bank m: $\text{LOANREL(Dummy)}_m^{\text{PublicDebt}}$ (one if there is a loan relationship with bank m in the last five years before the present debt underwriting transaction and zero otherwise), $\text{LOANREL(Number)}_m^{\text{PublicDebt}}$ (ratio of the number of loan deals with bank m to the total number of loan deals of the firm in the last five years before the current debt underwriting transaction), and $\text{LOANREL(Amount)}_m^{\text{PublicDebt}}$ (ratio of the dollar value of loan deals with bank m to the total dollar value of loan deals of the firm in the last five years before the current debt underwriting transaction). $\text{Lead-DEBTREL(Dummy)}_m^{\text{PublicDebt}}$ (one if there is a debt underwriting relationship in the lead underwriter capacity with bank m in the last five years before the present debt underwriting transaction and zero otherwise), $\text{Lead-DEBTREL(Number)}_m^{\text{PublicDebt}}$ (ratio of the number of debt underwriting deals in the lead underwriter capacity with bank m to the total number of debt underwriting deals of the firm in the last five years before the current debt underwriting transaction), and $\text{Lead-DEBTREL(Amount)}_m^{\text{PublicDebt}}$ (ratio of the dollar value of debt underwriting deals in the lead underwriter capacity with bank m to the total dollar value of debt underwriting deals of the firm in the last five years before the current debt underwriting transaction). $\text{Lead-EQUITYREL(Dummy)}_m^{\text{PublicDebt}}$ (one if there is an equity underwriting relationship in the lead underwriter capacity with bank m in the last five years before the present debt underwriting transaction and zero otherwise), $\text{Lead-EQUITYREL(Number)}_m^{\text{PublicDebt}}$ (ratio of number of the equity underwriting deals in the lead underwriter capacity with bank m to the total number of equity underwriting deals of the firm in the last five years before the current debt underwriting transaction), and $\text{Lead-EQUITYREL(Amount)}_m^{\text{PublicDebt}}$ (ratio of the dollar value of equity underwriting deals in the lead underwriter capacity with bank m to the total dollar value of equity underwriting deals of the firm in the last five years before the current debt underwriting transaction). PROCEEDS is the amount raised in USD millions for the debt underwriting transaction (reported coefficient has been divided by 1,000). $(\text{LOAN MKT SHARE})_m$ is the market share of bank m in the loan market in the year before the current debt underwriting transaction. Similar calculations estimate market shares for the debt underwriting and the equity underwriting markets. $(\text{TOP TIER-DEBT})_m$ and $(\text{TOP TIER-EQUITY})_m$ are dummy variables that equals one if the bank m is ranked in the top five debt and equity underwriters, respectively, and zero otherwise. $(\text{MID TIER-DEBT})_m$ and $(\text{MID TIER-EQUITY})_m$ are dummy variables that equals one if the bank m is ranked from 6th to 15th in debt and equity underwriting, respectively, and zero otherwise. $(\text{COMMERCIAL BANK})_m$ is a dummy variable that equals one if bank m had a Section 20 and/or investment banking subsidiary that was eligible to underwrite debt securities on the date of issuance and zero otherwise.

At the bottom of each panel we illustrate the economic impact of past lending, debt underwriting, and equity underwriting relationships on the probability of being chosen as the debt underwriter using the specification estimated in column 1. The first row reports the probability of a non-relationship bank ($\text{LOANREL(Number)}^{\text{PublicDebt}} = 0$) being chosen as the debt underwriter if all other variables are held equal to their mean. The second row reports the probability for a relationship bank ($\text{LOANREL(Number)}^{\text{PublicDebt}} = 1$) in the same way. Numbers in parentheses are standard errors corrected for heteroskedasticity and clustering (*** significant at the 1% level, ** significant at the 5% level, * significant at the 10% level).

	(1)	(2)	(3)	(4)	(5)
Const.	−6.27***	−7.06***	−6.98***	−5.96***	−6.27***
	(.20)	(.18)	(.17)	(.35)	(.20)
PROCEEDS	0.34***	0.19***	0.29***	1.22***	0.34***
	(0.11)	(0.06)	(0.06)	(0.24)	(0.11)
LOANREL(Dummy)$_{m}^{\text{PublicDebt}}$	0.66***				0.68***
	(0.09)				(0.11)
LOANREL(Number)$_{m}^{\text{PublicDebt}}$		1.22***			
		(0.12)			
LOANREL(Amount)$_{m}^{\text{PublicDebt}}$			0.86***		
			(0.18)		
(LOAN MKT SHARE)$_{m}$	4.51***	3.82***	5.5***	3.11***	4.59***
	(1.02)	(1.08)	(1.19)	(0.80)	(1.01)
Lead-DEBTREL(Dummy)$_{m}^{\text{PublicDebt}}$	2.27***			1.93***	2.29***
	(.09)			(0.07)	(0.10)
Lead-DEBTREL(Number)$_{m}^{\text{PublicDebt}}$		3.71***			
		(0.16)			
Lead-DEBTREL(Amount)$_{m}^{\text{PublicDebt}}$			3.08***		
			(0.13)		
(TOP TIER-DEBT)$_{m}$	2.30***	2.65***	2.75***	1.80***	2.30***
	(0.18)	(0.17)	(0.17)	(0.10)	(0.18)
(MIDDLE TIER-DEBT)$_{m}$	2.09***	2.26***	2.30***	1.52***	2.09***
	(0.16)	(0.15)	(0.15)	(0.08)	(0.16)
Lead-EQUITYREL(Dummy)$_{m}^{\text{PublicDebt}}$	0.94***			0.79***	0.94***
	0.08			0.07	0.08
Lead-EQUTYREL(Number)$_{m}^{\text{PublicDebt}}$		0.79***			
		(0.11)			
Lead-EQUTYREL(Amount)$_{m}^{\text{PublicDebt}}$			0.88***		
			(0.11)		
(TOP TIER-EQUITY)$_{m}$	0.96***	1.29***	1.24***	1.17***	0.96***
	(0.14)	(0.13)	(0.13)	(0.09)	(0.14)
(MIDDLE TIER-EQUITY)$_{m}$	0.66***	0.91***	0.93***	0.99***	0.67***
	(0.12)	(0.12)	(0.12)	(0.07)	(0.12)
LOANREL(Dummy)$_{m}$ × Lead-DEBTREL(Dummy)$_{m}$				0.29***	
				(0.11)	
LOANREL(Dummy)$_{m}$ × (1-Lead-DEBTREL(Dummy)$_{m}$)				1.83***	
				(0.07)	
Lead-DEBTREL(Dummy)$_{m}$ × (COMMERCIAL BANK)$_{m}$					−0.04
					(0.13)
Year dummies	Yes	Yes	Yes	Yes	Yes
Number of observations	77,350	77,350	77,350	77,350	77,350
Pseudo R^2	0.40	0.40	0.38	0.34	0.40

Impact of past relationships on the probability of being chosen as the lead debt underwriter using the column 1 specification

	Probability of being chosen (%)
LOANREL(Dummy)$_{m}^{\text{PublicDebt}} = 0$	0.29
LOANREL(Dummy)$_{m}^{\text{PublicDebt}} = 1$	0.55
Increase in probability	0.26
Lead-DEBTREL(Dummy)$_{m}^{\text{PublicDebt}} = 0$	0.28
Lead-DEBTREL(Dummy)$_{m}^{\text{PublicDebt}} = 1$	2.61
Increase in probability	2.33
Lead-EQUITYREL(Dummy)$_{m}^{\text{PublicDebt}} = 0$	0.31
Lead-EQUITYREL(Dummy)$_{m}^{\text{PublicDebt}} = 1$	0.79
Increase in probability	0.48

future debt underwriting mandates. Nevertheless, the economic impact of such cross-market relationships is also small.

We also explore the cumulative impact of having a lending relationship in conjunction with a prior underwriting relationship. Thus, we replace the LOANREL(Dummy)^{PublicDebt} variable in Eq. (10) by the two interaction terms LOANREL(Dummy)^{PublicDebt} × Lead-DEBTREL(M)^{PublicDebt} and LOANREL(Dummy)^{PublicDebt} × (1-Lead-DEBTREL $(M)^{\text{PublicDebt}}$). These interaction terms allow us to estimate the *incremental* impact that prior lending relationships have if a bank already has a prior debt underwriting relationship. As column 4 reports, LOANREL(Dummy)^{PublicDebt} × Lead-DEBTREL $(M)^{\text{PublicDebt}}$ has a positive and significant (at the 1% level) coefficient (0.29), which implies that a past lending relationship provides an extra benefit in terms of increasing the likelihood of winning future debt underwriting mandates over and above what a prior underwriting relationship provides.

Finally, in column 5 we test whether the identity of an underwriter is a significant factor in an issuer's choice. We segregate our choice set of potential underwriters between commercial banks and investment banks. Based on information from the Board of Governors of the Federal Reserve System, we create the dummy variable COMMERCIAL BANK, which equals one if the bank had a Section 20 and/or an investment banking subsidiary that was eligible to underwrite the debt security on the date when it was issued. To test if underwriter identity affects its selection, we include the interaction term Lead-DEBTREL(M)^{PublicDebt} × COMMERCIAL BANK in our underwriter selection model. The coefficient for this interaction term is insignificant, implying that commercial banks do not have a significant advantage in winning debt underwriting mandates over and above the effect that past lending and underwriting relationships provide. Overall, compared to the impact of relationships in the market for loans, their impact in the debt underwriting market is economically weaker.[45]

4.4.2. *Tests of Hypothesis 3 and equity underwriting*

The second investment banking product we examine is the lead underwriting mandate for issues of public equity. We segregate our sample of public equity issues into SEOs and IPOs. This partitioning also allows us to conduct tests of another aspect of the information production role of relationship lenders. Typically, IPO issuers suffer from a high degree of information asymmetry. Schenone (2004) notes, "... when firms go public, the market and the firm are asymmetrically informed about true value of the firm." Thus, an underwriter with a strong past lending relationship can provide credible certification about the true value of an IPO-issuing firm. Holding all else constant, we therefore expect that an IPO issuer is more likely to use its relationship lender as its equity underwriter than is an SEO issuer. We examine this in more detail below.

[45]We also use an alternative underwriting strength variable, $\text{RETAIN}_m^{\text{PublicDebt}}$, which takes the value of one if a bank m was retained as either the "Lead Underwriter" or as "Co-Manager" for that debt issue transaction, and zero otherwise. This more inclusive definition addresses the fact that even a second-tier underwriting role offers the bank incremental revenues. While the overall results (available upon request from the authors) are similar to those in Table 6, the coefficient for LOANREL(M)^{PublicDebt} is almost twice as large across all specifications. That is, the prior lending relationship variable now has a much stronger association with the probability of winning a lead underwriter or a co-manager role.

For SEOs we estimate the logit model

$$\begin{aligned}(\text{RETAIN})_m^{\text{lead-SEO}} = {} & \beta_0 + \beta_1(\text{PROCEEDS}) + \beta_2(\text{LOANREL(M)}_m^{\text{PublicEquity}}) \\ & + \beta_3(\text{Lead-EQUITYREL(M)}_m^{\text{PublicEquity}}) \\ & + \beta_4(\text{Lead-DEBTREL(M)}_m^{\text{PublicEquity}}) \\ & + \beta_5(\text{LOAN MKT SHARE})_m + \beta_6(\text{TOP TIER-DEBT})_m \\ & + \beta_7(\text{MID TIER-DEBT})_m + \beta_8(\text{TOP TIER-EQUITY})_m \\ & + \beta_9(\text{MID TIER-EQUITY})_m + \sum \beta_k(\text{CONTROL}_k). \qquad (11)\end{aligned}$$

Since an IPO is the first equity issue by a firm, prior *equity* underwriting relationships are not meaningful for IPO issuers. Also, since few IPO firms issue public debt prior to their IPO, debt underwriting relationships are not common. Thus, for IPOs we estimate the modified logit model

$$\begin{aligned}(\text{RETAIN})_m^{\text{Lead-IPO}} = {} & \beta_0 + \beta_1(\text{PROCEEDS}) + \beta_2(\text{LOANREL(M)}_m^{\text{PublicEquity}}) \\ & + \beta_4(\text{LOAN MKT SHARE})_m + \beta_5(\text{TOP TIER-EQUITY})_m \\ & + \beta_6(\text{MIDDLE TIER-EQUITY})_m \\ & + \sum \beta_k(\text{CONTROL}_k). \qquad (12)\end{aligned}$$

In both models, $(\text{RETAIN})_m$ is a dummy variable that takes a value of one if a bank m was retained as the "Lead Underwriter" for that transaction, and zero otherwise. Table 7 reports the results. In the first three columns we report the results for three alternative measures of prior lending and underwriting relationships. The coefficient for LOANREL, while positive, has a lower statistical significance (it is significant in two out of three specifications). The predicted probability of being retained as a lead SEO underwriter for a bank that did not have a prior lending relationship is 0.30% (holding all other variables constant at their respective means). This probability essentially remains unchanged at 0.31% if a bank did have a prior lending relationship (the results are somewhat stronger if continuous measures of relationship are used with the probability going up from 0.3% to 0.5%). These results suggest that a bank's past lending relationship with a borrower is not strongly associated with that bank's probability of being retained as a lead SEO underwriter by its relationship borrower.[46]

Similar to our test for debt underwriting, we explore the cumulative impact of having a lending relationship in conjunction with a prior equity underwriting relationship by replacing the $\text{LOANREL(Dummy)}^{\text{PublicEquity}}$ variable by the two interaction terms $\text{LOANREL(Dummy)}^{\text{PublicEquity}} \times \text{Lead-EQUITYREL(M)}^{\text{PublicEquity}}$ and $\text{LOANREL(Dummy)}^{\text{PublicEquity}} \times (1\text{-Lead-EQUITYREL(M)}^{\text{PublicEquity}})$, which isolate the

[46]A possible explanation for these results is that since equity underwriting is somewhat removed from traditional commercial banking business, a borrower may feel uncomfortable about rewarding the *lead* role in SEO underwriting to its relationship lender. However, it can still provide its relationship lender with incremental revenues by including it as a second-tier underwriter by awarding it a co-manager role. To test this, we use a broader measure of underwriting business, $\text{RETAIN}_m^{\text{SEO}}$, which equals one if bank m gets either the lead underwriter or a co-manager's role. Our results (not reported) show that past lending relationships are significantly associated with the ability to win some sort of underwriting role in SEOs (the probability of being retained as either lead or co-manager is 1.7% for a bank lacking past lending relationships and 2.9% for a relationship lender). However, the economic impact is still small.

Table 7
Impact of lending relationships on probability of getting future equity underwriting business-seasoned equity offerings (SEOs)

This table provides the logit regression estimates of the following equation:

$$\begin{aligned}(\text{RETAIN})_m^{\text{Lead-SEO}} = {} & \beta_0 + \beta_1(\text{PROCEEDS}) + \beta_2(\text{LOANREL(M)}_m^{\text{PublicEquity}}) \\ & + \beta_3(\text{Lead-EQUITYREL(M)}_m^{\text{PublicEquity}}) \\ & + \beta_4(\text{Lead-DEBTREL(M)}_m^{\text{PublicEquity}}) + \beta_5(\text{LOAN MKT SHARE})_m \\ & + \beta_6(\text{TOP TIER-DEBT})_m + \beta_7(\text{MIDDLE TIER-DEBT})_m \\ & + \beta_8(\text{TOP TIER-EQUITY})_m + \beta_9(\text{MIDDLE TIER-EQUITY})_m \\ & + \sum \beta_k(\text{CONTROL}_k).\end{aligned}$$

For each equity issue, we create the dummy variable $\text{RETAIN}_m^{\text{Lead-SEO}}$, which takes a value of one if a bank m was retained as the lead underwriter for that equity issue transaction and zero otherwise. For each equity underwriting deal i we create a choice set of at least 20 potential underwriters, creating at least 20 deal-underwriter pairs. The top 20 equity underwriters (based on market share) from the previous year and all commercial banks eligible to do equity underwriting in the previous year form the consideration set for each issuer in the current year. For each institution in a transaction-bank pair we estimate relationships across three markets: the bank loan market, the debt underwriting market, and the equity underwriting market. Within each market we use three different proxies of relationship strength for any bank m: $\text{LOANREL(Dummy)}_m^{\text{PublicEquity}}$ (one if there is a loan relationship with bank m in the last five years before the current equity underwriting transaction and zero otherwise), $\text{LOANREL(Number)}_m^{\text{PublicEquity}}$ (ratio of the number of loan deals with bank m to the total number of loan deals of the firm in the last five years before the current equity underwriting transaction), and $\text{LOANREL(Amount)}_m^{\text{PublicEquity}}$ (ratio of the dollar value of loan deals with bank m to the total dollar value of loan deals of the firm in the last five years before the current equity underwriting transaction). $\text{Lead-DEBTREL(Dummy)}^{\text{PublicEquity}}$ (one if there is a debt underwriting relationship in the lead underwriter capacity with bank m in the last five years before the present equity underwriting transaction and zero otherwise), $\text{Lead-DEBTREL(Number)}^{\text{PublicEquity}}$ (ratio of the number of debt underwriting deals in the lead underwriter capacity with bank m to the total number of debt underwriting deals of the firm in the last five years before the current equity underwriting transaction), and $\text{Lead-DEBTREL(Amount)}^{\text{PublicEquity}}$ (ratio of the dollar value of debt underwriting deals in the lead underwriter capacity with bank $m$to the total dollar value of debt underwriting deals of the firm in the last five years before the current equity underwriting transaction). $\text{Lead-EQUITYREL(Dummy)}^{\text{PublicEquity}}$ (one if there is an equity underwriting relationship in the lead underwriter capacity with bank m in the last five years before the present equity underwriting transaction and zero otherwise), $\text{Lead-EQUITYREL(Number)}^{\text{PublicEquity}}$ (ratio of the number of equity underwriting deals in the lead underwriter capacity with bank m to the total number of equity underwriting deals of the firm in the last five years before the current equity underwriting transaction), and $\text{Lead-EQUITYREL(Amount)}^{\text{PublicEquity}}$ (ratio of the dollar value of equity underwriting deals in the lead underwriter capacity with bank m to total dollar value of equity underwriting deals of the firm in the last five years before the current equity underwriting transaction). PROCEEDS is the amount raised in USD millions for the equity underwriting transaction (reported coefficient has been divided by 1,000). $(\text{LOAN MKT SHARE})_m$ is the market share of bank m in the loan market in the year before the current equity underwriting transaction. $(\text{TOP TIER-DEBT})_m$ and $(\text{TOP TIER-EQUITY})_m$ are dummy variables that equals one if bank m is ranked in the top five debt and equity underwriters, respectively, and zero otherwise. $(\text{MID TIER-DEBT})_m$ and $(\text{MID TIER-EQUITY})_m$ are dummy variables that equals one if bank m is ranked from 6th to 15th in debt and equity underwriting, respectively, and zero otherwise. $(\text{COMMERCIAL BANK})_m$ is a dummy variable that equals one if bank m had a Section 20 and/or investment banking subsidiary that was eligible to underwrite equity securities on the date of issuance and zero otherwise.

At the bottom of each panel we illustrate the economic impact of past lending, debt underwriting, and equity underwriting relationships on the probability of being chosen as the debt underwriter using the specification estimated in column 1. The first row reports the probability of a non-relationship bank ($\text{LOANREL(Number)}^{\text{PublicEquity}} = 0$) being chosen as the debt underwriter if all other variables are held equal to their mean. The second row reports the probability for a relationship bank ($\text{LOANREL(Number)}^{\text{PublicEquity}} = 1$) in the same way. Numbers in parentheses are standard errors corrected for heteroskedasticity and clustering (*** significant at the 1% level, ** significant at the 5% level,* significant at the 10% level).

	(1)	(2)	(3)	(4)	(5)
Const.	−6.78***	−6.79***	−6.76***	−6.83***	−6.77***
	(0.38)	(0.35)	(0.35)	(0.40)	(0.40)
PROCEEDS	0.16	0.31	0.33	0.16	0.16
	(0.21)	(0.21)	(0.21)	(0.21)	(0.21)
$\text{LOANREL(Dummy)}_{m}^{\text{PublicEquity}}$	0.02				−0.01
	(0.36)				(0.38)
$\text{LOANREL(Number)}_{m}^{\text{PublicEquity}}$		0.65*			
		(0.38)			
$\text{LOANREL(Amount)}_{m}^{\text{PublicEquity}}$			0.39**		
			(0.18)		
$\text{(LOAN MKT SHARE)}_{m}$	−20.13***	−21.98***	−19.46***	−19.78***	−23.14***
	(6.90)	(6.24)	(6.07)	(6.87)	(8.81)
$\text{Lead-DEBTREL(Dummy)}_{m}^{\text{PublicEquity}}$	1.34***			1.34***	1.33***
	(0.21)			(0.21)	(0.21)
$\text{Lead-DEBTREL(Number)}_{m}^{\text{PublicEquity}}$		1.89***			
		(0.28)			
$\text{Lead-DEBTREL(Amount)}_{m}^{\text{PublicEquity}}$			1.92***		
			(0.29)		
TOP TIER-DEBT	1.53***	1.65***	1.62***	1.53***	1.56***
	(0.34)	(0.33)	(0.33)	(0.33)	(0.34)
MIDDLE TIER-DEBT	0.92***	0.96***	0.93***	0.92***	0.91***
	(0.30)	(0.31)	(0.30)	(0.30)	(0.31)
$\text{Lead-EQUITYREL(Dummy)}_{m}^{\text{PublicEquity}}$	2.38***			2.42***	2.32***
	(0.22)			(0.23)	(0.24)
$\text{Lead-EQUITYREL(Number)}_{m}^{\text{PublicEquity}}$		2.97***			
		(0.27)			
$\text{Lead-EQUITYREL(Amount)}_{m}^{\text{PublicEquity}}$			2.97***		
			(0.26)		
TOP TIER-EQUITY	2.36***	2.54***	2.52***	2.39***	2.34***
	(0.43)	(0.43)	(0.43)	(0.44)	(0.43)
MIDDLE TIER-EQUITY	2.09***	2.14***	2.15***	2.12***	2.07***
	(0.37)	(0.37)	(0.37)	(0.38)	(0.37)
$\text{LOANREL(Dummy)}_{m} \times \text{Lead-EQUITYREL(Dummy)}_{m}$				−0.19	
				(0.50)	
$\text{LOANREL(Dummy)}_{m} \times \text{(1-Lead-EQUITYREL(Dummy)}_{m}\text{)}$				0.26	
				(0.38)	
$\text{Lead-EQUITYREL(Dummy)}_{m} \times \text{(COMMERCIAL BANK)}_{m}$					0.29
					(0.45)
Year dummies	Yes	Yes	Yes	Yes	Yes
Number of observations	12,310	12,310	12,310	12,310	12,310
Pseudo R^2	0.47	0.48	0.49	0.48	0.48

Impact of past relationships on the probability of being chosen as the lead SEO underwriter using the column 1 specification

	Probability of being chosen (%)
$\text{LOANREL(Dummy)}_{m}^{\text{PublicEquity}} = 0$	0.30
$\text{LOANREL(Dummy)}_{m}^{\text{PublicEquity}} = 1$	0.31
Increase in probability	0.01
$\text{Lead-DEBTREL(Dummy)}_{m}^{\text{PublicEquity}} = 0$	0.29
$\text{Lead-DEBTREL(Dummy)}_{m}^{\text{PublicEquity}} = 1$	1.09
Increase in probability	0.80
$\text{Lead-EQUITYREL(Dummy)}_{m}^{\text{PublicEquity}} = 0$	0.28
$\text{Lead-EQUITYREL(Dummy)}_{m}^{\text{PublicEquity}} = 1$	2.95
Increase in probability	2.67

incremental impact that prior lending relationships have if a bank already has a prior equity underwriting relationship with that issuer. As column 4 reports, $\text{LOANREL(Dummy)}^{\text{PublicEquity}} \times \text{Lead-EQUITYREL(M)}^{\text{PublicEquity}}$ has an insignificant coefficient (−0.19), implying that a past lending relationship provides no significant extra benefit in terms of increasing the likelihood of winning future equity underwriting mandates over and above what a prior underwriting relationship provides. The coefficient for $\text{LOANREL(Dummy)}^{\text{PublicEquity}} \times (1\text{-Lead-EQUITYREL(M)}^{\text{PublicEquity}})$ is also insignificant, thus, even when prior equity underwriting relationships is absent, a past lending relationship does not increase the likelihood of winning the SEO mandate significantly. In column 5 we test whether the identity of an underwriter is a significant factor in an issuer's choice. We segregate our choice set between commercial banks and investment banks. We create the dummy variable COMMERCIAL BANK, which equals one if the bank had a Section 20 and/or an investment banking subsidiary that was eligible to underwrite the equity security on the date when it was issued, and we include the interaction term $\text{Lead-EQUITYREL(M)}^{\text{PublicEquity}} \times \text{COMMERCIAL BANK}$ in our underwriter selection model. The coefficient for this interaction term is insignificant, implying that commercial banks do not have a significant advantage in winning equity underwriting mandates over and above that conferred by past lending and investment banking relationships.

As expected, the results for choice of lead IPO underwriter are different from SEOs. As Table 8 reports, prior lending relationships are associated with a significantly higher probability of winning the lead IPO underwriting role. As one can see at the bottom of Table 8, a bank that had been a lender in the past had a three-times higher probability of winning the future IPO underwriting business (increasing from 0.48% to 1.81%). However, as with the debt underwriting, the economic impact is much smaller compared to the impact of such relationships on the probability of winning future lending business.[47]

With respect to the other variables in the logit equation, equity underwriting reputation (TOP TIER-EQUITY) translates into a higher probability of being chosen for the equity underwriting role for both SEOs and IPOs.[48] While the effect of a prior equity underwriting relationship is relevant only for SEOs, similar to the results for debt underwriter selection (Table 6), we find that a prior equity underwriting relationship increases the probability of being retained as lead underwriter of an SEO from 0.3% to almost 3%.

Although lending relationships do have a positive (but economically small) impact on the probability of generating future investment banking business, overall, the impact of relationships seems to be considerably stronger in the loan market compared to the public debt or equity underwriting markets.

---

[47]When we use a broader measure of underwriting business, that is, $\text{RETAIN}_m^{\text{IPO}}$, which equals one if bank *m* gets either the lead underwriter or a co-manager's role, we find (results not reported) a significantly higher association between prior lending relationships and probability of winning an underwriter role in the IPOs. For IPOs, a relationship lender has a 13.46% probability of winning some sort of underwriting role in the IPO equity issue compared to a 2.03% probability for a bank lacking such a relationship.

[48]This is similar to the results of Krigman et al. (2001), who find that issuers often switch underwriters to graduate to more reputable underwriters

Table 8
Impact of lending relationships on probability of getting future equity underwriting business-initial public offerings (IPOs)

This table provides the logit regression estimates of the following equation:

$$
\begin{aligned}
(\text{RETAIN})_m^{\text{Lead-IPO}} = {} & \beta_0 + \beta_1(\text{PROCEEDS}) + \beta_2(\text{LOANREL(M)}_m^{\text{PublicEquity}}) + \beta_4(\text{LOAN MKT SHARE})_m \\
& + \beta_5(\text{TOP TIER-EQUITY})_m + \beta_6(\text{MIDDLE TIER-EQUITY})_m \\
& + \sum \beta_k(\text{CONTROL}_k).
\end{aligned}
$$

For each equity issue, we create the dummy variable $\text{RETAIN}_m^{\text{Lead-IPO}}$, which takes a value of one if a bank m was retained as the lead underwriter for that IPO equity issue transaction and zero otherwise. The model is a reduced version of the one estimated for SEOs in Table 7. We drop the investment banking relationship variables as these are not meaningful for firms conducting an IPO. At the bottom of each panel we illustrate the economic impact of past lending relationships on the probability of being chosen as the equity underwriter using the specification estimated in column 1. The first row reports the probability of a non-relationship bank ($\text{LOANREL(Number)}^{\text{PublicEquity}} = 0$) being chosen as the debt underwriter if all other variables are held equal to their mean. The second row reports the probability for a relationship bank ($\text{LOANREL(Number)}^{\text{PublicEquity}} = 1$) in the same way. Numbers in parentheses are standard errors corrected for heteroskedasticity and clustering (*** significant at the 1% level, ** significant at the 5% percent level, * significant at the 10% level).

	(1)	(2)	(3)
Const.	−6.25***	−6.23***	−6.23***
	(0.22)	(0.22)	(0.22)
PROCEEDS	0.27***	0.30***	0.29***
	(0.09)	(0.08)	(0.08)
$\text{LOANREL(Dummy)}_m^{\text{PublicEquity}}$	1.34***		
	(0.34)		
$\text{LOANREL(Number)}_m^{\text{PublicEquity}}$		1.52***	
		(0.39)	
$\text{LOANREL(Amount)}_m^{\text{PublicEquity}}$			1.44***
			(0.38)
$(\text{LOAN MKT SHARE})_m$	−11.2**	−10.39*	−10.27*
	(5.41)	(5.41)	(5.37)
TOP TIER-EQUITY	4.21***	4.18***	4.19***
	(0.24)	(0.24)	(0.24)
MIDDLE TIER-EQUITY	2.99***	2.97***	2.98***
	(0.24)	(0.24)	(0.24)
Year dummies	Yes	Yes	Yes
Number of observations	15,112	15,112	15,112
Pseudo R^2	0.24	0.24	0.23

Impact of past relationships on the probability of being chosen as the lead IPO underwriter using the column 1 specification

	Probability of being chosen (%)
$\text{LOANREL(Dummy)}_m^{\text{PublicEquity}} = 0$	0.48
$\text{LOANREL(Dummy)}_m^{\text{PublicEquity}} = 1$	1.81
Increase in probability	1.33

5. Conclusion

Our paper seeks to measure the direct benefits that a bank-borrower relationship generates for a lender. For lenders, the establishment of a relationship with a borrower allows for more efficient information production and processing in offering future loans and other information sensitive products. Consequently, a relationship lender should be more likely to secure the future business of its borrowers. We find that indeed, establishing a relationship with a borrower significantly increases the likelihood of winning this borrower's future loan business both statistically and economically. As predicted by theory, we find that the increased likelihood of winning future business is most powerful for those borrowers that suffer from the greatest degree of informational asymmetry. We also find a statistically strong, though economically weak, association between lending relationships and the probability of winning future debt and equity underwriting business from the same borrower. Again, consistent with theory, we find that firms conducting IPOs (in contrast to firms conducting SEOs) are significantly more likely to use their prior lenders as their equity underwriters.

Appendix A

A.1. Methodology for construction of relationship variables

The table below describes how various relationship measures are constructed. Panel A describes the methodology for constructing measures that capture the existence and extent of prior lending relationship. Panels B and C describe the methodology for constructing prior investment banking relationship measures

Relationship variable	Methodology
Panel A: Lending relationships-bank loan and investment banking markets	
Binary measures	
$\text{LOANREL(Dummy)}_m^{\text{BankLoans}}$	Equals one if a bank *m* had a prior lending relationship with the firm in at least one loan during the five-year window preceding the date of activation of the current loan
$\text{LOANREL(Dummy)}_m^{\text{PublicDebt}}$	Same as $\text{LOANREL(Dummy)}_m^{\text{BankLoans}}$, except the look-back window is from the date of debt issue
$\text{LOANREL(Dummy)}_m^{\text{PublicEquity}}$	Same as $\text{LOANREL(Dummy)}_m^{\text{BankLoans}}$, except the look-back window is from the date of equity issue
Continuous measures	
$\text{LOANREL(Amount)}_m^{\text{BankLoans}}$	Ratio of the dollar value of loans contracted by a firm with the lending bank *m* to the total dollar value of loans contracted by the firm during the five-year

	window preceding the date of activation of current loan
$\text{LOANREL(Amount)}_m^{\text{PublicDebt}}$	Same as $\text{LOANREL(Amount)}_m^{\text{BankLoans}}$, except the look-back window is from the date of debt issue for examining the impact of a lending relationship on the ability to attract underwriting of debt issues
$\text{LOANREL(Amount)}_m^{\text{PublicEquity}}$	Same as $\text{LOANREL(Amount)}_m^{\text{BankLoans}}$, except the look-back window is from the date of equity issue for examining the impact of a lending relationship on the ability to attract underwriting of equity issues
$\text{LOANREL(Number)}_m^{\text{BankLoans}}$	Ratio of the number of loans contracted by a firm with the lending bank *m* to the total number of loans contracted by the firm during the five-year window preceding the date of activation of current loan
$\text{LOANREL(Number)}_m^{\text{PublicDebt}}$	Same as $\text{LOANREL(Number)}_m^{\text{BankLoans}}$, except the look-back window is from the date of debt issue for examining the impact of a lending relationship on the ability to attract underwriting of debt issues
$\text{LOANREL(Number)}_m^{\text{PublicEquity}}$	Same as $\text{LOANREL(Number)}_m^{\text{BankLoans}}$, except the look-back window is from the date of equity issue for examining the impact of a lending relationship on the ability to attract underwriting of equity issues
Panel B: Investment banking relationships-debt underwriting market	
Binary measures	
$\text{Lead-DEBTREL(Dummy)}_m^{\text{PublicDebt}}$	Equals one if the bank *m* had underwritten at least one public debt issue (as the Lead underwriter) during the five-year window preceding the current debt issue
$\text{Lead-EQUITYREL(Dummy)}_m^{\text{PublicDebt}}$	Equals one if the bank *m* had underwritten at least one public equity issue (as the Lead underwriter) during the five-year window preceding the current debt issue
Continuous measures	
$\text{Lead-DEBTREL(Amount)}_m^{\text{PublicDebt}}$	Ratio of the dollar value of public debt issues of a firm underwritten by the bank *m* (as the Lead underwriter) to the total dollar value of public debt issues by the

	firm during the five-year window preceding the date of the current debt issue
Lead-DEBTREL(Number)$_m^{\text{PublicDebt}}$	Ratio of number of public debt issues of a firm underwritten by the bank *m* (as the Lead underwriter) to the total Number of public debt issues by the firm during the five-year window preceding the date of the current debt issue
Lead-EQUITYREL(Amount)$_m^{\text{PublicDebt}}$	Ratio of the dollar value of public equity issues of a firm underwritten by the bank *m* (as the Lead underwriter) to the total dollar value of public equity issues by the firm during the five-year window preceding the date of the current debt issue
Lead-EQUITYREL(Number)$_m^{\text{PublicDebt}}$	Ratio of number of public equity issues of a firm underwritten by the bank *m* (as the Lead underwriter) to the total Number of public equity issues by the firm during the five-year window preceding the date of the current debt issue
Panel C: Investment banking relationships-equity underwriting market	
Binary measures	
Lead-EQUITYREL(Dummy)$_m^{\text{PublicEquity}}$	Equals one if the bank *m* had underwritten at least one public equity issue (as the Lead underwriter) during the five-year window preceding the current equity issue
Lead-DEBTREL(Dummy)$_m^{\text{PublicEquity}}$	Equals one if the bank *m* had underwritten at least one public debt issue (as the Lead underwriter) during thefive-year window preceding the current equity issue
Continuous measures	
Lead-EQUITYREL(Amount)$_m^{\text{PublicEquity}}$	Ratio of the dollar value of public equity issues of a firm underwritten by the bank *m* (as the Lead underwriter) to the total dollar value of public equity issues by the firm during the five-year window preceding the date of the current equity issue
Lead-EQUITYREL(Number)$_m^{\text{PublicEquity}}$	Ratio of number of public equity issues of a firm underwritten by the bank *m* (as the Lead underwriter) to the total Number of public equity issues by the firm during the five-year window preceding the date of the current equity issue
Lead-DEBTREL(Amount)$_m^{\text{PublicEquity}}$	Ratio of the dollar value of public debt issues of a firm underwritten by the bank *m* (as the Lead underwriter) to the total

	dollar value of public debt issues by the firm during the five-year window preceding the date of the current equity issue
Lead-DEBTREL(Number)$_m^{\text{PublicEquity}}$	Ratio of number of public debt issues of a firm underwritten by the bank m (as the Lead underwriter) to the total Number of public debt issues by the firm during the five-year window preceding the date of the current equity issue

Appendix B

B.1. Descriptive statistics, relationship variables

The relationship measures are reported on an individual loan facility, debt issue transaction, and equity issue transaction basis. The bank loan market relationship measure on a particular loan facility is estimated by identifying the lead bank(s) on that facility and then searching over the prior five years to determine whether any of the lead bank(s) had been lead banks on any loans during this period. Thus, LOANREL(M)^{BankLoans} is estimated for all the lead banks on the current facility and the highest value across these is assigned as LOANREL(M)^{BankLoans} for that loan facility. A similar procedure is followed to estimate the relationship variables for debt and equity issue transactions.

	(1)	(2)	(3)
Panel A: Bank loan market-correlations across different relationship measures			
(1) LOANREL(Dummy)^{BankLoans}	1.00		
(2) LOANREL(Number)^{BankLoans}	0.89	1.00	
(3) LOANREL(Amount)^{BankLoans}	0.87	0.97	1.00

	(1)	(2)	(3)	(4)	(5)	(6)	(7)	(8)	(9)
Panel B: Public debt underwriting market-correlations across different relationship measures									
(1) Lead-DEBTREL(Dummy)^{PublicDebt}	1.00								
(2) Lead-DEBTREL(Number)^{PublicDebt}	0.60	1.00							
(3) Lead-DEBTREL(Amount)^{PublicDebt}	0.56	0.94	1.00						
(4) Lead-EQUITYREL(Dummy)^{PublicDebt}	0.23	0.41	0.46	1.00					
(5) Lead-EQUITYREL(Number)^{PublicDebt}	0.25	0.44	0.49	0.94	1.00				
(6) Lead-EQUITYREL(Amount)^{PublicDebt}	0.24	0.44	0.49	0.94	0.99	1.00			
(7) LOANREL(Dummy)^{PublicDebt}	−0.06	0.08	0.08	0.03	0.01	0.00	1.00		
(8) LOANREL(Number)^{PublicDebt}	−0.07	0.10	0.10	0.07	0.05	0.05	0.88	1.00	
(9) LOANREL(Amount)^{PublicDebt}	−0.07	0.09	0.10	0.06	0.04	0.03	0.91	0.98	1.00

	(1)	(2)	(3)	(4)	(5)	(6)	(7)	(8)	(9)
Panel C: Public equity underwriting market-correlations across different relationship measures									
(1) Lead-EQUITYREL(Dummy)^{PublicEquity}	1.00								
(2) Lead-EQUITYREL(Number)^{PublicEquity}	0.87	1.00							
(3) Lead-EQUITYREL(Amount)^{PublicEquity}	0.89	0.98	1.00						
(4) Lead-DEBTREL(Dummy)^{PublicEquity}	0.32	0.33	0.31	1.00					
(5) Lead-DEBTREL(Number)^{PublicEquity}	0.27	0.37	0.35	0.83	1.00				
(6) Lead-DEBTREL(Amount)^{PublicEquity}	0.29	0.37	0.35	0.86	0.99	1.00			
(7) LOANREL(Dummy)^{PublicEquity}	0.16	0.19	0.18	0.13	0.11	0.10	1.00		
(8) LOANREL(Number)^{PublicEquity}	0.15	0.20	0.18	0.09	0.06	0.04	0.89	1.00	
(9) LOANREL(Amount)^{PublicEquity}	0.15	0.20	0.18	0.10	0.08	0.06	0.94	0.97	1.00

Appendix C

C.1. Issues related to bank M&A activity

The high level of M&A activity in the U.S. banking industry during our sample period poses two issues that need to be addressed. The first issue is how to account for the relationships of banks that are acquired or merged. We assume that in the case of acquisitions, all the customer relationships of the bank being acquired are inherited by the acquiring bank. For mergers, the relationships of the merger partners are assumed to be inherited by the new post-merger entity. The second issue also arises from the significant consolidation of banking industry over our sample period. This affects the identity of the top 40 banks, the calculation of bank market share, as well as bank relationships. Several banks that existed in the earlier part of the sample ceased to exist later (due to mergers) or become relatively unimportant in terms of total loan market share in later years. For example, Manufacturers Hanover, which was one of the largest commercial banks in the late 1980s, merged with Chemical Bank in 1991. Clearly, for loan transactions on or before 1991, Manufacturers Hanover was an important bank that had a chance of securing the lending business. Post 1991, it no longer existed. Thus, it is clear that we need to account for the changing identities of potential lead banks for a given loan over time.

We use the Chemical-Manufacturers Hanover merger discussed above to illustrate how we address these methodological issues. As we mention before, all borrowers that had a lending relationship with either the old Chemical or the old Manufacturers Hanover are assumed to be relationship borrowers of the new Chemical Bank. The next issue is to determine the historical market share of a new bank resulting from a merger or acquisition if it is the first year of operation for this new entity. We address this in the following way: the historical market share of the new bank is simply imputed from the historical market share of the individual banks that merged (or the shares of the target and the acquiror in case of acquisition). Thus, 1992 was the first full operating year for the new Chemical Bank resulting from the merger between the old Chemical and the old Manufacturers Hanover. Since there is no history for this new bank, the historical market share is calculated by summing the 1991 market shares of the old Chemical and the old Manufacturer's Hanover. A related issue concerns the choice set of potential lenders in 1992. For illustrative purposes, assume no other mergers or acquisitions took place in 1991 and that both old Chemical and old Manufacturers Hanover were in the top 40 banks in 1991. Using the methodology we discuss earlier, both these banks would be in the choice set of potential lenders. However, neither of these two banks exist in 1992 due to the merger, while the new Chemical is very much a potential provider of loans in 1992. We address this issue by assuming in our calculations *as if* the new Chemical Bank existed in 1991. This imputed bank would have a market share equal to the sum of its two constituents as discussed above and the choice set in 1992 would consist of 39 banks instead of 40 as the two merger partners (in this example-the old Chemical and Manufacturers Hanover) are replaced by a single merged entity (in this example-the new Chemical Bank). If the merger was between a top 40 bank and a nontop 40 bank no adjustment is made; only the market share needs to be updated and the choice set would still consist of 40 banks.

References

Alford, A., Jones, J., Zmijeweski, M., 1992. Extensions and violations of the statutory SEC 10-K filing date. Unpublished manuscript. University of Chicago.

Barclay, M.J., Smith, C.W., 1995a. The maturity structure of corporate debt. Journal of Finance 50, 609–631.

Barclay, M.J., Smith, C.W., 1995b. The priority structure of corporate liabilities. Journal of Finance 50, 899–917.

Berger, A., 1999. The 'big picture' of relationship finance. In: Blanton, J.L., Williams, A., Rhine, S.L. (Eds.), Business Access to Capital and Credit. A Federal Reserve System Research Conference. pp. 390–400.

Berger, A., Udell, G., 1995. Relationship lending and lines of credit in small firm finance. Journal of Business 68, 351–381.

Berlin, M., 1996. For better and for worse: three lending relationships. Business Review. Federal Reserve Bank of Philadelphia November/December, 3–12.

Berlin, M., Mester, L.J., 1992. Debt covenants and renegotiations. Journal of Financial Intermediation 2, 95–133.

Berlin, M., Mester, L.J., 1999. Deposits and relationship lending. Review of Financial Studies 12, 579–607.

Bhattacharya, S., Chiesa, G., 1995. Proprietary information financial intermediation and research incentives. Journal of Financial Intermediation 4, 328–357.

Blackwell, D., Kidwell, D., 1988. An investigation of cost differences between public sales and private placements of debt. Journal of Financial Economics 22, 253–278.

Boot, A., 2000. Relationship banking: what do we know? Journal of Financial Intermediation 9, 7–25.

Boot, A., Greenbaum, S., Thakor, A., 1993. Reputation and discretion in financial contracting. American Economic Review 83, 1165–1183.

Burch, T.R., Nanda, V., Warther, V.A., 2005. Does it pay to be loyal? An empirical analysis of underwriting relationships and fees. Journal of Financial Economics 77, 673–699.

Carey, M., Post, M., Sharpe, S., 1998. Does corporate lending by banks and finance companies differ? Evidence on specialization in private debt contracting. Journal of Finance 53, 845–878.

Carlton, D.W., 1986. The rigidity of prices. American Economic Review 76, 637–658.

Dahiya, S., Puri, M., Saunders, A., 2003a. Bank borrowers and loan sales: new evidence on the uniqueness of bank loans. Journal of Business 76, 563–582.

Dahiya, S., Saunders, A., Srinivasan, A., 2003b. Financial distress and bank lending relationships. Journal of Finance 58, 375–399.

Dempster, A., Laird, N., Rubin, D., 1977. Maximum likelihood from incomplete data via EM algorithm (with discussion). Journal of Royal Statistical Society B39, 1–38.

Dennis, S., Mullineux, D., 2000. Syndicated Loans Journal of Financial Intermediation 9, 90–109.

Diamond, D., 1984. Financial intermediation and delegated monitoring. Review of Economic Studies 62, 393–414.

Diamond, D., 1991. Monitoring and reputation: the choice between bank loans and directly placed debt. Journal of Political Economy 99, 689–721.

Drucker, S., Puri, M., 2005. On the benefits of concurrent lending and underwriting. Journal of Finance 60, 2763–2799.

Eccles, R., Crane, D., 1988. Doing Deals—Investment Banks at Work. Harvard Business School Press, Boston.

Fama, E., French, K., 1992. Cross-section of expected stock returns. Journal of Finance 47, 427–465.

Greenbaum, S., Thakor, A., 1995. Contemporary Financial Intermediation. Dryden Press, New York.

Hoshi, T., Kashyap, A., Scharfstein, D., 1990. The role of banks in reducing the costs of financial distress in Japan. Journal of Financial Economics 27, 67–88.

Houston, J., Christopher, J., 1996. Bank information monopolies and the mix of private and public debt claims. Journal of Finance 51, 1863–1889.

James, C., 1987. Some evidence of the uniqueness of bank loans. Journal of Financial Economics 19, 217–235.

Kanatas, G., Qi, J., 2003. Integration of lending and underwriting: implications of scope economy. Journal of Finance 58, 1167–1191.

Klemperer, P., Padilla, A.J., 1997. Do firms' product lines include too many variables. RAND Journal of Economics 28, 472–488.

Krigman, L., Shaw, W.H., Womack, K.L., 2001. Why do firms switch underwriters? Journal of Financial Economics 60, 245–284.

Kroszner, R.S., Strahan, P., 2001. Throwing good money after bad? Board connections and conflicts in bank lending. NBER Working Paper No. 8694.

Leland, H., Pyle, D., 1977. Informational asymmetries, financial structure and financial intermediation. Journal of Finance 32, 371–387.

Levinthal, D., Fichman, M., 1988. Dynamics of interorganizational attachments: auditor-client relationships. Administrative Science Quarterly 33, 345–369.

Ljungqvist, A., Marston, F., Wilhelm, W.J., 2006. Competing for securities underwriting mandates: banking relationships and analysts recommendations. Journal of Finance 61, 301–340.

Lummer, S., McConnell, J., 1989. Further evidence on the bank lending process and the reaction of the capital markets to bank loan agreements. Journal of Financial Economics 25, 99–122.

Madan, R., Sobhani, R., Horowitz, K., 1999. Syndicated lending. PianeWebber Equity Research Report.

McLachlan, G., Krishan, T., 1997. The EM Algorithm and Extensions. Wiley, New York.

Megginson, W., Weiss, K., 1991. Venture capitalist certification in initial public offerings. Journal of Finance 46, 879–903.

Ongena, S., Smith, D., 1998. Banking relationships: a review. In: Harker, P., Zenios, S.A. (Eds.), The Performance of Financial Institutions. Cambridge University Press, Cambridge, UK, pp. 221–258.

Ongena, S., Smith, D., Michalsen, D., 2003. Firms and their distressed banks: lessons from the Norwegian banking crisis. Journal of Financial Economics 67, 81–112.

Petersen, M.A., Rajan, R.G., 1994. The benefits of lending relationships: evidence from small business data. Journal of Finance 49, 3–37.

Rajan, R.G., 1992. Insiders and outsiders: the choice between relationship and arm's length debt. Journal of Finance 47, 1367–1400.

Rajan, R.G., Winton, A., 1995. Covenants and collateral as incentives to monitor. Journal of Finance 50, 1113–1146.

Ramakrishnan, R., Thakor, A., 1984. Information reliability and a theory of financial intermediation. Review of Economic Studies 51, 415–432.

Schafer, J.L., 1997. Analysis of Incomplete Multivariate Data. Chapman & Hall, New York.

Schenone, C., 2004. The effect of banking relationships on the firm's IPO underpricing. Journal of Finance 59, 2903–2958.

Sharpe, S., 1990. Asymmetric information, bank lending and implicit contracts: a stylized model of customer relationship. Journal of Finance 45, 1069–1087.

Slovin, M.B., Shuska, M.A., Polonchek, J.A., 1993. The value of bank durability: borrowers as the bank stakeholders. Journal of Finance 48, 247–266.

Smith, C.W., Watts, R.L., 1992. The investment opportunity set and corporate financing, dividend and compensation policies. Journal of Financial Economics 32, 263–292.

Stein, J.C., 2002. Information production and capital allocation: decentralized vs. hierarchical firms. Journal of Finance 57, 1891–1921.

Strahan, P., 2000. Borrower risk and the price and nonprice terms of bank loans. Federal Reserve Bank of New York. Staff Paper No. 90.

Williams, R.L., 2000. A note on robust variance estimation for cluster-correlated data. Biometrics 56, 645–646.

Yasuda, A., 2005. Do bank relationships affect the firm's underwriter choice in the corporate-bond underwriting market? Journal of Finance 60, 1259–1292.

Lending Relationships and Loan Contract Terms

Sreedhar T. Bharath
Ross School of Business, University of Michigan

Sandeep Dahiya
McDonough School of Business, Georgetown University

Anthony Saunders
Stern School of Business, New York University

Anand Srinivasan
Department of Finance, NUS Business School and Risk Management Institute, National University of Singapore

We find that repeated borrowing from the same lender translates into a 10–17 bps lowering of loan spreads and that relationships are especially valuable when borrower transparency is low. These results hold using multiple approaches (propensity score matching, instrumental variables, and treatment effects model) that control for the endogeneity of relationships. We also provide a demarcation line between relationship and transactional lending. Spreads charged for relationship loans and nonrelationship loans are statistically identical if the borrower is in the largest 30% by asset size; has public rated debt; or is part of the S&P 500 index. Past relationships reduce collateral requirements and are also associated with obtaining larger loans. Our results imply that, even for firms that have multiple sources of outside financing, borrowing from a prior lender obtains better loan terms. (*JEL* D82, G3, G20, G21, G24, L14, N20)

Information asymmetry between lenders and borrowers has played a key role in the development of financial intermediation theory. If an owner/manager cannot credibly reveal the firm's future prospects, lenders must invest in costly information production and due diligence so as to assess the creditworthiness

Bharath acknowledges the research support of the Ross School of Business, University of Michigan. Srinivasan acknowledges the support of NUS research grants R-315-000-066-112 and R-315-000-066-133. The authors thank seminar participants at the University of Michigan, Boston College, Wharton School of Business, Indian School of Business, and Georgetown University. They thank conference participants at the Indian School of Business, participants at the Financial Intermediation Research Society conference 2008 in Anchorage, American Finance Association 2009 conference in San Francisco, Federal Reserve Bank of Chicago Conference, and 2006 Wharton Financial Intermediation Conference. They also thank Viral Acharya, Franklin Allen, Sumit Agarwal, Mark Carey, Doug Diamond, Mark Flannery, Anjan Thakor, and Tansel Yilmazer for their comments. All errors are those of the authors. Send correspondence to Sreedhar T. Bharath, Ross School of Business, Department of Finance, University of Michigan, Suite R3332, Ann Arbor, MI 48109; telephone: (734) 763-0485. E-mail: sbharath@umich.edu.

doi:10.1093/rfs/hhp064

of potential borrowers and to screen out unacceptably poor quality borrowers (adverse selection). Even if a firm is assessed as an acceptable credit risk, after making the loan the lender must expend resources in monitoring the borrower given the firm's incentives to invest suboptimally (borrower moral hazard). However, the information frictions caused by adverse selection and moral hazard can be mitigated if the lending is done by a single private lender such as a bank (Diamond 1984; Ramakrishnan and Thakor 1984; Fama 1985). These risk mitigation benefits are further magnified if the lending bank has had a strong past relationship with a borrower directly producing borrower-specific durable and reusable information (Boot 2000)[1] although an alternate view, with respect to lending relationships, can be found in Sharpe (1990) and Rajan (1992), who suggest that relationship borrowers may be "locked-in" due to information asymmetries between outside lenders and the borrower.

When a loan is shared among multiple lenders, as is the case of syndicated loans, there is an additional element of moral hazard between the lead lender, who is expected to be focal in monitoring the loan (Holmstrom and Tirole 1997), and other members of the syndicate. Nonlead lenders would likely anticipate less than optimal effort by the lead lender, given that it does not have exposure to the entire loan. We refer to this as "syndicate moral hazard," which results from information asymmetries *among lenders* and arises due to the lead bank's incentive to shirk from optimal monitoring. In contrast, "borrower moral hazard" results from an informational friction between the *lender and borrower* due to the borrower's incentives to divert cash flows for private benefit or to engage in excessive risk taking. Recent research has begun examining syndicate moral hazard.[2]

Our article adds to this literature by examining a large set of bank loans to publicly listed corporations. A key contribution of our article is to examine the impact of relationships in lowering information asymmetries both between lenders and borrowers, as well as between multiple lenders. Specifically, we examine how repeated borrowing from the same lender (which we call relationship borrowing) affects observed loan contract terms. A further contribution of this article is our estimation of the boundary between relationship and transactional lending. To the best of our knowledge, this is the first paper to estimate the cut-off point beyond which relationship lending becomes indistinguishable from transactional lending in that there are no apparent loan yield/spread benefits to the borrower from past lending relationships. We also examine how past lending relationships affect loan characteristics at different levels of syndicate moral hazard.

---

1 A borrower can benefit from a strong relationship with its lender in a number of ways. These include sharing confidential information such as details of R&D (Bhattacharya and Chiesa 1995); loan contracts that allow renegotiability (Berlin and Mester 1992; Boot, Greenbuam, and Thakor 1993); and the ability to smooth out loan pricing over multiple loans (Berlin and Mester 1998).

2 Sufi (2007) studies the effect of syndicate moral hazard on syndicate structure.

Lending Relationships and Loan Contract Terms

A number of studies of small, privately held borrowers have provided support for the benefits of relationship lending.[3] In this article, we extend this strand of literature by investigating the role of lending relationships for publicly listed, widely held firms. Our article differs from previous empirical studies of relationship lending on four dimensions. The first difference is that the firms in our sample have a much wider choice of financing options available, in that all have access to equity markets and a significant fraction to public debt markets. A rapid change in the capital market and increased competition among banks are more likely to impact these firms than private, closely held firms. While Petersen and Rajan (1995) argue that increased competition is likely to erode the benefits of relationship lending, Boot and Thakor (2000) provide a theoretical model that envisages banks engaging in relationship lending as well as "arms-length" transactional lending even as the competition increases. Our sample provides a natural universe to explore the empirical boundary between relationship and transactional lending.

The second difference is that our article focuses on firms borrowing in the syndicated loan market, where a loan is divided among more than one lender. Typically, one or a few lenders (denoted as the Lead Bank(s)) play a delegated monitoring role as described by Diamond (1984). Syndicate members differ in their ability to screen and monitor and the syndicate loan structure results in moral hazard for the lead bank, as it bears all the costs of monitoring the loan, but its share of the loan is less than 100%. Since the monitoring effort of the lead bank is unobservable, the other syndicate members anticipate "shirking" in the level of monitoring effort put in by the lead bank and ex ante demand higher spreads. Past relationships, which lower the cost of future monitoring, can be seen as a commitment to monitor and can mitigate this syndicate moral hazard problem. Our sample is well suited to test this.

The third difference is our use of a large cross-sectional variation in proxies for information opacity regarding the borrower (e.g., size, credit quality, analyst following, etc.). We use the term "information opacity" to capture the idea that higher opacity reflects the lower amount of publicly available information. Sufi (2007) provides a useful characterization of opacity ". . . of the degree to which a financial institution must investigate and monitor the borrower." For example, borrower size (as measured by the book value of assets) varies from $93 million at the 25th percentile to $1.6 billion at the 75th percentile. This variation allows us to test how past relationships affect loan contract terms at different levels of borrower information opacity and loan syndicate structure.

[3] These include Petersen and Rajan (1994), Berger and Udell (1995), Cole (1998), and Degryse and Van Cayseele (2000). Evidence from these studies is mixed. Petersen and Rajan (1994) find that while relationships do increase the *availability* of credit, the interest charged for loans is unaffected. Berger and Udell (1995) report that strong relationships lower both the interest charged, as well as collateral requirements. Cole (1998) reports that while *the duration of a relationship* did not affect the availability of credit, increasing *the scope of a relationship* as proxied by the purchase of multiple information-sensitive products (such as checking accounts) from a bank did increase the probability of getting loans from that bank. Degryse and Van Cayselee (2000) find similar results.

Fourth, unlike previous relationship papers that have viewed loan contract terms in an independent fashion, we allow for the joint determination of loan contract terms, specifically, the joint determination of loan spreads, loan maturity, and loan collateral requirements. Equally important, we also evaluate the endogeneity of relationship formation itself using three different approaches: propensity score matching (PSM), instrumental variables (IV) approach, and a treatment effects model approach. We believe that ours is among the first papers in relationship lending that uses all three approaches and documents the advantages and disadvantages of each.

To preview our results, we find that the benefits of relationship borrowing, measured by a reduction in the loan rate, become insignificant for the top 30% of the firms in our sample ranked by asset size. A similar dissipation of the benefits of relationship lending occurs once a firm has a public debt rating or is part of the S&P 500 index. We find that, on average, repeated borrowing from the same lender is associated with an almost 10–15 basis point (bp) reduction in loan spreads. This reduction is most pronounced for informationally opaque borrowers, consistent with relationships mitigating information asymmetry. We also segregate our loans into groups based on their potential for syndicate moral hazard between lead and nonlead lenders in the syndicate. Our results show that past relationships are significant commitments to monitor, as the presence of such relationships in high moral hazard syndicates is associated with lower spreads.

We also estimate the benefits of relationships using the PSM methodology. Specifically, this technique uses various observed borrower and loan characteristics to generate an index that measures how likely it is that a loan would be obtained from a relationship lender. Thus, for every relationship loan it is possible to find matching nonrelationship loans that had a similar propensity to use a relationship lender but did not. The difference in spreads between the relationship loan and matched nonrelationship loans allows us to measure the causal impact that relationships have on loan spreads. Our results are remarkably robust, and the difference in spreads ranges from 10 to 13 bps across different matching procedures. We also employed two additional methodologies to test for the importance of relationships. The first is an IV estimation using the distance between the borrower and the lender as an instrument that causes relationship formation. As the second, as an alternative to the IV approach, we employ a treatment effects model to control for the endogeneity of relationship formation. Both approaches demonstrate the benefits of relationships for loan spreads, consistent with our PSM findings.

Our results on nonprice terms of the loan (collateral and maturity) also find support for the hypothesis that relationships lower information asymmetry between lenders and borrowers. In particular, we find that relationships lower the likelihood that collateral will be pledged (consistent with reduction in adverse selection, as well as borrower moral hazard). We also find that relationships are associated with a shorter loan maturity for the lowest quality of borrowers. An interpretation of relationships as credible commitments to monitor is consistent with this finding, as a shorter maturity provides incentives for more frequent monitoring, which is likely to be less costly for a relationship lender.

While the importance of nonprice terms in debt contracts has been recognized in previous studies (e.g., Melnik and Plaut 1986), empirical evidence has often been limited by a focus on a single contract feature.[4] In reality, all the contract terms are likely to be interdependent. We address the econometric issues that arise if the price and nonprice terms are determined simultaneously.[5] We employ an IV approach, explicitly recognizing and testing for the endogeneity of contract terms such as the price, collateral, and maturity of a loan. We find that prior relationships continue to be associated with lower spreads, lower likelihood of collateral, and shorter maturity of the loan (for the lowest quality borrowers) in the joint specification.

Finally, we examine whether access to bank financing is related to borrower-lender relationships. Using the size of a loan facility (scaled by either the borrower's assets or the borrower's total long-term debt) as a proxy for access to debt, we find that a firm borrowing from its relationship lender is able to get a loan approximately 1–2% higher than a similar firm borrowing from a nonrelationship lender. Our article thus complements similar evidence for private, closely held borrowers reported by Petersen and Rajan (1994).

The remainder of the article is organized as follows. We discuss the theoretical predictions and testable implications in Section 1. Section 2 describes the data and our sample selection process. Our methodology and major results are presented in Section 3. We conclude in Section 4.

1. Theoretical Predictions and Tests

Since our article is empirical in nature, we first review the theoretical debate surrounding loan spreads, nonprice loan characteristics, and relationship lending. In doing so, we highlight how we propose to bring new and additional insights into this debate. As discussed in the introduction, information asymmetries between borrowers and lenders are an important element of financial intermediation theory. Further, in the case of syndicated loans, there is an additional element of moral hazard between the lead lender and other lenders. Below we explain in detail how lending relationships can mitigate the adverse selection problem, curb syndicate moral hazard, and lower borrower moral hazard.

Boot (2000) argues that relationship lending involves customer-specific information gathered over time through multiple interactions. Further, he argues

[4] For example, Berger et al. (2005a) examine the maturity of new loans, while Berger and Udell (1995) and Jiménez, Salas, and Saurina (2006) focus on the collateral requirements.

[5] Dennis, Nandy, and Sharpe (2000) are among the first to address the interrelationship between the price and nonprice terms of a loan contract. However, of the four contract features they consider, they analyze only two contract features together at one time. While the features within each set are assumed to be determined jointly, the two sets themselves are assumed to be independent and thus not true simultaneous systems.

that this information must be costly to produce, be proprietary to the lender(s), and be reusable. This definition implies that going back to one's past lender is likely to reduce adverse selection concerns, since previous transactions would have allowed the lender to generate proprietary inside information about the borrowers.

A second effect of relationship lending is to reduce the likelihood of syndicate moral hazard. In particular, not only does the relationship lender have lower information asymmetries with respect to the borrower, it also has a lower ongoing cost of monitoring the borrower relative to uninformed outside lenders. As a result, it can provide a more credible commitment to monitor the borrower. This commitment to monitor is especially important in syndicated loans where the lead bank does not fully internalize the benefits of its future monitoring effort. Thus, for syndicated loans, the nonlead participant banks can rationally expect a lead bank with a prior relationship to monitor more than a lead bank without a relationship.

A third effect of relationships, as a credible commitment to monitor, enables the lender to more effectively control the borrower, once a loan is made. In particular, borrower moral hazard is also mitigated and the borrower is discouraged from engaging in suboptimal investment and risk-shifting activities.

In what follows, we develop hypotheses to explore these relationship effects on loan spreads, collateral, maturity, and loan amount.

1.1 Effect of relationships on spreads

1.1.1 Effect of information asymmetries between lenders and borrowers.

As argued above, due to lower information asymmetries, the cost of providing future loans (and arguably other information-sensitive services such as securities underwriting) should be lower for a relationship lender. The relationship lender may choose to share, or pass on, these savings to its borrower in a number of ways such as through lower costs of borrowing, more flexible loan contract terms, or a combination of both. If a lender shares some of these benefits with its relationship borrower, then loan costs would be lower for a borrower that uses its relationship lender. Boot and Thakor (1994) also argue that rates charged for loans should decrease as a borrower-lender relationship matures. We call this the relationship benefit effect.

An alternate viewpoint regarding lending relationships (Sharpe 1990; Rajan 1992) posits that the relationship lender may actually distort investment decisions of the borrower and examines the possibility of the borrower being "locked-in." This lock-in effect would be most relevant only for borrowers with few or no alternative sources of financing beyond the relationship bank. Since most firms in our sample are publicly traded, and often have multiple bank relationships, the lock-in effect is likely to be small. However, we do explore the potential for such a lock-in for our sample as well.

We employ all-in-spread drawn (AISD) as the measure of the interest rate spread charged on a loan. AISD measures the interest rate spread on a loan (over LIBOR) plus any associated fees in originating the loan. Thus, AISD is an all-inclusive measure of loan price. Under the Boot and Thakor (1994) model, relationships should lower spreads. However, if the borrower is "informationally captured" (Sharpe 1990), such a lock-in can result in a relationship lender failing to pass on the benefits of lower information production/monitoring costs to its borrower. This would imply that relationship loans need not be significantly cheaper in terms of spreads charged relative to nonrelationship loans. Specifically, we test the following hypothesis:

Hypothesis 1 (H1). *Relationship loans, on average, carry a lower AISD compared to nonrelationship loans.*

The models of relationships (relationship benefits versus lock-in) also have quite sharp implications regarding the effect of information opacity on spreads. If the relationship benefit effect holds, then the amount of the benefit would depend on the relationship lender's potential to generate *proprietary* incremental information (and sharing this benefit with its borrower). The benefits may either come from a reduction in adverse selection or lower cost of future monitoring. The greater the information opacity, the greater will be its magnitude. On the other hand, with the lock-in effect, the greater the information opacity, the greater will be the borrower lock-in effect. We use multiple proxies to capture the relative degree of information opacity of a borrower (thus serving as a proxy for the potential to generate proprietary information or potential for lock-in). These include the size of a borrower's assets, access to public debt markets, inclusion in the S&P 500 index, number of analysts that follow the borrower, lagged discretionary accruals, and a microstructure measure of information asymmetry. We test to see whether relationship borrowers faced with higher information asymmetry have a greater reduction in spread (relationship benefit effect) or a lower reduction or even an increase in spread (lock-in effect) compared to nonrelationship borrowers. Accordingly, we test the following hypothesis:

Hypothesis 2 (H2). *The higher the information asymmetry faced by a large borrower, the greater the benefits of a relationship on its cost of borrowing.*

A natural implication of Hypothesis 2 is that if borrower transparency is high, the benefits of relationships can become insignificant. For such firms, banks may no longer offer relationship loans. Most theoretical models typically assume that nonrelationship or transactional lending is done in the capital market, while relationship loans are assumed to be provided by banks (Rajan 1992). However, in reality banks engage in both relationship lending as well as transactional lending. Boot and Thakor (2000) describe a model in which the banks and capital markets coexist, and banks may engage in relationship or transactional loans. A central result of their model is that there exists a critical level of borrower quality below which a bank would choose to provide relationship loans. For higher quality borrowers, the bank would offer transactional loans. If relationship loans are marked by lower spreads as argued in our Hypothesis 1 above, and the effect is greater for firms that are more informationally opaque as implied by Hypothesis 2, Boot and Thakor's (2000) model implies a third possible way to test for the impact of informational asymmetries among lenders and borrowers. In particular, we can estimate the critical point, in terms of borrower quality (i.e., *observable* measures of risk such as credit ratings and firm size), where there is a switch from relationship lending to transactional lending. The various measures of information opacity outlined earlier allow us to estimate the delineation point across different borrower characteristics (such as size) where the benefits of relationship borrowing (if any) become insignificant. We test the following hypothesis, which is conditional on finding a net relationship benefit effect.

Hypothesis 3 (H3). *There exists a borrower quality above which the benefits of relationships on loan rates are insignificant.*

1.1.2 Additional effect of syndicate moral hazard. Given that a large fraction of our loans are syndicated among multiple lenders, our data allow us to study the interaction of past lending relationships with moral hazard among multiple lenders. Holmstrom and Tirole (1997) show that in a setting that involves multiple lenders and where one lender (of a few) is expected to do the monitoring, the monitoring lender faces significant moral hazard, the intuitive idea being that the monitoring bank bears all the costs but shares only part of the benefits from engaging in such due diligence, and would rationally shirk from putting in the optimum effort. Ex ante, other lenders take these incentives into account and demand a higher rate to compensate them for the anticipated shirking by the monitoring bank.[6] Sufi (2007) tests the above model and finds that loan syndicates are structured to minimize this moral hazard problem. In particular, he finds that lending syndicates tend to be more concentrated and the lead bank retains a higher share of the loan for borrowers requiring high levels of monitoring. Thus, the observed syndicate structure is a reasonable proxy for the syndicate moral hazard faced by the lead bank. We use the two measures of moral hazard used by Sufi (2007), namely the share of loan retained by the lead bank and the Herfindahal index of loan shares. In addition, we also use the size of a syndicate to proxy for moral hazard. If a past lending relationship can be viewed as a commitment to monitor diligently future loans (and this commitment arises because the relationship bank faces a lower ongoing cost of monitoring than a comparable nonrelationship bank), its presence would

[6] A somewhat similar issue related to multiple lenders is discussed by Diamond (2004). He shows that for an appropriately structured debt contract, a large syndicate commits each lender in the syndicate to enforce the contract even when such enforcement is costly.

alleviate the moral hazard concerns of the syndicate participants, resulting in lower rates for such loans. Specifically, we test the following hypothesis:

Hypothesis 4 (H4). *Relationship loans would have a lower spread compared to nonrelationship loans in syndicates with high moral hazard.*

1.2 Effect of relationships on nonprice terms

Next, we focus on how nonprice terms are affected by lending relationships. Collateral and duration (maturity) of a loan are considered key loan contract features. We discuss collateral first. The use of collateral in debt contracts has been justified on two grounds: adverse selection and borrower moral hazard. While both arguments rely on information asymmetries, they provide opposite predictions of what type of borrowers would post collateral. The adverse selection models (Bester 1985; Besanko and Thakor 1987) argue that willingness to provide collateral serves as a credible signal of borrower quality. These models predict that better quality (i.e., low credit risk) borrowers would post collateral and obtain lower spreads for the loans. These models suggest that collateral and interest rate are substitute mechanisms. Borrower moral hazard models (Holmstrom and Tirole 1997; Stulz and Johnson 1985; Boot, Thakor, and Udell 1991) stress the ex ante incentives for asset substitution when firms take on risky debt. Holmstrom and Tirole sum it up concisely: "... Firms with low net worth have to turn to financial intermediaries, who can reduce the demand for collateral by monitoring more intensively. Thus, monitoring is a partial substitute for collateral ..." (p. 665). These incentives are strongest for the informationally opaque (presumably perceived as high credit risk) borrowers. In equilibrium, such borrowers can credibly commit to lower asset substitution by providing collateral. Thus, these models predict that the lowest quality borrowers are more likely to be required to provide collateral. However, the focus of our article is not on the determinants of collateral per se, but rather on the impact of relationships on the requirement of collateral. To the extent that relationships reduce adverse selection problems due to lower information asymmetry, the relationship lenders would not require collateral from their borrowers since they are not subject to this problem. On the other hand, if the borrower's moral hazard view of collateral is true (again, viewing relationships as a commitment to monitor), the relationship bank would not require as much collateral as an equivalent nonrelationship bank.[7] Thus, the effect of relationships on collateral is to imply a lower collateral requirement, both due to a reduction in adverse selection and due to a higher commitment to monitor. This yields our next hypothesis:

---

[7] Jiménez, Salas, and Saurina (2006) provide an extensive overview of this literature and provide empirical evidence that lower credit quality firms are significantly more likely to face collateral requirements.

Hypothesis 5 (H5). *The probability of using collateral as a loan contract nonprice term decreases if the loan is provided by a relationship lender.*

We also examine the maturity structure of loan contracts. While Flannery (1986) suggests that debt maturity would increase as borrower quality improves, Diamond (1991) predicts that corporate debt maturity would exhibit a nonmonotonic relationship with borrower quality. One of the central results of Flannery (1986) is that if transaction costs of debt issuance are high enough, borrowers with good future prospects can credibly convey their *unobservable* quality via choice of their debt maturity. Thus, Flannery's model predicts a linear relationship between borrower's unobservable credit quality and debt maturity—the better the (unobservable) future prospects of a firm, the shorter its debt maturity structure. Diamond uses a trade-off between information asymmetries and the liquidity risk of refinancing. On one hand, frequent refinancing necessitated by shorter maturity makes borrowing costs more sensitive to information, which is desirable for high-quality (high credit rating) firms. On the other hand, shorter maturity exposes a borrower to liquidity risk, that is, a temporary shock that can either cause the price of loans to go higher or make financing difficult to obtain. Diamond summarizes the key insight of his model as

> . . . For a borrower with a sufficiently good credit rating, this liquidity risk is outweighed by the effect of expecting future news to be favorable. For borrowers with lower ratings, the liquidity risk outweighs the information effect. . . . However, very low rated borrowers may have no choice but to choose short-term debt, despite the incentives for inefficient liquidation that it gives to lenders. The two types of borrowers that choose primarily short-term debt imply that the chosen debt maturity is not a monotonic function of the borrower's credit rating . . . empirical studies of maturity will measure a mixture of two effects. This could make inferences complicated. . . .

Based on the potential costs of a liquidity shock, Diamond's model predicts that the best quality firms (with high credit ratings) would *demand* short-term maturity debt while intermediate quality firms would opt for long-term debt. The lowest quality borrowers require intense monitoring and would thus be *supplied* with only short-term loans. How do borrowing relationships interact with the effect described above—namely information asymmetry, liquidity risk, as well as the demand-supply effects for higher and lower quality firms? In the model described by Flannery (1986), relationships would lower information asymmetries. As the need to signal quality through debt maturity becomes diminished due to better information sharing, strong relationships should result in longer maturity loans. In Diamond's model, such a reduction in adverse selection problem is only relevant for the high- and intermediate-quality borrowers, since debt maturity for these borrowers is largely demand driven. For high- and medium-quality borrowers, the reduction in information asymmetries due to past relationships leads to two opposing effects: on one hand, better information sharing removes the need to borrow short term to obtain favorable interest rates by the high-quality firms, thus predicting longer maturity for such borrowers. On the other hand, such reduction in information asymmetries also reduces the possibility of inefficient liquidation, which makes the shorter term debt more appealing for both high- and medium-quality firms. For the lowest quality firms, however, debt maturity is largely determined by supply factors. For these borrowers, Diamond's model predicts shorter debt maturity to enable more frequent monitoring by the lender. Past relationships reduce the cost of such frequent monitoring. Thus for low-quality borrowers, relationship lenders would offer shorter maturity since they face a lower monitoring cost. To summarize, the effects of relationships on debt maturity are likely to differ across different classes of borrower quality. This is captured in our next hypothesis:

Hypothesis 6 (H6). *For low-quality firms, relationship banks will commit to monitoring more by providing shorter maturity loans. For medium- and high-quality firms, relationships may either increase or decrease maturity.*

We also examine issues relating to the simultaneity of various loan contract terms in evaluating H5 and H6. Arguably, the interest rate (plus fees for AISD), collateral, and maturity on a loan are determined simultaneously. Most studies on debt contract terms have not considered simultaneity issues directly. We reestimate the relationship between the price and nonprice terms of loans using an IV framework. This approach requires an identification of relevant and valid instruments for collateral, maturity, and spreads. We employ a number of possible instruments to estimate our system and discuss them in Section 3.9.

A number of studies have documented the positive association between the length of a banking relationship and the availability of credit to a relationship borrower (Petersen and Rajan 1994; Degryse and Van Cayseele 2000). Hoshi, Kashyap, and Scharfstein (1990) report that for a sample of financially distressed Japanese firms, those with strong bank relationships were less likely to be credit constrained compared to the borrowers lacking strong banking relationships. These empirical findings provide support to the argument that a strong banking relationship is likely to increase access to financing for a borrower. As such, relationships reduce lender-borrower information asymmetries and the likelihood of syndicate moral hazard. We employ the size of loan facility (which we scale by either the borrower's assets or its existing long-term debt) as a proxy for access to financing. We formalize this benefit in our next hypothesis:

Hypothesis 7 (H7). *A borrower with a prior relationship with its lender would be able to obtain a larger loan amount compared to a similar borrower that does not have a prior relationship with its lender.*

2. Data and Sample Selection

Data on individual loan facilities is obtained from the Dealscan database maintained by the Loan Pricing Corporation (henceforth LPC).[8] LPC has been collecting information on loans to large U.S. corporations primarily through self-reporting by lenders, SEC filings, and its staff reporters. Strahan (1999) provides a good description of the LPC Dealscan database. While the LPC database provides comprehensive information on loan contract terms (LIBOR spread, maturity, collateral, etc.), it does not provide much information on borrowers. We manually match the borrowers in the LPC database with the merged CRSP and Compustat database following the procedure outlined in Bharath et al. (2007). We then use Compustat to extract data on accounting variables for the given company. We also extract the primary SIC code for the borrowers from Compustat and exclude all financial services firms (SIC codes between 6000 and 6999). To ensure that we only use accounting information that is publicly available at the time of a loan, we employed the following procedure: for those loans made in calendar year t, if the loan activation date is six months or later than the fiscal year ending month in calendar year t, we use the data of that fiscal year. If the loan activation date is less than six months after the fiscal year ending month, we use the data from the fiscal year ending in calendar year $t-1$.

Our sample period is from 1986 to 2003. Over this period, there was an extensive mergers and acquisitions activity in the U.S. banking sector. To construct a chronology of banking M&As, we used the Federal Reserve's National Information Center database and complemented it by hand-matching the data from the SDC mergers and acquisitions database, Lexis-Nexis, and the Hoover's corporate histories database. This allows us to trace lending relationships through time even if the original relationship lender disappears due to a merger or an acquisition.

To examine the impact that prior lending relationships have on the price and other terms of loan, we need to segregate our loans into those that are provided by a relationship lender and those that are provided by a nonrelationship lender. Following Dahiya, Saunders, and Srinivasan (2003), we construct the relationship measures for a particular loan i by searching all the previous loans (over the previous five-year window) of that borrower as recorded in the LPC database. We note the identity of all the *lead banks* on these prior loans, and if at least one of the lead banks for loan i had been a lead lender in the past, we classify loan i as a relationship loan. Since the identification of the "lead" bank (or banks) for a particular loan facility is the basic building block of classifying a loan as relationship or nonrelationship, we present a detailed discussion on this identification below.

[8] The LPC Dealscan database contains the data on loans made to large (mostly publicly traded) U.S. firms. It has been widely employed to study the private debt market. See, for example, Drucker and Puri (2005).

LPC's web-based product called LoanConnector provides a field labeled called "Lead Arranger Credit," which can take values of "Yes" or "No" for every bank. The banks that are classified as a lead-arranger credit hold a large fraction of the loan, on average about 58.88% over the entire sample period. In our examination of the data, we find that for most loans it is a single bank that is accorded the role of lead arranger credit by LPC. Thus, we classify such banks as lead banks. This mitigates the possibility that we may misclassify banks that are not relationship banks but make a large loan commitment. Sufi (2007) uses the field lead-arranger credit as the sole criterion for classifying a bank as a lead bank.

However, we need to account for the possibility that other roles may also represent banks that are also truly in a lead position. Therefore, we examine loan shares retained by banks in all the thirty-eight distinct roles in our sample. We identified the following roles where the bank retained a significant share of the loan (greater than 25%): agent, administrative agent, arranger, lead bank.[9] We designate banks that were retained in any of the above four roles as lead banks. Finally, sole lender transactions by construction have a clearly identified lead bank and we designate it as such. Thus our classification of what constitutes a lead bank is somewhat broader relative to Sufi (2007). For close to 90% of loans in the sample, our methodology results in a single bank being classified as the lead bank. We believe that this approach mitigates the problem of misclassification of relationship lenders.[10]

Next, for every facility, we construct three alternative measures of relationship strength by looking back and searching the past borrowing record of the borrower. We search the previous five years by starting from the activation date of that loan facility.[11] The relationship variable is denoted by *REL*(M), where M is one of the three alternatives measures. In the following paragraphs, we describe the process of constructing these relationship measures using a set of loans obtained by Owens Corning, one of the borrowers in our sample.

In June 1997, Owens Corning borrowed $2 billion from a syndicate of banks. The lead bank for the June 1997 issue was Credit Suisse. It was the only bank that was given lead-arranger credit for this deal. In addition, it was the only bank retained in one of the four roles that was considered to be a lead position. To estimate *REL*(M) for this $2 billion loan, we *look back* on the previous five years of borrowing history of Owens Corning up until the date of this loan to see

[9] The roles have evolved over time. In the early part of the sample, "agent" was frequently used for the lead bank; in the later years, "arranger" and "administrative agent" have become more common.

[10] We see some signs that syndication is becoming a specialist job, separable from being a relationship bank. We did find a new role titled "syndication agent," which appears frequently toward the end of the sample period but does not appear at all in the initial years. We exclude this role from the computation of our relationship measure.

[11] To be classified as either a relationship or a nonrelationship loan, we require that there be at least one loan in the five-year window prior to the loan being classified. If this condition is not met, we exclude the given loan from the sample of classified loans. This approach also implies that the first loan of any firm in the LPC database is not included in our analysis since by construction there can be no prior loans to allow the classification of the first loan as either relationship or nonrelationship.

if the lead bank of the current facility had provided loans in the past five years. LPC reported three loans taken by Owens Corning over this five-year look-back period. In September 1993, it borrowed \$475 million from a syndicate where Credit Suisse was the only bank retained that was given the lead-arranger credit and retained in the role of an agent. It borrowed another \$110 million from a syndicate led by Bank of New York in May 1994, where Bank of New York was given the lead-arranger credit and retained in the role of an agent. Then, in December 1995, it borrowed \$99.6 million where Credit Suisse was given lead-arranger credit and retained in the role of an agent. Thus, looking back from the point of the June 1997 loan, Owens Corning contracted three loans totaling \$684.6 million ($475 + 110 + 99.6$) in the five-year look-back period. Next, we describe the construction of various relationship measures for the June 1997 loan.

The first relationship strength variable is a binary measure of relationship and is designed to pick up the existence of prior lending by the same lender in the past. For a particular bank m, it is denoted by $REL(Dummy)_m$. In our example, *REL(Dummy)* would equal 1 for Credit Suisse. In case there were multiple lead banks retained, we pick the highest value of *REL(Dummy)* for all the lead banks and assign it to the loan. In our example, the June 1997 loan has $REL(Dummy) = 1$.

The other two measures of relationship strength are continuous. The first continuous measure of relationship strength is *REL(Amount)*. For bank m lending to borrower i, it is calculated as

$$REL(Amount)_m = \frac{\text{Amount of loans by bank } m \text{ to borrower } i \text{ in the last 5 years (\$)}}{\text{Total amount of loans by borrower } i \text{ in the last 5 years (\$)}}. \tag{1}$$

Again, this measure is calculated for each of the lead banks and the highest value across all lead banks is used in our analysis. Thus, in the case of the June 1997 loan to Owens Corning, $REL(Amount)_{Credit\ Suisse}$ is 0.84 ($\frac{475+99.6}{684.6}$).

The second continuous measure of relationship strength is *REL(Number)*. For bank m lending to borrower i, it is calculated as

$$REL(Number)_m = \frac{\text{Number of loans by bank } m \text{ to borrower } i \text{ in last 5 years}}{\text{Total number of loans by borrower } i \text{ in last 5 years}}. \tag{2}$$

In our example, *REL(Number)* would be 0.67 (calculated by dividing 2 by 3) for Credit Suisse. For loans with multiple lead banks, the highest *REL(Number)* is used.[12]

[12] To illustrate the process of estimating *REL* for a particular facility with multiple lead lenders, consider a loan facility that we need to assign a relationship measure to. Assume that this loan facility has two lead banks: bank A and bank B. To estimate whether this facility is a relationship loan, we first check the previous five years to see if *either* bank A or bank B has been a lender in the past. If this condition is true, *REL(Dummy)* for this facility

Table 1 provides the descriptive statistics for our data and segregates relationship and nonrelationship loans (i.e., loans from a bank that did not have a past relationship with the borrower). Panel A provides the calendar-time distribution of the loan sample. The low number of observations in the early years is largely due to an improvement in coverage in the LPC database over time.

Panel B of Table 1 illustrates the one-digit SIC classification of the borrowers. There is a strong concentration of loans in the manufacturing sector (SIC codes between 2000 and 3999). Panel C lists the primary purpose of the loan facility contracted, with loans for corporate purposes and debt repayment the most frequently reported purposes.

Following Drucker and Puri (2005), we use the LPC-reported "all-in-spread drawn" (AISD) as the measure of an interest rate for a loan. AISD is the coupon spread over LIBOR on the drawn amount plus the annual fee. Since the interest charged for a loan is affected by various loan-specific characteristics (maturity, loan size, etc.) and borrower-specific characteristics (borrower size, profitability, leverage, etc.), we obtain these variables from LPC and Compustat, respectively.

Table 2 reports the various sample summary statistics. The data are winsorized at the 1% and 99% levels to address the problem of extreme outliers. The median AISD is 212.5 bps. The median loan facility is $50 million. The median book value of assets for our sample of borrowers is $361 million. The high fraction of syndicated loans (79%) reflects the historical focus of LPC on collecting data on large syndicated loans. The average maturity for loan facilities is 43 months (median 36 months).

3. Methodology and Results

3.1 Univariate tests of H1

To examine if repeated borrowing from the same lender(s) affects loan contract terms, we first examine key loan features to see if these are significantly different for relationship versus nonrelationship loans to the borrowers.

In panel A of Table 3, we segregate the entire sample based on the existence of prior relationships to test if the loan contract terms reflect prior lending relationships. In the first column, we report key loan terms for loans taken from nonrelationship lenders. The second column provides the same information for relationship loans. These loan terms include loan price variables: all-in-spread drawn (AISD), all-in-spread-undrawn (AISU), upfront fee, and annual fee.[13]

is assigned the value 1 and 0 otherwise. The estimation of *REL(Number)* (and *REL(Amount)*) requires that we estimate it for both banks. If bank A has been the lead in one out of three loan facilities this borrower obtained in the previous five years, it would imply that *REL(Number)* is 1/3 = 0.333. Now we do the same calculations for bank B: it turns out that bank B has been the lead in two out of the same three loans. In that case, *REL(Number)* is 2/3 = 0.667. We assign the higher value (0.667) as the *REL(Number)* for that facility.

[13] AISU is the spread paid on the *undrawn* loan amount.

Table 1
Descriptive statistics of loan facilities

Panel A: Calendar time distribution of loans

Purpose	No relationship *REL(Dummy)* = 0	Relationship *REL(Dummy)* = 1	Total
1986	1	2	3
1987	68	48	116
1988	217	211	428
1989	252	317	569
1990	242	389	631
1991	276	447	723
1992	363	563	926
1993	412	737	1,149
1994	421	924	1,345
1995	359	1,018	1,377
1996	598	1,110	1,708
1997	618	1,497	2,115
1998	609	1,366	1,975
1999	548	1,272	1,820
2000	519	1,424	1,943
2001	474	1,270	1,744
2002	448	1,135	1,583
2003	375	1,102	1,477
Total	6,800	14,832	21,632

Panel B: Industry classification of borrowers

One-digit SIC code	No relationship *REL(Dummy)* = 0	Relationship *REL(Dummy)* = 1	Total
0	23	54	77
1	372	915	1,287
2	950	2,210	3,160
3	1,706	3,357	5,063
4	682	1,820	2,502
5	895	1,928	2,823
7	602	1,360	1,962
8	229	539	768
9	31	40	71
Total	5,490	12,223	17,713

Panel C: Loan purpose

Purpose	No relationship *REL(Dummy)* = 0	Relationship *REL(Dummy)* = 1	Total
Acquisition line	268	646	914
Corporate purposes	1,973	3,974	5,947
CP backup	190	1,483	1,673
Debt repayment	1,599	3,906	5,505
Debtor-in-possession	98	197	295
LBO/MBO	339	304	643
Recapitalization	165	297	462
Takeover	735	1,621	2,356
Working capital	1,066	1,813	2,879
Other	366	590	956
Total	6,799	14,831	21,630

Panels A through C provide the descriptive statistics for the sample of loan facilities. The statistics are reported separately for loans from relationship lenders *REL(Dummy)* = 1 and loans from nonrelationship lenders *REL(Dummy)* = 0. For any particular loan facility, *REL(Dummy)* equals 1 if any of the lead lenders for that loan facility had been a lead lender on any loans to that borrower in the five years preceding the loan facility.

Table 2
Summary statistics for key loan and borrower characteristics

Variable	*N*	Mean	Std. dev.	Min.	25th percentile	Median	75th percentile	Max
Panel A: Loan characteristics								
AISD (basis points)	26,955	216.63	139.89	17.50	100.00	212.50	300.00	630.00
AISU (basis points)	15,265	33.38	23.45	4.00	15.00	30.00	50.00	125.00
Fee upfront (basis points)	8,969	66.37	72.94	2.50	20.00	50.00	100.00	315.00
Fees annual (basis points)	6,634	19.52	25.63	1.33	7.50	12.50	24.50	100.00
Loan facility amount ($ millions)	31,384	190.0	500.0	0.5	13.0	50.0	180.0	2000.0
Maturity of loan (months)	28,335	43.2	28.36	3	17	36	60	120
Collateral	19,813	0.82	0.39	0.0	1.0	1.0	1.0	1.0
Syndicate	31,387	0.79	0.41	0.0	1.0	1.0	1.0	1.0
Panel B: Borrower characteristics								
Borrower assets ($ millions)	23,679	2,941.4	11,279.0	6.6	93.3	360.4	1,623.5	38,750.0
Coverage	22,604	40.18	731.51	0	2.4	4.83	10.05	309.40
Leverage	23,490	0.25	0.19	0	0.08	0.23	0.37	0.82
Profitability	23,838	0.14	0.13	0	0.06	0.12	0.19	0.62
Tangibility	23,596	0.34	0.23	0.02	0.16	0.29	0.50	0.90
Current ratio	22,578	2.08	2.50	0.32	1.14	1.66	2.41	8.86
Market-to-book	23,463	1.75	1.45	0.66	1.09	1.36	1.90	7.22
Investment grade	8,590	0.50	0.50	0.0	0.0	0.0	1.0	1.0
Not rated	31,387	0.73	0.45	0.0	0.0	1.0	1.0	1.0

The table provides summary statistics of various loan and borrower characteristics. Panel A reports key characteristics of the loan facilities, and panel B reports the same for borrower characteristics. AISD is the "all-in-spread drawn," which is the all-inclusive cost of a drawn loan to the borrower. This equals the coupon spread over LIBOR on the drawn amount plus the annual fee and is reported in basis points. Loan Facility Size is the dollar amount of loan facility in millions. AISU is the fee charged on the undrawn loan amounts. AISD, AISU, and Annual Fee are reported in basis points. Maturity is length in months between facility activation date and maturity date. Syndicate, Collateral, and Investment Grade are the percentage of facilities that have the stated attribute. To be classified as Investment Grade, the loan has to be rated BBB or above by S&P and zero otherwise. The descriptive statistics for Investment Grade are estimated for the subset of firms that are rated. Asset is the book value of assets of the borrower as reported in Compustat. Leverage is the ratio of book value of total debt to book value of total assets. Coverage is the ratio of EBITDA to interest expenses. Profitability is the ratio of EBITDA to sales. Tangibility is the ratio of NPPE to total assets. Current ratio is the ratio of current assets to current liabilities. Market-to-book is the ratio of (book value of assets − book value of equity + market value of equity) to the book value of assets. All values are winsorized at the 1% and 99% levels.

Table 3
Key price and nonprice loan contract terms—relationship vs. nonrelationship loans

	No relationship *REL(Dummy)* = 0 (A)	Relationship *REL(Dummy)* = 1 (B)	t-statistic (A)-(B) (z-statistic for Wilcoxon's sum test)
	Panel A: Loan characteristics		
AISD (bps)	238.97	187.47	23.86***
	(250.00)	(175.00)	(23.08***)
AISU (bps)	37.36	30.22	14.56***
	(37.50)	(25.00)	(17.43***)
Upfront fee (bps)	76.75	53.16	12.15***
	(50.00)	(30.00)	(14.58***)
Annual fee (bps)	23.52	17.07	8.16***
	(12.50)	(12.50)	(6.12***)
Facility size ($ millions)	125.00	271.00	−18.56***
	(40.00)	(100.00)	(−34.89***)
Maturity (months)	44.84	42.35	5.84***
	(36.00)	(36.00)	(5.02***)
Collateral	0.84	0.77	10.43***
	(1.00)	(1.00)	(10.38***)
Syndicate	0.78	0.90	−22.95***
	(1.00)	(1.00)	(−22.68***)
	Panel B: Borrower characteristics		
Total assets ($ millions)	2125.67	4074.99	−10.00***
	(279.82)	(714.03)	(−26.94***)
Coverage=(EBITDA/Interest)	36.64	33.50	0.27
	(4.38)	(5.06)	(−10.04***)
Leverage=LT Debt/Total assets	0.25	0.27	−7.24***
	(0.23)	(0.26)	(−8.59***)
Profitability=EBITDA/Sales	0.14	0.16	−9.69***
	(0.11)	(0.13)	(−13.08***)
Tangibility=NPPE/Total Assets	0.35	0.35	−2.30**
	(0.29)	(0.30)	(−10.80***)
Current ratio=CA/CL	1.96	1.90	2.50**
	(1.64)	(1.58)	(17.92***)
Market-to-book	1.68	1.73	−2.15**
	(1.31)	(1.39)	(−8.55***)
Investment grade	0.42	0.51	−6.22***
	0.00	1.00	(−6.20***)
Not rated	0.75	0.62	19.86***
	1.00	1.00	(19.68***)

Panel A segregates the entire sample into nonrelationship (*REL(Dummy)* = 0) and relationship (*REL(Dummy)* = 1) loans. The first two columns report the mean (medians in parentheses) values for various price and nonprice terms of loan contract. Panel B provides similar details for borrower-specific characteristics. The last column provides the t-statistic for difference in means (z-statistic for Wilcoxon's rank sum test). All values are winsorized at the 1% and 99% levels. ***, **, and * denote significance at the 1%, 5%, and 10% levels, respectively.

Other loan-specific features reported include loan facility size, maturity, and collateral (denoted as percentage of facilities secured). The last column reports the differences in mean (median) loan characteristics between relationship and nonrelationship loans. The results of univariate tests of differences in means and medians provide strong evidence that relationship loans enjoy significantly better loan price terms, as well as nonprice terms such as loan size and collateral requirement. Comparing AISD (the most comprehensive measure of the borrowing cost) for a company borrowing from a relationship lender, we find that on average, AISD is 52 bps lower compared to a borrower that does not have a prior relationship with the lender. This difference is significant at the 1% level.

AISU, upfront fees, and annual fees are all lower for relationship borrowers, and the difference is significant at the 1% level. Results for nonprice loan terms show similar effects. Typically, loans to relationship borrowers are less likely to be secured and are larger on average. Again these differences are significant at the 1% level and economically large. Thus, the price effects documented in the univariate tests are more consistent with the relationship benefit effect than "lock-in" effects.

While the univariate tests provide preliminary evidence that borrowers derive significant benefits from having strong relationships with their lenders, these results do not take into account potentially significant differences in borrower characteristics between the relationship borrower and nonrelationship borrower groups. It is likely that the relationship borrowers have fundamentally different characteristics. For example, banks may prefer to maintain relationships with borrowers with a track record of strong financial performance. To determine if borrowers using relationship lenders obtain better loan terms, we must first test whether the characteristics of the two groups (relationship and nonrelationship borrowers) are different, and whether these differences explain the difference observed in loan features across these two groups. We compare the borrower characteristics in the two groups. The results are reported in panel B of Table 3. The average size (as measured by the book value of assets) of a relationship borrower ($4,075 million) is almost twice the average size of a nonrelationship borrower ($2,126 million). This difference in size is significant at the 1% level. Firms borrowing from relationship banks also differ from those borrowing from nonrelationship banks across measures of leverage and profitability. For example, firms borrowing from relationship lenders have a higher EBITDA to sales ratio (16% versus 14%), higher long-term debt to assets ratio (27% versus 25%), and lower current ratios (1.90 versus 1.96). The higher leverage and lower current ratios of relationship borrowers suggest that these borrowers have better access to bank loans. Relationship loans are also more likely to have a credit rating and more likely to have an investment grade rating. These differences between the two borrower groups are statistically significant at the 1% level. Tests for difference in medians provide qualitatively similar results.

While the results of univariate tests suggest that firms benefit significantly by borrowing from relationship banks, these results also show that some of the key borrower characteristics that influence the cost of loans are systematically different across the relationship and nonrelationship borrowers. Consequently, we employ multivariate tests to better distinguish between relationship and performance effects on borrowing costs.

3.2 Multivariate tests of H1

Since the cost of borrowing is likely to depend on various loan-specific features such as loan size, maturity, etc., as well as on a borrower's historical performance, we use a regression model of the following form:

$$AISD = \beta_0 + \beta_1(REL(M)) + \sum \beta_i(Loan\_Characteristics_i) + \sum \beta_j(Borrower\_Characteristics_j) + \sum \beta_k(Control_k). \quad (3)$$

The variables are defined below:

- AISD: the dependent variable is "all-in-spread drawn" (AISD), which equals the coupon spread over LIBOR on the drawn amount plus the annual fee.
- *REL(M)*: this is the measure of relationship strength constructed by looking back and searching the past borrowing record of the borrower. As discussed earlier, we construct three different specifications for this variable.
- $Loan\_Characteristics_i$: various characteristics of loan facility are as described below:
  - LOG(MATURITY): the natural log of maturity of loan facility in months.
  - LOG(LOAN SIZE): the natural log of loan facility amount adjusted for inflation in year 2000 dollars.
  - COLLATERAL: a dummy variable that equals 1 if the loan facility was secured and 0 otherwise.
- $Borrower\_Characteristics_j$: various characteristics of the borrower are as described below:
  - LOG(ASSETS): the natural log of the book value of the assets of the borrower adjusted for inflation in year 2000 dollars. This controls for cross-sectional variation in borrower size in our sample.
  - LEVERAGE: ratio of the book value of total debt to the book value of assets.
  - LOG(1+COVERAGE): calculated as natural log of ratio $(1 + \frac{EBITDA}{Interest\ expenses})$.
  - PROFITABILITY: ratio of EBITDA to sales.
  - TANGIBILITY: ratio of property, plant, and equipment (PPE) to total assets.
  - CURRENT RATIO: ratio of current assets to current liabilities.
  - MARKET TO BOOK: calculated as the ratio of (book value of assets − book value of equity + market value of equity) to book value of assets.
- $Control_k$: these are other control variables and include dummy variables for the year of the loan facility, loan purpose, loan type, S&P senior unsecured debt rating with not-rated firms considered as a separate group, and the industry of the borrower (one-digit SIC code).

The results of this regression (Equation (3)) using *REL(M)* as the relationship measure are reported in Table 4. Regardless of which measure is used, the

Table 4
Effect of lending relationships on cost of borrowing

	(1)	(2)	(3)	(4)
Const.	903.21***	904.42***	903.82***	331.57***
	(22.76)	(22.95)	(22.89)	(19.40)
REL(Dummy)	−10.55***			−11.15***
	(2.44)			(2.47)
REL(Number)		−9.94***		
		(2.72)		
REL(Amount)			−10.15***	
			(2.68)	
Log(Maturity)	−18.07***	−17.91***	−17.95***	−18.58***
	(2.54)	(2.54)	(2.54)	(2.46)
Collateral	60.01***	59.99***	59.99***	58.82***
	(2.87)	(2.87)	(2.87)	(2.70)
Default spread				34.47***
				(1.90)
Log(Loan size)	−16.17***	−16.17***	−16.05***	−16.07***
	(1.56)	(1.55)	(1.55)	(1.23)
Log(Assets)	−9.71***	−10.06***	−10.05***	−9.55***
	(1.57)	(1.56)	(1.56)	(1.16)
Log(1+Coverage)	−23.91***	−23.93***	−23.91***	−24.19***
	(1.69)	(1.70)	(1.70)	(1.56)
Leverage	21.63**	21.21**	21.44**	23.92***
	(8.73)	(8.71)	(8.72)	(7.98)
Profitability	−44.03***	−43.68***	−44.00***	−41.86***
	(13.65)	(13.64)	(13.62)	(11.29)
Tangibility	−12.00*	−11.78*	−11.81*	−13.31**
	(6.73)	(6.76)	(6.76)	(5.29)
Current ratio	−2.71***	−2.71***	−2.71***	−2.45***
	(0.74)	(0.74)	(0.74)	(0.71)
Market-to-book	−1.13	−1.12	−1.12	−1.95**
	(0.96)	(0.96)	(0.96)	(0.92)
Obs.	13,158	13,158	13,158	13,158
R^2	0.57	0.57	0.57	0.56

The table provides the OLS estimates (corrected for heteroscedasticity and clustering) of the following equation:

$$AISD = \beta_0 + \beta_i(REL(M)) + \sum \beta_i(Loan\_Characteristics_i) + \sum \beta_j(Borrower\_Characteristics_j) + \sum \beta_k(Control_k).$$

The dependent variable AISD is the coupon spread over LIBOR on the drawn amount plus the annual fee in bps. *REL(M)* is the measure of relationship strength, estimated in three different ways: *REL(Dummy)* (1 if there is a relationship with any of the lead banks in the last five years before the present loan and 0 otherwise), *REL(Number)* (ratio of number of deals with the lead bank(s) to total number of loans borrowed by the firm in the last five years before the current loan), and *REL(Amount)* (ratio of the dollar value of deals with the lead bank(s) to the total dollar value of loans borrowed by the firm in the last five years before the current loan). For a facility with multiple lead banks, the maximum *REL(M)* value among all the lead banks is used. Maturity is the length in months between facility activation date and maturity date. Loan amount is the loan facility size in millions of real year 2000 dollars. Collateral is a dummy variable that equals 1 if the facility has the stated attribute and 0 otherwise. Log(Assets) is the natural log of book value of assets in real year 2000 dollars of the borrower as reported in Compustat. Leverage is the ratio of the book value of total debt to the book value of assets. Coverage is the ratio of EBITDA to interest expenses. Profitability is the ratio of EBITDA to sales. Tangibility is the ratio of NPPE to total assets. Current ratio is the ratio of current assets to current liabilities. Market-to-book is the ratio of (book value of assets − book value of equity+market value of equity) to the book value of assets. In addition to the variables reported, the regression also includes industry dummies based on the one-digit SIC code of the borrower, dummies for stated purpose of the facility, dummies for loan type, calendar year dummies, and dummies for the credit rating of the borrower, with not-rated firms considered a separate group. Numbers in parentheses are standard errors corrected for heteroscedasticity and firm-level clustering. Clustering at the deal level produces similar results. ***, **, and * denote significance at the 1%, 5%, and10% levels, respectively.

coefficient on the relationship variable is negative and significant at the 1% level. Standard errors used to assess significance are corrected for heteroscedasticity and firm-level clustering (Rogers 1993).[14] Holding all else constant, the cost of borrowing from a relationship lender is lower by almost 10 bps compared to borrowing from a nonrelationship lender. Given our univariate tests that show an approximately 50 bps difference between relationship and nonrelationship borrowers, the multivariate result implies that the relationship variable alone accounts for roughly 20% of that difference. As foreshadowed in our univariate results, the cross-sectional differences in borrower characteristics (relationship versus nonrelationship) explain much of the variation observed in spreads charged by lenders. For example, holding all else constant, a borrower at the 75th percentile of size (as measured by the book value of assets) would on average pay approximately 70 bps lower on a similar loan compared to a borrower at the 25th percentile of size. As expected, lower leverage, higher profitability, and higher current ratio are associated with significantly lower spreads charged on loans.

Interestingly, the negative (and significant) coefficient for maturity and the positive (significant) coefficient for collateral are inconsistent with the notion that these nonprice terms can be used as trade-off features for price terms. These results, however, conform with those reported by Berger and Udell (1990), who also find that borrowers that are required to post collateral are also more likely to be paying higher spreads.

In the first three columns of Table 4, we use year dummies to control for calendar-time effect, and in column 4, instead of year dummies we include the prevailing market default spread at the time of the loan. The default spread is measured as the difference between the yield on Moody's seasoned corporate bonds with a Baa rating and ten-year U.S. government bonds. In this specification, the coefficient for *REL(Dummy)* is −11.15 and is significant at the 1% level. The coefficient for default spread prevailing at the time of the loan is 34.47 and is also significant (at the 1% level).

3.2.1 Other robustness tests. We check the robustness of our results by reestimating our main specification (Equation (3)) in different ways. First, we drop all loan facilities classified as 364-day facilities in calculating *REL(Dummy)*.[15] These facilities arguably exist only because of bank capital regulation, and the set of borrowers that use them may be systematically different than other borrowers. The coefficient for the revised *REL(Dummy)* is now −10.25 (significant at the 1% level). This estimate is virtually identical to the original estimate of −10.55. In another exercise, we drop all loan facilities that appear

[14] Some loan facilities make up a single deal. Our analysis is done at the facility level. We also verified that clustering at the deal level produces similar results.

[15] All our results are robust to using *REL(Number)* or *REL(Amount)* in these tests, as well as all subsequent tests in the article. To conserve space, we do not report these results in detail, but they are available on request.

to be amendments of existing facilities, likely to be initiated by a borrower with improving credit prospects.[16] The coefficient for *REL(Dummy)* is now -12.80, which is significant at the 1% level.[17]

Overall, the multivariate results show that even after controlling for various loan, market, and borrower-specific characteristics, borrowing from relationship lenders is associated with significantly lower spreads, consistent with relationships providing benefits to borrowers.[18]

3.3 Endogeneity of relationship formation

3.3.1 Propensity score matching tests. A basic drawback of our relationship measure is that the decision to form a relationship or to break a relationship may be endogenous. The decision to form and stay in a relationship is to a certain extent determined by the borrower, which in turn is likely to be related to observed firm characteristics such as borrower size. Ideally, one would like to run an experiment with pairs of matched firms that are identical in all respects except relationships. One firm in each pair would borrow from a relationship lender while the other borrows from a nonrelationship lender. The observed difference in loan rates across all pairs would then be a robust estimate of the effect of past relationships on loan rates. While such an experiment is not feasible, econometric techniques can provide good matched samples based on observable characteristics. We employ the propensity score matching (PSM) technique described by Heckman, Ichimura, and Todd (1997, 1998). This methodology has been used by Drucker and Puri (2005), among others, in recent studies. Essentially, this technique estimates the predicted probability of group membership (e.g., probability of being in the treatment group versus the control group in a clinical drug trial) based on observed characteristics using a probit model. In our case, for each loan we use a number of loan and borrower characteristics to generate the probability of that loan being obtained from a relationship lender. Specifically, we estimate a probit model of the

[16] We searched the amendment comment field of every loan facility in the Dealscan database to check if the facility was an amended facility.

[17] These robustness results are available on request.

[18] A possible alternative explanation of our findings is that observed reduction in spreads simply reflects the lower transaction costs of lending to the same firm. If transaction costs are the sole determinant of relationship cost savings, then these savings should depend on the time elapsed between the current loan and the previous loan. Arguably, transaction cost savings are highest for loans that are made frequently and when the time between successive loans is short. Thus, the benefits of repeated borrowing should dissipate as the time from the first loan increases or if the loans are infrequent. For each loan in our sample, we create two measures to capture this idea of time between loans and frequency of loans. *Loan Index* equals the number of loans obtained by the borrower prior to the current loan. *Time to Last Loan* is the time measured in months between the current loan and the most recent loan. If the benefit of repeated borrowing from the same lender is due to reduced transaction costs, we should expect the benefits to decline as both *Loan Index* and *Time to Last Loan* increase. Specifically, if we interact the *REL* and one of these measures of time between loans, we should expect a positive and significant coefficient for the interaction term. On the other hand, if these benefits represent an enduring information advantage due to close relationships, the interaction term should be insignificant. To conserve space, we do not report the results of these specifications. We find that the interaction term is insignificant for both *Loan Index* and *Time to Last Loan*. This suggests that the benefits of lower spreads for repeated borrowing from the same lender are unlikely to be driven solely by lower transaction costs.

following form:

$$REL = \beta_0 + \sum \beta_i(Loan\_Characteristics_i) + \\ + \sum \beta_j(Borrower\_Characteristics_j) + \sum \beta_k(Control_k). \quad (4)$$

The dependent variable is *REL*, a dummy variable that equals 1 if there is a past relationship with any of the lead banks in the last five years before the present loan and 0 otherwise. The loan characteristics include log of loan size, and dummy variables for the type and purpose of the loan. Borrower characteristics include log of assets, profitability, tangibility, leverage, interest coverage, current ratio, market-to-book ratio, and borrower rating. Other controls include the one-digit SIC code of the borrower, term spread, and default spreads prevailing at the time of the loan origination. For each loan, we estimate predicted probability (i.e., propensity score) of it being a relationship loan. We then match each relationship loan with a set of nonrelationship loans that have propensity scores similar to that of the relationship loan. Heckman, Ichimura, and Todd (1997, 1998) describe the matched estimators we use. The NEAREST NEIGHBOR estimator chooses for each relationship loan, the n loans with closest propensity scores, and uses the arithmetic average of the AISD of n nonrelationship loans. (We use $n = 10$ and $n = 50$.) The GAUSSIAN and EPANECHNIKOV estimators use a weighted average of nonrelationship loans, with more weight given to nonrelationship loans with propensity scores that are closer to the relationship loan propensity scores. The GAUSSIAN estimator uses all nonrelationship loans, while for the EPANECHNIKOV estimator, we specify a propensity score bandwidth (h) that limits the sample of nonrelationship loans to be used for comparison. We specify that $h = 0.01$.

We report our results in Table 5, panel A. In column 1, we compute the mean AISD difference between relationship loans and nonrelationship loans by using the propensity score estimators to match them. Across all four matching specifications (NEAREST NEIGHBOR ($n = 10$), NEAREST NEIGHBOR ($n = 50$), GAUSSIAN, and EPANECHNIKOV), we find that spreads on relationship loans are 11–12 bps lower. These differences are significant at the 1% level (t-ratios are estimated using standard errors obtained by bootstrapping with fifty replications).

While column 1 of Table 5 provides estimates of relationship effects that are robust to endogeneity issues, we also need to address an additional concern. The group of loans we classify as nonrelationship loans includes two distinct subgroups. The first subgroup includes borrowers that had a prior lending relationship, but for the loan being classified, chose (or were forced) to obtain it from a nonrelationship lender. Such a loan denotes a break-up of an existing relationship. A second subgroup consists of loans where the borrower never formed a relationship in the past. Arguably these two types of nonrelationship loans may carry significantly different loan rates. For example, the decision

Lending Relationships and Loan Contract Terms

Table 5
Endogeneity of lending relationships

Panel A: Propensity score matching estimation

Estimator	1	2	3
NEAREST NEIGHBOR	−12.27***	−13.65***	−7.69
($n = 10$)	(2.93)***	(2.64)	(4.77)
NEAREST NEIGHBOR	−10.94***	−12.52***	−7.02*
($n = 50$)	(2.44)	(2.41)	(4.25)
GAUSSIAN	−11.16***	−12.56***	−8.64**
	(2.37)	(1.84)	(3.85)
EPANECHNIKOV	−10.95***	−12.53***	−7.82**
	(2.49)	(1.83)	(3.55)

Panel B: Instrumental variables regression estimation of effect of relationship on AISD

First Stage Regression		Instrumental variables estimation	OLS	IV
Constant	−4.552***	Constant	331.57***	422.16***
	(0.001)		(19.40)	(23.80)
Log(1+distance)	−0.058***	*REL(Dummy)*	−11.15***	−56.90**
	(0.011)		(2.47)	(25.14)
Log(Assets)	−0.002	Log(Maturity)	−18.58***	−15.40***
	(0.015)		(2.46)	(2.32)
Log(Loan size)	0.175***	Collateral	58.82***	71.41***
	(0.015)		(2.70)	(3.25)
Profitability	−0.108	Default spread	34.47***	35.71***
	(0.168)		(1.90)	(2.50)
Tangibility	−0.083	Log(Loan size)	−16.07***	−11.63***
	(0.082)		(1.23)	(2.01)
Leverage	0.443***	Log(Assets)	−9.55***	−12.59***
	(0.098)		(1.16)	(1.49)
Log(1+Coverage)	0.096***	Log(1+Coverage)	−24.19***	−24.12***
	(0.016)		(1.56)	(2.12)
Current ratio	0.010	Leverage	23.92***	55.56***
	(0.010)		(7.98)	(11.07)
Market-to-book	−0.007	Profitability	−41.86***	−57.85***
	(0.011)		(11.296)	(15.77)
Observations	16,074	Tangibility	−13.31**	−20.14***
Pseudo R^2	0.086		(5.29)	(7.27)
		Current ratio	−2.45***	−1.70**
			(0.71)	(0.80)
		Market-to-book	−1.95**	−3.23***
			(0.92)	(1.02)
		Obs.	13,158	13,158
		R^2	0.56	0.49
		First-stage F-statistic		128.18***

Panel C: Treatment effects model

	Relationship	AISD
Constant	−0.22	397.62***
	(0.33)	(18.05)
REL(Dummy)		−16.91***
		(4.07)
Log(1+Distance)	−0.055***	
	(0.01)	
Default spread	0.05*	35.86***
	(0.03)	(2.46)
Log(Loan size)	0.14***	−15.01***
	(0.02)	(1.47)

(continued overleaf)

Table 5
(Continued)

Panel C: Treatment effects model

	Relationship	AISD
Log(Assets)	0.04**	−12.19***
	(0.02)	(1.45)
Log(1+Coverage)	0.11***	−25.81***
	(0.02)	(1.86)
Leverage	0.559***	45.86***
	(0.11)	(9.67)
Profitability	−0.16	−57.34***
	(0.19)	(15.53)
Tangibility	−0.15*	−17.13**
	(0.09)	(7.17)
Current ratio	0.01	−1.81**
	(0.01)	(0.79)
Market-to-book	0.003	−3.13***
	(0.01)	(1.03)
Log(Maturity)		−12.79***
		(1.73)
Collateral		72.07***
		(3.04)
Obs.	13,158	13,158
ρ	0.042	
LR test of $\rho = 0 \chi^2(1) = 4.84$		
Probability $> \chi^2 = 0.028$		

Panel A reports the average difference in AISD of (i) relationship loans and nonrelationship loans; (ii) relationship loans and loans by borrowers who had lending relationships in the past but obtained the loan from a nonrelationship lender; and (iii) relationship loans and loans by borrowers who had no prior lending relationships. AISD is the coupon spread on the drawn amount plus the annual fee in bps. To examine mean AISD spread differences, we control for various borrower and lender characteristics. We compute propensity scores using the following probit model:

$$REL = \beta_0 + \sum \beta_i(Loan\_Characteristics_i) + \sum \beta_j(Borrower\_Characteristics\, j) + \sum \beta_k(Control_k).$$

The dependent variable is *REL(Dummy)*, a dummy variable that equals 1 if there is a past relationship with any of the lead banks in the last five years before the present loan and 0 otherwise. The loan characteristics include log of loan size, and dummy variables for the type and purpose of the loan. Borrower characteristics include log of assets, profitability, tangibility, leverage, interest coverage, current ratio, market-to-book ratio, and borrower rating. Other controls include one-digit SIC code of the borrower, term spread, and default spreads prevailing at the time of the loan origination. We use the following four estimators. The NEAREST NEIGHBOR estimator chooses for each relationship loan the n nonrelationship loans with closest propensity scores, and uses the arithmetic average of AISD for these loans. We use $n =$ 10 and $n = 50$. The GAUSSIAN and EPANECHNIKOV estimators use a weighted average of AISD of nonrelationship loans, with more weight given to nonrelationship loans with propensity scores that are closer to the relationship loan's propensity score. The GAUSSIAN estimator uses all the matched non-relationship loans, while for the EPANECHNIKOV estimator, we specify a propensity score bandwidth (h) that limits the sample of nonrelationship loans. We specify that $h = 0.01$. In column (1), we compute mean difference in AISD between relationship loans and nonrelationship loans by using the estimators to match relationship loans to nonrelationship loans. In column (2), we compute the mean difference in AISD between relationship loans and only those nonrelationship loans where the borrower had a relationship but chose to obtain the loan from a nonrelationship lender. In column (3), we compute the mean difference in AISD between relationship loans and only those nonrelationship loans where the borrowers did not have a past relationship. For all estimations, we present the sample averages. We report standard errors in parentheses that are computed by bootstrapping with fifty replications. Panel B provides the results of an instrumental variables (IV) estimation with log(1+distance) as an instrument for relationship. Distance is the spherical distance between the lead lender and the borrower. Panel C reports the results of a Treatment Effects Model. This table provides the results of the Treatment Effects Model using the following model:

$$\begin{aligned} AISD_i &= \beta_0 + \beta_1 Rel_i + \sum \beta_k (Control)_k + \epsilon_i \\ Rel_i^* &= \gamma_0 + \gamma_i log(1 + distance)_i + \sum \beta_j (Control)_j + u_i, \end{aligned}$$

where the observed decision is $Rel_i = 1$ if $Rel_i^* > 0$ and 0 otherwise, where ϵ and u are assumed to have a bivariate distribution with correlation ρ. The first column reports the estimation of relationship. The second column reports the estimation of effect of relationship on AISD. In addition to the variables reported, the regression also includes controls for the one-digit SIC code of the borrower, stated purpose of the facility, loan type, time, and credit rating of the borrower. ***, **, and * indicate significantly different than zero at the 1%, 5%, and 10% levels, respectively.

to switch or break up an existing relationship presents the new lender with an adverse selection problem (Detragiache, Garella, and Guiso 2000) and may result in higher loan spreads. To examine this issue in more detail, we divide our sample of nonrelationship loans into "break-ups" and "non-break-ups." For every nonrelationship loan, we look back on the most recent loan. If the most recent loan was a relationship loan, we classify the loan currently being examined as a break-up. If the prior loan was also a nonrelationship loan, we classify the loan currently being examined as a non-break-up.[19]

In column 2 of Table 5, we compute the mean AISD difference between relationship loans and only those nonrelationship loans where the borrower had a relationship but chooses to obtain the loan from a nonrelationship lender, thus breaking its existing relationship. In column 3, we compute mean AISD difference between relationship loans and only those nonrelationship loans where the borrowers did not have a past relationship. The benefit of maintaining a relationship versus breaking it is almost 13 bps and significant at the 1% level across all four specifications (column 2). The difference in spreads from borrowers who choose to stay in relationships compared to those borrowers who do not form relationships is lower (about 8 bps) and also significant (column 3).

Check for reliability of the PSM results. PSM estimators are not consistent estimators for treatment effects if the assignment to treatment is endogenous, i.e., if unobserved variables that affect the assignment process are also related to the outcomes. Also, the matching method is based on the conditional independence or unconfoundedness assumption, which states that the researcher should observe all variables simultaneously influencing the participation decision (propensity to form relationships, the treatment) and outcome variables (spreads). This is a strong identifying assumption and should be justified. If there are unobserved variables that simultaneously affect assignment to the treatment and the outcome variable, a hidden bias might arise to which matching estimators are not robust (Rosenbaum 2002). In order to estimate the extent to which such "selection on unobservables" may bias our qualitative and quantitative inferences about the effects of relationships on loan spreads, we conducted a sensitivity analysis as outlined in Rosenbaum (2002). The details of this analysis are described in the Appendix. Overall, results of this sensitivity analysis suggest that selection on unobservables is unlikely to weaken our results.

3.3.2 Instrumental variables estimation. A potential source of endogeneity is that there may be a common unobserved factor that drives both the formation of a relationship as well as the loan spread. Relationship is the main variable of interest in our empirical model where we seek to explain the cross-sectional

[19] This methodology implies that there would be some nonrelationship loans that cannot be classified into these two subgroups because the most recent loan is the first loan for the borrower in the LPC database and is thus unclassified. We exclude such loans from our analysis.

variation in observed loan spreads (AISD). To the extent that there are other borrower-specific characteristics that we do not control for that may explain both AISD and the existence of a relationship, our coefficient estimates are potentially biased. Unobserved credit quality is a possible factor, in the sense that a bank might tend to form relationships with firms of high credit quality (unobservable to the econometrician). Thus, lower loan spreads on relationship loans might not be because of incremental benefits of relationship lending as we have argued so far. It might simply be the result of the relationship variable proxying for unobservable higher credit quality of the borrower.

One potential solution is to use an instrument that is correlated with the relationship formation but does not affect the loan spreads directly except through relationships. We use the geographic distance between the borrower and its lead lender as an instrument for relationships. A number of papers have argued that information gathering and processing (which are at the heart of relationship lending theories) is more easily done when the physical distance between a lender and a borrower is shorter. For example, Berger et al. (2005b) describe this succinctly: "... being close to one's customers is likely to facilitate a loan officer's collection of soft information.... Being nearby might also help the loan officer to better understand the nuances of local business environment..." (p. 244). Coval and Moskovitz (2001) find that mutual fund managers' investments in firms that are physically close to the fund manager generate significantly higher returns and argue that this may arise due to better information: "Investors located near potential investments may have significant information advantages relative to the rest of the market..." (p. 839). Dass and Massa (forthcoming) also use the same argument of better information gathering/processing for physically closer borrowers and cast their lender-borrower relationship in terms of geographical distance.

These papers suggest that distance is likely to be correlated with propensity to form relationships. Other than its effect through the lending relationship, location should not have any impact on spreads.[20]

For each borrower, information on that firm's headquarters, i.e., city, state, and ZIP code, is taken from Compustat. For each loan, we locate the city in which the borrower has its headquarters and find the latitude and longitude of the city. We do a similar exercise for the headquarters of the lead bank.

With the longitude and latitude data for both the lender and the borrower, one can calculate the spherical distance between the two.[21] As discussed in Petersen and Rajan (2002), we use log(1+distance) to address the skewness in the distance variable. In the first-stage regression, we examine the determinants of a loan being a relationship or a nonrelationship loan. The results of this

[20] Shorter distance from the borrower increases the likelihood that lender and borrower would match up in the first place, leading to relationship formation. Lower costs of screening and monitoring a physically close borrower are probably the key driver of relationships formation, which in turn affects the spreads charged.

[21] Both Coval and Moskovitz (2001) and Dass and Massa (forthcoming) provide details of the estimating formula. We use the same methodology.

first-stage probit model are provided in panel B of Table 5. We argue that the propensity of forming a relationship would decrease as the physical distance between the borrower and the lender increases. Consistent with this, we find that the coefficient for log(1+distance) is negative (−0.058) and significant at the 1% level. These results suggest that log(1+distance) appears to be sufficiently correlated with relationships formation to be a viable instrument.

Since the dependent variable in the first stage *(REL)* is a binary variable, the first-stage probit is used to estimate the predicted probability of forming a relationship and this predicted probability is used as an instrument in the second-stage estimation. Wooldridge (2002) shows that this approach yields consistent coefficients, as well as correct standard errors. Panel B of Table 5 also provides the results of our IV regression. The first-stage F-statistic is 128.18 and rejects the null that the coefficients on the instruments are insignificantly different from zero, at the 1% level.

We reproduce the OLS estimates (from Table 4, column 4 in the article) and the IV results in panel B of Table 5. The coefficient of relationship is −56.90 (significant at the 5% level). Thus, the effect of relationship on loan spreads is about five times higher when it is instrumented using log(1+distance). Berger et al. (2005b) also use IV regressions to examine the impact of bank size on the exclusivity of bank-borrower relationships. Using instruments for bank size, they also find a large increase in coefficient for bank size compared to OLS estimates (approximately 5.5 times). The results of our IV regression suggest that relationships are associated with significant reduction in spreads for borrowers.

3.3.3 Treatment effects model. The unverifiable assumption in an IV estimation is that the instrument is uncorrelated with the error term in the outcome equation. Empirically, there is no way to prove that the instrument is not correlated with the error term, since the error is by definition unobservable. To assess the robustness of our conclusions from our IV tests, we employ an additional empirical strategy that involves estimating the effect of an endogenously chosen binary variable (relationship or nonrelationship) on another endogenous variable, which is continuous (AISD), conditional on two sets of independent variables. Our set-up can also be addressed using the treatment effects model as described in Maddala (1983) and Greene (2000). We can write this as

$$AISD_i = \mathbf{x}_i \beta + \delta REL_i + \epsilon_i . \tag{5}$$

Since REL_i is the endogenous variable, the binary decision to borrow from the relationship lender is modeled as the outcome of an unobserved latent variable REL_i^*, which is assumed to be a linear function of exogenous covariates $\mathbf{w}_i$ and a random component u_i. Specifically,

$$REL_i^* = \mathbf{w}_i \gamma + u_i . \tag{6}$$

Thus, the observed outcome is modeled as

$$REL_i = \begin{cases} 1, & \text{if } REL_i^* > 0 \\ 0, & \text{otherwise.} \end{cases}$$

The key assumption is that u and ϵ are bivariate normal with mean zero and covariance matrix:

$$\begin{bmatrix} \sigma^2 & \rho\sigma \\ \rho\sigma & 1 \end{bmatrix}.$$

The treatment effects model differs from the IV estimation in terms of assumptions made about the error term. As explained above, the IV approach assumes that the instrument used is uncorrelated with the error term and this assumption cannot be verified for a model that is exactly identified. The treatment effects model on the other hand assumes that the errors are bivariate normal—again this assumption cannot be empirically tested. Thus, both approaches have their strengths and weaknesses and we report results for both methodologies. We continue to use the log(1+distance) as before as an exogenous variable that affects the decision to borrow from a relationship lender in the vector $\mathbf{w}_i$. This helps us identify the system and we do not simply depend upon nonlinearities for identification. We report the results from the treatment effects model in panel C of Table 5. The first column provides the estimated effect of distance on relationship. The coefficient is −0.055 (significant at the 1% level), implying that the greater the distance between the borrower and the lender, the lower the likelihood of there being a relationship. The second column reports the endogeneity-adjusted estimate of a relationship on AISD. The coefficient is −16.91 (significant at the 1% level). The coefficient on the relationship variable is 1.5 times the size of the OLS estimate. Thus, after controlling for endogeneity, in a treatment effects model, we continue to find that past relationships are associated with significantly lower spreads.

We also report the estimated correlation between the error terms in the two equations, ρ, which equals 0.042, which is positive and significant at the 5% level. This signifies any unobserved factor(s) not captured in our specification, which causes matching between a firm and a relationship lender and also affects the observed spread, to be *positively* correlated. Of course, the treatment effects model is designed to explicitly take this correlation into account and provide the correct coefficients and standard errors. Thus, if unobserved credit quality causes both the formation/continuation of the relationship, as well as the observed spreads, the positive correlation implies that *lower* unobservable credit quality firms are more likely to borrow from relationship lenders. This result appears to alleviate a possible concern that banks might tend to build relationships with firms of unobservably higher credit quality (in which case ρ would have been *negative*).

The central issue addressed in this section relates to the potential endogeneity of the relationship variable itself. We addressed this issue in three different ways (PSM, IV estimation, and treatment effects model). Our results continue to show that relationships matter for loan spreads using all three methods that account for endogeneity. The results are in fact somewhat stronger after addressing the endogeneity issue.

3.4 Multivariate tests of H2

The multivariate tests in Section 3.2 suggest that there are significant benefits of relationships in terms of loan rates for our overall sample. The discussion in Section 1.1.1 suggests that this overall benefit should vary systematically across different types of borrowers, with a greater level of benefit accruing to more informationally opaque borrowers.

To test this, we propose the following model:

$$\begin{aligned} AISD = {} & \beta_0 + \beta_1(REL(M)) + \beta_2(Borrower\ Information\ Opacity) \\ & + \beta_3(REL(M)) \times (Borrower\ Information\ Opacity) \\ & + \sum \beta_i(Loan\_Characteristics_i) \\ & + \sum \beta_j(Borrower\_Characteristics_j) + \sum \beta_k(Control_k). \qquad (7) \end{aligned}$$

We employ six different measures of borrower information opacity in our tests: (1) *Log(Assets)*, (2) a dummy variable for not-rated firms, (3) inclusion in the S&P 500 index, (4) number of analysts following the firm, (5) a microstructure measure of information asymmetry, and (6) level of discretionary accruals.

The results are reported in Table 6. The coefficient for *REL(Dummy)* × *Log(Assets)* is 5.50 and is significant at the 1% level. The positive coefficient indicates that as firms become larger (less informationally opaque), the benefits of relationship lending decline, consistent with H2. Next, we use the existence of public bonds outstanding as a proxy for information opacity of the borrower. We create a dummy variable "*Not Rated*," which equals 1 if the firm does not have an S&P senior secured debt rating and 0 otherwise. The existence of an S&P debt rating is almost always associated with public debt outstanding.[22] Arguably, unrated firms face higher information asymmetries since they are not monitored by credit rating agencies. For such firms, borrowing from relationship lenders should be especially beneficial. The results reported in the second column of Table 6 show that the interaction term *REL(Dummy)* × *Not Rated* is −12.37 and is significant at the 1% level. This provides evidence in support of H2. We check also (in column 3 of Table 6) to see if the borrower is included in the S&P 500 index at the time of the loan. Firms that are part of this index are likely

[22] Cantillo and Wright (2000) report that the fraction of firms that *had* a bond rating but *did not* have public debt was less than 1%.

to be widely followed and can be considered informationally transparent. The interaction term is positive and significant, implying that there is no significant benefit for such firms if they borrow from relationship lenders, again consistent with the view that it is the informationally opaque borrowers that benefit from relationship lending. We also match the number of analysts (column 4) that issue earnings forecasts for a particular borrower at the time of the loan. We obtain these data from I/B/E/S. Firms that have few or no analysts covering them can be thought of as informationally opaque firms where the benefits of relationship borrowing would be large. Column 4 provides evidence consistent with this interpretation; the interaction term is positive and significant at the 1% level, suggesting relationship benefits decline, as more analysts follow the firm. Columns 5 and 6 employ additional proxies of information opacity, a

Table 6
Borrower information opacity and benefits of relationship

	(1)	(2)	(3)	(4)	(5)	(6)	(7)
Const.	927.16***	902.33***	436.46***	903.75***	909.74***	518.53***	903.09***
	(23.66)	(22.75)	(19.88)	(23.22)	(24.54)	(18.49)	(22.67)
REL(Dummy)	−43.77***	−2.35	−14.42***	−14.81***	−9.99***	−6.39*	−14.39***
	(8.94)	(3.65)	(2.72)	(3.07)	(2.71)	(3.50)	(2.74)
REL(Dummy) × Log(Assets)	5.50***						
	(1.37)						
REL(Dummy) × Not rated		−12.37***					
		(4.73)					
REL(Dummy) × S&P 500			26.94***				
			(6.27)				
REL(Dummy) × No. of analysts				0.93***			
				(0.30)			
REL(Dummy) × ASY					−3.23**		
					(1.65)		
REL(Dummy) × Accruals						−62.60*	
						(34.77)	
REL(Dummy) × Big-3 bank							22.98***
							(5.28)
S&P 500			−12.26				
			(8.17)				
No. of analysts				−0.89***			
				(0.32)			
ASY					2.14*		
					(1.29)		
Discretionary accruals						99.90***	
						(33.57)	
Big-3 bank							−20.59***
							(4.64)
Log(Maturity)	−18.27***	−18.06***	−18.07***	−18.16***	−18.49***	−20.05***	−18.04***
	(2.55)	(2.54)	(2.63)	(2.55)	(2.98)	(3.11)	(2.55)
Collateral	59.78***	59.80***	57.17***	59.82***	55.92***	57.64***	59.80***
	(2.86)	(2.86)	(2.90)	(2.86)	(3.14)	(3.46)	(2.86)
Log(Assets)	−13.53***	−9.73***	−10.35***	−9.31***	−8.72***	−7.88***	−9.81***
	(1.79)	(1.56)	(1.59)	(1.62)	(1.66)	(1.86)	(1.57)
Log(Loan size)	−16.15***	−16.15***	−16.71***	−16.10***	−17.70***	−17.89***	−15.89***
	(1.55)	(1.55)	(1.60)	(1.55)	(1.63)	(1.82)	(1.55)
Log(1+Coverage)	−23.52***	−23.76***	−24.48***	−23.70***	−25.40***	−29.09***	−23.84***
	(1.70)	(1.69)	(1.73)	(1.70)	(1.83)	(2.37)	(1.69)
Leverage	22.77***	22.04**	18.69**	21.27**	12.75	21.19**	21.13**
	(8.74)	(8.74)	(8.86)	(8.74)	(9.25)	(10.39)	(8.70)
Profitability	−43.81***	−44.26***	−43.08***	−43.49***	−41.30***	−16.89	−43.52***
	(13.61)	(13.64)	(14.40)	(13.70)	(15.62)	(16.71)	(13.61)
Tangibility	−12.10*	−11.95*	−2.35	−11.93*	−7.10	−6.32	−11.94*
	(6.69)	(6.73)	(6.91)	(6.72)	(7.11)	(7.70)	(6.73)
Current ratio	−2.65***	−2.72***	−2.73***	−2.68***	−3.13***	−3.09***	−2.71***
	(0.73)	(0.73)	(0.77)	(0.73)	(0.82)	(1.04)	(0.73)

(continued overleaf)

Table 6
(Continued)

	(1)	(2)	(3)	(4)	(5)	(6)	(7)
Market-to-book	−1.23	−1.15	−1.49	−1.07	−1.19	−1.06	−1.11
	(0.95)	(0.96)	(0.98)	(0.97)	(1.00)	(1.36)	(0.96)
Obs.	13,158	13,158	12,180	13,158	10,744	9,170	13,158
R^2	0.57	0.57	0.58	0.57	0.59	0.60	0.57

This table provides the OLS regression (corrected for heteroscedasticity and clustering) estimates of the following equation:

$$\begin{aligned} AISD = {} & \beta_0 + \beta_1(REL(M)) + \beta_2(Borrower\ Information\ Opacity) \\ & + \beta_3(REL(M)) \times (Borrower\ Information\ Opacity) \\ & + \sum \beta_i(Loan\_Characteristics_i) + \sum \beta_j(Borrower\_Characteristics_j) + \sum \beta_k(Control_k). \end{aligned}$$

The dependent variable AISD is the coupon spread on the drawn amount plus the annual fee in bps. *REL(Dummy)* equals 1 if there is a relationship with any of the lead banks in the last five years before the present loan and 0 otherwise. Maturity is length in months between facility activation date and maturity date. Loan Amount is the loan facility size in millions of real year 2000 dollars. Collateral is a dummy variable that equals 1 if the facility has the stated attribute and 0 otherwise. Log(assets) is the natural log of book value of assets of the borrower in millions of year 2000 real dollars as reported in Compustat. Leverage is the ratio of the book value of total debt to the book value of assets. Coverage is the ratio of EBITDA to interest expenses. Profitability is the ratio of EBITDA to sales. Tangibility is the ratio of NPPE to total assets. Current ratio is the ratio of current assets to current liabilities. Market-to-book is the ratio of (book value of assets − book value of equity+market value of equity) to the book value of assets. Borrrower information opacity is measured by six different proxies: Borrower's size (log of assets), if the borrower is not rated (not-rated dummy), if the borrower is in the S&P 500 index, number of analysts following the borrower firm, a microstructure measure of information asymmetry ASY developed by Bharath, Pasquareillo, and Wu (2009), and discretionary accruals computed according to Dechow and Dichev (2002). Big-3 bank is a dummy variable if the lead bank is either Citibank, JP Morgan Chase, or Bank of America. In addition to the variables reported, the regression also includes industry dummies based on the one-digit SIC code of the borrower, dummies for stated purpose of the facility, dummies for loan type, calendar year dummies, and dummies for the credit rating of the borrower, with not-rated firms considered a separate group. Numbers in parentheses are standard errors corrected for heteroscedasticity and firm-level clustering. Clustering at the deal level produces similar results. ***, **, and * denote significance at the 1%, 5%, and 10% levels, respectively.

microstructure measure of information asymmetry (as described in Bharath, Pasquareillo, and Wu 2009) and the level of discretionary accruals (Dechow and Dichev 2002). Higher levels for these measures imply a higher level of information asymmetry and correspondingly higher benefits from relationship borrowing and thus we expect the interaction term with *REL(Dummy)* to be negative. We find that the interaction terms are indeed negative and significant at the 5% and 10% levels, respectively. Taken together, the results reported in columns 1–6 of Table 6 provide strong empirical support for the hypothesis that repeated borrowing from the same lender is associated with a larger reduction in spreads for firms with higher information opacity.[23] These results are consistent with the view that relationships mitigate information asymmetry problems in contracting.

Our earlier results show that for borrowers that break with their past lending relationship, the loans carry a higher spread (Table 5, panel A). We also explore how break-ups interact with borrower opacity. We exclude all borrowers that

[23] The effect of lock-in on spreads would result in exactly the opposite pattern: firms with a higher information opacity should either have a lower cost saving or a higher spread relative to firms with a lower information opacity.

never form relationships. This leaves us with a sample in which all borrowers at some point had a lending relationship. We then create a dummy variable "Break" that takes the value of 1 if the borrower had a past relationship but chooses to get the loan from a nonrelationship lender (break of existing relationship) and zero otherwise. The discontinuation of the existing relationship is likely to affect the opaque firms most acutely as the new lenders lack the proprietary information that would have been accumulated by the existing relationship lender and the gains of which were shared with the borrower. Our results are consistent with this argument. The interaction term (Opacity × Break) is significant and increases in firm opacity for all six different measures of borrower opacity.[24]

A potential criticism of our results is related to the concentration of the loan syndication market. Three banks, Citibank, JP Morgan Chase, and Bank of America, dominate the market for syndicated loans. Arguably, these banks can show up as lead banks on loans where they may not have a relationship with the borrower but may simply appear as repeated lenders due to their sheer market share. The last column in Table 6 controls for this effect by including the dummy variable "*Big-3 Bank*," which equals 1 if any of the lead bank(s) is one of these three banks. The coefficient for *REL(Dummy)* is −14.39 (significant at the 1% level). These results imply that the lower rates on repeated borrowing from the same banks are not driven by the large market shares of the big-three banks. We employ two additional robustness tests. First, we drop all loan facilities where any of the big-three banks was involved in the role of the arranger. The coefficient for *REL(Dummy)* is −12.93 (significant at the 1% level). Second, we drop all facilities in which any of the big-three banks was involved in any capacity. The coefficient for *REL(Dummy)* is −15.07, which is significant at the 1% level. Thus, our results are robust to the exclusion of big-three banks.[25]

3.5 Multivariate tests of H3

As discussed in Section 1.1.1, Boot and Thakor (2000) posit that there should exist a critical point in terms of borrower quality below which banks engage in relationship lending and above which banks engage in transactional lending. Since several of our proxies for borrower information opacity (e.g., size) are also correlated with observable borrower quality (e.g., existence of credit rating), the empirical results in the previous section provide fairly robust support for the conjecture. Our results show that the benefits of relationship lending decrease with a decrease in borrower opacity. To examine this in further detail, we revisit the results in Table 6, column 1, where size as measured by total assets is used as a proxy for the borrower quality (the higher the size, the better the borrower quality). The economic significance of this result is best illustrated by comparing the coefficient of the interaction term with the coefficient for

[24] Detailed results of these robustness tests are available from the authors on request.

[25] Detailed results of these robustness tests are available from the authors on request.

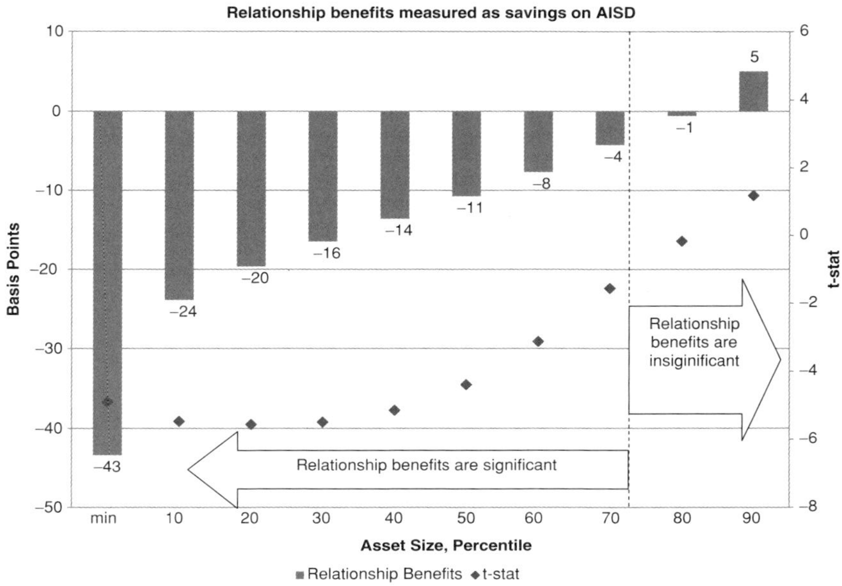

Figure 1
Relationship benefits and borrower size
This figure displays the price break in bps for a relationship borrower in each asset size decile compared to a similar borrower with no relationship in the same asset size decile. Asset size is measured in real year 2000 dollars. The estimate and statistical significance (*t*-stat.) is assessed using specification 1 of Table 6.

REL(Dummy), which is −43.77. This specification allows us to measure the extent and significance of benefit of repeated borrowing from the same lender for different sized borrowers. Ranked by the book value of assets, a borrower at the 10th percentile in our sample would have approximately \$37 million in assets. This translates into a relationship benefit of roughly −24 bps ($-43.77 + 5.50 \times \text{Log}(37)$). For the borrower at the 90th percentile level (asset size of \$7,134 million), the net relationship coefficient is +5.07 bps ($-43.77 + 5.50 \times \text{Log}(7, 134)$), which is statistically insignificant. This exercise allows us to map the relative benefits of relationship loans across the borrower size spectrum.

Figure 1 plots the coefficient of *REL(Dummy)* for different asset deciles and the *t-statistic* computed using the delta method for specification 1 in Table 6. The benefits of relationship decline as the borrower becomes larger and are statistically indistinguishable from zero for borrowers at the 70th percentile and above. This means for firms greater than \$1.31 billion in asset size (in year 2000 dollars), relationship benefits as reflected in spreads disappear. We also use the Brown, Durbin, and Evans (1975) test to examine whether two regimes exist in our spreads regression with respect to borrower quality. Using the Brown-Durbin-Evans test for the cumulative sum of square residuals, we find evidence that there are two regression regimes in our spreads regression and that the most likely point of the switch is around the 56th percentile in terms of borrower assets in year 2000 dollars (results not reported).[26] Along similar lines, using the results in Table 6, column 2, where firm quality is measured by the presence of a credit rating, the coefficient for the interaction term (*REL(Dummy)* $\times$ *Not Rated*) is -12.37 (significant at the 1% level). Thus, on average, a relationship loan carries an interest rate 15 bps lower (obtained by summing the coefficients of relationship and interaction terms) for a firm that does not have public bonds outstanding compared to a similar borrower that has access to public debt markets. If ratings of public debt are used as a measure of borrower quality in a Boot and Thakor (2000) setting, our results imply that benefits of relationship dissipate significantly once a firm issues public debt. A similar interpretation can be extended to several of the other information opacity measures. For example, the benefits of relationship lending are insignificant if the borrower is part of the S&P 500 index. The overall results of Table 6 along with Figure 1 provide support for the hypothesis that loans to firms above a certain quality threshold tend to be transactional loans while loans to firms of lower quality are relationship loans.

Our results show that for such high-quality firms (proxied by borrower size), there is no significant difference in loan spreads based on whether the loan is from a relationship lender or a nonrelationship lender. We describe such loans as "transactional loans" in this article.[27]

3.6 Multivariate tests of H4

The results so far are consistent with relationships addressing information asymmetry problems between lenders and borrowers. However, from the discussion in Section 1.1.2, we know that relationships can also be viewed as a commitment to monitor, and further, that this commitment will be especially

[26] Brown, Durbin, and Evans (1975) propose a method to evaluate the constancy of regression parameters for panel datasets. The null hypothesis is that there is no variation in all the regression parameters. The alternate hypothesis is that at least one of the regression parameters is not constant. Under the null hypothesis, the expected value of the regression residual (defined as a recursive residual) for the nth observation computed using parameter values estimated using the first $n-1$ observations is zero for all values of n. On the other hand, say the parameters switch at observation n. In that case, the expected value of the recursive residual for the nth observation using the parameter values computed using the first $n-1$ observation differs from zero. Using this insight, Brown, Durbin, and Evans (1975) suggest a test called the "Cumulative Sum of Square Residuals," which involves taking the sum of the square of the recursive residuals from sequential regressions consisting of the first "n" observations. Brown, Durbin, and Evans show that this scaled sum of recursive residuals has a beta distribution and derive critical values for the hypothesis of constant regression parameters. Kallberg, Liu, and Srinivasan (2004) test for the most likely location of a switch point in the quality of limited partnerships using this method. In the context of testing the implication of the Boot and Thakor (2000) model, we are interested principally in the constancy of the regression relationship over borrower quality. Thus, we are interested in evaluating the variation in regression parameters over borrower quality. To this end, we chose one of the main variables that we had earlier used to proxy for quality, namely size. We rank order the firms in our sample using asset size (in real 2000 dollars) and test for the constancy of regression parameters over variation in size. Figure 1 already provides strong and robust support for the nonconstancy of the importance of the relationship on spreads, when sorted by firm size. However, the use of a formal statistical model of nonconstant parameters can help us provide an independent method to verify that the benefits of relationships become insignificant as borrower size increases.

[27] Simply because there is no observed reduction in loan spreads does not imply by itself that these are transactional loans. After all, if there is no benefit to borrowing from a relationship bank, why do it? We acknowledge that such loans may or may not be part of a larger "relationship bundle," where the benefits may appear in other products that the borrower may purchase from the lender. We leave tests of this issue for future research.

valuable in syndicated loans where the lead bank has an incentive to reduce its monitoring effort by shirking. This syndicate moral hazard can exert an additional effect on the observed loan spreads.

To isolate the impact of syndicate moral hazard, we first focus on a subset of loans where this effect is not relevant. This subsample consists of loans where there was one reported lender. By construction, this sample lacks the moral hazard among lenders. The results are reported in column 1 of Table 7, panel A. It shows that relationships are associated with almost 18 bps lowering of observed loan spreads (significant at the 1% level). When we further restrict this single-lender subsample by requiring that the borrower has had a relationship with only one single lender through all of its prior loans, our results remain largely unchanged. The coefficient of *REL* is −14.44, which is significant at the 5% level (see column 2, panel A, Table 7). The set of relationship loans in this subsample, where the borrower has had only one, single bank relationship in the past and uses the same bank for the current loan, corresponds most closely to the theoretical scenario of "lock-in" envisaged in Sharpe (1990) and Rajan (1992). Even for this subsample, the relationship cost savings is comparable in magnitude to that obtained for the rest of the sample. The results in columns 1 and 2 indicate that relationships mitigate asymmetric information problems and that "lock-in" is not a significant issue for firms in our sample.

Next, we try to estimate the impact of bank (or syndicate) moral hazard among the syndicate members on loan spreads. Sufi (2007) shows that syndicates tend to be more concentrated and the lead lender(s) retain(s) a significantly higher share of the loan when the likelihood of borrower moral hazard is high. Thus, increasing loan share retained by the lead bank and higher loan HHI imply higher moral hazard concerns. However, data on how the loan facility is shared among banks are available for less than half the sample. Therefore, in addition to the observed shares, we use the size of the syndicate as an additional proxy for syndicate moral hazard. Borrowers that require a high level of monitoring would be most affected by the syndicate moral hazard issue. One could argue that the observed size of a syndicate could be related to the perceived moral hazard by the syndicate members, with larger syndicates indicating lower moral hazard.[28]

The last three columns of panel A of Table 7 provide empirical support for syndicate moral hazard playing a significant role in the determination of loan spreads. Larger syndicate size can be considered an ex post indication of low moral hazard among syndicate members, as seen in their willingness to join a large syndicate. We examine the role of relationship lending in the presence of syndicate moral hazard by including the log of syndicate size and an interaction term of *REL(Dummy)* and the log of syndicate size. If past relationships can be

[28] As noted earlier in Section 1.1.2, there is no prior empirical work that has established a clear link between larger syndicate size and lower moral hazard. Therefore, the results on use of syndicate loan size should be seen as a secondary proxy for syndicate moral hazard, the primary ones being lead bank allocation and Loan HHI.

Table 7
Role of relationships as a bank's commitment to monitor

Panel A

	(1)	(2)	(3)	(4)	(5)
Const.	569.22***	642.95***	898.58***	855.71***	834.47***
	(60.96)	(119.35)	(23.18)	(38.02)	(43.21)
REL(Dummy)	−18.19***	−14.44**	−20.27***	6.25	3.57
	(6.12)	(7.36)	(3.70)	(4.96)	(4.52)
REL(Dummy) × Log(Syndicate size)			8.59***		
			(2.02)		
Log(Syndicate Ssize)			−7.63***		
			(2.17)		
REL(Dummy) × Lead bank allocation				−0.26***	
				(0.09)	
Lead bank allocation				0.49***	
				(0.09)	
REL(Dummy) × Loan HHI					−0.002***
					(0.0008)
Loan HHI					0.005***
					(0.001)
Log(Maturity)	−16.21***	−19.15***	−17.82***	−15.39***	−14.67***
	(5.81)	(6.44)	(2.57)	(3.61)	(3.75)
Collateral	63.45***	64.70***	59.86***	60.82***	60.11***
	(7.75)	(8.53)	(2.88)	(3.62)	(3.72)
Log(Assets)	−21.10***	−17.00***	−9.82***	−15.50***	−15.33***
	(3.75)	(4.90)	(1.59)	(1.80)	(1.89)
Log(Loan size)	−20.29***	−25.61***	−15.34***	−11.37***	−10.49***
	(4.24)	(5.04)	(1.63)	(2.00)	(2.21)
Log(1+Coverage)	−15.07***	−13.89***	−23.58***	−24.18***	−24.24***
	(2.71)	(2.94)	(1.70)	(2.09)	(2.15)
Leverage	54.82**	43.82	22.12**	17.91	23.59**
	(22.46)	(26.75)	(8.73)	(11.40)	(11.89)
Profitability	−110.31***	−122.42***	−43.73***	−30.44*	−35.52**
	(42.47)	(43.45)	(13.58)	(16.50)	(16.94)
Tangibility	−30.57	−18.41	−11.93*	−13.92	−14.13
	(21.26)	(23.54)	(6.73)	(8.76)	(9.08)
Current ratio	−4.72**	−5.49**	−2.74***	−3.80***	−4.16***
	(2.12)	(2.23)	(0.73)	(1.22)	(1.24)
Market-to-book	0.12	0.52	−1.14	−1.14	−0.90
	(2.25)	(2.36)	(0.95)	(1.17)	(1.19)
Obs.	1,669	1,184	13,158	6,064	5,731
R^2	0.43	0.44	0.57	0.58	0.58

Panel B

	(1)	(2)	(3)	(4)
Const.	902.95***	911.75***	909.15***	909.43***
	(22.79)	(23.14)	(23.18)	(23.15)
REL(Dummy)	−1.83	−9.74***	−10.92***	−8.44***
	(3.45)	(3.11)	(2.44)	(2.88)
*REL(Dummy)**Collateral	−15.28***			
	(4.73)			
*REL(Dummy)**Covenant Index		−0.85		
		(1.68)		
Market-to-Book*Covenant Index			−3.00***	−2.22**
			(0.81)	(0.95)
*REL(Dummy)**Market-to-book*Covenant index				−1.16
				(0.75)

(*continued overleaf*)

Lending Relationships and Loan Contract Terms

Table 7
(Continued)

Panel B

	(1)	(2)	(3)	(4)
Covenant index		7.18***	11.22***	11.29***
		(1.87)	(1.90)	(1.91)
Log(Maturity)	−18.21***	−18.91***	−18.63***	−18.64***
	(2.55)	(2.53)	(2.52)	(2.52)
Collateral	70.72***	49.12***	49.13***	49.16***
	(4.72)	(3.65)	(3.65)	(3.64)
Log(Assets)	−9.58***	−9.45***	−9.81***	−9.77***
	(1.56)	(1.58)	(1.57)	(1.57)
Log(Loan size)	−16.22***	−16.69***	−16.44***	−16.47***
	(1.55)	(1.57)	(1.57)	(1.57)
Log(1+Coverage)	−23.79***	−24.30***	−24.18***	−24.20***
	(1.69)	(1.72)	(1.73)	(1.73)
Leverage	22.18**	17.78**	18.66**	18.87**
	(8.73)	(8.76)	(8.74)	(8.76)
Profitability	−43.74***	−44.63***	−44.83***	−44.69***
	(13.64)	(13.64)	(13.64)	(13.63)
Tangibility	−12.07*	−10.27	−10.54	−10.74
	(6.71)	(6.68)	(6.68)	(6.67)
Current ratio	−2.66***	−2.52***	−2.58***	−2.53***
	(.073)	(0.73)	(0.75)	(0.75)
Market-to-book	−1.11	−0.98	1.59	1.52
	(0.95)	(0.98)	(1.51)	(1.49)
Obs.	13,158	13,158	13,158	13,158
R^2	0.57	0.57	0.58	0.58

This table provides the OLS regression (corrected for heteroscedasticity and clustering) estimates of the following equation:

$$\begin{aligned} AISD = {} & \beta_0 + \beta_1(REL(M)) + \beta_2(Bank\ Monitoring\ Incentive) \\ & + \beta_3(REL(M)) \times (Bank\ Monitoring\ Incentive) \\ & + \sum \beta_i(Loan\_Characteristics_i) + \sum \beta_j(Borrower\_Characteristics_j) + \sum \beta_k(Control_k). \end{aligned}$$

The dependent variable AISD is the coupon spread on the drawn amount plus the annual fee in bps. *REL(Dummy)* equals 1 if there is a relationship with any of the lead banks in the last five years before the present loan and 0 otherwise. Maturity is the length in months between facility activation date and maturity date. Loan Amount is the loan facility size in millions of real year 2000 dollars. Collateral is a dummy variable that equals 1 if the facility has the stated attribute and 0 otherwise. Log(Assets) is the natural log of the book value of assets of the borrower in millions of year 2000 real dollars as reported in Compustat. Leverage is the ratio of book value of total debt to book value of assets. Coverage is the ratio of EBITDA to interest expenses. Profitability is the ratio of EBITDA to sales. Tangibility is the ratio of NPPE to total assets. Current ratio is the ratio of current assets to current liabilities. Market-to-book is the ratio of (book value of assets − book value of equity + market value of equity) to book value of assets. Syndicate moral hazard, i.e., the incentive to monitor the borrower, is measured by three different proxies: number of members in the syndicate, lead bank allocation of the loan in percent, and the loan concentration in the syndicate measured by the Herfindahl-Hirschmann index following Sufi (2007). Covenant index assumes the value between 0 and 5 with the presence of each of five different covenants coded as 1 and 0 otherwise and summed up (Bradley and Roberts 2004). In addition to the variables reported, the regression also includes industry dummies based on the one-digit SIC code of the borrower, dummies for stated purpose of the facility, dummies for loan type, calendar year dummies, and dummies for the credit rating of the borrower, with not-rated firms considered a separate group. Numbers in parentheses are standard errors corrected for heteroscedasticity and firm-level clustering. Clustering at the deal level produces similar results. ***, **, and * denote significance at the 1%, 5%, and 10% levels, respectively.

seen as credible commitments to monitor, such a commitment is likely to be less valuable where syndicate moral hazard is low (i.e., a large number of lenders are willing to join the syndicate). Overall, we find evidence consistent with this argument. Specifically, the coefficients on *REL* and the interaction term are −20.27 and 8.59, respectively (column 3 of Table 7). The combined effect of relationship is estimated by summing the coefficients for *REL(Dummy)* and the interaction term. For the smallest syndicate size of one lender, the interaction term is zero. For such a borrower, having a past relationship implies a relationship benefit of 20.27 bps. Since the median syndicate size is 2 for our sample, we consider the case of a loan that is provided by a syndicate that has the median size of our sample. Here the net effect of relationships is −14.31 bps ($-20.27 + 8.59 \times \ln(2)$). This result suggests that benefits of past relationships are lower when syndicate size increases (i.e., syndicate moral hazard is low). However, the overall effect of relationships at −14.31 bps is still statistically significant (p-value of 0.001).

Sufi (2007) shows that high syndicate moral hazard is associated with larger loan allocation to the lead bank and a higher Loan HHI. Again, we expect relationships to be of most value for loans where such moral hazard is high. The coefficients on *REL* and the interaction term between *REL* and lead bank allocation are 6.25 and −0.26, respectively (column 4 of Table 7, panel A). The combined economic and statistical effect of relationship is estimated by summing the coefficients for *REL(Dummy)* and the interaction term. The median lead bank allocation in our sample is 68.75. Thus, for the median loan facility, the total effect of a relationship is given by −11.86 bps ($6.25 - 0.26 \times 68.75$), which is significant at the 1% level (p-value of 0.001). Thus, a past relationship provides significant benefits but those benefits are especially powerful for loans where the lead bank retains a significantly large fraction since the interaction term is negative and significant. Consistent with this argument, assuming that the lead bank holds 0% of the loan (suggesting little or no syndicate moral hazard), we should expect little benefits from relationships as a commitment to monitor. This is indeed what we find when we substitute the lead bank allocation of 0% into the specification in column 4 of Table 7—the interaction term drops out and the coefficient for *REL* (which is 6.75 bps) is not significant. Column 5 uses the loan Herfindahl index as a measure of syndicate moral hazard. The coefficients for *REL* and *REL* × *Loan HHI* are 3.57 and −0.002. The median HHI in our sample is 6,250, implying a total relationship effect of −10.65 ($3.57 - 0.002 \times 6{,}250$), which is significant at the 1% level (p-value = 0.003). Again, this implies an overall beneficial impact of relationship which is especially pronounced for loans with high HHI (high syndicate moral hazard). If Loan HHI is close to zero (implying little syndicate moral hazard), the interaction term drops out and as expected the coefficient for *REL* is not significant since relationships are not particularly prized when syndicate moral hazard is very low.

We also test the relationship between observed loan spreads and syndicate moral hazard using propensity score matching (PSM). We need to divide our sample into high syndicate moral hazard and low syndicate moral hazard subgroups. For each loan where the entire loan is retained by the lead bank(s), we classify the given loan as the one with low syndicate moral hazard, since by definition there is no syndicate moral hazard for this set of loans. For the remaining subsample, we calculate the median lead bank allocation. We classify loans with a lead bank allocation higher than the median as those with a high syndicate moral hazard, and loans with a lead bank allocation below the median as those with low syndicate moral hazard. Using the PSM procedure, we create pairs of matched loans that are identical in all respects except that one loan in each pair would have a higher than median lead bank allocation, and the other loan in the same pair would have a lower than median lead bank allocation. Thus, for each pair, one loan (the one with a high lead bank allocation) will have high syndicate moral hazard, while the other loan (the one with a low lead bank allocation) will have low syndicate moral hazard. The observed difference in loan rates across all pairs (high-low syndicate moral hazard) allows us to test the effect of syndicate moral hazard on loan spreads. We should expect this difference to be positive and significant. We use four matching methodologies as described earlier in the article and we find a strong association between syndicate moral hazard and loan spreads, with high syndicate moral hazard loans having spreads of 6–10 bps higher than low syndicate moral hazard loans (significant at the 5% level or lower).[29]

We also test whether relationships play a meaningful role as a credible commitment to monitor. We focus on the subset of loans that are expected to have high syndicate moral hazard (i.e., loan syndicates where the lead bank allocation is higher than the sample median). For this group, we use a probit model to estimate the probability of borrowing from a relationship bank (same model as Table 5, panel A). The predicted probabilities allow us to create pairs of matched firms that are identical in all respects except for the relationship. One firm in each pair would have borrowed from its relationship lender while the other did not. The observed difference in loan rates across all pairs (relationship–no relationship) allows us to test the effect of relationships in a group that is preselected to have high moral hazard. If past relationships mitigate syndicate members' concerns of shirking by the lead bank, the difference in spreads between relationship and nonrelationship loans should be negative and significant. This is indeed what we find—for the high syndicate moral hazard group, relationship loans are 11–19 bps lower compared to matched nonrelationship loans and statistically significant.[30]

Finally, a typical loan provides a number of other contractual ways in which a lender can impact the "cost" of a loan to a borrower.[31] These include an

---

[29] The four matching estimators are the NEAREST NEIGHBOR ($n = 10$), NEAREST NEIGHBOR ($n = 50$), GAUSSIAN, and EPANECHNIKOV methods.

[30] These results are not reported but are available from the authors.

[31] We employ covenant intensity and collateral as contractual features that necessitate intensive borrower monitoring (Rajan and Winton 1995). We focus on the market-to-book ratio of borrowers as a measure of attractive growth

extensive use of covenants and requirements for collateral. For example, a lender can cut off credit if a covenant is violated without having to go to the extreme remedy of using foreclosure. By requiring collateral, a lender can commit to more rigorous monitoring.[32] In panel B of Table 7, we provide some limited evidence of past relationships being associated with a sharpening of effects of these contractual arrangements. In column 1, we interact *REL* with a dummy variable for collateral. While a requirement of collateral is associated with higher spreads, the presence of past relationships lowers the spread charged an average of 15 bps (significant at the 1% level). That is, collateral as a contractual device to mitigate borrower moral hazard is more effective in the presence of relationships, which serves as a commitment to monitor the borrower. We also construct a covenant index as described by Bradley and Roberts (2004). We focus on five specific covenants and assign one point to the index if that particular covenant condition is met. The covenants that we examine are Asset Sweep, Debt Sweep, Equity Sweep, Dividend Restriction, and presence of more than two financial ratio restrictions. Unlike Bradley and Roberts, we exclude the secured covenant since we capture it through our collateral dummy. In column 2, we report how covenant intensity affects loan spreads when the borrower has a prior borrowing relationship with the lender through the interaction of *REL(Dummy)* with covenant index. Again, while a higher number of covenants by itself is associated with higher loan spreads, a past relationship in the presence of a higher covenant index lowers the observed spread but the effect is not statistically significant. In the last two specifications (columns 3 and 4), we focus on borrowers that have attractive growth opportunities, as evidenced by high market-to-book ratios. Such borrowers are more credibly controlled via threats of credit cut-offs in the case of covenant violations. This is borne out by the negative and significant coefficient for the market-to-book and covenant index interaction term. In column 4, we report how this benefit evolves if the firm has a past relationship with its lender. While the coefficient on the three-way interaction term is negative, it is not significant.

3.7 Multivariate tests of H5

Next we focus on two specific *nonprice* terms of loan contracts: collateral requirements and loan maturity. First, we present our findings on how past relationships and collateral requirements are interrelated.

As discussed in Section 1.2, collateral can also serve as a credible signal of quality to address the adverse selection problem (Bester 1985; Besanko and Thakor 1987). Additionally, requiring collateral is a contractual mechanism to

opportunities. Arguably, a lender can control a growing borrower (i.e., firm with a high market-to-book ratio) by cutting off credit if a covenant is violated without having to resort to foreclosure (which is expensive for both the lender and borrower). For a low market-to-book firm, a lender may need to control such a firm by forcing a default, but this may impose costs on the lender as well. This illustrates that covenants and collateral can be especially useful contractual features for growing firms. Thus, relationships as a commitment to monitor would make the loan especially valuable (hence lower spreads ex ante) if covenants and collateral are present.

32 Collateral value may be sensitive to borrower actions (Rajan and Winton 1995).

control the borrower's moral hazard incentives. If past relationships address the adverse selection problem and are credible commitments to monitor, then such relationship loans may require less collateral. To test this, we run the following logit model:

$$
\begin{aligned}
Collateral = {} & \beta_0 + \beta_1(REL(M)) + \beta_2 Log(Loan\ Amount) + \beta_3(Leverage) \\
& + \beta_4(Tangibility) + \beta_5(Market\ to\ Book) \\
& + \beta_6(Loan\ Concentration) + \beta_7(Log(Maturity)) \\
& + \sum \beta_k(Control_k). \qquad (8)
\end{aligned}
$$

Collateral is a dummy variable that equals 1 if the loan was secured and 0 otherwise.[33]

We control for loan amount, maturity, leverage, tangibility of assets, market-to-book, loan concentration (measured as the fraction of the loan size to the sum of existing debt plus the loan size), and default risk. We also include industry, facility purpose, and calendar year dummies. We use loan concentration $(\frac{Loan\ Amount}{Existing\ Debt\ +\ Loan\ Amount})$ because if a particular loan facility is a significant portion of the firm's debt, it is more likely to be secured (Berger and Udell 1990; Boot, Thakor, and Udell 1991; Dennis, Nandy, and Sharpe 2000).[34]

Our results are reported in Table 8. The three columns provide estimates for each of the *REL* measures. Regardless of which measure of relationship we employ, the coefficient is negative and significant at the 1% level. Thus, a loan from a relationship lender is significantly less likely to require collateral. These findings are consistent with the arguments of Holmstrom and Tirole (1997), who suggest that if a lending relationship is a credible commitment to monitor, such loans are less likely to require collateral. These results are also consistent with Bester (1985), who suggests that the reduction in adverse selection by banking relationships would reduce collateral requirements. As reported in prior studies, we also find that loan facilities that are relatively large compared to existing debt are more likely to be granted on a secured basis. In particular, the coefficient for *Loan Concentration* is positive and significant at the 1% level.

We also address the concern about the endogeneity of relationship and collateral. It is possible that an unobserved factor influences both the decision to form relationships and the requirement for collateral. We use two econometric methods to address the endogeneity of relationship in the collateral estimation. In particular, we use a IV probit as well as bivariate probit methodologies. We use log(1+distance) as an instrument that determines relationships but not collateral. In the first stage, we use a probit model to estimate the probability

---

[33] For nearly one-third of our loan sample, LPC does not report whether the loans were secured by collateral or not. We treat such loans as unsecured. We also ran our tests by excluding all observations for which these data were missing. The results remain unchanged.

[34] We also calculate a loan concentration ratio in which we exclude lines of credit and debt repayment and the results are unchanged.

Table 8
Lending relationships and probability of pledging collateral

	(1)	(2)	(3)
Const.	−18.15***	−18.15***	−18.16***
	(0.62)	(0.63)	(0.63)
REL(Dummy)	−0.22***		
	(0.05)		
Rel(Number)		−0.26***	
		(0.06)	
Rel(Amount)			−0.25***
			(0.06)
Log(Loan size)	−0.47***	−0.47***	−0.47***
	(0.03)	(0.03)	(0.03)
Leverage	2.93***	2.96***	2.96***
	(0.27)	(0.27)	(0.27)
Tangibility	−0.48***	−0.48***	−0.48***
	(0.16)	(0.16)	(0.16)
Market-to-book	−0.12***	−0.12***	−0.12***
	(0.03)	(0.03)	(0.03)
Loan concentration	1.54***	1.57***	1.57***
	(0.16)	(0.16)	(0.16)
Log(Maturity)	0.25***	0.26***	0.25***
	(0.03)	(0.03)	(0.03)
Obs.	15,510	15,510	15,510
Pseudo R^2	0.26	0.26	0.26

This table provides the logit regression estimates (corrected for heteroscedasticity and clustering) of the following equation:

$$\begin{aligned} COLLATERAL = {} & \beta_0 + \beta_1(REL(M)) + \beta_2 Log(Loan\ Amount) + \beta_3(Leverage) + \beta_4(Tangibility) \\ & + \beta_5(Market\ to\ Book) + \beta_6(Loan\ Concentration) \\ & + \beta_7(Log(Maturity) + \beta_8(Not\ Rated) + \sum \beta_k(Control_k). \end{aligned}$$

The dependent variable COLLATERAL is a dummy variable that equals 1 if a loan facility is secured by collateral and 0 otherwise. *REL(M)* is the measure of relationship strength, estimated in three different ways: *REL(Dummy)* (equals 1 if there is a relationship with any of the lead banks in the last five years before the present loan and 0 otherwise), *REL(Number)* (ratio of number of deals with the lead bank(s) to total number of loans borrowed by the firm in the last five years before the current loan), and *REL(Amount)* (ratio of the dollar value of deals with the lead bank(s) to the total dollar value of loans borrowed by the firm in the last five years before the current loan). For a facility with multiple lead banks, the maximum *REL(M)* value among all the lead banks is used. The loan amount is the loan facility size in millions of real year 2000 dollars. Leverage is the ratio of book value of total debt to book value of assets. Tangibility is the ratio of NPPE to total assets. Market-to-book is the ratio of (book value of assets − book value of equity + market value of equity) to book value of assets. *Loan concentration* is the ratio of that loan facility amount to sum existing debt and the amount of loan facility. In addition to the variables reported, the regression also includes industry dummies based on the one-digit SIC code of the borrower, dummies for stated purpose of the facility, calendar year dummies, and dummies for the credit rating of the borrower, with not-rated firms considered a separate group. Numbers in parentheses are standard errors corrected for heteroscedasticity and firm-level clustering. Clustering at the deal level produces similar results. ***, **, and * denote significance at the 1%, 5%, and 10% levels, respectively.

of borrowing from a relationship lender. The predicted probability from this estimation is used as an instrument for the second-stage probit that estimates the effect of relationship on collateral. We find that the coefficient of the relationship variable for the IV estimation is −1.11 and it is significant at the 1% level (for comparison, the coefficient on relationships in a probit equation (not correcting for endogeneity) for collateral generates a coefficient of −0.13, significant at the 1% level). Note that the results reported in Table 8 use a logit specification where the coefficient for the relationship variable is −0.22, significant at the 1% level). In the bivariate probit model, the coefficient for the relationship variable in the collateral equation is −1.33, and it is significant at the 1% level. These results of the IV probit as well as of the bivariate probit suggest that relationships are associated with lower collateral requirements, even after controlling for the endogeneity of the relationship variable.[35]

3.8 Multivariate tests of H6

Next, we examine how past borrowing relationships affect (if at all) the maturity of the loan. As discussed in the theoretical section, the pure information asymmetry model by Flannery (1986) predicts relationships being associated with longer maturity debt while the Diamond (1991) model predicts that relationships could both increase or decrease debt maturity, depending on the credit rating of the firm. A factor complicating our estimation, especially in the context of the Diamond model, is that maturity is driven by borrower demand for high- and intermediate-credit-rated firms and by lender supply for low-rated firms. To get an insight into the loan maturity-customer relationship effect, we estimate several versions of the following basic model:

$$\begin{aligned}Log(Maturity) = {} & \beta_0 + \beta_1(REL(M)) + \beta_2(Log(Loan\ Amount)) + \beta_3(Leverage)\\ & + \beta_4(Log(Assets)) + \beta_5(Market\ to\ Book)\\ & + \beta_6(Log(Asset\ Maturity)) + \beta_7(Regulated) + \beta_8(Collateral)\\ & + \sum \beta_k(Control_k). \qquad (9)\end{aligned}$$

The dependent variable *Log*(*Maturity*) is the natural log of the stated maturity of the loan facility (measured as the length in months between the facility activation date and maturity date). We model the relationship between debt maturity and past banking relationships after controlling for variables that are known determinants for debt maturity (see Barclay and Smith 1995; Barclay, Marx, and Smith 2003). We control for firm size, leverage, market-to-book, and two additional variables that are unique to the maturity regressions. We use a measure of asset maturity that is defined as the weighted average of maturity of current assets and Net PPE.[36] The intuition behind this variable is that firms try to match their debt maturity to asset maturity. Hart and Moore (1994) describe a model of inalienability of human capital. This specificity of human capital makes the debt contracts hard to design since an entrepreneur can threaten to walk away from the project. They show that debt maturity can help address this problem. A key result of their model is that the optimal repayment path (debt maturity) would depend on the maturity structure of project payoffs and durability of assets. The model predicts that longer (shorter) life assets are likely to be financed by longer (shorter) term debt. Thus, using asset maturity as an explanatory variable for debt maturity is a reasonable assumption.

[35] For brevity, we do not report these results, but they are available on request from the authors.

[36] We follow the definition provided by Barclay, Marx, and Smith (2003) to estimate *Asset Maturity*, which equals $\frac{CA}{(CA+NPPE)} \times \frac{CA}{COGS} + \frac{NPPE}{(CA+NPPE)} \times \frac{NPPE}{Depreciation}$.

As another factor that might explain debt maturity, we include a dummy variable for regulated industries following Barclay and Smith (1995). This is because the higher regulatory oversight for these firms should result in lower agency costs of debt, which, in turn, should result in greater use of longer maturity debt. Alternatively, if these regulated firms have access to longer maturity debt from capital markets, it might result in greater use of shorter maturity bank debt. In addition, we also control for default risk using the credit rating dummies and include year dummies and dummies for debt type and debt purpose. In one of the specifications, instead of the year dummies, we also include a term spread measure defined as the difference in yields on ten-year and one-year U.S. government bonds prevailing at the time of loan origination. Brick and Ravid (1985, 1991) provide a model in which the firm value is increasing if it issues long-term debt when the yield curve is upward sloping. Their argument is based on the fact that tax savings are accelerated when a larger fraction of debt payment is allocated to long-term debt. This implies that maturity should be positively related to the term spread.

The results of these regressions are presented in Table 9. The first column reports the coefficient on *REL*. We find that the coefficient is negative and significant at the 1% level. However, the inference is clouded by the demand and supply effects as identified by Diamond (1991). To test if there exists any cross-sectional variation of relationship effects on loan maturity across firm quality, we decompose the *REL* variable into three parts by interacting it with dummy variables High, Middle, and Low. High equals 1 if the borrower is ranked in the highest tercile as ranked by assets. Middle and Low are defined similarly. Interacting *REL* with each of these variables is equivalent to running separate regressions for each of the three size subgroups. Our results are reported in column 2. We find that effects of relationship are most pronounced for the highest and the lowest terciles (where the relationship coefficient is negative and significant), while the mid-sized borrowers' debt maturity is not significantly affected by past relationships. In columns 3, 4, and 5, we use the credit rating of the borrower as the measure of quality. Column 3 reports the maturity regression results for the subsample of firms that lack a credit rating. Presumably, these firms can be viewed as being of the lowest quality. Column 4 reports the same regression for firms that do have a credit rating but are below the investment grade. These borrowers can be thought of as medium quality. Finally, in column 5 we tabulate maturity regression results for the subsample of investment grade-rated (high-quality) borrowers. Comparing the *REL* coefficient across these three groups shows a nonmonotonic relationship between repeated borrowing from the same lender and credit quality. The worst and the best quality borrowers appear to have much shorter maturity loans from their relationship lender compared to medium-quality firms. We interpret these results as follows: for the highest quality firms, relationship loans lower the cost of refinancing (liquidity risk) and therefore they demand even shorter loans from their relationship borrowers. For the lowest quality firms, the relationship

Lending Relationships and Loan Contract Terms

Table 9
Lending relationships and loan maturity

	(1)	(2)	(3)	(4)	(5)	(6)
Const.	2.58***	2.65***	3.42***	3.73***	2.57***	2.54***
	(0.10)	(0.10)	(0.23)	(0.23)	(0.13)	(0.10)
REL(Dummy)	−0.08***		−0.09**	−0.05*	−0.09***	−0.08***
	(0.02)		(0.04)	(0.03)	(0.02)	(0.02)
REL(Dummy) × High		−0.10***				
		(0.02)				
REL(Dummy)× Middle		−0.01				
		(0.02)				
REL(Dummy) × Low		−0.15***				
		(0.03)				
Log(Loan size)	0.14***	0.13***	0.09***	0.13***	0.14***	0.14***
	(0.009)	(0.009)	(0.02)	(0.02)	(0.01)	(0.009)
Leverage	0.41***	0.38***	0.36***	0.38***	0.39***	0.41***
	(0.04)	(0.04)	(0.11)	(0.08)	(0.05)	(0.04)
Log(Assets)	−0.05***	−0.05***	−0.03*	−0.08***	−0.03***	−0.05***
	(0.009)	(0.009)	(0.02)	(0.02)	(0.01)	(0.009)
Market-to-book	−0.005	−0.005	0.006	0.02	−0.008	−0.005
	(0.005)	(0.005)	(0.01)	(0.02)	(0.006)	(0.005)
Log (Asset maturity)	0.03***	0.04***	0.03	−0.04	0.06***	0.03***
	(0.01)	(0.01)	(0.02)	(0.02)	(0.01)	(0.01)
Regulated	−0.47***	−0.47***	−0.30***	−0.52***	−0.49***	−0.47***
	(0.06)	(0.05)	(0.06)	(0.13)	(0.10)	(0.06)
Collateral	0.12***	0.12***	0.26***	0.14***	0.08***	0.12***
	(0.02)	(0.02)	(0.06)	(0.03)	(0.02)	(0.02)
Term spread						0.0004**
						(0.0002)
Obs.	15,636	15,636	3,174	3,289	9,173	15,636
R^2	0.25	0.25	0.33	0.27	0.21	0.25

This table provides the OLS regression (corrected for heteroscedasticity and clustering) estimates of the following equation:

$$\begin{aligned} Log(Maturity) = {} & \beta_0 + \beta_1(REL(M)) + \beta_2(Log(Loan\ Amount)) + \beta_3(Leverage) + \beta_4(Log(Assets)) \\ & + \beta_5(Market\ to\ Book) + \beta_6(Log(Asset\ Maturity)) + \beta_7(Regulated) + \beta_8(Collateral) \\ & + \sum \beta_k(Control_k). \end{aligned}$$

The dependent variable Log(Maturity) is the natural log of the stated maturity of the loan facility (measured as the length in months between the facility activation date and maturity date). *REL(Dummy)* equals 1 if there is a relationship with any of the lead banks in the last five years before the present loan and 0 otherwise. Log(assets) is the natural log of the book value of assets of the borrower. Loan amount is the loan facility size. Leverage is the ratio of book value of total debt to book value of assets. Market-to-book is the ratio of (book value of assets − book value of equity + market value of equity) to book value of assets. Asset maturity is the weighted average of current assets divided by the cost of goods sold, and Net PPE divided by depreciation and amortization—as defined in Barclay, Marx, and Smith (2003). *Regulated Industry* is a dummy variable that equals 1 for firms in the utilities industry under the Fama-French (1997) industry classification and 0 otherwise. Term spread is the difference in yields between one-year and ten-year U.S. government bonds at the time of loan activation. In addition to the variables reported, the regression also includes industry dummies based on the one-digit SIC code of the borrower, dummies for the stated purpose of the facility, and calendar year dummies. Numbers in parentheses are standard errors corrected for heteroscedasticity and firm-level clustering. Clustering at the deal level produces similar results. ***, **, and * denote significance at the 1%, 5%, and 10% levels, respectively.

lenders commit to monitoring the firms more with shorter maturity loans. Given that monitoring costs for relationship lenders are likely to be lower, we expect relationship loans to have a shorter maturity for low-quality borrowers. These results are consistent with Diamond (1991). The last column reports the association between maturity and the prevailing term spread. We find a significant and positive association as predicted by the models of Brick and Ravid (1985, 1991).

3.9 IV estimation of price and nonprice features of loan facilities

Next, we address the issue of joint determination of price and nonprice terms of loans. Previous empirical studies have largely ignored the potential interaction and trade-offs among the price and nonprice terms of loans. To the extent that they are jointly determined, the true effects of relationships on these variables may be obscured. Melnik and Plaut (1986) model bank loans as a package of n contract terms that cannot be split and traded separately. Banks then offer an n-dimensional array of bundles from which to choose their contracts, and borrowers trade off contract terms in determining their optimal choice. This approach indicates that the price, maturity, and collateral terms of a bank loan contract may be interrelated. Consequently, we reestimate the model specifications above for the price and nonprice terms of loans using an IV framework. We describe the approach in detail below. As in Dennis, Nandy, and Sharpe (2000), we assume a unidirectional relationship between the price (AISD) term and nonprice (collateral requirement and maturity) terms. This assumed structure of joint determination needs some support. In particular, we are assuming that while maturity and collateral affect each other (bidirectional relationship), spread is only affected by maturity and collateral (unidirectional relationship). This structure reflects the loan syndication processes, as described in discussions with industry professionals. For example, the S&P Guide to Loan Markets (2006) describes the process in several discrete steps. Syndication starts by the borrower appointing the lead bank, which conducts due diligence and hammers out the nonprice loan features such as amount, collateral, maturity, and covenants with the borrower and leaves the final price (as yet) to be determined. At this stage, the lead bank would informally poll potential syndicate members to gauge the level of interest in the loan. This information is used to set the interest rate on the loan and it is launched for syndication. Thus, the loan syndication process has become increasingly similar to the "book-building" process used to sell publicly and privately placed bonds. This description of the syndication process makes our assumption of price being determined after all other nonprice terms have been settled quite realistic. The three-equation structural model can be described as

$$\begin{aligned} AISD &= \gamma_A(REL) + \gamma_{AC}(Collateral) + \gamma_{AM}(Log(Maturity)) \\ &\quad + X_A\beta_A + \epsilon_A \\ Collateral &= \gamma_C(REL) + \gamma_{CM}(Log(Maturity)) + X_C\beta_C + \epsilon_C \\ Log(Maturity) &= \gamma_M(REL) + \gamma_{MC}(Collateral) + X_M\beta_M + \epsilon_M. \end{aligned}$$

The γ_{ij} are the coefficients of interdependence effects. X_k are the exogenous variables that affect the kth dependent variable. The estimation of the system is complicated by the fact that while spreads and maturity are continuous variables, collateral is a discrete choice variable. We therefore follow Wooldridge (2002), who shows that estimating a logit equation for the discrete choice variable in the first stage and using the fitted value as an instrument for the discrete choice variable in the IV estimation leads to consistent estimates of the coefficients. We employ the two-stage least-squares (2SLS) method using instruments for our endogenous variables. Our choice of instruments is guided by existing theories of debt maturity, collateral, and price. We use prevailing default spread at the time the loan is made, as an instrument for observed spreads. Arguably, following the syndication process described by the industry professionals, contemporaneous default spreads should affect contracted loan spreads at the time of pricing (at which point, the other contract terms would have already been finalized). From the results reported earlier in column 4 of Table 4, we also know that default spreads are positively and significantly related to loan spreads.[37]

We also created another instrument that determines loan rates (based on our conversations with bankers): the average AISD of loans completed over the previous six months. This average captures the recent evolution in loan pricing and is a significant factor in pricing of new loans. The Loan Pricing Corporation in its promotional materials for Dealscan highlights the use of these data in banks' price setting. These data are called Pricing Grids and are an important primary market pricing benchmark. These grids enable lenders/borrowers to gauge current spread levels and follow pricing trends by rating, size, and industry. Thus, it is reasonable to argue that the lagged average spread on loans over the last six months is related to the current loan's AISD, but it is unlikely that past spread should affect this particular loan facility's nonprice terms such as collateral requirements. In our spread regression we have two loan-related endogenous variables, maturity and collateral, for which we need instruments. As described earlier, Hart and Moore (1994) argue that firms would attempt to match their debt maturity to the economic life of the assets. Barclay and Smith (1995) also use asset maturity as well as "regulated industry" dummy as key factors that affect the debt maturity structure of corporations. As an additional robustness check, following Brick and Ravid (1985, 1991), we also use the term spread as a factor that determines debt maturity. We use these variables as instruments for maturity. In addition, loan concentration is employed as an instrumental variable that affects collateralization of the debt. The latter is based on the evidence in Berger and Udell (1990), who report that the greater

[37] For the default spread to be a valid instrument, one has to assume that changes in default spreads are uncorrelated with changes in collateral requirement. In order to investigate this issue, we constructed the proportion of loans in our database each month that were collateralized. We regress the contemporaneous fraction of loans that are collateralized on default spread, term spread, and GDP growth. The latter two determinants were included, following (a) theoretical arguments by Kiyotaki and Moore (1997) that aggregate business cycles would determine the level of collateralization of loans and (b) empirical arguments by Jiminez, Salas, and Saurina (2006). We estimate an OLS as well as a generalized linear model (GLM). The default spread does not seem to be a determinant of the level of collateralization in both the OLS and GLM models. The coefficient on the default spread variable is insignificant and statistically indistinguishable from zero in all the specifications. Details of the test methodology and results are available on request.

the current loan borrowing relative to the size of the total debt, the greater the likelihood of a lender asking for collateral. Following Berger and Udell (1990), we estimate *Loan Concentration* $= \frac{\textit{Loan Amount}}{(\textit{Existing Debt} + \textit{Loan Amount})}$. As an additional robustness test, we also use the industry median tangibility ratio as a factor that affects collateralization, with industries whose assets have greater tangibility more likely to provide collateral.

The results of the IV estimation are presented in Table 10. Column 1 reports the OLS estimation for spreads (column 4 of Table 4). Columns 2 and 3 report the effect of past relationships on loan spreads controlling for the joint determination of maturity and collateral. The change of econometric specification produces some impact on the measured benefit of relationships to loan spreads. The coefficient for *REL(Dummy)* is −14.35 compared to −10.55 estimated in the simple OLS specification when we use default spreads as an instrument. Using average loan spreads over the previous six months yields a *REL(Dummy)* coefficient of −12.79, again significant at the 1% level. Thus, once we control for the endogeneity of various loan contract terms, our results show that borrowing from a relationship lender can reduce the cost of borrowing by up to 15 bps. These results are statistically significant at the 5% level. They are also economically significant as 15 bps represents an almost 6% savings on a median AISD of 212.5 bps.

In the IV regression of *Log(Maturity)*, we find that the effects of the relationship are negative and significant for the low-quality firms and positive and significant for the medium-quality firms. Both of these results are consistent with Diamond (1991). While the coefficient for the highest quality borrowers with relationships is negative as predicted, it is not statistically significant. The coefficient of collateral is positive and significant at the 1% level. This result confirms the prediction of Boot, Thakor, and Udell (1991), which implies that longer maturity loans are more likely to be collateralized.[38] The coefficient for *Asset Maturity*, our exogenous variable for the maturity regression, is positive and significant at the 1% level, implying that firms try to match loan maturity to asset maturity. The coefficient for *Regulated Industry* dummy, however, is negative; this is opposite of the results obtained by Barclay and Smith (1995). This difference is possibly due to the fact that we focus on bank loans while they examine public bond yields. Arguably, regulated firms borrow longer term from public debt markets and shorter term from banks.

Given that *Collateral* is a dichotomous variable, we use an IV probit model. Again as expected, the probability of having to post collateral is significantly lower (at the 1% level) for borrowers who obtain loans from their relationship lenders. All other variables enter with predicted signs. *Loan Concentration*, our exogenous measure of collateral requirements, has a positive and significant coefficient, suggesting that it is an appropriate instrument. In sum, the evidence

---

[38] Boot, Thakor, and Udell (1991) argue that "*dissipative costs*," i.e., likely loss in the value of collateral, are higher for a longer maturity loan. Thus, they predict that longer maturity loans would be characterized by a higher level of collateral.

Lending Relationships and Loan Contract Terms

Table 10
Instrumental variables estimation of loan spread, maturity, and collateral

	AISD			Log(Maturity)		Collateral	
Dependent variable	OLS	IV	IV	OLS	IV	Probit	IV Probit
REL(Dummy)	−10.55***	−14.35**	−12.79**			−0.13***	−0.07***
	(2.44)	(5.73)	(5.73)			(0.03)	(0.31)
*REL(Dummy)**High				−0.10***	−0.02		
				(0.02)	(0.03)		
*REL(Dummy)**Middle				−0.01	0.07***		
				(0.02)	(0.03)		
*REL(Dummy)**Low				−0.15***	−0.10***		
				(0.03)	(0.04)		
Log(Maturity)	−18.07***	−151.6***	−146.13***			0.15***	0.94***
	(2.54)	(42.70)	(42.04)			(0.02)	(0.15)
Collateral	60.01***	406.2***	408.2***	0.12***	1.67***		
	(2.87)	(68.09)	(64.94)	(0.02)	(0.97)		
Default spread		15.44***					
		(7.62)					
Average spread			0.68***				
			(0.11)				
Log(Asset maturity)				0.04***	0.65***		
				(0.01)	(0.15)		
Regulated				−0.47***	−0.24***		
				(0.05)	(0.77)		
Loan concentration						0.90***	1.00***
						(0.09)	(0.07)
Other controls		As in column 1 of Table 4	As in column 1 of Table 4		As in column 2 of Table 9		As in column 1 of Table 8
Tests of endogeneity:							
Durbin-Wu-Hausman's chi-sq. test	469.25	546.46		1170			
p-value	0.00	0.00		0.00			
Wald's chi-square test statistic						29.56	
p-value						0.00	

(*continued overleaf*)

Table 10
(Continued)

Dependent variable	AISD		Log(Maturity)	Collateral
Weak identification statistics:				
Cragg-Donald F-stat.	14.57	15.05		
Stock and Yogo (2005)				
critical value	11.03	11.03		
First-stage F-statistic			323.27	
Partial R-sqaure			8.16%	
Anderson's LR statistic	58.24	60.17	1289	
p-value	0.00	0.00	0.00	
Instrument exogeneity test:				
Hansen's J-statistic	4.132	3.967	0.001	
p-value	0.13	0.14	0.98	

This table provides estimations of the following system of equations using instrumental variables to estimate the impact of past relationships on Loan Spread, Maturity, and Collateral:

$$
\begin{aligned}
AISD &= \gamma_A(REL) + \gamma_{AC}(Collateral) + \gamma_{AM}(Log(Maturity)) + X_A\beta_A + \epsilon_A\\
Collateral &= \gamma_C(REL) + \gamma_{CM}(Log(Maturity)) + X_C\beta_C + \epsilon_C\\
Log(Maturity) &= \gamma_M(REL) + \gamma_{MC}(Collateral) + X_M\beta_M + \epsilon_M.
\end{aligned}
$$

AISD is the coupon spread over LIBOR on the drawn amount plus the annual fee. Log(maturity) is the natural log of the stated maturity of the loan facility (measured as the length in months between the facility activation date and maturity date). Collateral is a dummy variable that equals 1 if the loan was secured and 0 otherwise. *REL(Dummy)* is 1 if there is a relationship with any of the lead banks in the last five years before the present loan and 0 otherwise. Default spread is measured as the difference between the yields on Moody's seasoned corporate bonds with Baa rating and ten-year U.S. government bonds. Asset maturity is the weighted average of current assets divided by the cost of goods sold, and Net PPE divided by depreciation and amortization—as defined in Barclay, Marx, and Smith (2003). *Regulated industry* is a dummy variable that equals 1 for firms in the utilities industry under the Fama-French (1997) industry classification and 0 otherwise. *Loan concentration* is the ratio of that loan facility amount to sum existing debt and the amount of loan facility. The Durbin-Wu-Hausmann chi-square test is the test of the null hypothesis that maturity and collateral are indeed exogenous. The rejection of null implies they are endogenous. Wald's test provides a similar test for IV probit model for collateral. To test for instrument relevance, for AISD regression since we have two endogenous regressors, we estimate the Cragg-Donald statistic and compare it against critical values in Table 1 of Stock and Yogo (2005). For the Log(maturity) regression, we report the the first-stage F-statistic, as well as partial R^2 since it has only one endogenous variable. For both the AISD and Log(maturity) IV regressions, we report the Anderson LR test of the null hypothesis that our instruments and endogenous variables are not correlated. We reject the null (p-value $= 0.00$), implying that our instruments are correlated with the endogenous variables. Since we have two endogenous variables but four instruments for the spread equation, we are able to estimate the Hansen's J-statistic for overidentification restrictions. These are joint tests of the null hypothesis that the correct model is specified and the orthogonality conditions are met (correlations between the instruments and the error term is zero). Our test statistic does not reject the null for AISD and Log(maturity) regressions implying exogeneity of the instruments. For both AISD and Log(maturity) IV regressions, numbers in the parentheses are standard errors corrected for heteroscedasticity and firm-level clustering. For IV probit, cluster-corrected standard errors cannot be computed so we use bootstrapping with fifty replications to estimate the standard errors. ***, **, and * denote significance at the 1%, 5%, and 10% levels, respectively.

presented in Table 10 suggests that our results as to the benefits of prior relationships are robust to the simultaneous determination of contract terms. We also estimate the effects of relationship on price and nonpriced terms using different instruments to assess its robustness. These include Term-Spread for maturity, median industry tangibility ratio for collateral, and interest coverage for spreads. The results[39] are very similar to those reported in Table 10. Overall, the relationship effect remains robust to these alternate IV estimations, confirming our single equation results. We also perform a variety of econometric tests to assess the relevance and validity of our instruments. These tests and their results are described and summarized in the next subsection.

3.9.1 Tests of relevance and validity of instruments. We have used existing theoretical models and prior empirical research to motivate our instruments. However, our choice of instruments needs to be econometrically validated. The two key criteria that an instrument must meet are relevance (instrument is correlated with endogenous variable) and validity (instrument affects the dependent variable only through the endogenous variable). We conducted several tests that provide support for our instrument choices. The results of these tests are reported in the bottom panel of Table 10. For our spread regression, we confirm that collateral and maturity are indeed endogenous by estimating the Durbin-Wu-Hausman (DWH) chi-squared test. The null hypothesis for this test is that the two variables, maturity and collateral, are exogenous to spread. The rejection of the null implies that these variables are indeed endogenous and validates the IV approach. We obtain a chi-squared test statistic of 469.25 when we use default spread as the instrument for the observed spread, which strongly rejects the null (p-value $= 0.000$). Using average past spreads as an instrument, we obtain a chi-squared test statistic of 546.46 (p-value $= 0.000$). To test if our instruments are relevant, we conduct two tests to measure their strength. First, we calculate the Cragg-Donald statistic, which is 14.13 (for default spread as the instrument) and is higher than the 11.04 critical value reported by Stock and Yogo (2005) for an estimation with two endogenous variables. This implies that our instruments for maturity and collateral are relevant. Another test for the relevance of instruments is the Anderson LR test of the null hypothesis that correlations between the instruments and the endogenous variable are essentially zero. We obtain a test statistic value of 58.98, which strongly rejects the null (p-value $= 0.000$), implying that the instruments are strongly correlated with the endogenous variables. The results for using average spreads as instrument are very similar. Tests of the instrument's independence from an unobservable error process (validity) can only be ascertained if the number of instruments is higher than the number of endogenous variables so that the system of equations is overidentified. Since we have two endogenous variables but four instruments for the spread equation, we are able to estimate the Hansen's J-statistic for

[39] Available from the authors on request.

overidentification restrictions. These are joint tests of the null hypothesis that the correct model is specified and the orthogonality conditions are met (correlations between the instruments and the error term is zero). A rejection of the null calls both of these assumptions into question. For our spread regression, the Hansen J-statistic is 4.13, with a p-value of 0.13. Thus, we fail to reject the null hypothesis, which implies that our instruments are relevant and valid. We repeat all of these tests described so far, for the specification in which we use the average AISD of the loans in the last six months as an instrument for AISD. These results are reported in column 3 of Table 10 and are similar to those obtained using default spread as the instrument. We report a Hansen J-statistic of 0.001, with a p-value of 0.98 for the maturity regression, which shows that our instruments for collateral in the maturity equation are valid. Since the maturity equation has only one endogenous variable (collateral), we report the first stage F-statistic and the Shea partial R-squared statistic instead of the Cragg-Donald statistic. We obtain a first-stage F-statistic of 323.27, compared against the benchmark of 10 suggested by Staiger and Stock (1997) and a high partial R-squared statistic of 8.16%. These tests confirm the relevance of our instruments for collateral in the maturity equation. The Anderson LR statistic of 1,289 with a p-value of 0.000 rejecting the null (of zero correlation between the instrument and endogenous variable) further strengthens our conclusions. Finally, the DWH chi-squared test statistic of 1,170 with a p-value of 0.000 shows that collateral is indeed endogenous in the maturity equation. Since collateral is a dummy variable, we cannot apply the above tests of instrument relevance and validity.[40] However, we do report the results of the Wald test to see if maturity is exogenous in the collateral equation. The null hypothesis that maturity is exogenous is strongly rejected (p-value = 0.000). Collectively, these multiple tests provide econometric support for the relevance and validity of our instruments.

3.10 Multivariate tests of H7

An additional potential benefit for a relationship borrower is increased access to financing and even a number of publicly listed firms may be constrained in their ability to obtain debt financing. Furthermore, this constraint may be more binding for firms lacking strong borrowing relationships. Our univariate tests (panel B, Table 3) provide partial evidence for this when we compared the leverage ratios of firms borrowing from their relationship lender versus those borrowing from nonrelationship lenders. The relationship borrowers are significantly more leveraged than nonrelationship borrowers. However, these univariate tests do not control for various other loan and borrower characteristics. We use multivariate tests to better understand how past relationships are associated with availability of bank loans. Since credit availability cannot be

[40] We are not aware of any econometric tests for IV probit models.

observed directly, we construct a proxy that attempts to measure the incremental loan amount available for borrowing. This is estimated as the ratio of the loan amount being borrowed to the total assets of the borrower. To test if this ratio is related to the strength of relationships, we estimate a multivariate model of the following form:

$$\frac{Loan\ Amt.}{Assets} = \beta_0 + \beta_1(REL(M)) + \sum \beta_i(Loan\_Characteristics_i) + \sum \beta_j(Borrower\_Characteristics_j) + \sum \beta_k(Control_k). \quad (10)$$

The dependent variable $\frac{Loan\ Amt.}{Assets}$ is the ratio of the dollar amount of a loan facility to the total assets of the borrower. This ratio is the marginal amount of loan financing available to a borrower of a given size. A higher ratio implies better credit availability. The first three columns of Table 11 (panel A) report the effect of prior relationships on credit availability. We use multiple specifications for the relationship variable: *REL(Dummy)*, *REL(Amount)*, and *REL(Number)*. The coefficient for all specifications is positive and significant at the 1% level. The coefficient for *REL(Dummy)* is 0.008, which implies that on average, borrowing from a relationship lender would be associated with almost 1% larger loan availability (as a percentage of assets) compared to borrowing from a nonrelationship lender. In the last three columns of Table 11, we re-estimate our model using a different proxy for credit availability. We scale the loan amount by the existing total long-term debt of the borrower. The results are essentially unchanged. For example, the coefficient for *REL(Dummy)* is 0.02, implying a 2% increase in loan availability. Thus, we find that not only are relationship loans marked by better spreads and lower collateral, they also tend to be associated with greater credit availability.

4. Conclusion

The role of strong relationships between lenders and borrowers has been an active area of research. Theoretical models have generated a number of rich empirical implications both in terms of how past relationships may affect loan contracts in the future, as well as a set of borrower characteristics that would make relationships more (or less) important. We find that repeated borrowing from the same lender translates into a 10–17 bps lowering of loan spreads. Our results provide evidence that hypothesized economies in information production due to repeated interaction between the same lender and borrower are at least partly reflected in the price of loans. This result continues to hold across various methodologies that control for the endogeneity of the relationship formation. We also find that as the information opacity of a borrower increases, the observed reduction in the cost of borrowing due to a relationship becomes greater. These results also shed light on the boundary of relationship

Table 11
Lending relationships and access to loans

	(1)	(2)	(3)	(4)	(5)	(6)
Const.	0.63***	0.63***	0.63***	1.43***	1.42***	1.42***
	(0.03)	(0.03)	(0.03)	(0.06)	(0.06)	(0.06)
REL(Dummy)	0.008**			0.02***		
	(0.004)			(0.007)		
REL(Number)		0.009**			0.03***	
		(0.004)			(0.007)	
Rel(Amount)			0.01***			0.03***
			(0.004)			(0.007)
Log(Assets)	−0.06***	−0.06***	−0.06***	−0.10***	−0.10***	−0.10***
	(0.002)	(0.002)	(0.002)	(0.003)	(0.003)	(0.003)
Log(1+Coverage)	0.001	0.001	0.001	0.13***	0.13***	0.13***
	(0.002)	(0.002)	(0.002)	(0.005)	(0.005)	(0.005)
Log(Syndicate size)	0.06***	0.06***	0.06***	0.07***	0.07***	0.07***
	(0.002)	(0.002)	(0.002)	(0.004)	(0.004)	(0.004)
Profitability	0.13***	0.13***	0.13***	−0.34***	−0.34***	−0.34***
	(0.02)	(0.02)	(0.02)	(0.04)	(0.04)	(0.04)
Tangibility	−0.02**	−0.02**	−0.02**	−0.15***	−0.15***	−0.15***
	(0.01)	(0.01)	(0.01)	(0.02)	(0.02)	(0.02)
Current ratio	0.0002	0.0002	0.0002	−0.004	−0.004	−0.004
	(0.001)	(0.001)	(0.001)	(0.002)	(0.002)	(0.002)
Market-to-book	0.01***	0.01***	0.01***	0.008**	0.008**	0.008**
	(0.003)	(0.003)	(0.003)	(0.003)	(0.003)	(0.003)
Obs.	15,218	15,218	15,218	14,626	14,626	14,626
R^2	0.32	0.32	0.32	0.42	0.42	0.42

The first three specifications of this table provide the OLS estimates (corrected for heteroscedasticity) of the following equation:

$$\frac{\textit{Loan Amount}}{\textit{Assets}} = \beta_0 + \beta_1(\textit{REL(M)}) + \sum \beta_i(\textit{Loan\_Characteristics}_i) + \sum \beta_j(\textit{Borrower\_Characteristics}_j) + \sum \beta_k(\textit{Control}_k).$$

The next three specifications are essentially the same but the dependent variable is $\frac{\textit{Loan Amount}}{\textit{Long-Term Debt}}$. *REL(M)* is the measure of relationship strength, estimated in three different ways: *REL(Dummy)* (equals 1 if there is a relationship with any of the lead banks in the last five years before the present loan and 0 otherwise), *REL(Number)* (the ratio of number of deals with the lead bank(s) to the total number of loans borrowed by the firm in the last five years before the current loan), and *REL(Amount)* (the ratio of dollar value of deals with the lead bank(s) to the total dollar value of loans borrowed by the firm in the last five years before the current loan). For a facility with multiple lead banks, the maximum *REL(M)* value among all the lead banks is used. The loan amount is the loan facility size in millions of real year 2000 dollars. Profitability is the ratio of EBITDA to sales. Tangibility is the ratio of PPE to total assets. Current ratio is the ratio of current assets to current liabilities. Market-to-book is the ratio of (book value of assets − book value of equity + market value of equity) to book value of assets. In addition to the variables reported, the regression also includes industry dummies based on the one-digit SIC code of the borrower, dummies for stated purpose of the facility, calendar year dummies, and dummies for the credit rating of the borrower, with not-rated firms considered a separate group. Numbers in parentheses are standard errors corrected for heteroscedasticity and firm-level clustering. Clustering at the deal level produces similar results. ***, **, and * denote significance at the 1%, 5%, and 10% levels, respectively.

and transactional lending. We find that spreads charged for relationship loans and nonrelationship loans become indistinguishable if the borrower was in the top 30% when ranked by the asset size. Similar dissipation of relationship benefits occurs if the borrower has a rated public debt or is part of the S&P 500 index. The article uses the loan syndicate structure to examine the interaction of past relationships and syndicate moral hazard due to multiple lenders. The results in our article indicate that past relationships can mitigate syndicate moral hazard issues by serving as a commitment to monitor. We also find that relationship loans are significantly less likely to be secured by collateral, and our results on loan maturity are broadly consistent with Diamond (1991). Our results are robust to an estimation methodology that allows loan spread, collateral requirement, and loan maturity to be determined jointly using an IV approach. Finally, the relationship borrowers also obtain larger loans (scaled by the borrower's asset size or long-term debt) compared to nonrelationship borrowers. In sum, we report significant benefits of borrowing from relationship lenders even for *publicly traded* firms.

Appendix

Hidden Bias in Propensity Score Matching Results

In order to estimate the extent to which such "selection on unobservables" may bias our qualitative and quantitative inferences about the effects of relationships on loan spreads, we present the results of a Rosenbaum bounds sensitivity analysis (Rosenbaum 2002). The basic question is whether unobserved factors can alter inference about treatment effects (the effect of relationships on spreads). One wants to determine how strongly an unmeasured variable must influence the selection process of forming relationships to undermine the implications of the matching analysis. The bounding approach does not test the unconfoundedness assumption itself, because this would amount to testing that there are no (unobserved) variables that influence the selection into treatment. Instead, Rosenbaum bounds provide evidence on the degree to which any significance results hinge on this untestable assumption.

Let us assume that the relationships' participation probability is given by

$$P_i = P(x_i, u_i) = P(REL_i = 1|x_i, u_i) = F(\beta\, x_i + \gamma\, u_i), \tag{A1}$$

where x_i are the observed characteristics for borrower i, u_i is the unobserved variable, and γ is the effect of u_i on the participation decision. If our study is free of hidden bias, γ will be zero and the participation probability will be determined solely by x_i. However, if there is hidden bias, two borrowers with the same observed covariates x have different chances of receiving treatment. Let us assume that we have a matched pair of borrowers i and j and further assume that F is the logistic distribution. The odds that borrowers borrow from a relationship lender (receive treatment) are then given by $\frac{P_i}{(1-P_i)}$ and $\frac{P_j}{(1-P_j)}$, and the odds ratio is given by

$$\frac{P_i(1 - P_j)}{P_j(1 - P_i)} = \frac{\exp(\beta x_i + \gamma u_i)}{\exp(\beta x_j + \gamma u_j)}. \tag{A2}$$

If both borrowers have identical observed covariates as implied by the matching procedure, the x vector cancels out, implying that

$$\frac{P_i(1 - P_j)}{P_j(1 - P_i)} = \exp(\gamma(u_i - u_j)). \tag{A3}$$

But still, both borrowers differ in their odds of receiving treatment by a factor that involves the parameter γ and the difference in their unobserved covariates u. So, either if there are no differences in unobserved variables ($u_i = u_j$) or if unobserved variables have no influence on the probability of participating ($\gamma = 0$), the odds ratio is 1, implying the absence of hidden or unobserved selection bias. Sensitivity analysis now evaluates how changing the values of γ and

(u_i, u_j) alters inference about the treatment effect. We follow Rosenbaum (2002) and assume for simplicity that the unobserved covariate is a dummy variable with $u \in 0, 1$. He shows that the above discussion implies the following bounds on the odds ratio that either of the two matched borrowers will receive treatment:

$$\frac{1}{\exp(\gamma)} \leq \frac{P_i(1-P_j)}{P_j(1-P_i)} \leq \exp(\gamma). \tag{A4}$$

Both matched borrowers have the same probability of participating only if $\exp(\gamma) = 1$. Otherwise, if, for example, $\exp(\gamma) = 2$, borrowers who appear to be similar (in terms of x) could differ in their odds of receiving the treatment by as much as a factor of 2. In this sense, $\exp(\gamma)$ is a measure of the degree of departure from a study that is free of hidden bias.

Further, Rosenbaum (2002) develops a test statistic T (a Wilcoxon signed rank test statistic) for matched pairs where the outcome for the treatment is greater than the outcome for control. The ranks of these cases are summed and compared with the distribution of the test statistic under the null hypothesis that the treatment has no effect:

$$T = t(Z, r) = \left[\sum_{s=1}^{S} d_s \sum_{i=1}^{2} c_{si} Z_{si}\right], \tag{A5}$$

where Z is the variable that records which of each of the s pairs was treated, and r is the outcome for each case in the S pairs. Z_{si} equals 1 if a case is treated, and 0 otherwise; c is defined as follows:

$$c: \begin{cases} c_{s1} = 1, c_{s2} = 0, & \text{if } r_{s1} > r_{s2} \\ c_{s1} = 0, c_{s2} = 1, & \text{if } r_{s1} < r_{s2} \\ c_{s1} = 0, c_{s2} = 0, & \text{if } r_{s1} = r_{s2}. \end{cases}$$

Finally, d_s is the rank of $|r_{s1} - r_{s2}|$ with average ranks used for ties. As Rosenbaum (2002) shows in the case where the assignment to the treatment is not random, the above test statistic can be bounded. Under the assumption that a confounding variable u exists, the formula for T is the sum of S independent random variables where the sth pair equals d_s with probability

$$p_s = \frac{c_{s1}\exp(\gamma u_{s1}) + c_{s2}\exp(\gamma u_{s2})}{\exp(\gamma u_{s1}) + \exp(\gamma u_{s2})} \tag{A6}$$

and equals zero with probability $1 - p_s$. Define

$$p_s^+: \begin{cases} 0, & \text{if } c_{s1} = c_{s2} = 0 \\ \dfrac{\exp(\gamma)}{1+\exp(\gamma)}, & \text{if } c_{s1} \neq c_{s2} \end{cases}$$

and

$$p_s^-: \begin{cases} 0, & \text{if } c_{s1} = c_{s2} = 0 \\ \dfrac{1}{1+exp(\gamma)}, & \text{if } c_{s1} \neq c_{s2}. \end{cases}$$

Lending Relationships and Loan Contract Terms

Table A1
Rosenbaum bounds

	p-critical		Effect on spreads	
exp(γ)	Upper bound	Lower bound	Upper bound	Lower bound
1	0	0	−22.88	−19.06
1.05	0	0	−25.25	−16.63
1.1	0	0	−27.50	−14.29
1.15	0	0	−29.63	−12.05
1.2	0	0	−31.69	−9.88
1.25	0	6.70E-16	−33.63	−7.81
1.3	0	1.20E-10	−35.50	−5.79
1.35	0	9.80E-07	−37.25	−3.88
1.4	0	0.000609	−38.94	−2.00
1.45	0	0.038583	−40.56	−0.13
1.50	0	0.363088	−42.13	1.63

Rosenbaum (2002) shows that for a given value of γ, the null distribution of $T = t(Z, r)$ is bounded by two known distributions for T^+ and T^-, where

$$E(T^+) = \sum_{s=1}^{S} d_s p_s^+,$$

$$E(T^-) = \sum_{s=1}^{S} d_s p_s^-,$$

$$\mathrm{Var}(T^+) = \sum_{s=1}^{S} d_s^2 p_s^+(1 - p_s^+),$$

$$\mathrm{Var}(T^-) = \sum_{s=1}^{S} d_s^2 p_s^-(1 - p_s^-).$$

We can use these formulas to compute the significance level of the null hypothesis of no effect. For any specific γ, we compute

$$\frac{(T - E(T^+))}{\sqrt{\mathrm{Var}(T^+)}}, \frac{(T - E(T^-))}{\sqrt{\mathrm{Var}(T^-)}},$$

where T is the Wilcoxon signed rank statistic. These two values give the bounds of the significance level (p-values) of a one-sided test for no effect of the treatment (i.e., relationships).

Table A1 reports p-values from Wilcoxon signed rank tests for the average treatment effect (effect of relationship on spreads) on the treated while setting the level of hidden bias to a certain value exp(γ). The value of exp(γ) reflects our assumption about endogeneity in treatment assignment in terms of the odds ratio of differential treatment assignment due to an unobserved covariate (Equation (A3)). At each exp(γ), we calculate a hypothetical significance level "p-critical" (both a lower bound and an upper bound, corresponding to the bounds on the odds ratio), which represents the bound on the significance level of the treatment effect in the case of endogenous selection into treatment status. The method for calculating these variables has been outlined above. We do this for the matched pairs obtained using the nearest neighbor ($n = 10$) matching method. The results on the bounds are similar when calculated for other matching methods.

By comparing the Rosenbaum (2002) bounds on treatment effects at different levels of exp(γ) (the recommendation is to increase exp(γ) in steps of 0.05, starting from 1), we can assess the

Table A2
Examination of hidden bias n standard deviation in observed covariate required to justify an increase in odds ratio by a factor of 1.5 holding all other variables constant in the propensity score model

Variable	Odds ratio $\exp(\beta_k)$	Std. dev. s_k	Implied n
Assets	0.987	1.872	−16.55
Profitability	0.899	0.120	−31.73
Log(1+Coverage)	1.189	1.106	2.12
Leverage	2.194	0.189	2.73
Default spread	1.117	0.582	6.30

strength such unmeasured influences must have in order that the estimated treatment effects from propensity score matching would have arisen purely through nonrandom assignment. Intuitive interpretation of $\exp(\gamma)$ being equal to 1 is that unobservable factor(s) (hidden bias) has no effect on how each individual record (in our case each loan facility) is assigned to a treatment group (e.g., being classified as a relationship loan) or to a control group (e.g., being classified as a nonrelationship loan). For values of $\exp(\gamma)$ higher than 1, the implication is that the hidden bias is increasing the likelihood of being assigned to one group compared to being assigned to the other group.

Under the more stringent assumption of constant treatment effect, Rosenbaum (2002) also calculates the bounds on the point estimate of the treatment effect. This enables the researcher to frame the sensitivity analysis in terms of the interval of point estimates at a given confidence level. These results are shown in Table A1, under the column titled "Effect on spreads."

The critical level of $\exp(\gamma)$ at which we would have to question our conclusion of a negative effect of relationships on spreads is 1.50 (it is at this level that the confidence interval contains zero for the first time). A $\exp(\gamma)$ of 1.50 is attained if an unobserved covariate caused the odds ratio of treatment assignment to differ between treatment and control cases by a factor of about 1.50. It is important to recognize that these results are worst-case scenarios. A value for $\exp(\gamma)$ of 1.50 does not mean that there is no true negative effect of relationships on spreads. This result means that the confidence interval for the relationship effect on spreads includes zero, (a) if an unobserved variable caused the odds ratio of treatment assignment to differ between the treatment and control groups by 1.5, and (b) the unobserved variable's effect on outcome (spreads) has to be so strong as to almost perfectly determine whether the observed outcome (spread) would be bigger for the treatment case (relationship) in each pair of matched cases in the data, so as to overturn our inference and include zero in the confidence interval for the estimated effect. Note that in the case where a confounding variable had an equally strong effect on group assignment (treatment versus control) but only a weak effect on the outcome variable, the confidence interval for spreads would not contain zero.

To illustrate the magnitude of hidden bias that would cause us to revise our findings of causal effects of relationships on spreads, we equate the magnitude of hidden bias expressed by the specific level of $\exp(\gamma) = 1.50$ in terms of the equivalent effect of observed covariates for which we know the impact on assignment to treatment from our propensity score model. From the logistic regression model (with a covariate x_k with coefficient β_k and standard deviation s_k), for an n standard deviation in variable x_k, we know that the odds ratio is expected to change by a factor of $\exp(\beta_k * s_k * n)$, holding all other variables constant. By setting this equal to a factor of 1.5 (the change in odds ratio from $\exp(\gamma) = 1.5$ from $\exp(\gamma) = 1$), we can assess n for each observed covariate in the model. We do this for the covariates that are commonly thought to control for credit risk. This exercise yields Table A2.

This table indicates that implausibly high changes in observed credit risk covariates are necessary to increase the odds ratio by a factor of 1.5. For example, leverage will have to increase by at least 50% (i.e., 2.73 standard deviations) to increase the odds ratio of assignment by a factor of 1.5, which is the point at which we begin to question our results. Based on these results for observed covariates that affect credit risk, we conclude that it is unlikely such powerful unobserved covariates (over and above the long vector of observed covariates that we have controlled for) can be at work to challenge our estimates of the causal effect of relationships on spreads.

References

Barclay, M. J., and C. W. Smith. 1995. The Maturity Structure of Corporate Debt. *Journal of Finance* 50:609–31.

Barclay, M. J., L. M. Marx, and C. W. Smith. 2003. The Joint Determination of Leverage and Maturity. *Journal of Corporate Finance* 9:149–67.

Berger, A., and G. Udell. 1990. Collateral, Loan Quality and Bank Risk. *Journal of Monetary Economics* 25:21–42.

Berger, A., and G. Udell. 1995. Relationship Lending and Lines of Credit in Small Firm Finance. *Journal of Business* 68:351–81.

Berger, A., M. Espinosa-Vega, S. Frame, and N. Miller. 2005a. Debt Maturity, Risk, and Asymmetric Information. *Journal of Finance* 60:2895–923.

Berger, A., N. Miller, M. Petersen, R. Rajan, and J. Stein. 2005b. Does Function Follow Organizational Form? Evidence from the Lending Practices of Large and Small Banks. *Journal of Financial Economics* 76:237–69.

Berlin, M., and L. Mester. 1992. Debt Covenants and Renegotiations. *Journal of Financial Intermediation* 2:95–133.

Berlin, M., and L. Mester. 1998. Deposits and Relationship Lending. *Review of Financial Studies* 2:95–133.

Besanko, D., and A. Thakor. 1987. Collateral and Rationing: Sorting Equilibria in Monopolistic and Competitive Credit Markets. *International Economic Review* 28:601–689.

Bester, H. 1985. Screening vs. Rationing in Credit Market under Asymmetric Information. *Journal of Economic Theory* 42:167–82.

Bharath, S., S. Dahiya, A. Saunders, and A. Srinivasan. 2007. So What Do I Get? The Bank's View of Lending Relationships. *Journal of Financial Economics* 85:368–419.

Bharath, S., P. Pasquareillo, and G. Wu. 2009. Does Information Asymmetry Drive Capital Structure Decisions? *Review of Financial Studies* 22(8):3211–43.

Bhattacharya, S., and G. Chiesa. 1995. Proprietary Information, Financial Intermediation and Research Incentives. *Journal of Financial Intermediation* 4:328–57.

Boot, A. 2000. Relationship Banking: What Do We Know? *Journal of Financial Intermediation* 9:7–25.

Boot, A., A. Thakor, and G. Udell. 1991. Secured Lending and Default Risk: Equilibrium Analysis, Policy Implications, and Empirical Results. *Economics Journal* 101(406):458–72.

Boot, A., S. Greenbaum, and A. Thakor. 1993. Reputation and Discretion in Financial Contracting. *American Economic Review* 83:1165–83.

Boot, A., and A. Thakor. 1994. Moral Hazard and Secured Lending in an Infinitely Repeated Credit Market Game. *International Economic Review* 35:899–920.

Boot, A., and A. Thakor. 2000. Can Relationship Banking Survive Competition? *Journal of Finance* 55:679–713.

Bradley, M., and M. Roberts. 2004. The Structure and Pricing of Corporate Debt Covenants. Available at http://ssrn.com/abstract=466240.

Brick, I., and A. Ravid. 1985. On the Relevance of Debt Maturity Structure. *Journal of Finance* 40:1423–37.

Brick, I., and A. Ravid. 1991. Interest Rate Uncertainty and the Optimal Debt Maturity Structure. *Journal of Financial and Quantitative Analysis* 26:363–81.

Brown, R. L., J. Durbin, and J. M. Evans. 1975. Techniques for Testing for the Constancy of Regression Relationships over Time. *Journal of the Royal Statistical Society* 37:149–92.

Cantillo, M., and J. Wright. 2000. How Do Firms Choose Their Lenders? An Empirical Investigation. *Review of Financial Studies* 13:155–89.

Cole, R. A. 1998. The Importance of Relationships to the Availability of Credit. *Journal of Banking & Finance* 22:959–77.

Coval, J. D., and T. J. Moskowitz. 2001. The Geography of Investment: Informed Trading and Asset Prices. *Journal of Political Economy* 109(4):811–41.

Dahiya, S., A. Saunders, and A. Srinivasan. 2003. Financial Distress and Bank Lending Relationships. *Journal of Finance* 58:375–399.

Dass, N., and M. Massa. Forthcoming. The Bank-Firm Relationship: A Trade-Off between Better Governance and Greater Information Asymmetry. *Review of Financial Studies.*

Dechow, P., and I. Dichev. 2002. The Quality of Accruals and Earnings: The Role of Accrual Estimation Errors. *Accounting Review* 77(Supplement):35–59.

Degryse, H., and P. Van Cayseele. 2000. Relationship Lending within a Bank Based System: Evidence from European Small Business Data. *Journal of Financial Intermediation* 9:90–109.

Dennis, S., D. Nandy, and I. Sharpe. 2000. Determinants of Contract Terms in Bank Revolving Lines of Credit. *Journal of Financial and Quantitative Analysis* 35:87–109.

Detragiache, E., P. Garella, and L. Guiso. 2000. Multiple versus Single Banking Relationships: Theory and Evidence. *Journal of Finance* 55:1005–476.

Diamond, D. 1984. Financial Intermediation and Delegated Monitoring. *Review of Economic Studies* 62:393–414.

Diamond, D. 1991. Debt Maturity and Liquidity Risk. *Quarterly Journal of Economics* 106(3):709–37.

Diamond, D. 2004. Presidential Address, Committing to Commit: Short Term Debt When Enforcement Is Costly. *Journal of Finance* 59:1447–79.

Drucker, S., and M. Puri. 2005. On the Benefits of Concurrent Lending and Underwriting. *Journal of Finance* 60:2763–99.

Fama, E. 1985. What's Different about Banks? *Journal of Monetary Economics* 15(1):29–39.

Fama, E., and K. R. French. 1997. Industry Costs of Equity. *Journal of Financial Economics* 43:153–93.

Flannery, M. 1986. Asymmetric Information and Risky Debt Maturity Choice. *Journal of Finance* 41:19–37.

Greene, W. H. 2000. *Econometric Analysis*, 4th ed. Upper Saddle River, NJ: Prentice-Hall.

Hart, O., and J. Moore. 1994. A Theory of Debt Based on the Inalienability of Human Capital. *Quarterly Journal of Economics* 109:841–79.

Heckman, J., H. Ichimura, and P. Todd. 1997. Matching as an Econometric Evaluation Estimator: Evidence from Evaluating a Job Training Programme. *Review of Economic Studies* 64:605–54.

Heckman, J., H. Ichimura, and P. Todd. 1998. Matching as an Econometric Evaluation Estimator. *Review of Economic Studies* 65:261–94.

Holmstrom, B., and J. Tirole. 1997. Financial Intermediation, Loanable Funds, and the Real Sector. *Quarterly Journal of Economics* 112(3):663–91.

Hoshi, T., A. Kashyap, and D. Scharfstein. 1990. The Role of Banks in Reducing the Costs of Financial Distress in Japan. *Journal of Financial Economics* 27:67–88.

Jiménez, G., V. Salas, and J. Saurina. 2006. Determinants of Collateral. *Journal of Financial Economics* 81(2):255–81.

Kallberg, J., C. Liu, and A. Srinivasan. 2004. Limited Partnerships and Reputation Formation. *Journal of Financial and Quantitative Analysis* 39:631–59.

Kiyotaki, N., and J. Moore. 1997. Credit Cycles. *Journal of Political Economy* 105:211–48.

Melnik, A., and S. Plaut. 1986, Loan Commitment Contracts, Terms of Lending, and Credit Allocation. *Journal of Finance* 41:425–35.

Maddala, G. S. 1983. *Limited-Dependent and Qualitative Variables in Econometrics*. Cambridge: Cambridge University Press.

Petersen, M., and R. Rajan. 1994. The Benefits of Lending Relationships: Evidence from Small Business Data. *Journal of Finance* 49:3–37.

Petersen, M., and R. Rajan. 1995. The Effect of Credit Market Competition on Lending Relationships. *Quarterly Journal of Economics* 110:406–43.

Petersen, M., and R. Rajan. 2002. Does Distance Still Matter? The Information Revolution in Small Business Lending. *Journal of Finance* 57:2533–70.

Rajan, R. 1992. Insiders and Outsiders: The Relationship between Relationship and Arms Length Debt. *Journal of Finance* 47:1367–400.

Rajan, R., and A. Winton. 1995. Covenants and Collateral as Incentives to Monitor. *Journal of Finance* 50:1113–46.

Ramakrishnan, R., and A. Thakor. 1984. Information Reliability and a Theory of Financial Intermediation. *Review of Economic Studies* 51:415–32.

Rogers, W. 1993. Regression Standard Errors in Clustered Samples. *Stata Technical Bulletin* 13:19–23.

Rosenbaum, P. R. 2002. *Observational Studies*, 2nd ed. New York: Springer.

Sharpe, S. 1990. Asymmetric Information, Bank Lending and Implicit Contracts: A Stylized Model of Customer Relationships. *Journal of Finance* 45:1069–87.

Standard & Poor's. 2006. *A Guide to the Loan Market*.

Staiger, D., and J. Stock. 1997. Instrumental Variables Regression with Weak Instruments. *Econometrica* 65(3):557–86.

Stock J., and M. Yogo. 2005. Testing for Weak Instruments in Linear IV Regression. In D. W. K. Andrews and J. H. Stock (eds.), *Identification and Inference for Econometric Models: Essays in Honor of Thomas J. Rothenberg*, pp. 80–108. Cambridge: Cambridge University Press.

Strahan, P. 1999. Borrower Risk and the Price and Non-Price Terms of Bank Loans. Federal Reserve Bank of New York, Staff Paper No. 90. Available at http://ssrn.com/abstract=192769.

Stulz, R., and H. Johnson. 1985. An Analysis of Secured Debt. *Journal of Financial Economics* 14:501–21.

Sufi, A. 2007. Information Asymmetry and Financing Arrangements: Evidence from Syndicated Loans. *Journal of Finance* 62:629–68.

Wooldridge, J. M. 2002. *Econometric Analysis of Cross Section and Panel Data*. Cambridge, MA: MIT Press.

THE JOURNAL OF FINANCE • VOL. LVIII, NO. 1 • FEB. 2003

Financial Distress and Bank Lending Relationships

SANDEEP DAHIYA, ANTHONY SAUNDERS, and ANAND SRINIVASAN*

ABSTRACT

We use a unique data set of bank loans to examine the wealth effects on lead lending banks when their borrowers suffer financial distress. We find a significant negative announcement return for the lead lending bank when a major corporate borrower announces default or bankruptcy. Banks with higher exposure to the distressed firm have larger negative announcement-period returns. The existence of a past lending relationship with the distressed firm results in larger wealth declines for the bank shareholders. Finally, financial distress also has a significant negative effect on borrower's returns.

RECENT BANKING LITERATURE has focused increased attention on the costs and benefits of banking relationships (see Boot (2000)). In particular, existing empirical work has been aimed primarily at establishing and estimating the value of the relationships that borrowers have established with their bankers. Leading examples include James (1987; excess returns to borrowers on the announcement of new bank loans), Peterson and Rajan (1994; the role of the length of a relationship in determining the availability and pricing of bank credit), Puri (1996) and Gande et al. (1997; better pricing of newly issued securities when the underwriter also has a lending relationship). More recently, Dahiya et al. (2002) examine the value loss when bank relationships weaken by examining loan sale announcements. Thus, there is considerable evidence of value creation for the borrower, on initiation or renewal of a banking relationship. However, there is a paucity of studies that attempt to measure the value of such relationships for lending banks. Peterson and Rajan (1995) and Berlin and Mester (1998) suggest that banks have incentives to smooth out the interest charged on loans if they have repeated transactions with a borrower over a long period of time. This suggests that banks find it valuable to invest in and maintain long-term customer relationships. Nevertheless, the costs of such relationships to a bank are often ignored. In this paper, we attempt to fill this gap in the literature by examining the impact of a borrower's distress on its lead bank. The financial distress of a borrower should

*Dahiya is with Georgetown University, Saunders is with New York University, and Srinivasan is with the University of Georgia. This paper has benefited greatly from suggestions and comments from an anonymous referee as well as from Rick Green (the editor), Yakov Amihud, Ned Elton, Loretta Mester, David Yermack, Marc Zenner, and Kose John. We would like to thank Edward Altman, Mark Carey, and Edith Hotchkiss for providing the data used in this study.

reduce the value of any banking relationship. Specifically, we analyze the bank's share price reaction when one of a bank's corporate borrowers enters financial distress as reflected by a bond default and/or bankruptcy.

There are strong arguments for treating a borrower's distress announcement as a "no news" (or low cost) event for a bank. First, prudent banking norms limit the losses that a bank might suffer if any single borrower is unable to repay its debt, and typically a bank loan is secured and is senior debt.[1] Thus, the recovery rate on defaulted debt is likely to be fairly high for bank loans.[2] Second, banks are considered insiders with significant informational advantages. This implies that banks are likely to be better informed about the financial status of their borrowers and thus will be able to take steps to reduce their loan exposures before the news of a borrower's distress becomes public information. Last, in many instances, news of a borrower's distress is preceded by other public announcements such as a decline in its earnings, a cut in its dividends, and so forth, which may diminish the informational content of news regarding financial distress.

These effects have to be weighed against the hypothesis that a borrower's financial distress announcement is an "adverse news" event that has a negative impact on a bank's share price. First, there is a direct effect on the bank due to the expected losses because of the borrower's distress. This effect should be related to the exposure of the bank to the borrower. Second, there may also be indirect effects of the borrower's distress on the bank's stock price. Such indirect effects may arise from many sources. For example, multiplier or contagion effects may exist if the distress of one borrower is correlated across an industry (or region). That is, a firm's distress may convey information about an increased likelihood of distress of other borrowers in the same industry to which the bank may be exposed. In addition, the news of a corporate borrower's distress may be construed as a signal of poor loan initiation and management skills, with an accompanied loss of a bank's reputational values.[3] Last, bank regulators scrutinize banks' books to ensure that they meet the banking requirements of regulatory capital. A default or bankruptcy event is likely to increase this scrutiny and, therefore, will act as an additional "regulatory" tax on the bank.[4]

[1] Regulation also restricts loan exposures to a borrower to a maximum of 15 percent of the capital of the bank.

[2] Weiss (1990) studies 37 publicly traded firms and finds that secured creditors' claims are paid in full in most cases. To the extent that bank loans are secured, this suggests a fairly high recovery rate. Franks and Torous (1994), using a sample from 1983 to 1989, find that bank loans have recovery rates of about 85 percent. However, more recent evidence by Gupton, Gates, and Carey (2000) suggests a recovery rate of between 50 to 65 percent for bank loss in the event of default.

[3] The loss of reputational value may also be reflected in the unwillingness of other banks to enter into new loan syndications arranged by the lead bank. For example, Smith (1992) reports that Salomon Brothers lost over a third of it market value because of the treasury auction scandal in 1991. This loss of value, which amounted to over $1.5 billion, was well above the fines and other costs arising from expected legal and regulatory sanctions.

[4] Also, Benveniste, Singh, and Wilhelm (1993) find that the bankruptcy of Drexel Burnham resulted in positive returns for rival banks likely to benefit from this event.

The central hypothesis explored in this paper is whether the news of a corporate borrower's distress has a material economic impact on its lead bank. A group of studies has examined the impact on the lending banks' share price of the announcement of debt moratoriums by sovereign borrowers (see, e.g., Lamy, Marr, and Thompson (1986), Smirlock and Kaufold (1987), Grammatikos and Saunders (1990), and Musumeci and Sinkey (1990)). However, the evidence from these studies is mixed, with the majority of them finding negative reactions that are heterogeneous across banks.

Kracaw and Zenner (1996) examine bank share price reactions to nine highly leveraged firms that became financially distressed. They find a negative share price reaction for these banks, but one that was not statistically significant. However, these findings were for a very small sample of firms involved in highly leveraged transactions such as leveraged buyouts (LBOs) or recapitalizations. In contrast, our sample consists of a much larger number of firms (many of which are publicly traded) that faced financial distress and/or bankruptcy over a relatively lengthy sample period.

The rest of the paper proceeds as follows. Section I describes the sample selection and the data collection procedure. Section II describes the methodology. The empirical results and their interpretation are presented in Section III. We conclude with a brief summary of our main findings in Section IV.

I. Sample Selection and Data Collection

We define a firm to be financially distressed if it has insufficient cash flows to meet the payments on its debt.[5] This paper examines two types of financial distress announcements: (1) the default on a firm's public debt, and (2) the filing by a firm for bankruptcy protection under Chapter 11. Specifically, in all cases, we use a single date for default for each company, and this date is the first date of default of publicly traded debt as listed in the database on defaulted bonds produced by Altman.[6]

Gilson et al. (1990) (henceforth, GJL) and others use a broader set of events to define distress. In particular, while defaults constitute over 50 percent of the first event of distress in GJL, they also use reports of restructuring of debt, where the firm's creditors suffer some impairment on their claim due to an exchange of debt into equity or convertible securities, reduction of interest payments or

[5] Gilson, John, and Lang (1990), Wruck (1990), Franks and Torous (1994), Tashijian, Lease, and McConnell (1996), and Andrade and Kaplan (1998) study the effect of distress on the borrowing firm.

[6] We used data from "The Defaulted Bond Master Database" produced and updated by Altman (see, e.g., Altman and Kishore (1996)). This database includes defaults on medium- and long-term publicly traded bonds and debentures and does not include short-term debt or commercial paper defaults. This database covers over 1,000 defaults beginning in 1971. Default is defined as the issuer's inability to meet an interest or principal payment on the company's medium-term or long-term public debt, and the date on which this occurs is defined as the date of default.

principal, or extension of maturity. Such restructuring is termed as distressed restructuring. Towards the end of this paper, we study the effect of such distress events on our results. For the most part, our sample consists of distress events that occur subsequent to the sample period in GJL. Also, the borrower does not have to be a publicly traded firm to enter into our sample; rather, the only requirement is that the borrower have a bank loan outstanding.[7]

The impact of each of these announcements on a borrower's lead bank is estimated by calculating the abnormal returns for the bank's shareholders around the date of the relevant announcement. The study analyzes 71 cases of default and 101 cases of bankruptcy filings for a 10-year period, 1987 to 1996. We study the two events separately by constructing a sample of lead banks that had loans outstanding to firms on the date of their default and another sample of lead banks that had loans outstanding to firms on the date of their Chapter 11 filings. We also create a subsample of firms that are common to both samples. For this latter subsample, we first examine the impact of default and then that of subsequent bankruptcy. This allows us to control for the partial anticipation of bankruptcy induced by an earlier bond default. We repeat the same test for the subsample of distressed firms that either did not have any public debt outstanding or for whom the default and the bankruptcy events occurred simultaneously. This allows us to examine the informational content of a bankruptcy announcement without contamination due to a prior signal such as default.

To construct the sample of distressed firm announcement dates and the lending relationships of these firms, the following data were employed: (1) a comprehensive list of firms that defaulted on their public debt and the date of the default over the period 1987 to 1996, (2) a list of firms that filed for Chapter 11 and their filing date over the period 1987 to 1996, (3) details of bank loans made to distressed firms that were outstanding at the time of their default and/or bankruptcy.

The primary source for the list of defaults was an updated version of the Altman database used in Altman and Kishore (1996), and the primary source for the bankruptcies was Hotchkiss (1995).[8] These lists were cross-checked and supplemented with information from a variety of other sources. These included *The Bankruptcy Almanac*, published by New Generation Research, and various news sources, such as the Dow Jones News Retrieval Services and the Lexis-Nexis bankruptcy library.

We used data from the Loan Pricing Corporation Database (LPC)[9] to get details of loan transactions and the nature of the relationship between distressed firms and their banks. The LPC database contains detailed transaction-level information related to loan amount, start and expiration dates, terms and purpose of the loans, the name of the lead bank(s), and the syndicate's size. These details are especially advantageous in examining the impact of a borrower's distress on its lead bank. First, it allows for the identification of the lead bank(s) of a

[7] Tashijian et al. (1996) also do not require presence of public stock or private debt. However, they focus only on prepackaged bankruptcies.

[8] We thank Edith Hotchkiss and Ed Altman for sharing their data.

[9] We thank Mark Carey for providing help with the LPC data.

distressed firm. Second, the details of the loan transactions provide a rich cross section of loan attributes. Last, the start and the maturity dates allow us to determine whether a loan was outstanding at the time of distress.

The sample selection procedure was as follows: The names of the firms that defaulted on their bonds or filed for bankruptcy were hand matched with the list of loan borrowers in the LPC database. This allowed us to determine for which of these firms loan data were available.[10] This step yielded a list of 971 loan transactions involving borrowers that subsequently defaulted or filed for bankruptcy. This sample was further narrowed down to include only those transactions which were entered into before the date of the distress announcement and that had a contractual maturity date later than the date of the distress announcement. This step insured that we only included those transactions that could reasonably be assumed to be outstanding at the onset of financial distress. Using the default date as the date for distress, we obtained a sample of 174 transactions that could be assumed to be outstanding on the date of default. A similar procedure using the date of Chapter 11 filing as the distress date yielded a sample of 272 transactions. Next, we located the lead bank for these transactions by looking and searching for the words "arranger," "administrative agent," "agent," or "lead bank" in the lender role definition in the LPC database.[11] Finally, we used the names of all the commercial banks listed on CRSP in conjunction with the list of lead banks for the sample of firms that defaulted or filed for Chapter 11.[12] This step eliminated the transactions that had a foreign bank or a nonbank finance company as the lead lender.

The final sample consists of 123 transactions involving 71 borrowers that subsequently defaulted on their public debt and 174 transactions involving 101 borrowers that subsequently filed for bankruptcy. The 71 announcements of default represent 99 announcement events for the lead banks, while the 101 announcements of bankruptcy represent 130 announcement events. The higher number of bank events compared to the number of firms in distress occurs because some of the firms had multiple lead banks.

Sources of data on bank and borrower characteristics for the distressed borrowers' sample included the LPC database, Moody's manuals, and BANK COMPUSTAT. The size of the loan transaction, the purpose and terms of the deal, and the syndicate size were taken from the LPC database. The balance sheet data for

[10] The LPC database lists each credit facility as a separate record field. Thus, a single borrower may have multiple credit facilities from the same bank, or a single credit facility that is syndicated among multiple banks, or multiple facilities syndicated among multiple banks.

[11] The LPC database lists the role of the lead syndicate member as arrangers, co-arrangers, lead bank, agents, co-agents, documentation/credit agent, or lead manager. We looked for any of these role levels within a syndicate to assign the lead bank role. All the credit facilities included in the sample had a clear lead bank, as all syndicate members other than the lead bank were defined as participants in the credit facility.

[12] A number of loans were made by the subsidiaries of the main bank holding company. For this study, we use the stock price reaction of the bank holding company. Also, some of the banks merged or were taken over after the loan was made, but before the company filed for bankruptcy. In those instances, the announcement effect of bankruptcy is measured on the merged/acquirer bank.

lead banks, where available, was obtained from BANK COMPUSTAT data tapes. Where the information was not available, it was supplemented by information taken from Moody's bank manuals. The information on bank holding companies was obtained from Moody's bank manuals.

In Panel A of Table I we provide the distribution of the sample by the year of the bankruptcy and default announcement. Most of the financial distress announcements are clustered in the years 1990 to 1993. This is in line with the timing of the economic recession of the 1990 to 1991 period, when more cases of financial distress are to be expected. More than 70 percent of the defaults and bankruptcies occur in the 1990 to 1993 period.

In panel B, we document the characteristics of the lender banks. There are 22 different banks for the sample of 71 firms that defaulted on their public debt (36 banks for 101 firms that filed for Chapter 11). We also report the mean ratio of total transaction size to the equity of the lead bank in the year before the date of distress. This ratio is 19.02 percent (median 6.08 percent) for the banks of defaulting firms (mean 12.1 percent, median 2.7 percent for the banks of firms filing for Chapter 11). The absolute level of this ratio should be interpreted with care as it represents the ratio of the aggregate transaction size to the lead bank's equity. This is not the bank's actual exposure, as that would depend on the share of the

Table I

Descriptive Statistics of the Sample

This table presents the descriptive statistics of the credit transactions and the lead banks of the borrowers that experienced financial distress over the period 1987 to 1996. The sample is categorized by the year of onset of financial distress; i.e., default on public debt or filing for chapter 11 (in Panel A), the number of lead banks involved (in Panel B), the size and type of transaction (in Panel C), and the specific structure of the credit transaction (in Panel D).

Panel A: Distribution of the sample by year of announcement

Year of financial distress	Number of defaults	Number of bankruptcies
1987	2	1
1988	1	1
1989	3	7
1990	16	16
1991	27	32
1992	11	22
1993	3	11
1994	2	4
1995	6	6
1996	0	1
Total (1987–1996)	71	101

Panel B: Lender characteristics

	Default	Chapter 11 filing
Number of bank announcement events	99	130
Number of different banks involved	22	36
Average transaction size to bank equity ratio (median)	19.02% (6.8%)	12.10% (2.7%)
Average loan loss reserve ratio (median)	2.3% (2.05%)	2.08% (2.05%)

Table I.—*continued*

Panel C: Mean (median) statistics for the credit transactions

Transaction Type	Default			Chapter 11		
	No. of Trans-actions	Trans-action size ($ mm)	Syndicate size	No. of Trans-actions	Trans-action size (mm)	Syndicate size
Debt repayment/ consolidation	26	208 (145)	10.4 (5.5)	45	156 (80)	9.9 (6)
General corporate purposes	21	236 (100)	9.2 (6)	36	162 (50)	7.4 (4)
Working capital	25	161 (110)	8.2 (7)	31	128 (78)	7 (2)
Takeover acquisition	17	962 (200)	22.1 (7)	18	912 (212)	20.8 (8)
Leveraged buyout	16	616 (327)	25.9(17)	14	380 (357)	20 (8)
Recapitalization	10	919 (370)	33 (19.5)	10	816 (287)	29 (15)
Others	8	167 (112)	10.8 (5)	20	101 (53)	5 (1.5)
TOTAL	123	415 (195)	15.2 (7)	174	280 (260)	11.4 (4)

Panel D: Additional information on the structure of credit transactions

	Default	Chapter 11 filing
	Mean (Median)	Mean (Median)
Premium over LIBOR ($n = 88; 96$)	2.05% (2.50%)	1.91% (2.00%)
Premium over US prime ($n = 110; 151$)	1.24% (1.50%)	1.17% (1.37%)
Commitment fee ($n = 74; 88$)	0.46% (0.50%)	0.42% (0.50%)
Up-front fee ($n = 59; 81$)	1.21% (1.15%)	1.02% (0.87%)

transaction size retained by the lead bank, since most of these transactions are syndicated among other participating banks and nonbank finance companies. Also, each transaction is made up of multiple facilities, not all of which may be fully drawn-down. While this ratio is not an exact estimate of the bank's exposure to the distressed firm, it is a proxy for the upper limit of a bank's exposure.[13]

In Panel C, we provide the descriptive statistics at the aggregate loan transaction level. Our full sample consists of 123 transactions involving firms that defaulted and 174 transactions involving firms that filed for Chapter 11. All of these loan transactions had a contractual life that overlapped the date of default/bankruptcy by the borrowing firm. The mean (median) transaction size of $415 million ($195 million) for the default sample is larger than the mean (median) transaction size of $280 million ($260 million) for the bankruptcy sample. We also partition our sample by the stated purpose of the transaction. The large proportion of the lending is for the purposes of LBOs, recapitalizations, takeovers, and working capital. Although takeover/acquisition, leveraged buyouts, and

[13] Indeed, a bank faces reputational losses, in addition to the size of loan retained, should a syndicate led by that bank make losses. The mean ratio of loan loss reserves to the total assets of the lead banks for the year before the year of distress is 2.3 percent (median 2.05 percent) for the sample of lead banks of defaulting firms, and 2.1 percent (median 2.05 percent) for the banks of bankrupt firms.

recapitalizations account for less than one-fourth of the number of transactions, they account for over 60 percent of the total dollar value. These transactions are also fairly large. For example, in the case of the sample of firms that declared bankruptcy, the mean transaction size for takeover/acquisition is $912 million (median $212 million), for LBOs $380 million ($357 million), and for recapitalizations $816 million ($287 million). In comparable studies of LBOs and recapitalizations, Kaplan (1989) has a mean (median) transaction size of $524 million ($254 million), and Muscarella and Vetsuypens (1990) have a mean (median) value of $250 million ($105 million). Relatively large syndicates finance these transactions. The mean size of the syndicate involved in a transaction to finance takeover/acquisitions is 20.8 (median 8), while that for LBOs is 20 (median 8), and for recapitalizations 29 (median 15). The transactions providing the day-to-day regular financing for working capital and general corporate purposes account for over 45 percent of the transactions by number, but constitute less than 25 percent of the total dollar value. This is reflected in the mean transaction size for working capital, $128 million (median $ 78 million), and for general corporate purposes, $157 million ($50 million). The mean syndicate size for working capital is 7 (median 2), and 7.1 (median 4) for general corporate purposes.

Additional information about the structure of the sample of transactions is presented in Panel D of Table II. For the sample of firms filing for Chapter 11, on

Table II

Cumulative Abnormal Returns for the Lead Banks on the Announcement of Financial Distress by Their Borrowers

Cumulative abnormal return (CARs) for the lead banks of the firms facing financial distress over the period 1987 to 1996. Panel A describes the share performance of lead bank(s) around the date of default by the borrower, and Panel B describes the same around the date of chapter 11 filing. The sample of firms that defaulted on their public debt and the date of default are obtained from the Altman database of defaulted bonds, and the sample of firms that filed for chapter 11 is compiled from multiple sources including Hotchkiss (1995), DJNR, the *Bankruptcy Almanac*, and Lexis bankruptcy library. CARs are calculated using the Center for Research in Security Prices (CRSP) database.

Event Window	ACAR	*t*-statistic	Median CAR	Wilcoxon *z*-statistic
Panel A: Abnormal returns for the lead banks when borrowers default on public debt ($N = 99$)				
11-day window [− 8, 2]	− 3.766%	− 5.327***	− 2.547%	− 3.886***
7-day window [− 4, 2]	− 1.922%	− 3.445***	− 1.158%	− 3.084***
5-day window [− 2, 2]	− 1.750%	− 3.769***	− 1.522%	− 3.192***
3-day window [− 1, 1]	− 0.857%	− 2.459**	− 0.719%	− 2.513**
Panel B: Abnormal returns for the lead banks when borrowers file for chapter 11 ($N = 130$)				
11-day window [− 8, 2]	− 1.832%	− 3.303***	− 1.305%	− 2.165**
7-day window [− 4, 2]	− 1.089%	− 2.437**	− 0.686%	− 2.003**
5-day window [− 2, 2]	− 0.911%	− 2.131**	− 0.350%	− 2.268**
3-day window [− 1, 1]	− 0.492%	− 1.367	− 0.386%	− 1.391

***Significant at the one percent level
**Significant at the five percent level
*Significant at the 10 percent level

average, the borrower paid a premium of 1.89 percent (median 2 percent) over LIBOR and 1.16 percent (median 1.25 percent) over the U.S. prime rate. Commitment fees on the unused portion of the lending facility are 0.43 percent and the up-front fees are 1 percent. The statistics for the sample of defaulting firms are similar. The loan rates are lower for our sample compared to those reported by Kracaw and Zenner (1996) for their sample of nine highly leveraged transactions.

II. Test Methodology

The basic null hypothesis is:

H_0: The announcement of a firm's financial distress is a "no news" event for the firm's lead bank(s).

The alternative hypothesis is:

H_1: The announcement of a firm's financial distress is an "adverse news" event for the firm's lead bank(s).

A simple way to examine the reaction of a bank's stock price to the announcement of a borrower's financial distress is to employ a standard event study methodology to study the movements in the bank's stock return around the date of the announcement of financial distress by the borrower. However, the use of the default announcement or Chapter 11 filing as the study event poses some problems. These announcements are usually preceded by many other announcements and news stories that foreshadow the subsequent announcement of default and/or bankruptcy. Thus, the traditional narrow event window of two or three days is unlikely to capture the entire stock price reaction of a bank lender. A typical chronology of the release of various distress-related announcements is illustrated by Figure 1.

The release of relevant information prior to the actual event is well illustrated by the chronology of news items that appeared before the default and bankruptcy of Columbia Gas Systems, which suffered a long period of financial deterioration before finally filing for bankruptcy.

- June 20, 1991—Columbia Gas Systems suspends dividends and calls for renegotiations with its gas suppliers. The firm said that potential losses on existing contracts exceed $1.1 billion. (*Wall Street Journal*)
- June 21, 1991—Columbia Gas Systems defaulted on $15 million of commercial paper and other short-term notes. (*Wall Street Journal*)

1	2	3	4
Dividend cuts, Earnings decline	Default on debt, Credit rating change	Chapter 11 filing	Plan of reorganization is confirmed

Figure 1. Typical chronology of distress-related news information. The figure provides a typical time-line illustration of how different classes of distress-related news stories are announced.

- June 25, 1991—Columbia Gas Systems defaulted on an additional $10 million of short term notes. (*Wall Street Journal*)
- July 9, 1991—Columbia Gas Systems defaulted on $14 million of commercial paper. (*Wall Street Journal*)
- July 22, 1991—Columbia Gas Systems defaulted on $15 million of short-term debt. (*Wall Street Journal*)
- August 1, 1991—Columbia Gas Systems files for bankruptcy. (*Wall Street Journal*).

The long drawn-out nature of the distress process makes the use of the standard two- or three-day event window unsuitable for this study.[14] To fully capture the impact of the deterioration in the bank–borrower relationship more usefully, we use four different event windows: 11 days, 7 days, 5 days, and the traditional 3 days, to measure the market's reaction to the news of a borrower's default and bankruptcy on its lead bank. (We also examined event windows of 15 and 21 days; the results are essentially identical and are not reported).

We calculate the announcement abnormal returns for banks using the market model methodology as detailed in Mikkelson and Partch (1986) and James (1987). The parameters of the market model are estimated by regressing the firm's common stock returns for the period 200 days before the event date, to 50 days before the event date on the rate of return on CRSP's dividend inclusive, equal-weighted index for NYSE/AMEX/Nasdaq stocks. The abnormal return is computed as the difference between the observed return and the estimated return from the market model. Cumulative abnormal returns (CAR) are the sum of abnormal returns for the days in the relevant event window. Tests of significance are based on standardized abnormal returns and CARs. In the last section of the paper, we also examine the effect of distress on the borrower using an event study in a manner similar to GJL and others. We use the equally weighted index as the benchmark and a similar estimation period for the borrowing firms.

III. Empirical Results

A. Stock Price Response to the News of Financial Distress

If the announcement of its borrowers' financial distress is a no news event for the lead bank, we do not expect to find any abnormal movement in the stock price of the bank around the date of the announcement. However, if the distress is an adverse news event, then negative wealth effects for the lead bank's shareholders are expected. The results presented below are largely consistent with the adverse news hypothesis.

[14] The date of default in the Altman database for Columbia Gas Systems was July 31, 1991 (see footnote 6). This date also corresponds to the date on which the company's senior and subordinated debt were downgraded to the default rating status of D by S&P.

Specifically, Table II, Panel A, presents the average stock price response of the lead banks to the announcements of public debt defaults of their borrowers. For the 11-day period starting 8 days before the news of default and lasting until 2 days after, the average cumulative abnormal return (ACAR) is −3.77 percent, which is significant at the 1 percent level (t-statistic = −5.39). −Narrowing the event window to 7 days and further to 5 days leaves the results unchanged. For the traditional event window of 3 days (−1, 0, +1), the ACAR is −0.86 percent, which is still significant at the 5 percent level (t-statistic = −2.45). Thus, the news of borrowers' defaulting on their public debt is received as significant adverse news by the shareholders of the lead lending banks.

In Table II, Panel B, we repeat the event study for a different sample of firms for whom the onset of financial distress is proxied by the date of their filing for Chapter 11 bankruptcy. The direction of the results is similar to the default sample—again, the announcement has a negative effect on the lead bank's share price. However, the scale of the stock price reaction is much lower on the news of bankruptcy than on bond default. The 11-day ACAR is −1.83 percent, which is significant at the 1 percent level (t-statistic = −3.30). This is roughly half of the size of the price reaction that banks suffer on the news of default. (The results are similar for 7-day and 5-day windows). For the 3-day window, the ACAR is negative but statistically insignificant.[15]

Overall, the tests for the aggregate sample of banks provide strong evidence for the adverse news hypothesis especially on the announcement of bond defaults. However, there is considerable variation in the size of credit transactions and the size of the lending banks. Although the details of individual bank exposures are not public knowledge, an informationally efficient market would react more severely to the distress announcement of a borrower in which the lead bank had a relatively high exposure compared to a bank with a relatively low exposure. We examine the impact of exposure levels on the magnitude of the lead bank's stock price reaction next.

B. Stock Price Response of High versus Low Exposure Banks

If the individual share of each bank in each loan transaction were known, we would be able to determine the exact dollar amount that the lead bank has directly exposed to the distressed firm. Unfortunately, we only have data on the aggregate size of each loan transaction. To differentiate the banks with high exposure from those with low exposure, we calculate the following

[15] We also performed a nonparametric Wilcoxon signed rank test for differences between the abnormal returns. This test has two principal advantages over parametric tests like the t-test and the z-test: (1) It uses only the rank of the returns ordered in terms of the magnitude and sign and does not use the magnitude of the return; therefore, it is robust to the presence of outliers; and (2) it does not make assumptions about the distribution of abnormal returns. If the two sets of data are identically distributed, then the sum of ranks of the two sets should be close to each other. The difference in the sum of ranks can be used to test for differences in the sample mean of the two data sets. In virtually all cases (See Table II, column 5), the direction and the level of statistical significance of the results of this test are consistent with those obtained in the t-tests.

exposure ratio for each bank j to a given borrowing firm k:

$$Exp_j = \frac{\sum_{i=1}^{T} Transacamount_{ij}^{k}}{Bankcap_j}, \tag{1}$$

where for each borrower k, $Transacamount_{ij}$ is the dollar amount of transaction i; for which bank j was the lead bank, T is the total number of loan transactions that lead bank j has outstanding at the time of distress to the borrower, and $Bankcap_j$ is the capital of the bank j as reported for the year before the year of borrower's distress.

Thus, Exp_j provides a proxy for the bank's exposure to the distressed borrower. We divide the default sample into the two subsamples based on this ratio: banks with exposure ratios higher than the median of 6.84 percent and banks with exposure levels lower than the median. This is repeated for the bankruptcy sample (median exposure ratio 2.78 percent). In Table III, we report the results of the event study for these subsamples. We find that the price reaction is much more negative and significant for the subsample of highly exposed banks. This holds true for both the news of a bond default as well as for bankruptcy. Panel A compares the ACAR for the high exposure banks and the low exposure banks around the date of default by the bank's borrower. The 11-day ACAR is −5.48 percent for the high exposure banks, which is approximately twice as large as the ACAR of −2.09 percent for the low exposure banks. The ACAR is negative and statistically significant for the high exposure banks across all event windows, yet while it is also negative for the low exposure banks, it is not statistically significant. We also test whether the difference between the ACAR for the two groups is statistically significant. The last column in panel A reports the t-statistics for the difference between high exposure and low exposure banks. The differences between the two groups are significant for all event windows.

Panel B reports the same results for the price reaction around the date of Chapter 11 filings. The results are similar to the ones reported in Panel A. The 11-day ACAR for the high exposure banks is −2.95 percent (t-statistic = −3.49). Low exposure banks, on the other hand, have an ACAR of −0.72 percent (t-statistic = −1.17). Varying the length of the event window to 7, 5 or 3 days leaves the results largely unchanged, as the high exposure banks suffer a price reaction much larger than that for the banks with low exposure. However, the statistical significance of the difference between the two groups is much weaker. As reported in the last column, the difference between the two groups is only significant for the 11-day window.

Finally, some of the firms in our bankruptcy sample are included in the sample of defaulting firms. This may diminish the true effect of the bankruptcy announcement for these firms, as the news of their bankruptcy may have already been anticipated by the news of their bond default. Thus, the chronological order of various distress announcements may have an important bearing on how the market reacts to news regarding distressed borrowers. We investigate this in the next section.

Table III

Cumulative Abnormal Returns for the Higher and Lower Exposure Lead Banks on Announcement of Financial Distress by Their Borrowers

Average Cumulative Abnormal Return (ACARs) for the lead bank(s) of the firms facing financial distress over the period 1987 to 1996. The figures in parentheses below each ACAR represent the ± statistic that tests if the given ACAR is significantly different from zero. Panel A compares the share performance of higher exposure lead banks with that of lower exposure lead bank(s) around the date of default by the borrower, and Panel B describes the same around the date of Chapter 11 filing by the borrower. The exposure is defined as the ratio of aggregate transaction size divided by the lead bank's equity as reported for the latest year before borrowers' financial distress. The sample of firms that defaulted on their public debt and the date of default are obtained from the Altman database of defaulted bonds, and the sample of firms that filed for Chapter 11 is compiled from multiple sources including Hotchkiss (1995), DJNR, the *Bankruptcy Almanac*, and Lexis bankruptcy library. CARs are calculated using the Center for Research in Security Prices (CRSP) database.

Event Window	ACAR for higher exposure banks	ACAR for lower exposure banks	*t*-statistic for Difference
Panel A: ACAR for the lead banks around the date of default by the banks' borrowers			
11-day window [– 8, 2]	– 5.485%	– 2.081%	– 2.035**
	(– 5.517)***	(– 2.034**)	
7-day window [– 4, 2]	– 3.212%	– 0.792%	– 2.374**
	(– 4.125)***	(– 0.763)	
5-day window [– 2, 2]	– 3.086%	– 0.441%	– 2.784***
	(– 4.559)***	(– 0.790)	
3-day window [– 1, 1]	– 1.829%	0.098%	– 2.697***
	(– 3.692)***	(– 0.202)	
Panel B: ACAR for the lead banks around the date of Chapter 11 filing by the banks' borrowers			
11-day window [– 8, 2]	– 2.946%	– 0.719%	– 1.701*
	(– 3.499)***	(– 1.173)	
7-day window [– 4, 2]	– 1.855%	– 0.321%	– 1.624
	(– 2.909)***	(– 0.536)	
5-day window [– 2, 2]	– 1.268%	– 0.554%	– 0.979
	(– 2.127)**	(– 0.886)	
3-day window [– 1, 1]	– 0.894%	– 0.095%	– 1.418
	(– 1.739)*	(– 0.201)	

***Significant at the 1 percent level
**Significant at the 5 percent level
*Significant at the 10 percent level

C. Reaction to the News of Default Prior to Bankruptcy

The sample of borrowing firms filing for bankruptcy can be divided into two subsamples depending on whether or not there was a bond default prior to the bankruptcy. We construct a subsample of 33 firms that defaulted on their public debt at least seven days prior to filing for bankruptcy. The remaining 68 firms either did not have any public debt outstanding or their default and bankruptcy announcements occurred on the same day.

For the subsample of 33 firms, the announcement of a Chapter 11 filing would be partially anticipated because of their prior default on public debt. Thus, the expectation of bankruptcy would already have been incorporated (in part) in the bank's share price by the time bankruptcy was actually announced. For the subsample of 68 firms, however, the news of the bankruptcy would still have significant informational content. This is supported by the results reported in Table IV. Panel A presents the ACAR of the banks for the first subsample (33 firms) on the announcement of default, while Panel B reports the ACAR results for the

Table IV

Cumulative Abnormal Returns for the Lead Banks for the Sub-sample of Borrowers Filing for Bankruptcy

Average Cumulative Abnormal Return (ACARs) for the lead bank(s) of the firms that defaulted on their bonds at least seven days prior to filing for bankruptcy over the period 1987 to 1996. Panels A and B describe the share performance of the lead banks of the firms that defaulted on their public debt at least seven days before filing for bankruptcy. Panel A presents the ACAR around the date of default and Panel B describes the same around the date of bankruptcy by the borrowers. Panel C describes the performance of lead banks for the subsample of bankrupt firms that either did not have public debt outstanding or the default and bankruptcy announcement was made simultaneously. The sample of firms that defaulted on their public debt and the date of default are obtained from the Altman database of defaulted bonds, and the sample of firms that filed for chapter 11 is compiled from multiple sources including Hotchkiss (1995), DJNR, the *Bankruptcy Almanac*, and Lexis bankruptcy library. CARs are calculated using the Center for Research in Security Prices (CRSP) database.

Event window	ACAR	*t*-statistic
Panel A: ACAR for the lead banks on the date of default for their borrower firms that subsequently filed for bankruptcy ($N = 51$)		
11-day window [−8, 2]	−2.812%	−3.011***
7-day window [−4, 2]	−1.929%	−2.787***
5-day window [−2, 2]	−1.291%	−2.256**
3-day window [−1, 1]	−0.669 %	−1.561
Panel B: ACAR for the lead banks on the date of bankruptcy by the firms in Panel A sample ($N = 51$)		
11-day window [−8, 2]	−0.187%	0.358
7-day window [−4, 2]	−0.163%	0.083
5-day window [−2, 2]	−0.321%	0.008
3-day window [−1, 1]	0.0409%	0.611
Panel C: ACAR for the lead banks on the date of bankruptcy by the firms that had no public debt or the default and bankruptcy occurred simultaneously ($N = 79$)		
11-day window [−8, 2]	−2.894%	−4.267***
7-day window [−4, 2]	−1.686%	−3.193***
5-day window [−2, 2]	−1.293 %	−2.739***
3-day window [−1, 1]	−0.836%	−2.243**

***Significant at the one percent level
**Significant at the five percent level
*Significant at the 10 percent level

same 33 firms in the event of their subsequent bankruptcy filing. As reported in Panel A, the announcement returns are −2.81 percent for the 11-day window on the news of the bond default, which is significant at the one percent level (*t*-statistic = −3.01). The results are directionally similar for the 7-, 5-, and 3-day windows. However, when these same firms declare bankruptcy (Panel B), the ACAR for the lead banks is only −0.19 percent for the 11 days around the date of their Chapter 11 filing, failing to reject the null hypothesis (*t*-statistic = 0.358). The results are similar for event windows of shorter length. These results imply that prior news of a bond default significantly reduces the informational content (for banks) of subsequent bankruptcy announcements by their borrowers.

In Panel C, we report the results for the subsample of bankrupt firms that either did not have any public debt or for whom default and the bankruptcy occurred simultaneously. For these firms, there is no default signal of distress prior to their declaration of bankruptcy. In the absence of any prior default news, we find a bankruptcy announcement return for banks of −2.89 percent for the 11-day window, which is significant at the one percent level (*t*-statistic = −4.27). The results are robust to different lengths of the event window, which continue to be negative and significant. Thus, when there is no prior bond default, the bankruptcy announcement of a firm has a significantly negative impact on the market value of its lead lending bank.[16]

D. *Multivariate Tests*

Our results so far show that the shareholders of a lead bank suffer a wealth decline when there is unanticipated news of financial distress by their major borrowers. In this section, we seek to confirm our univariate findings and to investigate other factors that may potentially affect bank abnormal returns around distress announcements. Specifically, there is considerable variation in the characteristics of the banks and the loans in our sample, as well as in macroeconomic conditions, which may have had an impact on how the market reacted to news of a borrower's distress. To examine the impact of these factors on announcement period returns for banks lending to distressed firms, we estimate a regression model that takes the following form:

$$\begin{aligned}\mathrm{CAR_j} &= \beta_0 + \beta_1 \mathrm{RELATIONSHIP}_j + \beta_2 \mathrm{EXPOSURE_j} + \beta_2 \mathrm{RECESSION}_j \\ &\quad + \Sigma\beta_k \mathrm{CNTRLVAR}_{jk}, \qquad (2)\end{aligned}$$

[16] It should be noted that once news of a prior default becomes public, the reputational losses as well as the possibility of additional regulatory scrutiny are realized. Such losses could very well incorporate the possibility of a bankruptcy and subsequent losses in that process. Even though the recovery rates are high, there is still a large amount of uncertainty in the amount to be recovered. Using recent evidence, Gupton et al. (2000) suggest that mean bank loan value in default is 69.5 percent for senior secured debt and 52.1 percent for senior unsecured debt. However, loss given default values have a large variance with the lowest 10th percentiles of recoveries at 39.2 percent for senior secured debt and 5.8 percent for senior unsecured debt.

where:

- CAR_j is the dependent variable is the 11-day cumulative abnormal return for bank j around the date of bankruptcy (or bond default) by the bank's borrower. (For the borrowers that are common to the default and bankruptcy samples, the earlier of the two events is used.)
- $RELATIONSHIP_j$ is a dummy variable that takes on the value one if bank j had been the lead bank in lending (making previous loans) to the distressed borrower before its default/bankruptcy. This variable captures the existence of a prior bank-borrower relationship.
- $EXPOSURE_j$ is a measure of the exposure of bank j to the distressed borrower as defined by equation (1) earlier.
- $RECESSION_j$ is a dummy variable that takes the value of one if the distress occurs between the dates of July 1, 1990, and March 31, 1991 (the peak-to-trough business contraction dates as defined by the National Bureau for Economic Research.)
- $CNTRLVAR_{jk}$ is a set of control variables for loan and bank characteristics. These include the following.
  - LOAN LOSS RESERVE is the loan loss reserve of the bank divided by the bank capital in the year prior to the distress date.
  - LOAN LOSS RESERVE DIFFERENCE is the difference of the bank's loan loss reserves for the year of the distress date and its loan loss reserves for the year prior to the distress date divided by the bank capital in the year prior to distress.
  - BANKSIZE is the natural log of the total assets of the bank as reported for the year prior to the date of distress.
  - LBO is a dummy variable that takes the value of one if the loan purpose was for a leveraged buyout.
  - CREDIT SPREAD is the spread of the loan over LIBOR at the time of loan origination.
  - MULTIPLE BANK DUMMY is set to one when the borrower involved in the distress event has multiple lead banks.
  - PRIOR DISTRESS DUMMY is set to one when the first event of distress was not a default on public debt or a bankruptcy (e.g., it was a debt restructuring) and we can identify the exact date.[17]
  - INDUSTRY: A set of dummy variables to control for the borrower's industry.

E. Regression Results

Higher loan exposures should put a lending bank at risk of losing a greater proportion of its capital base, and thus risk insolvency or closure if the borrower is unable to repay its loans. This implies a negative relationship between announcement period returns and the bank's degree of exposure. This is indeed the case in Models 1 and 3 in Table VA.

[17] See the earlier papers of Gilson et al. (1990) for a definition of distress that includes debt restructuring.

Table VA

Regressions Relating the Cumulative Abnormal Return for the Lead Bank around the Date of Financial Distress to the Lender and Borrower Characteristics

The OLS regression of cumulative abnormal returns (CAR) for the 11-day window around the dates of distress (bankruptcy in case there is no prior news of distress, default if it occurs before bankruptcy). The independent variables include the following: RELATIONSHIP is a dummy variable that takes the value one if the bank provided credit to the firm in the past. EXPOSURE is a ratio of the aggregate sum of all credit facilities extended to the distressed firm by the lead bank to the total equity of the lead bank as reported for the year before the year of distress. RECESSION DUMMY is a dummy variable that is one if the date of distress is between July 1, 1990, and March 31, 1991. LBO is a dummy variable that takes the value one if the loan transaction was for the purpose of leveraged buyout. In addition to the variables reported, the regression also includes industry dummies based on the one-digit SIC code of the borrower. Numbers in the parentheses are standard errors.

Variable	(1)	(2)	(3)
INTERCEPT	0.0139	0.0171	0.0181
	(0.0191)	(0.0172)	(0.0172)
EXPOSURE	– 0.0434*		– 0.0295*
	(0.0149)		(0.0165)
RELATIONSHIP		– 0.0379***	– 0.0343***
		(0.0114)	(0.0121)
RECESSION DUMMY	– 0.0556***	– 0.0521***	– 0.0517***
	(0.0179)	(0.0167)	(0.0166)
LBO DUMMY	0.0256	0.0269	0.0266
	(0.0215)	(0.0184)	(0.0184)
N	156	156	156
Adj. *R* Sq.	0.10	0.13	0.14

***Significant at the one percent level
**Significant at the five percent level
*Significant at the 10 percent level

As discussed in the introduction, if the bank had been involved with the borrower in a lending relationship prior to its distress, the relationship is likely to have been of value and the dissolution of such a relationship is likely to be costly to the bank.[18]

Thus, we expect that banks, which had a prior lending relationship with a distressed borrower, will be more adversely impacted by the onset of distress. To measure this effect, an indicator variable, RELATIONSHIP, is used, which equals one if the bank has been involved in a lending relationship with the distressed firm prior to its distress or bankruptcy.

The regression results reported in Table VA provide strong support for the argument that prior relationships are valuable. Distress of a borrower with a past

[18] Slovin, Shushka, and Polonchek (1993) document significant value loss for the *borrowers* of a *bank* (Continental Illinois) when it was facing distress. Others such as Lummer and McConnell (1989) find that loan renewals result in positive abnormal returns for borrowers. Our study examines this impact in the other direction, that is, the effect of a borrower's distress on the lender.

Table VB

Regressions Relating the Cumulative Abnormal Return for the Lead Bank around the Date of Financial Distress to the Lender and Borrower Characteristics

The OLS regression of cumulative abnormal returns (CAR) for the 11-day window around the dates of distress (bankruptcy in case there is no prior news of distress, default if it occurs before bankruptcy). See Table V A or Section III Subsection D for the definitions of the exposure, relationship, recession, and LBO variables. BANKSIZE is the natural log of the total assets of the lead bank as reported for the year prior to the year in which distress occurs. The LOAN LOSS RESERVE is the loan loss reserve of the bank in the year prior to the date of distress divided by the bank's capital in that year. The difference between the loan loss reserve of the bank at the end of the year of the first distress event (default or bankruptcy) and the loan loss reserve in the year before the distress event divided by the bank's capital in the year before distress is the LOAN LOSS RESERVE DIFFERENCE. EXP × LLRD is the interaction of the exposure and the loan loss difference variables. CREDIT SPREAD is the spread of the loan over LIBOR at the time the loan was issued. The PRIOR DISTRESS DUMMY takes a value of one if the first distress event was not a default or a bankruptcy and the company experienced financial distress as defined in Gilson, John, and Lang (1990). The MULTIPLE BANK DUMMY takes a value of one when the borrower has multiple lead banks. In addition to the variables reported, the regression also includes industry dummies based on the one-digit SIC code of the borrower. Numbers in the parentheses are standard errors.

Variable	(1)	(2)	(3)	(4)
INTERCEPT	0.0072	0.0034	0.0184	−0.0236
	(0.0217)	(0.0222)	(0.0174)	(0.0408)
RELATIONSHIP	−0.0340***	−0.0336***	−0.0337***	−0.0308***
	(0.012)	(0.0121)	(0.0121)	(0.0123)
RECESSION DUMMY	−0.0554***	−0.0564	−0.0509***	−0.0722***
	(0.0166)	(0.0165)	(0.0166)	(0.0273)
LBO DUMMY	0.0253	0.0253	0.0272	0.0415*
	(0.0182)	(0.0182)	(0.0184)	(0.0203)
LOAN LOSS RESERVE	0.0278	0.0379		
	(0.0303)	(0.0326)		
LOAN LOSS RESERVE		0.0394		
DIFFERENCE (LLRD)		(0.0449)		
LLRD × EXP			0.0797*	
			(0.0442)	
BANKSIZE				0.0003
				(0.0002)
CREDIT SPREAD				−0.0131
				(0.0117)
PRIOR DISTRESS DUMMY				−0.0055
				(0.0122)
MULTIPLE BANK DUMMY				−0.0056
				(0.0124)
N	156	156	156	153
Adj. *R* Sq.	0.14	0.14	0.14	0.14

***Significant at the one percent level
**Significant at the five percent level
*Significant at the 10 percent level

relationship with the bank is relatively more costly for the bank. Specifically, the coefficient for the prior relationship variable (RELATIONSHIP) is negative and significant at the one percent level as reported in models 2–3, Table VA.

One possible concern about these relationship results is that they are driven by a few transactions that have large negative returns. Out of the total sample of 156 transactions, 68 transactions involved borrowers and banks that had prior relationships. These 68 transactions involved 62 different firms and 13 different banks. Moreover, the ACAR (recorded over 11 days) for this subsample with prior relationships was − 5.04 percent and that for the subsample without prior relationships was − 0.81 percent. The difference in these abnormal returns was significantly different from zero at the one percent level of significance. Thus, both the univariate and multivariate tests suggest that the existence of a prior relationship is important in impacting the scale of the valuation effect on a bank with loans outstanding to a distressed borrower.[19]

The RECESSION dummy variable controls for the different macroeconomic conditions prevailing at the time of the announcement of distress. Our sample period, 1987 to 1996, includes the 1990 to 1991 economic recession. The negative and significant coefficient for the recession dummy variable is consistent with the view that the news of financial distress has a larger negative impact on the lending banks during a period of economic contraction.[20]

Next, in Table VB, we investigate the effect of other bank and firm specific variables on the abnormal returns of the leading bank. In particular, our previous univariate and multivariate results suggest that one source of the loss to banks is the direct loss arising from the size of their loan exposure to the distressed borrower. To investigate this effect further, we use data on loan loss reserves in the regression. These are reserves that banks are required to set aside against expected or anticipated future losses on their loan portfolio. Thus, anticipation of a distress event should result in an increase of the banks' loan loss reserve ratio in the period prior to distress. If a bank has built up sufficient reserves, it is less likely to fail as a result of borrower defaults.[21] As such, we should find that banks that have built up loan loss reserves prior to default should be less negatively impacted by news of distress events.[22] Model 1 in Table VB tests this possible relationship. As can be seen, the loan loss reserve variable is positive but insignificant. In Model 2, we test if additions to the reserve have any impact on the abnormal returns. Other authors such as Grammatikos and Saunders (1990)

[19] The studies by Lummer and McConnell (1989) used only existence of a prior relationship in evaluating the stock price reaction. Other authors such as Peterson and Rajan (1994) and Berger and Udell (1995) also use the duration of the relationship as a measure of the strength of the relationship. Unfortunately, the LPC data is censored, starting only from the beginning of 1987 and, therefore, we cannot measure the duration of the relationship.

[20] One possible reason for this is that recovery rates, including the value of collateral such as real estate, are likely to be lower in recessions and contractions.

[21] Loan loss reserves can be viewed as a first line of defense against losses (i.e., expected losses), while capital reserves can be viewed as the second line of defense, that is, against unexpected losses.

[22] We thank the referee for suggesting this.

found that additions to the loan loss reserve by banks were viewed favorably by the market. This variable is also found to be positive but insignificant. Lastly, we interact the difference in loan loss reserves with the exposure variable. We find that this variable has a positive and significant effect, suggesting that banks that have larger exposures and increase their loan loss reserves in anticipation of financial distress of one of their borrowers tend to have less negative abnormal returns than banks that do not.[23]

We also controlled for the LBO loans and the borrower's industry by the inclusion of a set of dummy variables. Except for the LBO dummy, which was significantly positive in one model, none of these control variables had regression coefficients that were statistically significant in Tables VA and VB.

F. Robustness Checks

As mentioned earlier, our definition of distress is somewhat more restrictive than that used in the study by GJL. To test the robustness of our findings, we collected data on the first date of distressed restructuring of the borrowers in our sample (see Section I for a definition of a distressed restructuring). We go back two years prior to the first date of distress as defined in this study (which is a public default or bankruptcy) to find a date when (or if) the borrower attempted to restructure its debt. We used the Lexis-Nexis libraries on public news and bankruptcy for this search. We focused only on those restructuring events where it was clear from the related news story that the attempted restructuring of debt was due to financial difficulties. In several cases, the restructuring event coincided with the default or bankruptcy date. In those cases where the company attempted to restructure its debt before default or bankruptcy (and we can identify the exact date when this happened), we set the PRIOR DISTRESS DUMMY to 1 in the multivariate tests in Table VB, Model 4; otherwise, the dummy is given a value of zero. As can be seen, while the sign of the dummy is negative, it is not statistically significant in our sample.

We control for bank-specific characteristics with the variables BANKSIZE. On one hand, one might expect the importance of any individual corporate loan default to be relatively small, because larger banks are likely to be more diversified. On the other hand, the borrowers of larger banks tend to be bigger and more widely followed companies. The distress announcement of such a borrower may cause a larger negative reaction for a larger bank as the market revises its assessment of the quality of the bank's overall loan portfolio and efficiency of the bank as a "delegated monitor" (see, e.g., James (1987)). As can be seen from Table VB, Model 4, the bank size variable was found to be insignificant.

The coefficient on the CREDIT SPREAD variable (the spread on the loan over LIBOR at the time of loan origination) should proxy for the bank's ex ante expectation of the borrower's risk before the distress event. As can be seen, inclusion of

[23] One complicating factor is that banks appear to use the loan loss reserve not only as a fund to insulate against future losses but also to smooth earnings. See Collins, Shackelford, and Wahlen (1995), Beaver and Engel (1996), and Wall and Koch (2000) for evidence on such smoothing.

the credit spread on the loan made by the bank prior to distress had no significant explanatory effect on the size of the lending bank's CAR at the time of distress.

A potential problem in our multivariate test results is that each event of distress for a given borrower may result in multiple events in our regression if the given borrower had multiple lead banks. To control for this, we created a MULTIPLE BANK DUMMY for those distress events where the borrower had multiple lead banks (dummy equal to 1) and those where it had a single lead bank (dummy equal to 0). As can be seen from Table VB, Model 4, this dummy appears to be insignificant. Indeed, univariate tests of the difference in ACARs between these two categories (i.e., multiple bank lending versus single bank lending) indicated that these two sets of ACARs were not statistically different from each other.[24]

Finally, our findings, while supportive of the adverse information hypothesis, may be confounded, in part, by some other event that negatively affects both the value of the bank and the borrowing firm, but has nothing (directly) to do with the distress itself. A good example of such confounding events is an increase in prime lending rates (see Park, Nabar, and Saunders (1993) for evidence of the effect of prime rate changes on bank returns). To account for this, we collected data on prime rate increases that occurred during the 11-day event window around distress announcements. Excluding events contaminated by prime rate increases had no effect on our results.[25]

G. Borrower Returns

Thus far, we have examined the returns to the borrower's lead banks around the distress dates. A natural line of inquiry would be to examine the effect of distress on the borrower itself. If adverse information about the borrower is indeed the cause of the negative return experienced by the bank, the borrower should also experience negative abnormal returns during the event window period. We estimate borrower returns using the methods suggested by GJL, employing an estimation period from 250 days before the announcement date to 50 days before the announcement date. Since a number of the companies in our sample were private and many had been delisted before the bankruptcy event, the number of borrowers for which these returns are available is smaller than the size of our full sample. Out of the 33 borrowers in the default subsample, 23 subsequently filed for bankruptcy. Thus, our borrower sample consists of many firms that failed to restructure their debt and therefore filed for bankruptcy.

[24] It should be noted that the returns of the two banks, although based on the same distress event, are unlikely to be identical. First, the banks' loan exposures are likely to be different. Second, their sizes will generally be different. Last, each individual bank may or may not have a prior relationship with the borrower. Therefore, the same default or bankruptcy event can have different wealth implications for the different lead banks.

[25] We thank the referee for pointing this out. We focus only on events where there is an increase in prime rates, as a decrease in prime rates is unlikely to cause negative returns to banks or their borrowers. These three events were excluded in the estimation of Model 4 in Table VB.

These results (Table VI, Panels A and B) suggest that the borrowers experienced large negative abnormal returns around the events of both default and bankruptcy. In Panel C, we present evidence on abnormal returns from debt restructuring, in those cases when the first distress event was not a default or a bankruptcy. As can be seen, these events also have significantly negative effects on borrower returns. Our results for the borrower returns (whether because of default or bankruptcy or distressed restructuring) are similar in magnitude to those obtained by GJL. For example, GJL find two-day returns of − 16.7 percent for firms that file for bankruptcy. We find a one-day return of − 13.4 percent for firms that file for bankruptcy. Similarly, GJL find that firms that ultimately file for Chapter 11 have a negative return of − 6.3 percent at the first announcement

Table VI

Cumulative Abnormal Returns for Borrowers on their Announcement of Financial Distress

Cumulative abnormal return (CARs) for the borrower firms facing financial distress over the period 1987 to 1996. Panel A describes the share performance of firm around the date of its default on public debt, and Panel B describes the same around the date of chapter 11 filing. Panel C shows the abnormal return around the date of the first restructuring, provided this restructuring was not a default or a bankruptcy. Average cumulative abnormal return (ACAR) and *t*-statistics are calculated using methods similar to Gilson, John, and Lang (1990) and Tashijian, Lease, and McConnell (1996). The sample of firms that defaulted on their public debt and the date of default is from Altman (1996), and the sample of firms that filed for chapter 11 is compiled from multiple sources including Hotchkiss (1995), DJNR, the *Bankruptcy Almanac*, and Lexis bankruptcy library. CARs are calculated using the Center for Research in Security Prices (CRSP) database.

Event window	Number of firms	ACAR	*t*-statistic
Panel A: Abnormal returns for the borrowers when they default on public debt			
11-day window [− 8, 2]	33	− 10.209%	− 5.674***
7-day window [− 4, 2]	33	− 7.378%	− 4.840***
5-day window [− 2, 2]	33	− 4.910%	− 3.786***
1-day window [day 0]	33	− 2.420%	− 5.306***
Panel B: Abnormal returns for the borrowers when they file for chapter 11			
11-day window [− 8, 2]	43	− 22.462%	− 9.488***
7-day window [− 4, 2]	43	− 21.739%	− 9.034***
5-day window [− 2, 2]	43	− 18.568%	− 8.714***
1-day window [day 0]	43	− 13.357%	− 17.236***
Panel C: Abnormal returns for the borrowers when they announce distressed restructuring before the default or bankruptcy			
11-day window [− 8, 2]	31	− 6.683%	− 4.690***
7-day window [− 4, 2]	31	− 8.145%	− 6.512***
5-day window [− 2, 2]	31	− 8.696%	− 7.958***
1-day window [day 0]	31	− 5.752%	− 9.362***

***Significant at the one percent level
**Significant at the five percent level
*Significant at the 10 percent level

of distress. The borrowers that announced a debt restructuring in our sample had a one-day negative return of – 5.75 percent.[26, 27]

More importantly, we also find that the borrowers themselves had significant negative ACARs within the same event window that their lead lender banks had negative abnormal returns. Thus, the linkage between borrower distress and the negative abnormal returns of their lead banks is made stronger. In the bank event study, we found that the default event had a strong negative effect on the bank return while the bankruptcy event (when preceded by a default) had a weaker effect. For borrowers, we find that both default and bankruptcy events (as well as distressed restructurings) result in large negative abnormal returns. This suggests that these events generally had material news effects for both the borrowing firms and the banks. Perhaps, not surprisingly, the effect on borrowing firms' stock returns is larger (in percentage terms) due to the greater loss exposure of equity holders in distressed firms. By contrast, bank stockholders hold relatively senior debt claims on the borrowing firm, and, as such, normally have priority over the borrowing firm's equity holders.

IV. Conclusion

The risk of loan default is the one of the most important risks faced by banks. While there have been studies examining the impact of sovereign loan defaults on the stock prices of lending banks, a similar exercise has not been undertaken to analyze the impact of defaults/bankruptcy announcements of corporate borrowers on lending banks. The small size of any individual corporate loan relative to the size of a bank, the relatively high recovery rate for senior secured bank loans, and the prior anticipation of a borrower's financial difficulties, aligned with the role of the bank as an insider or "delegated monitor," all imply that the news of any single corporate distress might not have a significant impact on the lending bank's share price. Alternatively, industry and geography-wide correlations among distressed firms, the loss of valuable customer relationships, and the cost of lost reputation and increased regulatory scrutiny because of a borrower's distress imply that the news of a default or a bankruptcy might have a materially adverse impact on the share price of the lead lending bank.

This paper is the first large-sample documentation of the wealth effects for lead bank shareholders when bank borrowers face financial distress. For a lead bank, the news of default of a corporate borrower is associated with an average decline of 3.8 percent in its stock returns over an 11-day period surrounding the date of default. News of a corporate bankruptcy is associated with a decline in bank stock returns of 1.8 percent over a similar 11-day window. When banks are ranked according to their exposures to distressed firms, the price decline for the low exposure banks is insignificant, while that for the high exposure banks is large and significant. Our multivariate tests also indicate that exposure of a

[26] We thank the referee for suggesting this entire section.
[27] All of these borrowers did not subsequently file for Chapter 11.

bank significantly affects the size of the (negative) abnormal returns on the announcement of distress.

We also find that prior banking relationships are valuable for lenders. On average, abnormal returns to banks, on the announcement of a borrower's financial distress, are significantly and negatively related to existence of a prior past borrowing relationship with that borrower. Finally, we find that the announcement of distress also has a significantly negative effect on borrower returns in our sample. This is consistent with the results of prior studies looking at the effect of distress on borrowers.

References

Altman, Edward, and Vellore Kishore, 1996, Almost everything you wanted to know about the recoveries on defaulted bonds, *Financial Analysts Journal*, Nov./Dec, 57–64.

Andrade, Gregor, and Steven Kaplan, 1998, How costly is financial (not economic) distress? Evidence from highly leveraged transactions that became distressed, *Journal of Finance* 53, 1443–1493.

Beaver, William H., and Ellen E. Engel, 1996, Discretionary behavior with respect to allowances for loan losses and the behavior of security prices, *Journal of Accounting and Economics* 22, 177–206.

Benveniste, Lawrence M., Manoj Singh, and William J. Wilhelm Jr., 1993, The failure of Drexel Burnham Lambert: Evidence on the implications for commercial banks, *Journal of Financial Intermediation* 3, 104–137.

Berger, Allen N., and Gregory F. Udell, 1995, Relationship lending and lines of credit in small firm finance, *Journal of Business* 68, 351–381.

Berlin, Mitchell, and Loretta Mester, 1999, Deposits and relationship lending, *Review of Financial Studies* 12, 579–607.

Boot, Arnoud, 2000, Relationship banking: What do we know? *Journal of Financial Intermediation* 9, 7–25.

Collins, Julie H., Douglas A. Shackelford, and James M. Wahlen, 1995, Bank differences in the coordination of regulatory capital, earnings, and taxes, *Journal of Accounting Research* 33, 263–291.

Dahiya, Sandeep, Manju Puri, and Anthony Saunders, 2002, Bank borrowers and loan sales: New evidence on the uniqueness of bank loans, *Journal of Business*, forthcoming.

Franks, Julian R., and Walter N. Torous, 1994, A comparison of financial recontracting in distressed exchanges and Chapter 11 reorganizations, *Journal of Financial Economics* 35, 349–370.

Gonde, Amar, Manju Puri, Anthony Saunders, and Ingo Walter, 1997, Bank underwriting of debt securities: Modern Evidence, *Review of Financial Studies* 10, 1175–1202.

Gilson, Stuart, Kose John, and Larry Lang, 1990, Troubled debt restructurings: An empirical study of private reorganizations of firms in default, *Journal of Financial Economics* 27, 315–354.

Grammatikos, Theoharry, and Anthony Saunders, 1990, Addition to bank loan-loss reserves: Good news or bad news?, *Journal of Monetary Economics* 25, 289–304.

Gupton, Greg M., Daniel Gates, and Lea V. Carty, 2000, Bank loan loss given default, *Moody's Investors Service Global Credit Research* Special Comment, November.

Hotchkiss, Edith, 1995, Post-bankruptcy performance and management turnover, *Journal of Finance* 50, 3–21.

James, Christopher, 1987, Some evidence of the uniqueness of bank loans, *Journal of Financial Economics* 19, 217–235.

Kaplan, Steven, 1989, The effects of management buyouts on operating performance and value, *Journal of Financial Economics* 24, 217–254.

Kracaw, William A., and Marc Zenner, 1996, The wealth effects of bank financing announcements in highly leveraged transactions, *Journal of Finance* 51, 1931–1946.

Lamy, Robert E., Wayne Marr, and G. Rodney Thompson, 1986, The Mexican debt crisis, the IMF, and the efficiency of bank share prices, *Studies in Banking and Finance* 3, 203–217.

Lummer, S., and John McConnell, 1989, Further evidence on the bank lending process and the capital market response to bank loan agreements, *Journal of Financial Economics* 25, 99–122.

Mikkelson, Wayne, and Megan Partch, 1986, Valuation effects of securities offerings and the issuance process, *Journal of Financial Economics* 15, 31–60.

Muscarella, Chris J., and Michael R. Vetsuypens, 1990, Efficiency and organizational structure: A study of reverse LBOs, *Journal of Finance* 45, 1389–1413.

Musumeci, James J., and Joseph H. Sinkey, 1990, The international debt crisis, investor contagion, and bank security returns in 1987: The Brazilian experience, *Journal of Money, Credit and Banking* 22, 209–220.

Park, Sang Yong, Prafulla Nabar, and Anthony Saunders, 1993, Prime rate changes: Is there an advantage in being first, *Journal of Business* 66, 69–92.

Peterson, Mitchell A., and Raghuram G. Rajan, 1994, The benefits of lending relationships: Evidence from small business data, *Journal of Finance* 49, 3–37.

Peterson, Mitchell A., and Raghuram G. Rajan, 1995, The effect of credit market competition on lending relationships, *Quarterly Journal of Economics* 110, 407–443.

Puri, Manju, 1996, Commercial banks in investment banking: Conflict of interest or certification role? *Journal of Financial Economics* 40, 373–401.

Slovin, Myron B., Marie E. Sushka, and John A. Polonchek, 1993, The value of bank durability: Borrowers as the bank stakeholders, *Journal of Finance* 48, 247–266.

Smirlock, Michael, and Howard Kaufold, 1987, Bank foreign lending, mandatory disclosure rules, and the reaction of bank stock prices to the Mexican debt crisis, *Journal of Business* 60, 347–364.

Smith, Clifford W., 1992, Economics and ethics: The case of Salomon Brothers, *Journal of Applied Corporate Finance* 5 (2), 23–38.

Tashijian, Elizabeth, Ronald C. Lease, and John J. McConnell, 1996, Prepacks: An empirical analysis of prepackaged bankruptcies, *Journal of Financial Economics* 40, 135–162.

Wall, Larry D., and Timothy W. Koch, 2000, Bank loan loss accounting: A review of the theoretical and empirical evidence, *Federal Reserve Bank of Atlanta Economic Review* Second Quarter, 1–19.

Weiss, Lawrence A., 1990, Bankruptcy resolution: Direct costs and violation of priority of claims, *Journal of Financial Economics* 27, 285–314.

Wruck, Karen H., 1990, Financial distress, reorganization, and organizational efficiency, *Journal of Financial Economics* 27, 419–444.

Sandeep Dahiya
Georgetown University

Manju Puri
Duke University and National Bureau of Economic Research

Anthony Saunders
New York University

Bank Borrowers and Loan Sales: New Evidence on the Uniqueness of Bank Loans*

This article examines the information content of the sale announcement of a borrower's loans by its lending bank. We find significant negative stock returns for the borrower on the loan sale announcement, particularly for subpar loan sales, where the bank's information advantage is greatest. Further, a large proportion of these borrowers file for bankruptcy after the loan sale. The evidence supports the hypothesis that the news of a bank loan sale conveys negative certification, which is validated by the subsequent performance of the firms whose loans are sold. We also find that the selling banks are not significantly affected.

> An original lender on a $150 million Bradlees credit reportedly sold a $5 million piece of the revolver in a hurry last week, according to traders familiar with the situation, sending the message to some traders that the lenders most familiar with Bradlees are not comfortable with the company's situation. Because a long-term lender dumped the paper, and urgently, traders said they suspect the lender knew something they did not. (*Bank Letter* 1995)

I. Introduction

The secondary loan market for loans includes two broad categories. The first is the primary, or syndicated, loan market, in which portions of a loan are placed with a number of banks, often in conjunction with, and as part of, the loan origination process (usually referred to as the sale of participations). The second category is the seasoned, or secondary, loan sale market in which a bank subsequently sells off an ex-

* We would like to thank the referee for helpful comments and participants at the AFA conference and our discussant, Allen Berger, for valuable comments. We also thank Sreedhar T. Bharath, Ali Burak Guner, and Lei Yu for excellent research assistance.

(*Journal of Business,* 2003, vol. 76, no. 4)

0021-9398/2003/7604-0003$10.00

isting loan (or part of a loan). While a number of reasons for seasoned loan sales have been identified in the previous literature, there have been no empirical studies of the effects of such sales on the returns of those borrowers whose loans are sold or on the banks selling the loans.[1]

Conventional wisdom has long held that loan sales by banks—especially loans of customers who have established long-term customer relationships with that bank—would have a negative information effect regarding the borrowing firm. This effect would result from the special, or unique, role of banks as "insiders" to the borrowing firms, such that a decision to sell a customer's loan would be taken as revealing to the market hitherto private (negative) information regarding a borrower's financial condition.[2] Indeed, while the effect of loan sales on borrowers has been untested prior to this article, such an effect might be expected given the findings of James (1987), Lummer and McConnell (1989), Best and Zhang (1993), and Billett, Flannery and Garfinkel (1995), among others, that new loans and loan renewals carry (positive) private information to the outside equity market about a borrowing firm's financial condition.[3] In a recent paper, James and Smith (2000) provide a comprehensive review of the past and recent research on the special nature of bank loan financing. Overall, they show that research to date finds a robust, favorable impact of bank loan announcements on borrowers' stock returns in contrast with the insignificant or negative response of investors to the announcement of most other forms of new security issuance (e.g., public debt and equity).

While the positive impact of news announcing the formation of a bank lending relationship is well established, there is a paucity of studies examining the impact of the termination (or reduction) of a banking relationship on a borrower's stock returns and the borrowers' long-run performance in the postsale period.[4] In this article we employ a previously unutilized information source to identify loan sale events. In particular, we focus on sales of seasoned subpar loans, where the information effects of bank sales are likely to be

1. See, e.g., James (1988) and Pennacchi (1988), who model the effects of loan sales on a bank's capital position and its underinvestment problem.

2. The special information-producing and monitoring functions of banks have been discussed by Campbell and Kracaw (1980), Diamond (1984), and Fama (1985).

3. James (1987) finds a significant positive impact of announcement of bank loan agreements; Lummer and McConnell (1989) document a positive impact of favorable loan renewals, while nonrenewals are accompanied by negative returns for the borrowers. Billet et al. (1995) show that the impact of loan announcements is positively related to the quality of the lender. Best and Zhang (1993) document evidence that the stock market reaction is strongest for those borrowers for whom the quality of publicly available information is the poorest. Related to this evidence, Puri (1999) models theoretically, and Puri (1996) and Gande et al. (1997) find empirically, a positive effect for the prices of new securities when the bank is both the lender and underwriter, suggesting that the bank's certification role exists even in situations where there may be confounding effects because of the bank's multiple roles.

4. Slovin, Shuska, and Polonchek (1993) examine the impact of the possible termination of lending relationships by examining the stock returns of borrowers of Continental Illinois Bank during the bank's financial problems. Dahiya, Saunders, and Srinivasan (2000) examine the impact of borrower distress on the lending bank when the lending relationship is likely to terminate following the announcement of default or bankruptcy filing by the borrower of the bank.

highest, and test the effects of such sales on borrowers' returns. We conducted two set of tests. First, we tested for and find a significant negative impact of loan sale announcements on borrowers' stock returns, which complements the established finding that the announcement of new lending relationships (or their continuation) has a positive effect on a borrower's stock returns. Our finding is both consistent with and extends the existing literature on this dimension. Second, we examined whether the negative information contained in the loan sale announcement is validated by the long-term performance of firms whose loans are sold. We find that almost half of those firms whose loans are sold file for bankruptcy within 3 years of the loan sale announcement. Interestingly, these firms are not the worst-performing firms in their industry at the time of the loan sale, suggesting that publicly available information alone might have been insufficient for outside investors to preidentify the degree of weakness of the firms whose loans were sold and that the bank's loan sale announcement contained valuable negative private information.

We are also interested in the factors that influence a bank's decision to sell its loans. One possibility identified in the theoretical literature is that bank loan sales are motivated by a bank's desire to mitigate "regulatory taxes" such as capital requirements (see, e.g., Pennacchi 1988). Moreover, loan sales may reflect the loan origination and distribution abilities of a bank. Consequently, we examine the motivation for a bank to sell loans as well as the effect of a loan sale announcement on the selling bank's equity returns.

The outline of the article is as follows: Section II discusses data sources and sample selection. Section III presents the results of tests on the effects of loan sales on borrower returns and the link between loan sales and the long-run viability of the firm. Section IV presents tests analyzing the effects of loan sales on the selling bank's returns and the characteristics of those banks that sell loans. Section V presents some robustness checks. Section VI summarizes and concludes.

II. Data and Sample Selection

The bank loan sales market is an over-the-counter, wholesale market in which transactions are arranged through a network of dealers. Historically, trades took many weeks to complete; however, dealers now work for completion of trades with a $T + 10$ day horizon.[5] Typical sellers of bank loans are large, wholesale money centers (e.g., Citibank) and overseas banks (e.g., ING Barings). Typical buyers of bank loans are smaller regional banks, foreign banks, and vulture funds (including hedge funds), as well as insurance companies (see, e.g., Miller 1998). Key sources of information about the market are trade newsletters and screen services such as Bloomberg that list and identify loan sales. Our test design requires identifying loans that are traded in the secondary

5. Interviews with loan traders reveal an increased standardization in the custody, settlement, and payment procedures surrounding loan sales in recent years.

market and locating the date of actual sale of a loan by a bank in order to conduct the event study. We use two market newsletters, *Bank Letter* and *Gold Sheets,* as the primary data sources. To identify the secondary market sale of a bank loan by one of the lenders, we check for loan sale news stories in *Bank Letter. Bank Letter* is a weekly publication, produced by Institutional Investor, Inc., which publishes a number of other well-known newsletters such as *Bond Week, Derivatives Week,* and *Corporate Financing Week.*[6] *Bank Letter* is the primary "trade rag" that carries news of the sales of bank loans by banks, and the date of *Bank Letter* publication provides us with the event date to conduct the event study. *Gold Sheets* is a publication of Loan Pricing Corporation, which provides information about new loan originations and the terms of these loans. *Gold Sheets* is widely used by practitioners, and recently by some academics. While it carries no news stories of loan sales, it does carry secondary market loan price quotes (not the actual trades) of a large number of loans. Thus, *Gold Sheets* allows us to generate the universe of borrowers whose loans attract a price quote in the secondary market. From our discussion with traders, these two publications are the most widely followed newsletters in the secondary loan market.

The main period of our study is 1995–98. (In Sec. VI, we look at an augmented sample period 1995–2000.) For the 1995–98 period in *Gold Sheets,* we found a total of 215 U.S. borrowers whose bank loans attracted a secondary market price quote that was published for the first time. *Gold Sheets* report the price quotes for the loans under two distinct categories. The first category is classified as "Par Loans" and includes all loans that are quoted at or very close to 100% of face value. The second category, termed "distressed loans" or "subpar loans," comprises loans where the bid quote is significantly below the face value (usually 80% or below of the face value) or loans where the the borrower is in default.

Of the 215 loans, 162 were par loans and the rest (53 loans) were subpar or distressed loans. While *Gold Sheets* provides us with a fairly good estimate of the total universe of loans being traded in the secondary market, we were unable to identify the exact date on which the loan sale took place for the first time, as the newsletter does not carry news of loan sale announcements. The loan sale announcement dates were obtained from reading the weekly issues of *Bank Letter*. We found 101 news stories of loan sale announcements for U.S. corporate borrowers (an additional six news stories involved non-U.S. borrowers for a total of 107 loan sale news announcements). This list also included multiple sale announcements for the same borrower. For example, there were 11 separate loan sale announcements for Mobilemedia in the period from August 12, 1996, to August 18, 1997. Taking the multiple announcements into account, the 101 announcements involved 58 different borrowers. To examine the information impact of the loan sale announcement, we carried out an event study on borrowers' stock returns around the date of loan

6. *Bank Letter* has recently been renamed *Loan Market Week.*

sale announcements. As a first step, all borrowers for which announcements of loan sales were published in *Bank Letter* were identified. We then searched the Center for Research in Security Prices (CRSP) daily price database for a match to those firms whose loans had been sold, so as to determine the availability of an equity price history around the date of announcement of a loan sale. This procedure reduced the sample of 58 borrowers to 29 firms for which sufficient stock price data existed. Since these loan sales are not classified as par or nonpar, we used the following procedure to classify these borrowers as either par or subpar. The loans were classified subpar if *Gold Sheets* listed the loan as nonpar within 2 months of the loan sale. Similarly if *Gold Sheets* listed it as par within 2 months of loan sale, we classified it as par. If the loan sold did not appear in *Gold Sheets* within 2 months of sale, we looked at the price range mentioned in the loan sale story in *Bank Letter,* and if the price was below 80% of the face value, we classified it as subpar, and par otherwise. Finally, if no price is mentioned, we tried to determine from news stories if the firm was facing repayment difficulties, and we classified it as subpar if such repayment difficulties were reported. Of the 29 firms we were able to classify 13 as par loans and 15 as subpar loans. (For one firm—Checkers Drive In Restaurants—no information was available, and we were unable to assign it as either par or subpar, so we excluded it from the analysis.) Appendix table A1 provides the details of the main sample.

As a second step we conducted an event study on the whole sample of 29 loan sale announcements to examine the impact of such announcements on a borrower's stock return. Next, we split this sample into par and subpar loans since we expected bank informational effects to be stronger in subpar firms. However, comparing our sample with the total number of traded loans listed in *Gold Sheets,* it seems clear that our sample captures only a small proportion of all par loan sales (13 as compared with 162 par loans mentioned in the *Gold Sheets*) but does capture a larger proportion of subpar loan sales (15 as compared with 53 subpar loans in *Gold Sheets*). Since the informational effects for which we were looking are likely to be strongest in subpar loan sales, where we have a more representative sample of such traded loans, we focus primarily on these firms in this article. Hereafter, the 15 subpar firms whose loan sale announcements appeared in *Bank Letter* will be referred to as the *Bank Letter* sample, and the 53 subpar firms that generated a secondary market bid price quote will be referred to as the *Gold Sheets* sample. Of the 15 firms in the *Bank Letter* sample, 13 are also in the *Gold Sheets* sample; thus, the *Bank Letter* sample is effectively a subsample of the *Gold Sheets* sample of subpar firms.

In order to examine the operating performance of the firms in the period before the loan sale was made, we computed financial characteristics (performance measures) of these firms using data for the year prior to the year in which the loan sale took place. We calculated three operating rations for the borrowing firm. Return on assets was calculated by dividing earnings before interest, taxes, depreciation, and amortization (EBITDA; Compustat data item no. 13) by the book value total assets (Compustat data item no. 6). The second operating ratio that we used was total leverage, which is computed by dividing book value of current liabilities and long-term debt (sum of Compustat item nos. 5 and 9) by the book value of total asset. Finally, we calculated investment intensity, which is the ratio of capital expenditure (Compustat data item no. 128) divided by the book value of total assets.

The borrowing firms whose loans were sold come from a number of industries; in order to account for industry-wide effects, we adjusted each borrowing firm's performance measures by median industry performance. For example, to calculate the industry-adjusted return on assets, we calculated this ratio for all firms in the Compustat files that had the same four-digit Standard Industrial Classification (SIC) code as the sample firm and took the median of these ratios.This median return on assets for the industry was then subtracted from the return on assets for the sample firm (for the same year). This procedure was carried out for all the nonpar firms in both samples so as to compute the industry-adjusted return on assets for every firm.

To analyze the long-term performance of the sample of loan sale firms (in the postloan sale period), we focused on the survival rate of these firms after an announcement of sale of their loan was made. To determine if any of the subpar firms in the *Bank Letter* as well as the *Gold Sheets* samples filed for bankruptcy after a bank announced the sale of a firm's loan, we followed a two-step procedure. As a first step we matched all the firms whose loans were sold against the list of firms filing for Chapter 11 in the *Bankruptcy Datasource.*[7] This step allowed us to identify the firms that went bankrupt subsequent to the loan sale announcement. As a second step, we searched the Dow Jones News Retrieval Service for any stories that contained the sample firm's name and the words "Chapter 11" or "bankruptcy" to confirm if the news of the bankruptcy was reported in the public media. This step is a robustness check to ensure that we identified all firms that filed for bankruptcy after a loan sale. While for the event study our sample is limited to subpar loans, where we have both the loan sale date as well as the CRSP stock prices, we can feasibly measure long-term performance for the entire sample of subpar loans appearing in *Gold Sheets,* from the date that the first loan price appears. We report the long-run survival rate for the firms in both the *Bank Letter* and the *Gold Sheets* samples. We find that the survival rates are similar across the two samples.

III. Test Methodology and Results

We employ the event study methodology as outlined in Mikkelson and Partch (1986) to estimate the impact of a bank loan sale announcement on the stock

7. The Bankruptcy Datasource is a database produced by New Generation Research, Boston. It is available through Securities Data Corporation as well as Lexis-Nexis. It is a comprehensive source of data on Chapter 11 filings (since 1988) by all firms that have public securities (debt or equities) outstanding and have more than $10 million in assets.

return of the borrowing firm. The abnormal returns are computed around the date of publication of *Bank Letter* in which the loan sale announcement first appeared. The abnormal return for common stock of borrower j on day t is defined as

$$AR_{jt} = R_{jt} - (\alpha_j + \beta_j R_{mt}). \tag{1}$$

Expression R_{jt} is the continuously compounded rate of return for borrower j on day t, and R_{mt} is the continuously compounded rate of return for the CRSP's dividend-inclusive, value-weighted index for New York Stock Exchange/American Stock Exchange/NASDAQ stocks. The coefficients α_j and β_j are estimated by regressing R_{jt} for the period from 200 trading days before the event date (defined as the date of publication of *Bank Letter* announcing the loan sale) to 51 trading days before the event date on R_{mt}. The abnormal returns are computed for each day in the event period that begins 50 trading days before the announcement and ends 30 trading days after the announcement.

The average abnormal return on event day t for a sample of size N is

$$AR_t = \frac{1}{N}\sum_{j=1}^{N} AR_{jt}. \tag{2}$$

Tests of significance are based on standardized abnormal returns. Standardized errors for firm j on day t are defined as

$$SAR_{jt} = \frac{AR_{jt}}{S_{jt}}, \tag{3}$$

where

$$S_{jt} = \left\{ V_j^2 \left[1 + \frac{1}{ED} + \frac{(R_{mt} - \bar{R}_m)^2}{\sum_{k=1}^{ED} (R_{mk} - \bar{R}_m)^2} \right] \right\}^{1/2}. \tag{4}$$

Expression V_j^2 is the residual variance for borrower j from the market model regression in equation 1, ED is the estimation period (150 trading days) used in the market model regression, R_{mt} is the market return on day t, and $\bar{R}_m$ is the mean market return over the estimation period. The average standardized abnormal return for day t is

$$ASAR_{jt} = \frac{1}{N}\sum_{j=1}^{N} SAR_{jt}. \tag{5}$$

Under the assumption that individual daily abnormal returns are distributed normally, SAR_{jt} follows a Student-t distribution with $ED - 2$ degrees of freedom. Cumulative abnormal returns (CAR_{T_1,T_2}) are the sum of abnormal returns

TABLE 1 **Cumulative Abnormal Returns for the Firms on the Announcement of Sale of Their Loan by Their Bank**

Event Window	CAR (%)	z-Statistic
A. Abnormal returns for the firms around the date of first loan sale announcement (N = 29):		
7-day window (−4, 2)	−4.70	−2.55**
5-day window (−2, 2)	−4.50	−3.53***
3-day window (−1, 1)	−1.74	−3.60***
B. Abnormal returns for the firms around the date of first subpar loan sale announcement (N = 15):		
7-day window (−4, 2)	−8.11	−3.84***
5-day window (−2, 2)	−7.04	−4.27***
3-day window (−1, 1)	−1.61	−3.56***
C. Abnormal returns for the firms around the date of first par loan sale announcement (N = 13):		
7-day window (−4, 2)	.66	.69
5-day window (−2, 2)	.15	.16
3-day window (−1, 1)	−.97	−1.21

NOTE.—Cumulative abnormal returns (CARs) exist for 29 firms around the date of first announcement of sale of their loan by their lender. The CARs are calculated using the Center for Research in Security Prices database using the methodology outlined in Mikkelson and Partch (1986). Panel A provides the event study results for the entire sample of 29 borrowers. Panel B provides the event study results for the subsample of 15 subpar loan sales. Panel C provides the event study results for the subsample of 13 par loan sale firms. (One borrower—Checkers Drive In Restaurant Inc.—cannot be classified as either par or subpar and, hence, is not included in either panel B or panel C.)

* Significant at 10% level.

** Significant at 5% level.

*** Significant at 1% level.

for the event window beginning with trading day T_1 and ending with T_2, and they are given by

$$CAR_{T_1,T_2} = \frac{1}{N}\sum_{j=1}^{N}\sum_{t=T_1}^{T_2} AR_{jt}. \tag{6}$$

The test statistic for the null hypothesis that $CAR_{T_1,T_2} = 0$ is given by

$$Z_{T_1,T_2} = \sqrt{N}(ASCAR_{T_1,T_2}), \tag{7}$$

where the average standardized cumulative abnormal return ($ASCAR_{T_1,T_2}$) is calculated as follows:

$$ASCAR_{T_1,T_2} = \frac{1}{N}\sum_{j=1}^{N}\sum_{t=T_1}^{T_2} SAR_{jt}/(\sqrt{T_2 - T_1 + 1}). \tag{8}$$

The results for the event study are reported in table 1. Panel A reports the cumulative abnormal returns (CAR) for the entire sample of 29 loan sale announcements around the date of first announcement of a loan sale. Panel B reports the results of the event study for the 15 borrowers that we classify as subpar, while panel C describes the same for the 13 borrowers classified as par. (One borrower could not be classified as either par or nonpar and is excluded for the analysis.) As can be seen, for various event windows (7, 5, and 3 days) the results reported in table 1 provide strong evidence of a negative news effect surrounding a bank loan sale announcement. From table 1, panel

A, for a 3-day window surrounding the full sample of 29 loan sale announcements, the average abnormal return for the borrowers whose loans were sold was −1.74%, which is significant at the 1% level. However, this negative news impact is not the same across subpar and par loan sales. As reported in panel B, the impact of the news of a loan sale is much larger and more significant if the loan sale involves a subpar borrower. This result holds true across all event windows. Moreover, as shown in panel C, the negative abnormal return effect is statistically insignificant at conventional levels for the loan sale announcements involving par borrowers. Overall, these results are consistent with a bad news (information) effect arising from loan sales, in particular those of subpar borrowers, which is the converse of the good news effect of new loan announcements or renewals (see, e.g., James 1987).

Our next test examines whether the negative information that the market surmises from a loan sale announcement is validated by the borrowing firm's subsequent performance. If the market perceives that the bank's inside information about the firm's future prospects is unfavorable, since the bank has decided to sell the loan rather than continue its lending relationship with the firm at its current level, then a logical consequence would be that such a firm's performance would worsen subsequent to the loan sale.

Perhaps the starkest and simplest measure of poor performance is whether a firm goes bankrupt. We collect data to examine if and when a firm filed for bankruptcy (under Chapter 11 of the U.S. bankruptcy code) for a period of 3 years subsequent to the date of the loan sale announcement. This test has the additional advantage of allowing us to use the entire sample of 53 subpar loan sales obtained from *Gold Sheets* as well as the 15 subpar loan sales firms from *Bank Letter* used in the event study tests above. Overall, we find that a large number of our sample firms (close to half of the firms for whom loan sales occurred) file for bankruptcy within 3 years of the date of the first loan sale announcement.[8] Table 2, panel A, shows that 32% of the firms whose loans were quoted as subpar filed for bankruptcy within 1 year of the first bid price quote reported by *Gold Sheets,* an additional 8% within 2 years, and a further 2% within 3 years. In aggregate, 42% of the *Gold Sheets* subpar sample firms filed for bankruptcy within 3 years of their loan first being announced for sale.

Although the bankruptcy filing rate appears to be high, there may be a concern that this rate reflects industry or economy wide factors. To control for such effects, we carry out a robustness test. For each firm whose loan attracted a price quote, we obtain the four-digit SIC classification from Compustat. If the firm is not listed in the Compustat database, we search the Dealscan database for any loans made to that borrower. The Dealscan database is maintained by Loan Pricing Corporation and contains details of over 60,000

8. We can evaluate the long-term performance for 3 years only for loans sold up through 1997. For the loans sold in 1998, we are examining performance only for 2 years. This implies that we slightly understate the likelihood of bankruptcy.

TABLE 2 **Incidence of Financial Distress for the Sample of Firms for Which an Outstanding Bank Loan Attracted a Subpar Bid between January 1995 and December 1998**

Incidence of Chapter 11 Filing	Less than 12 Months after the Loan Sale Announcement	12–24 Months after the Loan Sale Announcement	24–36 Months after the Loan Sale Announcement	More than 36 Months after the Loan Sale Announcement
A. Subpar loans reported in *Gold Sheets* (N = 53):				
No. of firms filing for Chapter 11:	17 (32)	4 (8)	1 (2)	0 (0)
	Same Year as the Year of Loan Price Quote	1 Year after the Year of Loan Price Quote	2 Years after the Year of Loan Price Quote	3 Years or More after the Year of Loan Price Quote
B. All firms with the same SIC as the firms in panel A (N = 751):				
No. of firms filing for Chapter 11:	23 (3.1)	12 (1.6)	10 (1.3)	15 (2.0)
C. All firms in panel A that are in the bottom quartile of their industry as ranked by EBITDA/total assets (N = 191):				
No. of firms filing for Chapter 11:	9 (4.7)	5 (2.6)	4 (2.1)	3 (1.6)

NOTE.—EBITDA = earnings before interest, taxes, depreciation, and amortization; SIC = Standard Industrial Classification. Percentages of samples are in parentheses. The information on filing for Chapter 11 is obtained from Bankruptcy Datasource and Dow Jones News Retrieval Services. Panel A provides the incidence of bankruptcy for the entire sample of 53 firms for which a loan sale price quote appears in the *Gold Sheets* and is classified as subpar. Panel B reports incidence of bankruptcy for the sample of all firms that are in the same industry as the firms whose loan price quote appeared in *Gold Sheets*. Panel C reports the results for the subset of firms in panel B and consists of those firms that fall in the bottom quartile in their industry as ranked by the ratio of EBITDA to total assets.

private loans made to U.S. borrowers. Apart from loan-specific details such as amount, terms, and maturity, the database also provides borrower-specific information, including primary SIC code. We were able to obtain information on 47 of our 53 borrowers.

Next we compiled a list of these firms that included their SIC classification and the year in which the first loan price quote for that borrower appeared in *Gold Sheets*. Since some of the borrowers are from the same industry or had their first loan price quoted in the same year, there is some duplication in this list. We eliminated multiple observations of the same industry by including each industry only once. If there were multiple borrowers from an industry, we picked the year in which an industry borrower's loan was quoted in *Gold Sheets* for the first time. This year is defined as the base year for that industry.

Next, for each industry observation, we generated the list of all firms with the same four-digit SIC code that are in the Compustat database for the year immediately preceding the base year. If there were fewer than three firms that matched the borrower's industry group, we generated all the firms with same three-digit SIC code. This step generates a plausible universe of all firms in the same industry as the firm that attracted the first loan price quote in that industry. We trace all firms in each industry for any incidence of Chapter 11 filing in the 3 years subsequent to the year of loan sale activity. This exercise allows us to generate the bankruptcy incidence in the industries to which the loan sale borrowers belonged. The results presented in table 2, panel B, show that the frequency of bankruptcy is 3% in the year in which the first loan sale price quote appeared, and for the year following the loan sale activity it is 1.6%. This is substantially lower then the results reported in table 2, panel A.

One can argue that the bankruptcy rate is likely to be higher among firms that are showing poor financial performance. Hence, we repeated the same exercise with a subset of those firms that fall in the bottom quartile of their industry as ranked by their operating performance. We calculated the ratio of EBITDA to total assets for all firms. Those firms for which this ratio is in the bottom 25% of the industry were included in the sample of poorly performing firms in that industry. As expected, the bankruptcy filing rate is higher for this subsample, with the frequency of bankruptcy being 4.7% in the year in which the first loan price quote appeared and 2.6% for the first year following the loan sale activity. As the results in table 2, panel C, show, the bankruptcy rate is substantially lower than the rates reported in panel A.[9]

These results of subsequent poor performance, combined with our results of the negative stock price reaction at the time of the seasoned nonpar loan sale announcement, are further evidence consistent with the view that banks play a special, or unique, role as monitors (or corporate insiders) and that

9. These tests were repeated for the subsample of firms for which CRSP data and a precise loan sale date are available from *Bank Letter*. We examined the frequency of bankruptcy filings by the 15 subpar firms that were the basis of our earlier event study test and compared these rates to the filing rate in their industries. The results are very similar to those reported in table 2.

TABLE 3 **Industry-Adjusted Performance Characteristics for the Sample of Subpar Loan Firms**

Financial Ratio (*N* = No. of Firms with Data Available)	Industry-Adjusted Mean	*t*-Statistic	Industry-Adjusted Median	*z*-Statistic
A:				
Return on assets (*N* = 30)	−.1175	−1.31	−.0228	−2.30**
Investment intensity (*N* = 29)	−.0002	−.02	−.0058	−1.17
Total leverage (*N* = 29)	.1829	3.65***	.1683	3.36***
B:				
Return on assets (*N* = 14)	−.0114	−1.04	−.0023	−.75
Investment intensity (*N* = 14)	−.0017	−.462	−.0029	−.25
Total leverage (*N* = 14)	.1751	4.09***	.1988	2.92***

NOTE.—The financial information is for the last fiscal year prior to the year in which the loan sale took place and is obtained from Compustat. The table reports the financial characteristics for the sample of subpar loan sales from *Gold Sheets* (panel A) and *Bank Letter* (panel B). The ratios are reported on an industry-adjusted basis, which is calculated as the difference between the relevant ratio (e.g., return on assets) of the sample firm and the median ratio (e.g., return on assets) for those firms operating in the same four-digit Standard Industrial Classification code as the sample firm. Return on assets is defined as the ratio of earnings before interest, taxes, depreciation, and amortization to total assets. Investment intensity is the ratio of the capital expenditure to the total assets. Total leverage is the ratio of the sum of long-term debt and current liabilities to the total assets. Also reported are the *t*-statistics and *z*-statistics for the null hypothesis that the mean and median are equal to zero.

* Significant at 10% level.
** Significant at 5% level.
*** Significant at 1% level.

announcements about bank lending decisions convey hitherto private information to the capital market at large (see, e.g., Fama 1985; James 1987).

A natural question, however, is whether the ex post performance of these firms is correlated to their ex ante performance prior to the loan sale, that is, whether we could have anticipated the poor performance of these firms even without the announcement of the sale of a loan. Related to this is another question: What are the (publicly available) financial characteristics of those firms whose loans are sold at the time of the loan sale? To evaluate this question, we collated information on the financial characteristics of those firms whose loans were sold in the year prior to the loan sale.

Table 3 provides some financial and operating performance measures for the sample of borrowing firms whose loans were sold over the 1994–98 period. Panel A documents these measures for the sample of nonpar firms obtained from *Gold Sheets,* while panel B presents similar results for the *Bank Letter* sample. These performance measures are reported on an industry-adjusted (median) basis. Specifically, financial ratios were calculated for all firms with the same four-digit SIC code as that of the borrowing firm whose loan was sold, and the median financial ratio (for the industry) was then subtracted from the financial ratio of the borrowing firm. Three such financial ratios are shown in table 3. As can be seen, firms whose loans were sold appear to have performed below the industry median in the year preceding the loan sale. In particular, they had a lower return on assets, a higher level of debt (as measured by the ratio of book liabilities to total assets), and a lower degree of investment

TABLE 4 Within-Industry Distribution of Selected Financial Characteristics for the Two Samples of Subpar Loan Sales

Industry Quartile (N = No. of Firms with Available Data)	Quartile 1	Quartile 2	Quartile 3	Quartile 4
A. Sample of subpar loan sales from *Gold Sheets*:				
Return on assets (N = 30)	7	12	9	2
	(23.3)	(40.0)	(30.0)	(6.7)
Investment intensity (N = 29)	6	12	6	5
	(20.7)	(41.4)	(20.7)	(17.2)
Total leverage (N = 29)	3	3	7	16
	(10.3)	(10.3)	(24.2)	(55.2)
B. Sample of subpar loan sales from *Bank Letter*:				
Return on assets (N = 14)	1	6	7	0
	(7.1)	(42.9)	(50.0)	(0)
Investment intensity (N = 14)	2	5	4	3
	(14.3)	(35.7)	(28.6)	(21.4)
Total leverage (N = 14)	1	1	4	8
	(7.1)	(7.1)	(28.6)	(57.2)

NOTE.—For each firm in the two samples, financial data are gathered for all firms with the same four-digit Standard Industrial Classification code in Compustat for the year before the year of sale for the sample collected from *Bank Letter* and for the year before the year in which the first price quote is reported in *Gold Sheets* for the *Gold Sheets* sample. The relevant financial ratio is calculated for every firm in that industry to get the distribution of the ratio and to determine in which quartile the sample firms lies. Quartile 1 is the bottom 25% of the industry, quartile 2 is the bottom 25%–50% of the industry, quartile 3 is the top 50%–75% of the industry, and quartile 4 is the top 25% of the industry. Return on assets is defined as the ratio of earnings before interest, taxes, depreciation, and amortization to total assets. Investment intensity is the ratio of the capital expenditure to the total assets. Total leverage is the ratio of the sum of long-term debt and current liabilities to the total assets. The percentage of firms of the total sample in each category is given in parentheses.

intensity (measured by capital expenditures to total assets) compared with the median firm in the same industry.

Nevertheless, we wished to examine further whether these are the poorest performing firms in their respective industry, that is, whether, on an ex ante basis, we would have expected these firms to have poor future viability (i.e., file for bankruptcy). For example, if our loan sale sample firms were in the bottom quartile of their industry, an astute investor might reasonably anticipate that some of these firms would go bankrupt or exit the industry regardless of a bank's decision to sell the firm's loans. Table 4 compares the financial performance of the two nonpar loan samples to their respective peer industry groups. Specifically, for the year immediately preceding the loan sale announcement, we calculated a set of financial ratios (as publicly available proxy measures of performance) for all firms that have the same four-digit SIC codes as each borrower whose loan was sold. This allows us to generate a distribution for each financial ratio within the loan sale firm's industry. Surprisingly, we find that the firms whose loans were sold are not the worst performers in their respective industries across all performance measures, nor were they always concentrated in the bottom decile or even the bottom 25% (quartile). As table 4 shows, for two of the three accounting measures, return on assets and investment intensity, the majority of the sample firms lie in the second quartile (twenty-fifth to fiftieth percentile). The results are similar across both the sample of nonpar borrowers obtained from *Gold Sheets* (panel A) and the sample obtained from *Bank Letter* (panel B). This suggests that publicly available financial information alone may have been insufficient for outside investors to clearly distinguish, or preidentify, the degree of weakness of the firms whose loans were sold and that publicly announced loan sale decisions by banks appear to have provided valuable (hitherto private) information to outside investors regarding the true financial condition of these firms.

IV. The Effect of Loan Sales on Bank Stock Returns

The decision to sell a loan may also contain information about the quality of bank loan portfolios. Indeed, loan sales may be interpreted favorably by the market as a reflection that the average quality of a bank's remaining portfolio will improve—given its incentive to sell off, or divest, its poorer quality loans. However, in selling such loans the bank has to assess the potential cost of such sales, which might harm its relationship with the borrower whose loan is sold (as well as potential borrowers who may be concerned that their loans will be sold in the future)[10] or its reputation with investors who buy the loans sold by the bank (should they deteriorate further in quality). Plus, a loan sale might signal that the bank's management in general has exhibited poor judgment in its lending decisions or that its capital position is weak. To examine the net effects of a loan sale on a selling bank, we conducted an event study for those banks announcing the sale of loans. We are limited by the fact that *Bank Letter* news stories announcing loan sales do not always mention the identity of the selling bank. The quote below provides a typical loan sale announcement: "A Musicland lender auctioned off $11 million in bank debt late last week, with bids in the high 70s, according to market sources" (*Bank Letter* 1997).

For the total of 107 loan sale announcements originally collected from *Bank Letter,* we were able to identify the loan-selling institution in 58 cases. Of these, 25 sale announcements were made by foreign financial institutions and 33 were made by U.S. financial institutions. The lenders mentioned in these 33 U.S. financial institution announcements were then matched to the CRSP daily stock price database. Two lenders did not have stock price information,[11] and two announcements involving Fleet Bank were made on the same day and, thus, were included as a single announcement, leaving us with 30 bank loan sale announcement dates. Finally, we removed the three loan sales made by investment banks, leaving 27 U.S. commercial bank loan sellers.[12] The

10. It is not unusual for borrowers to attempt the curtailment of secondary trading in their loans. In an extreme case, one borrower made it a part of the loan agreement by specifying 11 past lenders to which it did not want its loan to be sold (see *Bank Letter* 1998).

11. These were nonbanking firms (Goldman Sachs and Heller Financial).

12. Results remain unchanged if we include the three investment banks. The results for the subsample of three investment banks are similar to those reported for the sample of 27 banks.

TABLE 5 Cumulative Abnormal Returns for the Banks on the Announcement of Sale of Their Loan

Event Window	CAR (%)	z-Statistic
A. Abnormal returns for the banks (all announcements) ($N = 27$):		
7-day window (−4, 2)	−.09	−.08
5-day window (−2, 2)	−.05	−.10
3-day window (−1, 1)	.59	1.41
B. Abnormal returns for the banks of subpar loan sales ($N = 15$):		
7-day window (−4, 2)	−.54	−.40
5-day window (−2, 2)	−.12	−.06
3-day window (−1, 1)	.25	.67

NOTE.—In panel A, we report the cumulative abnormal return (CARs) for 27 loan sale announcements by U.S. banks. Panel B reports the CARs for the U.S. banks for the 15 subpar loan sales subsample. The CARs are calculated using the Center for Research in Security Prices database.

results of the event study on selling banks' returns are reported in table 5, panel A. We also looked at the subset of loan sale announcements involving the 15 nonpar borrowers that were examined in the "borrower"-related tests described in tables 1–5. This subset yielded 15 clearly identifiable U.S. bank lenders. The loan sale announcement effects for these 15 banks are reported in table 5, panel B.

The results of table 5 indicate that, on average, the sale of loans by banks does not appear to have any net (new) impact on the selling banks' stock returns (i.e., there is no evidence of any net costs or benefits to the selling banks' shareholders). This result holds true for the whole sample for which the bank seller could be identified (panel A) as well as the subsample of nonpar loan sales (panel B).

Nevertheless, it is of interest to examine the characteristics that differentiate between those banks that engage in loan sales and those that do not, especially as some have argued that an important motivation for loan sales is to improve a bank's solvency position, such as the bank's regulatory capital ratio (see, e.g., Pennacchi 1988). As discussed above, for the event study examining a bank's own share price reaction to a sale of a loan, we were able to identify 27 unique loan sale event dates. Since some banks announced multiple sales in the same year, these multiple loan-selling banks were treated as a single observation in the same year. This resulted in a final sample of 19 distinct bank-loan sale years. We obtained key financial characteristics for each of the selling banks for the year before the loan sale announcement from a variety of sources, including Bank Compustat, annual reports, and 10-K filings. These included size denoted by total assets (Bank Compustat data item no. 36), tier-1 capital (data item no. 48), reserves for bad loans (data item no. 78), and net income (data item no. 161). We use these to construct the operating measures described in table 6. For each bank sale year we generated the list of all banks in the Bank Compustat by using the following four-digit SIC codes: 6020 (commercial banks), 6021 (national commercial banks), 6022 (state commercial banks), and 6029 (commercial banks). We then calculated

TABLE 6 **Within-Industry Distribution of Selected Financial Characteristics for the Two Samples of Subpar Loan Sales**

Industry Quartile (N = No. of Banks with Available Data)	Quartile 1	Quartile 2	Quartile 3	Quartile 4
Total assets (N = 19)	0	0	1	18
	(0)	(0)	(5.3)	(94.7)
Tier 1 capital (N = 19)	17	1	0	1
	(89.5)	(10.5)	(0)	(0)
Reserves for bad loans/total assets (N = 19)	3	1	8	7
	(15.8)	(5.3)	(42.2)	(36.7)
Net income/total assets (N = 19)	4	4	8	3
	(21.0)	(21.0)	(42.2)	(15.8)

NOTE.—For each selling bank, financial data are gathered for all financial institutions with four-digit Standard Industrial Classification codes equal to 6020 (commercial banks), 6021 (national commercial banks), 6022 (state commercial banks), and 6029 (commercial banks [NEC]) in Bank Compustat for the year before the year of sale for the sample collected from *Bank Letter*. The relevant financial ratio is calculated for every banking firm to get the distribution of the ratio and to determine in which quartile the selling bank lies. Quartile 1 is the bottom 25% of the industry, quartile 2 is the bottom 25%–50% of the industry, quartile 3 is the top 50%-75% of the industry, and quartile 4 is the top 25% of the industry. The percentage of firms of the total sample in each category is given in parentheses.

the ratios described in table 6 for these banks, giving us the distribution for each ratio of the banking industry as a whole. Banks involved in loan sales are large banks, with 18 out of 19 selling banks to be found in the top 25% of the banking firms ranked by total assets. Most of the loan-selling banks also fall in the bottom quartile of banks ranked by their tier-1 capital, which is consistent with Pennacchi's (1988) hypothesis that a prime incentive for loan sales is to boost a bank's capital ratios (although it is worth noting that none of the banks were below the Bank for International Settlements statutory 4% minimum requirement). In addition, more than three-quarters of the banks fall in the top 50% of banks ranked according to the bad loan reserves to total asset ratio. Finally, the selling banks are evenly distributed across the four quartiles if the ranking is done according to net income to total assets ratio. Overall, it appears that loan-selling banks are, on average, of poorer quality than are nonselling banks.

V. Additional Robustness Tests

Our main sample consists of all news stories from 1995–98. Our sample ended in 1998 so that we could look at the long-term performance of those firms whose loans were sold. However, while we cannot examine the long-term performance of more recent loan sales, it is possible to extend our event study to include more recent loan sales (so as to examine the robustness of our event study results). Accordingly, we gathered additional data on loan sale news stories for 1999 and 2000 from *Bank Letter/Loan Market Week*.

Another robustness check is to examine whether there were other events

TABLE 7 Cumulative Abnormal Returns for the Firms on the Announcement of Sale of Their Loan by Their Bank for the Augmented Sample from 1995 to 2000

Event Window	CAR (%)	*z*-Statistic
A. Abnormal returns for the firms around the date of first loan sale announcement ($N = 44$):		
7-day window (−4, 2)	−4.11	−1.75*
5-day window (−2, 2)	−3.86	−2.63***
3-day window (−1, 1)	−1.30	−2.65***
B. Abnormal returns for the firms around the date of first subpar loan sale announcement ($N = 25$):		
7-day window (−4, 2)	−7.84	−2.95***
5-day window (−2, 2)	−6.70	−3.47***
3-day window (−1, 1)	−1.24	−2.12**
C. Abnormal returns for the firms around the date of first par loan sale announcement ($N = 18$):		
7-day window (−4, 2)	2.12	1.07
5-day window (−2, 2)	1.36	.42
3-day window (−1, 1)	−.70	−1.36

NOTE.—Cumulative abnormal return (CARs) exist for 44 firms around the date of first announcement of sale of their loan by their lender. The CARs are calculated using the Center for Research in Security Prices database using the methodology outlined in Mikkelson and Partch (1986). Panel A provides the event study results for augmented sample of 44 borrowers in the period 1995–2000. Panel B provides the event study results for the subsample of 25 subpar loan sales. Panel C provides the event study results for the subsample of 19 par loan sale firms. (One borrower—Checkers Drive In Restaurant Inc.—cannot be classified as either par or subpar and, hence, is not included in either panel B or panel C.)

* Significant at 10% level.
** Significant at 5% level.
*** Significant at 1% level.

taking place at the same time as the loan sale that may have affected the event study results. Accordingly, we did a news search on ABI/Inform for all news events in the event-study window. We ruled out observations where there was news of losses or defaults, a cut or suspension of dividends, a credit rating cut, a CEO selling a major equity stake, a lawsuit being filed, and takeover-target-related news. As a result of these checks, we dropped three observations from our original sample and added 18 new observations from the 1999–2000 period. This yielded a total sample of 44 loan sales, of which 25 are subpar, 18 are par loan sales, and one cannot be classified.

With respect to the event study for the augmented sample (1995–2000) for borrowers for whom the loan sale is announced, our results are very similar to those shown in table 1 for 1995–98. The augmented results are reported in table 7. Overall, we find a significantly negative stock price reaction to loan sale announcements, which is larger and more significant for subpar loan sales. Moreover, the signs and scale of abnormal returns closely mirror those in table 1.

By adding 1999 and 2000, we were able to augment our original sample of 27 by an additional six banks that were clearly identifiable and for which CRSP data were available. Thus, we had a larger sample of 33 banks. We continued to find insignificant abnormal returns for selling banks with the larger sample.[13]

Finally, it might be of interest to examine the wealth effects for the "buyers" of the bank loans that are sold. As shown in the appendix, only in a limited number of cases do we know the identity of the buyer. Specifically, for the augmented sample of 44 loan sales, we have information (and CRSP data) for the buyers in eight cases. We conducted an event study to test for cumulative abnormal returns for buyers on the loan sale announcement. Perhaps not surprisingly, given the small sample size, we found insignificant cumulative abnormal returns for this group.

VI. Summary and Conclusions

This is the first article to evaluate empirically the effects of secondary loan sales by banks on both borrowers as well as bank stock returns. Using loan sales announcements reported in the publication *Bank Letter,* we find evidence of a negative effect of loan sales by banks on borrowers' returns. This effect is strongest for the sale of subpar loans. This result is consistent with a strong certification effect of loan sales. Specifically, the sale of a loan appears to carry a signal to the capital market that is the mirror image of the findings of James (1987), Lummer and McConnell (1989), and others regarding the (positive) news effect of loan initiations. This result adds further support to the view that banks play a special, or unique, role in diffusing hitherto private information to outside investors regarding the performance of borrowing forms. We also find that 42% of the firms whose loans are sold file for bankruptcy within 3 years of the announcement of a loan sale by their bank lender. While cross-sectional tests confirmed that borrowers whose loans are sold are generally in a weaker financial and operating condition than a matched control group of firms whose loans are not sold, the sale of a loan appears to convey to the market additional (material) information about the relative degree of weakness of the borrowing firm whose loan is sold.

Finally, we examined the effects of a loan sale on the selling bank itself, since the sale of a loan may convey new information to the market regarding the quality of a selling bank's loan portfolio as well as affect, among other things, its reputation and relationships with other loan customers and investors. Interestingly, the sale of a loan by a bank carried no significant impact on its own stock return, although loan sales appear to be made by generally weaker banks.

13. Results are not reported in tables but are available from the authors on request.

Appendix

TABLE A1

Par/Subpar	Borrower Name	Selling Bank	Buyer	S&P Rating	Indicated Price (per $100)	Indicated Amount (in $Millions)
N.A.	Checkers Drive In Restaurant	Original lenders	Galileo Fund	Not rated	N.A.	35
Subpar	American Pad & Paper	Nations Bank/Chase	N.A.	Not rated	94	40
Subpar	American Rice	Original lenders	N.A.	Not rated	90	21
Subpar	APS Holdings	Bank of America	N.A.	Not rated	91.5	20
Subpar	Boston Chicken	Bankers Trust	N.A.	CC	86	10
Subpar	Bradlees	Original lenders	N.A.	B+	85.25	5
Subpar	Caldor	Mitsubishi Trust/ United Jersey Bank	Lehman/JP Morgan	Not rated	85	33.5
Subpar	Edison Brothers	Original lenders	N.A.	Not rated	N.A.	N.A.
Subpar	Fleming Company	Boatmen's Bank	N.A.	BB−	93.5	23
Subpar	FPA Medical Management	Lehman	N.A.	CCC−	33	50
Subpar	Morrison Knudsen	Mellon Bank	Merrill Lynch	Not rated	82.5	25
Subpar	Musicland	Comerica Bank	Amroc Investments	CCC+	70	15
Subpar	Paragon Trade Brands	Original lenders	N.A.	Not rated	85	20
Subpar	Philip Services	Credit Lyonnais	Goldman Sachs	Not rated	94	50
Subpar	Today's Man	Fleet	N.A.	Not rated	66	7
Subpar	Trans World Entertainment	Fleet Bank	N.A.	Not rated	72–82	30
Par	Arch Communications Group	Original lenders	N.A.	B−	NA	N.A.
Par	Brylane	Wells Fargo	N.A.	Not rated	99.8125	13
Par	Fred Meyer	N.A.	N.A.	Not rated	98	4
Par	IVAX	Sakura Bank	N.A.	Not rated	95	17
Par	Kmart	National City Bank	N.A.	BBB	95	10.5
Par	Lucent Technologies	Goldman Sachs	N.A.	A	100.75	30
Par	Marvel Entertainment Group	Citibank	N.A.	B−	94	9
Par	MobileMedia	Original lenders	N.A.	B−	99.75	20
Par	Nextel	Original lenders	Retail Investor	CCC−	97	15
Par	Reebok International	Original lenders	N.A.	A−	99.75	70
Par	Service Merchandise	Original bankers	Goldman Sachs, Merrill	BB	93.125	40
Par	Shoney's	CIBC	Goldman Sachs	Not rated	94.5	100
Par	Time-Warner	Japanese lenders	N.A.	BBB−	99.125	10

References

Bank Letter. 1995. Original lender dumps block of Bradlees debt. *Bank Letter* 19, no. 24 (June 19).
Bank Letter. 1997. Musicland auction attracts bids in high 70s. *Bank Letter* 21, no. 3 (January 27).
Bank Letter. 1998. Nextel blackballs 11 banks. *Bank Letter* 22, no. 11 (March 16).
Best, R., and Zhang, H. 1993. Alternative information sources and the information content of bank loans. *Journal of Finance* 48:1507–22.
Billet, M. T.; Flannery, M. J.; and Garfinkel, J. A. 1995. The effect of lender identity on a borrowing firm's equity return. *Journal of Finance* 50:699–718.
Campbell, T., and Kracaw, W. 1980. Information production, market signaling, and the theory of intermediation. *Journal of Finance* 35:863–82.
Dahiya, S.; Saunders, A.; and Srinivasan, A. 2003. Financial distress and the bank lending relationship. *Journal of Finance* 58:375–99.
Diamond, D. W. 1984. Financial intermediation and delegated monitoring. *Review of Economics Studies* 51:393–414.
Fama, E. 1985. What's different about banks. *Journal of Monetary Economics* 15:29–36.
Gande, A.; Puri, M.; Saunders, A.; and Walter, I. 1997. Bank underwriting of debt securities: Modern evidence. *Review of Financial Studies* 10:1175–1202.
James, C. 1987. Some evidence of the uniqueness of bank loans. *Journal of Financial Economics* 19:217–35.
James, C. 1988. The use of loan sales and standby letters of credit by commercial banks. *Journal of Monetary Economics* 22:395–422.
James, C., and Smith, D. C. 2000. Are banks still special? New evidence on their role in the corporate capital-raising process. *Journal of Applied Corporate Finance* 13:52–63.
Lummer, S., and McConnell, J. 1989. Further evidence on bank lending process and capital market response to bank loan agreements. *Journal of Financial Economics* 25:52–63.
Mikkelson, W., and Partch, M. 1986. Valuation effects of security offerings and the issuance process. *Journal of Financial Economics* 15:31–60.
Miller, S. 1998. The development of the leveraged loan asset class. In F. Fabozzi (ed.), *Bank Loans: Secondary Market and Portfolio Management*. New Hope, Pa.: Fabozzi Associates, pp. 1–23.
Pennacchi, G. 1988. Loan sales and cost of bank capital. *Journal of Finance* 43:375–96.
Puri, M. 1996. Commercial banks in investment banking: Conflict of interest or certification role? *Journal of Financial Economics* 40:373–401.
Puri, M. 1999. Commercial banks as underwriters: Implications for the going public process. *Journal of Financial Economics* 54:133–63.
Slovin, M. B.; Shuska, M. A.; and Polonchek, J. A. 1993. The value of bank durability: Borrowers as the bank stakeholders. *Journal of Finance* 48:247–66.

Nadia Massoud
University of Alberta

Anthony Saunders
New York University

Barry Scholnick
University of Alberta

The Impact of ATM Surcharges on Large versus Small Banks: Is There a Switching Effect?*

This paper uses a unique database to test the effect of ATM surcharges on larger versus smaller banks. Only nonbank ("foreign") users of ATMs pay ATM surcharges. Customers thus face incentives to switch accounts from smaller banks to larger banks in order to avoid high ATM surcharges. We find that, after we control for other bank factors, higher ATM surcharges result in a greater market share of deposits of larger banks and a lower market share for smaller banks, results that are consistent with customer switching. However, smaller banks can positively affect their market share by establishing larger ATM networks.

I. Introduction

In April 1996 member banks of shared automatic teller machine (ATM) networks (Cirrus, Plus, etc.) were allowed by these networks to impose surcharges on nonbank (also referred to as "foreign") customers using

* We would like to acknowledge the financial support of the Social Sciences and Humanities Research Council of Canada, the National Research Program on Financial Services and Public Policy at York University, the Salomon Center for the Study of Financial Institutions at New York University, and the School of Business, University of Alberta. We are grateful to Tony Hayes of Dove Consulting Inc. for making the Dove ATM survey data available to us. We thank Dan Bernhardt, Stephane Crétien, Rob Engle, Bill Greene, Tim Hannan, Randall Morck, Steven Ongena, and an anonymous referee for their suggestions. We thank our research assistants Faris Mohammad and Yuseph and Osama Montaser. Contact the corresponding author, Barry Scholnick, at barry.scholnick@ualberts.ca.

[*Journal of Business*, 2006, vol. 79, no. 4]

0021-9398/2006/7904-0015$10.00

their ATMs.[1] This regulatory change has resulted in a public policy debate over whether the ability to impose ATM surcharges benefits large banks and hinders small banks. Several consumer interest groups (e.g. Public Interest Research Group [PIRG] 1999) have argued that ATM surcharges create an incentive for bank customers to switch from smaller banks with smaller ATM networks to larger banks with larger ATM networks. The reason is that only nonbank (foreign) customers pay the ATM surcharge so that a customer belonging to a large bank with many ATMs would be less likely to have to pay ATM surcharges because of free access to this larger network.

The PIRG, for example, has made the argument, regarding the period following the 1996 liberalization, that "large banks in particular were eager to take advantage of their size . . . when competing against smaller banks. The new fees gave the large banks the golden opportunity to advertise that they had far more ATMs than smaller banks, which meant that their customers would have to pay fewer fees for using "foreign" banks' ATMs" (2001, 1). In a survey of 106 ATMs in New York State in 2002, this group found that 42% of the ATMs they examined displayed advertisements in which the surcharge is disclosed to foreign customers, encouraging these foreign ATM users to "switch their accounts to the bank that owns the ATM to avoid fees." The bank-owned ATMs that included the "switching" advertisements in their surcharge disclosures include Citibank, Fleet Bank, HSBC, and Key Bank (PIRG 2002).[2]

An indication of the importance of ATM surcharges to both banks and consumer lobby groups is the extent of recent litigation around this issue. A case involving the rights of cities or states to impose ATM surcharge bans has recently reached the U.S. Supreme Court. This followed the attempt by the City of San Francisco and other cities to impose bans on ATM surcharges. In May 2003 the U.S. Supreme Court upheld the ruling of lower courts, which denied cities and states the right to impose ATM surcharge bans (*City of San Francisco et al. v. the Bank of America et al.* [no. 02-1404, 5/27/2003]).

A theoretical explanation regarding the incentive for banks to set high ATM fees is provided by Massoud and Bernhardt (2002). Using a spatial model,

1. Other fee revenues include a fee charged to a bank's own customer who uses another bank's ATMs (a so-called foreign fee) as well as interchange fees paid by the customer's bank to the ATM owner when the bank's own customer uses the owner's ATM. The latter fee is usually set by the network and is constant across all banks in a network. Other fees that may be paid or charged include an own-bank ATM fee (which is rare), a point of sale fee, a card fee, and a switch fee (see Stavins 2000, 15). It should be clarified that the ATM network of importance in this paper is the bank's own ATMs, since switching can take place by depositors either at other banks in the same ATM network (e.g., Cirrus or Plus) or at banks at another ATM network. Foreign users in either the same network or other networks are subject to the same surcharge for using another bank's ATMs.

2. A public policy concern has also been raised about the negative effects of bank merger policy liberalization on small banks. However, Berger et al. (1998) find no support for this in the case of small business lending. On the other hand, it has also been argued that branching and merger restrictions have often favored smaller banks (see, e.g., Palia 1994; Economides, Hubbard, and Palia 1996).

they endogenize both the pricing of ATM services by banks and the choice of home bank and ATM use by customers. They show that banks impose especially high ATM surcharges on nonmembers (higher than the price they charge for their member customers) because each bank wants to encourage more customers to establish deposit accounts with it. That is, surcharges raise the costs of nonaffiliation with the ATM-supplying bank and encourage switching of accounts. In a variant spatial model, Bernhardt and Massoud (2004) show that banks strategically overprovide their ATM network. This raises the attraction of establishing an account with the bank, increases the bank's potential customer base for the sale of other bank products, and enables banks to extract rents more efficiently from their member customers.[3]

The aim of this paper is to empirically examine whether the ability to impose ATM surcharges has indeed benefited larger banks and hindered smaller banks. We use a unique new panel database, which provides us with bank-level data on ATM surcharges, the size of ATM networks, and the percentage of foreign (i.e., nonbank) users of ATMs who have to pay the surcharge. Using this database, we examine the impact that ATM surcharges and ATM network size have on the market share of deposits of larger and smaller banks. We also motivate our study by conducting an event study test of the market reaction to the announcement that banks would be allowed to charge their own ATM surcharges.

While there has been some recent theoretical research on the effects of ATM pricing, a significant impediment to empirical work on this issue has been the lack of data availability. Indeed in his recent literature review, McAndrews (2003) comments that a large amount of empirical work still remains to be conducted on ATMs, including the empirical question of whether "larger banks can use ATMs and surcharges to disadvantage smaller rivals in competition for depositors" (156).

In this paper, we develop testable hypotheses from the existing theoretical literature on ATMs, in particular the models of Massoud and Bernhardt (2002) and Bernhardt and Massoud (2004). As discussed above, these papers consider the possibility that ATM surcharges can affect banks' profitability, both directly and indirectly, through a so-called customer switching effect. The direct effect on profitability stems from the direct revenue generated from "foreigners" (i.e., non–bank customers) paying higher ATM surcharges. The indirect effect results from customers at smaller banks with relatively few ATMs switching their deposit accounts to larger banks with a larger number of ATMs in order to avoid paying ATM surcharges. The higher the surcharge at larger

3. Massoud and Bernhardt (2002) also explore how bank size affects ATM pricing. They show that the strategic pricing impacts are greater for larger banks. The intuition behind this result is that because, spatially, consumers are more likely to be near a large bank's ATM, an increase in the large bank's ATM surcharge leads to a greater incentive for smaller bank customers to switch their accounts to larger banks to save on ATM fees. This finding is consistent with PIRG's (2001) concerns that "a surcharging is part of the big bank's anti-competitive strategy to squeeze out smaller banks and credit unions by encouraging their customers to switch their accounts to banks with larger ATM networks."

banks, the greater incentive customers have to switch to that bank in order to avoid paying the higher surcharges. If switching occurs from smaller to larger banks, then higher ATM surcharges should enhance the market share of bank products (e.g., deposits) of larger banks and reduce the market share of deposits of smaller banks.

One of the key implications of the Massoud and Bernhardt (2002) model is the argument that consumers will switch banks in order to avoid ATM surcharges. This argument is implicitly based on the premise that the switching costs involved in changing banks are low enough to allow consumers to switch. The issue of switching costs has been extensively debated in the theoretical literature (e.g., Matutes and Padilla 1994). One of the key contributions of this paper is that it enables us to provide new empirical evidence on the extent of the switching costs involved in changing banks. If we find that banks are able to affect the market share of their deposits by setting a particular ATM surcharge level, then this implies that some switching has occurred and, in turn, that switching costs may not be sufficiently high so as to impede depositors changing banks in response to the imposition of ATM surcharges.

We first motivate the importance of the ATM surcharge issue to banks by using an event study to examine the announcement effect of surcharge liberalization on publicly traded banks. We examine both the day of the original announcement of the policy change and the day of the announcement that the policy implementation had occurred, and we find strong evidence that larger banks had significantly positive abnormal returns whereas smaller banks had either significantly negative abnormal returns or insignificant abnormal returns. This result implies that the market expected a relatively favorable effect on large bank returns and market share relative to smaller banks in the post-1996 period as a result of ATM surcharge liberalization.

We then use our panel database for individual bank ATM surcharges over the 1996–2001 period to examine the actual impact of an increase in surcharge levels. While the direct effect of high surcharges on a bank's revenue will depend on the price elasticity of demand of customers to using ATMs of a foreign bank,[4] the overall effect of the ATM surcharge on a bank's deposit market share will reflect the degree of switching that occurs by customers who move their accounts (and related bank product demands) to the higher-surcharge bank in order to avoid paying the larger ATM surcharges imposed on "foreign" users.

We find that the level of ATM surcharges is positively related to the market share of deposits of larger banks in the following year. On the other hand, we find that for smaller banks the level of the surcharge is negatively related to their market share in the following year. This is consistent with bank customers switching accounts from smaller to larger banks to avoid paying surcharges at larger banks. However, we also find that smaller banks can affect

4. If the demand function is inelastic, an increase in surcharge will have a positive direct effect on bank revenues. If the demand curve is elastic, it will have a negative effect on bank revenues.

their market share of deposits in the following year by adopting a larger ATM network. Our results thus indicate that larger banks (which already have large ATM networks) are able to generate a larger market share of deposits by setting ATM surcharges at a higher level, whereas smaller banks are able to influence their market share of deposits only by establishing larger ATM networks.

These results are robust across a large variety of econometric specifications, including fixed and random effects panel models and Tobit models. Furthermore, we examine two additional specifications to account for possible endogeneity issues. These are three-stage least-squares (3SLS) models and the log-log panel specification, which tests the model in terms of rates of change.

Section II reviews the previous literature on ATM pricing. Section III assesses the ex ante materiality of the 1996 liberalization of ATM surcharges by examining the market reaction to these announcements. Section IV discusses our hypotheses. Section V describes our panel database, Section VI describes the methodology, and Section VII discusses the empirical results. Finally, Section VIII is a summary and conclusion. Appendix A describes in detail the ATM data employed in this study provided by Dove Consulting Group, Appendix B outlines a theoretical model that provides an economic motivation for the hypotheses tested in the paper, and Appendix C provides details of the 3SLS models used.

II. Previous Literature on ATMs and ATM Pricing

Following the dramatic increase in the number of banks applying a surcharge to their foreign customers, there has also been an increase in research on this issue. Massoud and Bernhardt (2002), McAndrews (2002), and Bernhardt and Massoud (2004) have developed theoretical models that introduce and analyze the idea of the indirect (or switching) effect of ATM surcharging on bank profitability. Other research (e.g., Prager 1999, 2001; Stavins 2000; Hannan et al. 2003) has examined empirically various elements of ATM pricing. A recent literature survey on the economics of ATMs is provided by McAndrews (2003)

Prager (2001) examines whether small banks are disadvantaged by ATM surcharges, but she uses state and city market-level (metropolitan statistical area) data rather than the bank-level data used here. Furthermore, Prager's study covers a period prior to the liberalization of ATM surcharging (and the dramatic growth in ATMs) that occurred after 1996.

Other empirical papers in the literature (e.g., Hannan et al. 2003) attempt to identify factors that determine whether a bank sets a surcharge or not. The empirical questions posed by Hannan et al.—the factors determining whether or not a bank imposes a surcharge—were clearly of importance in the context of their 1997 database, when only about half of the banks in their survey imposed ATM surcharges. However, the very large increase in the proportion of banks using ATM surcharges since then (88% of all banks and 98% of large banks had ATM surcharges in 2001[5]) leads us to ask a different question in this paper: what has been the impact of the surcharge level on bank outcomes and, in particular, on market share of deposits of small versus large banks after the surcharge liberalization?

An important element of this paper concerns the attempts by banks to increase their customer base and strengthen their relationships with their customers by making their ATM networks more attractive. This paper thus contributes to the growing literature on relationship banking, which describes how banks build relationships with customers. Recent papers in this literature include Berger and Udell (1995) and Berlin and Mester (1999).[6]

III. Event Study Evidence: How Did the Market React to ATM Surcharge Liberalization?

Before we trace the long-term impact of the post-1996 liberalization of surcharges on bank market share, it is important to establish the materiality of the news of this liberalization on both large and small banks. Specifically, what were the market's (and equity investors') ex ante expectations regarding the potential impact? To the extent that the market (investors) factored in both direct and indirect effects, the more likely it is that the announcement had a material effect on bank stock returns.

To examine this question we conduct event studies of the impact of the various announcements regarding the liberalization of ATM surcharges on bank returns and, in particular, the relative impact of this announcement on large versus small banks. On November 27, 1995, an announcement was made by VISA indicating that in the future banks would be allowed to set their own ATM surcharges. This was quickly followed by similar announcements by other network providers. On April 1, 1996, Cirrus and Plus (which is controlled by VISA) were the first networks to actually announce that they had implemented the ATM surcharge liberalization.

To examine the announcement effects of the proposed (November 27, 1995) and actual (April 1, 1996) surcharge liberalization, we examine first whether there are differences in abnormal returns from portfolios of larger and smaller banks and second whether, with a seemingly unrelated regression (SUR) approach, abnormal returns from individual banks are related to the asset sizes of those banks.

Firstly, using standard event study methodology, we calculated abnormal returns for two portfolios of banks: (i) a portfolio of big banks (with asset size on the event date exceeding $1 billion) and (ii) a portfolio of small banks

5. Data are taken from the Federal Reserve Report to Congress of Retail Fees of Depository Institutions (Hannan 2002).

6. For detailed discussions of customer relationship effects in a different context, see Ongena and Smith (2001) and Bae, Kang, and Lim (2002). Mester, Nakamura, and Renault (2003) also show that there is a link between customer checking accounts and the information they generate and other services (such as the provision of loans).

TABLE 1 **Test of Market Reaction to Removing the ATM Surcharge Ban Using Portfolios of Larger and Smaller Banks**

	Larger Banks (Assets > $1B)		Smaller Banks (Assets ≤$1B)	
Window	Abnormal Return	Patell *Z*-Test	Abnormal Return	Patell *Z*-Test
	A. Abnormal Return on Event Day of Announcement Freeing Constraints on ATM Surcharges (November 27, 1995)			
(−5, +5)	1.90%	3.965***	−1.43%	−1.488*
(−1, 0)	.42%	1.718**	.03%	.43
(−1, +1)	.31%	.855	−.41%	−.892
(0, 0)	.58%	3.425***	−.01%	.644
(0, +1)	.47%	1.751**	−.46%	−1.067
Number of banks	126		196	
	B Abnormal Return on Event Day of the Effective Date of Removing the Ban of ATM Surcharges (April 1, 1996)			
(−5, +5)	.07%	.013	−.66%	−1.532*
(−1, 0)	.49%	2.942***	−.77%	−4.044***
(−1, +1)	.46%	2.291**	−.95%	−3.595***
(0, 0)	.66%	5.559***	−.16%	−1.931**
(0, +1)	.63%	3.795***	−.33%	−1.725**
Number of banks	142		229	

NOTE.—The table presents the results of event study tests for the event on November 27, 1995 (the first announcement of removing the ban of ATM surcharge) (panel A), and the event on April 1, 1996 (the actual date of removing the ban) (panel B). The model is $R_{i,t} = \alpha_i + \beta_i R_{M,t} + \varepsilon_{i,t}$, where $R_{i,t}$ is the equally weighted return of the portfolio of all the banks in the ith portfolio (either larger [assets > $1 billion] or smaller [assets ≤ $1 billion] banks) at time t; $R_{M,t}$ is the market return at time t. The event study tests examine how equity prices for a sample of publicly traded banks responded to the announcement that banks would no longer face restrictions on imposing ATM surcharges. The results indicate that the market believed ex-ante that large banks would benefit from this regulatory change and that small banks would lose. Data are taken from all banks in the Compustat Bank File that have event day returns data available from the Center for Research in Security Prices (CRSP) data set. Asset size is determined from Compustat as of 1995 and 1996. Return on market model with equally weighted index. The market model is estimated over 255 days in length, ending 10 days before the event day.

* Significant at 10%.

** Significant at 5%.

*** Significance at 1%.

(with asset size on the event date of less than or equal to $1 billion). Our choice of a cutoff of asset size of $1 billion is the same cutoff used by the Federal Reserve as its definition of "large banks" in the context of its report to Congress on ATM surcharges (see, e.g., Hannan 2001, 2002).

The parameters of the market model were estimated over a one-year (255-day) period ending 10 days before the event day.[7] We use both a one-factor and a two-factor model (which includes daily interest rate changes, as well as market returns) in order to account for possible interest rate effects on bank returns (see, e.g., Flannery and James 1984). To test the significance of the announcement day abnormal returns ($AR(n)$), we used the Patell Z test. For each of the two event days we examine a large variety of windows around the event date. As can be seen from table 1, the market expected a very

7. Our results are also robust to change of the end date for the market model to a longer period, i.e., 49 days.

different impact for the portfolio of larger versus smaller banks. In panel A of table 1 we report the abnormal returns for larger and smaller banks for five different event windows, (−5, +5), (−1, 0), (−1, +1), (0, 0), and (0, +1), where the event day is day 0, and a negative number indicates days before the event day and a positive number indicates days after the event day. In all the windows examined except (−1, 0), we find that larger banks had a significantly positive abnormal return. For the small banks we find that there is a negative abnormal return for the (−5, +5) window, with the rest being insignificantly different from zero. In panel B of table 1, we examine the abnormal returns for larger and smaller banks on the day of the implementation of the surcharge policy change, April 1, 1996. Once again our results show that for all the windows examined except (−5, +5), there was a significant positive abnormal return for the larger banks. For all five of the windows examined we find a significant negative abnormal return for the smaller banks. These results thus indicate that the market generally believed that these regulatory changes would benefit larger banks and hinder smaller banks.[8]

In order to check the robustness of these event study results, we also examine whether the impact of the abnormal returns of individual banks (rather than the portfolios used above) on our two event days is related to the size of the banks. Using an SUR methodology, we are able to determine the abnormal return for each individual bank in our sample for each of the different event windows around our event dates (see table 2 for summary statistics). We then regress these abnormal returns against the asset size of each bank. A significant positive relationship between bank-specific abnormal returns and asset size will indicate that as banks get bigger the market expects them to enjoy a greater benefit from the ability to impose their own ATM surcharges.

Our results from these regressions of bank-specific abnormal returns and asset size are reported in table 3. Once again we examine abnormal returns from five different event windows, for both event days. With the exception of the (−1, 0) event window, we find a significant positive relationship between asset size and bank-specific abnormal return for all the other event windows around both event days. These results strongly support the hypothesis that the market believed that the larger the bank, the greater the positive impact an ability to strategically impose independent ATM surcharges would have.[9]

Having established that the equity markets did expect that the liberalization of ATM surcharges would benefit larger banks and not smaller banks, we now turn to an evaluation of whether this actually occurred in the post-1996 period.

8. These results are robust for both the one-factor and the two-factor models.
9. Our results are robust across both the one-factor and the two-factor models.

TABLE 2 **Summary Statistics for Cumulative Abnormal Returns for Individual Banks Using SUR**

Cumulative Abnormal Returns (Window)	Observations	Mean	Standard Deviation	Minimum	Maximum
			A. November 27, 1995		
(−5, +5)	261	−.00134	.05285	−.35727	.163845
(−1, 0)	261	.001844	.024622	−.094	.148256
(−1, +1)	261	−.00136	.026501	−.0995	.144261
(0, 0)	261	.002065	.022213	−.05894	.188725
(0, +1)	261	−.00114	.027302	−.18501	.18473
			B. April 1, 1996		
(−5, +5)	304	.004231	.040265	−.15095	.143407
(−1, 0)	304	.002451	.025991	−.11955	.109091
(−1, +1)	304	.001951	.028837	−.10611	.117737
(0, 0)	304	.0035	.027328	−.15171	.12288
(0, +1)	304	.003	.028437	−.11559	.120601

NOTE.—The table provides summary statistics for abnormal return for a sample of traded banks for two events. Panel A presents the summary statistics of abnormal return for the event on November 27, 1995, the first announcement of the intention of removing the ATM surcharge ban on April 1 1996. Panel B presents the summary statistics of abnormal return for the event on April 1, 1996, the actual date of removing the ATM surcharge ban. To obtain estimates of bank-specific abnormal return, we use the SUR approach. We estimate a model of the realized daily stock return for each bank on a measure of the realized daily return market index, nominal daily yield on 90-day Treasury bill, and a set of daily dummies $D_{k,t}$, where $k = -\tau, -\tau + 1, \ldots, 0, \ldots, \tau - 1, \tau$, which take the value of one for days inside the event window and zero outside the window;

$$R_{i,t} = \alpha_i + \beta_i R_{M,t} + \vartheta_i r_t + \sum_{k=-\tau}^{\tau} \mu_{i,k} D_{k,t} + \varepsilon_{i,t},$$

where $R_{i,t}$ is the realized daily stock return for the ith bank at time t; $R_{M,t}$ is the market return at time t. The coefficient $\mu_{i,k}$ measures the daily abnormal returns inside the event window. For the variables reported in the table, we start the estimation 380 days prior to the start of the event window of 10 days. Sums of daily return abnormal return estimates of over various window yield cumulative abnormal return $\text{CAR}_i(l, q)$.

IV. Testable Hypotheses

In the reminder of the paper we test the following three hypotheses. A theoretical justification for these is shown in Appendix B. On the basis of the discussion of these models we can examine three testable hypotheses.

HYPOTHESIS 1. The higher a bank's ATM surcharge, the lower the proportion of its users will be foreign users, that is, those who have to pay the higher surcharge.

HYPOTHESIS 2. The higher the ATM surcharge of a bank, the larger the market share of deposits as customers switch to that bank to avoid paying the surcharges.

HYPOTHESIS 3. The larger the size of a bank's ATM network, the larger the market share of deposits as customers switch to that bank to avoid paying surcharges.

These three hypotheses are discussed in more detail below.

TABLE 3 The Impact if Bank Asset Size on Bank-Specific Cumulative Abnormal Returns for the Events of Removing the ATM Surcharge Ban

	Constant		Log of Assets		
Window	Coefficient	Standard Error	Coefficient	Standard Error	R^2
	A. OLS Regression of Bank-Specific Cumulative Abnormal Return for November 27, 1995, on Asset Size (N = 260)				
(−5, +5)	−.089	.013***	.0124	.0019***	.1473
(−1, 0)	−.006	.0067	.0011	.0009	.0055
(−1, +1)	−.01608	.0072**	.0021	.001**	.0172
(0, 0)	−.0094	.0061	.0016	.0008**	.0144
(0, +1)	−.01949	.0074***	.0026	.001***	.0250
	B. Regression of Bank-Specific Abnormal Return for April 1, 1996, on Asset Size (N = 284)				
(−5, +5)	−.013	.01	.0025	.001*	.012
(−1, 0)	−.0071	.0061	.0013	.0008	.009
(−1, +1)	−.0096	.01	.0016	.001*	.01
(0, 0)	−.012	.007*	.0021	.001**	.017
(0, +1)	−.0146	.0071**	.0025	.001***	.0229

NOTE.—The table presents the results for estimating an ordinary least squares (OLS) model between bank asset size and bank specific cumulative abnormal return $CAR_i(l, q) = \varphi + \delta asset_i + \eta$, where $CAR_i(l, q)$ is the cumulative abnormal return for bank i from day l to day q, and asset is the natural logarithm of bank-specific assets. Panel A presents OLS results for the event on November 27, 1995, the first announcement of removing the ATM ban on April 1, 1996. Panel B presents OLS estimates for the event on April 1, 1996, the effective date of removing the ban. To obtain estimates of abnormal return, using the SUR approach (see Flannery and James [1984] for more on the SUR methodology), we estimate a two-factor model of the realized daily stock return for each bank on a measure of the realized daily return market index, a daily interest rate for one-year Treasury bills, and a set of daily dummies.See also the note to table 2. Data are taken from all banks in the Compustat Bank File that have event day returns data available from the CRSP data set. Asset size is determined from Compustat as of 1995 and 1996. Return on market model with equally weighted index.

* Significance at 10%.
** Significance at 5%.
*** Significance at 1%.

A. *The Impact of ATM Surcharges on Foreign Usage*

Our initial hypothesis relates to the impact of ATM surcharges on the percentage of foreign users of ATMs—who are the only customers who have to pay surcharges. Standard economics, as well as the Massoud and Bernhardt (2002) and Bernhardt and Massoud (2004) models, indicates that the higher the price of this service, the lower the proportion of surcharge-paying foreign customers who use the service, relative to customers who do not pay. Thus we predict a negative relationship between the level of the ATM surcharge and the percentage of foreigners who use ATMs at a particular bank.

It should be noted that a negative coefficient on the relationship between ATM surcharges and foreign percentage is consistent only with the hypothesis that a customer's behavior does indeed respond when ATM surcharges are imposed. Foreign usage could decline, however, either because customers switch or move to banks with larger ATM networks or, alternatively, because they simply do not access foreign ATMs as frequently as they did prior to ATM surcharge increases.

B. The Impact of ATM Surcharges on the Market Share for Deposits

Our second testable hypothesis examines the relationship between the level of ATM surcharges and the market share of deposits. The switching effect argues that a bank may be able to induce noncustomers to switch their deposit accounts to that bank by setting a high ATM surcharge. The customers who are most likely to switch are those who are most likely to use the bank's ATM network but would have to pay the high surcharge if they remained a foreign customer.

The key distinction between larger and smaller banks is that if a larger bank (with a larger ATM network) increased its ATM surcharge, there are likely to be more foreign customers who use that larger network because of the increased convenience of that network and thus face an incentive to switch their deposit accounts to that bank. In other words, a higher ATM surcharge set by a larger bank should result in a larger market share of that bank. On the other hand, if a smaller bank set a higher ATM surcharge, it is not clear that there will be many, if any, foreign customers who would face an incentive to switch to the smaller bank. Indeed smaller banks may lose market share relative to larger banks if depositors are switching to larger banks.

An important factor to consider when attempting to empirically capture switching behavior is that there is likely to be a lag between a bank setting an ATM surcharge and a customer deciding to switch deposit accounts to that bank. It is for this reason that in all our empirical estimates we measure the relationship between the ATM surcharge in year t and deposit market share in the following year (year $t + 1$).

C. The Impact of ATM Network Size on Market Share for Deposits

Our third testable hypothesis concerns the relationship between the ATM network size and the market share of deposits. We argue here that the more extensive the ATM network of a bank, given any ATM surcharge, the more likely it will be for customers to switch to that bank because they are attracted by the convenience of that bank's larger ATM network, and in order to avoid paying the ATM surcharge for the use of that network.

Once again, because of the lag between the establishment of a given ATM network size and a customer's decision to switch to another bank, we empirically examine the relationship between ATM network size in time t and deposit market share in the following year (year $t + 1$).

V. Data

A major impediment to the empirical testing of the various predictions from the theoretical literature is a lack of data on ATMs. In this paper we make use of a very rich new database made available to us by Dove Consulting of Boston (the 1999 and 2002 ATM Deployer Studies). These data provide specific details by bank and year regarding level of ATM surcharge, ATM network size, percent use of a bank's ATM network by foreigners, and other pertinent ATM-related data. The panel database covers a large number of banks of different sizes over six years. An indication of the richness of this database is that our paper is the first to be able to include data on the foreign percentage of ATM users—a key variable for determining the impact of ATM surcharges on ATM usage. Our paper is also the first to utilize bank-level panel data to examine this issue.

For each of the banks in the Dove survey, we also collected additional data from a variety of sources. For example, we collected balance sheet data for each of these banks from the Federal Reserve Call Reports (Statements of Condition and Income). We also collected market share data from the Federal Reserve database on the market share of deposits. Considerable time and effort were expended in matching these different data from the different databases across different banks and across different years. We eliminate from our database all data in which a bank merger has occurred since this will affect our measure of market share. Appendix A provides a detailed description of the data used in this study.

The Dove data are based on survey data generated by Dove Consulting in two reports on ATM deployment and pricing: the first in 1999 and the second in 2002. As discussed in Appendix A, not every variable was available each year, and the sample of banks differed over the 1999 and 2002 surveys. Nevertheless, the richness of these data across both larger and smaller banks allows us to examine the hypotheses outlined above.

In terms of our hypotheses described above, we have two dependent variables of interest, the foreign percentage (hypothesis 1) and the market share of deposits (hypotheses 2 and 3). Since switching is likely to occur with a lag, we analyze the impact of surcharge or network size in the current year (year t) on market share one year ahead (year $t + 1$). Our two key explanatory variables are the ATM surcharge and the ATM network size. Our data for ATM surcharge, ATM network size, and foreign percentage are taken from the Dove surveys. Our data on market share of deposits are taken from Federal Reserve data on bank market share, which measure the percentage of a bank's total deposits in the state in which the bank is located.

We add to these independent variables a variety of control variables, which are taken from Call Report data as well as the Dove surveys. The Call Reports used were those that most closely matched the dates of the Dove surveys. The variables derived from Call Reports were a measure of bank risk (the bank capital-asset ratio) and two measures of bank size (bank assets and number of employees). We also include as a control variable a yearly measure for the average certificate of deposit interest rate. This measure reflects the opportunity cost of holding cash (which can influence the use of ATMs) as well as changes over the business cycle. Thus when we examine the determinants of market share, for example, we are able to control for the variables that usually explain bank market share, including bank assets, bank employees, and a bank's capital ratio. Thus if we find significant coefficients on ATM surcharge and ATM network size, it implies that these factors influence market share while controlling for the other bank-level variables.

As additional control variables we also included the Dove measure of geographic dispersion of a bank's ATM network. This is a relatively rough measure used by Dove, in which they simply divide the United States into seven regions (plus one region for "international"), and identifies whether a bank has ATMs in each region and outside the United States (internationally), making eight possible regions in all. The geographic dispersion variable reflects the number of these regions over which a bank locates its ATMs.

As in the case of our event study results reported above, we differentiate between larger and smaller banks on the basis of whether the bank assets are above or below $1 billion. This is the same cutoff used by the Federal Reserve when describing ATM surcharges in its Annual Report to Congress of Retail Fees of Depository Institutions (see, e.g., Hannan 2001, 2002).

VI. Empirical Methodology

In order to examine the different relationships described above, we use four different empirical methodologies in order to check for the robustness of our results. Our first set of tests are panel data tests across individual banks and across time (six years). We utilize traditional panel data techniques including fixed effects and random effects estimation.[10]

Our second set of tests involves Tobit estimation. In our models the dependent variables are measured as a percentage (i.e., either foreign percentage or market share of deposits). In order to account for the fact that the dependent variable is bounded between zero and 100%, we use Tobit analysis. In order to account for the panel data nature of our models, we also include bank-level dummies in our Tobit models to capture bank-level fixed effects.

One issue that may affect the interpretation of our results is the issue of endogeneity, particularly in the case in which our dependent variable is market share of deposits. It could be argued, for example, that a high market share of deposits may cause a bank to set a high ATM surcharge. One important issue to note in this regard is that all our empirical tests have the dependent variable of market share measured at year $t + 1$ (the following year) with the independent variables (e.g., ATM surcharge) measured contemporaneously (year t). It would be hard to make the case that future (one-year-ahead) market share *causes* the current ATM surcharge. Nevertheless, in order to control for any remaining endogeneity issues, we utilize two further model specifications: a panel log-log specification and a 3SLS specification.

Our third specification, the panel log-log specification, focuses on the effect of a percentage change in ATM surcharges on percentage changes in foreign

10. To determine the most appropriate panel model, we employ the Hausman test statistic. The null hypothesis under the Hausman test statistic is whether the random effects model is appropriate. Where the Hausman test indicates that the random effects model is appropriate, we report the random effects model. If not, we report the fixed effects model.

usage and market share.[11] One advantage of looking at percentage changes in ATM surcharges rather than levels is that the level of ATM surcharges may be affected by more extraneous factors, compared to ATM surcharge percentage changes. That is, the percentage change in the ATM surcharge may better control for the potential endogeneity problems.[12] In addition, it provides insights into how increases in the ATM surcharge, rather than just the level of the surcharge, affect bank customer behavior.

The fourth specification seeks to control for potential endogeneity problems by estimating a four-equation 3SLS system. Once again we include bank-level dummy variables (fixed effects) in each equation of this system to account for the panel nature of our data. The four dependent variables in our system are market share of depositors (one year ahead), foreign percentage, ATM surcharge, and ATM network size. By capturing all these equations simultaneously in a 3SLS system, we are able to account for possible endogeneity in the relationship between bank strategic variables (ATM surcharge and network size) and outcomes (market share of deposits and foreign percentage).[13] Details of the 3SLS system are provided in Appendix C.

VII. Results

As described above, we are interested in three particular relationships: (i) the impact of the ATM surcharge on foreign percentage usage, (ii) the impact of the ATM surcharge on one-year-ahead market share, and (iii) the impact of ATM network size on one-year-ahead market share. As discussed above, in order to examine the robustness of our results, we provide estimates of these relationships using four econometric methodologies: (i) standard panel models with either fixed or random effects, (ii) Tobit models with bank fixed effects, (iii) a log-log specification with either fixed or random effects, and (iv) a 3SLS system with bank fixed effects. The panel, Tobit, and log-log results for the foreign usage model are reported in table 4; the panel, Tobit, and log-log results for the market share model in table 5; and the 3SLS results with all four equations in table 6. For each of our tests we report results for both larger banks, which have assets above \$1 billion, and smaller banks, which have assets of less than \$1 billion. For larger banks, the results for all our hypotheses are robust across all four econometric specifications; for smaller banks our results are robust across most of our econometric specifications.

11. As in the case of the panel-level specification, we also use the Hausman test in the log-log specification to determine whether the fixed or random effects panel model is more appropriate.

12. We also examined a change on change specification. Unfortunately, too many observations were lost to make the results statistically meaningful.

13. As described above, we measure the impact of ATM surcharge and ATM network size on market share in the following year (lead). In our 3SLS system we measure the market share lead when market share is a dependent variable and the market share (contemporaneous) when market share is an independent variable.

TABLE 4 The Determinants of Foreign Percent

	Panel Model		Tobit Model		Log-Log Model	
Variable	Coefficient	Standard Error	Coefficient	Standard Error	Coefficient	Standard Error
	A. Larger Banks (Assets > $1B)					
Surcharge	−15.76	4.17***	−15.76	2.66***	−.476	.127***
Number of ATMs	.00	.01	.00	.00	−.019	.051
Geographic dispersion	−9.83	3.14***	−9.83	2.00***	−.065	.096
Bank capital ratio	−4.65	1.95**	−4.65	1.24***	−.159	.187
Bank assets	.00	.00	.00	.00**	−.007	.063
Number of employees	.00	.00	.00	.00	−.042	.057
CD rate	−1.07	1.78	−1.07	1.13	−.012	.200
Constant	117.29	23.03***	242	43.6***	4.611	1.214***
Sample size	101		101		92	
R^2	.03		.33		.285	
Hausman test	19.82(.01) fe				8.12(.321) re	
Log likelihood			−269.54			
LR χ^2			264.21***			
	B. Smaller Banks (Assets ≤ $1B)					
Surcharge	4.49	4.98	6.27	3.81	−.494	.261*
Number of ATMs	−.01	.03	.08	.13	.653	.182***
Geographic dispersion	2.41	3.73	6.20	9.22		
Bank capital ratio	.11	.39	−.47	1.01	.350	1.259
Bank assets	.00	.00**	.00	.00	−.126	.601
Number of employees	.00	.00	.00	.00	−.051	.0565
CD rate	−1.61	2.89	−7.99	3.24**	−.381	.692
Constant	47.32	19.39**	54.59	75.94	4.491	13.168
Sample size	64		64		62	
R^2	.15		.32		.0092	
Hausman test	4.83(.57) re				11.92 (.064) fe	
Log likelihood			-189.65271			
LR χ^2			181.84***			

NOTE.—The table estimates the model of eq. (C1) in App. C. The dependent variable, foreign percentage, measures the percentage of ATM users who have to pay the ATM surcharge because they are nonmembers (nondepositors) of the bank. Members of the bank do not have to pay the ATM surcharge. A negative coefficient on the surcharge variable indicates that the higher the surcharge, the lower the proportion of ATM users who pay the surcharge. For the Hausman tests, for panel and log-log models, re indicates use of random effects and fe indicates use of fixed effects. p-values are in parentheses. Tobit models include bank-level fixed effects. In the log-log panel models all variables are logged.

* p-value of 10%.

** p-value of 5%.

*** p-value of 1%.

A. The Impact of ATM Surcharge on Foreign Percentage Usage

Hypothesis 1 developed above indicates that a higher ATM surcharge level should reduce the proportion of customers who pay a surcharge (foreigners); that is, we expect a negative coefficient on the relationship between ATM surcharge and foreign percentage usage. This should apply to both large and small banks and indicates that ATM surcharge levels do affect customer behavior. Our empirical specification is

TABLE 5 The Determinants of Market Share in Year $t + 1$

Variable	Panel Model Coefficient	Panel Model Standard Error	Tobit Model Coefficient	Tobit Model Standard Error	Log-Log Model Coefficient	Log-Log Model Standard Error
			A. Larger Banks (Assets > $1B)			
Surcharge	1.40	.71**	1.58	.58***	.248	.121**
Number of ATMs	.00	.00	.00	.00	.001	.093
Geographic dispersion	.22	.51	.59	.46	.243	.249
Bank capital ratio	−.21	.20	−.20	.18	−.354	.226
Bank assets	.00	.00	.00	.00	.135	.064**
Number of employees	.00	.00***	.00	.00***	.047	.061
CD rate	−.01	.15	.00	.12	−.015	.093
Constant	8.92	2.74***	−3.83	3.34	−1.112	1.269
Sample size	171		171		159	
R^2	.04		.56		.1582	
Hausman test	6.88(.44) re				38.5 (.00) fe	
Log likelihood			−278.38			
LR χ^2			704.89***			
			B. Smaller Banks (Assets ≤ $1B)			
Surcharge	−1.66	.94*	−1.73	.72**	.150	.402
Number of ATMs	.23	.04***	.23	.03***	−.010	.113
Geographic dispersion	NA		−19.14	2.15***	.093	.588
Bank capital ratio	.11	.06*	.11	.05**	−.901	.506*
Bank assets	.00	.00*	.00	.00**	−.021	.340
Number of employees	−.11	.03***	−.12	.02***	.600	.357*
CD rate	−.53	.27*	−.60	.21***	−.051	.393
Constant	18.57	3.79***	89.47	12.0***	−1.627	5.502
Sample size	106		106		91	
R^2	.014		.29		.30	
Hausman test	70.40(.00) fe				1.84 (.933) re	
Log likelihood			-172.68			
LR χ^2			143.66***			

NOTE.—The table estimates the model of eq. (C2) in App. C. The dependent variable, market share of deposits, is measured as a percentage deposit market share that a bank has in the state in which a bank is located. A positive (negative) coefficient on the surcharge or number of ATM variables indicates that the higher the ATM surcharge or ATM network size, the higher (lower) the market share of deposits will be in the following year. Also see the note to table 4.

* *p*-value of 10%.

** *p*-value of 5%.

*** *p*-value of 1%.

$$\begin{aligned}\text{Foreign Percentage}_{i,j} = {} & \theta_{0,j} + \theta_{1,j}\text{Surcharge}_{i,t,j} \\ & + \theta_{2,j}\text{Number of ATMs}_{i,t,j} \\ & + \theta_{3,j}\text{Geographic Dispersion}_{i,t,j} \\ & + \theta_{4,j}\text{Capital Ratio}_{i,t,j} + \theta_{5,j}\text{Assets}_{i,t,j} \\ & + \theta_{6,j}\text{Employees}_{i,t,j} + \theta_{7,j}\text{CD rate} + u_{i,j} + e_{i,t,j}, \qquad (1)\end{aligned}$$

where i denotes bank, t denotes time, j denotes portfolio (larger or smaller bank), and $u_{i,j}$ represents the bank-specific residual. We report panel, Tobit, and log-log results for the foreign percentage relationship in table 4 and the

TABLE 6 **3SLS results, Four Equations Solved Simultaneously**

Independent Variable	Larger Banks (Assets > \$1B) Coefficient	Larger Banks Standard Error	Smaller Banks (Assets ≤ \$1B) Coefficient	Smaller Banks Standard Error
	Dependent Variable: Market Share of Depositors (Lead)			
Surcharge	10.18	2.03***	−1.82	1.05*
Number of ATMs	.00	.00	.22	.05***
Geographic dispersion	.72	.84	−4.61	1.22***
Bank capital ratio	.08	.49	.18	.10*
Bank assets	.00	.00**	.00	.00
Number of employees	.00	.00	.01	.01
CD rate	1.19	.56**	−.25	.32
Constant	−12.96	15.17	NA	
χ^2	5,419.27***		869.09***	
	Dependent Variable: Foreign Percentage			
Surcharge	−14.27	7.21**	15.45	22.55
Number of ATMs	.02	.01	−1.52	.95
Geographic dispersion	−10.25	2.93***	40.97	25.28
Bank capital ratio	−4.68	2.06**	−1.16	1.70
Bank assets	.00	.00	.00	.00
Number of employee	.00	.00	.17	.21
CD rate	.32	2.32	1.31	6.61
Constant	166.18	65.12**	NA	
χ^2	880.49***		2,051.5***	
	Dependent Variable: Surcharge			
Number of ATMs	.00	.00***	−.04	.02**
Market share of depositors	.05	.01***	1.70	.99*
Geographic dispersion	.01	.07	1.83	.82**
Constant	−1.33	.42***	−6.01	4.01
χ^2	1,306.86***		116.68***	
	Dependent Variable: Number of ATMs			
Surcharge	679.97	130.62***	−18.25	8.14**
Market share of depositors	−33.36	11.98***	36.85	23.77
Employee numbers	.02	.00***	.04	.09
Bank assets	.00	.00***	.00	.00
Account fee	.37	.34	−.17	.29
Constant	−1,124.87	234.65***	489.97	9.38***
χ^2	9,202.34***		15,565.21***	

NOTE.—In order to control for any possible endogeneity in the results of tables 4 and 5, we run a four-equation 3SLS system in which (in addition to foreign percentage and market share [lead]), ATM surcharge and ATM network size are also endogenous. We include bank-level fixed effects in all of the four equations. NA denotes that the variable could not be estimated because of lack of dispersion.

* *p*-value of 10%.

** *p*-value of 5%.

*** *p*-value of 1%.

results for this relationship from the 3SLS procedure in table 6 (the ATM surcharge variable in the foreign percentage equation). In general, our results are robust across all four econometric methodologies used. We find a significant negative relationship between the level of ATM surcharges and the foreign usage of larger banks, and no significant relationship at the 5% level for smaller banks.[14] These results indicate that if larger banks set their ATM surcharges at relatively higher levels, a lower proportion of foreign users (who have to pay the surcharge) will use those ATMs. This indicates that for the larger banks at least, customers will reduce their demand for using foreign ATMs if the surcharge level is high.

There are a number of possible reasons why we do not find evidence of a strongly significant negative relationship for smaller banks. Foreign customers may be insensitive to changes in ATM surcharges if they do not usually access the foreign ATMs of smaller banks because such banks have very few ATMs in their network. Alternatively, foreigners may be insensitive to small bank ATM surcharges if small banks are located in isolated locations with few alternatives, in which case a higher surcharge level would not decrease the proportion of foreigners using that ATM.

Our finding that, for large banks, foreign customers will reduce their demand when the surcharge level is higher indicates that these customers are indeed price sensitive to ATM surcharges and that ATM surcharges can indeed affect customer behavior. We now examine whether ATM surcharges can actually result in customers switching between banks.

B. The Impact of the ATM Surcharge on the Market Share of Deposits

Hypothesis 2 above argued that the level of the ATM surcharge would positively affect the market share of deposits if foreign users were persuaded to shift their deposits to a bank with the higher surcharge level in order to avoid paying that surcharge. Our empirical specification is

$$\begin{aligned}\text{Market Share}(t+1)_{i,j} = {} & \psi_{0,j} + \psi_{1,j}\text{Surcharge}_{i,t,j} \\ & + \psi_{2,j}\text{Number of ATMs}_{i,t,j} \\ & + \psi_{3,j}\text{Geographic Dispersion}_{i,t,j} \\ & + \psi_{4,j}\text{Capital Ratio}_{i,t,j} + \psi_{5,j}\text{Assets}_{i,t,j} \\ & + \psi_{6,j}\text{Employees}_{i,t,j} + \psi_{7,j}\text{CD rate} \\ & + \eta_{i,j} + \varepsilon_{i,t,j},\end{aligned} \tag{2}$$

where i denotes bank, t denotes time, j denotes portfolio (larger or smaller bank), and $u_{i,j}$ represents the bank-specific residual. The coefficient on surcharge in this equation is important for the hypothesis described in this sub-

14. The coefficient of ATM surcharge is significantly negative at the 10% level in the log-log model for the smaller banks.

section, whereas the coefficient on number of ATMs is important for testing our third hypothesis in subsection *C*.

Our panel, Tobit, and log-log results for this relationship are reported in table 5, and our 3SLS results are reported in the market share equation in table 6.

We find in all four econometric specifications that, for larger banks, there is a significant positive relationship between the ATM surcharge and the market share in the following year, after controlling for other bank variables. For smaller banks there is a significantly negative relationship in three out of the four specifications. The relationship for smaller banks is statistically insignificant with the log-log specification. One possible reason for this is that the smaller bank sample is weakened by the relatively larger loss of observations of those banks with zero ATM surcharges (since the log of zero is undefined). Alternatively, smaller banks' market shares are affected by the absolute level of the ATM surcharge rather than the percentage change in that level.

Our findings for the larger banks are consistent with the argument that those larger banks that set their ATM surcharge levels high will increase their market share by inducing foreign users of their ATMs to switch their deposit accounts into those banks in order to avoid paying higher surcharges.

The negative coefficient on the relationship between the level of the ATM surcharge and market share in the following year for smaller banks indicates that if smaller banks establish high ATM surcharges, they will not be able to persuade depositors to switch to that bank. Indeed, the lower market share of smaller banks is consistent with smaller bank customers switching to larger banks and increasing the larger bank's relative market shares.

C. The Impact of ATM Network Size on the Market Share of Deposits

Hypothesis 3 above argued that the larger the number of ATMs in a bank's network, given any surcharge level, the greater the incentive for a customer to switch to that bank in order to access the convenience of that ATM network without paying the ATM surcharge. Our results for the panel, Tobit, and log-log estimates are reported in table 5 and for the 3SLS estimates in the market share (lead) equation of table 6. For larger banks we find that the number of ATMs in a bank's network has no significant impact on its market share. For smaller banks, however, we find that the more extensive the ATM network provided, the greater the bank's market share, although from the log-log panel specification we find that a (small) percentage change in network size does not induce a positive percentage change in bank market share.

The results for the smaller banks are of particular interest, especially in light of the results reported above that smaller banks are not able to affect their market share through the level of their ATM surcharge. Our results indicate that smaller banks, however, are able to positively affect their market share by establishing a larger ATM network—thus attracting customers who will find the convenience of larger ATM networks attractive.

There may be a variety of reasons explaining why for larger banks the number of ATMs is not a significant determinant of market share. It may be that customers already assume that larger banks have large ATM networks, without actually considering the specific number of ATMs in each network. It is not clear whether customers actually know the number of ATMs of, for example, Citibank, but they will believe that it is a “large” and thus convenient network. For a small local bank, on the other hand, it seems plausible that customers will be able to judge the number of ATMs provided in a local market and make judgments as to whether to switch to or from that bank based on those perceptions.

These results have important strategic policy implications for smaller banks. They show that smaller banks, which are not able to attract switchers by raising ATM surcharges, can raise their market share through more extensive ATM provision.

VIII. Summary and Conclusion

This paper has examined whether allowing banks to set their ATM surcharge in an unconstrained fashion benefits large banks relative to small banks. The issue of whether customers may switch their accounts from smaller banks to larger banks in order to avoid paying high ATM surcharges at the larger banks has been central to much of the policy discussion on ATM surcharges as well as the theoretical discussion on this topic. This paper is the first to empirically address this issue by using disaggregated bank-level data on ATM surcharge pricing. We are able to conduct this study because of our access to a newly available and very rich data source on ATMs, made available by Dove Consulting.

In order to motivate the importance of this issue, we show first that on the days of the announcement and implementation of ATM surcharge liberalization, publicly traded large banks experienced a significantly positive abnormal stock return reaction, whereas the market valuation of small banks had either an insignificant or a significantly negative abnormal return reaction. This is an indication that the market expected such policy changes to benefit larger banks and hinder smaller banks.

We then examine if such expectations were justified by examining how ATM surcharges and ATM network size affected the market share of deposits of larger and smaller banks in the period after ATM surcharge liberalization. We build a new panel database made up of bank-level ATM data from Dove, market share data from the Federal Reserve, and balance sheet data from Call Reports. We show first that a high ATM surcharge level will result in a lower percentage of (surcharge-paying) foreigners using ATMs. This is an indication that ATM surcharges can affect customer behavior. Second, if the level of surcharges is high for both larger and smaller banks, larger banks will have a significantly larger market share of deposits in the following year and smaller banks will have a significantly smaller market share in deposits in the following year. We interpret this finding to be consistent with a customer switching effect, implying that customers will shift their deposits from smaller to larger banks in order to avoid paying ATM surcharges. We also found that increases in the ATM surcharge had effects on larger banks' market share directionally similar to those found with the level tests. For smaller banks, however, the level of ATM surcharge, rather than its percentage change, appears to affect customer behavior. Finally, we show that while smaller banks cannot positively affect their market share through ATM surcharges, they can potentially affect it by establishing a more extensive ATM network.

Appendix A

Data Issues: The Panel Data Base

An important aspect of this paper lies in the uniqueness of the ATM data set employed in our tests. This data set was purchased from Dove Consulting, Boston, and includes bank-level data on a range of variables that have not previously been used in the empirical ATM literature. In particular, the data include a measure of the percentage of ATM users for different banks who are foreigners, that is, those who pay ATM surcharges. We spent considerable effort in matching the Dove survey data with other bank-level data used in the paper, including Call Reports (Report of Condition and Income) taken from the Federal Reserve's Web site as well as Federal Reserve market share data.

The data base provided by Dove Consulting is taken from two separate surveys of ATM providers: one taken in 1998 and the second in 2001. (The Dove reports themselves were published in 1999 and 2002, respectively.) In each case data were collected from each bank in the sample for the preceding three years, generating a six-year sample that spans 1996–2001. The two surveys are not identical across the two time periods; thus some data are available for some subset of the time period only. For example, while each of the two Dove surveys asked respondents for information on a variety of variables for each of the preceding three years, this was not the case for the foreign percentage variable. The first survey conducted during 1998 did ask for these data for each of the preceding three years; however, the second survey asked the respondents for these data only for the final year of that survey (i.e., 2001). In other words, in some of our empirical tests, for example, those that require the use of the foreign percentage variable, we use a data set made up of a given set of banks for each of 1996, 1997, and 1998 and different banks in 2001.

A further issue with our data concerns how the banks were asked to report their ATM surcharges over the preceding three years. In the case of both the 1998 and 2001 surveys, banks were asked to provide data on their ATM surcharges at the time of the survey. They were also asked to provide the date of the last change of the surcharge and how much that change was (in dollars and cents). This information is enough to create a partial historical record of surcharges charged by each bank. For example, if the date of the previous surcharge change occurred prior to the three-year period covered by the survey, then we are able to use the value of the surcharge in the final year of the survey for all the previous three years. Similarly, if the most recent surcharge change occurred during the preceding three years, we are able to infer surcharges after that date. However, we would not be able to infer surcharges outside the three-year window of each data set. In cases in which we are not able to infer the surcharge amount from the data, we do not use the data.

Another variable employed is the measure of geographic dispersion of a bank's ATM network. Dove divides the United States into seven regions and identifies whether each bank (in each year) has an ATM in one of those regions plus whether ATMs are held internationally (making eight regions). The seven U.S. regions identified were New England, Mid-Atlantic, Southeast, South, Midwest, Mountain and Pacific. The geographic dispersion variable takes a value between one and eight, where the value of the variable reflects the sum of the regions in which a bank locates its ATMs. For example, if geographic dispersion is equal to one, it indicates an ATM presence in only one region; if it is higher than one, it indicates presence in more than one region. In table A1 we provide a summary of the panel data used in the paper.

TABLE A1 Panel Data: Descriptive Statistics

Variable	Observations	Mean	Median	Standard Deviation
	A. Larger Banks (Asset Size > $1B)			
Foreign percentage (%)[a]	107	34.49	32.00	12.66
Market share of deposits (%)[c]	184	9.77	8.01	9.35
ATM surcharge ($)[a]	176	1.31	1.50	.47
Number of ATMs[a]	185	994	366	2,068
Geographic dispersion (1–8 regions)[a]	187	2.13	1.00	1.61
Capital ratio (%)[b]	184	8.16	7.81	2.30
Assets ($M)[b]	184	38,100.00	9,870.00	91,700.00
Number of employees[b]	187	9,989	3,983	21,503
CD rate[d]	187	5.37	5.46	.92
	B. Smaller Banks (Asset size ≤ $1B)			
Foreign percentage (%)[a]	83	42.30	45.00	18.99
Market share of deposits (%)[c]	144	.59	.21	2.16
ATM surcharge ($)[a]	128	1.16	1.00	.47
Number of ATMs[a]	144	68	11	329
Geographic dispersion (1–8 regions)[a]	147	1.19	1.00	.86
Capital ratio (%)[b]	147	11.03	9.48	7.36
Assets ($M)[b]	147	336.00	198.00	290.00
Number of employees[b]	131	161	102	364
CD rate[d]	147	5.45	5.47	.74

[a] Source: Dove Consulting Inc. ATM surveys.
[b] Source: Call Reports bank balance sheets.
[c] Source: Federal Reserve market share data.
[d] Source: Federal Reserve interest rate data.

Appendix B

Theoretical Underpinnings: The Impact of ATM Surcharges and ATM Network Size

This appendix provides a theoretical framework that contributes to the development of the hypotheses tested in this paper. We utilize the theoretical framework of Massoud and Bernhardt (2002) and Bernhardt and Massoud (2004) to analyze the impact of ATM surcharge and ATM network size on bank market share (and thus on bank profitability).

In Bernhardt and Massoud (2004), a spatial game is considered between two banks, A and B. Each bank is associated with a distinctive spatial line of length Q, and each bank chooses the density of its ATM network on a distinctive line where ATM services can be obtained.

There is a measure n of bank customers. Customers are distinguished by how much they value one bank intrinsically. The relative valuation for bank A is uniformly distributed over the range $[-m, m]$. In addition to providing bank deposits and other products, banks provide ATM services for members and nonmembers (so-called foreign users). First, customers establish a bank account at a local bank. Customers are then hit with a bank-specific location shock that is uniformly distributed over the range $[0, Q]$. Each customer receives incremental utility M from consuming bank services. The transportation cost of acquiring a service is Td, where d is the distance traveled to the closest ATM and T is an incremental transportation cost. Each bank chooses an ATM service fee to members and nonmembers, $P^j(\delta)$, where $\delta = 1$ for members, $\delta = 0$ for nonmembers, and j is bank A or bank B.[15] Here bank product charges (F^j) are broadly defined to include returns from investing in assets (e.g., making loans) backed by relatively low-cost deposits. Stavins (2000) among others argues that the fee banks charge their own customers for using their own ATM machines is invariably zero, so that ATM fees here are isomorphic to a bank's ATM surcharges on foreign users.

A. Timing of the Game

In stage 1, banks maximize profits by choosing the density of their ATM locations and the prices charged for different services (e.g., ATM surcharge to foreign users). In stage 2, each customer chooses a bank at which to establish an account. In stage 3, each customer receives a bank-specific location shock[16] and chooses where to obtain his or her ATM service (this is a simple one-shot game).

The expected profit function of bank A is[17]

$$\pi_A = N_A F^A + N_B y^A(0)[p^A(0) - C_{\text{ATM}}] - \alpha_A C_\alpha, \tag{B1}$$

where N_j is the number of bank j's customers, C_{ATM} is the marginal cost of providing ATM services to nonmembers, C_α is the cost of installing each ATM machine, $y^A(0)$ is the proportion of foreigners as customers (i.e., bank B customers in this game

15. Here members are the depositors who hold deposit accounts at the bank.

16. A location shock introduces mobility into the game, as a representation of real-life conditions faced by bank customers.

17. For simplicity, we consider a reduced form of the profit function in which the in-branch service fee and the ATM service fees for members are set equal to their marginal cost.

using bank A's ATMs), α_A is ATM density chosen by bank A, and $p^A(0)$ is the ATM surcharge fee bank A charges bank B customers. The first term in equation (B1) is the bank's profit from members' use of bank products such as deposits and loans, the second term is the profit from nonmembers (i.e., foreigners) who use bank A's ATM services, and the last term is the cost of installing the ATM network.

When a bank chooses its optimal ATM surcharge, it takes into consideration how that surcharge would directly affect its profitability, which depends on foreign customers' demand elasticity, as well as the indirect effects on its profitability as a result of switching. That is, the effect of ATM pricing on a bank's profitability can be decomposed into two effects: a direct effect and an indirect effect. Using the dynamic programming technique, we can solve for the equilibrium outcome of the model. To motivate our hypothesis, in the next sections in this appendix, we focus on the strategic action of banks to maximize their profits.

B. Bank Surcharge: The Direct and Indirect Effects

The effects of a marginal change in the ATM surcharges on a bank's profitability are shown by the following first-order condition:

$$\frac{\partial \pi_A}{\partial p^A(0)} = \frac{\partial N_A}{\partial p^A(0)} F^A + \frac{\partial N_B}{\partial p^A(0)} y^A(0)[p^A(0) - C_{\text{ATM}}] + N_B \left\{ \frac{\partial y^A(0)}{\partial p^A(0)} [p^A(0) - C_{\text{ATM}}] + y^A(0) \right\}, \tag{B2}$$

where $\partial N_A / \partial p^A(0) > 0$, $\partial N_B / \partial p^A(0) < 0$, and $\partial y^A(0)/\partial p^A(0) < 0$.

The first two terms in equation (B2) show the indirect effect of ATM surcharges on bank A's profitability, where $[\partial N_A / \partial p^A(0)]F^A$ is the increase in bank account membership and bank service purchases induced by a marginally higher surcharge times the bank product charges or profit extracted from other bank product provision, and

$$\frac{\partial N_B}{\partial p^A(0)} y^A(0)[p^A(0) - C_{\text{ATM}}]$$

is the loss in surcharge revenues from those foreign customers (i.e., bank B customers in this model) who switch bank membership to bank A as a result of the increase in ATM surcharges.[18] The third and last term in equation (B2),

$$N_B \left\{ \frac{\partial y^A(0)}{\partial p^A(0)} [p^A(0) - C_{\text{ATM}}] + y^A(0) \right\},$$

shows the direct effect of ATM surcharges on bank A's profitability, which is the impact of increasing ATM surcharges on surcharge profits from (foreign) customers who continue to establish bank accounts at competing bank B.

The third and last term in equation (B2), or the direct effect, can be rewritten in terms of nonmembers' ATM demand elasticity, ξ:

$$y^A(0) N_B \left[-\xi \frac{p^A(0) - C_{\text{ATM}}}{p^A(0)} + 1 \right].$$

18. The bank does not impose a surcharge to its own members (depositors).

The sign of this term depends on

$$\text{sign}\left[-\xi\frac{p^A(0) - C_{\text{ATM}}}{p^A(0)} + 1\right].$$

If this term is nonnegative,

$$-\xi\frac{p^A(0) - C_{\text{ATM}}}{p^A(0)} + 1 \geq 0,$$

then it implies that $\xi \leq p^A(0)/[p^A(0) - C_{\text{ATM}}]$ and $p^A(0)/[p^A(0) - C_{\text{ATM}}] > 1$. Given that in general an oligopoly operates in a price region such that the elasticity exceeds one,[19] then the inequality $1 < \xi \leq p^A(0)/[p^A(0) - C_{\text{ATM}}]$ should hold, which implies that ATM profits are positively related to ATM surcharges.

Note also that $\partial N_A/\partial p^A(0) > 0$ shows that an increase in the ATM surcharge increases a bank's customer base because of switching and $\partial y^A(0)/\partial p^A(0) < 0$ shows that an increase in the ATM surcharge reduces a bank's market share of nonmember (foreign) customers.

C. ATM Intensity: The Direct and Indirect Effects

The effects of a marginal change in the ATM intensity (also referred to as ATM network size) on a bank's profitability is shown by the following first-order condition:

$$\frac{\partial \pi_A}{\partial \alpha_A} = \frac{\partial N_A}{\partial \alpha_A}F^A + \frac{\partial N_B}{\partial \alpha_A}y^A(0)[p^A(0) - C_{\text{ATM}}] + N_B\frac{\partial y^A(0)}{\partial \alpha_A}[p^A(0) - C_{\text{ATM}}] - C_\alpha, \tag{B3}$$

where $\partial N_A/\partial \alpha_A > 0$, $\partial N_B/\partial \alpha_A < 0$, and $\partial y^A(0)/\partial \alpha_A > 0$. The first two terms in equation (B3) show the indirect effect of ATM intensity on bank A's profitability, where $(\partial N_A/\partial \alpha_A)F^A > 0$ is the increase in bank account membership and bank service purchases induced by a marginally higher ATM intensity times the bank product charges or profit extracted from other bank product provision, and

$$\frac{\partial N_B}{\partial \alpha_A}y^A(0)[p^A(0) - C_{\text{ATM}}] < 0$$

is the loss in surcharge revenues from those foreign customers who switch bank membership to bank A because of the increase in ATM intensity. The last term in equation (B3),

$$N_B\frac{\partial y^A(0)}{\partial \alpha_A}[p^A(0) - C_{\text{ATM}}] > 0,$$

shows the direct effect of ATM intensity on bank A's profitability, which is the impact of higher ATM intensity on increasing surcharge profits from (foreign) customers who continue to establish bank accounts at competing bank B.

19. Tirole (1994, 66) shows that when the elasticity of demand is less than one, the monopolist's revenue—and his profits—is decreasing in quantity. Our model is one of oligopoly, i.e., bank A and bank B, but the results will hold for any non–perfectly competitive market for banking services. Given barriers to entry into the U.S. banking industry, it is not unreasonable to view the U.S. banking industry as imperfectly competitive.

Note also that $\partial N_A/\partial \alpha_A > 0$ shows that an increase in the ATM intensity increases a bank's customer base because of switching and $\partial y^A(0)/\partial \alpha_A > 0$ shows that an increase in the ATM intensity increases a bank's market share of nonmember (foreign) customers.

Appendix C

The Structure of the 3SLS Model

Our four-equation system used in our 3SLS model in table 6 is as follows:

$$\begin{aligned}\text{Foreign Percentage}_{i,j} = {} & \theta_{0,j} + \theta_{1,j}\text{Surcharge}_{i,t,j} \\ & + \theta_{2,j}\text{Number of ATMs}_{i,t,j} \\ & + \theta_{3,j}\text{Geographic Dispersion}_{i,t,j} \\ & + \theta_{4,j}\text{Capital Ratio}_{i,t,j} + \theta_{5,j}\text{Assets}_{i,t,j} \\ & + \theta_{6,j}\text{Employees}_{i,t,j} + \theta_{7,j}\text{CD rate} + u_{i,j} + e_{i,t,j},\end{aligned} \tag{C1}$$

$$\begin{aligned}\text{Market Share}(t+1)_{i,j} = {} & \psi_{0,j} + \psi_{1,j}\text{Surcharge}_{i,t,j} \\ & + \psi_{2,j}\text{Number of ATMs}_{i,t,j} \\ & + \psi_{3,j}\text{Geographic Dispersion}_{i,t,j} \\ & + \psi_{4,j}\text{Capital Ratio}_{i,t,j} + \psi_{5,j}\text{Assets}_{i,t,j} \\ & + \psi_{6,j}\text{Employees}_{i,t,j} + \psi_{7,j}\text{CD rate} \\ & + \eta_{i,j} + \varepsilon_{i,t,j},\end{aligned} \tag{C2}$$

$$\begin{aligned}\text{Surcharge}_{i,t,j} = {} & \lambda_{0,j} + \lambda_{1,j}\text{Number of ATMs}_{i,t,j} + \lambda_{2,j}\text{Market Share}_{i,t,j} \\ & + \lambda_{3,j}\text{Geographic Dispersion}_{i,t,j} + \omega_{i,j} + \gamma_{i,t,j},\end{aligned} \tag{C3}$$

$$\begin{aligned}\text{Number of ATMs}_{i,t,j} = {} & \mu_{0,j} + \mu_{1,j}\text{Surcharge}_{i,t,j}\ \mu_{2,j}\text{Market Share}_{i,t,j} \\ & + \mu_{3,j}\text{Employee}_{i,t,j} + \mu_{4,j}\text{Asset}_{i,t,j} + \mu_{5,j}\text{Fee}_{i,t,j} \\ & + \alpha_{i,j} + \nu_{i,t,j}.\end{aligned} \tag{C4}$$

In the 3SLS system, equations (C1) and (C2) are the same equations used in the single-equation estimates of these models reported in tables 4 and 5. Equations (C3) and (C4) are included in order to account for any possible endogeneity of ATM surcharge and ATM network size in equations (C1) and (C2). To ensure that the 3SLS model is identified, we introduced a new variable that influences the number of ATMs. This new variable is the fees earned from other bank accounts and is taken from Call Report data. The argument for its inclusion in equation (C4) is that the higher the account fees a bank earns, the greater the incentive to provide ATMs in order to encourage switching. As can be seen from table 6, however, the coefficient on this variable is insignificant. The key conclusion from the estimation of this 3SLS system is that the 3SLS results from equations (C1) and (C2) in the system are generally consistent with those found for the single-equation results reported in tables 4 and 5.

References

Bae, Kee-Hong, Jun-Koo Kang, and Chan-Woo Lim. 2002. The value of durable bank relationships: Evidence from Korean banking shocks. *Journal of Financial Economics* 64, no. 2: 181–214

Berger, Alan, and Gregory Udell. 1995. Relationship lending and lines of credit in small firm finance. *Journal of Business* 68, no 3:351–81

Berger, Allen, Anthony Saunders, Joseph Scalise, and Gregory Udell. 1998. The effects of bank mergers and acquisitions on small business lending. *Journal of Financial Economics* 50, no. 2:187–229.

Berlin, Mitchell, and Loretta Mester. 1999. Deposits and relationship lending. *Review of Financial Studies* 12, no 3:579–607.

Bernhardt, Dan, and Nadia Massoud. 2004. Endogenous ATM location and pricing. Working paper, University of Alberta, School of Business, Department of Finance.

Economides, Nicholas, Glenn Hubbard, and Darius Palia. 1996. The political economy of branching restrictions and deposit insurance: A model of monopolistic competition among small and large banks. *Journal of Law and Economics* 39, no. 2:667–704.

Flannery, Mark, and Christopher James. 1984. Market evidence on the maturity of bank assets and liabilities. *Journal of Money, Credit and Banking* 16, no. 4:435–45.

Hannan, Timothy H. 2001. Retail fees of depository institutions, 1994–1999. *Federal Reserve Bulletin* (January): 1–11.

———. 2002. Retail fees of depository institutions, 1997–2001. *Federal Reserve Bulletin* (September): 405–13.

Hannan, Timothy H., Elizabeth K. Kiser, Robin A. Prager, and James J. McAndrews. 2003. To surcharge or not to surcharge: An empirical investigation of ATM pricing. *Review of Economics and Statistics* 58, no. 4:990–1002.

Massoud, Nadia, and Dan Bernhardt. 2002. Rip-off ATM surcharges. *Rand Journal of Economics* 33, no. 1:96–115.

Matutes, Carmen, and A. Jorge Padilla. 1994. Shared ATM networks and banking competition. *European Economic Review* 38, no. 5:1130–38.

McAndrews, James J. 2002. A model of ATM pricing: Foreign fees and surcharges. Mimeo, Federal Reserve Bank of New York.

———. 2003. Automated teller machine network pricing: A review of the literature. *Journal of Network Economics* 2, no. 2:146–58

Mester, Loretta, Leonard I. Nakamura, and Micheline Renault. 2003. Checking accounts and bank monitoring. Working Paper no. 1-3, Federal Reserve Bank of Philadelphia.

Ongena, Steven, and David C. Smith. 2001. The duration of bank relationships. *Journal of Financial Economics* 61, no. 3:449–75

Palia, Darius. 1994. Recent evidence of bank mergers. *Financial Markets, Institutions and Instruments* 26, no. 5:36–59.

PIRG (Public Interest Research Group). 1999. Big banks. Bigger fees: The 1999 PIRG bank fee survey. http://www.pirg.org/reports/consumer/bankfees/bank99.pdf.

———. 2001. A brief history of ATMs. http://www.stopatmfees.com/newpage3.htm.

———. 2002. ATMs always taking money. http://www.nypirg.org/consumer/atm/2002/intro.htm.

Prager, Robin. 1999. ATM network mergers and the creation of market power. *Antitrust Bulletin* 44, no. 2:349–63.

———. 2001. The effects of ATM surcharges on small banking organizations. *Review of Industrial Organization* 18, no. 2:161–73.

Stavins, Joanna. 2000. ATM fees: Does bank size matter? *New England Economic Review* (January/February): 13–24.

Tirole, Jean. 1994. *The theory of industrial organization*. 7th ed. Cambridge, MA: MIT Press.

V. Banks and Risk Management

THE JOURNAL OF FINANCE • VOL. XLV, NO. 2 • JUNE 1990

Ownership Structure, Deregulation, and Bank Risk Taking

ANTHONY SAUNDERS, ELIZABETH STROCK, and NICKOLAOS G. TRAVLOS*

ABSTRACT

This paper investigates the relationship between bank ownership structure and risk taking. It is hypothesized that stockholder controlled banks have incentives to take higher risk than managerially controlled banks and that these differences in risk become more pronounced in periods of deregulation. In support of this hypothesis, we show that stockholder controlled banks exhibit significantly higher risk taking behavior than managerially controlled banks during the 1979–1982 period of relative deregulation.

IN THIS PAPER WE analyze the relationship between risk taking by banking firms and their ownership structures. In particular, we concentrate on the potential conflict of interest over risk taking between managerially controlled banks (defined as banks whose managers hold a relatively small proportion of the banks' stock and act in their own utility-maximizing interests) and stockholder controlled banks (defined as banks whose managers hold a relatively large proportion of the bank's stock and act in the stockholder's value-maximizing interest).

This conflict of interest is important partly because others have already documented an inverse relationship between *non*-bank firm risk taking and the degree of managerial control[1] and partly because of the presence of a third party or set of agents ("bank regulators") who by their actions define the general set of rules and regulations regarding bank risk taking. Specifically, by changing the regulatory environment, for example toward activity and interest rate deregulation and/or closure rule forbearance, any conflicting risk taking incentives of stockholders and managers can be accentuated and the degree of risk taking by stockholder controlled banks increased. Thus, we expect to find ownership structure having a more powerful effect on the risk characteristics of banks in periods of deregulation relative to periods of regulation.

* Saunders is Professor of Finance, Graduate Business School, New York University and Research Advisor, Federal Reserve Bank of Philadelphia. Strock and Travlos are Assistant Professors of Finance, Wallace E. Carroll School of Management, Boston College. The authors would like to thank Linda Allen, Yakov Amihud, George Aragon, Mitch Berlin, James Brickley, Chris James, Lucille Mayne, Loretta Mester, John G. Preston, Steve Raymar, Ithzak Swary, Greg Udell, and Jerry Viscione and would like to acknowledge the helpful comments of two anonymous referees. This study was completed while Strock was the recipient of a Boston College Research Fellowship. Saunders would like to acknowledge financial support provided by a Salomon Brothers Fellowship, a Bank and Financial Analysts Fellowship, and a Senior Yamaichi Research Fellowship. Travlos acknowledges financial support from the Boston College Research Council. The research assistance of Avi Peled and Jean Lee is gratefully appreciated.

[1] See Amihud and Lev (1981) and Agrawal and Mandelker (1987), for example.

In Section I the conflict of interest between managers and stockholders over the degree of bank risk taking is briefly described. In Section II a model is specified that links measures of bank risk to a measure of the ownership structure of the bank and a set of other control variables. In Section III tests are conducted on the model to determine the empirical relationship between these capital market measures of bank risk and ownership structure, as well as on the sensitivity of this relationship to changing regulatory regimes. Finally, Section IV is a summary and conclusion.

I. The Conflicting Risk Preferences of Bank Stockholders and Managers

A. Stockholders

The incentive for limited liability stockholders to increase the risk of the firm by increasing leverage has been widely noted. (See Galai and Masulis (1976), for example.) In particular, to the extent that debtholders (depositors) can only monitor and control stockholders' actions imperfectly and ex post, stockholders can increase the value of their equity *call* options by increasing the risk of the underlying assets of the bank (firm). In addition, Merton (1977), Marcus and Shaked (1984), and Ronn and Verma (1986), among others, have argued that the current system of levying fixed-price (risk-insensitive) deposit insurance premia results in a *put*-option-like subsidy to bank stockholders—the value of which also increases with bank risk.

However, the ability of a bank's stockholders to maximize the value of their call and put options by increasing risk depends in part on the preferences of the bank's managers (see below) and on the costs, constraints, and restrictions imposed on bank risk taking by regulators (see Buser, Chen, and Kane (1981)).[2] In periods of bank activity deregulation and forbearance over closure rules, bank stockholders, ceteris paribus, have greater incentives (and ability) to increase risk taking than when regulations are tight and strictly enforced.

B. Managers

The risk taking incentives of bank managers will depend on the degree to which their best interests or preferences are tied to those of value-maximizing stockholders. If managers' wealth is largely in nondiversifiable human capital (bank-specific) form, they may act in a *risk-averse* rather than a value-maximizing manner (see Kane (1985) and Benston et al. (1986)), in which case their optimal degree of risk taking would be less than that desired by stockholders. However, by giving managers stock or stock options in the banking firm, their interest will become more closely aligned with those of stockholders, as long as their increased *non*-human wealth investment in the firm is not so large as to make them increasingly sensitive to the (potentially undiversifiable) nonsystematic risk of the bank. To the extent that the latter effect is present, this would

[2] Buser, Chen, and Kane (1981) view such restrictions as akin to implicit deposit insurance premiums that get more stringent as bank risk taking increases.

tend to mitigate the value of managerial stock-ownership plans as incentive conflict control devices.[3]

II. Testable Hypotheses on the Relationship between Risk and Ownership Structure

In this and the following section we test the following *two* hypotheses:

H1: Stockholder controlled banks are more risky than managerially controlled banks.

H2: Risk taking differences between stockholder and managerially controlled banks increase during periods of relative deregulation.

To test H1 and H2 we specify the following model:

$$\sigma_i = f(O_i, FL_i, OL_i, S_i), \tag{1}$$

where σ_i is the risk of the ith bank, O_i is the ownership structure of the ith bank, FL_i is the financial leverage of the ith bank, OL_i is the operating leverage of the ith bank, and S_i is the size of the ith bank.

This model differs from Demsetz and Lehn (1985), who view σ_i (risk) as *exogenous* and ownership structure as *endogenous* in a test methodology (for non-bank firms) similar to equation (1). In their view of the world, the noisier (the more risky) the environment the greater the incentive for stockholder-owners to change the control structure of the firm toward greater stockholder control. Our view, especially for banks, is that financial portfolios are much more flexible in the short term than ownership structures. That is, transaction costs of stockholders changing ownership structures endogenously, e.g., through the market for corporate control, should outweigh the transaction costs of changing the structure of bank (financial) portfolios to alter risk—such as changing the composition of a bank's deposits, loans, and securities. Hence, in the *short term* at least, risk taking can be viewed as an endogenous decision of the bank impacted by its ownership structure, other control variables, and the regulatory environment.[4]

The variables in equation (1) were measured as follows:

Bank Risk (σ_i)

As in Amihud and Lev (1981), we concentrate on capital market measures of firm (bank) risk. It was assumed that a two-index market model was the appropriate return-generating process for bank stock returns. (See, for example, Flannery and James (1984), Sweeney and Warga (1986), and Kane and Unal (1988).) The *two*-index market model suggests four different capital market measures of risk: σ_s (total return risk), σ_ε (nonsystematic risk), β_m (market risk),

[3] The importance of managers' exposure to nonsystematic risk of the firm as a result of stock ownership plans will depend on the extent to which managers' *non*-human wealth is invested in the firm's stock and therefore on the limits to their ability to diversify their *non*-human wealth.

[4] We measure risk taking and ownership structures over the relatively short one-year period, whereas Demsetz and Lehn measure capital market risk of a five-year period.

and β_I (interest rate risk). A high β_I coefficient (in absolute terms) is *consistent* with a bank mismatching the duration of its assets and liabilities, i.e., being exposed to greater interest rate risk—see Flannery and James (1984). The measure of unexpected changes in interest rates is the same as that used in Sweeney and Warga (1986) and Kane and Unal (1988), i.e., the daily change in yields. Two alternative interest rate series are used: DRI's 3-month Treasury bill (bond equivalent) yield and 10-year note yield series. Thus, we estimate a series of β_I's for both short (S) and long (L) rates for each bank. The two-index market model is estimated using daily CRSP file stock data for each bank, the CRSP equally weighted market index, and DRI interest rate data each year over the period of analysis. Thus, for each bank (a sample of 38), we generate an 8-year time series for σ_s, σ_ε^S, β_m^S, β_I^S, σ_ε^L, β_m^L, and β_I^L, where the superscripts S and L indicate estimates derived from (alternatively) a two-index model with short rates (S) or long rates (L) as the second factor.[5]

Ownership Structure (O_i)

We measure the degree of stockholder control by the proportion of stock held by banking firm managers (*PROP*),[6] measured each year for each bank from bank proxy statement data. As discussed in Section I, by increasing managers' stock ownership in the firm their risk taking incentives become more closely aligned to those of stockholders as long as their ownership stake is not so large a proportion of their *non*-human wealth as to make them overly concerned with (averse to) the nonsystematic risk of the bank.[7] Thus, it is hypothesized (H1) that *PROP* should be positively related to σ_i.

Financial Leverage (FL_i)

Following Lev (1974), highly leveraged firms tend to exhibit greater stock return variance. To control for this leverage effect, we used the bank's book value of capital to assets ratio (*KA*) since this is the leverage measure most commonly monitored by regulators and outside investors. A high *KA* (low leverage ratio) should be negatively related to bank risk.

[5] We also examined various accounting measures of interest rate and credit risk, but, in general, these performed poorly.

Brickley and James (1986) argue that, because the value of deposit insurance guarantees rises during periods of deregulation and regulator forbearance, capital market risk measures tend to underestimate the true level of asset risk. If this is so, then a finding of a relationship between capital market risk measures and ownership structure—during a period of relative deregulation—probably underestimates the strength of the true relationship. That is, the tests are biased against us finding such a relationship.

[6] Specifically, *PROP* is estimated as the number of shares beneficially held by executives and directors plus the number of shares related to their unexercised options divided by the total number of shares outstanding plus the number of shares related to unexercised options.

[7] Clearly, whether the incentives toward risk taking resulting from managerial stock-ownership plans outweigh the disincentives is an empirical question that should be reflected in the explanatory power of the *PROP* variable.

Operating Leverage (OL_i)

Mandelker and Rhee (1984), among others, have argued that operating leverage acts in an analogous fashion to financial leverage in increasing firm risk. The most commonly used proxy of operating leverage, and the one used in this study, is the ratio of fixed assets (assumed to mimic fixed costs) to total assets. This ratio (*FAA*) is expected to be positively related to our risk measures.

Bank Size (S_i)

The larger a bank the greater should be its potential to diversify its asset risk. Alternatively, the larger the banking firm the more information that is likely to be collected by financial analysts and the lower the information risk from holding its stock. (See Banz (1981).) Finally, investors may believe that regulators are unwilling to let larger banks fail, in which the value of implicit failure guarantees rise with bank size. Each of these three effects suggests that size (measured here by total assets (*TA*)[8]) and risk should be negatively related.[9]

The Regulatory Environment

As discussed in this paper's introduction, regulators define the general constraints and regulations on bank risk taking behavior. In periods of deregulation and regulator forbearance, the ability of stockholders to maximize the value of their call and put options by greater risk taking is enhanced. Consequently, it was hypothesized (H2) that *PROP* should have a more powerful effect on bank risk taking in a deregulated subperiod.

The period 1979–1982 is widely acknowledged to have been a period of significant interest rate and bank activity deregulation as well as increased regulator forbearance. Specifically, the Fed changed its monetary policy operating targets away from interest rates toward *non*-borrowed reserve target in (October) 1979 and maintained this policy until (October) 1982. This led to a considerable increase in interest rate volatility over this period. (See Saunders and Urich (1988).) Moreover, in 1980 and 1982 through, respectively, the DIDMCA and Garn-St. Germain Acts, comprehensive bank deregulation packages were passed by Congress. Further, the 1980–1982 period was one of increased regulator

[8] We reran all the tests using the market value of bank equity as an alternative proxy for size without any substantive effect on the results. (The Pearson correlation coefficient between total assets and the market value of bank equity was .93.)

[9] Sensitivity tests were also conducted by adjusting the total assets figures in the financial and operating leverage measures by an average annual loan sales measured from the figure reported in Schedule L of the *Call Report* over 1983–1985. This adjustment has no substantive effect on the results.

We also experimented with different proxies for the market for corporate control: in particular, dummy variables for the willingness of a bank's headquarter state to allow multi-bank holding company acquisitions and/or interstate branching. However, there was insignificant variability in the data (because of the concentration of banks in a relatively small number of states) for these variables to be informative.

forbearance regarding enforcement of bank closure rules. (See Brickley and James (1986).)

Rather than prespecifiying the 1979–1982 period as one of relative deregulation and the pre-1979 and post-1982 periods as ones of relative regulation, we conducted sensitivity tests using the switching regressions methodology of Goldfeld and Quandt (1972, 1973). For our 1978–1985 sample period, this methodology suggested two switch dates and three regimes, 1978, 1979–1982, and 1983–1985.

III. Empirical Results

This relationship among bank risk, ownership structure, and other control variables is first estimated using the following cross-section time-series regression for 38 bankholding companies over the 8-year period 1978–1985.[10]

$$RISK_{it} = a_0 + a_1\, PROP_{it} + a_2 KA_{it} + a_3 FAA_{it} + a_4 TA_{it} + u_{it}, \qquad (2)$$

where

$RISK_{it}$ = one of seven different capital market risk measures (σ_s, σ_ε^S, β_m^S, β_I^S, σ_ε^L, β_m^L, and β_I^L) for bank i in year t, $i = 1 \cdot\cdot\cdot\cdot 38$ and $t = 1 \cdot\cdot\cdot\cdot 8$;

$PROP_{it}$ = the percentage of stock owned by officers and directors in bank i in year t;

KA_{it} = the book value of capital-assets ratio of bank i in year t;

FAA_{it} = the ratio of *fixed* assets to total assets (operating leverage) of bank i in year t;

TA_{it} = the total assets of bank i in year t.

The regression results for the whole sample period are shown on the first line of each panel in Table I.

Consider first the coefficient on the *PROP* variable. It was hypothesized (H1) that this coefficient should be positively related to bank risk. The results for Table I offer some support for this hypothesis. Of the seven different capital market measures, three coefficients are significant and positive at the 1% level: those for σ_s (total return risk), σ_ε^S (unsystematic risk from the two-index model with short-term rates as the second factor), and σ_ε^L (unsystematic risk from the two-index model with long-term interest rates as the second factor). Interestingly, the relationship between *systematic* market risk (either β_m^S or β_m^L) and *PROP* is insignificant. This is *consistent* with discretionary risk taking being reflected in the *nonsystematic* risk of the bank rather than its *systematic* risk—as might be expected. Further, the results also imply that discretionary risk taking is not reflected in the interest rate exposure coefficients (β_I^S and β_I^L).

While these results may be of some comfort to well-diversified investors who

[10] The accounting data reflect the aggregated ratios for bank(s) comprising the holding company; i.e., it is constructed from the *Call Report* data for individual banks. This has the advantage of excluding holding company assets that are not directly related to the underlying banks. For a few sample banks, some annual observations were lost because proxy data were incomplete and/or banks within the group merged.

Table I

Estimated Coefficients and t-Values (in Parentheses) from Regressing Different Risk Measures of Banking Firms on Ownership Structure and Other Control Variables, Years 1978–1985

$$RISK_{it} = a_0 + a_1\, PROP_{it} + a_2\, KA_{it} + a_3\, FAA_{it} + a_4\, TA_{it} + u_{it}$$

For each risk measure (Panels A through G), the explanatory variables are defined as follows: $PROP_{it}$ is the proportion of outstanding common stock shares held by officers and directors (including shares relating to unexercised stock options) for bank i in year t, KA_{it} is the ratio of book value of capital to assets for bank i in year t, FAA_{it} is the ratio of fixed assets to total assets for bank i in year t, and TA_{it} is the total assets for bank i in year t.

Panel A: Coefficient estimates when $RISK_{it}$ is measured as σ_s, the standard deviation of daily stock returns for bank i in year t

Time Period	Intercept	*PROP*	*KA*	*FAA*	*TA*	R^2	*F*-Statistic	*P*-Value	Number of Observations
1978–1985	.0159	.0152	−.0271	.0225	2.15E-05	.074	4.99	.001	256
	(7.65)	(4.26)	(−.65)	(.35)	(1.71)				
1978	.0124	.0129	−.0062	.0118	3.57E-05	.232	2.04	.116	32
	(3.57)	(2.49)	(−.10)	(.10)	(1.19)				
1979–1982	.0164	.0196	−.0478	.0695	2.31E-05	.199	8.32	.0001	139
	(7.31)	(5.51)	(−1.03)	(.99)	(1.54)				
1983–1985	.0148	.0019	.0532	−.0922	4.65E-06	.007	.15	.963	85
	(2.33)	(.16)	(.42)	(−.64)	(.18)				

Panel B: Coefficient estimates when $RISK_{it}$ is measured as σ_ε^S, the standard error of residuals for bank i in year t from the two-index market model using short-term interest rates

Time Period	Intercept	*PROP*	*KA*	*FAA*	*TA*	R^2	*F*-Statistic	*P*-Value	Number of Observations
1978–1985	.0139	.0152	−.0068	.0351	8.07E-06	.080	5.42	.0003	256
	(6.82)	(4.33)	(−.17)	(.57)	(.66)				
1978	.0104	.0134	.0095	.0310	2.08E-05	.270	2.49	.067	32
	(3.15)	(2.71)	(.16)	(.27)	(.73)				
1979–1982	.0141	.0195	−.0210	.0694	1.18E-05	.234	10.24	.0001	139
	(6.83)	(5.98)	(−.49)	(1.07)	(.86)				
1983–1985	.0134	.0020	.0630	−.0715	−1.24E-05	.008	.15	.961	85
	(2.10)	(.17)	(.49)	(−.49)	(−.48)				

Table I—*Continued*

Panel C: Coefficient estimates when $RISK_{it}$ is measured as β^S_m, the beta coefficient of the CRSP equally weighted market index for bank i in year t from the two-index market model using short-term interest rates

Time Period	Intercept	*PROP*	*KA*	*FAA*	*TA*	R^2	*F*-Statistic	*P*-Value	Number of Observations
1978–1985	.7679	.0029	−2.5840	.2984	.0060	.298	26.66	.0001	256
	(6.56)	(.01)	(−1.10)	(.08)	(8.54)				
1978	.9012	−.3163	−6.2710	−3.3876	.0043	.522	7.37	.0004	32
	(4.21)	(−.99)	(−1.64)	(−.45)	(2.34)				
1979–1982	1.0246	.1992	−8.8017	5.3412	.0030	.188	7.75	.0001	139
	(6.78)	(.83)	(−2.83)	(1.13)	(2.95)				
1983–1985	.9106	−.0359	−.9293	−10.2483	.0075	.521	21.77	.0001	85
	(3.73)	(−.08)	(−.19)	(−1.86)	(7.64)				

Panel D: Coefficient estimates when $RISK_{it}$ is measured as β^S_I, the beta coefficient of daily changes in short-term interest rates for bank i in year t from the two-index market model

Time Period	Intercept	*PROP*	*KA*	*FAA*	*TA*	R^2	*F*-Statistic	*P*-Value	Number of Observations
1978–1985	−.0060	−.0051	.1178	−.0621	−4.72E-05	.040	2.60	.037	256
	(−1.67)	(−.81)	(1.60)	(−.55)	(−2.13)				
1978	−.0164	−.0192	.1951	.0630	.0001	.149	1.18	.341	32
	(−1.62)	(−1.27)	(1.08)	(.18)	(1.46)				
1979–1982	−.0059	−.0012	.0449	.1772	−3.15E-05	.118	4.48	.002	139
	(−1.97)	(−.24)	(.73)	(1.89)	(−1.58)				
1983–1985	−.0144	.0001	.4416	−.5341	−.0001	.112	2.53	.046	85
	(−1.23)	(.00)	(1.89)	(−2.03)	(−2.30)				

Panel E: Coefficient estimates when $RISK_{it}$ is measured as σ^L_ϵ, nonsystematic risk measured similarly to σ^S_ϵ with the exception of using long-term interest rates

Time Period	Intercept	*PROP*	*KA*	*FAA*	*TA*	R^2	*F*-Statistic	*P*-Value	Number of Observations
1978–1985	.0142	.0155	−.0110	.0288	6.79E-06	.081	5.51	.0003	256
	(6.94)	(4.41)	(−.27)	(.46)	(.55)				

Table I—*Continued*

Panel E: Coefficient estimates when $RISK_{it}$ is measured as σ_ϵ, nonsystematic risk measured similarly to σ_ϵ with the exception of using long-term interest rates

Time Period	Intercept	*PROP*	*KA*	*FAA*	*TA*	R^2	*F*-Statistic	*P*-Value	Number of Observations
1978	.0105	.0135	.0090	.0307	2.00E-05	.272	2.53	.064	32
	(3.16)	(2.73)	(.15)	(.26)	(.70)				
1979–1982	.0146	.0200	−.0291	.0585	9.33E-06	.236	10.35	.0001	139
	(7.04)	(6.08)	(−.68)	(.90)	(.68)				
1983–1985	.0134	.0020	.0638	−.0707	−1.29E-05	.008	.16	.958	85
	(2.08)	(.16)	(.50)	(−.49)	(−.50)				

Panel F: Coefficient estimtes when $RISK_{it}$ is measured as β_m^L, market risk measured similarly to β_m^S with the exception of using long-term interest rates

Time Period	Intercept	*PROP*	*KA*	*FAA*	*TA*	R^2	*F*-Statistic	*P*-Value	Number of Observations
1978–1985	.7893	.0644	−3.0291	−.2121	.0054	.259	21.95	.0001	256
	(6.74)	(.32)	(−1.29)	(−.06)	(7.61)				
1978	.9252	−.0926	−6.0870	−6.5798	.0034	.457	5.69	.002	32
	(4.29)	(−.29)	(−1.58)	(−.88)	(1.85)				
1979–1982	1.0796	.2174	−9.7628	4.2278	.0021	.166	6.65	.0001	139
	(7.10)	(.90)	(−3.12)	(.89)	(2.10)				
1983–1985	.8992	.0637	−1.1523	−9.1401	.0070	.490	19.21	.0001	85
	(3.75)	(.14)	(−.24)	(−1.69)	(7.27)				

Panel G: Coefficient estimates when $RISK_{it}$ is measured as β_I^L, interest rate risk measured similarly to β_I^S with the exception of using long-term interest rates

Time Period	Intercept	*PROP*	*KA*	*FAA*	*TA*	R^2	*F*-Statistic	*P*-Value	Number of Observations
1978–1985	−.0271	−.0065	.4031	.3900	−.0001	.151	11.18	.0001	256
	(−3.74)	(−.51)	(2.72)	(1.73)	(−2.95)				
1978	−.0092	.0753	.3154	−1.3275	−.0002	.160	1.28	.302	32
	(−.29)	(1.62)	(.57)	(−1.22)	(−.86)				
1979–1982	−.0366	−.0303	.4933	.8074	−.0001	.247	10.98	.0001	139
	(−3.80)	(−1.99)	(2.49)	(2.68)	(−1.49)				
1983–1985	−.0100	.0229	.1822	−.0373	−.0002	.173	4.20	.004	85
	(−.77)	(.94)	(.70)	(−.13)	(−3.26)				

can diversify nonsystematic risk away, regulators are (or should be) concerned with the *total* insolvency risk of a bank reflected by both its σ_s and its σ_ε. This has interesting implications for bank examination and surveillance. Specifically, given limited examination resources, our results suggest that regulators might allocate greater time and effort toward monitoring stockholder, rather than managerially, controlled banks; i.e., ownership structure might be used as a flag determining examination frequency.

With respect to the three control variables, KA_{it}, FAA_{it}, and TA_{it}, the results are rather mixed. Both the *KA* and *FAA* variables are generally insignificant, while the *TA* variable is insignificantly related to total and residual risk (σ_s, σ_ε^S, σ_ε^L) but positively related to β_m^S and β_m^L and *negatively* related to β_I^S and β_I^L.[11] These results imply that bank size has different and offsetting effects on bank market and interest rate risk exposures. That is, larger banks appear to be more sensitive to general market movements but are better able to diversify their interest rate risk exposure.

Regulatory Regimes

As discussed above, we hypothesize (H2) that the manager-stockholder conflict over the degree of risk taking should be exacerbated under periods of deregulation. The switching regression procedure identified three different regimes over the 1978–1985 period which seemed to accord with our a priori expectations regarding periods of relative deregulation (1979–1982) and periods of relative regulation (1978 and 1983–1985). These results are shown on lines, 2, 3, and 4 of each panel in Table I.

As can be seen, the overall relationship between risk and ownership structure is still strongest for the total return risk (σ_s) and nonsystematic risk measures (σ_ε^S and σ_ε^L). Both the point estimate and the *t*-value for the *PROP* variable are more positive in the 1979–1982 period than in either the 1978 or the 1983–1985 period.[12]

To examine the extent to which risk changes in 1979–1982 period were attributable to the *PROP* variable—i.e., were consistent with stockholders being better able to exploit their put and call risk taking incentives—rather than being due to other factors, we ran the following tests on the *PROP* variable for 1978 vs. 1979–1982, 1979–1982 vs. 1983–1985, and 1978 vs. 1983–1985. Specifically, to test (for example) the change in *PROP* between 1978 and 1979–1982, we ran

$$RISK_{it} = a_0 + a_1 PROP_{it} + a_2 KA_{it} + a_3 FAA_{it} + a_4 INTP12_{it} + a_5 TA_{it} + u_{it}, \qquad (3)$$

[11] The Pearson correlation coefficient between bank size (*TA*) and *PROP* was −.29.

[12] In general, the model fitted poorly for 1983–1985. This led us to test for other variables that might be excluded; these included dummy variables for money center banks, time trend dummies, and time interactive dummies. None appeared to offer a ready explanation for the poor fit of the model in this period. However, one possible explanation is that, following increased regulator forbearance surrounding the failure of Continental Illinois in 1984, capital market risk measures considerably underestimated true asset risk given presumptions that big banks were too large to fail. That is, deposit insurance guarantees rose to such an extent that it weakened the link between stock return risk and the risk of the bank's underlying assets.

where

$$INTP12_{it} = PROP_{it} * DUMP12$$

and

$$DUMP12 = 0 \text{ if } 1978,$$

$$DUMP12 = 1 \text{ if } 1979\text{–}1982.$$

Hence, $a_1 + a_4$ is the coefficient on *PROP* for 1979–1982, or a_4 is the *incremental* coefficient relating ownership structure to risk in the 1979–1982 period.

The results, not reported here, show that, in five out of seven cases (σ_s, σ_ε^S, β_m^S, β_I^S, and σ_ε^L), the null hypothesis of *no* change in the risk-ownership structure relationship ($a_4 = 0$) could be rejected. The coefficient a_4 was significantly positive at the 5% level, indicating that the effect of *PROP* on risk taking significantly increased in the 1979–1982 subperiod. However, the null hypothesis could not be rejected for the 1979–1982 vs. 1983–1985 subperiods and in only two cases for 1978 vs. 1983–1985. The results are therefore generally consistent with a change in the risk-ownership structure relationship in the 1979–1982 period only.

Finally, these results are not meant to imply that PROP was the only, or even the major, factor explaining the increase in bank risk in the 1979–1982 period but rather that they are consistent with ownership structure being a contributing factor to the increase in risk taking in this subperiod.

IV. Summary and Conclusion

This paper investigates the relationship between bank ownership structure and risk taking. It is argued that, unlike non-banking firms, the presence of regulators may either accentuate or mitigate bank risk taking incentives. In particular, it is hypothesized that stockholder controlled banks would have call and put option-type value-maximizing incentives to take risks compared to more risk-averse managerially controlled banks (H1) and that risk taking differences between stockholder and managerially controlled banks should become more transparent in periods of deregulation (H2). Using capital market measures of risk and the proportion of stock owned by managers (as a proxy for ownership structure), it is found that there is some support for both H1 and H2.

These results also have an important implication as far as bank failure avoidance is concerned. Specifically, to better monitor bank risk taking in a period of limited examination resources and deregulation, the FDIC and other regulators should increase the relative frequency of examination for stockholder controlled banks. Moreover, changes in ownership structure could be employed as useful early warning flags for bank examiners.

REFERENCES

Agrawal, A. and G. N. Mandelker, 1987, Managerial incentives and corporate investment and financing decisions, *Journal of Finance* 42, 823–837.

Amihud, Y. and B. Lev, 1981, Risk reduction as a managerial motive for conglomerate mergers, *Bell Journal of Economics* 12, 605–617.

Banz, R. W., 1981, The relationship between return and market value of common stock, *Journal of Financial Economics* 9, 3–18.

Benston, G., R. Eisenbeis, P. Horvitz, E. Kane, and G. Kaufman, 1986, *Perspectives on Safe and Sound Banking: Past, Present, and Future* (MIT Press, Cambridge, MA).

Brickley, J. A. and C. M. James, 1986, Access to deposit insurance, insolvency rules and the stock returns of financial institutions, *Journal of Financial Economics* 16, 345–371.

Buser, S. A., A. H. Chen, and E. J. Kane, 1981, Federal deposit insurance, regulatory policy and optimal bank capital, *Journal of Finance* 36, 51–60.

Demsetz, H. and K. Lehn, 1985, The structure of corporate ownership: Causes and consequences, *Journal of Political Economy* 93, 1155–1177.

Flannery, M. J. and C. M. James, 1984, The effect of interest rate changes on the common stock returns of financial institutions, *Journal of Finance* 39, 1141–1153.

Galai, D. and R. Masulis, 1976, The option pricing model and the risk factor of stock, *Journal of Financial Economics* 3, 53–81.

Goldfeld, S. M. and R. E. Quandt, 1972, *Nonlinear Methods in Econometrics* (North Holland Publishing Company, Amsterdam).

——— and R. E. Quandt, 1973, The estimation of structural shifts by switching regressions, *Annals of Economic and Social Measurement* 2, 475–485.

Kane, E. J., 1985, The gathering crisis in federal deposit insurance (MIT Press, Cambridge, MA).

——— and H. Unal, 1988, Change in market assessments of deposit-institution riskiness, *Journal of Financial Services Research* 1, 207–229.

Lev, B., 1974, On the association between operating leverage and risk, *Journal of Financial and Quantitative Analysis* 9, 627–642.

Mandelker, G. N. and S. G. Rhee, 1984, The impact of degrees of operating and financial leverage on systematic risk of common stock, *Journal of Financial and Quantitative Analysis* 19, 45–57.

Marcus, A. J. and I. Shaked, 1984, The valuation of FDIC deposit insurance using option price estimates, *Journal of Money, Credit, and Banking* 16, 446–460.

Merton, R. C., 1977, Analytic derivation of the cost of deposit insurance and loan guarantees, *Journal of Banking and Finance* 1, 3–11.

Ronn, E. and A. K. Verma, 1986, Pricing risk adjusted deposit insurance: An option based model, *Journal of Finance* 41, 871–896.

Saunders, A. and T. Urich, 1988, The effects of shifts in monetary policy and reserve accounting regimes on bank reserve management behavior in the federal funds market, *Journal of Banking and Finance* 12, 523–536.

Sweeney, R. J. and A. O. Warga, 1986, The pricing of interest rate risk: Evidence from the stock market, *Journal of Finance* 41, 393–410.

ELSEVIER Journal of Banking & Finance 22 (1998) 1249–1282

Journal of BANKING & FINANCE

Credit spreads in the market for highly leveraged transaction loans

Lazarus A. Angbazo [a,1], Jianping Mei [b], Anthony Saunders [c,*]

[a] *Department of Finance, Purdue University, USA*
[b] *Department of Finance, New York University, USA*
[c] *Leonard Stern School of Business, Salomon Brothers Center, New York University, 44 West 4th Street, New York, NY 10012, USA*

Abstract

This paper is an empirical exploration of the determinants of the required credit spreads on highly leveraged transaction (HLT) loans. The analysis uses a multi-factor spread model to estimate the movement of loan spreads relative to spreads required in the (competing) corporate bond market as well as the significance of loan-specific characteristics in determining loan spreads. The empirical estimates are based on the Loan Pricing Corporation's database which consists of over 4000 loan transactions between 1987 and 1994. We find a positive HLT loan spread sensitivity to changes in spreads in the corporate bond market, but this sensitivity is significantly less than unity; indicating that the HLT loan market and high yield public debt market are not fully integrated. Furthermore, there is evidence that lenders augment, rather than substitute, loan yield spreads with additional fees for syndication, commitment and cancellation risks. In general syndicated loans have lower yield spreads than other HLT loan types. © 1998 Published by Elsevier Science B.V. All rights reserved.

JEL classification: G21

Keywords: Loans; Debt; Yield spread; Leverage; High-yield bands

* Corresponding author. Tel.: +1 212 998 0711; fax: +1 212 995 4220; e-mail: asaunder@stern.nyu.edu

[1] Chase Manhattan Bank. This paper was completed while this author was on the finance faculty at Purdue University.

0378-4266/98/$ – see front matter
PII: S0378-4266(98)00065-X

1. Introduction

The objective of this paper is to examine the determinants of credit risk spreads on loans. Although there are a number of theoretical models of credit spread determinants the empirical literature is sparse. [2] This is largely due to the fact that information on loan spreads (or bank private debt) has not been publicly available until recently. In this paper we employ the Loan Pricing Corporation's (LPC) database on highly leveraged loans (HLT) to examine the factors that impact the required spreads on these loans.

Economic theory suggests that if financial markets are efficient, comparable forms of financing will be priced to reflect the law of one price, adjusted for risk, transaction costs and embedded options. Rational borrowers will not pay a higher rate than is available on a substitutable form of financing. Similarly, rational investors will be unwilling to accept different risk-adjusted returns from similar investments.

Interestingly, one aspect of the pricing of HLT loans is that there appears to be a persistent spread between the yields in the HLT loan market and the high yield bond market (see Fridson, 1995). Price differences or spreads will exist to the extent that they reflect market imperfections. One imperfection is the difference in borrower/investor access to the loan market compared to the bond market caused by regulatory and institutional barriers. The difficulties of bringing to the market high yield bond offerings of a size of less than $100 million implies that the bond market has a barrier to entry which may be reflected in price disparities in the loan and bond markets. Furthermore, regulatory restrictions on commercial banks, insurance companies, and thrift investments in below-investment grade corporate bonds as well as maturity constraints that preclude bond purchases by prime rate funds, exemplify barriers to access on the investor side. These constraints could affect the liquidity of the below-investment grade bond market, increasing price differences across loan and bond markets.

This paper explores the determinants of the ex ante credit spreads on HLT loans by estimating the systematic movements in loan spreads, relative to the spreads required in the "competing"corporate bond market. The objective is to determine the degree of divergence between HLT loan and bond yield spreads. We use the yields on (i) investment grade corporate bonds rated Baa by Moody's and (ii) Merrill Lynch's All-High-Yield Bond index yield to test the degree of market divergence. The results show a loan yield spread sensitivity towards changes in spreads in the corporate Baa bond market and the high yield ("junk") bond market that while positive, is significantly less than unity,

[2] See Fisher (1959), Boardman and McEnally (1981), Roberts and Viscione (1984), and Saunders (1997, Ch. 10), for a review.

indicating that the HLT loan spreads do not move in direct tandem with spreads of either the corporate Baa bonds or junk bonds. Nevertheless, these data also show that there is greater degree of HLT loan pricing convergence with the corporate Baa bond market than with the junk bond market.

The paper also estimates the impact of loan specific characteristics on HLT loan spreads based on a multi-factor model. Specifically, the divergence in loan-bond yield spreads may be tied to various characteristics or factors including the loan amount, use of loan proceeds, maturity, collateralization, syndication and type of loan. In addition, borrower characteristics such as size and the ex ante credit rating of the borrower as well as the role of the originating bank may all influence the pricing of new-issue loans and the pricing discrepancy observed relative to the competing corporate bond market.

The paper is organized as follows: In Section 2, we examine the basic characteristics of the HLT market. In Section 3, we discuss the sample. In Section 4, a credit spread model is specified. Section 5 reports the empirical results and Section 6 concludes.

2. Institutional characteristics of HLT loans

The development of the market for HLT loans can be traced to the growth over the past decade in commercial lending transactions to finance mergers and acquisitions, leveraged buyouts, and related transactions. One measure of the growth in HLTs is that between January 1987 and September 1994, LPC reported that there were 4122 deals, with a combined dollar amount (in new-issue loans) estimated at $593.5 billion.

While HLTs are now a significant portion of outstanding commercial credits, the nature of these loans, the market participants (including borrowers, originating banks and participating investors), and the interest and fee structures are not well documented.

2.1. HLT criteria

The criteria for classification of a loan as an HLT were in dispute prior to October 1989, when highly-leverage-transaction guidelines were laid out by the Office of the Comptroller of Currency, the Federal Reserve Board, and the Federal Deposit Insurance Corporation (1989, 1990). These criteria defined HLT loans as:

- all loan financings used for buyouts, acquisitions, recapitalizations;
- all loan financings which: (i) double the borrower's liabilities and result in a leverage ratio (total liabilities/total assets) higher than 50%; or (ii) increase the leverage ratio higher than 75%;

- all loan financings that are designated as an HLT by the syndication agent;
- all loan financing to subsidiaries of HLT companies, even if the subsidiary does not meet the HLT definitions above.

The underlying regulatory guidelines exclude debtor-in-possession financing for businesses in Chapter 11 bankruptcy reorganization. Furthermore, some loans are excluded if they meet certain performance criteria, even if the borrower's leverage ratio continues to exceed 75%.

Due to a review prompted by the recession and a perceived credit crunch during 1991–1992, bank regulators (i.e., the Federal Reserve, the FDIC, and the Comptroller of Currency) phased out the requirement that banks disclose the total amount of loans to highly leveraged companies in their financial statements as of 30 June 1992. This decision reflected regulators' findings that large banks were not overexposed to HLTs and that they posed little threat to either the bank insurance fund or bank capital reserves. There was also a desire to prevent bank examinations from impeding the availability of credit to borrowers. However, the Securities and Exchange Commission (SEC) has required the continuation of HLT loan exposure disclosures. [3] Given that the LPC database is constructed from loan information filed with the SEC, the sample reflects the HLT designation required by the SEC which is identical to the reporting requirements of bank regulators.

2.2. HLT loan features

High-leverage-transaction loans have traditionally being originated by banks and syndicated to other banks in the secondary market for loans. However, in recent years, these loans have become attractive to a larger class of investors. The high ex ante interest rates associated with these loans are only one reason for their increased attractiveness, especially, compared to high yield ("junk") bonds. [4] In Table 1 the key features of HLT loans relative to junk bonds are summarized. In general, HLT loans have a senior priority position over subordinated bondholders with respect to repayment of interest and principal. Because of their senior position in the capital structure, borrowers usually repay HLT loans ahead of all other debt obligations. Furthermore, these loans are normally secured by pledges of specific collateral either in the form of assets or the equity of the borrower. HLT bank loans also tend to have shorter maturities, averaging 4.4 years (53 months) compared to an average maturity of 10 years for high yield debt.

[3] See *The New York Times,* 22 January 1992, Section D, Column 1, p. 17.

[4] For a discussion on the background on senior bank loans in general and highly-leveraged transaction loans in particular, see Carlson and Fabozzi (1992) and Ross et al. (1990).

Table 1
HLT bank loans versus high-yield bonds

HLT bank loans	Junk bonds
Senior[a]	Subordinated
Secured	Unsecured
Short maturity[b] (Ave. 4.4 years)	Long maturity (Ave. 10 years)
Quarterly interest in cash	Semiannual interest, sometimes not in cash
First claim on cash flows and specific claims on assets	Junior claim on cash flows and no specific claims on assets
Scheduled principal amortization schedules	None
Specified asset sale requirement	None
Strong financial covenants	–
Floating-rate-based	Fixed-rate-based

This table summarizes the major differences in the characteristics of highly-leveraged-transaction bank loans and high yield (junk) fixed income instrument. Other differences are that HLT bank loans require more burdensome documentation (at least until June 1992), involve higher transaction costs, create more potential conflicts of interest, and impose more severe restrictions on eligible investors or investable loans (i.e. revolving or term loans).

[a] This includes contractual and structural seniority. The contractual seniority results from the actual terms agreed to by the different classes of lenders under various indentures. Structural seniority occurs by placing the debt in the operating subsidiary and securing this debt with the subsidiary's specific assets. If the loan is made to the holding company, seniority is conferred by guaranteeing the loan by a subsidiary's equity pledged as security. Contractual seniority typically allows senior lenders to block interest and principal payments to subordinated lenders for a specified "blockage period".

[b] This results in less repayment risk compared to subordinated fixed income. This is further lessened by scheduled amortization.

There are also important differences with respect to pricing conventions and financial covenants between HLT loans and high yield debt. Loans are usually floating-rate based and typically allow borrowers to select a pricing formula linked to the Prime rate, LIBOR, or a Certificate of Deposit rate (CDs), plus a credit spread. Borrowers are also often free to change the base index on any rollover date (usually semiannually). Finally, HLT debt (as bank issued private debt) generally has more stringent protective covenants than public debt such as high yield bonds (see Carey et al., 1994).

2.3. HLT loan market participants

The growth in leveraged loan transactions may be explained in part by an increasing shift by banks from the origination of loans, as long term investment vehicles, to their origination for distribution to others through loan sales or through participations. Through these loan sales and participations, originating banks can increase the volume of their lending while simultaneously diversifying firm, interest rate and geographic risks, improving liquidity, and enhancing their ability to comply with capital requirements and lending concentration restrictions. The most important of the originating banks are US money center and large regional banks, many of whom sell participations to a group of buyers beyond their correspondent banks, including smaller banks, non-bank financial institutions such as General Electric Capital Corporation, foreign banks and investment banks. [5]

More specifically, the major purchasers of loans and loan participations can be classified into two groups: (passive) portfolio investors and active strategic buyers. Portfolio investors include US banks and foreign branches, agencies of foreign banks, insurance firms, pension and mutual funds. These firms purchase HLT loans in anticipation of earning attractive rates of return on senior debt. Foreign banks and smaller banks invest for product and geographic diversification to overcome the effects of restrictions on interstate banking.

Strategic buyers of loans and participations invest in HLT loans with the objective of subsequently owning or obtaining a large controlling position in a borrower or its subsidiary. These investors include vulture funds which specialize in purchasing distressed loans for bargaining in a restructuring deal.

Table 2 provides a listing of the top selling institutions in leveraged loan transactions over the past decade. The LPC database lists the originating lender (and major participants) for 4122 deals. An institution is classified as a "lead" lender if it retains primary administrative, monitoring, and contract enforcement responsibilities. These banks also typically retain the largest stake in the loan. Some banks perform administrative oversight duties, although these are relatively minor, and their share ownership in the loan is smaller, on average, than lead banks. These banks are generally referred to as loan managers. A third group is referred to as participants, to reflect the fact that they do not perform special functions other than being signatories to the original loan agreement.

The top 20 lead banks in Table 2 are ordered by the number of transactions. Citibank was the top originator with 323 HLT deals, with an average deal size of $203.36 million, over half of which was sold in participation agreements with other firms (53.0%). The bank's share represents about 11.23% of the total amount of HLT loans issued, a figure that is second only to the 11.43% reported by (the since-merged) Manufacturers Hanover Trust (MHT). In 190 of the 4122 deal sample, MHT was the lead bank with the highest average deal size of $356.99 million. The table also shows that Bank of America retains the largest portion of HLT deals, with an average of 70.9% share per deal. Overall, the top 20 institutions are lead lenders in 2573 (or 62.42%) deals, which in dollar terms represents 66.13% of the HLT outstanding. Second-tier institu-

[5] See Ch. 25 in Saunders (1997) and Gorton and Pennacchi (1995) for a description of recent trends in the loan sales market.

Table 2
Top 20 lenders in HLT bank loans

Institution	No.of deals lead	Average deal size (US $)	Average deal share (%)	Percentage of total $$
Citi Bank	323	206361808	46.0	11.23
Chemical Banking	249	111750856	47.1	4.69
Bankers Trust	231	151923233	52.7	5.91
Chase Manhattan Bank	195	101898445	38.0	3.35
Manufacturers Hanover Trust	190	356998146	29.5	11.43
Bank of Boston	135	73315436	60.8	1.67
Nova Scotia Bank	133	193081432	23.8	4.33
Nations Bank	128	93608317	50.9	2.02
Wells Fargo	118	158458830	40.8	3.15
Bank of America	107	117080903	70.9	2.11
CIBC	103	107635783	57.6	1.87
Continental Illinois	99	62091672	39.1	1.04
Secucity Pacific NB	94	138562191	39.2	2.19
Tor-Dominion Banks	88	270934305	39.0	4.02
Banque Paribas	83	51426371	53.5	0.72
First Chicago	70	161423925	61.2	1.90
LTCB Ltd.	63	223309524	22.8	2.37
Bank of Montreal	60	111272800	32.7	1.12
Bank of New York	53	81617241	57.1	0.37
Barclays Bank Plc	51	196094960	23.5	1.69

This table shows the top 20 Lead banks by the number deals, average deal size, average deal share, and share of total HLT loan originated. The lead bank is the primary lender as identified in the Gold Sheet announcement. The sample is based on 4122 deals announced between January 1987 and December 1994. For the total sample, the number of deals led by Lead banks range from 1 to 323, while the average share of the Lead banks ranges from 0% to 100%. The next 20 leading Lead banks and number of deals led are : Morgan Guaranty (48), General Electric Capital Corp. (45), Credit Lyonnais (44), Citicorp (40), NatWest Banks USA (38), TCB (34), CiticorpUSA (31), Heller Financial (30), First Interstate (26), Sumitomo Bank Ltd. (25), ABN AMRO (24), Mellon Bank (24), INT-Neder (23), BTCom (20), Creditan (20), Harris Trust Bank (20), Marine Midland (20), NBD Bank (20), and Swiss Bank Corp. (19). These banks account for 12.70% of all HLT origination's.

tions (i.e., the next 20 leading "lead" firms) accounted for a further 12.70% of the amounts originated.

3. Sample description

3.1. General description of sample

The sample is based on 4122 HLT deals reported by LPC between January 1987 and September 1994, with a total volume of new issue HLT loans of

$593.5 billion. The LPC database is compiled from the LPCs weekly Gold Sheets which cover the loan syndication market borrowers, loan amounts, facility type, maturity, credit rating, credit spreads, fees, as well as lenders' shares and role (lead manager, loan manager, etc.). Gold Sheets are in turn constructed from loan information filed with the Security Exchange Commission (SEC) covering large corporate, middle market, and international loans with sizes varying from $100,000 to over $13 billion.

We show the annual volume of new issue HLT bank loans stratified by HLT designation in Fig. 1. The first three years of the sample covering 1987–1989 is characterized by HLT growth from $50 billion in 1987 to over $150 billion by 1989. However, after 1990 the annual volumes of new HLT loans started to fall, partly due to a decline in mergers and LBO activity and partly due to increased regulation of HLT loan by bank supervising authorities after October 1989. Although bank regulators' requirement regarding HLT loan disclosures ceased on 30 June 1992, the SEC has required the continuation of such disclosures.

HLT loan characteristics, for new issues during 1987–1994 period, are shown in Table 3 by loan type, HLT designation (i.e., purpose), by industry type of the borrower (based on the one digit SIC code), and by lender role. For the full sample, the average loan size is $145.8 million, with loans ranging in size from as low as $234,000 to $13.6 billion. The maturity of these loans averages 53.38 months, but ranges between 1 and 204 months. Approximately 94.5% of the loans are syndicated with the lead lenders retaining a share averaging 51.42%. This indicates that originating lenders generally retain only about half of these loans in their portfolio. Contrary to popular perception, only 21.3% of these loans are secured by a pledge of assets. The corporate rating of the borrower is almost always below investment grade, with 98.6% of the ratings at the time of the deal below Standard and Poor's BBB rating. Borrower size, as measured by sales in the year immediately preceding the deal, ranges from $440,000 to $21.35 billion, with average sales of $843.08 million.

3.2. Loan type, HLT designation, and industry groups

In general HLT loans may be allocated to term loan or revolving facilities. Term loans are installment loans which cannot be reborrowed once repaid. These funds are typically drawn down at one time, but occasionally do have a takedown or delayed take-down period. Another feature is that the loan principal is usually amortized, although the loan may be prepaid without additional fees. Attributes of term loans and their differences with revolving facilities are highlighted in Panel A of Table 3. Term loans constitute about 37.28% of all new issues and on average are larger in size ($154.5 million), and have longer maturities (65.7 months).

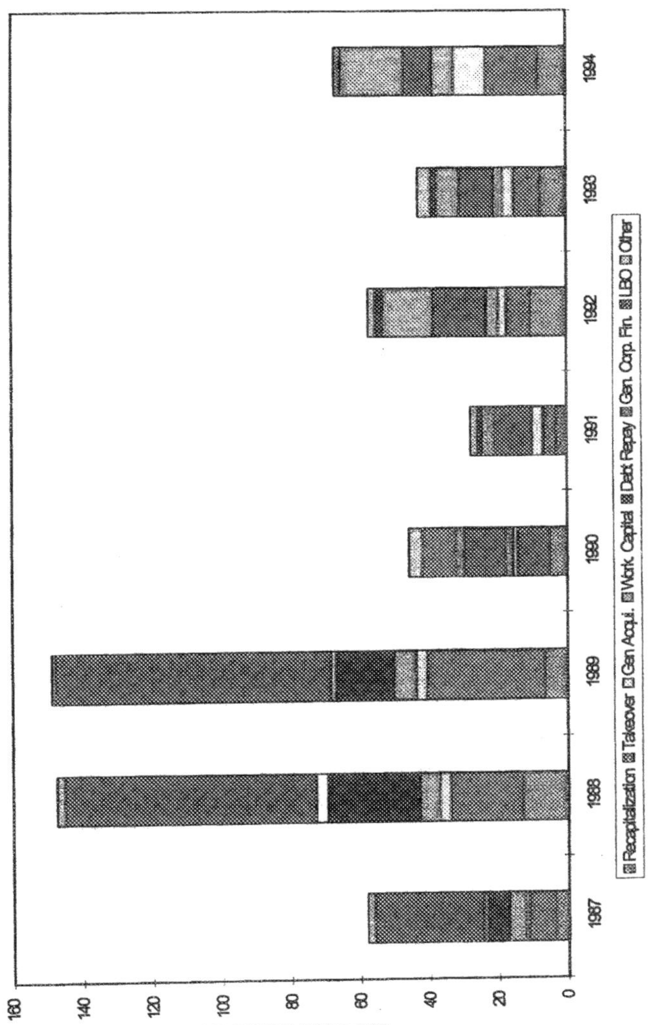

Fig. 1. Volume of new issue HLT loans.

Revolving facility loans may be drawn down (up to the commitment amount), repaid and reborrowed any number of times. An interest fee is charged on the outstanding loan amount as is a commitment fee (on any commitment unused) and a facility fee (on the total commitment amount available). These loans comprise 46.43% of the HLT total, are relatively smaller in size ($107.33 million), and have shorter maturities (51.6 months) than term loans. There are statistically no differences in the level of syndication, the proportion of loans secured, the share retained by the originating lenders, or the corporate ratings of the borrowers between revolving loans and term loans.

The final category of loans, classified as "other" in Table 3, comprises of very short-term facilities such as bridge loans, 365-day facility, and demand loans. This loan group, which also includes loans made to support letters of credit (or bankers acceptances), tends to be larger, with an average size of $292.5 million, shorter-term (27.94 months), less frequently syndicated, but more often secured, compared to both term loans and revolving facilities. Borrowers' security is large and their credit ratings are generally below investment grade.

The LPC database also provides the primary designation of each loan. Table 3 Panel B shows that the most common use of loan proceed is debt repayment (22.10% of the sample which includes all facilities for refinancing or consolidation of existing debt prior to maturity). Approximately 99.5% of these loans are below investment grade. On average, LBO loans (15.62% of the sample) are the largest sized (an average of $315.12 million), and are made to the biggest firms (mean sales of $1.4645 billion).

The shortest maturity loans are for working capital needs such as funding inventory purchases (12.44% of the sample). These loans also have the smallest deal size ($68.6 million on average). Loans for recapitalizations comprise 8.76% of the sample and are used to support changes in a corporate borrowers' capital structure. These loans are often made simultaneously with a debt or equity offering. Recapitalization loans have the lowest syndication rate but are most often secured. General corporate loans are a catch-all purpose loan category that can be used for various activities related to general operations, purchases or working capital. A unique characteristic of these loans is the lack of security, with only about 12.8% being secured. Originating lenders retain their greatest shares (60.2%) in these loan categories.

General acquisition loans (also called "hunting lines") comprise 6.3% of the sample, and may be differentiated from takeover loans in that these loans are designated for unspecified asset acquisitions, while takeover loans are used to support purchase of specific assets or a company. The average loan size and maturity of general acquisition loans is less than that of takeover loans. In addition lenders tend to syndicate a higher proportion of takeover loans. Finally, loan characteristics by industry group and lender role are shown in Table 3, panels C and D, respectively.

Table 3
Summary statistics of HLT bank loans

	Percentage of total[a]	Loan size ($millions)	Maturity (months)	Percentage syndicated	Percentage secured	Borrower size sales ($millions)	Percentage below investment grade	Primary lender share (%)
Panel A: By type of loan[b]								
Total	100	145.8	53.38	94.5	21.3	843.08	98.6	51.42
		(401.3)	(29.41)			(1771.8)		(34.05)
Revolver	46.43	107.33	51.6	94.7	22.15	761.10	98.82	50.6
		(235.3)	(25.93)			(1587.1)		(33.3)
Term	37.28	154.5	65.7	95.3	20.17	833.5	98.6	50.5
		(370.2)	(26.2)			(1864.8)		(33.7)
Other	12.08	292.5	27.94	92.6	24.0	1298.0	97.7	51.25
		(856.5)	(29.17)			(2217.9)		(35.6)
Panel B: By loan purpose[c]								
Recap.	8.76	154.9	58.2	90.5	41.6	1048.6	98.2	53.7
		(259.0)	(24.4)			(1614.5)		(35.2)
Take over	16.72	152.7	58.3	96.8	27.0	751.8	99.0	46.60
		(359.9)	(30.6)			(1453.8)		(30.9)
Gen. acqui.	6.30	90.6	53.9	94.3	19.2	353.4	98.3	56.1
		(133.9)	(29.2)			(991.7)		(33.0)
Working cap.	12.44	68.6	44.2	91.2	18.8	779.8	99.5	59.9
		(109.5)	(26.6)			(1806.4)		(33.4)
Debt repay.	22.10	118.9	55.9	96.3	17.9	705.8	99.5	45.0
		(231.7)	(25.7)			(1469.2)		(31.6)
Gen. corp.	14.58	85.2	44.8	93.7	12.8	614.3	97.5	60.2
		(291.6)	(26.0)			(1419.1)		(36.12)

Table 3 (Continued)

	Percentage of total[a]	Loan size ($millions)	Maturity (months)	Percentage syndicated	Percentage secured	Borrower size sales ($millions)	Percentage below investment grade	Primary lender share (%)
LBO	15.62	315.12	56.9	96.0	20.4	1464.5	98.0	43.6
		(821.3)	(33.9)			(2764.8)		34.3
Panel C: By industry classification[d]								
Agriculture	4.70	157.4	56.0	91.1	24.0	2045.4	100.0	55.8
		(354.2)	(31.9)			(3535.0)		(33.7)
Mining	0.53	149.6	60.9	88.4	34.6	1836.9	100.0	58.0
		(211.2)	(35.6)			(1818.6)		(28.5)
Construction	3.85	122.2	47.2	92.0	15.2	442.6	95.8	73.3
		(268.1)	(27.4)			(724.1)		(32.8)
Manufacturing	0.82	71.4	46.8	94.2	37.1	177.4	100.0	52.1
		(86.1)	(34.6)			(107.4)		(25.5)
Transportation	38.96	139.68	55.3	95.8	22.0	727.3	98.2	46.3
		(440.9)	(27.8)			(1371.6)		(32.4)
Wholesale	13.27	197.3	58.5	96.5	16.6	693.4	99.4	49.4
		(553.1)	(32.5)			(1774.1)		(32.2)
Retail	3.42	141.4	47.03	93.7	13.2	729.6	100	64.01
		(564.9)	(26.9)			(1720.6)		(33.6)
Finance/Insur.	11.64	173.5	50.8	94.2	18.8	1773.4	98.6	49.3
		(303.6)	(28.1)			(2819.5)		(35.5)
Services	9.26	128.9	48.0	92.7	22.6	462.3	98.0	53.5
		(405.3)	(31.0)			(1553.31)		(34.8)
Public administration	12.88	106.96	50.5	92.7	26.4	624.92	99.9	56.8
		(201.1)	(28.0)			(1025.8)		(36.5)
Panel D: By lender role								
Lead lender[e]	35.80	152.9	52.3	85.56	57.24	878.7	98.5	51.5
		(474.7)	(30.74)			(1,969.8)		(33.7)

Manager[f]	1.26	333.96	57.04	82.69	44.23	1,078.03	100	45.03
		(546.6)	(28.50)			(1,335.9)		(42.07)
Participant[g]	62.93	135.1	53.75	99.96	0.07	750.3	98.6	23.74
		(366.1)	(28.68)			(1,413.86)		(53.71)

This table presents summary statistics (average) and standard deviation on selected non-price characteristics of new issue HLT bank loans originated during the period January 1987–December 1994. Figures in parentheses are standard deviations.

[a] The sum of observations in each subgroup may not add up to 100% in each panel because certain deals are not classified into specific categories.

[b] See text for loan types.

[c] See text for HLT designation.

[d] See text for industry groupings.

[e] Includes lender roles such as arranger, CO-arranger, administrative agent, agent and CO-agent. These origination's lenders retain the largest commitment remain the primary monitors of the borrowers.

[f] These banks retain a smaller share in the commitment to lend and play a secondary role in servicing and monitoring. These are identified as lead manager, CO-lead manager, manager, CO-manager and senior manager.

[g] These banks do not perform any special roles except to be signatories to the original loan agreement.

3.3. Credit spreads and fee structure

A leveraged loan transaction typically involves two types of revenues to a banker; interest and fees. Interest revenues usually are based on one or more floating rate-index plus a credit spread. In Table 4, we show the distribution of the three most commonly-used indices by the year of loan origination. These

Table 4
HLT loan credit spreads versus corporate yield spreads

Year	*N*	HLT spread	Baa spread	Junk bond spread
Panel A: 6-month LIBOR index				
1987	214	238.48	320.50	509.90
1988	590	250.64	251.65	467.81
1989	578	237.37	93.29	447.04
1990	379	250.79	206.99	751.52
1991	331	258.59	402.83	832.05
1992	505	254.01	507.73	749.93
1993	501	245.55	435.76	643.36
1994	706	234.92	369.78	540.12
Total	3804	247.02	316.32	598.43
Panel B: Prime index				
1987	222	139.92	242.95	432.35
1988	610	149.55	143.08	359.24
1989	556	144.16	73.58	280.17
1990	364	140.61	33.09	577.62
1991	275	140.68	148.81	578.03
1992	405	133.15	273.99	516.19
1993	303	121.75	180.39	388.53
1994	294	103.10	170.63	340.98
Total	3029	136.49	130.44	412.93
Panel C: 6-month CD-index				
1987	85	253.74	359.51	548.91
1988	210	257.58	282.55	498.71
1989	170	253.74	109.26	463.01
1990	68	257.50	215.48	760.00
1991	49	253.06	407.99	837.21
1992	51	249.56	525.31	767.51
1993	29	239.92	397.29	658.08
1994	20	235.63	393.23	563.58
Total	682	253.82	329.31	617.88

This table shows the distribution (mean) of credit spreads for HLT bank loans by the different indices of the pricing options. The sample consists of all HLT deals reported by LPC's data base, for the period 1987–1994.

include the Prime rate, 6-month LIBOR, and 6-month Certificate of deposit (CD) rates. (Note that since the loans are frequently priced off of more than one of the indexes, as alternative choices for borrowers, the sum of the proportions of the loans based on the Prime, LIBOR, and CD rates exceeds 100%.)

In Panel A we show that about 92.28% of the loans have the 6-month LIBOR rate benchmark. The credit spread (above the libor) was widest in 1991 at 258.59 basis points and narrowest in 1994 (234.92 basis points); by comparison, the average yield spreads on corporate Baa and junk bonds are 316.32 and 298.43 basis points, respectively. In Panel B, we show that 73.5% of HLT loans in the sample have the lead bank's Prime rate as the benchmark rate. The average spread of the loans over the prime is 136.49 basis points, compared to an average 130.44 and 412.13 basis points for the corporate Baa and the All-High-Yield bond indexes, respectively. The prime-based interest rate "float-s"only to the extent that banks change their rates. The least frequently-used option is the CD-based pricing, with only about 16.54% all the loans issued during the period. It is interesting to see that the yield spreads on Baa and junk bonds vary quite a lot over time, while the spreads on HLT loans are somewhat "sticky" with less variation over time (Fig. 2).

The second source of revenue is derived from fees. In Table 5, a description of fee structures and their distribution is shown. Upfront fees are one time fees which are collected at deal closing time to compensate the originating bank for providing immediacy and for the risk of not being able to sell participations in the loans made. The average upfront fee is 55.714 basis points. Annual fees are annual charges against the commitment amount for loan administration costs; commitment fees compensate for providing the line of credit (a callable option from which the borrower can draw), while the cancellation fee is charged against termination or commitment reduction. A letter of credit fee may also be charged. Table 5 shows that the fees are charged regularly and the cross-sectional variation in the size of the fees is fairly large. In general, the correlation among these fees is positive and statistically significant, indicating that lenders use these fees in a complementary, rather than an offsetting, fashion.

4. The determinants of loan spreads

4.1. A theoretical model

In this paper, we use an augmented multi-factor model to model the determinants of the ex ante yield spread on loans. We assume that yield spreads are determined by the following model:

$$y_{it} = X_{it}\beta_i + Z_{it}\gamma + \varepsilon_{it}, \qquad (1)$$

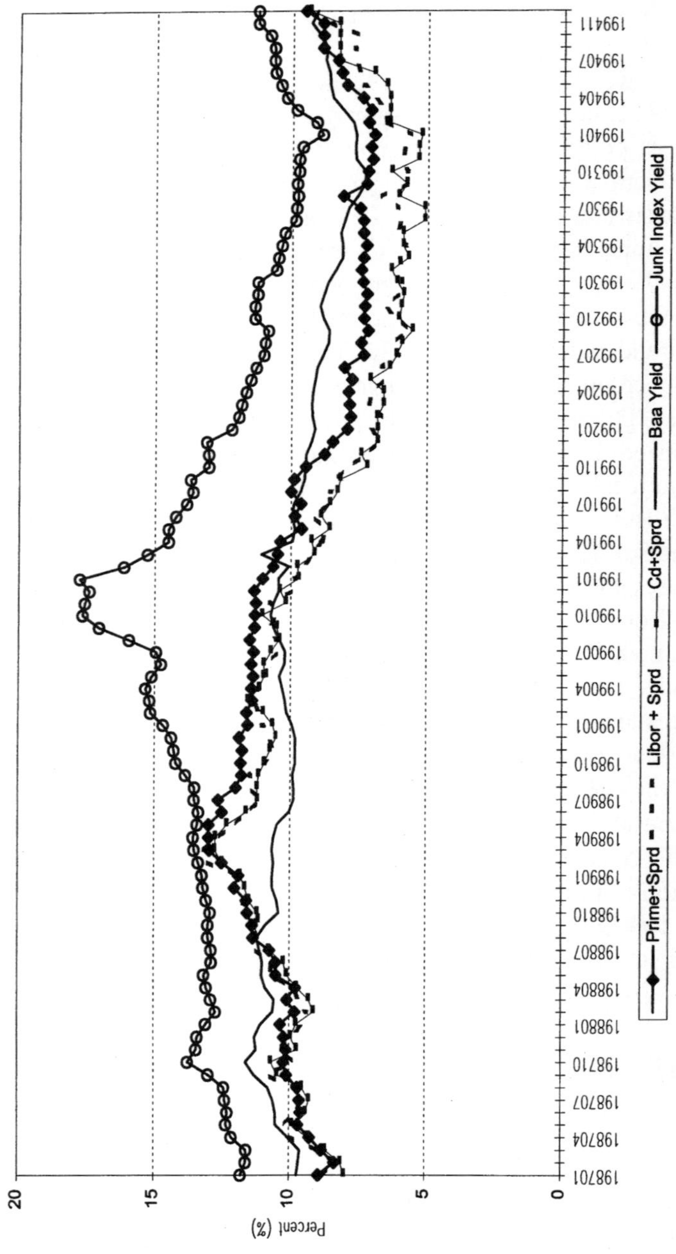

Fig. 2. New issue HLT loan vs. coroporate bond rates.

Table 5
Distribution of HLT bank loan fees

	Fee type	N	Mean	Std dev.	Minimum	Maximum	
Panel A: 1987–1994	Upfront fee	4122	55.714	84.545	0	570	
	Annual fee	4122	3.723	11.926	0	212	
	Commitment fee	4122	23.96	25.274	0	300	
	Cancellation fee	4122	5.584	33.592	0	800	
	LC (Letter of Credit)	4122	39.901	82.97	0	375	
	Year	N	Upfront	Annual	Commitment	Cancellation	LC
Panel B: Average fees by year	1987	238	85.2	4.3	28.5	8.6	27.5
	1988	661	91.2	4.7	32.1	6.2	42.9
	1989	651	73.2	4.5	26	4.3	29.4
	1990	422	47.3	3	21.9	8.1	39.3
	1991	353	46.9	5	21.2	7.2	49.6
	1992	532	46.7	2.9	21.9	3.8	55.5
	1993	520	34	3.5	20.9	5.6	43.8
	1994	745	30.1	2.4	19.5	4.2	32.2
		Upfront	Annual	Commitment	Cancellation	LC	
Panel C: Correlation coefficients	Upfront	1.0000					
		0.0000					
	Annual	0.0796	1.0000				
		0.0001	0.0000				
	Commitment	0.1345	0.0148	1.0000			
		0.0001	0.0000	0.0000			
	Cancellation	0.1055	0.0270	0.0513	1.0000		
		0.0001	0.0837	0.0010	0.0000		
	LC	0.0333	0.0505	0.3396	0.0465	1.0000	
		0.0326	0.0012	0.0001	0.0028	0.0000	

This table provides a distribution of the fee structure of the HLT bank loans. The sample is based on 4122 deals reported by LPC between 1978 and 1994. Panel A provides the distribution aggregated over the 8-year period. Panel B provides the average fee for each year. Panel C provides the correlation matrix. All fee amounts are in basis point spreads.

where y_{it} is the loan yield spread over a benchmark market index rate at time of origination (time t). X_{it} is a 2×1 vector which includes the Baa yield spread and junk bond yield spread over the benchmark rate at time t. These spreads vary according to the date of origination of the loan over the 1987–1994 period. The coefficient β_i is the ith loan's spread sensitivity to the spreads of the two corporate bonds (i.e., Baa and junk). Z_{it} is a vector of loan-specific characteristics, while γ measures the impact of these loan-specific characteristics on HLT loan spreads.

The intuition underlying the model is that a loan's yield spread is determined, in part, by its systematic relationship (β_i) to the spreads required in (competing) corporate bond markets. That is, the Baa bond (and junk bond) yield spread reflects required credit risk compensation for a competing benchmark corporate bond. The higher a loan's systematic risk exposure, the higher its ex ante loan spreads or risk premium.

However, β_i is incapable of capturing all the determinants of a borrower's credit risk. Thus, we allow loan-specific characteristics to affect loan pricing. This essentially assumes that (β_i, Z_{it}) span the same pricing space as the underlying systematic risk exposure factors. This use of firm-specific variables as proxies for factor loadings has been used recently by Fama and French (1992, 1995), Berk (1995) and Mei (1993). Nevertheless, Eq. (1) is not directly estimable in a cross-section of loan spreads, since β_i is not observable and varies across individual loans. Thus, we estimate the following regression:

$$y_{it} = X_{it}\overline{\beta} + Z_{it}\gamma + \eta_{it}, \tag{2}$$

where $\overline{\beta}$ is the population mean of the β_i sensitivity coefficients. In Appendix A, we show the conditions under which the OLS estimator of Eq. (2) is statistically unbiased and consistent.

The $\overline{\beta}$ in Eq. (2) measures the average loan sensitivity towards changes in spreads in the corporate bond (Baa or junk debt) market. If these loans are of a similar credit quality and maturity as the benchmark bond, we would expect the loan β_i to be close to one. [6] This is similar in spirit to equity pricing, where we would expect, in a cross-sectional regression similar to that of Eq. (2), with a well diversified sample of stocks, that the beta should be close to one if the market portfolio is used as X_{it}.

4.2. Empirical determinants

As discussed above, HLT loans may be priced based either off the Prime, LIBOR, or CD rates. The dependent variable we use in the regressions that follow is the ex ante (percentage) credit spreads which is calculated as

---

[6] The quality and maturity differences are directly accounted for through Z_{it}, the vector of loan-specific characteristics.

$$\text{spread} = \frac{\text{Loan rate} - \text{Base rate}}{\text{Base rate}} \tag{3}$$

at time of origination. Here the base rate is the monthly average Prime, 6-month LIBOR, or 6-month CD rate at the time of loan origination (as reported by the Federal Reserve). The independent variables which are used to explain the percentage spread are described below (listed in Table 6).

4.2.1. The independent variables

The independent variables fall into five categories: the bond market yield spread, loan characteristics, borrower characteristics, lender role, and HLT designation.

BaaYield: It represents the ex ante yield on the portfolio of corporate bonds with Moody's corporate rating of Baa at time of loan origination obtained from federal Reserve Statistical Release H15.

Junkb_Yield: It represents the ex ante yield on Merrill Lynch's All-High-Yield ("junk") bond portfolio index obtained from Bloomberg Information Services.

Ln(Sales): It represents borrower size, as measured by the natural logarithm of total sales in the year immediately preceding the closing of the deal.

Ln(Amount): It represents the natural logarithm of the loan commitment amount at origination.

Syndicate: This is a dummy variable equal to 1 (0 otherwise) if the loan is syndicated.

Secured: This is a dummy variable equal to 1 (0 otherwise) if the loan is secured by a pledge of specific assets (or equity) of the borrower.

Maturity: It is represented by three dummy variables based on the maturity of the loan. LOWMAT is 1 (0 otherwise) if the loan's contractual maturity is 60 months or less; MEDMAT is 1 (0 otherwise) if maturity is greater than 60 months but less than 180 months; HIMAT is 1 (0 otherwise) if the maturity is greater than 180 months.

Lender Role: Three dummy variables reflect the role of the originating lender. AGENT-LEAD is 1 (0 otherwise) if the originating bank is the lead lender. This group is usually identified in the LPC database by titles such as arranger, co-arranger, administrative agent, agent or co-agent. MANAGER is a dummy variable equal to 1 (0 otherwise) if the primary lender has a lower level of commitment or syndication risk. This is identified in the LPC database as the bank being a lead manager, co-lead manager, manager, co-manager, senior manager. Finally, PARTICIPANT is a dummy variable equal to 1 (0 otherwise) if originating lender performs no specific role other than being a signatory to the original loan agreement and funding a share of the loan.

Loan type: Stands for three dummy variables based on the type of the loan. TERM is 1 (0 otherwise) if the loan is a term loan; REVOLVER is 1

Table 6
Description of independent variables

Variable	Description
BAAYIELD	Ave. ex ante yield of Moody's Baa corporate bonds over the base rate (Prime, Libor, or CD rates); e.g. (Baa-Prime)/Prime
JUNKB_YIELD	Ave. ex ante yield on All-High-Yield ("Junk") bonds over the base rate (Prime, Libor, or CD rates); e.g. (JUNK-Prime)/Prime
LN (SALES)	Natural logarithm of borrower sales revenue
LN (AMOUNT)	Natural logarithm of loan amount
SYNDICATE	Dummy variable equal 1 (0 otherwise) if the loan is underwritten by a syndicate of banks
LOWMAT	Dummy variable equal 1 (0 otherwise) if loan matures in $\leqslant 60$ months
MEDMAT	Dummy variable equal 1 (0 otherwise) if loan matures between 60 and 180 months
UNRATED	Dummy variable equal 1 (0 otherwise) if borrower's bond rating outstanding is unrated
INVGRD	Dummy variable equal 1 (0 otherwise) if borrower's bond rating is S&P BBB and above
BB-B	Dummy variable equal 1 (0 otherwise) if borrower's bond rating is S&P BB-B
CCC-D	Dummy variable equal 1 (0 otherwise) if borrower's bond rating is S&P CCC-D
AGENT-LEAD	Dummy variable equal 1 (0 otherwise) if primary lender's role is agent (including administrative) or lead bank or manager
MANAGER	Dummy variable equal 1 (0 otherwise) if primary lender's role is a CO-agent, arranger or CO-arranger
PARTICIPANT	Dummy variable equal 1 (0 otherwise) if primary lenders role is a participant
SECURED	Dummy variable equal 1 (0 otherwise) if the loan is secured
TERM	Dummy variable equal 1 (0 otherwise) if the loan is a term loan
REVOLVER	Dummy variable equal 1 (0 otherwise) if the loan is a revolving loan
OTHER	Dummy variable equal 1 (0 otherwise) if loan is a standby, demand, bridge or other loan agreement
RECAPITAL-IZATION	Dummy variable equal 1 (0 otherwise) if loan purpose is recapital-ization
TAKEOVER	Dummy variable equal 1 (0 otherwise) if loan purpose is acquisition with specific collateral
GEN. ACQUISI-TION	Dummy variable equal 1 (0 otherwise) if loan purpose is for general acquisition program
WORKING CAPITAL	Dummy variable equal 1 (0 otherwise) if loan purpose is working capital
DEBT REFINANCE	Dummy variable equal 1 (0 otherwise) if loan purpose is to repay existing debt
GEN.CORP FINANCE	Dummy variable equal 1 (0 otherwise) if loan purpose is general corporate purpose
LBO	Dummy variable equal 1 (0 otherwise) if loan purpose is for leveraged-buy-out

This table contains a description of all the independent variables used in the cross-sectional analysis of the determinants of the ex ante yield of highly-leveraged-transactions bank loans. All data pertain to the sample of 4122 loans originated in 1987–1994.

(0 otherwise) if the loan is a revolving facility; and OTHER is 1 (0 otherwise) if the loan is a short-term facility such as demand, bridge, standby LC or bankers' acceptances loans.

Corporate rating: This represents corporate debt ratings (based on Standard and Poor's Classification) of the outstanding debentures of the borrower at the time of the loan transaction. INVGRD is 1 (0 otherwise) if the borrower is investment grade (BBB and above in Standard and Poor's rating); NOGRD is 1 (0 otherwise) if the borrower is unrated; SUBGRD is 1 (0 otherwise) if the borrower is below-investment grade but within the range BB-B. SPECUGRD is 1 (0 otherwise) if the borrower is a speculative issue with a rating between CCC and D.

HLT designation: Seven dummy variables reflect the designated purposes of the leveraged loan. These dummy variables are Recapitalization, Takeover, General Acquisition, Working Capital, Debt Refinancing, and General Corporate Purposes, and Leverage-Buy-Outs (LBO).

4.3. Discussion of empirical determinants

The objective of the analysis is to model the determinants of the ex ante spreads (and fees) of new issue HLT loans relative to the ex ante yield spreads in the competing corporate bond markets as well as specific loan characteristics or features. The ex ante market yield spreads are the yield spreads on corporate bonds rated Baa by Moody's (taken from the Federal Reserve System H.15 release) and the yield spread on Merrill Lynch's All-High-Yield bond index (obtained from Bloomberg).

A loan feature that may be an important determinant of spreads is the size of the loan. Larger loans tend to be associated with large public borrowers and there is more public information available regarding such borrowers. As such, default risk may be lower than for smaller loans; leading to a lower yield spread. Alternatively, a larger loan size can lead to enhanced credit risk concentration at the originating bank (to the extent that the bank cannot syndicate/sell-off all of the loans). That is, the lender is exposed to a higher level of borrower-specific risk. This suggests a higher loan yield spread may be demanded by the originating lender. Therefore, one might expect either a negative or positive relationship between borrower size and loan yield spreads.

The ex ante credit rating of the borrower is clearly an important factor in determining the risk and price of a new-issue loan. One would expect that higher credit rated corporations will have lower default risk and hence lower yield spreads. Credit quality differences may be even more important, after the bank regulators' disclosure requirements were phased out, as the incentives for lending to highly indebted borrowers may have increased. Longer maturity loans should be expected to have a higher risk of principal repayment compared to the short-term loans (this should lead to higher yields); see Flannery

(1986). A revolving facility provides an on-going line of credit that may be drawn down, repaid and re-borrowed many times over the life of the line. Compared to the fixed term loan facilities, the revolver is more likely to be associated with takedown risk. This should lead to higher required yield spreads (see Ho and Saunders, 1983).

If the loan is underwritten by a syndicate, it is more likely to be successfully distributed to other lenders until the lead bank's target share is reached. This is equivalent to a reduction in syndication risk for the originating bank and to a reduction in firm-specific risk associated with individual loans. This suggests that one should expect lower yield spread on syndicated loans. [7] If a loan is secured by a pledge of specific assets or equity of the borrower, the risk of principal and interest default is likely to be lower, leading to lower yield spreads. [8]

The role of the primary or originating lender is used to differentiate commitment levels and a bank's exposure to syndication, commitment, and cancellation risks. An agent-lead bank by definition has a higher commitment level and thus greater credit risk exposure. This should lead to a higher required yield spread. Offsetting this effect is the fact that a lead bank has the primary responsibility for monitoring and covenant enforcement. As such the uncertainty associated with the loan is reduced–leading to a lower spread. [9]

Finally, the relationship between loan proceed use (designation) and loan spreads will be influenced by differences in the lenders' ability to extract higher rates of return for different use of proceeds. In otherwords, the purpose of the loan has useful information content beyond the signals about credit-worthiness that are conveyed in loan origination announcements (see James (1987) and Lummer and McConnell (1989)). In the tests, seven categories of proceed use are included. Loans for financing acquisition may earn higher yields than general corporate loans because lenders are able to charge higher rates for providing immediacy. [10] Loans for debt refinancing or recapitalization are viewed as

[7] Note, however, that the originating banks may earn fees associated with syndication. These are more likely to be reflected in upfront or commitment fees, rather than in higher yields.

[8] However, arguably only high risk borrowers have to pledge collateral. As such collateral may be viewed as a signal of being a higher (rather than lower) risk.

[9] In Diamond (1984, 1991), it is shown that direct lender–borrower liaison will result in costly or inadequate information production, either because of duplication of effort, if each lender monitors, or a free-rider problem in which no lender acts. However, if a delegated monitor has primary responsibility for monitoring and enforcing loan contracts on behalf of the whole syndicate, the uncertainty associated with a borrower is reduced, and this should lead to a lower risk default.

[10] Megginson et al. (1995) show that lending syndicates are able to extract higher loan rates for financing transactions where the borrower needs to acquire financing quickly (e.g., takeover and leveraged buyout). In another study, Kracaw and Zenner (1994) show that there are significant differences in borrowing firms' abnormal returns at the announcement of bank financing of LBOs compared to announcements of bank financing for recapitalizations.

negative NPV investments since they are usually utilized for defensive purposes in corporate control contests (Denis, 1990). This should lead to higher yield spreads. Debt refinancing and recapitalization loans can be viewed as renewals which provide positive signals about the borrower's prospects. Lenders may be able to earn a higher yield through higher rates or from equity-kicker features that allow lenders to share in upside returns with borrowers.

5. Empirical results

Various specifications of the yield spread model are reported in Tables 7–12 and are based on LIBOR, Prime and CD benchmark rates to generate spreads. Discussions of results focus mainly on the LIBOR-based model since most HLT loans (92.28%) are priced-off of the 6-month LIBOR. [11]

5.1. Loan-bond price divergence

One consistent finding from the regression tests with the different model specifications is that the ex ante corporate bond yield spread variable (Baa-Yield) has a positive and generally significant impact on loan yield spreads. However, we find this sensitivity is much smaller than one ($\beta = 0.299$). While quality characteristics/factors and institutional features may impact the degree of divergence (see Section 5.2), the finding that β is significantly less than one could in part be due to "loan interest spread stickiness", i.e., a time lag on the part of banks to adjust loan spreads to reflect changing spreads in the corporate debt markets. It is worth noting that the "spread stickiness" referred to here is different from the general interest rate stickiness examined in previous studies (e.g., Berger and Udell, 1992; Mester and Saunders, 1995). Here we are not talking about stickiness with respect to the general level of interest rates or bank rates (e.g., prime rate), but rather with respect to changes in yield spreads, i.e., to changes in the risk premium. Table 7 also shows a mean β for junk bonds which is significantly smaller than that of the corporate Baa bond, suggesting that there is relatively greater price divergence between the HLT loan and junk bond markets than between the HLT loan an corporate bond markets [12].

[11] However, where there are important differences with the Prime and CD rates models, the differences are noted appropriately.

[12] We also ran the regression with Baa yield or junk bond yield only. The results are quite similar. We find the $\overline{\beta}$ for Baa yields is larger than the for junk bond, but they are both less than 1. We also computed the t-statistic for the linear hypothesis that the coefficients on BaaYield and Junkb_Yield are equal to 1. In both cases the hypothesis that the coefficient is equal to 1 is rejected. The t-statistic is 40.44 for the BaaYield and 68.75 for Junkb_Yield, both of which are significant.

Table 7
The convergence of HLT loan and corporate bond prices

	Spread (LIBOR)	Spread (Prime)	Spread (CD)
INTERCEPT	0.327	−0.009	0.183
	(10.060)*	(−0.451)	(3.383)*
BAAYIELD	0.299	0.116	0.222
	(18.264)*	(8.411)*	(8.748)*
JUNKB_YLD	0.048	0.044	0.083
	(3.636)*	(3.744)*	(4.161)*
LN(SALES)	−0.002	0.005	−0.001
	(−1.040)	(4.639)*	(−0.163)
LN(AMOUNT)	−0.006	0.001	−0.006
	(−2.871)*	(0.320)	(−0.183)
SECURED	0.032	0.007	0.006
	(5.887)*	(2.043)*	(0.750)
MEDMAT	0.013	0.008	0.011
	(2.893)*	(2.937)*	(1.724)**
INVGRD	−0.047	−0.017	−0.015
	(−2.743)*	(−1.530)	(−0.841)
SYNDICATE	−0.009	0.017	0.021
	(−0.912)	(2.642)*	(4.161)*
N	3050	2582	572
R^2	0.6878	0.1465	0.7657

This table shows estimates of the relationship of the ex ante yield spread on HLT loans and the required spreads in the competing Baa corporate and high-yield-bond market. The regression estimates in each column reflect the three pricing options available. Figures in parenthesis are *t*-ratios. The effects of loan and borrower characteristics are reflected through secured (SECURED), loan size (LN(AMOUNT)), maturity (MEDMAT), corporate rating (INVGRD), and borrower size (LN(SALES)). The syndication variable is a dummy variable (SYNDICATE) takes the value of 1 (0 otherwise) if the loan is underwritten by two or more lenders.
* Indicates significance at 5%.
** Indicates significance at 10%.

5.2. Loan specific effects and lender characteristics

In this section we summarize the findings regarding the effects of other loan characteristics on the HLT spreads. Borrower size (Ln(Sales)) is insignificant, but loan size (Ln(Amount)) is negative and significantly correlated with ex ante yields, indicating that larger loans have a borrowing cost advantage. We also find that longer maturity loans (MEDMAT) generate higher yields. Loans which are secured by a pledge of assets (SECURED) have higher, rather than lower, yields. On average, secured issues generate 3.2 basis points in higher expected yields, which is statistically significant. [13] This confirms the view (see

[13] Note however that in the CD regression, secured loans are associated with lower yields (about 2.0 basis points) on average.

Battacharya and Thakor, 1993) that collateral backing signals a more (rather than less) risky borrower.

The coefficient for loan syndication versus sole-lender (SYNDICATE) is negative but insignificant. The sign of the coefficient can be interpreted as (weak) evidence in support of the hypothesis that syndicated lending lowers the risk of an unsuccessful distribution of loans. The syndicated loan sample is also disaggregated into three subcategories reflecting the existence of different incentives for lenders to monitor and, if necessary, to enforce contract terms. In Table 8, we substitute the SYNDICATE variable with two interactive dummy variables. The first interactive dummy variable is SYNDICATE × LEAD – the interaction between SYNDICATE and AGENT-LEAD. This variable is included to measure the effect on yield spreads when there is a lead lender within the syndicate who retains the largest share. If the incentive to monitor is correlated with the share of the loan retained as well as with the lender's designation, this variable should have a negative sign, consistent with a reduction of credit risk. The second interactive variable SYNDICATE × MANAGER measures the effect of reduced monitoring incentives when the originating bank retains a lower share. [14] The role of MANAGER is associated with a lower share in the loan retained, and therefore with narrower oversight authority (and monitoring incentives). This variable is predicted to have a more positive effect on credit spreads than SYNDICATE × LEAD. [15] By comparison, syndicated loans where both SYNDICATE × LEAD and SYNDICATE × MANAGER dummies are zero should have a relatively higher spread.

In Table 9, we report estimates from a multivariate regression of the ex ante yield spreads with several modifications to the models estimated in Tables 7 and 8. First, since credit rating is important, we include a broader set of credit ratings in order to exploit the additional information that may be implied by the ratings differences. Specifically, three credit rating dummies for unrated issues (UNRATED), sub-investment issues (BB-B), and speculative issues (CCC-D) are included. The estimated coefficients are all positive, with the largest being for the speculative issues.

The use of the loan proceeds is also more finely partitioned, with six out of seven dummy variables included (where the dummy for general corporate financing is excluded to avoid linear dependency). All dummy variables are positive with the exception of general acquisition loans. The positive signs for

[14] Also a lower share would be consistent with an enhanced moral hazard risk to loan buyers since there is an incentive for an originating bank (with private information) to sell more of bad loans (retaining a lower share) than good loans.

[15] SYNDICATE × PARTICIPANT is excluded since it is linearly dependent with the other two interaction variables.

1274 L.A. Angbazo et al. / Journal of Banking & Finance 22 (1998) 1249–1282

Table 8
The influence of lender role and commitment

	Spread (LIBOR)	Spread (Prime)	Spread (CD)
INTERCEPT	0.328	−0.005	0.187
	(10.093)*	(−0.238)	(3.484)*
BAAYIELD	0.306	0.114	0.233
	(17.748)*	(7.828)*	(8.437)*
JUNKB_YLD	0.043	0.046	0.074
	(3.063)*	(3.662)*	(3.382)*
LN(SALES)	−0.002	0.005	0.001
	(−1.164)	(4.776)*	(0.010)
LN(AMOUNT)	−0.006	0.001	0.001
	(−2.962)*	(0.693)	(0.058)
SECURED	0.365	0.006	0.012
	(5.889)*	(1.373)	(1.241)
MEDMAT	0.125	0.009	0.011
	(2.857)*	(3.086)*	(1.726)**
INVGRD	−0.046	−0.016	−0.015
	(−2.683)*	(−1.513)	(−0.884)
SYNDICATE × LEAD	−0.007	−0.001	−0.012
	(−1.190)	(−0.216)	(−1.265)
SYNDICATE × MANAGER	0.043	−0.005	−0.026
	(2.084)*	(−0.351)	(−0.665)
N	3050	2582	572
R^2	0.6887	0.1442	0.7660

This table provides estimates of the influence of the role and share retained by the originating bank in a syndicate. The regression estimates in each column reflect the three pricing options available. Figures in parenthesis are t-ratios. LEAD lenders are the agent or originating banks who retain the largest commitment and maintain the primary servicing and monitoring responsibilities. MANAGER lenders retain a smaller share but play a secondary monitoring role. PARTICIPANT lenders are joint originators/signatories to the original loan agreement but do not perform any other roles. These are passive lenders. The interactive variable SYNDICATE × LEAD reflects the influence of an agent bank with primary oversight on yields of a syndicated loan. SYNDICATE × MANAGER reflects a lower level of commitment on the part of agent bank. The effects of loan and borrower characteristics are reflected through the ex ante Baa corporate bond market yield (BAAYIELD), Merrill Lynch's All-High-Yield bond yield (JUNKB_YLD), secured (SECURED), loan size (LN(AMOUNT)), maturity (MEDMAT), corporate rating (INVGRD) and borrower size (LN(SALES)).

* Indicates significance at 5%.

** Indicates significance at 10%.

takeover and acquisition loans are consistent with evidence in Megginson et al. (1995) that banks are able to extract higher yields for providing immediacy (e.g. transactions in which quick financing is needed). Similarly, the higher yield spreads associated with debt repayment and recapitalization loans support the view that these loans are negative NPV investments (Denis, 1990). In general, the positive coefficients suggest that lenders are able to extract higher yields to compensate for high risk exposure than under general corporate fi-

Table 9
Effect of credit rating and loan designation

Variable	Spread (LIBOR)	Spread (Prime)	Spread (CD)
INTERCEPT	0.363	0.034	0.275
	(10.621)*	(1.567)	(4.965)*
BAAYIELD	0.271	0.112	0.241
	(14.976)*	(7.455)*	(8.628)*
JUNKB_YLD	0.053	0.052	0.078
	(3.825)*	(4.161)*	(3.536)*
LN (SALES)	−0.003	0.004	−0.002
	(−1.983)*	(3.770)*	(−0.786)
LN (AMOUNT)	−0.007	−0.001	−0.002
	(−3.789)*	(−0.791)	(−1.320)
SECURED	0.026	0.001	0.007
	(4.319)*	(0.158)	(0.761)
MEDMAT	0.003	0.003	0.010
	(0.550)	(0.966)	(1.430)
UNRATED	0.036	0.004	−0.031
	(5.532)*	(1.087)	(−2.271)*
BB-B	0.028	0.005	0.029
	(3.983)*	(1.168)	(2.226)*
CCC-D	0.176	0.103	−0.054
	(6.406)*	(5.136)*	(−1.002)
SYNDICATE × LEAD	−0.005	−0.001	−0.011
	(−0.772)	(−0.246)	(−1.176)
SYNDICATE × MANAGER	0.043	−0.003	−0.001
	(2.113)*	(−0.196)	(−0.015)
RECAPITALIZATION	0.076	0.051	0.066
	(9.271)*	(9.258)*	(4.486)*
TAKE OVER	0.021	0.031	0.025
	(2.814)*	(6.252)*	(2.013)*
WORKING CAPITAL	0.019	0.017	0.025
	(2.531)*	(3.284)*	(1.939)**
DEBT REPAYMENT	0.018	0.020	0.014
	(2.864)*	(4.468)*	(1.243)
GEN. ACQUISITION	0.020	0.011	0.035
	(2.055)*	(1.512)	(1.975)*
LBO	0.055	0.041	0.038
	(6.809)*	(8.011)*	(3.107)*
REVOLVER	−0.016	−0.019	−0.003
	(−2.364)*	(−4.578)*	(−0.262)
TERM	0.007	−0.006	0.004
	(0.931)	(−1.251)	(0.327)
N	3050	2582	572
R^2	0.7072	0.2039	0.7815

This table gives the estimates of determinants of the ex ante yield on HLT bank loans. The dependent variable in each regression is the ex ante yield premium or credit spread as a percentage of the bench mark rate index. The independent variables reflect corporate and junk bond yield, loan size, maturity, secured status, syndication, loan purpose and type, lender role and corporate size and rating. Figures in parenthesis are the t-ratios.

* Indicates statistical significance at 5%.

** Indicates statistical significance at 10%.

nancing loans. An interesting piece of evidence is that revolving loans have a lower yield spread than term loans, the latter are generally larger in size and have a longer maturity.

5.3. Effect of fees

Table 10 presents regression estimates of the relationship between fees and the ex ante yield premium of HLT loans, controlling for loan characteristics. The fee variable is included to examine whether fees and spreads are potential substitute or complementary sources of revenues for originating banks. If fees and loan spreads are substitutes then a negative relationship should be expected between fees and yield spreads.

Fees are specified as a percentage of the underlying facility expressed in basis points, and refer to upfront, commitment, cancellation, and letter of credit (LC) fees. We present here only the results for upfront fees as the relationship with the spread is similar for the other fees.

The main result is that upfront fees have a positive and significant coefficient in the HLT yield spread regression, which is inconsistent with the hypothesis that loan rates and fees are substitutes. That is , banks do not appear to charge lower loan rates with the expectation of extracting higher upfront fees from borrowers. We explored this relationship further by analyzing the characteristics of borrowers who were charged upfront fees compared to those who were not charged fees. Table 11 indicates that, on average, upfront fees are charged on larger loans, and the loans are often designated for LBO financing. Our finding is consistent with recent empirical evidence that lenders are able to extract relatively higher gross returns on loans for takeover and leverage buyouts (see Megginson et al., 1995; Kracaw and Zenner, 1994). In general, our results provide evidence that one way banks extract higher returns on riskier loans is through the incidence of upfront fees in addition to higher loan rates, more security, and shorter maturity. [16]

5.4. Deregulation of HLT lending

Table 12 presents results of the impact of the easing of bank regulators' reporting requirements on HLT lending. Regression coefficients are estimated for two periods corresponding to regulation (January 1987–June 1992), and post-regulation (July 1992–September 1994). The regulation period represents the period in which banks were required to disclose the total amount of loans with HLT designation (see Section 2.1). This reporting requirement was phased

[16] When we include these variables in the regressions with upfront fees, the coefficients of the upfront fees are still significant.

Table 10
Relationship of ex ante yield spreads and upfront fees

Variable	Spread (LIBOR)	Spread (Prime)	Spread (CD)
INTERCEPT	0.371	0.041	0.275
	(10.044)*	(1.890)**	(4.956)*
BAAYIELD	0.271	0.112	0.241
	(15.044)*	(7.544)*	(8.597)*
JUNKB_YLD	0.054	0.052	0.079
	(3.892)*	(4.220)*	(3.583)*
LN(Sales)	−0.004	0.004	−0.002
	(−2.180)*	(3.579)*	(−0.817)
LN(Amount)	−0.008	−0.001	−0.004
	(−4.098)*	(−1.180)	(−1.343)
MEDMAT	0.003	0.003	0.010
	(0.602)	(1.119)	(1.437)
SECURED	0.023	−0.001	0.007
	(3.748)*	(−0.289)	(0.720)
UNRATED	0.039	0.006	−0.029
	(5.928)*	(1.456)	(−2.189)*
BB-B	0.031	0.008	0.029
	(4.417)*	(1.766)**	(2.236)*
CCC-D	0.164	0.086	−0.057
	(5.979)*	(4.303)*	(−1.050)
SYNDICATE × LEAD	−0.005	−0.003	−0.012
	(−0.920)	(−0.688)	(−1.263)
SYNDICATE × MANAGER	0.040	−0.004	−0.005
	(1.971)*	(−0.264)	(−0.124)
RECAPITALIZATION	0.072	0.048	0.065
	(8.740)*	(8.784)*	(4.398)*
TAKE OVER	0.018	0.028	0.024
	(2.457)*	(5.829)*	(1.987)*
WORKING CAPITAL	0.018	0.016	0.025
	(2.375)*	(3.130)*	(1.934)*
DEBT REPAYMENT	0.020	0.020	0.015
	(2.831)*	(4.440)*	(1.338)
GEN. ACQUISITION	0.047	0.011	0.036
	(2.069)*	(1.569)	(2.043)*
LBO	0.047	0.036	0.036
	(5.749)*	(6.886)*	(2.953)*
REVOLVER	−0.014	−0.018	−0.002
	(−2.105)*	(−4.154)*	(−0.183)
TERM	0.008	−0.004	0.004
	(1.171)	(−0.895)	(0.369)
UPFRONT FEES	1.449	1.074	0.411
	(5.515)*	(6.681)*	(1.009)
N	3050	2582	572
R^2	0.7101	0.2175	0.7819

This table estimates the relationship between the ex ante yield and upfront fees. The dependent variable in each regression is the ex ante premium or credit spread as a percentage of the bench mark rate index. The control variables reflect corporate and junk bond yield, loan size, maturity, secured status, syndication, loan purpose and type, lender role and corporate size and rating. Figures in parenthesis are the t-ratios.

* Indicates significance at 5%.

** Indicates significance at 10%.

Table 11
Characteristics of HLT borrowers stratified by incidence of upfront fees

	Firms without fees	Firms with fees
Borrower sales size ($millions)	717.25	895.05
Loan size ($millions)	120.17	171.7
Loan maturity (months)	55.03	51.3
Pct. of loan serviced	14.70	28.50
Pct. of borrowers with speculative credit rating – (CCC-D)	2.25	6.8
Pct. of loans for LBOs	10.10	22.04
Pct. of loans which are standby or demand loans	9.83	14.7

out to prevent regulation from impeding credit creation toward the end of 1991–1992 credit crunch. The computed F-statistic, for the null hypothesis of stable parameters across time, $F(18, 3039) = 14.0433$, is statistically significant at the 5% level, rejecting the hypothesis of a stable structural model determining spreads during the pre- and post-"regulatory" periods.

Specifically, loan yield spreads were slightly more sensitive to junk bond yield spreads movements than corporate Baa yield spread movements in the post-deregulation period. By contrast, during the period of regulation, loan yield spreads were more sensitive to Baa yield spread ($\beta = 0.281$) than to junk bond yield spreads ($\beta = 0.023$). [17] The relative sizes of the coefficients on Baa yield and junk bond yield variables were more similar in absolute value in the post-regulation period, perhaps reflecting the improved credit quality of the junk bonds. [18] The spreads on HLT loans also appear to have declined in recent years (i.e., spreads during regulation were an average 2.53%, compared to 2.42% in the post-regulation period).

6. Conclusion

In this paper, we employ the Loan Pricing Corporation's database on HLT loans to analyze the determinants of ex ante yield spreads. The data base consists of 4122 deals between 1989–1994, with a combined dollar amount (in new-issue loans) estimated at $593.5 billions. The results show that, on average, HLT loan yield spread sensitivity to yield spreads in the Baa corporate

[17] As in Section 5.1, we also computed t-statistics for the linear hypothesis that the coefficient on BaaYield and Junkb_Yield variables are equal to 1. Across the two subperiods – regulation (January 1987–June 1992) and post-regulation (post-June 1992) – the computed t-statistics reject the hypothesis of unit coefficients for both variables.

[18] The correlation coefficient between BaaYield and Junkb_Yield in the regulation is 0.8708 compared to 0.9073 in the post-regulation period.

Table 12
Deregulation of HLT lending

Variable	Full sample	1987–1992	1992–1994
INTERCEPT	0.371	0.253	0.636
	(10.044)*	(8.976)*	(7.746)*
BAAYIELD	0.271	0.281	0.111
	(15.044)*	(18.529)*	(1.407)
JUNKB_YLD	0.054	0.023	0.173
	(3.892)*	(2.091)*	(3.066)*
LN(Sales)	−0.004	0.003	−0.015
	(−2.180)*	(2.185)*	(−4.166)*
LN(Amount)	−0.008	−0.006	−0.013
	(−4.098)*	(−3.645)*	(−2.960)*
MEDMAT	0.003	0.004	0.005
	(0.602)	(0.996)	(0.490)
SECURED	0.023	−0.003	0.027
	(3.748)*	(−0.426)	(2.346)*
UNRATED	0.039	0.008	0.019
	(5.928)*	(1.142)	(1.047)
BB-B	0.031	0.012	0.033
	(4.417)*	(1.939)**	(1.683)**
CCC-D	0.164	0.112	0.142
	(5.979)*	(3.014)*	(3.124)*
SYNDICATE × LEAD	−0.005	−0.031	0.025
	(−0.920)	(−5.432)*	(2.368)*
SYNDICATE × MANAGER	0.040	−0.020	0.080
	(1.971)*	(−1.044)	(2.188)*
RECAPITALIZATION	0.072	0.035	0.081
	(8.740)*	(4.261)*	(5.444)*
TAKE OVER	0.018	0.008	0.009
	(2.457)*	(1.283)	(0.599)
WORKING CAPITAL	0.018	0.004	0.024
	(2.375)*	(0.576)	(1.595)
DEBT REPAYMENT	0.020	0.011	0.015
	(2.831)*	(1.826)	(1.228)
GEN. ACQUISITION	0.047	0.027	−0.001
	(2.069)*	(2.605)*	(−0.076)
LBO	0.047	0.023	0.137
	(5.749)*	(3.481)*	(4.449)*
REVOLVER	−0.014	−0.021	−0.003
	(−2.105)*	(−3.791)*	(−0.220)
TERM	0.008	−0.014	0.048
	(1.171)	(−2.460)*	(2.974)*
UPFRONT FEES	1.449	1.742	2.988
	(5.515)*	(8.548)*	(4.118)*
N	3050	1848	1181
R–2	0.7101	0.6852	0.4195
SUM OF SQUARES	128.189	31.267	42.504
Mean Spread	14.0433*		
CHOW TEST F(18,3039)			

This table shows the determinants of the ex ante yield on HLT loans to test for a parametric shift after deregulation of HLT lending. The dependent variable is the ex ante premium or credit spread as a percentage of the benchmark rate index. The independent variables reflect loan size, maturity, collateral, syndication, loan purpose and type, lender role and size and rating.

* Indicates significance at 5%.

** Indicates significance at 10%.

bond market and junk bond market has been positive, but significantly less than unity; indicating that pricing in the HLT loan and corporate bond markets diverge. Interestingly, we find that over the whole sample period that loan yields are more sensitive to movements in investment grade bond (Baa) yield spreads than junk bond yield spreads.

Our study also finds several other important borrower quality characteristics that are important determinants of HLT loan spreads. In particular, there is evidence that lenders augment, rather than substitute, loan yield spreads with additional fees for syndication, commitment and cancellation risks. Moreover, syndicated loans have lower yield spreads and spreads are further lowered by the presence of a lead lender who retains a large share (and thus retains broad monitoring responsibilities).

The use of loan proceeds are also important determinants of HLT loan spreads. Specifically, loans for acquisitions and debt restructurings have relatively larger yield spreads to compensate for immediacy (i.e., transactions that require quick financing), and for increased borrower leverage. Term loans which are generally larger in size and have longer maturities also have larger yield spreads than revolving loan facilities. We also found that secured loans generate higher expected yields, confirming the view that more risky loans require collateral to be pledged. Finally, HLT spreads on average appear to have fallen in the post-July 1992 (deregulation period) and to be relatively more closely linked to movements in junk bond yield than in the pre-July 1992 period.

Acknowledgements

We thank Ed Altman and Manju Puri for useful comments and suggestions, Martin Fridson for providing data on Merrill Lynch All High-Yield-Bonds, Beverly Christenson and Christopher Balian for valuable research assistance. All remaining errors are ours. LAA gratefully acknowledges financial support from the Center for International Business Education and Research (CIBER), Purdue University.

Appendix A

Assume loan pricing is determined by the following linear pricing equation:

$$y_i = x_i\beta_i + z_i\gamma + \varepsilon_i, \tag{A.1}$$

where $\beta_i \sim N(\overline{\beta}, \sigma_\beta^2)$, and β_i is uncorrelated with x_i and z_i. Under the above condition, the OLS estimator,

$$\hat{\Upsilon} = \begin{pmatrix} \hat{\beta} \\ \gamma \end{pmatrix} = [(XZ)'(XZ)]^{-1}(XZ)'Y \tag{A.2}$$

is an unbiased estimator of $\begin{pmatrix} \overline{\beta} \\ \gamma \end{pmatrix}$.

Proof.

$$\begin{aligned} \mathrm{E}(\hat{\Upsilon}) &= \mathrm{E}[(XZ)'(XZ)]^{-1}(XZ)'\left[\left((XZ)\begin{pmatrix} \overline{\beta} \\ \gamma \end{pmatrix} + \varepsilon\right) + \begin{bmatrix} x_1(\beta_1 - \overline{\beta}) \\ \vdots \\ x_N(\beta_N - \overline{\beta}) \end{bmatrix}\right] \\ &= \begin{pmatrix} \overline{\beta} \\ \gamma \end{pmatrix} + \mathrm{E}[(XZ)'(XZ)]^{-1}(XZ)\begin{bmatrix} x_1(\beta_1 - \overline{\beta}) \\ \vdots \\ x_N(\beta_N - \overline{\beta}) \end{bmatrix} \\ &= \begin{pmatrix} \overline{\beta} \\ \gamma \end{pmatrix} + (XZ)'(XZ)^{-1}(XZ)'\begin{bmatrix} \mathrm{E}x_1(\beta_1 - \overline{\beta}) \\ \vdots \\ \mathrm{E}x_N(\beta_N - \overline{\beta}) \end{bmatrix} \\ &= \begin{pmatrix} \overline{\beta} \\ \gamma \end{pmatrix}. \end{aligned} \tag{A.3}$$

By the same token, it is also easy to show that under fairly general assumptions, the above OLS estimator is also consistent.

References

Berger, A., Udell, G., 1992. Some evidence on the empirical significance of credit rationing. Journal of Political Economy 100 (5), 1047–1077.

Berk, J., 1995. A critique of size-related anomalies. Review of Financial Studies 8, 275–286.

Bhattacharya, S., Thakor, A.V., 1993. Contemporary banking theory. Journal of Financial Intermediation 3, 2–50.

Boardman, C.M., McEnally, R.W., 1981. Factors affecting seasoned corporate bond prices. Journal of Financial and Quantitative Analysis 16, 207–226.

Carlson, J.H., Fabozzi, F.J., 1992. The Trading and Securitization of Senior Bank Loans. Probus Publishing Company.

Carey, M. et al., 1994. The economics of private placements: A new look. Financial Markets, Institutions and Instruments 2 (3).

Diamond, D., 1984. Financial intermediation and delegated monitoring. Review of Economic Studies 51, 393–414.

Diamond, D., 1991. Monitoring and reputation: The choice between bank loans and directly placed debt. Journal of Political Economy 99 (4), 689–721.

Denis, D., 1990. Defensive changes in corporate payout policy: Share repurchases and special dividends Journal of Finance 45, 1433–1456.

Fisher, L., 1959. Determinants of risk premiums on corporate bonds. Journal of Political Economy 76, 217–237.

Flannery, M., 1986. Asymmetric information and risky debt maturity choice. Journal of Finance XLI, 19–37.

Fridson, M.S., 1995. Why the leveraged loan and high yield bond markets must converge. The Journal of Global High Yield Bond Research, May/June.

James, C., 1987. Some evidence on the uniqueness of bank loans. Journal of Financial Economics, 217–235.

Famà, E., French, K., 1992. The cross-section of expected returns. Journal of Finance 47, 427–465.

Fama, E., French, K., 1995. Size and book-to-market factors in earnings and returns. Journal of Finance 50, 131–157.

Kracaw, W.A., Zenner, M., 1994. The wealth effects of bank financing announcements in highly leveraged transactions. Working paper, Pennsylvania State University.

Gorton, G.B., Pennacchi, G.G., 1995. Banks and loan sales: Marketing non-marketable assets. Journal of Monetary Economics 35 (3).

Ho, T., Saunders, A., 1983. Fixed-rate loan commitments, takedown risk, and the dynamics of hedging with futures. Journal of Financial and Quantitative Analysis 18, 499–516.

Lummer, S.L., McConnell, J.J., 1989. Further evidence on the bank lending process and the capital market response to the bank loan agreements. Journal of Financial Economics 25, 99–122.

Mei, J., 1993. A semiautoregression approach to arbitrage pricing theory. Journal of Finance 48, 599–620.

Megginson, W.L. et al., 1995, Syndicated loan announcements and the market value of the banking firm. Journal of Money, Credit and Banking 27 (2).

Mester, L.J., Saunders, A., 1995. When does the prime rate change. Journal of Banking and Finance 19, 743–764.

Roberts, G.S., Viscione, J.A., 1984. The impact of seniority and security covenants on bond yields: A note. Journal of Finance 39, 1597–1602.

Ross, P.H. et al., 1990. HLT bank loans: A new market for relative value investors. Salomon Brothers High Yield Research.

Saunders, A., 1997. Financial Institution Management: A Modern Perspective. Irwin.

EDWARD I. ALTMAN
AMAR GANDE
ANTHONY SAUNDERS

Bank Debt versus Bond Debt: Evidence from Secondary Market Prices

This paper uses a new data set of daily secondary market prices of loans to analyze the specialness of banks as monitors. Consistent with a monitoring advantage of loans over bonds, we find the secondary loan market to be informationally more efficient than the secondary bond market prior to a loan default. Specifically, we find that secondary market loan returns Granger cause secondary market bond returns prior to a loan default. In contrast, secondary market bond returns do not Granger cause secondary market loan returns prior to a loan default.

JEL codes: G14, G21, G22, G23, G24
Keywords: bonds, default, loans, monitoring.

BANKS, WHICH LEND to corporations, are considered "special" for several reasons, including reducing the agency costs of monitoring borrowers.[1]

1. See Saunders and Cornett (2008) for a comprehensive review of why banks are considered special.

We thank the editor (Deborah Lucas) and two anonymous referees for their valuable comments and suggestions. Our paper has benefited from helpful comments from Cliff Ball, Mark Carey, Sandeep Dahiya, Mark Flannery, Edith Hotchkiss, Craig Lewis, Ron Masulis, Manju Puri, Hans Stoll, and the seminar participants at the Western Finance Association annual meeting, the American Economic Association annual meeting, the Bank Structure Conference of the Federal Reserve Bank of Chicago, the Financial Management Association annual meeting, and at Vanderbilt University. We also thank Steve Rixham, Vice President, Loan Syndications at Wachovia Securities, for helping us understand the institutional features of the syndicated loan market, and Ashish Agarwal, Victoria Ivashina, and Jason Wei for research assistance, and the Loan Pricing Corporation (LPC), the Loan Syndications and Trading Association (LSTA), and Standard & Poor's (S&P) for providing us data for this study.

EDWARD I. ALTMAN *is the Max L. Heine Professor of Finance, Department of Finance, Stern School of Business, New York University* (*E-mail:* ealtman@stern.nyu.edu). AMAR GANDE *is an Assistant Professor of Finance, Finance Department, Edwin L. Cox School of Business, Southern Methodist University* (*E-mail:* agande@cox.smu.edu). ANTHONY SAUNDERS *is John M. Schiff Professor of Finance, Department of Finance, Stern School of Business, New York University* (*E-mail*: asaunder@stern.nyu.edu).

Received March 26, 2007; and accepted in revised form December 15, 2009.

Journal of Money, Credit and Banking, Vol. 42, No. 4 (June 2010)

Several theoretical models highlight the unique monitoring functions of banks (e.g., Diamond 1984, Ramakrishnan and Thakor 1984, Fama 1985). These studies generally argue that banks have a comparative advantage as well as enhanced incentives (relative to bondholders) in monitoring debt contracts. For example, Diamond (1984) contends that banks have scale economies and comparative cost advantages in information production that enable them to undertake superior debt-related monitoring. Ramakrishnan and Thakor (1984) show that banks as information brokers can improve welfare by minimizing the costs of information production and moral hazard. Fama (1985) argues that banks, as insiders, have superior information due to their access to inside information whereas outside (public) debt holders must rely mostly on publicly available information.

The theoretical models described earlier view bank loans to be largely illiquid; that is, a bank makes a loan and holds it until maturity. One possible explanation for this behavior is that the selling of loans could generate a moral hazard problem for the buyer because the bank could retain higher quality loans and sell its "lemons." However, as Gorton and Pennacchi (1995) show, this moral hazard problem can be mitigated if the bank retains a portion of the originated loan as is common in most loan syndications.

In this paper, we examine whether the monitoring advantage of bank loans relative to public bonds persists in the presence of an active secondary market for bank loans, that is, not only when loans are sold by the originating bank to other agents but also when these loans are then traded in an active secondary market. We argue that the bank advantages and incentives to monitor are likely to be preserved even in the presence of loan sales in the secondary market for several reasons. First, discussions with industry experts reveal that the lead arranger bank, which typically holds the largest share of a syndicated loan (see Kroszner and Strahan 2001), retains a large proportion for "relationship reasons" and avoidance of the lemons problem discussed earlier. As suggested by Gorton and Pennacchi (1995), since the lead arranger bank retains a portion of the loan for "relationship reasons," the moral hazard problem is likely to be mitigated as well. Second, the syndicate structure of bank loan origination and the repeated nature of loan syndications ensures incentive compatibility among syndicate members to maintain their reputations over time by not indulging in loan sales that are subject to moral hazard problems. Finally, Drucker and Puri (2009) show empirically that only loans that are subject to a lower moral hazard actually trade on the secondary market.

Taken together, the above evidence suggests that moral hazard concerns relating to loan sales may well be mitigated, even in the presence of an active secondary market for bank loans. Consequently, the monitoring advantage of bank loans relative to public bonds is likely to persist in the presence of an active secondary market for bank debt.

Given the continued incentives (and their abilities as "insiders") of banks to monitor loans they originate, we test a direct implication of the monitoring or informational advantage of bank loans over public bonds prior to a loan default. Specifically, we test whether loan returns Granger cause bond returns and whether bond returns do not Granger cause loan returns prior to a loan default by a borrower. The presence of an active secondary market for bank loans makes it possible to conduct such an empirical test of banks' continuing "specialness."

Our study is the first to investigate the monitoring advantage of loans over bonds prior to a corporate borrower's loan default using Granger causality tests. While a few studies have examined the lead–lag relationship of stocks relative to those of bonds based on Granger causality tests, none have examined the lead–lag relationship of loans relative to those of bonds, largely due to the unavailability (at least until now) of secondary market prices of loans.[2] Our study therefore casts light on this important gap in the literature. Specifically, using a new data set of secondary market daily prices of loans from November 1, 1999 to October 31, 2007, we conduct Granger casuality tests to examine the informational efficiency of the secondary market for loans as compared to that for bonds, prior to a corporate borrower's loan default.

We find evidence consistent with a continuing monitoring advantage of loans over bonds prior to a corporate loan default. Indeed, we find strong evidence that loan returns Granger cause bond returns prior to a firm defaulting on its loans. In contrast, we find no evidence that bond returns Granger cause loan returns prior to the loan default.

The results of our paper have important implications regarding the relative monitoring advantage of loans (and bank lenders) versus bonds (and bond investors), and the benefits of loan monitoring for other financial markets, such as the bond market.

The remainder of the paper is organized as follows. Section 1 briefly describes the growth of the secondary market for bank loans. Section 2 describes our data and sample selection. Section 3 presents our testable hypothesis. Section 4 summarizes our empirical results, and Section 5 concludes.

1. THE GROWTH OF THE SECONDARY MARKET FOR BANK LOANS

The secondary market for loans has grown rapidly during the past decade. The market for loans typically includes two broad categories, the first is the primary or syndicated loan market, in which portions of a loan are placed with a number of banks, often in conjunction with, and as part of, the loan origination process (usually referred to as the sale of participations). The second category is the seasoned or secondary loan sales market in which a bank subsequently sells an existing loan (or part of a loan). We explore the latter category of the loan sales market in this study.

2. The lead–lag relationship of the bond market relative to the stock market has received increasing attention in recent years. For example, Kwan (1996) finds, using daily data, that stock returns lead bond returns, suggesting that stocks may be informationally more efficient than bonds, while Hotchkiss and Ronen (2002) find, using higher-frequency (intraday) data, that the informational efficiency of corporate bonds is similar to that of the underlying stocks. Also, see Angbazo, Mei, and Saunders (1998) for evidence on the sensitivity of credit spreads in the highly leveraged transaction loan market to those of the corporate bond market.

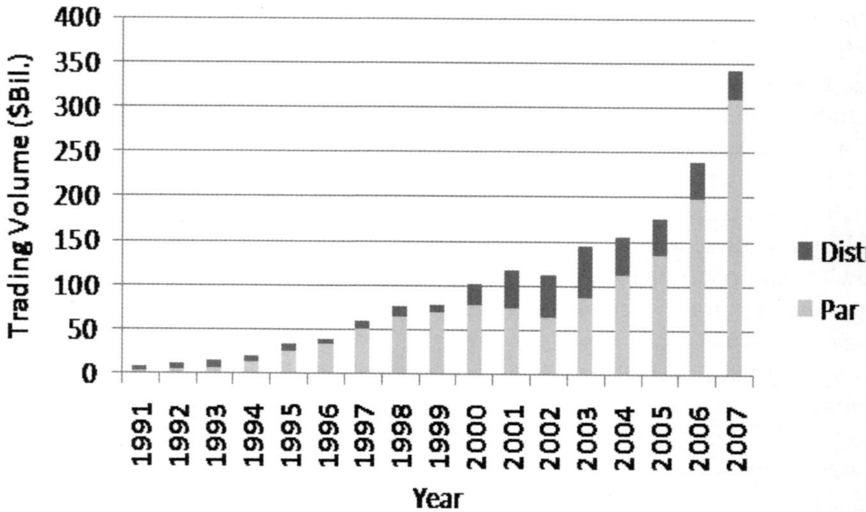

FIG. 1. Secondary Loan Market Volume.
Source: Reuters LPC Traders Survey.

Banks and other financial institutions have sold loans among themselves for over 100 years. Even though this market has existed for many years, it grew slowly until the early 1980s when it entered a period of spectacular growth, largely due to expansion in highly leveraged transaction (HLT) loans to finance leveraged buyouts (LBOs) and mergers and acquisitions (M&As). With the decline in LBOs and M&As in the late 1980s after the stock market crash of 1987, the volume of loan sales fell to approximately $10 billion in 1990. However, since then the volume of loan sales has expanded rapidly, especially as M&A activity picked up again.[3] Figure 1 shows the rate of growth in the secondary market for loans from 1991 to 2007. Note that secondary market loan transactions have exceeded $100 billion a year since 2000.

The secondary loan sales market is sometimes segmented based on the type of investors involved on the "buy side," for example, institutional loan market versus retail loan market. An alternative way of stratifying loan trades in the secondary market is to distinguish between the "par" loans (loans selling at 90% or more of face value) and "distressed" loans (loans selling at below 90% of face value). Figure 1 also shows an increasing proportion of distressed loan sales, reaching approximately 42% of the total loan sales in 2002. However, the proportion of distressed loan sales has come down to more moderate levels post-2002.

3. Specifically M&A activity increased from $190 billion in 1990 to $500 billion in 1995, and to over $1,800 billion in 2000 (Thomson Financial Securities Data Corporation).

2. DATA AND SAMPLE SELECTION

The sample period for our empirical analysis is from November 1, 1999 to October 31, 2007. Our choice of sample period is driven by data considerations. That is, our empirical analysis requires secondary market daily prices of loans, which were not available prior to November 1, 1999. In addition, since the required data were not available from a single source, we use multiple sources of data to construct a data set for our empirical analysis. Furthermore, since these multiple data sources do not have a unique identifier, we manually match using the company name and other identifying variables, such as date. We next describe the construction of our data set from these multiple sources of data.

We start with the database of daily secondary market loan prices. This is a new database from the Loan Syndications and Trading Association (LSTA) and Loan Pricing Corporation (LPC), supplied to over 100 institutions managing over $200 billion in bank loan assets under the name "Secondary Market Pricing Service" (SMPS). This database contains daily bid and ask price quotes aggregated across dealers. Each loan has a minimum of at least two dealer quotes and a maximum of over 30 dealers, including all top loan broker-dealers.[4] These price quotes are obtained on a daily basis by LSTA in the late afternoon from the dealers. The items in this database include a unique loan identification number (LIN); name of the issuer (Company); type of loan, for example, term loan (Facility); date of pricing (Pricing Date); average of bid quotes (Avg Bid); number of bid quotes (Bid Quotes); average of second and third highest bid quote (High Bid Avg); average of ask quotes (Avg Ask); number of ask quotes (Ask Quotes); and average of second and third lowest ask quotes (Low Ask Avg).

For our empirical analysis, we also need daily secondary market bond prices. However, we need the nine-character bond cusip assigned by Standard & Poor's to each bond to obtain daily secondary market bond prices from the data sources mentioned below. We manually search the Fixed Income Securities Database (FISD) using the name of the issuer in the SMPS database to match with the name of the issuer in FISD to extract the relevant nine-character bond cusips.

We use two data sources for bond prices over two nonoverlapping subperiods that together span our entire sample period. The main reason for doing this is an alternative comprehensive database of bond prices, known as "Trade Reporting and Compliance Engine" (TRACE) became available during the later part of the sample period as a result of an improvement in bond market transparency.[5] The first data source for daily bond prices is the *Salomon* (now Citigroup) Yield Book (YB). We extract daily bond

4. Since LSTA and LPC do not make a market in bank loans and are not directly or indirectly involved in the buying or selling of bank loans, the LSTA/LPC mark-to-market pricing service is believed to be independent and objective.

5. The National Association of Securities Dealers (NASD) phased-in the dissemination of bond transaction information through its TRACE initiative—in particular, prices—starting with an initial set of investment grade bonds (about 500) in July 2002. The coverage was expanded to the full universe of bonds (including high yield bonds) in October 2004.

prices from the YB database from November 1, 1999 to June 30, 2002 for all the companies in the SMPS database using their nine-character bond cusips from FISD. The second data source for daily bond prices is the TRACE database. We extract end of day bond prices from TRACE from July 1, 2002 to October 31, 2007 for all the companies in the SMPS database using their nine-character bond cusips from FISD. We use the same data source in computing daily bond returns. For example, bond returns calculated from TRACE start on July 2, 2002 since the first available bond price in TRACE is on July 1, 2002.

Our loan defaults data come from Portfolio Management Data (PMD), a business unit of Standard & Poor's that has been tracking loan defaults in the institutional loan market since 1995. We have confirmed with the data provider that these loan defaults correspond to a missed interest or a principal payment rather than a technical violation of a covenant. We manually match the company names from the loan defaults database with the company names from the SMPS database for our empirical analysis.

Finally, we obtain information on security-specific characteristics (for the purpose of reporting some descriptive statistics of our sample), such as size, maturity, seniority, collateral, and covenants from the Dealscan database of the LPC for loans and from the FISD for bonds. As before, due to the absence of a unique identifier that ties the databases together, we merge these databases with the others by manually matching based on the company name from the SMPS database.

3. TESTABLE HYPOTHESIS

Above, we have argued that banks as "insiders" have continued skills and incentives to monitor their loans to a borrower even in the presence of an active secondary market for bank loans. The resulting monitoring advantage of bank loans relative to public bonds implies that secondary market loan prices will reflect any additional information from such continued bank loan monitoring. In contrast, secondary market bond prices do not reflect such "inside" information simply because bond investors do not have similar inside informational access to a borrowing firm.

It could be argued that bond investors may be able to access secondary market loan prices and thus piggyback on the incremental benefits of bank monitoring. Nevertheless, even if that were to be the case, a bond investor would still effectively lag a loan investor in terms of new information. Consequently, the monitoring advantage of bank loans relative to public bonds leads to the following testable hypothesis:

Secondary market loans are informationally more efficient than secondary market bonds prior to a loan default date.

We empirically examine the above hypothesis in Section 4.1 through Granger-causality tests based on vector autoregression (VAR) models of the daily returns in the secondary market for loans and bonds. Specifically, we analyze whether loan returns Granger cause bond returns and whether bond returns do not Granger cause loan returns prior to a loan default date.

TABLE 1

DESCRIPTIVE STATISTICS

	Loans		Bonds		Difference	
Variable	Mean	*t*-stat	Mean	*t*-stat	Mean	*t*-stat
MATURITY (months)	60.98	30.63***	67.56	18.65***	−6.58	1.59
AMOUNT ($ million)	501.29	14.79***	408.88	21.57***	92.41	2.38**
SENIOR (fraction)	1.00	nm	0.95	56.98***	−0.05	−3.07***
SECURED (fraction)	0.70	20.43***	0.03	2.49**	0.67	18.06***
COVENANT SCCORE (0–4)	1.62	14.11***	2.99	46.63***	−1.37	−10.46***

NOTE: This table presents descriptive statistics of the 176 matched loan-bond pairs (based on the name of the borrower), making it a total of 352 observations. MATURITY stands for the remaining maturity (in months) of the loan or the bond, as on the loan default date of the same company. AMOUNT stands for the amount of the loan or bond issue (in $ millions). SENIOR and SECURED each take a value of one if a loan or a bond is classified likewise and zero otherwise. COVENANT SCORE is the sum of four dummy variables that represent four loan/bond covenants as described in Smith and Warner (1979) and Bagnani et al. (1994), namely, INVCOV = 1 for restrictions on investments, DIVCOV = 1 for restrictions on dividends, FINCOV = 1 for restrictions of financing, and PAYCOV = 1 for covenants modifying payoff to investors. ** and *** stand for statistical significance at the 5% and 1% levels, respectively, using a two-tailed test, and nm refers to "not meaningful."

4. EMPIRICAL RESULTS

Table 1 presents descriptive statistics of matched loan-bond pair data (based on the name of the borrower). Loans typically have a shorter maturity and are larger (in terms of issue size) than bonds. Moreover, as is well known, loans are more senior and are more secured than bonds.[6]

We compute a daily loan return based on the midprice quote of a loan, namely, the average of the bid and ask price of a loan in the loan price data set.[7] That is, a one-day loan return is computed as today's midprice divided by yesterday's midprice of a loan minus one. The daily bond returns are computed based on the prices of a bond in the bond price data set in an analogous manner. During the July 2002–October 2007 sample period, where we use the TRACE bond transaction data, we compute daily returns based on the last recorded price on any particular day.

4.1 Informational Efficiency of Loans versus Bonds

We investigate the informational efficiency of loans versus bonds using Granger causality tests (see Granger 1969 and Sims 1972 for details). Empirically, we follow the Hotchkiss and Ronen (2002) methodology, by conducting Granger causality tests based on VAR models for the daily returns in the secondary market for loans and bonds. Specifically, we equally weight secondary market loan returns and secondary market bond returns of matched loan-bond pairs (based on the name of the borrower),

6. The relevance of collateral in debt financing is well established in the literature. For example, Berger and Udell (1990, 1995) document that collateral plays an important role in more than two-thirds of commercial and industrial loans in the United States. John, Lynch, and Puri (2003) study how collateral affects bond yields. Also, see Dahiya, Saunders, and Srinivasan (2003) for more evidence on the value of monitoring to a borrower.

7. We calculate returns based on the midprice to control for any bid–ask "bounce." See, for example, Stoll (2000) and Hasbrouck (1988) for more details.

and examine whether secondary market loan returns Granger cause secondary market bond returns or whether secondary market bond returns Granger cause secondary market loan returns during the preloan default period, that is, the time period leading up to a loan default, such as [−244, −11], where day 0 refers to a loan default date. For robustness, we consider several alternative preloan default periods, such as [−244, −6], [−244, −1], [−122, −11], [−61, −11], and find that our results (discussed later in this section) are invariant to the exact definition of the preloan default period.

To test the null, that secondary market loan returns do not Granger cause secondary market bond returns, following Hotchkiss and Ronen (2002), we rely on a bivariate VAR model (equation (1)), and estimate by ordinary least squares (OLS):

$$RB_t = c_1 + \sum_{i=1}^{j} a_{1,i} RB_{t-i} + \sum_{i=1}^{j} b_{1,i} RL_{t-i} + \nu_{1,t}. \quad (1)$$

Similarly, to test the null that secondary market bond returns do not Granger cause secondary market loan returns, we rely on a similar bivariate VAR model (equation (2)):

$$RL_t = c_2 + \sum_{i=1}^{j} a_{2,i} RL_{t-i} + \sum_{i=1}^{j} b_{2,i} RB_{t-i} + \nu_{2,t}, \quad (2)$$

where RB_t are the equally weighted secondary market bond returns, RL_t are the equally weighted secondary market loan returns, as and bs are OLS coefficient estimates, cs are the regression constants, ν_ts are the disturbance terms, and j is the lag length. We then conduct F-tests of the null hypothesis that secondary market loan returns do not Granger cause secondary market bond returns using equation (3), and of the null hypothesis that secondary market bond returns do not Granger cause secondary market loan returns using equation (4):

$$H_0 : b_{1,i} = 0, \forall i, \quad (3)$$

$$H_0 : b_{2,i} = 0, \forall i. \quad (4)$$

Following Hamilton (1994) we test equations (3) and (4) using lag lengths from 1 to 10 days.[8] We do not make any assumption as to which of these lag lengths is optimal, and draw inferences based on the overall evidence, rather than based on a specific lag length.

Table 2 summarizes the results of the Granger causality tests prior to a loan default. We find strong evidence that secondary market loan returns Granger cause secondary

8. For a similar approach, see Kwan (1996) who uses a lag length of 1 in analyzing the informational efficiency of stocks versus bonds. Our approach uses a range of lags from 1 to 10, and is focused on the informational efficiency of loans versus bonds.

TABLE 2

GRANGER CAUSALITY TESTS USING A BIVARIATE VAR

Panel A. Expanded versions of the preloan default period

	Preloan default period [−244, −11]		Preloan default period [−244, −6]		Preloan default period [−244, −1]	
Null hyp.	Loan returns do not Granger cause bond returns	Bond returns do not Granger cause loan returns	Loan returns do not Granger cause bond returns	Bond returns do not Granger cause loan returns	Loan returns do not Granger cause bond returns	Bond returns do not Granger cause loan returns
Lags	*F*-statistic	*F*-statistic	*F*-statistic	*F*-statistic	*F*-statistic	*F*-statistic
1	5.17**	0.28	4.57**	0.28	6.46**	0.56
2	4.97***	0.13	3.81**	0.18	3.96**	0.27
3	4.47***	0.13	3.02**	0.17	3.07**	0.23
4	3.46***	0.32	2.33*	0.37	2.33*	0.29
5	3.15***	0.26	2.04*	0.30	1.99*	0.23
6	2.69**	0.47	1.82*	0.46	1.69	0.46
7	2.58**	0.50	1.93*	0.45	1.78*	0.47
8	2.39**	0.80	1.75*	0.86	1.60	0.84
9	2.12**	0.85	1.55	0.92	1.41	0.93
10	1.95**	0.81	1.38	0.85	1.42	0.85

Panel B. Reduced versions of the preloan default period

	Preloan default period [−244, −11]		Preloan default period [−121, −11]		Preloan default period [−61, −11]	
Null hyp.	Loan returns do not Granger cause bond returns	Bond returns do not Granger cause loan returns	Loan returns do not Granger cause bond returns	Bond returns do not Granger cause loan returns	Loan returns do not Granger cause bond returns	Bond returns do not Granger cause loan returns
Lags	*F*-statistic	*F*-statistic	*F*-statistic	*F*-statistic	*F*-statistic	*F*-statistic
1	5.17**	0.28	8.10***	6.16**	4.93**	3.23*
2	4.97***	0.13	4.52**	3.30**	3.69**	1.98
3	4.47***	0.13	3.68**	2.03	2.93*	1.52
4	3.46***	0.32	4.31***	1.66	3.51**	1.30
5	3.15***	0.26	3.76***	1.17	2.56**	0.99
6	2.69**	0.47	3.11***	1.16	2.04*	1.35
7	2.58**	0.50	2.65**	1.20	1.72	1.17
8	2.39**	0.80	2.52**	1.27	1.91*	0.96
9	2.12**	0.85	2.36**	1.25	1.84*	0.93
10	1.95**	0.81	2.45**	1.63	2.70**	1.61

NOTE: This table summarizes the results of Granger causality tests. Following Hotchkiss and Ronen (2002), we use equally weighted loan returns and bond returns of 176 matched loan-bond pairs (based on the name of the borrower) prior to a loan default date of the same company. Specifically, we conduct an F-test of the null hypothesis that the loan returns do not Granger cause the bond returns as shown in equation (3). Similarly, we also conduct an F-test of the null hypothesis that the bond returns do not Granger cause the loan returns as shown in equation (4). In Panel A, we present results separately for expanded versions of the preloan default period, namely, [−244, −11], [−244, −6] and [−244, −1], and in Panel B, we present results separately for the reduced versions of the preloan default period, namely, [−244, −11], [−121, −11] and [−61, −11], where day 0 refers to the loan default date. *, **, and *** stand for statistical significance of the reported F-statistic (in rejecting the null hypothesis of no Granger causality) at the 10%, 5%, and 1% levels, respectively.

market bond returns, independent of the number of lags. For example, the F-statistic for the null hypothesis that daily secondary market loan returns have no explanatory power for the daily secondary market bond returns during the [−244, −11] preloan default period (see equation (3)) in Panel A of Table 2 is 4.97 at a lag length of 2 and 3.15 at a lag length of 5; both imply that the null hypothesis in equation (3) is rejected at the 1% level. This evidence suggests that the secondary market loan returns Granger cause secondary market bond returns prior to a loan default date.

In contrast, we find no evidence that secondary market bond returns Granger cause secondary market loan returns. For example, the F-statistic for the null hypothesis that daily bond returns have no explanatory power for loan returns during the $[-244, -11]$ preloan default period (see equation (4)) in Panel A of Table 2 is 0.13 at a lag length of 2 and 0.26 at a lag length of 5; both imply that the null hypothesis in equation (4) cannot be rejected at any reasonable level of significance. This evidence suggests that secondary market bond returns do not Granger cause secondary market loan returns prior to a loan default date.

In summary, we find strong evidence supporting the informational efficiency hypothesis specified in Section 3. That is, consistent with a monitoring advantage of loans over bonds, we find evidence that secondary market loan returns Granger cause secondary market bond returns, whereas secondary market bond returns do not Granger cause secondary market loan returns prior to a loan default. We next examine the robustness of this finding to different definitions of the preloan default period, and in the extent to which this finding is influenced by sample companies with multiple loans or bonds.

Preloan default period. Our result that prior to a loan default, secondary market loan returns Granger cause secondary market bond returns whereas secondary market bond returns do not Granger cause secondary market loan returns, is based on a preloan default period defined as $[-244, -11]$, where day 0 refers to a loan default date. We now examine whether this result changes if we change the definition of the preloan default period.

First, we examine whether we obtain the same result if we expand the length of the preloan default period from $[-244, -11]$ to $[-244, -6]$ and $[-244, -1]$. Panel A of Table 2 presents, in addition to the results corresponding to $[-244, -11]$, the results for the expanded versions of the preloan default period (i.e., $[-244, -6]$ and $[-244, -1]$)). The results for the $[-244, -6]$ and $[-244, -1]$ periods are qualitatively similar to that of the $[-244, -11]$ period.

Second, we examine whether we obtain the same result if we reduce the length of the preloan default period from $[-244, -11]$ to $[-121, -11]$ and $[-61, -11]$. Panel B of Table 2 presents the results for the reduced versions of the preloan default period (i.e., $[-121, -11]$ and $[-61, -11]$) for comparison with that of $[-244, -11]$. Once again, the results are qualitatively unchanged. In particular, while loan returns Granger cause bond returns at almost all lag lengths, bond returns do not Granger cause loan returns, with the exception of the first two lags. Hence, for the remainder of the analysis, we focus only on the expanded versions of the preloan default period, namely, $[-244, -11]$, $[-244, -6]$, and $[-244, -1]$.

Multiple loans or bonds for the same company. Given that some companies in our sample have multiple loans or bonds, equally weighting returns in our Granger causality tests implicitly results in a proportionately larger weight for such companies. To that extent, one could argue that our major result, that prior to a loan default,

TABLE 3

GRANGER CAUSALITY TESTS USING A BIVARIATE VAR (ACCOUNTS FOR MULTIPLE LOANS OR BONDS OF THE SAME BORROWER)

	Preloan default period [−244, −11]		Preloan default period [−244, −6]		Preloan default period [−244, −1]	
Null hyp.	Loan returns do not Granger cause bond returns	Bond returns do not Granger cause loan returns	Loan returns do not Granger cause bond returns	Bond returns do not Granger cause loan returns	Loan returns do not Granger cause bond returns	Bond returns do not Granger cause loan returns
Lags	F-statistic	F-statistic	F-statistic	F-statistic	F-statistic	F-statistic
1	0.27	0.26	0.16	0.04	1.37	0.12
2	0.23	2.79*	0.37	2.92*	1.97	1.61
3	1.42	1.96	0.52	2.08	2.03	1.16
4	1.71	1.46	1.81	1.54	3.61***	0.85
5	2.86**	1.74	2.58**	1.78	3.78***	1.93*
6	2.34**	1.52	2.27**	1.56	3.12***	2.01*
7	2.07**	1.31	1.97*	1.34	2.72***	1.78*
8	1.80*	1.22	1.75*	1.27	2.44**	1.68
9	1.78*	1.23	1.74*	1.24	2.28**	1.59
10	2.40**	1.16	2.21**	1.19	2.67***	1.52

NOTE: This table summarizes the results of Granger causality tests. Following Hotchkiss and Ronen (2002), we use equally weighted loan returns and bond returns of 176 matched loan-bond pairs (based on the name of the borrower) prior to a loan default date of the same company. If a company has multiple loan-bond pairs, we choose the loan-bond pair that has the maximum number of observations among all the loan-bond pairs for the same company in the equal weighting across companies, thus ensuring that every company receives the same weight in constructing the portfolio returns. Specifically, we conduct an F-test of the null hypothesis that the loan returns do not Granger cause the bond returns as shown in equation (3). Similarly, we also conduct an F-test of the null hypothesis that the bond returns do not Granger cause the loan returns as shown in equation (4). We present results separately for the expanded versions of the preloan default period, namely [−244, −11], [−244, −6], and [−244, −1], where day 0 refers to the loan default date. *, **, and *** stand for statistical significance of the reported F-statistic (in rejecting the null hypothesis of no Granger causality) at the 10%, 5%, and 1% levels, respectively.

secondary market loan returns Granger cause secondary market bond returns, whereas secondary market bond returns do not Granger cause secondary market loan returns, may be disproportionately driven by companies with multiple loans or bonds.

To address whether our result is susceptible to the above-mentioned bias, we modify our Granger causality analysis by selecting a single loan-bond pair for each company before we equally weight the returns. Specifically, for companies with multiple loan-bond pairs, we select the loan-bond pair that has the most number of total (i.e., bond plus loan) return observations during the preloan default period. We then equally weight the returns as before. Thus, our modified analysis ensures that each company gets an equal weight in the Granger causality analysis, independent of whether or not it has multiple loans or bonds that are traded.

We modify our analysis as described above and rerun the regression analysis for the expanded versions of the preloan default period, namely, [−244, −11], [−244, −6], and [−244, −1] of Table 2. The results of the modified analysis are presented in Table 3. The results are once again qualitatively similar to those in Table 2. That is, prior to a loan default, there is a substantial amount of evidence of loan returns Granger causing bond returns, whereas there is very little evidence of bond returns Granger causing loan returns.

Based on the above evidence, we conclude that the secondary loan market is informationally more efficient than the secondary bond market prior to a loan default date and that this conclusion is independent of the specific definition of the preloan default period and is not entirely driven by sample companies that have multiple loans or bonds.

5. CONCLUSIONS

Using a new data set of secondary market prices of corporate loans, we find the secondary loan market to be informationally more efficient than the secondary bond market prior to a loan default. Specifically, we find that secondary market loan returns Granger cause secondary market bond returns prior to a loan default. In contrast, secondary market bond returns do not Granger cause secondary market loan returns prior to a loan default.

Overall, our results have important implications regarding the continuing specialness of banks as monitors and the benefits of loan monitoring for other financial markets, such as the bond market.

LITERATURE CITED

Angbazo, Lazarus A., Jianping Mei, and Anthony Saunders. (1998) "Credit Spreads in the Market for Highly Leveraged Transaction Loans." *Journal of Banking and Finance,* 22, 1249–82.

Bagnani, Elizabeth S., Nikolaos T. Milonas, Anthony Saunders, and Nickolaos G. Travlos. (1994) "Managers, Owners, and the Pricing of Risky Debt: An Empirical Analysis." *Journal of Finance,* 49, 453–77.

Berger, Allen N., and Gregory F. Udell. (1990) "Collateral, Loan Quality, and Bank Risk." *Journal of Monetary Economics,* 25, 21–42.

Berger, Allen N., and Gregory F. Udell. (1995) "Relationship Lending and Lines of Credit in Small Firm Finance." *Journal of Business,* 68, 351–81.

Dahiya, Sandeep, Anthony Saunders, and Anand Srinivasan. (2003) "Financial Distress and Bank Lending Relationships." *Journal of Finance,* 58, 375–99.

Diamond, Douglas W. (1984) "Financial Intermediation and Delegated Monitoring." *Review of Economic Studies,* 51, 393–414.

Drucker, Steven, and Manju Puri. (2009) "On Loan Sales, Loan Contracting, and Lending Relationships." *Review of Financial Studies,* 22, 2835–72.

Fama, Eugene F. (1985) "What's Different about Banks?" *Journal of Monetary Economics,* 15, 29–39.

Gorton, Gary, and George G. Pennacchi. (1995) "Banks and Loan Sales: Marketing Nonmarketable Assets." *Journal of Monetary Economics,* 35, 389–411.

Granger, Clive W. J. (1969) "Investigating Causal Relations by Econometric Models and Cross-Spectral Methods." *Econometrica,* 37, 424–38.

Hamilton, James D. (1994) *Time Series Analysis.* Princeton, NJ: Princeton University Press.

Hasbrouck, Joel. (1988) "Trades, Quotes, Inventories, and Information." *Journal of Financial Economics,* 22, 229–52.

Hotchkiss, Edith S., and Tavy Ronen. (2002) "The Informational Efficiency of the Corporate Bond Market: An Intraday Analysis." *Review of Financial Studies,* 15, 1325–54.

John, Kose, Anthony W. Lynch, and Manju Puri. (2003) "Credit Ratings, Collateral, and Loan Characteristics: Implications for Yield." *Journal of Business,* 76, 371–409.

Kroszner, Randall S., and Philip E. Strahan. (2001) "Throwing Good Money after Bad? Board Connections and Conflicts in Bank Lending." NBER Working Paper No. 8694.

Kwan, Simon H. (1996) "Firm-specific Information and Correlation between Individual Stocks and Bonds." *Journal of Financial Economics,* 40, 63–80.

Ramakrishnan, Ram T. S., and Anjan V. Thakor. (1984) "Information Reliability and a Theory of Financial Intermediation." *Review of Economic Studies,* 51, 415–32.

Saunders, Anthony, and Marcia M. Cornett. (2008) *Financial Institutions Management: A Risk Management Approach,* 6th ed. New York, NY: McGraw-Hill Publishers.

Sims, Christopher A. (1972) "Money, Income and Causality." *American Economic Review,* 62, 540–52.

Smith, Clifford W., and Jerold B. Warner. (1979) "On Financial Contracting: An Analysis of Bond Covenants." *Journal of Financial Economics,* 7, 117–61.

Stoll, Hans R. (2000) "Friction." *Journal of Finance,* 55, 1479–514.

Journal of Monetary Economics 25 (1990) 289–304. North-Holland

ADDITIONS TO BANK LOAN-LOSS RESERVES
Good News or Bad News?*

Theoharry GRAMMATIKOS

Graduate School of Business, University of Wisconsin, Madison, WI 57306, USA

Anthony SAUNDERS

Stern School of Business, New York University, New York, NY 10006, USA

Received January 1989, final version received February 1990

This paper examines the effects of Citicorp's and succeeding banks' loan-loss reserve announcements in 1987. It was found that while the average effect on bank stock return portfolios was weak, the effect on individual bank returns was heterogeneous. Tests were undertaken to determine which bank-specific variables explained the latter result. Two significant variables were the size of a banks' LDC debt exposure and its position in LDC rescheduling committees.

1. Introduction

Since the Mexican and Brazilian debt payment suspensions of August–September 1982, the major U.S. banks have been placed in the dilemma of whether to refinance Less Developed Countries' (LDC) debt through rescheduling of old loans and providing new money packages or to write off some of these loans as losses. Until 1987, the primary approach to meeting the LDC debt problem was through new money and rescheduling. However, following the Brazilian suspension of interest payments in February 1987, major U.S. banks appeared to change their strategy. Beginning with Citicorp in May 1987, a number of banks announced significant additions to their loan-loss reserves (LLR) in preparation to charging off some of this debt. In this paper, we analyze the information content of these LLR additions.[1] Specifically, the study's objectives are to determine (i) the average stock return

*Anthony Saunders would like to acknowledge financial support from a Bank and Financial Analysts Association Fellowship and a Yamaichi Senior Research Fellowship. We would also like to thank an anonymous referee, Yakov Amihud, George Benston, Mitch Berlin, George Kaufman, Rich Lang, Ithzak Swary, Rex Thompson, and Greg Udell for their helpful comments on earlier versions of this paper, and Bruce Johnson for providing the release times of banks' announcements on the Dow Jones News Broad Tape.

[1] It should be noted that the findings of this study are specific to the LLR additions in response to the Brazilian interest suspension. They may not be generalizable to LLR additions in other quarters or years.

responses of U.S. banks to the LLR-related announcements and (ii) to explain the observed cross-sectional variation in return responses by banks to their own and Citicorp's LLR addition announcements.

Two separate events are analyzed. The first is the announcement by Citicorp that it was adding $3 billion to its loan-loss reserve to meet expected future charge-offs on its LDC debt. The second set of events is the succeeding announcements by 34 other banks of their own LDC-debt-related loan-loss reserve additions. In section 2, the nature of the accounting, regulatory, and tax rules governing the size and composition of bank LLRs are very briefly described. Section 3 discusses some theoretical reasons why U.S. banks' LLR additions in 1987 may have either positive or negative implications for stockholder returns. The data and methodology for testing (i) the average announcement effects of these events and (ii) the cross-sectional variation of these effects are described in section 4. The results are presented in section 5 and section 6 is a conclusion.

2. The nature of bank loan-loss reserves

U.S. banks use a reserve accounting method to meet expected future charge-offs. Stockholder funds are moved into a loan-loss reserve which is then used to charge off loans over future periods [see Buynak (1987)].

Prior to the Tax Reform Act (TRA) of 1986, banks received a favorable tax break by adding funds to their LLR even if these reserve additions were not immediately matched by charge-offs of bad loans. Since 1987, however, additions to the LLR can only be expensed in the same year when the loan is actually charged off. Thus, banks now face a time value opportunity loss by having to delay the expensing (and reduction in taxes) to a period when the loan is actually charged off. Moreover, the TRA reduced the corporate tax rate from 46% to 34%.[2] In the post-1986 tax environment, therefore, additions to LLRs have potentially less favorable tax implications compared to the pre-1986 situation.

Finally, the LLR is a key component of bank capital for the purpose of calculating a bank's capital adequacy ratio.[3] In general, in assessing capital adequacy, bank examiners expect a bank to charge off 100% of its bad loans and 50% of its doubtful loans. This is usually done by examiners deducting these expected losses from the bank's LLR and recalculating its primary capital to assets ratio net of the required charge-offs. If a bank's capital to assets ratio is then judged to be too low (e.g., vis-a-vis the 5.5% norm), the

[2]However, the reduction in the nominal rate did not necessarily reduce banks' effective tax rates. Indeed, bank effective tax rates seem to have been *much* lower than statutory tax rates. For example, Tax Analysts (1987) report an average effective tax rate of 12.33% for the banks in our sample.

[3]The other major components of primary capital are retained earnings and common stock.

bank is usually required to infuse additional capital and add to reserves in the future. If the bank fails to do this, various regulatory actions can follow, including, in the extreme case, cease and desist orders or even closure.

3. Theoretical considerations

In this section it is argued that any given unexpected additions to a bank's LLR for LDC loans will be valued differently by equity holders due to differences in bank capital adequacy positions, tax positions, LDC loan exposure positions, and bargaining positions. Thus LLR additions should have heterogeneous effects across banks.

3.1. Regulatory cost effect

If investors believe that by adding to LLR today a bank will charge off more loans in the future, LLR additions may be perceived as implying future regulatory costs or burdens on the bank. Future charge-offs (COs) will be expected to lower the bank's future capital ratio and raise regulatory costs in the form of increased surveillance by regulators and/or costs of raising additional equity to comply with regulatory imposed minimum capital standards. More specifically, the lower a bank's existing capital ratio, the higher the expected future regulatory costs that should be expected from a given LLR addition.

3.2. Tax effect

By adding to LLRs, investors may anticipate current and future charge-offs and tax breaks as the charge-offs are expensed. For tax purposes, COs can be used to offset current taxable income or carried back three years to past income and forward years to future income. Therefore, a bank's ability to enjoy tax breaks depends on its current, past, and expected future taxable income and its tax rate. In general, the lower its current and expected taxable income and the lower its effective tax rate, the weaker the tax effect.

3.3. Information effects

Banks are required to establish a LLR based on their actuarially fair judgments as to the probability of future loans COs. As stated above, this behavior is monitored by other 'insiders' such as regulators and bank examiners. Outside investors, such as stockholders, base their judgments as to the *optimal* size of a bank's LLR on all publicly available information. This may include all public reports as well as prices quoted in the secondary market for different countries' debt. However, bank examiners' reports are strictly available to insiders only. If insiders, such as managers and bank examiners, have better information than outsiders, an unexpected addition to a LLR may provide new signals to outside investors regarding the true value of a bank's loan portfolio.

One can readily conceive of an information framework in which LLR additions might be taken as *bad* news by investors and another in which LLR additions may be taken as *good* news. First, consider a situation in which the only *inside* (private) information that bank managers possess is over the quality of their bank's LDC loans. In this framework, any bank that unexpectedly raises loan-loss reserves is sending a *bad* information signal to outside investors in the market. However, assume instead that the bank holds two types of assets, LDC loans and 'other loans', and bank managers have private information about the high quality and expected earnings on investing more in the 'other loan' portfolio (i.e., it has many attractive loan opportunities). Freeing the bank portfolio from existing bad LDC loan investments and any new money commitments by adding to LLRs may be perceived by outsiders as a signal that the bank is reorienting its balance sheet towards these good other loans, thereby generating more than compensating returns for the bank in the future. Thus, an LLR addition against bad LDC loans may be interpreted by outsiders as a good signal regarding the *future* prospects of the bank. In this framework, the better the privately known future investment opportunities available to 'other loans', the larger will be the optimal amount of LLR additions the bank reports today.

3.4. Bargaining power effect

By making unexpectedly large additions to its LLR, a bank may be announcing its intention to change its bargaining strategy. Rather than meeting LDC payment difficulties with new money packages that either extend or increase its exposure, adding to the bank's LLR explicitly acknowledges an increased probability of borrower default. That is, it weakens the power of the LDC borrower to threaten default in future debt rescheduling negotiations. For smaller banks, LLR additions may be a response to a change in the bargaining strategies of large banks.

It has been noted by James (1988) and Krugman (1987) that a bargaining power effect would be particularly important for the *large* U.S. banks that make up the core of 'old' LDC lending syndicates and that provided most the the 'new money' loans to help the LDCs maintain their interest and/or principal payments on old loans [see also the *Wall Street Journal* (WSJ) 5/20/87]. Before the new bargaining strategy, small fringe banks often had a *free ride* enjoying lower probability of default on old loans as a result of the new money LDC loans provided by the big banks. By adding to LLRs, the probability of default faced by large banks is increased. However, this may be offset by savings in new money loans. Small banks, in contrast, simply find that an increase in the probability of default has occurred with no savings in new money if they were not participating in new money programs. This suggests a heterogeneous bargaining power effect which may benefit large or major bargainer banks but not necessarily small or fringe banks.

4. Data and methodology

To examine the effects of the U.S. banks' LLR additions on stockholder wealth, we analyze the following events triggered by the Brazilian interest suspension on 2/20/87. The first event is the Citicorp announcement of 5/20/87, adding $3 billion to its LLR against its LDC debt exposure. As Huizinga (1989) argues, Citicorp's announcement may have created a new *expected* reserve norm of 25% of LDC debt exposure for other LDC debt exposed banks (see also WSJ 5/20/87 and 5/28/87). In addition, it may have indicated a new or different bargaining strategy towards accepting losses on old loans rather than making more new money loans to keep interest payments current. The second set of events are 34 individual bank announcements of *actual* LLR additions following Citicorp's announcement and ending with J.P. Morgan's addition on 7/9/87. To the extent that actual announced additions deviated from expected additions (i.e., if the new levels were unexpected), an additional stockholder response might be expected for these banks.

It is important to note that the period 5/20/87 to 7/9/87 does not contain any actual first-quarter earnings announcements by those banks adding to LLRs nor, with the exception of J.P. Morgan, any second-quarter earnings announcements. However, along with the LLR announcements, there were also managerial forecasts of second-quarter earnings. Later, we attempt to disentangle the individual bank LLR announcement from the earnings forecast announcement effects. The 35 reserve adding banks are shown in the appendix. The sample includes 130 banks trading on the New York Stock Exchange (NYSE), the American Stock Exchange (AMEX), and the Over the Counter (OTC) markets whose returns are available in the CRSP tapes. The sample contains 256 daily return observations for each bank over the period 10/1/86 to 10/5/87. This period is sufficiently long to cover the events analyzed and to generate market model estimates.

The *first* set of tests examines the *average* return effects of the LLR-related announcements on the returns of different *portfolios* of bank stocks. Specifically, the 130 banks were placed into three equally-weighted nonoverlapping portfolios: (i) 11 money center banks,[4] (ii) 46 other banks with LDC debt

[4]The Money Center banks are those defined by *Salomon Brothers Bank Stock Research*. These banks are Bank of New York, Bankers Trust, Chemical, Chase Manhattan, Irving Bank, Citicorp, J.P. Morgan, Manufacturers Hanover, Horizon Bankcorp, Bank America, First Chicago. It might be noted that two of these banks did not add to their LLRs over our period of study (Irving Bank and Horizon Bankcorp).

exposure, and (iii) 73 banks *without* LDC exposure as a control group. In addition, a fourth equally-weighted portfolio was constructed consisting of the 34 banks that added to their LLR following Citicorp's announcement.

The *second* set of tests looks at individual bank return reactions to LLR announcements. As noted in section 3, the information, regulatory cost, tax, and bargaining effects are probably heterogeneous across banks and these differential effects are likely to be confounded when analyzing returns on equally-weighted portfolios. The effects of these announcements are examined within the multivariate regression framework used by Binder (1985) and Saunders and Smirlock (1987) among others. This approach allows one to discriminate for different cross-sectional announcement effects across banks, while allowing for contemporaneous correlations among individual bank returns. Moreover, it allows for the evaluation of many events (announcements) over a period of time.

The basic multivariate regression model takes the following form:

$$\begin{aligned} R_{1t} &= b_{10} + b_{11}R_{mt} + b'_{11}R_{mt-1} + \Phi_{10}D_0 + \Phi_{11}D_1 + \Phi_{12}D_{12} + \varepsilon_{1t}, \\ &\vdots \\ R_{nt} &= b_{n0} + b_{n1}R_{mt} + b'_{n1}R_{mt-1} + \Phi_{n0}D_0 + \Phi_{n1}D_1 + \Phi_{n2}D_{n2} + \varepsilon_{nt}, \end{aligned} \tag{1}$$

where

R_{jt} = return of bank (or bank portfolio) j ($j = 1, \ldots, n$) on day t ($t = 1, 2, \ldots, 256$),
R_{mt} = return on the equally-weighted market index on day t,
R_{mt-1} = return on the equally-weighted market index on day $t-1$,
b_{j1} = the beta coefficient,
b'_{j1} = the lagged beta coefficient used to correct for nonsynchronous trading problems [see Scholes and Williams (1977)],
D_0 = 1 on the announcement of the Brazilian Interest Suspension (2/20/87) and the following day (2/21/87), = 0 otherwise,
D_1 = 1 on the announcement of Citicorp's LLR addition (5/20/87), = 0 otherwise,
D_{j2} = 1 on the announcement of bank j's LLR addition (see appendix), = 0 otherwise,

It should be noted that if the individual bank announcement appeared in the Dow Jones News Service after the close of trading for the day, a one-day announcement dummy is used for the following day (which is also the day of announcement in the WSJ). If the announcement was made before the close of the day's trading, a two-day announcement dummy is used (i.e., the day of the Dow Jones release and the following day which is also the WSJ announcement day). The appendix shows whether a one- or a two-day announcement dummy is used in each case.

The *third* set of tests seeks to disentangle the underlying reasons behind banks' different price reactions to Citicorp's announcement as well as to banks' own (noncontemporaneous) LLR addition announcements. Following the discussion in section 3, four independent variables are used to explain differential reactions to Citicorp's announcement across banks: the bank's primary capital to assets ratio as a proxy of the regulatory cost effect, the proportion of its LDC loans to total assets as a proxy of the information signalling effect,[5] its effective tax rate as a proxy of the tax effect, and finally, a size variable based on total assets as a proxy of the bargaining power. Further, as an alternative proxy for the bargaining power effect, a dummy variable is also used for those banks that have been the lead or major bargainers in recent LDC debt rescheduling negotiations. The list of banks leading rescheduling committees for LDC debt reschedulings was obtained from the credit department of J.P. Morgan (see table 1). The variable $DUMMY_j$ is set equal to the number of times a bank is identified as leading a rescheduling committee. The effective tax rates for 1986 were obtained from *Tax Analysts* (1987).[6] Since tax rates were available for only 65 banks, the cross-sectional tests are limited to those banks. All financial statement variables were obtained from bank annual reports and 10-Ks as of 12/31/86. The following cross-sectional relationship is hypothesized for Citicorp's announcement (the predicted signs are shown in brackets):

$$\hat{\Phi}_{j1} = \beta_0 + \underset{[+,-]}{\beta_1(EXP_j)} + \underset{[+]}{\beta_2(CRATIO_j)} + \underset{[+]}{\beta_3(T_j)}$$

$$+ \underset{[+]}{\beta_4 \begin{pmatrix} DUMMY_j \\ \text{or} \\ SIZE_j \end{pmatrix}} + u_j, \tag{2}$$

where

EXP_j = LDC loans/total assets (as of 12/31/86),
$CRATIO_j$ = primary capital/total assets (as of 12/31/86),
T_j = effective tax rate (as of 1986),
$SIZE_j$ = total assets (as of 12/31/86),
$DUMMY_j$ = number of rescheduling committees a bank leads.

[5]Following James (1988) LDC debt exposure includes loans to Argentina, Brazil, Chile, Columbia, Mexico, Philippines, and Venezuela.

[6]To estimate effective tax rates, Tax Analysts make various adjustments to both the reported tax expense and pre-tax income. For example, state income taxes, extraordinary gains/losses, and gains/losses from minority interests are excluded from income. The tax expense is adjusted for both permanent items (such as tax-exempt income, investment credit, etc.) and quasi-permanent items (such as accelerated depreciation, leasing transactions, etc.). For more detailed information see Tax Analysts (1987, pp. 3–12).

Table 1

Banks leading rescheduling committees for LDC debt.[a]

Bank	Countries	*DUMMY*
Citicorp	Brazil, Mexico, Argentina, Peru, Uruguay	5
Chase Manhattan	Venezuela, Yugoslavia	2
Manufacturers Hanover	Chile, Philippines	2
Bank America	Costa Rica, Bolivia	2
Chemical	Columbia	1
Bankers Trust	Panama (leading lender)	1
Lloyds[b]	Ecuador	na
Bank of Nova Scotia[b]	Jamaica	na
Societe Generale and BNP[b]	Paraguay (leading lenders)	na

[a]*Source:* Credit department of J.P. Morgan.
[b]These non-U.S. banks are not in the sample used in this study.

The traditional approach utilizes a cross-sectional regression of eq. (2) to draw inferences about the relation between abnormal returns and the hypothesized effects. However this approach may lead to invalid inferences if there is cross-sectional correlation and heteroscedasticity in the bank return processes from which the abnormal returns are estimated. Sefcik and Thompson (1986) describe an alternative approach that permits valid inferences about cross-sectional regression parameters [see also Schipper, Thompson, and Weil (1987)].

For Citicorp's announcement, this procedure involves two steps. First, four portfolios of banks are constructed with weights such that each portfolio loads on *only one* of the four proxy variables and has a *zero* net value for the other three proxy variables. For example, the first portfolio identifies the LDC exposure with a total portfolio value of unity, while the other three portfolios have zero LDC exposure (i.e., the weights sum to zero). The matrix of weights, X, used to form the four orthogonal portfolios is

$$X = (F'F)^{-1}F', \tag{3}$$

where

X = a 4×65 matrix of portfolio weights,
F = a 65×4 matrix of individual bank variables such that $F_j = (EXP_j, CRATIO_j, SIZE_j, T_j)$.

Second, the portfolio returns are regressed on the market return and event dummy variables as in model (1), excluding the individual bank announcements, D_{j2}. This method accounts fully for cross-sectional disturbance heteroscedasticity and interdependence. Moreover, since by design the portfolios are orthogonal to each other, any multicollinearity problems among the independent variables are eliminated.

We are also interested in the differential reaction of individual bank returns to their own LLR addition announcement (i.e., those that followed Citicorp's announcement). In this case, because these 34 individual announcements are not contemporaneous, we do not employ the Sefcik and Thompson (1986) methodology. With noncontemporaneous announcements, cross-sectional regressions can provide valid inferences if disturbances do not violate the standard OLS assumptions.[7]

In all cases where banks announced their actual LLR addition they also provided earnings forecasts for the second quarter. Such managerial forecasts, if different from analysts' expectations, may also have provided unexpected news to the market and have affected stock prices. Consequently, to analyze any additional *unexpected* information due to the actual LLR announcement by individual banks (relative to the 'norm' expected or established by the Citicorp announcement) as well as any unexpected earnings effect, we ran the following cross-sectional regression:

$$\hat{\Phi}_{j2} = \beta_0 + \beta_1(EXP_j) + \beta_2(CRATIO_j) + \beta_3(T_j) + \beta_4(SIZE_j) + \beta_5(ULLR_j) + \beta_6(UE_j) + u_j, \qquad j=1,\dots,34. \tag{4}$$

where

$$ULLR_j = \frac{LLR - 0.25\ (\text{Bank } j\text{'s LDC loans})}{\text{Market value of equity}},$$

$$UE_j = \frac{\text{Management's forecasted earnings} - \text{Analysts' forecasted earnings}}{\text{Market value of equity}}$$

Following Christie (1987), the surprise variables, $ULLR_j$ and UE_j, are deflated by the market value of equity (in our case as of 12/31/86). The most recent analysts' forecasts just before the LLR addition announcement were obtained from IBES and Value Line to estimate two alternative measures of earnings surprise. Finally, to estimate the reserve surprise, the actual LLRs are measured after the reserve addition announced by banks, while for expected LLRs we use the 25% LDC loan exposure 'norm' established by Citicorp.[8] Moreover, as a *sensitivity* test an alternative LLR expectations model was also tried where the announced LLR additions were assumed to be specific to

[7]However, since certain announcements were made on the same day (see appendix), some cross-sectional dependence may still be present.

[8]All management forecasted earnings and most actual LLRs (after the reserve additions) were obtained from the WSJ announcements. In a few cases the second variable was estimated from banks' annual reports and 10-Ks.

Table 2

The average effects of the reserve addition announcements on the values (percent returns) of bank portfolios (standard errors in parentheses).

$$R_{jt} = b_{j0} + b_{j1} R_{mt} + b'_{j1} R_{mt-1} + \Phi_{j0} D_0 + \Phi_{j1} D_1 + \Phi_{j2} D_2 + \varepsilon_{jt}.^{a}$$

Bank portfolios	Φ_{j1}	Φ_{j2}	R^2
11 money center	−0.091 (0.862)	0.009 (0.203)	0.367
46 with LDC exposure	0.219 (0.379)	0.111 (0.089)	0.626
73 without LDC exposure	−0.199 (0.345)	0.023 (0.081)	0.613
34 reserve adding	0.255 (0.463)	0.132 (0.109)	0.619

[a] Φ_{j1} = coefficient measuring the effect of Citicorp's reserve addition, Φ_{j2} = coefficient measuring the effect of reserve additions by individual banks.

Brazil. In this case, the norm set for other banks by Citicorp's LLR addition was 63% of their Brazilian loan exposures.

5. Empirical findings

Table 2 shows the first set of results using nonoverlapping equally-weighted portfolios of 11 money center, 46 LDC debt exposed, and 73 non-LDC debt exposed banks. The 34 reserve-adding banks were also analyzed in a separate portfolio. These portfolio regressions employ one dummy, D_1, for Citicorp's announcement and *one* dummy, D_2, that is set at one whenever one of the other 34 banks announced a LLR addition. As seen in table 2, the *average* effects of Citicorp's and the individual banks' LLR additions are insignificantly different from zero at the 10% level for all bank portfolios. Nevertheless, as noted in section 3 individual bank effects are likely to be heterogeneous.

Specifically, to examine the differential effects across banks, our second set of tests estimates the full system of equations specified in model (1) on the 35 reserve-adding banks (including Citicorp) using the Seemingly Unrelated Regressions (SUR) methodology proposed by Zellner (1982). These results are shown in table 3.

Citicorp showed a strong and significant positive stock price reaction upon its LLR announcement (Φ_{j1}) indicating good news, as did Bank of Boston, Republic New York, and J.P. Morgan upon Citicorp's announcement. However, four other banks had a significantly negative return adjustment. Finally, six individual bank announcements were received as good news and another six as bad news. The results clearly suggest heterogeneous effects of these

Table 3

The effects of the announcement of bank reserve additions on the values (percent return) of individual banks.[a]

Bank name	Citicorp's announcement Φ_{j1}	Individual bank announcement Φ_{j2}
Citicorp	5.490[b]	na
Norwest Corp	0.286	3.452[b]
Chase Manhattan Corp	1.432	1.196
Security Pacific Corp	0.934	0.668
Merchants National Corp	−0.637	−2.932[d]
Mercantile Bancorporation	−0.798	7.666[b]
Bank of Boston Corp	3.603[c]	−3.436[c]
BankAmerica Corp	−2.194	−1.180
First Interstate Bancorp	0.032	1.262
Chemical Banking Corp	−2.348[d]	−0.278
Shawmut National Corp	0.792	−1.278
First Chicago Corp	−0.537	0.985
Wells Fargo & Co	−0.490	−1.858[d]
Mellon Bank Corp	0.544	4.151[b]
Northern Trust Corp	0.135	3.661[b]
Bankers Trust New York	2.098	−0.421
Manufacturers Hanover	−3.555[b]	0.763
Republic New York Corp	2.133[d]	1.243
Marine Midland	−1.156	9.699[b]
Bank of New England	−0.222	−1.089
First Wisconsin Corp	−0.268	−0.208
First Wachovia Corp	1.344	1.054
Continental Illinois	−1.850	−6.836[b]
Comerica Inc	0.107	0.434
Signet Banking Corp	−2.070[d]	−3.290[b]
First Bank System Inc	−1.203	−0.510
Banc One Corp	−2.072[d]	−0.585
Ameritrust Corp	0.061	−1.641
National City Corp	−0.206	−2.049[c]
Bank of New York Co Inc	−1.072	0.893
First Republicbank Corp	0.597	−1.859
First Union Corp (N.C.)	0.702	0.679
Fidelcor	1.430	−0.878
Huntington Bancshares	1.992	−0.383
Morgan (J.P.) & Co	2.998[c]	2.910[b]

[a] The system weighted R^2 is 0.1019.
[b] Significant at the 1% level for a two-tailed test.
[c] Significant at the 5% level for a two-tailed test.
[d] Significant at the 10% level for a two-tailed test.

LLR-related announcements on bank returns. Indeed, the null hypotheses of equality in the dummy coefficients across banks ($H_1: \Phi_{11} = \cdots = \Phi_{n1}$ and $H_2: \Phi_{12} = \cdots = \Phi_{n2}$) could be rejected at the 1% level using an F-test.

The next set of tests seeks to explain why we observe such heterogeneous reactions across banks. As noted in section 4, for the Citicorp announcement we employ the Sefcik and Thompson (1986) methodology on 65 banks to

Table 4

The cross-sectional variation of bank responses to Citicorp's reserve addition: Portfolios weighted by banks' economic characteristics (time-series regressions estimated on four weighted portfolios; standard errors in parentheses).

	Bargaining power proxied by	
Portfolio weighting basis	Relative bank size	Dummy for major bargaining banks[a]
1) LDC exposure	−0.3972[b] (0.1555)	−0.2514[c] (0.1419)
2) Capital ratio	−0.0692 (0.0716)	−0.0134 (0.0736)
3) Bargaining power proxy	0.0084[b] (0.0025)	0.0106[b] (0.0035)
4) Relative tax rate	0.0035 (0.0024)	0.0044[c] (0.0024)

[a]This variable is equal to the number of times a bank leads a LDC rescheduling committee (see table 1).
[b]Significant at the 1% level for a two-tailed test.
[c]Significant at the 10% level for a two-tailed test.

examine the separate effects of the regulatory cost proxy (capital to assets ratio), the information signalling proxy (LDC debt exposure), the tax effect proxy (tax rate), and the bargaining power effect proxy (bank size or bargainers' dummy).[9] These results are presented in table 4.

As discussed earlier, managers may have private information about the quality of their LDC loan portfolio. Consequently, announcing additions to LLR may be perceived by investors as signalling a decline in the quality of this loan portfolio and an increase in the expected size of future loan charge-offs. The results in table 4 imply that the larger a bank's exposure, the more *negatively* Citicorp's announcement was perceived by the market. They also suggest that the equally-weighted portfolio or average return effect tests (table 2) masked the apparently heterogeneous LDC exposures among banks which are reflected by the Sefcik and Thompson methodology.

The other significant explanatory variable is the variable reflecting bargaining power, either relative bank size or bargaining dummy. As argued earlier, large banks provided most of the loans in 'new money' packages which were used to pay interest on old loans. As a result, relatively smaller banks often had a free ride. Citicorp's LLR addition was perceived as setting the stage for

[9]The measurement units of the four independent variables can be set to any convenient value. The level chosen determines the units in which the portfolio parameters are expressed. In our case, the level of LDC exposure is set at unity for the LDC exposed portfolio. The LDC exposed portfolio event parameters can then be interpreted as a return shift per unit of LDC exposure. The size and tax variables are divided by the average value across all banks. Thus, the size portfolio parameters, for example, can be interpreted as a return shift per unit of average bank size [see footnote 18 in Schipper, Thompson, and Weil (1987)].

a new bank bargaining strategy – being willing to accept a higher probability of default instead of providing more 'new money' packages. Consistent with a bargaining power effect and independent of the effect of LDC loan exposure, the relative size (and bargaining dummy) variable is significantly positive.

The variable reflecting tax effects is positive in both sets of weighted portfolios and weakly significant when using the bargainers' dummy. This indicates expectations of small benefits from the tax breaks as banks charge off their bad loans. These small expected benefits are probably due to banks' low effective tax rates. Indeed, the average effective tax rate for our sample banks was only 12.33%.[10] Finally, the capital ratio variable is insignificant suggesting that investors in low capital to asset ratio banks did not perceive unfavorable regulatory cost repercussions stemming from Citicorp's announcement.

The final set of tests seeks to examine whether there was any *additional* information content present when, following the Citicorp announcement, 34 other banks announced reserve additions. As discussed earlier, if these actual reserve additions deviated from those expected after the Citicorp announcement, there may have been additional news content for these banks' stockholders. However, since banks announcing LLR additions provided management earnings forecasts at the same time, it is necessary to control for any earnings surprise (unexpected change in forecasted earnings) as well as LLR surprise. Table 5 displays the results of the cross-sectional regression model (4) used to explain the variation in the reactions of the 34 banks to their own LLR announcements. The earnings surprise variable, whether we use the IBES or Value Line forecasts, and LDC exposure are the only variables with systematically significant *t*-values. The reserve surprise variables, whether measured by the total LDC exposure norm or the Brazil debt exposure norm are insignificant, consistent with individual banks' reserve announcements conforming to the standard established by Citicorp's May 20th announcement.[11] Unfortunately, as can be seen from the correlation matrix of the independent variables, the LDC exposure and the earnings surprise variables are highly collinear, so that these individual coefficient 'effects' should be interpreted with caution.

6. Summary and conclusion

This paper has examined whether additions to bank LLRs following the Brazilian interest suspension on its debt in February 1987 were viewed as good

[10] It might also be noted that banks with assets of $5 billion or more had a negative return on assets in 1987 [see Federal Reserve Bulletin, July 1989, p. 469]. Given the limited carryback provisions of the 1986 tax law, any tax shield benefits may have to be delayed into the future lowering their present values.

[11] In fact, six banks met the 25% norm, another fourteen banks exceeded the norm slightly (25%–35%), and for only two banks the LLR was set at below the 25% norm established by Citicorp.

Table 5

The cross-sectional variation of bank responses to their own LLR addition announcement (cross-sectional regressions estimated on 34 banks (observations); standard errors in parentheses).

$$\hat{\Phi}_{j2} = \beta_0 + \beta_1 EXP_j + \beta_2 CRATIO_j + \beta_3 T_j + \beta_4 SIZE_j + \beta_5 ULLR_j + \beta_6 UE_j + u_j.^{a}$$

Earnings forecasting service	Constant	LDC exposure	Capital ratio	Tax rate	Assets $\times 10^{-5}$	Reserve surprise	Earnings surprise	Adjusted R^2
A. LLR Norm of 25% of LDC Debt								
IBES	−1.655	118.743[c]	54.258	−1.167	−3.222	0.212	9.790[b]	0.297
	(3.615)	(47.849)	(51.939)	(0.782)	(3.052)	(0.703)	(3.148)	
Value Line	0.832	114.081[c]	15.550	−1.509[c]	−2.967	0.297	10.440[b]	0.496
	(3.562)	(43.168)	(51.572)	(0.565)	(2.681)	(0.682)	(2.688)	
B. LLR Norm of 63% of Brazil Debt								
IBES	−0.662	102.520[d]	45.927	−1.077	−2.746	−0.125	8.437	0.296
	(4.491)	(50.503)	(57.312)	(0.761)	(2.966)	(0.490)	(5.211)	
Value Line	3.992	82.838[d]	−12.511	−1.554[c]	−2.435	−0.330	7.583[d]	0.503
	(4.810)	(47.800)	(60.308)	(0.565)	(2.652)	(0.493)	(4.381)	

C. Correlation Matrix for the IBES Forecasts and a Norm of 25% of LDC Debt

	Cap ratio	Tax	Assets	Reserves	Earnings
LDC exposure	−0.468[b]	−0.352[c]	0.628[b]	−0.540[b]	−0.761[b]
Capital ratio		0.032	−0.442[b]	0.067	0.504[b]
Tax rate			0.006	0.269[d]	0.308[c]
Assets				−0.335[c]	−0.448[b]
Reserve surprise					0.335[c]

[a] $\hat{\Phi}_{j2}$ = coefficient on individual bank reserve addition dummy, $ULLR_j = (LLR_j - 0.25$ (Bank j's LDC loans)/(Market value of equity), UE_j = (Management's forecasted earnings − Analysts' forecasted earnings)/(Market value of equity).

[b] Significant at the 1% level for a two-tailed test.

[c] Significant at the 5% level for a two-tailed test.

[d] Significant at the 10% level for a two-tailed test.

or bad news by stockholders. It was argued that LLR additions could be viewed as good or bad news because of a number of different economic effects that follow or are associated with such announcements. Specifically, there might be an information signalling effect, a tax effect, a regulatory cost effect, and a bargaining power (or bargaining strategy) effect. As a result, it was argued that we might expect to see heterogeneous effects across bank returns to both the Citicorp and individual bank LLR announcements.

Using the SUR methodology, it was found that these announcements did indeed have a heterogeneous effect across banks. Thus, while Citicorp's LLR announcement had a significant positive effect on its own returns, it had a diverse effect on other bank returns. However, these diverse effect could be partly explained by the size of a bank's LDC debt exposure (consistent with the information signalling effect) and its relative size or position in LDC rescheduling committees (consistent with a bargaining effect). Finally, the individual LLR additions that followed Citicorp's announcement appear to have contained no new (unexpected) LLR-related information to the market.

Appendix

Table 6

Announcement dates in the Wall Street Journal.

Date	Bank name	Additions to reserves
2/20	Brazil suspended interest payments (67 bil loans)	
5/20	Citicorp	$3 bil
5/27	Norwest	200 mil
5/28	Chase Manhattan	1.6 bil
6/2	Security Pacific	500 mil
6/3	Mercantile Bancorp	75 mil
6/3	Merchants National Corp	30 mil
6/4	Bank of Boston	300 mil
6/9	BankAmerica	1.1 bil
6/12	Chemical New York	1.1 bil
6/12	First Interstate Banco	750 mil
6/15[a]	First Chicago Corp	800 mil
6/15	Shawmut Corp	69 mil
6/16	Mellon Bank Corp	415 mil
6/16	Wells Fargo	400 mil
6/17	Bankers Trust	700 mil
6/17[a]	Manufacturers Hanover	1.70 bil
6/18	Marine Midland	400 mil
6/18	Republic New York Corp	100 mil
6/19[a]	Bank of New England Corp	107 mil
6/19[a]	First Wisconsin Corp	96 mil
6/19	First Wachovia Corp	50 mil
6/23	Continental Illinois	500 mil
6/24[a]	First Bank System	160 mil
6/24	Signet Banking Corp	75 mil
6/24[a]	Comerica	36 mil
6/25	Ameritrust	78.1 mil
6/25[a]	Banc One	54 mil
6/30[a]	Bank of New York	135 mil
6/30[a]	Fidelcor	30 mil
6/30	First Union Corp	25 mil
6/30	First Republicbank	325 mil
6/30	National City Corp	55 mil
7/1[a]	Huntington Bancshares	25 mil
7/9	J.P. Morgan	875 mil

[a] The announcement appeared on the Dow Jones News Broad Tape *before* the close of trading on the *previous day*. For these banks a two-day announcement period is used, the WSJ date and the previous day. For all other banks the announcement in the Broad Tape appeared either on the same day with the WSJ or *after* the close of trading on the previous day. In these cases a one-day announcement period (the WSJ date) is used.

References

Binder, J.J., 1985, Measuring the effects of regulation with stock price data, Rand Journal of Economics 16, 167–183.

Buynak, T.M., 1987, How will tax reform affect commercial banks?, Federal Reserve Bank of Cleveland Economic Review, June, 24–33.

Christie, A.A., 1987, On cross-sectional analysis in accounting research, Journal of Accounting and Economics 9, 231–258.

Federal Reserve Bulletin, July 1989 (Board of Governors of the Federal Reserve System, Washington, DC).

Huizinga, H., 1989, The commercial bank claims on developing countries: How have banks been affected?, in: I. Husain and I. Diwan, eds., Dealing with the debt crisis (World Bank, Washington, DC) 129–143.

James, C., 1988, Heterogeneous creditors and the market value of bank LDC loan portfolios, Working paper, Sept. (University of Oregon, Eugene, OR).

Krugman, P., 1987, International debt strategies in an uncertain world, in: G. Smith and J. Cuddington, eds., International debt strategies in an uncertain world (World Bank, Washington, DC).

Salomon Brothers, 1988, Review of bank performance (New York, NY).

Saunders, A. and M. Smirlock, 1987, Intra- and inter-industry effects of bank securities market activities: The case of discount brokerage, Journal of Financial and Quantitative Analysis 22, 467–482.

Schipper, K., R. Thompson, and R. Weil, 1987, Disentangling interrelated effects of regulatory changes on shareholder wealth: The case of motor carrier deregulation, Journal of Law and Economics 30, 67–100.

Scholes, J. and J. Williams, 1977, Estimating betas from nonsynchronous data, Journal of Financial Economics 4, 309–327.

Sefcik, S. and R. Thompson, 1986, An approach to statistical inference in cross-sectional models with security abnormal returns as dependent variable, Journal of Accounting Research 24, 316–334.

Tax Analysts, 1987, Effective corporate tax rates: 1986 (Arlington, VA).

Wall Street Journal, 1987, Citicorp sharply lifts loss reserves, putting its rivals on the spot: The move gives it leverage in third world but may hurt banks' united front, May 20th.

Wall Street Journal, 1987, Chase increases loan reserve by $1.6 billion: Bank puts 2nd-period loss at $1.4 billion and cites foreign-loan problems, May 28th.

Zellner, A., 1982, An efficient method of estimating seemingly unrelated regressions and tests for aggregation bias, Journal of the American Statistical Association 77, 348–368.

Viral V. Acharya
London Business School and Centre for Economic Policy Research

Iftekhar Hasan
Rensselaer Polytechnic Institute

Anthony Saunders
New York University

Should Banks Be Diversified? Evidence from Individual Bank Loan Portfolios*

We study the effect of loan portfolio focus versus diversification on the return and the risk of 105 Italian banks over the period 1993–99 using data on bank-by-bank exposures to different industries and sectors. We find that diversification is not guaranteed to produce superior performance and/or greater safety for banks. For high-risk banks, diversification reduces bank return while producing riskier loans. For low-risk banks, diversification produces either an inefficient risk-return trade-off or only a marginal improvement. Our results are consistent with a deterioration in the effectiveness of bank monitoring at high risk-levels and upon lending expansion into newer or competitive industries.

I. Introduction

Should financial institutions (FIs) and banks be focused or diversified? Does the extent of focus or di-

* We acknowledge the Interbank Deposit Protection Fund of Italy and the Italian Bankers' Association for providing us with the data set employed in this paper; to Cristiano Zazzara and Marco Pellegini for their help in acquisition, translation, and understanding of this publicly available data set; to Emilia Bonaccorsi di Patti for help with classification of banks into consortium banks; and the Bank for International Settlements (BIS) for provision of data on stock market indices for Italy. We thank Linda Allen, Enrica Detragiache, Mike Fishman, Dario Focarelli, Patrick Frazer, Reint Gropp, Robert Hauswald, Bernd Hofmann, Philip Lowe, Fabio Panetta, Mitch Petersen, N. R. Prabhala, Paola Sapienza, Henri Servaes, Paolo Volpin, the seminar participants at 2003 American Finance Association meetings, BIS, Cambridge, Ente Einaudi Bank of Italy, the 2002 Federal Reserve Bank of Chicago conference on Bank Structure and Competition, Indian Institute of Management (IIM) Ahmedabad, IIM Bangalore, INSEAD, Industrial Credit and Investment Corporation of India Research Centre, London Business School, London School of Economics, Oxford, and Rutgers, and an anonymous referee, for very useful comments. Acharya acknowledges the support of BIS toward this project during July 2001. Hasan acknowledges the support of the Bank of Finland. The views expressed are exclusively those of the authors. Contact the corresponding author, Viral V. Acharya, at vacharya@london.edu

[*Journal of Business*, 2006, vol. 79, no. 3]

0021-9398/2006/7903-0012$10.00

versification affect the quality of their loan portfolios? Does diversification, based on traditional portfolio theory wisdom, lead to greater safety for FIs and banks? In this paper, we undertake an empirical investigation of these questions. The evidence we present suggests that, in contrast to the recommendations of traditional portfolio and banking theories, diversification of bank assets is not guaranteed to produce superior return performance and/or greater safety for banks.

There are several reasons why the focus versus diversification issue is important in the context of FIs and banks. First, FIs and banks face several (often conflicting) regulations that create incentives either to diversify or to focus their asset portfolios, such as the imposition of capital requirements that are tied to the risk of assets, branching and asset investment restrictions, and so forth. Hence, from a policy standpoint, it is interesting to ask whether FIs and banks benefit or get hurt from diversification of their loan portfolios.

In addition, the very nature of an intermediary's business activities makes the question of focus versus diversification an interesting economic issue to explore. FIs and banks act as delegated monitors in the sense of Diamond (1984) and acquire proprietary information about the firms they lend to, as noted by Fama (1980, 1985) and James (1987) and as modeled by Sharpe (1990) and Rajan (1992). The quality of monitoring and information acquisition is, however, an *endogenous* choice of FIs and banks. This choice is governed by the extent of agency conflict between equity holders (bank owners) and creditors of an FI. As explained below, this agency conflict is affected by the "downside riskiness" or insolvency risk of the FI and by the extent of the FI's focus or diversification.

We define portfolio downside risk or insolvency risk to mean the likelihood that the FI's asset returns will be lower than a given threshold (i.e., the level of deposits in the bank's capital structure), an event that constitutes a "default" or an economic insolvency. For the sake of illustration, consider the extreme case in which the FI's insolvency risk is extremely high; then on an expected basis most benefits from monitoring accrue only to its creditors (uninsured depositors and providers of borrowed funds). In this case, bank owners have little incentive to monitor. All else being equal, the FI's underinvestment in monitoring will be more severe the greater its risk of failure. Under such an incentive structure, can FIs and banks monitor their loans effectively as they expand into different industries and segments of the loan markets? How does the decision to be focused or diversified affect their monitoring incentives and the endogenous quality (i.e., the risk and the return) of their loans?

In this paper, we analyze two empirical relationships directly linked to this focus versus diversification debate. First, we explore the relationship between bank return and risk and the degree of bank focus (diversification). In particular, we are interested in how the returns of banks vary with the level of diversification at different bank risk levels and whether this relationship is linear or nonlinear. Second, we seek to explore how the entry of banks via lending into new sectors (i.e., an increase in their diversification) affects their risk. For example, diversification into new sectors may lower monitoring effectiveness and increase bank risk.

To answer these questions, we examine data on the asset and loan portfolio compositions of individual Italian banks during the period 1993–99. The choice of Italian banks is driven by the availability of detailed data on the industrial and sectoral composition of their balance sheets. By contrast, in the United States, publicly available data on bank loan portfolios are restricted to call reports that do not contain such "fine" asset decompositions. In particular, U.S. regulators do not provide a breakdown of individual (or aggregate) bank lending to specific industries or industrial sectors. Instead, the general level of disaggregation is highly coarse in nature, specifically into household-sector loans, commercial and industrial loans, and so forth. In the paper, we employ several measures of downside risk of banks (both expected and unexpected) based on their availability and measurability from the data.

Our results are consistent with a theory that predicts a deterioration in the effectiveness of bank monitoring at high levels of risk and upon lending expansion into newer or competitive industries. Our most important finding is that both industrial and sectoral loan diversification reduce bank return while endogenously producing riskier loans for high-risk banks in our sample. For low-risk banks, these forms of diversification either produce an inefficient risk-return trade-off or produce only a marginal improvement.

Some of these issues have been examined at a theoretical level in a paper by Winton (1999). Traditional arguments based on Diamond (1984) suggest that banks should be as diversified as possible. This precludes any agency problem between bank owners and bank creditors. In practice, however, banks cannot fully diversify all their risks. Winton presents a theoretical framework that allows for a residual agency problem between bank owners and bank creditors and investigates the merit of the proverbial wisdom of not putting all one's eggs in one basket.[1] The model provides a number of testable empirical hypotheses that are central to the focus versus diversification debate in banking.

The issue of focus versus diversification has not been addressed thoroughly in an empirical context for financial institutions and banks, although it has a long history in the corporate finance literature.[2] Our findings, compared to

1. Winton motivates the issue by comparing the following two pieces of advices: "It's the part of a wise man to keep himself today for tomorrow and not venture all his eggs in one basket" by Miguel de Cervantes (*Don Quixote de la Mancha*, 1605), and "Behold the fool saith 'Put not thine eggs in one basket'—which is but a manner of saying, 'Scatter your money and attention'; but the wise man saith 'Put all your eggs in one basket and watch that basket'" by Mark Twain (*Pudd'nhead Wilson*, 1894).

2. Using more aggregated measures of bank diversification, Hughes et al. (1996), Berger and DeYoung (2001), and Saunders and Wilson (2001) examine geographical diversification. Caprio and Wilson (1997) examine cross-country evidence for a relationship between on–balance sheet concentration and bank insolvency. Klein and Saidenberg (1998) present portfolio simulations to compare lending by multibank bank holding companies and their pro forma "pure-play" benchmark banks. Berger, Demsetz, and Strahan (1999) find that consolidation in the financial services industry has been consistent with greater diversification of risks on average but with

the extant literature, are based on a finer measure of bank focus that relies on individual loan portfolio composition of banks. In addition to being complementary to this literature, our findings have important and direct implications for the optimal size and scope of banks. While traditional banking theory based on a delegated monitoring argument recommends that it is optimal for a bank to be fully diversified across sectors or "projects" (see, e.g., Boyd and Prescott, 1986), our results suggest that there are diseconomies of scope that arise through weakened monitoring incentives and a poorer-quality loan portfolio when a risky bank expands into additional industries and sectors. This complements the agency theoretic analysis of the boundaries of a bank's activities as proposed in Cerasi and Daltung (2000), Berger et al. (2001), and Stein (2002).[3] From a normative standpoint, our results sound a cautionary note to the adoption of regulatory mechanisms that encourage bank-level portfolio and/or activity diversification, or attempt to measure credit portfolio risk through traditional diversification measures.

Section II describes the data underlying our tests of the relationship between bank performance (return as well as risk) and bank diversification (focus). In Section III, we present our empirical results. Finally, Section IV provides concluding remarks.

II. Data

A. *Data Sources*

Data for the industrial, asset, and geographic decompositions of the portfolios of Italian banks in our study are taken from the regulatory reports submitted by these banks to the Bank of Italy, the Italian Bankers' Association, and the Interbank Deposit Protection Fund of Italy. The latter is the Italian equivalent of the U.S. Federal Deposit Insurance Corporation. Our sample starts with a database of 105 primarily commercial banks that reported their asset portfolio and other data during the entire 1993–99 period. The sample period starts in 1993 since the banking law of August 27, 1993 (Consolidating Act), marked a regime shift in the Italian banking structure. It revolutionized the Italian banking system by encouraging the emergence of full-service financial institutions in that it eliminated the distinction between specialized lending institutions (medium- and long-term credit) and retail banks (short-term credit).

A complete list of all banks and those that are publicly traded during our sample period is shown in Appendix table A1, along with the average size

little or no cost efficiency improvements. DeLong (2001) finds that bank mergers in the United States that are focusing in terms of geography and activity produce superior economic performance relative to those that are diversifying. Finally, Stiroh (2002) finds that during the period from the late 1970s to 2001, a greater reliance on noninterest income by U.S. banks, particularly on trading revenue, is associated with higher risk and lower risk-adjusted profits at the individual bank level.

3. Berger et al. (2001) and Stein (2002) tie incomplete contracting between loan officers and their superiors to the inability of large banks to process "soft" information about their borrowers. This potentially leads to diseconomies of scale for FIs and banks.

of each bank over the sample period. These 105 banks constitute over 80 percent of the total banking assets of Italy. These data are aggregated at the level of the bank holding company, wherever applicable. A few of the banks in our sample undertook acquisitions of other banks. The data set, however, does not provide any details as to which these acquiring banks were and which banks they acquired. Furthermore, the data set does not include foreign bank operations in Italy. Over our sample period, the foreign bank penetration of the Italian banking market was weak largely because of the prohibition on foreign banks from accepting deposits of Italian residents.

In terms of size, eight of these 105 banks are "very large" (as defined by the Bank of Italy), seven are "large," 15 are "medium," and the remaining 75 are "small." In terms of geographical scope of banking activities, nine of these banks are "national," 18 are "regional," 13 are "intraregional," 10 are "local," and the remaining 55 are "provincial." Finally, 34 of these banks are publicly traded, 62 of them were state-owned at the beginning of 1993,[4] and 70 of them were not members of a consortium or a bank holding group. Whenever our analysis employs measures of performance based on stock market data, we are constrained to focus on the publicly traded sample only. In Section III.*D*, we also examine separately the robustness of our analysis to state ownership and membership in a consortium or a bank holding company.

While there are natural differences between the banking sectors of any two countries, there are several dimensions along which the Italian banking system is similar to that in the United States: (1) In contrast to other banking systems in continental Europe, Italy has a large number of banks (about 850 at the beginning of our sample), giving rise to a less concentrated banking system like that of the United States. (2) The branching restrictions on banks in Italy were removed in 1990 as they were in the United States in the mid-1990s. (3) There has been a wave of consolidation in the banking system in 1990s mirroring that in the United States. (4) The banking system comprises a few very large banks and a large number of medium- to small-sized banks as in the United States. However, Italy differs from the United States in that some of its banks are state-owned, although state ownership has been steadily declining over the past decade following the Amato-Carli law.[5]

These stylized facts and the use of Italian banking data to address other important economic issues such as the benefit of relationship banking (Degatriache, Garella, and Guiso 2000) and the effect of bank mergers on loan contracts (Sapienza 2002) lead us to believe that our results would generalize to banking sectors of other countries, including the United States.[6]

4. We are very grateful to Paola Sapienza for supplying us the state ownership dummy for our sample based on her work on Italian banks in Sapienza (2002).

5. Our results are found to hold also for the privately owned sample of banks (see Sec. III.*D*).

6. Descriptions of the Italian banking sector can be found in Degatriache et al. (2000) and Sapienza (2002). Industry perspectives on the developments of the Italian banking system can also be found in BNP Paribas (2001) and Goldman Sachs (2001).

For each bank in our sample, data are available to calculate the following portfolio decompositions:

1. A disaggregated industrial sector decomposition based on each bank's top five industrial sector exposures, with a sixth exposure comprising the sum of the remaining exposures. While the exposures could be to any of the 23 industries listed below, the data provide disaggregated information only about the top five exposures. The set of 23 industries are (1) agricultural, forestry, and fishing products; (2) energy products; (3) iron and noniron material and ore; (4) ores and products based on nonmetallic minerals; (5) chemicals; (6) metal products apart from machinery and means of conveyance; (7) agricultural and industrial machinery; (8) office, electronic data processing machinery, and others; (9) electric material; (10) transport; (11) food products, beverages, and tobacco-based products;, (12) textile, leather, shoes, and clothing products; (13) paper, publishing, and printing products; (14) rubber and plastic products; (15) other industrial products; (16) construction; (17) services trade and similar; (18) hotel and public firms products; (19) internal transport services; (20) sea and air transport; (21) transport-related services; (22) communication services; and (23) other sales-related services. Note that in aggregate these exposures (collectively defined in the data as nonfinancial and household exposures) constitute the dominant part of each bank's portfolio.
2. A broad asset sector decomposition based on exposures to (1) sovereigns, (2) other governmental authorities, (3) nonfinancial corporations, (4) financial institutions, (5) households, and (6) other counterparties.

Note that the size of bank lending to a particular sector or industry in our data set is net of loans that are already classified as either doubtful or nonperforming. Also, our data set does not provide more detailed loan-by-loan or borrower-by-borrower information within these decompositions.

The financial statement variables and capital structure variables are obtained from the Bank of Italy and Bankscope data bases. Stock market data items for the 34 banks that are publicly traded were taken from the Datastream and Milan Stock Exchange information bases on Italian banks. A few banks had to be discarded from the sample because of missing values of relevant variables, for example, doubtful and nonperforming loans.

B. Construction of Herfindahl Indices

We measure focus (diversification) by employing a Hirschman Herfindahl index (HHI) measure. HHI is the sum of the squares of exposures as a fraction of total exposure under a given classification. In our case, we construct two different kinds of HHIs, which consist of industrial and household sector HHIs, more simply referred to as industrial sector HHIs (I-HHI) and broad asset sector HHIs (A-HHI).

Since we have data only for the top five industry exposures for each bank, our measure of I-HHI for a bank is also based on these five top industries in which loans were made by that bank. As stressed before, we would like to employ, if possible, the exposure to all industries while calculating I-HHI for a bank. Unfortunately, our data provide only the top five exposures, ranked by their amounts. For most banks in our sample, the top five exposures cover over 70%–80% of the total size of the loan portfolio. The sixth exposure in our computation of I-HHI considers the remaining portion of the industrial loan portfolio. For this sixth exposure, we employed two conventions: (1) where the sixth exposure is treated as a separate "hypothetical" industry and (2) where the sixth exposure is treated as being equally divided among the remaining 18 industries. Our results turned out to be insensitive to this choice, as is to be expected given that the top five exposures constitute, on average, a large proportion (over 70%) of the total exposure of a bank. Hence, we report results with I-HHI computed using the sixth exposure as a hypothetical industry. Thus, if the proportional exposures to six industries are X_1, X_2, X_3, X_4, X_5, and X_6, respectively, then I-HHI equals $\sum_{i=1}^{6}(X_i/Q)^2$, where $Q = \sum_{i=1}^{6} X_i$. Note that the HHI has a maximum of one when all loans are made to a single industry.

The A-HHI is the sum of the squared exposures (measured as a fraction) in the form of sovereign loans, other governmental loans, nonfinancial sector loans, financial sector loans, household sector loans, and other loans.

C. *Balance Sheet and Stock Market Variables*

We employ the following (annual) variables obtained from the balance sheet and stock market data for the banks in our sample over the period 1993–99:

Return measures:

- ROA: return on assets measured as net income/assets;
- SR: stock return measured as the return over the current year, that is, as the return from the end of the previous year to the last day of the current year.

Risk measures:

- DOUBT: the doubtful and nonperforming assets ratio measured as doubtful and nonperforming loans/assets;[7]
- PROVISION: the ratio of loan loss provisions to assets, which can also be interpreted as an ex ante measure of the level of expected losses.

In addition, we also seek to establish the robustness of our results with the following measures of unexpected losses:

- STDOUBT: the sample standard deviation of DOUBT for each bank;

7. Note that realized losses can be interpreted as capturing the level of expected losses.

- STDRET: the monthly stock return volatility for each publicly traded bank based on monthly stock return data;
- IDIOSYNCRATIC: the component of monthly stock return volatility for each publicly traded bank that is not explained by the market return proxied by the Milano Italia Borsa general index, a weighted arithmetic average of all stocks listed on the Milan Stock Exchange (Borsa Valori di Milano).[8]

Control variables:

- SIZE: asset size of the bank (in millions of dollars calculated using the spot exchange rate between the U.S. dollar and Italian lira at the point of measurement);
- EQRATIO: capital ratio of the bank measured as equity (book value)/assets, the approximate equivalent of the bank's tier 1 capital ratio; this is essentially equivalent to one minus (book value) debt to assets ratio for the bank;
- BRRATIO: branch ratio measured as number of bank branches (excluding headquarters)/assets; note that this is simply the inverse of a measure of average branch size;
- EMPRATIO: employee ratio measured as number of employees/assets.

Table 1 presents the univariate statistics (mean, median, standard deviation, minimum, and maximum) for these variables and for Herfindahl indices for all the banks over the sample period 1993–99. Note that the mean (median) bank's size is about US$12 billion ($3 billion) or 20 trillion (5 trillion) Italian lira, the mean (median) capital ratio is 8.732% (8.113%), and the mean (median) ratio of doubtful and nonperforming loans to assets is 5.234 (3.199).[9] The average industrial and asset sectoral focus measures (I-HHI and A-HHI) are low, suggesting a significant degree of diversification in these areas.

Table 2 completes the descriptive statistics by presenting the correlation matrix among these variables. As table 2 illustrates, the measures of focus, I-HHI and A-HHI, are not highly correlated, the correlation being 0.26. This suggests the possibility that the effects of these different diversification measures on bank risk-return performance may be different. Further, there is

8. It is conceivable to come up with an alternative measure of the risk of a bank that is based on the returns (profitability), variability of returns, and the correlation of returns for different industries a bank lends to. For Italy, Morgan Stanley Capital indices (MSCI) provide industry-by-industry returns. However, the classification of industries therein does not map onto the classification of industries employed in our data set. Hence, we use only bank return and bank risk measures available at the aggregate level for the bank. By contrast, the focus (diversification) measures are computed for each bank using disaggregated industry-by-industry exposures of each bank. We believe that measuring bank focus in this manner gives a reasonable first-order approximation since over our sample period, Italian banks derived, on average, between 60% and 70% of their revenues from their lending related activities (see BNP Paribas 2001).

9. The 1990s were a particularly difficult period for many Italian banks and industries (see BNP Paribas 2001; Goldman Sachs 2001; Sapienza 2002, 2004).

TABLE 1 **Univariate Descriptive Statistics: 105 Italian Banks, 1993–99**

Variable/Ratio	Mean	Median	Standard Deviation	Minimum	Maximum
ROA (%)	.927	.982	.852	−5.962	2.958
ROE (%)	8.76	11.60	29.30	−6.229	37.75
SR: stock return (%)	20.95	10.37	41.76	−24.01	129.30
Industrial sector I-HHI	.237	.231	.038	.181	.793
Asset sector A-HHI	.371	.352	.098	.197	.875
Geographical sector G-HHI	.947	.895	.099	.315	1.000
SIZE: asset size:					
Dollars (millions)	11,894	3,080	22,674	376	152,596
Italian lira (billions)	19,614	5,033	37,426	592	248,578
EQRATIO: equity to asset ratio (%)	8.732	8.113	3.76	.604	31.80
BRRATIO: branch to asset ratio	.022	.221	.010	0	.06185
EMPRATIO: employment expenses to assets ratio (%)	1.855	.018	.611	.232	4.636
DOUBT: doubtful and nonperforming loans to assets ratio (%)	5.234	3.199	5.632	0	44.43
STDOUBT: standard deviation of DOUBT	14.853	9.760	10.856	2.760	28.564
STDRET: standard deviation of SR	6.745	13.04	11.204	1.701	41.86
Systematic risk	6.673	8.471	11.580	.060	27.358
Idiosyncratic risk	4.941	6.256	10.006	.017	18.241
Provision for loan losses to assets ratio (%)	.601	.640	2.098	.105	5.267

NOTE.—The definitions of all variables and also a description of how they are computed appear in Sec. II.

significant variation in all the variables we employ, and the correlations suggest a relationship between return measures (ROA, ROE, and SR) and the balance sheet control variables (SIZE, EQRATIO, BRRATIO, EMPRATIO).

Panel A of table 3 presents the year-by-year quintiles of the focus measures.[10] What is important for our tests is that the focus measures not only exhibit variability in the overall sample and through time, but also do so for individual banks through time. For our data, we find that the time-series standard deviation of I-HHI (A-HHI), averaged across all banks, is about 0.016 (0.051), which is about half as large as the overall sample standard deviation of I-HHI (A-HHI), which is 0.038 (0.099). This implies that there

10. Note that App. A and tables 1, 2, and 3 (panel A) also provide statistics for the geographic focus (G-HHI) computed as the sum of the squared exposures (measured as a fraction) to domestic (Italian) loans, European Union loans, and rest of the world loans. However, the average geographical focus (G-HHI) in table 1 is quite high, capturing the fact that most banks in our sample lent to domestic Italian firms. Furthermore, panel A of table 3 shows that G-HHI is equal to one for about 25% of the sample in each year. This reflects the fact that relatively smaller Italian banks have no loan exposures outside of Italy (see App. A). Since our data set does not provide a disaggregation of loans within Italy into different regions of Italy, we focus below only on I-HHI and A-HHI, the industrial and asset sectoral focus measures. Goldman Sachs (2001) and Sapienza (2002, 2004) also provide corroborating evidence on the level of geographical focus of Italian banks during this period.

TABLE 2 **Bivariate Descriptive Statistics: Correlation Coefficients for 105 Italian Banks, 1993–99**

Variable/ Ratio	ROA	ROE	SR	I-HHI	A-HHI	G-HHI	SIZE	EQ	BR	EMP	DOUBT	STDRET	SYSTEMATIC	IDIOSYNCRATIC
ROA	1.00													
ROE	.621	1.00												
SR	.294	.144	1.00											
I-HHI	−.001	.062	.124	1.00										
A-HHI	.144	.083	.193	.257	1.00									
G-HHI	.134	.037	.162	−.307	−.024	1.00								
SIZE	−.225	−.101	−.155	.205	−.115	−.589	1.00							
EQRATIO	.422	.146	.112	.009	.236	.084	−.321	1.00						
BRRATIO	.139	.038	.002	−.366	−.294	.425	−.400	.133	1.00					
EMPRATIO	.087	−.009	−.319	−.384	−.365	.356	−.278	.167	.743	1.00				
DOUBT	−.418	−.266	−.075	−.061	−.041	.099	.003	−.063	−.116	−.134	1.00			
STDRET	.245	.116	.697	.197	.126	.038	−.006	.044	−.044	−.275	−.201	1.00		
SYSTEMATIC	.162	.081	.336	.075	.105	.030	−.005	.028	−.028	−.256	−.134	.793	1.00	
IDIOSYNCRATIC	.182	.103	.606	.132	.116	.028	−.005	.039	−.041	−.195	−.182	.836	.439	1.00

Note.—All correlation coefficients greater than 0.08 in magnitude are statistically significant at least at the 10% confidence level.

TABLE 3 Quantiles Values: 105 Italian Banks, 1993–99

	Mean	Minimum	10th Percentile	25th Percentile	50th Percentile	75th Percentile	90th Percentile	Maximum
				A. Focus Measures				
I-HHI	**.2375**	**.1812**	**.2039**	**.2130**	**.2304**	**.2528**	**.2819**	**.7938**
1993	.2397	.1868	.1996	.2127	.2333	.2563	.2871	.5000
1994	.2395	.1812	.2059	.2160	.2320	.2501	.2859	.3994
1995	.2327	.1854	.2054	.2117	.2276	.2433	.2732	.3346
1996	.2362	.1845	.2047	.2130	.2319	.2508	.2828	.3213
1997	.2358	.1905	.2040	.2147	.2303	.2529	.2721	.3235
1998	.2424	.1849	.2051	.2125	.2321	.2556	.2801	.7938
1999	.2363	.1874	.2012	.2111	.2299	.2571	.2784	.3598
A-HHI	**.3715**	**.1975**	**.2666**	**.3108**	**.3521**	**.4094**	**.4964**	**.8759**
1993	.4181	.2564	.3185	.3017	.3954	.4517	.5540	.7049
1994	.3557	.2199	.2688	.2982	.3369	.3782	.4589	.8759
1995	.3423	.1975	.2573	.2928	.3345	.3704	.4343	.6665
1996	.3346	.2108	.2483	.2846	.3264	.3670	.4149	.7138
1997	.3410	.2129	.2535	.2934	.3268	.3669	.4445	.7247
1998	.4124	.2169	.3028	.3421	.3947	.4604	.5517	.8000
1999	.4011	.2364	.2982	.3391	.3808	.4369	.5222	.7833
G-HHI	**.9477**	**.3155**	**.8169**	**.9424**	**.9957**	**1**	**1**	**1**
1993	.9542	.3778	.7981	.9564	.9987	1	1	1
1994	.9634	.3138	.8747	.9569	.9981	1	1	1
1995	.9529	.3155	.8408	.9471	.9966	1	1	1
1996	.9393	.4850	.7959	.9240	.9942	1	1	1
1997	.9406	.4811	.7944	.9434	.9948	1	1	1
1998	.9418	.4680	.8116	.9338	.9929	.9989	1	1
1999	.9412	.4278	.8278	.9259	.9919	.9983	1	1

TABLE 3 *(Continued)*

	Mean	Minimum	10th Percentile	25th Percentile	50th Percentile	75th Percentile	90th Percentile	Maximum
				B. Risk Variables				
DOUBT	**5.23**	**.00**	**.84**	**2.77**	**5.63**	**6.19**	**10.06**	**44.43**
1993	3.66	.23	1.22	1.96	2.99	4.22	6.72	14.72
1994	4.96	.21	1.52	2.45	3.75	6.17	9.73	24.06
1995	5.91	.00	1.71	3.24	4.44	7.75	11.68	24.09
1996	6.48	.00	1.70	2.89	4.45	8.00	12.84	34.15
1997	6.36	.00	1.70	2.58	4.44	7.68	10.60	36.91
1998	6.70	.19	1.55	2.71	4.53	7.14	11.27	40.94
1999	6.51	.09	1.38	2.59	4.18	6.98	10.62	44.43
STDOUBT	**14.85**	**2.76**	**4.96**	**6.35**	**9.76**	**17.50**	**24.91**	**28.56**
PROVISION	**.60**	**.10**	**.21**	**.39**	**.64**	**1.75**	**2.12**	**5.26**
1993	.60	.10	.18	.25	.68	.95	1.44	3.94
1994	.62	.09	.19	.27	.72	.74	1.76	4.86
1995	.68	.12	.19	.33	.78	.80	2.21	4.94
1996	.71	.13	.21	.35	.84	.94	2.28	5.08
1997	.78	.14	.22	.36	.88	.95	2.46	5.25
1998	.83	.14	.24	.35	.84	1.04	2.51	5.26
1999	.85	.15	.26	.36	.86	.96	2.60	5.14
STDRET	**6.75**	**1.70**	**3.63**	**8.45**	**13.04**	**27.17**	**39.84**	**41.86**
1993	7.01	1.74	4.01	7.85	11.23	25.83	38.82	35.31
1994	6.08	1.70	4.65	7.97	14.53	25.71	30.61	31.35
1995	8.21	1.79	3.97	8.16	14.91	26.02	34.80	37.92
1996	5.45	1.72	2.41	8.51	12.50	26.91	37.05	40.04
1997	10.20	1.86	2.68	7.03	19.82	30.87	36.83	41.86
1998	6.75	1.76	2.04	7.16	11.73	31.08	35.48	39.72
1999	5.77	1.70	2.76	6.91	12.61	31.63	37.99	38.43

IDIOSYNCRATIC	**4.94**	**.02**	**2.17**	**3.94**	**6.26**	**8.99**	**12.02**	**18.24**
1993	4.99	.17	2.05	3.06	6.42	7.46	10.28	16.45
1994	4.51	.13	2.16	2.87	5.56	8.02	10.04	17.02
1995	5.08	.95	1.88	3.76	5.94	9.24	12.65	16.24
1996	4.42	.09	2.00	2.99	5.43	8.77	11.07	15.96
1997	4.75	.31	2.15	3.56	5.98	9.03	11.65	17.06
1998	5.48	.86	3.24	4.54	7.12	10.74	14.81	18.24
1999	5.07	.02	2.95	4.36	8.09	10.01	14.08	18.08

is time-series variability in the focus measures at the level of an individual bank that is comparable to the variability in the focus measures in the cross section. We explore this issue in some more detail later.

Finally, panel B of table 3 contains the year-by-year quintiles of various risk measures. As is clear from the table, 1993–99 represents a turbulent period for Italian banks: losses measured as doubtful loans to assets ratio (DOUBT) reached values above 10% for about 10% of the sample in each year, and maximum values ranged from 15% to 45%. Overall, the latter half of the sample period appears to have more stable values of DOUBT. Doubtful loans trended upward between 1993 and 1996 as a result of the lingering effects of the 1992–93 crisis, reflecting in part the increased fragility of state-owned enterprises, rising risk from exporting companies, and problems affecting the construction industry and the service sector. With the exception of the period of the Russian and Asian crises, the doubtful loans to assets ratio stabilized after 1997. In further evidence, new allowances to loan loss provisions, an ex ante measure of risk in contrast to realized doubtful loans, also followed a similar pattern over the sample period (see BNP Paribas 2001). Other risk measures, including overall stock return volatility (STDRET) and idiosyncratic stock return volatility (IDIOSYNCRATIC), exhibit similar behavior, demonstrating the high levels of riskiness of many banks in the sample. Our sample period thus provides potential insights regarding countries with banking systems subject to similarly stressful periods.

III. Effect of Focus on Bank Performance

To study the overall effect of a bank's focus (diversification), we study its effect on both bank return and bank risk. If focus produces an increase in bank return and a decrease in bank risk, then we interpret this result as implying that focus improves bank performance and thus, by implication, that increased diversification would decrease bank performance. On the other hand, if focus results in a decrease in bank return and an increase in bank risk, then we conclude that focus weakens bank performance; that is, increased diversification would improve bank performance. When bank return and bank risk either both increase or both decrease, the overall effects on bank performance are ambiguous and cannot be determined without taking a stand on what constitutes an "efficient" risk-return trade-off. To partially address the issue concerning the endogeneity of focus measures, we consider the relationship between focus in year $t - 1$ on performance measures in year t. We complement this analysis with an important robustness check that employs focus measures in year t as well but treats them as *endogenously* determined variables.

A. *The Effects of Focus on Bank Return at Different Levels of Bank Risk*

Before examining the relationship between bank returns and focus, at different levels of bank risk, we first consider the following linear regression to understand the average relationship between bank returns and focus:

$$\text{Return}_{it} = \alpha_{i0} + \alpha_1 \times \text{I-HHI}_{it-1} + \alpha_2 \times \text{A-HHI}_{it-1} + \sum_{s=1995}^{1999} \kappa_s \text{TIME}_s + \epsilon_{it}. \quad (1)$$

We wish to test whether diversification is better for bank returns ("don't put all your eggs in one basket") or, by implication, whether focus (increased HHI) is harmful to bank returns:

$$\alpha_1 < 0,\ \alpha_2 < 0. \quad (2)$$

As noted earlier, Return_t is proxied by two variables: (i) ROA and (ii) SR. Throughout the paper, regressions are run by pooling observations across all banks and across all years and including time dummies (TIME_s) for 1995–99 as well as bank-specific fixed effects (except when their inclusion in the specification would lead to a multicollinearity problem).

The bank-specific fixed effects help us control for bank characteristics not captured in our specifications (assuming that they do not change dramatically over time). Furthermore, for bank fixed effects to sufficiently control for the fact that we are using pooled time-series data for each bank, we require that enough banks switch between diversification and focus. As observed earlier, the time-series standard deviation of focus measures for an individual bank, averaged across all banks, is about half as large as the overall sample standard deviation of focus measures. Furthermore, if we focus attention on the extremes, then only one bank features in the top 10 focused banks in all years, and only two banks feature in the top 10 diversified banks in all years, when focus and diversification are measured using A-HHI. The corresponding numbers when measurement is done using I-HHI are zero and three, respectively. The numbers are virtually the same if one were to compare these deciles in 1993 and 1999, suggesting that the composition of these deciles in 1993 and 1999 is essentially different. These statistics confirm that there is sufficient time-series variation in an individual bank's industrial and asset sector diversification.

The time dummies help us control, among other things, for the possible effect of change in macroeconomic conditions. Ideally, we would also like to isolate the linkage between diversification and performance that is specific to the bank's own activities such as its expertise in screening and monitoring from a possible mechanical linkage arising from a response of the bank's loan portfolio composition to the demand for loans in different industries. To be specific, if an industry a bank is lending to does relatively well compared to other industries, the bank may optimally lend greater credit to this industry and appear focused as well as performing better at the same time. A possible control for this would be the relative performance of the industries over time, proxied, for example, by the MSCI for Italian industries. Unfortunately, the industry classification of loans employed in our data does not map nicely into the one employed by MSCI data.

In addition, we employ the following control variables for each bank: log of its size LN(SIZE), its equity to assets ratio EQRATIO, its branch to assets ratio BRRATIO, and its employment expense to assets ratio EMPRATIO, all measures in year t. Note that since we use log of SIZE as the explanatory variable and simultaneously employ time fixed effects, the measurement of SIZE in U.S. dollars or Italian lira does not affect the coefficient on LN(SIZE): fluctuations in the dollar-lira exchange rate from the beginning of one year to the next affect only the coefficients on time fixed effects. Finally, we adjust returns for risk by employing the risk measure DOUBT_{t-1}, the ratio of its doubtful and nonperforming loans to assets, also as an explanatory variable.

We then test whether, in contrast to the specification in equation (1), the return-focus relationship depends on the level of bank risk. The return-focus relationship may in fact depend in a nonlinear way on bank risk (see, e.g., Winton 1999). From traditional portfolio theory, we know that diversification increases the central tendency of the distribution of a loan portfolio. However, when debt is risky and the central tendency of distribution is low relative to the level of debt, diversification can in fact increase the probability of bank insolvency. This would occur, for example, if the downside risk of bank loans is substantial. For the sake of illustration, figure 1 plots the cumulative probability function for two normal distributions with different standard deviations and with a common mean of zero. Suppose that these distributions (suitably scaled) correspond to two possible distributions for realization on bank loans. Suppose further that the level of debt varies along the x-axis.

If the level of debt is to the left of zero (under a suitable scale), for example, at $x = -1$, then a decrease in standard deviation, by reducing the likelihood of events in the left tail of the distribution (the "insolvency" states), reduces the probability of default. However, if the level of debt is to the right of zero, for example, at $x = 1$, then a decrease in standard deviation, by reducing the likelihood of events in the right tail of the distribution (the "no-default" states), in fact increases the probability of default. The left-skewed nature of a typical loan portfolio's return distribution implies that the level of debt, in fact, may not need to be too high for this effect to arise. Thus there may be an *inverted* U-shaped relationship between return and diversification as the level of risk increases from low to high. And, by implication, the relationship between return and focus may be a U-shaped function of the level of risk.

An additional impact reinforcing the U-shaped (nonlinear) hypothesis is the conflict of interest between bank owners and bank creditors. Specifically, an increase in the probability of insolvency reduces the incentives of bank owners to monitor their loans. If the loan portfolio has high downside risk (i.e., a high probability of asset returns falling below deposits, making the bank insolvent), then an improvement in loan monitoring and, in turn, in loan quality produces greater benefits to the creditors than to the bank owners. Since the

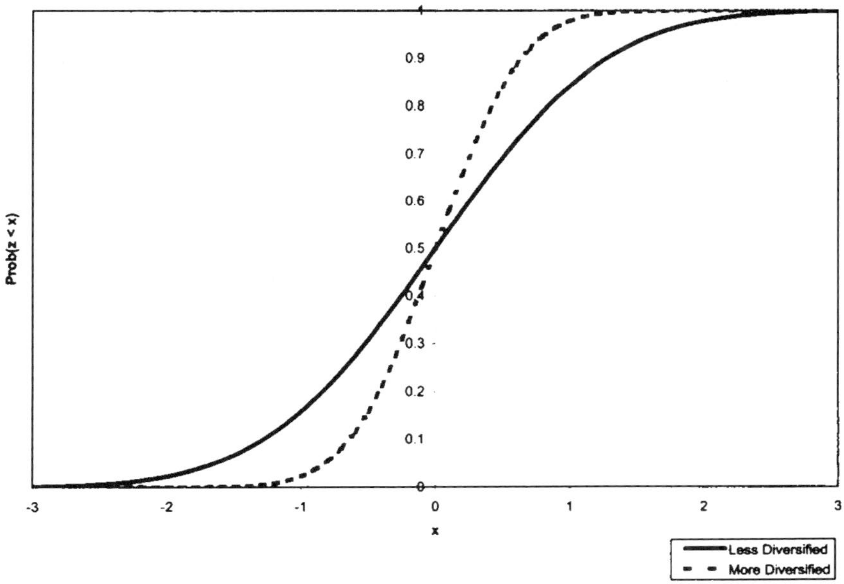

FIG. 1.—The effect of diversification (focus) on the probability of failure. The figure plots the cumulative probability function, $\text{Prob}(z < x)$, for two normal distributions with different standard deviations and with a common mean of zero. The thick line denoted as "less diversified" has a standard deviation of 1.0, whereas the dashed line denoted as "more diversified" has a lower standard deviation of 0.5. For the sake of illustration, z is treated as the distribution of bank returns and x as the level of bank debt (under a suitable scale). If the level of debt x is to the left of the central tendency of zero, e.g., at $x = -1$, then a decrease in standard deviation, by reducing the likelihood of events in the left tail of the distribution (the "default" states), reduces the probability of default. However, if the level of debt x is to the right of zero, e.g., at $x = 1$, then a decrease in standard deviation, by reducing the likelihood of events in the right tail of the distribution (the "no-default" states), in fact increases the probability of default.

cost of monitoring is borne by the bank owners (the residual claimants), it follows that if the loan portfolio has high downside risk, then an increase in diversification leads to weaker incentives for bank owners to monitor loans. This, in turn, leads to lower bank returns.

To try to capture the implied U-shaped (nonlinear) nature of the return-focus relationship as a function of bank risk, we modify equation (1) by introducing interaction terms between the focus measures and our measure of risk, the nonperforming and doubtful loans (RISK) as well as risk squared

($RISK^2$). That is,

$$\begin{aligned}\text{Return}_{it} = {} & \alpha_{i0} + \alpha_1 \times \text{I-HHI}_{it-1} + \alpha_2 \times \text{A-HHI}_{it-1} + \eta \times C_{it-1} \\ & + \beta_0 \times \text{RISK}_{it-1} + \beta_{11} \times \text{I-HHI}_{it-1} \times \text{RISK}_{it-1} \\ & + \beta_{12} \times \text{I-HHI}_{it-1} \times \text{RISK}^2_{it-1} \\ & + \beta_{21} \times \text{A-HHI}_{it-1} \times \text{RISK}_{it-1} \\ & + \beta_{22} \times \text{A-HHI}_{it-1} \times \text{RISK}^2_{it-1} \\ & + \sum_{s=1995}^{1999} \kappa_s \text{TIME}_s + \epsilon_{it}, \end{aligned} \tag{3}$$

where C_{it-1} is a vector representing the non–risk control variables stated above. Under this specification, the effect of focus on returns is quadratic in risk. For example, for industrial focus, I-HHI (where we have suppressed the bank-specific index i),

$$\frac{d(\text{Return})}{d(\text{Focus})} = \alpha_1 + \beta_{11} \times \text{RISK} + \beta_{12} \times \text{RISK}^2. \tag{4}$$

If, for example, the effect of a bank's focus on its returns is U-shaped in risk, then

$$\beta_{11} < 0,\ \beta_{12} > 0,\ \beta_{21} < 0,\ \beta_{22} > 0. \tag{5}$$

As stated above, we employ different measures of bank RISK in the regression above: the ratio of doubtful and nonperforming loans to assets, DOUBT_{t-1}, the standard deviation of DOUBT, STDOUBT, and loan loss provisions to assets ratio, PROVISION_{t-1}. While DOUBT is a measure of realized losses, STDOUBT and PROVISION are potentially more attractive as ex ante measures of unexpected and expected bank insolvency risk, respectively. Note that there is only one value of STDOUBT for a bank over the entire period. Hence, the time index in RISK_{t-1} is not relevant when risk is proxied by STDOUBT. In general, the risk measures we employ are based on discretionary actions of bank owners. To eliminate any bias arising from this, we also employ for the publicly traded sample two stock return–based measures of unexpected bank risk: the total stock return volatility of a bank, STDRET, and its idiosyncratic volatility, IDIOSYNCRATIC.

Table 4 presents the results for regressions of bank returns on focus specified in equations (1) and (3) with ROA as the bank return and DOUBT, STDOUBT, and PROVISION as the risk measures.[11] Overall, the view that focus reduces bank returns (and thus diversification increases bank returns) is rejected for

11. Note that all standard errors reported in the tables are corrected using White's adjustment for heteroscedasticity, and examination of lags did not reveal any significant autocorrelation problem in our data.

both measures of loan portfolio focus: industrial and household focus (I-HHI) and broad asset sector focus (A-HHI), as reflected by the positive and statistically significant (mostly at the 5% confidence level) coefficients on these measures in columns 1 and 2. The inclusion of control variables in column 2 significantly enhances the explanatory power of equation (1). The control variables for a bank's capital ratio and the risk of its loans (doubtful and nonperforming loans to assets ratio) are strongly significant in their effect on ROA.

Columns 3–5 of table 4 test whether the return-focus relationship is nonlinear in the level of bank risk, thus linking the cross-sectional effect of focus on returns to the level of bank risk (see eq. [3]). Interestingly, these results provide support for a U-shaped relationship between focus and returns as a function of the level of risk of the bank. The coefficients on the interaction terms, $HHI_{t-1} \times RISK_{t-1}$ and $HHI_{t-1} \times RISK^2_{t-1}$, are negative and positive, respectively, and are statistically significant (in some cases at the 5% and in all but one case at the 10% levels). This holds for both measures of focus, I-HHI and A-HHI, and for all three measures of bank risk, DOUBT, STDOUBT, and PROVISION. Computation of F-statistics to test the statistical significance of the linear and quadratic terms, separately and jointly, revealed that the coefficients on these terms are statistically significant (at a 99% confidence level) in contributing to the explanatory power of the regressions in columns 3–5 of table 4. As noted before, this U-shaped relationship is consistent with a weakening of bank monitoring incentives, on an increase in diversification, in the case in which the downside or insolvency risk of the bank is high.

In table 5, we repeat these tests with SR as the bank return measure. In addition, we employ stock return–based measures of bank risk. The sample size is smaller for the stock return–based measures of bank returns since only 34 out of our 105 banks are publicly traded. The control variables for a bank's capital ratio and the risk of its loans, which were strongly significant in their effect on ROA, have a less significant impact on the bank's SR. The coefficients on I-HHI and A-HHI in columns 1 and 2, corresponding to estimation (1), are strongly significant.

Overall, the U-shaped relationship finds some support with SR as the measure of bank return. Most coefficients on the linear and quadratic interaction terms, $HHI_{t-1} \times RISK_{t-1}$ and $HHI_{t-1} \times RISK^2_{t-1}$, are significant or marginally significant, but a few are insignificant. The U-shaped relationship fares relatively better when bank risk is proxied by DOUBT, STDOUBT, PROVISION, or IDIOSYNCRATIC, compared to STDRET as the proxy for bank risk. In terms of signs, all coefficients have the correct signs except the linear terms with STDRET as the risk measure, which are found to be positive. Note, however, that a positive sign of the linear coefficients provides even further evidence that the effect of diversification on bank returns is not positive. Moreover, once we control for endogeneity of focus measures, the coefficients always take correct signs and are statistically significant. However, before

TABLE 4 **Test for Nonmonotonicity in Effect of Focus on Bank Returns on Assets: 105 Italian Banks, 1993–99**

	ROA_t				
	(1)	(2)	(3)	(4)	(5)
Intercept	.006	.001	.023	.018	−.008
	(1.71)***	(1.85)***	(1.03)	(1.29)	(1.54)
$I\text{-}HHI_{t-1}$	.013	.002	.008	.015	.001
	(2.01)**	(1.93)***	(1.97)**	(1.98)**	(1.62)
$A\text{-}HHI_{t-1}$	.002	.004	.016	.019	.015
	(2.96)*	(2.16)**	(2.68)**	(2.28)**	(2.05)**
$LN(SIZE)_{t-1}$		−.002	−.001	−.001	−.002
		(1.87)***	(1.03)	(.80)	(1.31)
$EQRATIO_{t-1}$		.089	.086	.075	.028
		(10.37)*	(6.35)*	(6.22)*	(5.16)*
$BRRATIO_{t-1}$		.072	.032	.021	.116
		(1.81)***	(1.78)***	(1.39)	(1.53)
$EMPRATIO_{t-1}$		−.093	−.063	−.267	−.065
		(1.44)	(1.21)	(1.60)	(1.33)
$DOUBT_{t-1}$		−.065	−.096		
		(3.87)*	(2.01)**		
STDOUBT				−.047	
				(1.80)***	
$PROVISION_{t-1}$					−.085
					(1.73)***
$I\text{-}HHI_{t-1} \times DOUBT_{t-1}$			−1.020		
			(1.82)***		
$A\text{-}HHI_{t-1} \times DOUBT_{t-1}$			−.046		
			(1.89)***		
$I\text{-}HHI_{t-1} \times (DOUBT_{t-1})^2$			7.391		
			(2.16)**		
$A\text{-}HHI_{t-1} \times (DOUBT_{t-1})^2$			2.906		
			(1.87)***		
$I\text{-}HHI_{t-1} \times STDOUBT$				−1.319	
				(1.69)***	
$A\text{-}HHI_{t-1} \times STDOUBT$				−.517	
				(1.88)***	
$I\text{-}HHI_{t-1} \times (STDOUBT)^2$				8.776	
				(1.75)***	
$A\text{-}HHI_{t-1} \times (STDOUBT)^2$				5.320	
				(2.04)**	
$I\text{-}HHI_{t-1} \times PROVISION_{t-1}$					−.764
					(1.80)***
$A\text{-}HHI_{t-1} \times PROVISION_{t-1}$					−2.552
					(2.19)**
$I\text{-}HHI_{t-1} \times (PROVISION_{t-1})^2$					3.754
					(1.52)
$A\text{-}HHI_{t-1} \times (PROVISION_{t-1})^2$					6.420
					(1.87)***
1995	.001	.014	.016	.001	.001
	(1.61)	(1.39)	(1.31)	(1.40)	(1.49)
1996	.002	.002	.001	.015	.008
	(2.09)**	(.95)	(1.18)	(1.71)***	(1.63)
1997	−.001	−.001	−.001	−.001	−.001
	(.73)	(2.14)**	(2.14)**	(.68)	(1.35)
1998	.002	.002	.001	.015	.009
	(1.84)***	(1.08)	(1.20)	(.70)	(1.03)
1999	−.001	−.003	−.002	−.022	−.014
	(1.36)	(1.99)**	(1.90)***	(1.69)**	(1.85)***
Adjusted R^2	.0229	.3612	.4055	.4003	.4129

TABLE 4 ***(Continued)***

	ROA$_t$				
	(1)	(2)	(3)	(4)	(5)
F-statistics	3.28*	38.64*	40.25*	44.39*	36.76*
Number	604	604	604	604	604

NOTE.—This table presents the results for the test of whether the relationship between bank return and bank focus is positive on average (eq. [1]) and whether it is nonlinear and U-shaped in bank risk (eq. [3]). The *t*-statistics in parentheses are corrected for heteroscedasticity using White's correction. The coefficients on bank-specific fixed effects are not reported for the sake of brevity.

* Statistically significant at the 1% level.

** Statistically significant at the 5% level.

*** Statistically significant at the 10% level.

proceeding to this endogeneity correction, we discuss the magnitude of the effects documented so far, in particular of the U-shaped relationship between focus and returns as the level of bank risk changes.

To understand the economic significance of the U-shaped relationship, we plot the marginal effect *d*(Return)/*d*(Focus) for different values of RISK for both measures of focus, I-HHI and A-HHI, and for different measures of Return and RISK. In figures 2*a* and 3*a*, we employ ROA as the return measure and employ DOUBT and STDOUBT as the risk measures, respectively. In figures 2*b*, 3*b*, 4*a*, and 4*b*, we employ SR as the return measure and employ DOUBT, STDOUBT, STDRET, and IDIOSYNCRATIC as the risk measures, respectively. In all plots, the marginal effect is plotted for both I-HHI (thick line) and A-HHI (dotted line). The range of the RISK proxy is measured over the spectrum covered by that proxy for the Italian banks in our sample over the period 1993–99 (panel B of table 3).

Consider figures 2*a* and 3*a*. These graphs are based on estimated coefficients from table 4, columns 3 and 4, respectively. As can be seen in these plots, *d*(ROA)/*d*(I-HHI) is close to zero at low risk values, is small and negative at moderate risk levels (5–10% for DOUBT and 2–14% for STDOUBT), and is positive and sharply rising at high risk levels. The spectrum of high risk levels in which the effect is positive and sharply rising consists of the highest risk decile (about 10% of the sample in each year) in the case of DOUBT and the highest quartile (about 25% of the sample) in the case of STDOUBT.[12]

A natural question to ask is whether these observations are outliers that should be ignored. In fact, it turns out that these observations cannot be treated as mere outliers and discarded for banking systems under stress. As mentioned earlier, the 1990s were a particularly difficult period for many Italian banks and industries. We examined, for example, the sets of banks in each year with a DOUBT ratio in the top 10% of DOUBT ratios across all banks in that year. Importantly, we found that many banks experienced fluctuations in their

12. The fact that these high-risk banks constitute a significant portion of our total sample in each year is consistent with the observation that the 1990s were a particularly difficult period for many Italian banks (and industries), resulting in significantly high nonperforming loan ratios for many banks (see also BNP Paribas [2001], Goldman Sachs [2001], and Sapienza [2002, 2004] for corroborating evidence).

TABLE 5 Test for Nonmonotonicity in Effect of Focus on Bank Stock Returns: 105 Italian Banks, 1993–99

	SR_t						
	(1)	(2)	(3)	(4)	(5)	(6)	(7)
Intercept	−.422	−.097	−.089	−.072	.052	−.082	−.037
	(2.65)**	(1.99)**	(1.74)***	(1.88)***	(1.69)***	(1.79)***	(.81)
I-HHI_{t-1}	.013	.052	.085	.058	.021	.039	.018
	(3.16)*	(2.99)*	(3.23)*	(3.06)*	(2.47)**	(2.82)**	(2.46)**
A-HHI_{t-1}	.192	.104	.071	.050	.044	.076	.027
	(4.02)*	(3.63)*	(3.37)*	(3.78)*	(2.64)**	(2.99)*	(2.52)**
LN(SIZE)_{t-1}		−.073	−.114	−.127	−.032	−.002	−.001
		(.81)	(.58)	(1.39)	(1.06)	(1.53)	(1.12)
EQRATIO_{t-1}		.003	.006	.013	.076	.047	.067
		(.65)	(1.03)	(1.45)	(.74)	(1.05)	(1.15)
BRRATIO_{t-1}		.135	.131	.146	.104	.103	.108
		(1.71)***	(1.70)***	(1.53)	(1.54)	(1.57)	(1.62)
EMPRATIO_{t-1}		−2.825	−2.829	−.814	−.384	−.648	−.204
		(2.40)**	(1.63)	(1.35)	(1.80)***	(2.30)**	(1.52)
DOUBT_{t-1}		−1.03	−1.759				
		(.18)	(.46)				
STDOUBT				−1.184			
				(.41)			
PROVISION_{t-1}					−.072		
					(2.02)**		
STDRET_{t-1}						.0276	
						(2.41)**	
$\text{IDIOSYNCRATIC}_{t-1}$							−.884
							(1.92)***
$\text{I-HHI}_{t-1} \times \text{DOUBT}_{t-1}$			−.491				
			(1.67)***				
$\text{A-HHI}_{t-1} \times \text{DOUBT}_{t-1}$			−1.091				
			(1.62)				
$\text{I-HHI}_{t-1} \times (\text{DOUBT}_{t-1})^2$			5.064				
			(1.90)***				

A-HHI$_{t-1}$ × (DOUBT$_{t-1}$)^2	6.041				
	(1.99)**				
I-HHI$_{t-1}$ × STDOUBT		−.276			
		(1.50)			
A-HHI$_{t-1}$ × STDOUBT		−.275			
		(1.67)***			
I-HHI$_{t-1}$ × (STDOUBT)^2		4.083			
		(1.42)			
A-HHI$_{t-1}$ × (STDOUBT)^2		3.748			
		(1.90)***			
I-HHI$_{t-1}$ × PROVISION$_{t-1}$			−.256		
			(1.44)		
A-HHI$_{t-1}$ × PROVISION$_{t-1}$			−.905		
			(1.78)***		
I-HHI$_{t-1}$ × (PROVISION$_{t-1}$)^2			2.562		
			(1.70)***		
A-HHI$_{t-1}$ × (PROVISION$_{t-1}$)^2			4.094		
			(2.36)**		
I-HHI$_{t-1}$ × STDRET$_{t-1}$				1.329	
				(1.48)	
A-HHI$_{t-1}$ × STDRET$_{t-1}$				3.062	
				(1.76)***	
I-HHI$_{t-1}$ × (STDRET$_{t-1}$)^2				5.743	
				(.51)	
A-HHI$_{t-1}$ × (STDRET$_{t-1}$)^2				8.053	
				(1.06)	
I-HHI$_{t-1}$ × IDIOSYNCRATIC$_{t-1}$					−.641
					(1.89)***
A-HHI$_{t-1}$ × IDIOSYNCRATIC$_{t-1}$					−.524
					(2.33)**
I-HHI$_{t-1}$ × (IDIOSYNCRATIC$_{t-1}$)^2					3.082
					(1.60)
A-HHI$_{t-1}$ × (IDIOSYNCRATIC$_{t-1}$)^2					2.081
					(1.83)***

TABLE 5 *(Continued)*

	SR_t						
	(1)	(2)	(3)	(4)	(5)	(6)	(7)
1995	.091	−.001	−.001	.001	.002	.067	.028
	(.92)	(1.42)	(1.48)	(1.52)	(1.30)	(1.17)	(1.66)***
1996	.053	.018	.017	.013	.025	.036	.025
	(.54)	(1.97)**	(1.90)**	(2.01)**	(2.26)**	(.95)	(1.29)
1997	−.021	−.001	−.001	−.006	−.003	−.014	−.007
	(.98)	(.58)	(.50)	(.48)	(.97)	(1.06)	(1.22)
1998	.032	.014	.014	.014	.007	.035	.029
	(2.86)**	(.82)	(.76)	(.69)	(1.06)	(2.31)**	(2.00)**
1999	−.051	−.049	−.049	−.059	−.035	−.039	−.014
	(3.54)*	(2.58)**	(2.41)**	(2.14)**	(2.01)**	(2.46)**	(2.05)**
Adjusted R^2	.0658	.2846	.3082	.2958	.2937	.2895	.2603
F-statistics	7.33*	14.10*	12.43*	11.86*	10.54*	12.06*	9.80*
Number	152	152	152	152	152	152	152

NOTE.—This table presents the results for the test of whether the relationship between bank return and bank focus is positive on average (eq. [1]) and whether it is nonlinear and U-shaped in bank risk (eq. [3]). The t-statistics in parentheses are corrected for heteroscedasticity using White's correction. The coefficients on bank-specific fixed effects are not reported for the sake of brevity.

* Statistically significant at the 1% level.

** Statistically significant at the 5% level.

*** Statistically significant at the 10% level.

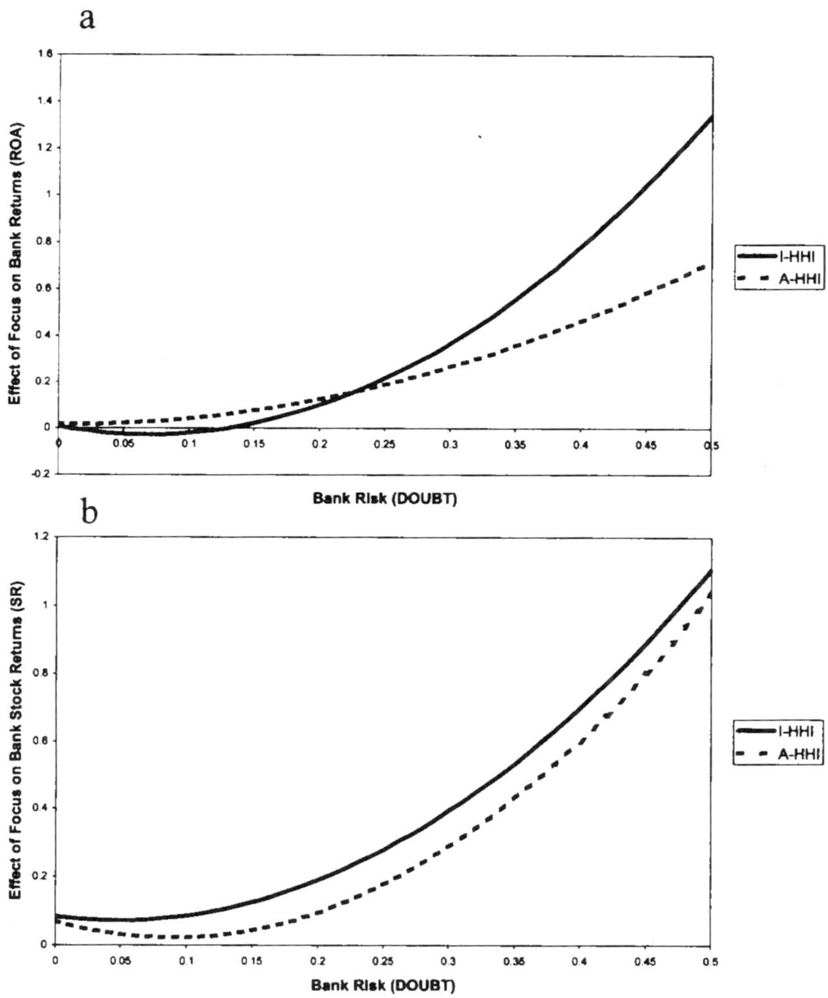

FIG. 2.—Economic significance of the relationship between bank return and bank focus, which is nonlinear as a function of bank risk. *a*, Nonmonotonicity in effect of focus on ROA as a function of DOUBT. *b*, Nonmonotonicity in effect of focus on SR as a function of DOUBT. The figure plots the marginal effect *d*(Return)/*d*(Focus) as specified in eq. (4), the underlying specification for which is eq. (3). The marginal effect is plotted for both focus measures, I-HHI and A-HHI. The coefficients used to plot the relationships are obtained from table 4 and table 5. For each figure, the range of respective risk variable is taken to be between 0% and an upper bound that covers the minimum and the maximum values over our sample period (see panel B of table 3). The definitions of all variables and also a description of how they are computed are presented in Sec. II.

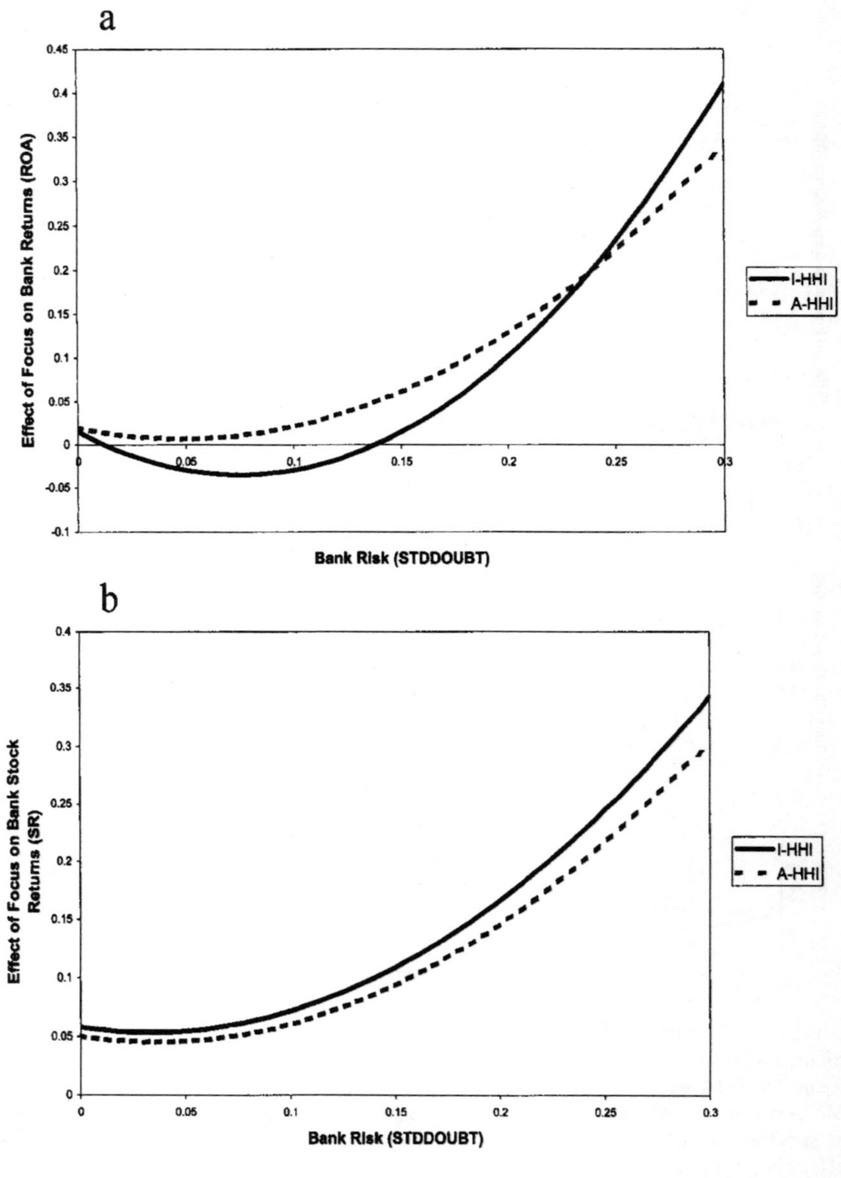

FIG. 3.—Economic significance of the relationship between bank return and bank focus, which is nonlinear as a function of bank risk. *a*, Nonmonotonicity in effect of focus on ROA as a function of STDDOUBT. *b*, Nonmonotonicity in effect of focus on SR as a function of STDDOUBT. See also the legend to fig. 2.

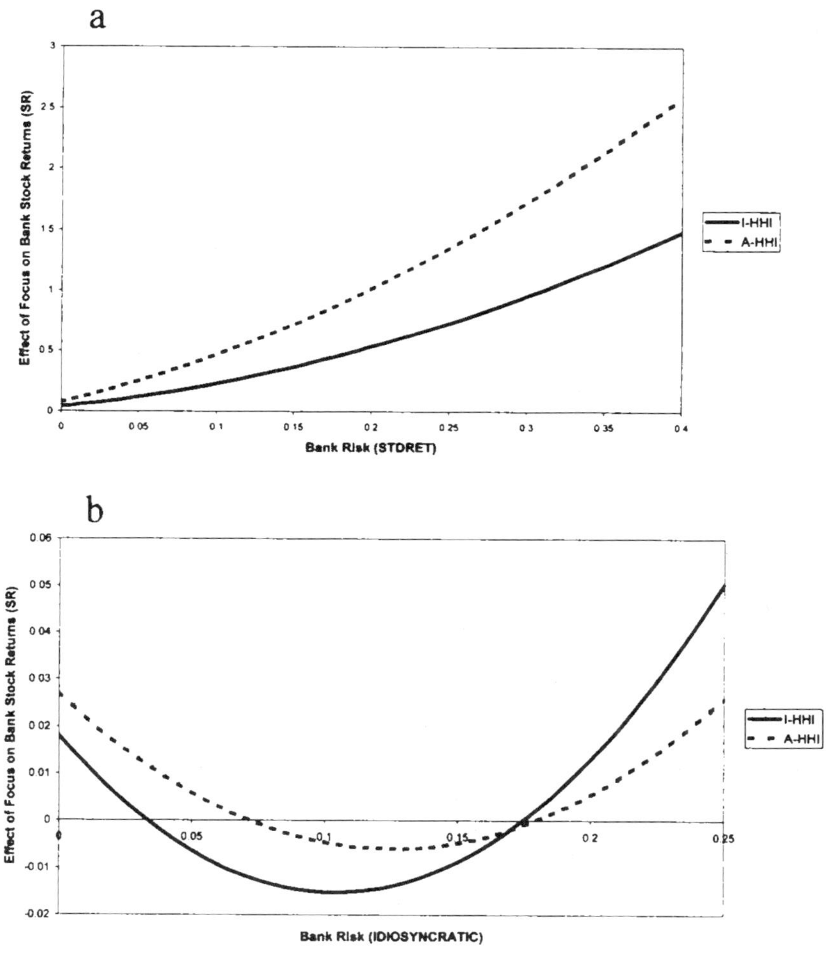

FIG. 4.—Economic significance of the relationship between bank return and bank focus, which is nonlinear as a function of bank risk. *a*, Nonmonotonicity in effect of focus on SR as a function of STDDRET. *b*, Nonmonotonicity in effect of focus on SR as a function of IDIOSYNCRATIC. See also the legend to fig. 2.

DOUBT values from being very low to very high. This is captured in the high values of STDOUBT, the standard deviation of DOUBT, in table 1 and panel B of table 3. However, different banks experienced these fluctuations *at different points during the sample period*. Eliminating observations with high DOUBT values would thus amount to retaining only those data points for each bank that correspond to low or moderate values of DOUBT. Moreover, if the top 10% observations of DOUBT were omitted in each year, this would correspond to omission of over 25 banks (about one-fourth of our sample size of 105 banks) across different years.[13] That is, banks with the highest values of DOUBT in any given year are not necessarily the same banks with the highest values of DOUBT in other sample years.

Thus it appears that diversification across industries and asset sectors is not particularly beneficial for the bank returns and may in fact be especially costly for high-risk banks. For example, for a bank with DOUBT of 25% in the previous year, the effect of increasing industrial focus from 0.16 (approximately equally exposed to six industries) to 0.20 (approximately equally exposed to five industries) is to increase its next year's ROA by approximately 0.80%. Note that such a bank lies in the highest DOUBT decile. A similar increase in focus for a bank with a standard deviation of DOUBT of 20% results in an increase in its return of approximately 0.40%. Such a bank lies in the seventy-fifth–ninetieth percentile region of STDOUBT in our sample. Given that the mean ROA is 0.93% with a standard deviation of 0.85% in our sample (table 1), these effects are clearly economically important.[14] A similar conclusion is drawn from figures 2*b*, 3*b*, 4*a*, and 4*b*, where SR is employed as the return measure and the risk measures employed are DOUBT, STDOUBT, STDRET, and IDIOSYNCRATIC, respectively.

13. To be even more precise, there are only three common banks in the top decile of DOUBT between years 1993 and 1999 (BP Dell'irpinia, CR Teramo, and Banco di Sicilia), and similarly only three common banks in the bottom decile of DOUBT between these years (BP Commercio and Industria, CR Ravenna, and CR Rimini). This reflects the fact that these deciles are essentially composed of different banks in the years 1993 and 1999 and, more generally, during the interim period.

14. We also explored the following question: Is the U-shaped relationship between return and focus, as a measure of risk, a spurious econometric outcome due to the quadratic specification employed? To answer this question, we considered the following piecewise linear relationship:

$$\begin{aligned}\frac{d(\text{Return})}{d(\text{Focus})} = {} & \alpha + \beta_1 \times \text{Dummy}(3\% \leq \text{DOUBT} < 6\%)\\ & + \beta_2 \times \text{Dummy}(6\% \leq \text{DOUBT} < 10\%)\\ & + \beta_3 \times \text{Dummy}(10\% \leq \text{DOUBT} < 15\%)\\ & + \beta_4 \times \text{Dummy}(15\% \leq \text{DOUBT} < 25\%)\\ & + \beta_5 \times \text{Dummy}(\text{DOUBT} \geq 25\%).\end{aligned}$$

We considered similar piecewise linear relationships for risk measures other than DOUBT. If the U-shaped relationship is robust, then the sum of α and the β's associated with relatively lower levels of DOUBT should be negative and decreasing (increasing in magnitude) but the sum of α and β's should eventually be positive and increasing as higher and higher DOUBT observations are considered. This is precisely what the estimated coefficients reveal. For example, in the case of industrial focus (I-HHI), we find that $0 > \alpha + \beta_1 > \alpha + \beta_2 > \alpha + \beta_3$ and $\alpha + \beta_3 < \alpha + \beta_4 < 0 < \alpha + \beta_5$. The coefficients estimated for asset focus (A-HHI) and for other proxies for risk (STDOUBT, PROVISION, STDRET, and IDIOSYNCRATIC) reveal a similar pattern. This gives us confidence that the nonlinear relationship between returns and focus as a function of risk is not purely an artifact of our quadratic specification. These results are contained in table 13 and are available from the authors on request.

B. Endogeneity of Focus Measures

In our tests so far, we employed focus measures with a lag; that is, we considered the effect of Focus_{t-1} on Return_t. This helps to partially address the endogeneity issue. Arguably, it is appropriate for ROA_t, since any monitoring-related effects of focus may get captured in book returns only with a lag. However, this is less justifiable in the case of stock returns since they will reflect contemporaneous information as to the expected effects of any focus changes (assuming these changes are publicly observable). Hence, it is important to consider the effects of Focus_t on Return_t. Furthermore, the fact that diversified banks seem to be either underperforming or certainly not dominating the focused banks begs the question as to why some banks are undertaking performance-destroying (or value-destroying) diversification. These questions pertain to the issue of the endogeneity of bank focus measures: Specifically, if a bank has some latent characteristic that induces it to be focused and simultaneously results in greater bank returns, then estimations of equation (3) will likely produce biased estimates.[15] We address this endogeneity issue next.

To account for the possible endogeneity of focus measures, we estimate a simultaneous equations system in which Return_t and Focus_t are both treated as variables to be explained and the error terms of the two equations in the system are allowed to be correlated with each other. This is essentially a seemingly unrelated regression (SUR) approach (see Theil 1971; Johnson 1972; Maddala 1977). In order to prevent the system from growing too large in terms of the number of coefficients to be estimated and, in turn, to retain statistical power in the estimation, we alternately treat one of the two focus measures, I-HHI_t and A-HHI_t, as endogenous in year t and the other as its exogenous value in year $t-1$. When treating I-HHI_t (A-HHI_t) as endogenous, we employ A-HHI_{t-1} (I-HHI_{t-1}) as an explanatory variable only for Return_t and not for I-HHI_t (A-HHI_t). This ensures that the order conditions for identifying the system are satisfied.

For the endogenous determination of Focus_t, we considered a number of independent explanatory variables as instruments:

- LN(SIZE): natural logarithm of the asset size of the bank.
- NATIONAL DUMMY: This takes on a value of one if the bank is classified as "national" (in a geographic sense) by Bank of Italy and zero otherwise. The dummy is one for the nine "very large" banks of our sample (see App. A). Eight of these banks are also money center banks.
- PRIVATE DUMMY: This is one for all banks that are not publicly

15. Campa and Kedia (2002), Graham, Lemmon, and Wolf (2002), Maksimovic and Phillips (2002), and Villalonga (2004) examine the endogeneity of the decision to focus or diversify for corporations and question, on both empirical and economic grounds, the analysis of the "diversification discount" in the corporate finance literature that ignores the endogeneity issue.

traded, 71 out of 105 in our sample, and zero for the remaining 34 banks.

- STATE-OWNED DUMMY: This is one for 62 banks in our sample that are state-owned at the beginning of 1993 as classified by Sapienza (2002).
- GROUP DUMMY: This takes on a value of one for all banks that are "a part of a bank group or a consortium" and zero otherwise. There are 35 consortium banks in our sample.
- DEPOSIT TO ASSET RATIO: This is the ratio of all deposits of the bank to its overall asset base. It is included with a lag; that is, DEPOSIT TO ASSET RATIO$_{t-1}$ is an explanatory variable for Focus$_t$.
- AVERAGE Focus$_t$: When I-HHI$_t$ (A-HHI$_t$) is treated as endogenous, this variable is average I-HHI (A-HHI) across all banks in year t.

The ex ante rationale for the use of these instruments is as follows. A large body of banking literature has shown a positive relationship between diversification and size. The standard arguments are based either on the finiteness of good projects or on diminishing returns to scale within an industry, and on the risk avoidance induced by relatively high franchise values of large banks. National banks and money center banks may have greater size and scope by definition and thus intrinsically may be more diversified. Private banks, state-owned banks, and consortium banks may have an objective function, and, in turn, a focus or diversifying strategy, that differs from their publicly owned counterparts. For example, private banks may face less corporate governance scrutiny than public banks, state-owned banks may be forced to lend to certain sectors or industries to fulfill state objectives (see Sapienza 2002), and consortium banks may be following a collective focus or diversifying strategy conceived at the level of the consortium. Banks with a high deposit to assets ratio may not be well diversified on the liability side and perhaps rely significantly on "core" deposits. The need to focus or diversify for these banks will differ from that of banks well diversified on the liability side, for example, those with greater access to the purchased funds market. Finally, average focus across all banks in a given year potentially captures macroeconomic conditions and the regulatory environment, not fully captured through other instruments.

Table 6 provides a summary of the bank characteristics and the instruments for the focused and the diversified subsample. In each year t from 1994 to 1999, banks were divided into two groups, focused and diversified, on the basis of whether their HHI measure in year t is below or above the median. Using univariate analysis, the table shows the industrially focused group of banks to have a higher return on assets and on equity, a greater asset sector focus (higher A-HHI), a larger size, a smaller ratio of employees to assets, and a smaller doubtful loans to assets ratio. Publicly traded banks, banks that are not state-owned, and banks that are part of a consortium group are more likely to be industrially focused than diversified. While the overall pattern is somewhat similar for an asset sector–focused group of banks, this group of

TABLE 6 Properties of Focused and Diversified Banks

	Based on I-HHI Median		Based on A-HHI Median	
	Focused	Diversified	Focused	Diversified
ROA_{t-1}	.967	.865	.892	.937
ROE_{t-1}	10.711	6.613	9.391	7.965
$I\text{-}HHI_{t-1}$	.261	.213	.241	.234
$A\text{-}HHI_{t-1}$	.402	.348	.420	.333
$G\text{-}HHI_{t-1}$	.923	.967	.941	.949
$SIZE_{t-1}$	16,978	6,811	9,341	14,178
$EQRATIO_{t-1}$	8.596	8.871	9.024	8.469
$BRRATIO_{t-1}$	.020	.026	.022	.023
$EMPRATIO_{t-1}$	2.872	3.616	3.107	3.374
$DOUBT_{t-1}$	3.758	5.282	4.123	4.910
DEPOSIT $RATIO_{t-1}$	72.899	75.661	74.100	74.462
National dummy	.327	.306	.278	.352
Publicly traded dummy	.385	.162	.333	.217
State-owned dummy	.546	.710	.397	.636
Group dummy	.328	.269	.309	.329

NOTE.—This table provides a summary of the bank characteristics and the instruments for the focused and the diversified samples. In each year t from 1994 to 1999, banks are divided into two groups, focused and diversified, on the basis of whether their HHI measure in year t is below or above the median. Specifically, banks are sorted into focused and diversified groups for each year t and the year $t-1$; characteristics of banks thus sorted in each group are averaged over time. The sorting is done first for I-HHI and next for A-HHI. The last four rows indicate the mean value of the dummy for respective variables indicating proportion of banks in the category.

banks is smaller in size compared to an asset sector–diversified group and is less likely to be from the set of national banks. Overall, the table suggests that the set of instruments identified above should have explanatory power for the endogeneous focus or diversification choice of banks.

The simultaneous system of equations resulting from the choice of these instruments is presented below when $I\text{-}HHI_t$ is treated as endogenous (other specifications we estimate will be described later):

$$\begin{aligned}\text{Return}_{it} = {} & \alpha_{i0} + \alpha_1 \times \text{I-HHI}_{it} + \alpha_2 \times \text{A-HHI}_{it-1} + \eta \times C_{it-1} \\ & + \beta_0 \times \text{RISK}_{it-1} + \beta_{11} \times \text{I-HHI}_{it} \times \text{RISK}_{it-1} \\ & + \beta_{12} \times \text{I-HHI}_{it} \times \text{RISK}^2_{it-1} \\ & + \beta_{21} \times \text{A-HHI}_{it-1} \times \text{RISK}_{it-1} \\ & + \beta_{22} \times \text{A-HHI}_{it-1} \times \text{RISK}^2_{it-1} \\ & + \sum_{s=1995}^{1999} \kappa_s \text{TIME}_s + \epsilon_{iRt}, \end{aligned} \tag{6}$$

$$\begin{aligned}\text{I-HHI}_{it} = {} & \gamma_i + \theta \times C_{it-1} + \delta \times \text{RISK}_{it-1} + \omega \times Z_{it-1} \\ & + \sum_{s=1995}^{1999} \kappa_s \text{TIME}_s + \epsilon_{iIt}, \end{aligned} \tag{7}$$

where C_{t-1} is a vector representing the control variables (LN(SIZE), EQRATIO, BRRATIO, EMPRATIO, and STATE-OWNED DUMMY), Z_{t-1} is a vector representing the instrumental variables (NATIONAL DUMMY, PRIVATE DUMMY, DEPOSIT TO ASSET RATIO$_{t-1}$, GROUP DUMMY, and AVERAGE I-HHI$_t$), and the error terms ϵ_{Rt} and ϵ_{It} may be correlated. Note that LN(SIZE) is included in the control variables and thus serves as a potential instrument for the focus measures. Furthermore, in contrast to the specifications examined in tables 4 and 5, STATE-OWNED DUMMY is also included as a control variable for explaining returns. This is to allow for a possible direct effect of state ownership on bank returns due to inefficiencies, such as higher overheads, looser expense controls, and wasteful bureaucracy, that are more likely to plague state-owned banks. Time dummies and bank-specific fixed effects are included in determining both Return$_t$ and I-HHI$_t$ (except when their inclusion leads to a multicollinearity problem). Under the specification of equations (6) and (7), the effect of focus on returns continues to remain quadratic in risk. Formally,

$$\frac{d(\text{Return}_t)}{d(\text{I-HHI}_t)} = \alpha_1 + \beta_{11} \times \text{RISK} + \beta_{12} \times \text{RISK}^2 \tag{8}$$

and

$$\frac{d(\text{Return}_t)}{d(\text{A-HHI}_{t-1})} = \alpha_2 + \beta_{21} \times \text{RISK} + \beta_{22} \times \text{RISK}^2, \tag{9}$$

where we have suppressed the bank-specific index i.

The results are reported in table 7 (for ROA in panel A and for SR in panel B). In panel A, estimated coefficients are reported for ROA$_t$ and I-HHI$_t$ in columns 1 and 2, with risk measures being DOUBT and STDOUBT, respectively. Columns 3 and 4 report the estimated coefficients for ROA$_t$ and A-HHI$_t$. In panel B, the risk measures are STDRET and IDIOSYNCRATIC. Results with other risk measures are not reported for considerations of space. Examining the coefficients on the linear and quadratic interaction terms between focus and risk, we find that the results corrected for the endogeneity of focus provide even stronger and more consistent evidence in support of the U-shaped relationship. Indeed, all coefficients have the correct sign and are statistically significant at the 10% confidence level or better. The implied marginal effects of focus on return, as risk is varied, are plotted in figures 5*a*, 5*b*, 6*a*, and 6*b*. These correspond to results in columns 1 and 2 of panel A of table 7 and columns 1 and 2 of panel B, respectively, where industrial focus I-HHI$_t$ is treated as endogenous, and are the counterparts of figures 2*a*, 3*a*, 4*a*, and 4*b*, respectively. The marginal effects when A-HHI$_t$ is treated as endogenous are not plotted for considerations of space.

Most notably, all the marginal effects are U-shaped. In particular, the statistical significance of the effect with SR as the return measure and STDRET as the risk measures, which were relatively weak earlier (col. 6 of table 5 and

TABLE 7 **Simultaneous (SUR) Estimation of Effect of Focus on Bank Return Treating Focus as Endogenous Variable**

	A. Return on Assets							
	(1)		(2)		(3)		(4)	
	ROA_t	$I\text{-}HHI_t$	ROA_t	$I\text{-}HHI_t$	ROA_t	$A\text{-}HHI_t$	ROA_t	$A\text{-}HHI_t$
Intercept	.140	.316	.145	.356	.027	.317	.031	.289
	(6.07)*	(8.02)*	(6.03)*	(7.82)*	(1.18)	(8.73)*	(1.12)	(8.62)*
$I\text{-}HHI_t$ (cols. 1, 2),	.001		.001		.006		.005	
$I\text{-}HHI_{t-1}$ (cols. 3, 4)	(1.73)***		(1.80)***		(1.87)***		(1.84)***	
$A\text{-}HHI_{t-1}$ (cols. 1, 2),	.013		.015		.013		.011	
$A\text{-}HHI_t$ (cols. 3, 4)	(1.84)***		(1.86)***		(2.35)**		(2.00)**	
$LN(SIZE)_{t-1}$	−.001	−.007	−.002	−.005	−.001	−.007	−.001	−.005
	(.84)	(3.75)*	(.73)	(3.55)*	(1.09)	(1.94)***	(1.19)	(1.96)**
$EQRATIO_{t-1}$	.043	−.096	.044	−.074	.074	.181	.054	.157
	(5.49)*	(2.35)**	(5.00)*	(2.46)**	(5.82)*	(1.75)***	(6.66)*	(1.71)***
$BRRATIO_{t-1}$	.154	.092	.126	.052	.310	−1.636	.354	−.991
	(1.78)***	(1.06)	(1.87)***	(.99)	(1.73)***	(2.14)**	(1.61)	(1.96)**
$EMPRATIO_{t-1}$	−.050	−.010	−.046	−.007	−.054	−.165	−.105	−.235
	(1.47)	(.71)	(1.42)	(.78)	(1.23)	(.98)	(1.33)	(.52)
$DOUBT_{t-1}$	−.012	−.015			−.076	−.158		
	(1.88)***	(3.68)*			(2.40)**	(2.05)**		
STDOUBT			−.031	−.025			−.037	−.016
			(1.68)***	(2.79)**			(1.70)***	(2.40)**
$I\text{-}HHI_t \times DOUBT_{t-1}$	−1.245				−1.008			
	(1.78)***				(1.90)***			
$A\text{-}HHI_{t-1} \times DOUBT_{t-1}$	−.026				−.028			
	(2.42)**				(2.17)**			
$I\text{-}HHI_t \times (DOUBT_{t-1})^2$	5.245				5.646			
	(1.92)***				(1.74)***			

TABLE 7 *(Continued)*

	(1)		(2)		(3)		(4)	
	ROA_t	$I\text{-}HHI_t$	ROA_t	$I\text{-}HHI_t$	ROA_t	$A\text{-}HHI_t$	ROA_t	$A\text{-}HHI_t$
$A\text{-}HHI_{t-1} \times (DOUBT_{t-1})^2$	1.313				1.374			
	(1.69)***				(1.77)***			
$I\text{-}HHI_t \times STDOUBT$			−.481				−1.059	
			(1.88)***				(1.69)***	
$A\text{-}HHI_{t-1} \times STDOUBT$			−1.434				−1.911	
			(1.70)***				(1.80)***	
$I\text{-}HHI_{t-1} \times (STDOUBT)^2$			5.430				5.095	
			(2.30)**				(1.81)***	
$A\text{-}HHI_{t-1} \times (STDOUBT)^2$			7.931				7.325	
			(1.96)**				(2.12)**	
National dummy		−.015		−.018		−.005		−.014
		(1.98)**		(2.00)**		(1.92)***		(2.02)**
Private dummy		−.024		−.026		−.041		−.026
		(2.52)**		(2.49)**		(4.00)*		(3.25)*
DEPOSIT TO ASSET $RATIO_{t-1}$		−.012		.015		−.056		−.045
		(1.09)		(1.03)		(.52)		(.87)
State-owned dummy	.001	.016	.005	.018	.001	.001	.004	.005
	(.95)	(2.09)**	(1.62)	(2.15)**	(.80)	(2.39)**	(1.65)	(2.14)**
Group dummy		−.003		−.005		−.001		−.002
		(.83)		(.66)		(1.18)		(1.05)
Avg. $I\text{-}HHI_t$ (cols. 1, 2), Avg. $A\text{-}HHI_t$ (cols. 3, 4)		.005		.003		.001		.002
		(1.17)		(.99)		(.72)		(1.06)
1995	.012	−.005	.006	.016	.009	−.005	.005	−.005
	(1.61)	(.53)	(1.44)	(1.61)	(1.59)	(1.03)	(1.38)	(1.06)
1996	.010	−.003	.005	.016	.004	−.002	.005	−.005
	(1.49)	(.47)	(1.37)	(1.44)	(1.42)	(1.27)	(1.26)	(1.30)
1997	−.004	−.013	−.005	−.007	−.002	−.008	−.005	−.007
	(2.50)**	(1.45)	(2.14)**	(1.56)	(2.35)**	(1.90)***	(2.13)**	(1.98)**

	SR,	I-HHI,	SR,	I-HHI,	SR,	A-HHI,	SR,	A-HHI,
1998	.001	−.005	.003	.003	.001	−.004	.001	−.005
	(.71)	(1.08)	(.81)	(.98)	(.61)	(1.23)	(.66)	(1.57)
1999	−.004	−.011	−.006	−.006	−.004	−.015	−.005	−.027
	(2.01)**	(2.26)**	(1.97)**	(2.04)**	(1.97)**	(2.08)**	(2.01)**	(2.14)**
System-weighted R^2	.4003		.3848		.4231		.3940	
Cross-model covariance	.017***		.018***		.014***		.015***	
Cross-model correlation	.024**		.026**		.023**		.024**	
Number	604		604		604		604	

B. Stock Return

	(1)		(2)		(3)		(4)	
	SR_t	$I\text{-}HHI_t$	SR_t	$I\text{-}HHI_t$	SR_t	$A\text{-}HHI_t$	SR_t	$A\text{-}HHI_t$
Intercept	.026	.220	.025	.328	.025	.304	.029	.335
	(1.05)	(6.34)*	(1.45)	(8.29)*	(1.36)	(6.92)*	(1.48)	(8.36)*
$I\text{-}HHI_t$ (cols. 1, 2), $I\text{-}HHI_{t-1}$ (cols. 3, 4)	.015		.015		.005		.012	
	(1.94)***		(1.83)***		(1.90)***		(1.88)***	
$A\text{-}HHI_{t-1}$ (cols. 1, 2), $A\text{-}HHI_t$ (cols. 3, 4)	.019		.025		.015		.017	
	(2.12)**		(2.49)**		(1.88)***		(2.32)**	
$LN(SIZE)_{t-1}$	−.002	−.006	−.008	−.005	−.004	−.017	−.016	−.006
	(1.50)	(2.90)**	(1.35)	(2.99)*	(1.28)	(2.84)**	(1.48)	(2.91)*
$EQRATIO_{t-1}$	.080	−.183	.068	−.154	.079	−.178	.054	−.156
	(1.32)	(1.94)***	(1.03)	(2.14)**	(1.27)	(2.00)**	(1.07)	(2.15)**
$BRRATIO_{t-1}$	.107	−.132	.111	−.106	.094	−.148	.086	−.108
	(1.70)***	(2.20)**	(1.65)	(2.09)**	(1.09)	(2.30)**	(1.29)	(2.20)**
$EMPRATIO_{t-1}$	−1.066	−.163	−1.124	−.178	−.858	−.106	−.981	−.155
	(1.44)	(.95)	(1.30)	(1.04)	(1.60)	(1.08)	(1.60)	(.90)
$STDRET_{t-1}$	−.095	−.152			−.065	−.125		
	(2.00)**	(2.02)**			(2.47)**	(2.48)**		
$IDIOSYNCRATIC_{t-1}$			−.043	−.024			−.075	−.029
			(2.41)**	(2.11)**			(2.29)**	(2.36)**

TABLE 7 (*Continued*)

	(1)		(2)		(3)		(4)	
	SR_t	I-HHI_t	SR_t	I-HHI_t	SR_t	A-HHI_t	SR_t	A-HHI_t
I-HHI_{t-1} × $STDRET_{t-1}$	−.875				−.010			
	(1.71)***				(1.77)***			
A-HHI_{t-1} × $STDRET_{t-1}$	−.342				−.021			
	(1.84)***				(2.03)**			
I-HHI_{t-1} × $(STDRET_{t-1})^2$	4.821				4.860			
	(1.97)**				(1.85)***			
A-HHI_{t-1} × $(STDRET_{t-1})^2$	1.090				1.324			
	(1.83)***				(1.75)***			
I-HHI_{t-1} × $IDIOSYNCRATIC_{t-1}$			−.056				−.044	
			(1.79)***				(1.98)**	
A-HHI_{t-1} × $IDIOSYNCRATIC_{t-1}$			−.044				−.038	
			(2.00)**				(1.85)***	
I-HHI_{t-1} × $(IDIOSYNCRATIC_{t-1})^2$			1.552				1.165	
			(1.82)***				(1.71)***	
A-HHI_{t-1} × $(IDIOSYNCRATIC_{t-1})^2$			2.024				2.540	
			(2.00)**				(1.96)**	
National dummy		−.005		−.005		−.005		−.006
		(1.87)***		(1.85)***		(1.92)***		(1.95)***
Private dummy		−.038		−.041		−.032		−.041
		(4.01)*		(3.96)*		(3.79)*		(3.55)*
DEPOSIT TO ASSET $RATIO_{t-1}$		−.053		−.052		−.046		−.061
		(.16)		(3.17)*		(.86)		(3.55)*
State-owned dummy	−.003	.003	−.001	.005	−.002	.005	−.002	.008
	(.60)	(2.35)**	(.66)	(1.94)***	(.62)	(2.12)**	(.68)	(2.04)**
Group dummy		−.013		−.013		−.010		−.016
		(3.05)*		(3.29)*		(3.11)*		(3.34)*
Avg. I-HHI_t (cols. 1, 2), Avg. A-HHI_t (cols. 3, 4)		.001		.001		.002		.002
		(.73)		(.74)		(.70)		(.93)

1995	.012	−.004	.016	−.010	.018	−.005	.013	−.009
	(1.27)	(.90)	(1.18)	(1.06)	(1.27)	(1.08)	(1.48)	(1.32)
1996	.006	−.005	.005	−.009	.005	−.005	.007	−.005
	(1.50)	(1.26)	(1.26)	(1.21)	(1.18)	(1.50)	(1.21)	(1.48)
1997	−.005	−.017	−.002	−.016	−.013	−.015	−.025	−.012
	(1.48)	(1.59)	(1.44)	(1.33)	(1.51)	(1.44)	(1.78)***	(1.55)
1998	.018	−.009	.010	−.005	.015	−.016	.013	−.019
	(1.69)***	(1.51)	(1.66)***	(1.45)	(1.67)***	(1.63)	(1.59)	(1.60)
1999	−.006	−.016	−.001	−.019	−.016	−.012	−.004	−.010
	(1.93)***	(1.97)**	(1.78)***	(2.00)**	(1.81)***	(2.09)**	(1.85)***	(2.16)**
System-weighted R^2	.2967		.3192		.3176		.3297	
Cross-model covariance	.0320		.0303		.0365		.0318	
Cross-model correlation	.0418		.0442		.0403		.0406	
Number	152		152		152		152	

NOTE.—This table presents the results for the test of whether the relationship between bank return and bank focus is positive on average (eq. [1]) and whether it is nonlinear and U-shaped in bank risk (eq. [3]) for 105 Italian banks over the sample period 1993–99. The results are corrected for endogeneity of focus measures I-HHI$_t$ and A-HHI$_t$. In cols. 1 and 2, I-HHI is treated as endogenous. In cols. 3 and 4, A-HHI is treated as endogenous. The specification is a simultaneous system of equations as in eqq. (7) and (8). The t-statistics in parentheses are corrected for heteroscedasticity using White's correction. The coefficients on bank-specific fixed effects are not reported for the sake of brevity.

* Statistically significant at the 1% level.

** Statistically significant at the 5% level.

*** Statistically significant at the 10% level.

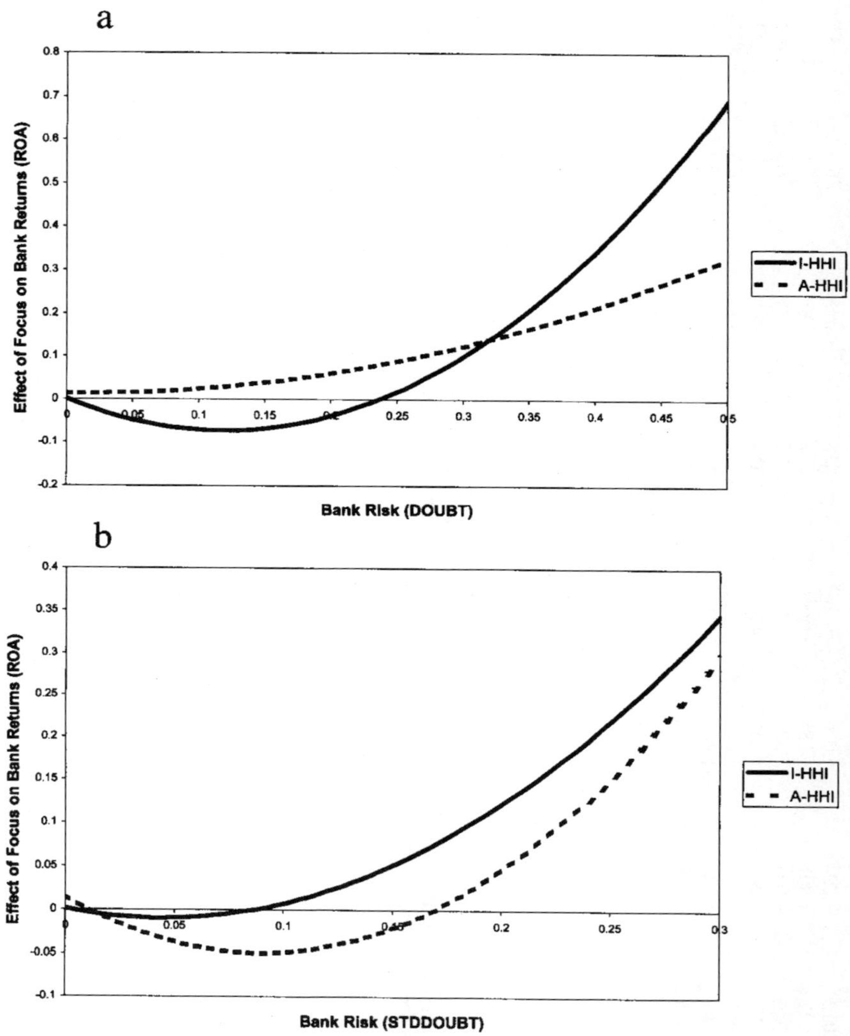

FIG. 5.—Economic significance of the relationship between bank return and bank focus, which is nonlinear as a function of bank risk. *a*, Nonmonotonicity in endogeneity-corrected effect of focus on ROA as a function of DOUBT. *b*, Nonmononotonicity in endogeneity-corrected effect of focus on ROA as a function of STDDOUBT. The figure plots the marginal effect *d*(Return)/*d*(Focus) as specified in eq. (4), the underlying specification for which is the simultaneous system of eqq. (6) and (7). The marginal effect is thus corrected for the endogeneity of focus measures, as described in Sec. III.*B*. In each plot, the marginal effect is plotted for both focus measures, I-HHI and A-HHI. The coefficients used to plot the relationships are obtained from panel A of table 7, cols. 1 and 2. For each figure, the range of respective risk variable is taken to be between 0% and an upper bound that covers the minimum and the maximum values over our sample period (see panel B of table 3). The definitions of all variables and also a description of how they are computed are presented in Sec. II.

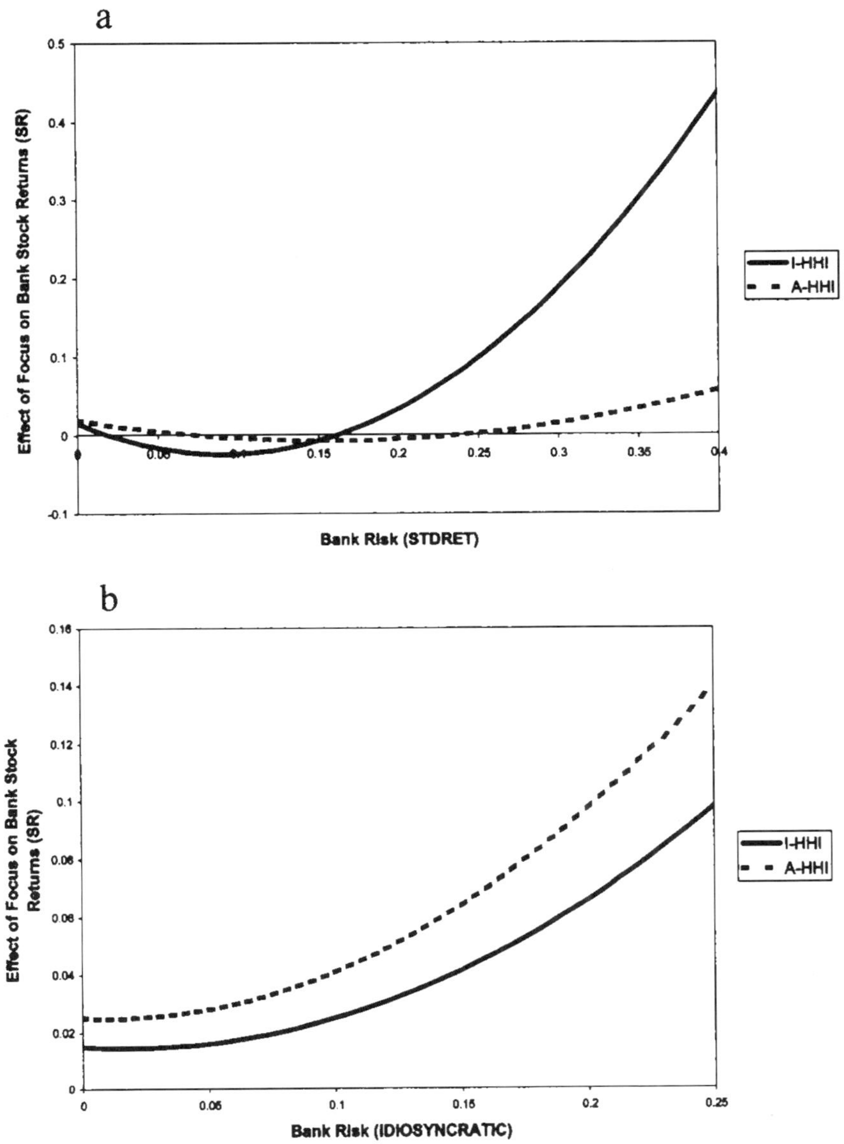

FIG. 6.—Economic significance of the relationship between bank return and bank focus, which is nonlinear as a function of bank risk. *a*, Nonmonotonicity in endogeneity-corrected effect of focus on SR as a function of STDRET. *b*, Nonmonotonicity in endogeneity-corrected effect of focus on SR as a function of IDIOSYNCRATIC. The coefficients used to plot the relationships are obtained from panel B of table 7, cols. 1 and 2. Also see the the legend to fig. 5.

fig. 4*a*), are now stronger and the coefficients have the expected signs. Similarly, the positive effect with SR as the return measure and IDIOSYNCRATIC as the risk measure, which spanned only a small range of risk values (col. 7 of table 5 and fig. 4*b*), is now uniformly positive after the endogeneity correction.

It is also of interest to examine the estimated coefficients in the endogenous determination of focus measures. The effects overall are similar for both focus measures, I-HHI (cols. 1 and 2) and A-HHI (cols. 3 and 4). Large banks and national or money center banks are more diversified as reflected by the negative sign on LN(SIZE) and NATIONAL DUMMY in the focus regressions. Interestingly, private banks are more diversified than public banks, an effect that is quite strong statistically. All else being equal, state-owned banks are more focused, consistent with Sapienza's (2002) conclusion that these banks have an objective that is geared toward supporting specific industries, often at subsidized rates. The deposit to assets ratio and average focus of all banks in the given year do not seem to have any incremental effect, whereas being part of a consortium has a statistically insignificant effect for industrial focus but a negative effect on asset sector focus.

Interestingly, the effect of past losses or risk ($DOUBT_{t-1}$, STDOUBT, $STDRET_{t-1}$, and $IDIOSYNCRATIC_{t-1}$) on focus is always negative and significant. This implies that, all else being equal, banks that are overall risky or have recently experienced higher losses or increases in their stock return volatility choose to focus less, that is, diversify more. This lends support to the need for the endogeneity correction we have employed: If banks that choose to diversify (focus) are precisely the ones that are loss-making (profit-making) or risky (safe), then a negative relationship between return and diversification arises even in the absence of any direct causal effect of diversification on return. In other words, the negative relationship between return and diversification may be "spurious" in that it simply reflects which banks select to diversify and which banks choose to focus. The results in table 7 show convincingly, however, that even though this selection problem is present in our sample, it is not solely responsible for the relationship between diversification and return. The empirical relationship confirmed in table 7 confirms that some of the diversified banks, especially the riskier ones, might benefit from choosing to increase their focus instead.

Overall, our results lend empirical support for diversification (focus) having a small benefit (cost) at low bank risk levels, and in fact, hurting (helping) bank returns at very high risk levels. We find this to hold for both industrial and asset sectoral focus, for return on bank assets as well as stock returns of banks, and for a variety of accounting and stock return–based measures for unexpected and expected bank risk. It is important to note, however, that examining bank returns is only one side of the trade-off between return and risk. Next, we examine the other side of the trade-off, the effect of the decision to focus (diversify) on bank loan risk.

C. The Relationship between Focus and Risk: The Effect of Expanding the Loan Portfolio in New Areas

In order to study the effect of focus (diversification) on bank monitoring effectiveness and, in turn, on the quality of bank loan portfolios as banks expand the scope of their loan portfolios, we consider first the risk of bank loans as a dependent variable in the regression

$$\text{RISK}_{it} = \mu_{i0} + \mu_1 \times \text{I-HHI}_{it-1} + \mu_2 \times \text{A-HHI}_{it-1} + \xi \times C_{it-1} + \sum_{s=1995}^{1999} \kappa_s \text{TIME}_s + \epsilon_{it}, \tag{10}$$

where, as before, C_{t-1} are the non–risk control variables augmented to include past returns (ROA_{t-1} or SR_{t-1}), and risk is proxied by the variable DOUBT_t, STDRET_t, or IDIOSYNCRATIC_t. If an increase in focus (increase in HHI) reduces the risk of bank loan portfolios, then

$$\mu_1 < 0, \ \mu_2 < 0. \tag{11}$$

There are at least three reasons why this might arise. First, banks may lack the monitoring expertise in lending to a new sector when learning costs are present. Second, when the loan sector to which banks migrate is already being supplied with credit by other banks, new bank entrants may be subject to adverse selection and a "winner's curse" effect.[16] This suggests that diversification could lower returns on bank loans and increase the risk of failure to a greater degree when the sectors into which the bank expands are subject to greater competition. Third, diversification can cause a bank to grow in size, subjecting it to agency-based scale inefficiencies.

Consequently, entering into "new" loan sectors may adversely affect bank loan portfolio quality (increase risk). Note that we use the qualifier "newer" for those industries in which previous exposures of the bank have been relatively small or nonexistent (rather than being newer in the sense of technological or productive aspects of the industry such as dot.com firms). To test this relationship, we construct two variables, NEW_t and FRACNEW_t, defined as follows:

- NEW_t: This dummy variable is one in year t for a bank if its top five industries (ranked by loan exposure amounts) in the nonfinancial and household parts of the loan portfolio in year t include an industry not contained in its top five industries in year $t - 1$, and zero otherwise.[17]

16. Several papers have discussed the adverse effect of competition on bank loan quality. These include Gehrig (1998), Dell'Arricia, Friedman, and Marquez (1999), Winton (1999), Boot and Thakor (2000), and Hauswald and Marquez (2002) for theory and Shaffer (1998) for empirical results.

17. We have also employed a variant of this variable in which we used the past three years to check whether an industry in year t was not contained in the bank's prior top five industry exposures.

In essence, this captures whether a bank has had recent experience in lending to all its top industries, "recent experience" being interpreted as the bank having had a substantial exposure to these industries in the past few years.

- FRACNEW_t: This variable measures the fraction of the loan portfolio of a bank in year t that consists of exposures to "new" industries, newness of an industry being defined as in the description of the variable NEW_t above.

Finally, we also introduce an additional variable, COMP_t, that measures the extent of competition a bank faces in lending for its top five industries, defined as follows.

- COMP_t: For bank i, COMP_t is measured as $\Sigma_{j=1}^{5} [1 - (X_{ij}/R_j)]$, where $R_j = \Sigma_{i=1}^{N} X_{ij}$, the total exposure across all banks (1 through N) to industry j. Note that COMP is higher for bank i if its exposure to the (top five) industries it lends to is smaller compared to the exposure of other banks to the same set of industries; that is, it has a smaller share of lending to these industries.

If COMP_t is high for a bank, we interpret that it is likely to face greater competition, and adverse selection or winner's curse problems, when it seeks to expand its loans to these industries. Note that COMP is a measure of loan-side competition faced by banks in the aggregate lending market. Our data do not allow us to compute a local version of this measure or a measure of local competition based on deposit taking. The lending-based measure of competition should, however, be more appropriate for the adverse selection hypothesis.[18]

To test whether the hypothesis concerning deterioration of the quality of a loan portfolio (increase in bank risk) occurs upon entry into "newer" industries (i.e., reduced focus), we modify regression (10) along two dimensions. First, we introduce NEW_t, FRACNEW_t, and COMP_{t-1} as explanatory variables for RISK_t. Second, we introduce interaction terms between these three variables

18. Recall that our data provide only the top five industry exposures of a bank. This means that our measure of competition in an industry is necessarily imperfect: it excludes competing banks whose exposure in that industry is not one of the top five industry exposures. Suppose that the ratio of the total exposure of the banking sector to an industry calculated using our data to the actual total exposure to that industry were the same for all industries. In this case, the bias in the COMP measure is systematic and would not affect our estimates. Suppose instead that this ratio varies across industries but in a perfectly random fashion across all industries over time. This would constitute a "pure noise" measurement error in COMP, biasing its estimate toward zero and making it difficult for our tests to find any effect of competition on bank risk. However, if the variation in the ratio across industries is systematically high for some industries and low for others, then our tests might identify an effect even when none exists. Without knowing the entire loan portfolio composition of all banks in our sample, it is difficult to know the exact nature of the measurement error (or bias) in COMP.

and the two focus measures I-HHI$_{t-1}$ and A-HHI$_{t-1}$.[19] The resulting specification is

$$\begin{aligned}\text{RISK}_{it} = {} & \mu_{i0} + \mu_1 \times \text{I-HHI}_{it-1} + \mu_2 \times \text{A-HHI}_{it-1} + \xi \times C_{it-1} \\ & + \nu_{10} \times \text{NEW}_{it} + \nu_{20} \times \text{FRACNEW}_{it} + \nu_{30} \times \text{COMP}_{it-1} \\ & + \nu_{11} \times \text{I-HHI}_{it-1} \times \text{NEW}_{it} + \nu_{12} \times \text{A-HHI}_{it-1} \times \text{NEW}_{it} \\ & + \nu_{21} \times \text{I-HHI}_{it-1} \times \text{FRACNEW}_{it} \\ & + \nu_{22} \times \text{A-HHI}_{it-1} \times \text{FRACNEW}_{it} \\ & + \nu_{31} \times \text{I-HHI}_{it-1} \times \text{COMP}_{it-1} \\ & + \nu_{32} \times \text{A-HHI}_{it-1} \times \text{COMP}_{it-1} + \sum_{s=1995}^{1999} \kappa_s \text{TIME}_s + \epsilon_{it}. \end{aligned} \tag{12}$$

Consider the marginal effect of NEW$_t$ on RISK$_t$. We obtain

$$\frac{d(\text{RISK}_t)}{d(\text{NEW}_t)} = \nu_{10} + \nu_{11} \times \text{I-HHI}_{t-1} + \nu_{12} \times \text{A-HHI}_{t-1}, \tag{13}$$

where we have suppressed the bank-specific index i. The null hypothesis is that $d(\text{RISK}_t)/d(\text{NEW}_t)$ is positive and is increasing in bank diversification or decreasing in bank focus. The reason is that for a well-diversified bank, the effect of entry into new industries is primarily one of spreading its monitoring resources more widely. By contrast, for a focused bank, the effect of entry into new industries is beneficial from a traditional diversification standpoint and is also less harmful from the standpoint of a deterioration in monitoring quality since, even with an additional industry, the bank remains relatively specialized. That is, the constant term ν_{10} is positive and the interaction term coefficients ν_{11} and ν_{12} are negative. The hypothesis with respect to the marginal effect of FRACNEW$_t$ and COMP$_{t-1}$ on RISK$_t$ take similar forms yielding the overall hypotheses[20]

$$\nu_{j0} > 0, \ \nu_{j1} < 0, \ \nu_{j2} < 0, \quad j = 1, 2, 3. \tag{14}$$

Table 8 presents empirical evidence on how the decision to focus or diversify endogenously affects the risk of bank loan portfolios by reporting the results of tests of equations (10)–(12) above. The first three columns in table 8 correspond to the entire sample in which the risk measure employed is doubtful and the nonperforming loans to assets ratio DOUBT$_t$, and the last six columns

19. We draw the reader's attention here to the fact that the variables NEW, FRACNEW, and COMP had either statistically insignificant or economically insignificant effects on return measures when added to the specification in Sec. III*A*. Hence, these variables were omitted.

20. Note that if diversification has an effect on bank risk due to (agency) costs associated with any corresponding increase in the bank size or increase in the number of branches or employees, then such effects should be at least partially captured through the coefficients in the regressions on the control variables: LN(SIZE), BRRATIO, and EMPRATIO.

TABLE 8 Test for Effect of Focus on Bank Loan Risk

	Dependent Variable								
	$DOUBT_t$			$STDRET_t$			$IDIOSYNCRATIC_t$		
Variable	(1)	(2)	(3)	(1)	(2)	(3)	(1)	(2)	(3)
Intercept	.103	.082	.075	.082	.075	.089	.076	.079	.072
	(1.99)**	(1.85)***	(1.83)***	(1.72)***	(1.68)***	(1.74)***	(1.71)***	(1.69)***	(1.75)***
$I\text{-}HHI_{t-1}$	−.028	−.016	−.020	−.038	−.042	−.050	−.018	−.022	−.035
	(3.09)*	(2.82)**	(2.61)**	(2.04)**	(2.13)**	(2.14)**	(2.14)**	(2.35)**	(2.05)**
$A\text{-}HHI_{t-1}$	−.061	−.051	−.051	−.022	−.018	−.012	−.068	−.056	−.049
	(2.57)**	(2.48)**	(2.41)**	(1.99)**	(1.92)***	(1.88)***	(2.31)**	(2.24)**	(2.14)**
$LN(SIZE)_{t-1}$		−.009	−.016		−.017	−.013		−.010	−.011
		(1.74)***	(1.64)		(1.61)	(1.74)***		(1.50)	(1.42)
$EQRATIO_{t-1}$		−.051	−.062		−.059	−.046		−.032	−.039
		(1.84)***	(1.88)***		(1.90)***	(1.97)***		(1.49)	(1.17)
$BRRATIO_{t-1}$		−.601	−.625		−.586	−.533		−.011	−.024
		(1.99)**	(1.94)**		(2.18)**	(1.85)***		(1.44)	(1.29)
$EMPRATIO_{t-1}$		−.763	.740		.504	.616		.071	.084
		(1.54)	(1.46)		(1.08)	(1.06)		(1.49)	(1.33)
ROA_{t-1} or SR_{t-1}		−.042	−.041		−.024	−.053		−.031	−.027
		(1.36)	(1.22)		(1.06)	(1.85)***		(1.55)	(1.48)
NEW			.017			.019			.013
			(1.74)***			(1.53)			(1.90)***

FRACNEW			−.022			.067			.028
			(1.28)			(1.42)			(1.66)***
$COMP_{t-1}$			.023			.026			.025
			(1.89)***			(1.96)**			(2.07)**
$IHHI_{t-1}$ × NEW			−.030			−.022			−.026
			(1.67)***			(1.70)***			(1.79)***
$AHHI_{t-1}$ × NEW			−.031			−.025			−.015
			(1.85)***			(1.78)***			(1.82)***
$IHHI_{t-1}$ × FRACNEW			−.007			−.015			−.022
			(1.08)			(1.27)			(2.00)**
$AHHI_{t-1}$ × FRACNEW			−.001			−.024			−.019
			(1.30)			(1.15)			(1.35)
I-HHI_{t-1} × $COMP_{t-1}$			−.018			−.014			−.027
			(1.99)**			(2.02)**			(1.74)***
A-HHI_{t-1} × $COMP_{t-1}$			−.027			−.038			−.026
			(2.14)**			(2.13)**			(1.98)**
Adjusted R^2	.0279	.2416	.2829	.0307	.2119	.2576	.0301	.2515	.3309
F-statistics	10.14*	9.25*	10.17*	5.39*	6.55*	6.80*	3.96*	5.46*	6.23*
Number	604	604	604	152	152	152	152	152	152

NOTE.—This table presents the results for the effect of bank focus, entry into newer industries, and competition faced by a bank in lending on bank risk for 105 Italian banks over the sample period 1993–99. Col. 1 tests the specification with only the focus measures (eq. [11]), col. 2 adds to this specification the control variables, and col. 3 tests the specification that further includes the effect of entry into newer industries and of competition faced in lending (eq. [13]). The t-statistics in parentheses are corrected for heteroscedasticity using White's correction. The coefficients on year dummies and bank-specific fixed effects are not reported for the sake of brevity.

* Statistically significant at the 1% level.

** Statistically significant at the 5% level.

*** Statistically significant at the 10% level.

correspond to the publicly traded sample in which the risk measures employed are stock return volatility $STDRET_t$ and its idiosyncratic component $IDIOSYNCRATIC_t$. In each panel of three columns, the first two columns correspond to the test of hypothesis (11) and the third column corresponds to the test of hypothesis (14).

From columns 1 and 2 in each panel of table 8, we observe that the effect of both industrial and asset sectoral focus on bank risk is negative and statistically significant. The effect is also economically significant. For example, for risk measure $DOUBT_t$, the effect of increasing a bank's industrial focus from 0.16 (approximately equally exposed to six industries) to 0.33 (approximately equally exposed to three industries) in year $t - 1$ is to decrease the bank's year t doubtful and nonperforming loans to assets ratio by approximately 0.51%. Note that the average DOUBT value in the sample period is 5.23% with a standard deviation of 5.63%. The effect is of similar magnitude for stock return–based volatility measures.

Furthermore, the above effect persists even after we control for endogeneity of the focus measures. In table 9, we consider a simultaneous equations estimation of $RISK_t$ and $Focus_t$. The focus specification we test for the presence of endogeneity is identical to that of Section III.*B*, and, as can be seen, the coefficients on both focus terms, I-HHI and A-HHI, are always negative and statistically significant.

Finally, column 3 in table 8 reveals that when a bank enters "new" industrial sectors, loan risk increases at a rate that is increasing in the extent of diversification of the bank. That is, the direct coefficient on NEW_t is always positive (though only marginally significant), and the coefficient on interaction terms between NEW_t and the two focus measures is negative and significant. For highly diversified banks (low I-HHI and A-HHI), the effect of moving into new industries is to increase bank risk (e.g., increase in DOUBT of 0.5% at the lowest values of I-HHI and A-HHI in the sample). For moderate diversification, the effect is close to zero (e.g., at average values of I-HHI and A-HHI in the sample). Finally, for highly focused banks, moving into new industries in fact reduces bank risk. The variable $FRACNEW_t$, the fraction of bank loan portfolio in the newer industries, has no substantial effect on bank risk.

Stronger than the effect of entry into newer industries is the effect of competition that a bank faces in lending (in the five largest industries it has loan exposures to). The direct coefficient on $COMP_{t-1}$ is positive and significant. This suggests that banks facing greater competition have riskier portfolios. This could be due either to the negative effect of competition on profits, which in turn provides risk-shifting incentives (see Allen and Gale 2000), or the effect of market competition on charter values (see Keeley 1990). In terms of economic magnitudes, consider the simple example of two banks that are otherwise identical but one is a leader in one of its top five industries, holding an 80% share. The other bank is a relatively smaller loan player in this same industry, which does, however, belong to its own top five industries in terms of exposure amounts, holding the remaining 20% share of the market. The difference in competition faced by these two banks contributes to the difference in their doubtful loans to assets ratio of $[(1.0 - 0.2) - (1.0 - 0.8)] \times 2.3\% = 1.38\%$, where 2.3% is the estimated coefficient on COMP_{t-1} in column 3 of the DOUBT panel in table 8.

Furthermore, the risk-increasing effects of competition are greater the more diversified banks are. The coefficients on the interaction terms between COMP_{t-1} and focus measures, I-HHI_{t-1} and A-HHI_{t-1}, are both negative and statistically significant. In other words, an increase in focus, that is, a decrease in diversification, reduces risk more when the competition that the bank faces in its loan sectors is higher. This interaction effect is, however, economically small compared to the direct effects of focus measures on bank risk and the direct effect of competition on bank risk as well as the interaction effect of focus measures and entry into newer industries.

These results provide some evidence suggesting that the quality of monitoring by banks is poorer in newer industries and that banks face greater adverse selection when they expand into industries that have been previously penetrated by their competitors. This also suggests that if banks take the effect of lending competition into account and are value-maximizing, then they should choose to diversify (if at all) into industries with lower penetration by other banks, as proposed by Boot and Thakor (2000). In a recent paper, Hauswald and Marquez (2002) also demonstrate that bank incentives to concentrate informational resources are increasing in the degree of adverse selection they face in the market, which in turn would be greater if banks expand by lending more to industries in which (lending) competition is strong.[21]

D. Additional Robustness Tests and Results

State-owned versus private banks.—Sapienza (2002) finds that the objective functions of state-owned Italian banks differ from those of private Italian banks. State-owned banks charge lower interest rates than privately owned banks to similar or identical firms, even if the company is able to borrow more from privately owned banks. Further, she finds that state-owned banks mostly favor firms located in depressed areas and large firms. This makes it plausible that a part of the inefficiency arising from diversification may simply be due to the presence of state-owned banks in our sample. As a check, we employed the same classification of state-owned and private Italian banks employed by Sapienza (2002) and reexamined our hypotheses for the private (not state-owned) bank sample. On the basis of the available classification at the beginning of 1993, 34 banks in our sample were privately owned. The qualitative nature and the significance of our results remain unaffected by

21. It is also possible that the ex ante screening by banks suffers as well in newer industries, as theoretically shown by Hauswald and Marquez (2002), amplifying the effect of ex post poor monitoring. However, our data do not allow us to distinguish between these two possible channels. This appears to be a fruitful goal to pursue in future research should more micro-level data on bank lending and monitoring practices become available.

TABLE 9 Simultaneous (SUR) Estimation of Effect of Focus on Bank Loan Risk Treating Focus Measures as Endogenous Variables

	(1)		(2)		(3)		(4)	
	$DOUBT_t$	$I\text{-}HHI_t$	$STDRET_t$	$I\text{-}HHI_t$	$DOUBT_t$	$A\text{-}HHI_t$	$STDRET_t$	$A\text{-}HHI_t$
Intercept	.098	.133	.075	.081	.077	.321	−.085	−.081
	(1.77)***	(3.50)*	(1.73)***	(3.49)*	(1.74)***	(6.62)*	(.74)	(.85)
$I\text{-}HHI_t$ (cols. 1, 2), $I\text{-}HHI_{t-1}$ (cols. 3, 4)	−.012		−.044		−.008		−.016	
	(1.70)***		(2.14)**		(1.71)***		(1.90)***	
$A\text{-}HHI_{t-1}$ (cols. 1, 2), $A\text{-}HHI_t$ (cols. 3, 4)	−.013		−.025		−.012		−.013	
	(1.97)**		(1.86)***		(1.90)***		(1.79)***	
$LN(SIZE)_{t-1}$	−.038	−.042	−.083	−.016	−.031	−.018	−.070	−.011
	(.66)	(3.11)*	(.70)	(3.28)*	(.89)	(2.86)*	(.81)	(1.43)
$EQRATIO_{t-1}$	.070	−.825	.005	.643	.073	−.714	.004	.575
	(1.88)***	(.70)	(1.15)	(.91)	(1.80)***	(1.03)	(1.01)	(.81)
$BRRATIO_{t-1}$	−.053	.086	−.027	−.010	−.030	.025	−.027	−.045
	(1.89)***	(1.17)	(1.77)***	(1.15)	(1.76)***	(1.06)	(1.81)***	(1.40)
$EMPRATIO_{t-1}$	−.013	−.045	−.060	−.047	−.700	−.053	−.096	−.055
	(.51)	(.82)	(1.29)	(1.18)	(1.09)	(.97)	(1.07)	(1.31)
$DOUBT_{t-1}$	−.054	−.155			−.146	−.091		
	(1.37)	(3.38)*			(1.05)	(2.72)**		
$STDRET_{t-1}$			.609	−.091			.007	−.086
			(1.12)	(2.07)**			(1.25)	(1.85)***
ROA_{t-1}	−.011	.074			−.010	.090		
	(1.08)	(1.55)			(.90)	(1.80)***		
SR_{t-1}			.003	−.013			.001	−.007
			(.97)	(1.39)			(1.08)	(1.21)
National dummy		−.041		−.044		−.020		−.040
		(1.91)***		(1.92)***		(1.67)***		(1.74)***
Private dummy		−.026				−.022		
		(2.95)*				(2.90)*		
DEPOSIT TO ASSET $RATIO_{t-1}$		−.038		−.010		−.020		−.016

		(.81)		(1.81)***		(.89)		(1.48)
State-owned dummy	−.019	.004	−.016	.023	−.020	.005	−.015	.026
	(1.82)***	(2.31)**	(1.78)***	(2.59)**	(1.80)***	(2.29)**	(1.85)***	(3.71)*
Group dummy		−.004		−.007		−.007		−.018
		(1.16)		(3.00)*		(1.51)		(3.61)*
Avg. I-HHI, (cols. 1, 2), Avg. A-HHI, (cols. 3, 4)		.005		.023		.003		.005
		(1.41)		(1.28)		(1.13)		(1.54)
1995	−.004	−.005	−.003	−.014	−.005	−.005	−.006	−.008
	(1.46)	(1.25)	(1.26)	(1.43)	(1.46)	(1.44)	(1.21)	(1.45)
1996	.005	−.006	.005	.005	.007	−.005	.009	.007
	(1.57)	(1.49)	(1.18)	(1.23)	(1.45)	(1.60)	(.80)	(1.40)
1997	−.006	−.0075	.004	.008	−.008	−.005	.008	.010
	(.80)	(.86)	(.86)	(1.05)	(.69)	(.97)	(1.00)	(1.58)
1998	−.016	−.002	−.003	−.015	−.012	−.004	−.006	−.005
	(1.38)	(1.23)	(1.18)	(1.49)	(1.42)	(1.49)	(1.30)	(1.38)
1999	−.018	−.017	−.016	−.015	−.013	−.016	−.015	−.007
	(1.89)***	(1.91)***	(1.30)	(1.79)***	(1.88)***	(1.73)***	(1.44)	(1.44)
System-weighted R^2	.3028		.3917		.3290		.3073	
Cross-model covariance	.0322		.0249		.0387		.0278	
Cross-model correlation	.0485		.0382		.0409		.0304	
Number	604		152		604		152	

NOTE.—In cols. 1 and 2, I-HHI is treated as endogenous. In cols. 3 and 4, A-HHI is treated as endogenous. The specification is a simultaneous system of equations analogous to eqq. (7) and (8), eq. (7) being replaced by eq. (11). The *t*-statistics in parentheses are corrected for heteroscedasticity using White's correction. The coefficients on bank-specific fixed effects are not reported for the sake of brevity.

* Statistically significant at the 1% level.

** Statistically significant at the 5% level.

*** Statistically significant at the 10% level.

restricting our analysis to this smaller sample: (i) both focus measures improve bank returns on average, and the effect of focus on returns is U-shaped as a function of bank risk; (ii) both focus measures reduce bank risk.[22]

National versus intraregional and local banks.—The measure of focus and diversification employed in our paper concerns the asset side of the bank balance sheet; that is, it is based on a bank's loan exposures to different industries and sectors. The effect of changes in focus or diversification might affect money center banks differently since they do not rely as heavily on core (local) deposits. To check for links between asset-side focus and performance while controlling for the liability structure of banks, we employed the classification of banks in our sample into national banks and nonnational (i.e., intraregional or local) banks. Eight out of nine national banks in our sample were also identified as money center banks. Estimation of the effects of focus (diversification) on return (tables 4 and 5) and on risk (table 8) separately for the sample of national banks and the rest of the banks produced qualitatively similar patterns for both samples. This confirms that our results are not driven by the presence of the large, national banks.[23]

Consortium banks.—Another feature of certain Italian banks in our sample reflects the fact that they are "part of a bank group or a consortium." Since bank strategy to focus or diversify might be determined at a consortium-wide level, it might be deemed as more appropriate to measure return and risk of such banks also at a consortium-wide level. Consequently, we estimated the effects of focus (diversification) on return (tables 4 and 5) and risk (table 8) separately for the subsample of banks that are not a part of a bank group or consortium. There were 70 such banks in our sample. While the overall pattern remains qualitatively unaffected, we find that in fact, the harmful effect of diversification on risk is actually more pronounced.[24]

Large banks.—One final concern could be that a few big and well-diversified banks in our sample, especially Banco di Napoli, Banco di Sicilia, and Banca Popolare di Novara, had large negative shocks to their profits in the first half of our sample period and their bad loans increased dramatically, primarily for regulatory and institutional reasons. We do include bank size as a control variable, but to be absolutely sure that these observations are not driving our results, we reran our regressions two different ways: (1) by excluding these three banks from the sample altogether and (2) by introducing

22. These results are contained in tables 10, 11, and 12, available from the authors on request. Note that the classification of Italian banks into state-owned and private banks in Sapienza (2002) is based on their ownership as at the beginning of 1993. While there have been changes in the state vs. private ownership of some Italian banks since then (in particular, a decline in the number of state-owned banks; see Goldman Sachs [2001]), we have been unable to obtain a comprehensive data set that provides these changes.

23. These results are contained in tables 14, 15, and 16, available from the authors on request. We also classified banks into two samples depending on whether their deposits to assets ratio was greater or smaller than the median deposits to assets ratio in each year. This classification produced results similar to those obtained from division of the sample into national and nonnational banks. The corresponding tables 17, 18, and 19 are also available on request.

24. These results are contained in tables 20, 21, and 22, available from the authors on request.

an interaction term between the size variable and time dummies. The exclusion of these three banks hardly affects the quantitative or the qualitative nature of our results, and the interaction between size and time effects is almost always insignificant.[25]

E. Overall Effects of Diversification on Bank Performance

Combining the empirical findings of tables 3–8 regarding the effects of diversification (focus) on bank returns and bank loan portfolio risk, we summarize our results in terms of their implications for the benefits of loan portfolio diversification as follows:

	Moderately Risky Banks	Highly Risky Banks
Industrial or sectoral diversification	Return unaffected or ↑ marginally	Return ↓ significantly
	Risk ↑ ⇒ Decreased performance OR Effect on performance ambiguous	Risk ↑ ⇒ Decreased performance

Note that an up arrow means an increase and a down arrow means a decrease.

We conclude the following for our sample of banks:

1. Industrial loan diversification does not result in an efficient trade-off between risk and return. Specifically, loan portfolio return is close to being unaffected or increased by a small amount with diversification for low to moderate insolvency risk banks and deteriorates with diversification for high insolvency risk banks, whereas loan risk for banks increases with diversification. This implies an overall deterioration in performance of high insolvency risk banks from greater diversification.
2. Broad asset sector diversification appears to affect bank performance in an adverse manner analogous to industrial diversification.
3. The effect of industrial and asset sector diversification on banks with moderate insolvency risk levels cannot be assessed without taking a stand on how much bank return should increase per unit increase in bank risk.[26]

Crucially, a robust finding that emerges from our results is that the conventional wisdom of not putting all of one's eggs in a single basket cannot be applied uniformly to all banks. That is, diversification per se is no guarantee of superior performance or greater bank safety and soundness, which is a major goal of regulatory policy.

25. These results are contained in tables 23–28, available from the authors on request.

26. In practice, many banks use a risk-adjusted return on capital framework to determine whether such loans are beneficial. Commonly the return per unit of risk of the loan should exceed some cost of capital benchmark specified by the bank such as the after-tax ROE of the bank.

IV. Conclusion

In this paper, we have examined the effects of a bank's decision to focus (diversify) on its return and risk. Understanding these two effects enables us to derive conclusions about the overall effects of focus (diversification) on a bank's performance. Indeed, we believe that this is the first paper to employ measures of focus (diversification) based on relatively micro-level data, that is, industrial and sectoral exposures in individual bank asset portfolios.

Driven by the availability of data, our tests are based on a unique data set of 105 Italian banks over the sample period 1993–99. While data limitations mean that our results need to be interpreted with caution, they do suggest some implications for the optimal size and scope of banks. While traditional banking theory based on a delegated monitoring argument (see, e.g., Boyd and Prescott 1986) recommends that the optimal organization of a bank is one in which it is as diversified as possible, our results suggest that, empirically, there seem to be diseconomies of diversification for a bank that expands into industries in which it faces a high degree of competition or lacks prior lending experience. Our results suggest that these diseconomies arise in the form of a worsening of the credit quality of loan portfolios simultaneously with a fall in bank returns (perhaps due to worse monitoring, adverse selection, higher overheads, or some combination of these factors).

Such diseconomies imply that the optimal industrial organization of a banking sector might be one that comprises several focused or specialized banks instead of a large number of diversified banks, an outcome that may also be attractive from a systemic risk standpoint as noted by Shaffer (1994) and Acharya (2001). Finally, our results potentially explain the results of DeLong (2001), who finds that bank mergers that are focusing (in terms of activity and geography) produce superior economic performance relative to those that are diversifying.

Appendix

TABLE A1 Banks in Our Sample over the Period 1993–99

					Average Asset Size 1993–99				
Italian Bank	Publicly Traded	State Owned	Size	Type	Billions of Lira	Millions of Dollars	Average I-HHI	Average A-HHI	Average G-HHI
1st Banc. S. Paolo Torino SP		Yes	Very large	National	210,140.62	127,697.41	.256	.333	.747
Banca di Roma	Yes		Very large	National	151,531.03	92,116.38	.205	.402	1.000
Carispa Prov. Lombarde SPA		Yes	Very large	National	147,173.38	88,961.87	.242	.295	.865
B. Ca. Commerciale Italiana	Yes	Yes	Very large	National	144,846.22	87,582.60	.292	.373	.581
B. Ca. Naz. le del Lavoro SPA	Yes	Yes	Very large	National	142,746.88	86,629.62	.291	.321	.811
Credito Italiano	Yes	Yes	Very large	National	107,569.79	65,935.05	.288	.337	.702
Banca Monte Paschi Siena	Yes	Yes	Very large	National	107,493.46	64,653.49	.228	.266	.872
Banco di Napoli SPA	Yes	Yes	Very large	National	78,937.00	48,283.50	.221	.289	.868
Rola Banca 1473 SPA	Yes		Large	Intraregional	61,427.64	36,928.96	.257	.288	.741
Banco di Sicilia SPA		Yes	Large	Intraregional	49,912.07	30,238.15	.237	.232	.950
B. Ca. Pop. di Novara	Yes		Large	National	39,659.93	24,109.91	.247	.390	.915
B. Ca. Pop. di Milano	Yes		Large	Intraregional	38,731.39	23,473.00	.277	.373	.772
Carispa di Torino SPA		Yes	Large	Intraregional	37,885.21	23,048.44	.246	.350	.781
B. Ca. Naz. le Agricoltura	Yes		Large	Intraregional	35,772.62	21,764.49	.234	.383	.786
Deutsche Bank SPA			Large	Intraregional	31,907.99	19,286.35	.253	.362	.810
Cariverona Banca SPA		Yes	Large	Intraregional	31,616.59	19,186.40	.271	.349	.912
B. Ca. Pop. di Bergamo-Credito Varesino	Yes		Large	Intraregional	31,452.00	19,013.32	.240	.348	.966
Banca Toscana	Yes		Large	Intraregional	25,275.43	15,357.70	.245	.356	.996
Carispa in Bologna SPA		Yes	Large	Intraregional	24,080.17	14,610.17	.228	.324	.947
Cr. Parma e Piacenze SPA		Yes	Large	Intraregional	23,607.37	14,443.26	.230	.340	.909
Banca Antoniana-Pop. Veneta			Medium	Regional	21,711.34	13,083.25	.244	.428	.985
BP Verona/Pop. Verona-S. Gim. E S. Pros	Yes		Medium	Regional	21,823.51	13,075.80	.254	.352	.965

TABLE A1 (*Continued*)

Italian Bank	Publicly Traded	State Owned	Size	Type	Average Asset Size 1993–99: Billions of Lira	Average Asset Size 1993–99: Millions of Dollars	Average I-HHI	Average A-HHI	Average G-HHI
Carispa di Firenze SPA		Yes	Medium	Regional	18,676.78	11,350.44	.226	.325	.994
Carispa Padova Rovigo SPA		Yes	Medium	Regional	18,132.87	10,990.80	.235	.427	.999
B. Ca. Pop. Emilia Romagna	Yes		Medium	Regional	18,128.69	10,943.33	.254	.372	.957
Mediocredito Lombardo SPA		Yes	Medium	Regional	17,711.59	10,688.70	.253	.687	.993
Banca Carige SPA	Yes	Yes	Medium	Regional	17,288.69	10,479.00	.250	.325	.974
Banco di Sardegna SPA	Yes	Yes	Medium	Regional	17,021.80	10,348.93	.206	.265	.900
Centrobanca		Yes	Medium	Regional	15,756.71	9,576.32	.305	.487	.945
Efibanca		Yes	Medium	Regional	15,470.99	9,414.93	.324	.417	.884
Credito Bergamasco	Yes		Medium	Regional	12,937.12	7,848.34	.261	.390	.902
Banca Mediocredito SPA		Yes	Medium	Regional	12,633.36	7,638.04	.249	.325	.997
B.R.E. Banca		Yes	Medium	Regional	11,714.61	7,110.85	.242	.312	.997
B. Agricola Mantovana	Yes		Medium	Regional	11,432.56	6,898.42	.245	.386	.962
Banca delle Marche		Yes	Medium	Regional	11,141.62	6,752.06	.212	.321	1.000
Interbanca	Yes	Yes	Medium	Regional	11,013.61	6,678.02	.298	.412	.919
B. Ca. Pop. di Lodi	Yes		Medium	Regional	10,647.84	6,413.13	.239	.360	.897
B. Ca. Pop. di Brescia	Yes		Medium	Regional	9,981.72	5,921.20	.241	.361	.996
B. Pop. Com. IO. Industria	Yes		Medium	Regional	9,420.45	5,684.98	.242	.491	.917
Carispa di Venezia SPA		Yes	Medium	Regional	8,141.56	4,930.30	.223	.344	.926
B. Pop. Etruria e Lazio	Yes		Medium	Regional	7,758.24	4,704.56	.234	.444	.999
Credito Emiliano SPA	Yes	Yes	Small	Intraregional	11,468.50	6,889.18	.235	.346	.935
Banca Sella SPA			Small	Provincial	6,150.18	3,706.60	.312	.359	.909
B. del Salento-C.P. Sal. SPA			Small	Provincial	5,820.58	3,507.56	.218	.344	.911
Banca Fideuram SPA	Yes		Small	Provincial	5,515.31	3,369.71	.213	.430	.999
B. Pic. Lo Cred. Valtellinese	Yes		Small	Provincial	5,473.48	3,297.29	.219	.385	.959
Banca di Legnano	Yes		Small	Provincial	4,391.87	2,665.17	.252	.347	.978
Credito Artigiano	Yes		Small	Provincial	3,962.57	2,384.90	.257	.500	.973
B. Chiavari Riv Ligure SPA	Yes		Small	Provincial	3,834.23	2,330.64	.210	.291	.958

B. Desio e della Brianza	Yes		Small	Provincial	3,458.57	2,094.03	.226	.454	1.000
B. Agric. Pop. Ragusa			Small	Provincial	3,391.94	2,052.50	.261	.396	1.000
B. Ca. Trento e Bolzano			Small	Provincial	3,241.00	1,966.21	.233	.360	.973
Banca di Piacenza			Small	Provincial	3,033.98	1,841.55	.221	.399	1.000
Mediocredito Centrale SPA		Yes	Small	Provincial	10,685.48	6,426.76	.296	.528	.417
B. Ca. Pop. di Sondrio	Yes		Small	Provincial	8,300.64	5,012.77	.235	.456	.974
B. Ca. Pop. di Vicentina			Small	Provincial	8,030.56	4,843.56	.261	.486	.977
Cassamarca SPA		Yes	Small	Provincial	6,101.02	3,699.20	.217	.306	.849
Biverbanca SPA		Yes	Small	Provincial	5,780.94	3,499.32	.230	.370	.970
Carispa Bolzano SPA		Yes	Small	Provincial	5,782.34	3,491.64	.202	.371	.994
Banca Pop. di Ancona SPA			Small	Provincial	5,746.32	3,466.38	.223	.328	1.000
Carispa di Lucca SPA		Yes	Small	Provincial	5,201.22	3,155.62	.200	.323	.991
Ca. Ri. Tro SPA		Yes	Small	Provincial	5,088.15	3,088.71	.208	.308	.993
Carispa Trieste-Banca SPA		Yes	Small	Provincial	4,635.64	2,816.87	.229	.349	.991
Banca Mediterranea SPA			Small	Provincial	4,577.49	2,802.25	.210	.288	1.000
Carispa di Perugia SPA		Yes	Small	Provincial	4,399.06	2,671.11	.239	.327	.998
B. Ca. Pop. Friuladria			Small	Provincial	4,168.56	2,514.32	.247	.408	.999
Carispa Pistoia Pescia SPA		Yes	Small	Provincial	4,045.06	2,462.67	.213	.311	.999
B. P. Puglia e Basilicata			Small	Provincial	4,034.06	2,436.34	.207	.243	.985
Carispa di S. Miniato SPA		Yes	Small	Provincial	3,963.08	2,417.15	.235	.354	.977
Carispa Udine e PN SPA		Yes	Small	Provincial	3,617.26	2,191.54	.242	.367	.988
Carispa di Asti SPA		Yes	Small	Provincial	3,599.16	2,181.40	.213	.356	.999
Carispa di Pisa SPA		Yes	Small	Provincial	3,562.14	2,163.15	.203	.376	.984
B.C.C. di Roma			Small	Provincial	3,547.50	2,142.55	.225	.362	.722
Banca Pop. Irpinia			Small	Provincial	3,507.99	2,135.68	.199	.438	1.000
Banca Pop. Alto Adige			Small	Provincial	3,411.25	2,060.46	.244	.406	.962
Tercas-C.R. Teramo SPA		Yes	Small	Provincial	3,354.14	2,034.38	.219	.324	.998
Carispa di Ferrara SPA		Yes	Small	Provincial	3,237.85	1,966.96	.200	.309	1.000
Carispa della Spezia SPA		Yes	Small	Provincial	3,112.11	1,887.49	.214	.273	1.000
Carispa di Rimini SPA		Yes	Small	Provincial	2,093.01	1,759.66	.215	.368	.980
B. Ca. Pop. di Intra-SCPARL	Yes		Small	Provincial	2,807.94	1,692.76	.212	.374	.971
B. Ca. Pop. di Cremona	Yes		Small	Provincial	2,778.12	1,686.39	.281	.411	1.000
B. Pop. Luino e Varese-SPA	Yes		Small	Provincial	2,763.59	1,677.24	.228	.438	.999
Carispa di Alessandria SPA		Yes	Small	Provincial	2,698.53	1,641.21	.212	.302	1.000
Carispa di Forli' SPA		Yes	Small	Provincial	2,636.64	1,596.49	.244	.352	1.000
Carispa di Ravenna SPA		Yes	Small	Provincial	2,541.91	1,539.31	.235	.328	.993
Carispa di Cesena SPA		Yes	Small	Provincial	2,483.27	1,518.21	.207	.327	1.000

TABLE A1 (*Continued*)

Italian Bank	Publicly Traded	State Owned	Size	Type	Average Asset Size 1993–99: Billions of Lira	Average Asset Size 1993–99: Millions of Dollars	Average I-HHI	Average A-HHI	Average G-HHI
B. Pop. di Abbiategrasso-SPA			Small	Provincial	2,363.16	1,445.37	.235	.507	.999
Med. Tren.-Alto Adi. SPA		Yes	Small	Provincial	2,312.20	1,403.63	.314	.620	1.000
Carispa Prov. Chieti SPA		Yes	Small	Provincial	2,264.49	1,384.76	.217	.343	1.000
Cr. Pescara Loerto SPA		Yes	Small	Provincial	2,217.55	1,349.76	.231	.360	1.000
Carispa di Fermo SPA		Yes	Small	Provincial	2,158.86	1,313.52	.223	.309	1.000
Banca Monte Parma SPA		Yes	Small	Provincial	2,140.66	1,297.52	.203	.419	.999
Carispa di Rieti SPA		Yes	Small	Provincial	2,112.70	1,292.20	.208	.256	1.000
Carispa di Savona SPA		Yes	Small	Provincial	2,129.53	1,292.03	.209	.298	.998
B. Ca. Pop. di Spoleto SPA			Small	Provincial	2,086.80	1,264.85	.222	.268	1.000
Carispa di Gorizia SPA		Yes	Small	Provincial	2,059.13	1,251.80	.231	.288	.997
Carispa Prov. Viterbo SPA		Yes	Small	Provincial	1,963.78	1,194.85	.198	.374	.987
Irfis-Med. Sicilia SPA		Yes	Small	Provincial	1,901.04	1,155.97	.274	.652	.997
Carispaq-SPA		Yes	Small	Provincial	1,853.71	1,135.98	.230	.337	1.000
Cred. Fond. Toscana SPA		Yes	Small	Provincial	1,849.07	1,126.50	.236	.280	.997
Banca Pop. Udinese			Very small	Local	1,991.05	1,207.66	.267	.402	.995
Carispa Ascoli Piceno SPA		Yes	Very small	Local	1,957.42	1,187.36	.210	.257	1.000
B. Ca. di Valle Camonica			Very small	Local	1,820.57	1,102.95	.228	.383	.999
Carispa Terni e Narni SPA		Yes	Very small	Local	1,374.69	834.76	.216	.243	1.000
Carispa Civitavecchia SPA		Yes	Very small	Local	687.87	426.94	.218	.273	1.000

References

Acharya, V. 2001. A theory of systemic risk and design of prudential bank regulation. Working paper, London Business School.
Allen, F., and D. Gale. 2000. *Comparing financial systems*. Cambridge, MA: MIT Press.
Berger, A., R. Demsetz, and P. Strahan. 1999. The consolidation of the financial services industry: Causes, consequences, and implications for the future. Working paper, Board of Governors of the Federal Reserve System, Washington, DC.
Berger, A., and R. DeYoung. 2001. The effects of geographic expansion on bank efficiency. Working paper, Board of Governors of the Federal Reserve System, Washington, DC.
Berger, A., N. Miller, M. Petersen, R. Rajan, and J. Stein. 2001. Does function follow organizational form? Evidence from the lending practices of large and small banks. Working paper, University of Chicago.
BNP Paribas. 2001. Italian banking's metamorphosis. *Conjuncture*, no. 11 (December), pp. 2–13.
Boot, A., and A. Thakor. 2000. Can relationship banking survive competition? *Journal of Finance* 55, no. 2:679–713.
Boyd, J., and E. Prescott. 1986. Financial intermediary coalitions. *Journal of Economic Theory* 38:211–32.
Campa, J. M., and S. Kedia. 2002. Explaining the diversification discount. *Journal of Finance* 57, no. 4:1731–62.
Caprio, G., and B. Wilson. 1997. On not putting all the eggs in one basket: The role of diversification in banking. Working paper, World Bank, Washington, DC.
Cerasi, V., and S. Daltung. 2000. The optimal size of a bank: Costs and benefits of diversification. *European Economic Review* 44, no. 9:1701–26.
Degatriache, E., P. Garella, and L. Guiso. 2000. Multiple versus single banking relationships: Theory and evidence. *Journal of Finance* 55, no. 3:1133–61.
Dell'Arricia, G., E. Friedman, and R. Marquez. 1999. Adverse selection as a barrier to entry in the banking industry. *Rand Journal of Economics* 30:515–34.
DeLong, G. 2001. Stockholder gains from focusing versus diversifying bank mergers. *Journal of Financial Economics* 59, no. 2:221–52.
Diamond, D. 1984. Financial intermediation and delegated monitoring. *Review of Economic Studies* 59:393–414.
Fama, E. 1980. Banking in the theory of finance. *Journal of Monetary Economics* 9, no. 1:39–58.
———. 1985. What's different about banks? *Journal of Monetary Economics* 15:29–39.
Gehrig, T. 1998. Screening, cross-border banking and the allocation of credit. *Research in Economics* 52:387–407.
Goldman Sachs. 2001. Banks: Italy. *Global Equity Research* (September).
Graham, J., M. Lemmon, and J. Wolf. 2002. Does corporate diversification destroy value? *Journal of Finance* 57, no. 2:695–720.
Hauswald, R., and R. Marquez. 2002. Competition and strategic information acquisition in credit markets. Working paper, University of Maryland.
Hughes, J., W. Lang, L. Mester, and C. Moon. 1996. Safety in numbers? Geographic diversification and bank insolvency risk. Working paper, Federal Reserve Bank of Philadelphia.
James, C. 1987. Some evidence on the uniqueness of bank loans. *Journal of Financial Economics* 19:217–36.
Johnson, J. 1972. *Econometric methods*. 2nd ed. New York: McGraw-Hill.
Keeley, Michael C. 1990, Deposit insurance, risk and market power in banking. *American Economic Review* 80:1183–1200.
Klein, P., and M. Saidenberg. 1998. Diversification, organization, and efficiency: Evidence from bank holding companies. Working paper, Federal Reserve Bank of New York.
Maddala, G. S. 1977. *Econometrics*. New York: McGraw-Hill.
Maksimovic, V., and G. Phillips. 2002. Do conglomerate firms allocate resources inefficiently? *Journal of Finance* 57, no. 2:721–67.
Rajan, R. 1992. Insiders and outsiders: The choice between relationship and arms length debt. *Journal of Finance* 47:1367–1400.
Sapienza, P. 2002. The effects of banking mergers on loan contracts. *Journal of Finance* 57, no. 1:329–68.
———. 2004. The effects of government ownership on bank lending. *Journal of Financial Economics* 72, no. 2:357–84.

Saunders, A., and B. Wilson. 2001. An analysis of bank charter value and its risk constraining incentives. *Journal of Financial Services Research* 19 (April/June): 185–95.

Shaffer, S. 1994. Pooling intensifies joint failure risk. *Research in Financial Services* 6:249–80.

———. 1998. The winner's curse in banking. *Journal of Financial Intermediation* 4:158–87.

Sharpe, S. 1990. Asymmetric information, bank lending, and implicit contracts: A stylized model of customer relationships. *Journal of Finance* 55:1069–87.

Stein, J. 2002. Information production and capital allocation: Decentralized vs. hierarchical firms. *Journal of Finance* 57, no. 5:1891–1921.

Stiroh, K. 2002. Diversification in banking: Is noninterest income the answer? Working paper, Federal Reserve Bank of New York.

Theil, H. 1971. *Principles of econometrics*. New York: Wiley.

Villalonga, B. 2004. Diversification discount or premium? New evidence from the business information tracking series. *Journal of Finance* 59, no. 2:479–506.

Winton, A. 1999. Don't put all your eggs in one basket? Diversification and specialization in lending. Working paper, University of Minnesota.